MORAL DEVELOPMENT AND BEHAVIOR

MORAL DEVELOPMENT AND BEHAVIOR

Theory, Research, and Social Issues

THOMAS LICKONA, Editor
State University of New York at Cortland

Consulting Editors:

Gilbert Geis
University of California at Irvine

Lawrence Kohlberg
Harvard University

HOLT, RINEHART AND WINSTON
New York   Chicago   San Francisco   Atlanta
Dallas   Montreal   Toronto   London   Sydney

Library of Congress Cataloging in Publication Data

Main entry under title:

Moral development and behavior: theory, research,
and social issues.

    Bibliography: p. 364
    Includes index.
    1. Ethics—Addresses, essays, lectures.
2. Social ethics—Addresses, essays, lectures.
3. Moral education—Addresses, essays, lectures.
I. Lickona, Thomas
BJ21.M58   170   75–29471
ISBN: 0–03–002811–6

Contributors

Justin Aronfreed
Urie Bronfenbrenner
Roger V. Burton
H. J. Eysenck
James Garbarino
Gilbert Geis
James Gilligan
Martin L. Hoffman
Ted L. Huston
Lawrence Kohlberg
Chuck Korte
Thomas Lickona
Robert M. Liebert

Alan Lockwood
James C. Mancuso
Harriet N. Mischel
Walter Mischel
John Monahan
Bert S. Moore
Rita Wicks Poulos
James R. Rest
D. L. Rosenhan
Herbert D. Saltzstein
Theodore R. Sarbin
Robert L. Selman
Elizabeth Léonie Simpson

Bill Underwood

*To my
mother and father*

Preface

In his Pulitzer Prize-winning book *The Best and the Brightest* (1969), David Halberstam quotes a passage written one month after the Bay of Pigs by Chester Bowles, Undersecretary of State with the then new Kennedy Administration; Bowles wrote in his private diary,

> The question which concerns me most about this new Administration is whether it lacks a genuine sense of conviction about what is right and what is wrong . . .
>
> Anyone in public life who has strong convictions about the rights and wrongs of public morality, both domestic and international, has a very great advantage in times of strain, since his instincts on what to do are clear and immediate. Lacking such a framework of moral conviction . . . he is forced to lean almost entirely upon his mental processes; he adds up the plusses and minuses of any question and comes up with a conclusion. Under normal conditions, when he is not tired or frustrated, this pragmatic approach should successfully bring him out on the right side of the question.
>
> What worries me are the conclusions that such an individual may reach when he is tired, angry, frustrated, or emotionally affected. The Cuban fiasco demonstrates how far astray a man as brilliant and well intentioned as Kennedy can go who lacks a basic moral reference point.

More than a decade since Bowles wrote those prophetic words, and after the moral agonies of the longest war in American history, the question of morality in public life is still very much with us. Consider the following statements:

> I carried out my orders. . . . Where would we have been if everyone had thought things out in those days?

> I was not the one to stand up in a meeting and say that this should be stopped . . . in all honesty, because of the group pressure that would ensue . . .

> I was there to follow orders, not to think.

The first statement was made by Adolf Eichmann; the last two are taken from the Proceedings of the U.S. Senate Committee on Presidential Campaign Activities and were made by Watergate defendants (Pfeiffer, *New York Times*, June 30, 1974).

At a time when national consciousness of the need for moral referents is perhaps greater than ever before, so is the need for understanding the origins and nature of moral reasoning and behavior. How does a person become moral? What is a conscience? What does it mean to be "a person of principle"? What factors influence the way people really behave in moral situations, not simply how they think? What can parents and society do to help children grow into morally mature adults? What do we now know about moral development and behavior, and what remains to be learned?

This book is an attempt to answer these questions. It brings together a distinguished group of scholars whose work, combined with the issues of the times, has helped to move morality to the forefront of social science. During the last decade, the surge of interest in moral development has been everywhere evident: at conventions, among graduate students, and in the research and theoretical literature. The present volume is a measure of that interest and an effort to stimulate still wider and deeper probing into this critical sphere of human functioning.

The appeal of the chapters is meant to be broad. They represent the viewpoints of cognitive-developmental psychology, psychoanalysis, psychobiology, social learning theory, social psychology, education, clinical psychology, political psychology, and social ecology. Morality emerges from this multiplicity of perspectives as one of the major interdisciplinary crossroads. It offers a broad integrative framework for dealing with a wide range of theoretical and empirical concerns in the study of both child development and adult behavior: violence, altruism, criminality, cooperation, honesty, child-rearing, self-control, situational variations in behavior, modeling, the influence of heredity versus experience, bystander response to emergencies, social and political attitudes, personality functioning, and the impact of culture on socialization, to name just a few. And while this volume as a whole testifies to the centrality of morality in human behavior, it also includes a psychiatrist's counterargument that morality is, and should be, dead.

The book is divided into four parts. Part 1 is an *Introduction*, intended to help the reader organize the wealth of theory and research in the field around eight basic questions confronting a science of morality. Part 2, *Theoretical Perspectives*, sets forth eight distinctively different theoretical views of how moral development occurs. Part 3 deals with *Research*; it critically examines findings in selected areas of moral functioning, pinpoints methodological problems, and suggests new methods for the study of morality. Part 4, *Morality and Social Issues*, looks at the moral dimensions of important social issues and attempts to derive intervention strategies from the accumulated theory and research about moral behavior.

As the book (four years in the making) finally sees the light of print, I owe many thanks: to the contributors, first of all, for the care with which they approached their subjects and for their receptiveness to editorial suggestions; to Gil Geis and Larry Kohlberg, the book's consulting editors, for wise counsel and for helping to review or edit manuscripts; to Ted Sarbin and Jim Mancuso for encouraging the idea of such an enterprise and to Ted for his suggestions about how to trim the book down to its present size; to Morris Eson for encouraging my interest as a graduate student in the study of moral development; to Debby Doty at Holt for supporting the book proposal and to Kathy Nevils for the huge amount of work a Project Editor does to turn a manuscript into a finished book; to Carol Herold and Linda Hammond for assistance with the typing; to Ted Huston both for helping me conceive this undertaking on a

Canadian vacation back in the summer of 1971 and for sharing his knowledge of the editor's role in such a project; to my sons Mark and Matthew—Mark for his patience with a father often anchored to his desk, and Matthew for not pulling apart my typewriter ribbon sooner than he did; and to my wife Judith, for her expert editorial suggestions on my own and other chapters, for assistance with the myriad details of getting a book off, and for countless discussions that have helped to stimulate and shape my thinking about morality.

Good reading.

Cortland, New York   *Thomas Lickona*
October 1975

Contents

The old-fashioned school regarded obedience to authority the one essential; the new ideal regards insight into the reasonableness of moral commands the chief end. It is said, with truth, that a habit of unreasoning obedience does not fit one for the exigencies of modern life, with its partisan appeals to the individual and its perpetual display of grounds and reasons, specious and otherwise, in the newspapers. The unreasoning obedience to a moral guide in school may become in after life unreasoning obedience to a demagogue or to a leader in crime.

William T. Harris
Editor's introduction to
The Moral Instruction of Children,
Washington, D.C., July 1892.

MORAL DEVELOPMENT AND BEHAVIOR

PART 1

INTRODUCTION

CHAPTER 1

Critical Issues in the Study of Moral Development and Behavior

Thomas Lickona

It is axiomatic that in any field of inquiry you need good questions to get good answers. This chapter is an effort to identify the questions that have guided the study of morality, to examine the contrasting answers offered by the contributors to this volume, and to provide a set of basic issues that can be used to organize the wealth of theory, research, and prescriptions for social intervention that follow.

What Is the Meaning of "Morality" and "Moral Development"?

A recent book on moral education (Sizer & Sizer, 1970) begins with an ancient question put to Socrates by Meno: "Can you tell me, Socrates, whether virtue is acquired by teaching or by practice; or if neither by teaching nor practice, then whether it comes to man by nature, or in what other way?" Socrates answered, "You must think I am very fortunate to know how virtue is acquired. The fact is that far from knowing whether it can be taught, I have no idea what virtue is" (p. 11).

Socrates' intention, we can assume,

was to force his questioner to confront an issue that remains the starting point for any consideration of morality: What is the good or the moral? All the essays in this volume touch on this question either explicitly or implicitly. How it is answered has profound implications for every other aspect of one's conception and investigation of moral thought and behavior.

One approach is to try to steer clear of philosophical entanglements and simply equate morality with social conditioning. Thus in Chapter 6 H. J. Eysenck defines conscience as a "conditioned reflex," an anxiety-based avoidance of acts that have been punished by society. Berkowitz (1964) gives a parallel definition of moral values as "evaluations of action believed by members of a given society to be 'right'" (p. 44). But to identify morality with conformity is to be forced to take the position that a loyal Nazi was behaving morally. Clearly, *moral judgments*—the revulsion against such historic barbarities as Nazism and against the willingness of experimental subjects to follow orders to inflict cruel punishment (Rosenhan, Moore, & Underwood, Chap. 13), as well as standards of justice that hold an Eichmann or a Calley accountable to laws of respect for human life and dignity regardless of the demands of their superiors—reveal a profound sense that what is "moral" is more than, different from, what is simply "social." Allport (1955) speaks of another inadequacy of equating morality with the residue of social training:

If conscience were merely a matter of self-punishment for breaking an established habit taught with authority, then we could not account for the fact that we often discard codes imposed by parents and by culture, and devise codes of our own. . . . It is the generic self-guidance that keeps conscience alive and applicable to new experience (p. 71).

William Sloan Coffin, Jr. (1973), writing in *The New York Times* about Watergate, makes fundamentally the same point in a different way. Coffin says that he wishes that he had taught Jeb Magruder, his former ethics student at Williams College and one of the convicted defendants in the Watergate scandal, that it is the great *individual* consciences of history—men like Jesus, Socrates, Thoreau, and Gandhi—rather than the mass mind, that "best represent the universal conscience of mankind." The lesson of Watergate, Coffin writes, is that to do evil one need not be an evil person, "only a nice guy who is not yet a good man" (p. 39).

The fact that mere compliance with social expectations does not define the upper reaches of human morality is also acknowledged by writers such as Aronfreed in Chapter 3 and Mischel and Mischel in Chapter 5. These authors have sought to integrate social-learning theory with what is known about the complexities of cognitive-moral development. Aronfreed, for example, distinguishes between "internalized control of conduct," which is nonevaluative, and control involving "moral decision-making." He welcomes Piaget and Kohlberg's moral judgment work as an "antidote to a behavioristic paradigm in which an act is regarded as

'moral' by virtue of its conformity to an external norm." Similarly, Mischel and Mischel take account of the individual's capacity to "construct" (generate) a great range of moral and immoral behaviors in a way that is active and personal rather than passive and stereotyped. In the new social-learning matrix of interacting social and cognitive factors, however, the meaning of "moral" remains obscure. Mischel and Mischel quote Pascal's comment that "Evil is never done so thoroughly or so well as when it is done with a good conscience"; and they observe that "history is replete with atrocities that were justified by invoking the highest principles and that were perpetrated upon victims who were equally convinced of their own moral principles." Confronted with these gloomy observations, the reader must surely ask, Why bother? If moral principles are so ambiguous or elastic as to be used for great evil as well as for good, then why study them, let alone work to stimulate their development?

A better, or at least a more basic, question would be, What is a moral principle? Lawrence Kohlberg is virtually the only contemporary psychologist to embrace philosophy as essential to defining what is moral as the first required step in the study of moral development. He argues that only the "epistemological blinders" of logical positivism and behaviorism (equating knowing with learning and learning with behavior) have kept psychologists from seeing that "the concept of morality is itself a philosophical (ethical) rather than a behavioral concept" (Kohlberg, 1971a, p. 152). To define "the distinctively moral," Kohlberg turns in Chapter 2 to the "moral categories analyzed by moral philosophy." This line of analysis leads him to the conclusion that "the most essential structure of morality" is the principle of justice, and that "the core of justice is the distribution of rights and duties regulated by concepts of equality and reciprocity." In a speech on educating for justice, Kohlberg (1970) distinguishes between a moral principle and a concrete rule of action:

Justice is not a rule or a set of rules; it is a moral principle. By a moral principle we mean a mode of choosing which is universal, a rule of choosing which we want all people to adopt always in all situations. We know it is all right to be dishonest and steal to save a life because it is just, because a man's right to life comes before another man's right to property. We know it is sometimes right to kill, because it is sometimes just. The Germans who tried to kill Hitler were doing right because respect for the equal values of lives demands that we kill someone murdering others in order to save their lives. There are exceptions to rules, then, but no exception to principles. A moral obligation is an obligation to respect the right or claim of another person. A moral principle is a principle for resolving competing claims, you versus me, you versus a third person. There is only one principled basis for resolving claims: justice or equality. Treat every man's claim impartially regardless of the man. A moral principle is not only a rule of action but a reason for action. As a reason for action, justice is called respect for persons.[1]

Morality based on the principle of justice, Kohlberg (1969a) points out, "is not fanatical; it does not sacrifice other persons to one's own beliefs and ideals" (p. 27). To act justly, with respect for persons, is to "act so as to treat each person as an end [as having unconditional value], rather than as a means" (Kohlberg, 1971a, p. 210). Kohlberg explains that the principle of justice as respect for persons is "higher than the law" because the claims of law and social contract may be deduced from it. Moral philosophy is thus used to define the endpoint of moral development as being justice, and to provide the moral concepts (rights, duties, welfare, liberty, rules, social order, etc.) to analyze observed developmental progress toward the highest form of justice (Kohlberg's Stage 6). To the extent that actual development moves through sequential "stages of principles" or modes of moral reasoning toward the postulated endpoint of fully universalized justice, the initial philosophical definition

of morality gains at least "partial validation" (Kohlberg, 1971a, p. 154).

At the less mature levels of moral reasoning, where justice or "being fair" is not yet fully abstracted or differentiated from particular social beliefs and practices and generalized to all persons impartially, the individual can stay within the boundaries of his low-level principles and get away with being hurtful or unjust to particular persons or groups. The principles of conventional moral reasoning, for example, which draws its morality from the values and rules of the group, have

a vast amount of "stretch" to absorb arbitrary but socially authoritative content. . . . A Stage 3 conservative racist may "stretch" what is "nice" or "loving" to absorb a great deal of racist behavior, as he may stretch "maintaining social order" or "giving people their just due" (Kohlberg, 1971a, p. 177).

This does not mean that "people can do anything in the name of moral principles and so morality doesn't matter," but that different levels of moral principles permit different kinds of actions. Richard Peters (1970), a philosopher, writes that moral principles "cannot prescribe precisely what we ought to do, but at least they rule out certain courses of action and sensitize us to features of a situation which are morally relevant" (pp. 34–35). Kohlberg's Stage 5, for example, would not rule out shocking the "learner" in Milgram's (1963) experiments (in order to keep the social contract with the experimenter) or preclude dropping the atomic bomb on Hiroshima and Nagasaki (to end the war sooner and "save a million lives"); Stage 6 would.

One may argue, as philosophers do, about the matter of which moral principles define the "ultimate good," or endpoint of development, but it seems much less arguable that some definition of morality is certainly needed to be able to define and study its development. The effort to define the moral, however, leads directly to a second major issue on which social scientists are sharply divided.

Are Some Moral Principles or Stages Higher or Better Than Others?

Kohlberg (1971a) has argued at length that it is logically possible to move from his description of what moral stage development *is* to a statement of what such development *ought to be*. By this logic, the chronologically later stages are higher or better, and their development should be fostered. Chapters 3, 5, and 19 address Kohlberg's is-to-ought assertion and flatly deny its validity. In Chapter 3 Aronfreed writes that "aside from the sheer cognitive power that is obviously required for a respondent's formulation of the higher stage, the reasons which are offered for such a system of classification do not go persuasively beyond a commitment to a philosophical position." Similarly, in Chapter 5 Mischel and Mischel approvingly cite philosopher Alston's argument (1971) that a given moral stage—even one which is logically dependent on an earlier stage as a prerequisite—is not necessarily morally superior to its predecessor.

Is the objection here specifically to the moral hierarchy that Kohlberg has formulated, or to a scientist's assertion of *any* moral hierarchy? The latter seems to be the case. In Chapter 19 Mancuso and Sarbin exhort their social science colleagues to

avoid the trap of believing that a psychologically later-developing form of behavior approaches an approximation of an ultimately good behavior. . . . While we might yearn to see a society of persons who understand rules within a morality of reciprocity, the fact that this kind of morality develops later in the course of psychological growth does not show that once we have achieved it, we are farther along the road to ultimate goodness. The prescription to achieve a morality or reciprocity has no more of an a priori obligation than does the prescription to obey authority.

In the same spirit, Mischel and Mischel (Chapter 5) caution that

sophisticated social science versions of stratification systems which categorize people in terms of their overall level of morality, unless carefully moderated, can lead to an elitism that is empirically unjustified as well as socially hazardous . . . perhaps the greatest challenge to social science will be to discover the optimal conditions that can help each person realize himself in the ways he construes as best within the great range of capacities open to him.

These lines of reasoning have much appeal both to ethical tolerance and to the strain of intellectual relativism that runs strong in American social science. But what logical problems are masked by that appeal? At the same time that Mischel and Mischel's essay rejects "moral stratification systems," it deplores the fact that people tend to be facile at using "a wide variety of self-deceptive mechanisms . . . to facilitate and excuse the most horrendous acts . . . and extraordinarily cruel aggressions." By what criteria are acts to be judged horrendous or cruel? If one does attempt to construct moral criteria that would identify horrendous acts as well as good ones, can "stratifications" or levels of morality be avoided? And if, within such a moral hierarchy, some actions are defined as evil or as less good or just than others, can one then urge social science to "help each person realize himself in the ways *he* construes as best within the great range of capacities open to him" (italics added)? Those capacities in many persons include a capability for inflicting suffering on others en route to their own "self-realization." An unqualified prescription for social science to help each person achieve his self-chosen end could be taken as reducing the scientist to a technological servant of any individual or society, however perverted its moral means or goals.

Mischel and Mischel, of course, could point out that for *all* persons to be able to attain their self-defined goals would automatically restrict the freedom of any one individual to coerce or injure others. To recognize this, however, is to recognize that a morality that respects the rights of others is superior to a morality that does not, and to concede logically that individuals' development of such a higher morality is a necessary condition for the kind of society whose members each have a fair chance at the pursuit of happiness or fulfillment. The failure of many persons to develop this level of moral regard for the rights of others—and the failure of society to demand it—has led to unchecked social evils (e.g., the poisoning of air and water and the production of unsafe products) of the sort that Geis and Monahan catalog in Chapter 20 in their attack on unfettered and unaccountable power.

The logical impossibility of taking a value-neutral approach to the study of morality is equally apparent in Chapter 19, in which Mancuso and Sarbin give their views on jurisprudence. While arguing that "the behavior scientist should avoid lending support to the ultimate validity of certain classes of ethical behaviors," they strongly urge jurisprudence to reject "outworn formist and mechanist paradigms" in favor of a "contextualist" approach. It is this last approach that will consider "the total ecology of rule-following conduct," including the lawmaker's efficacy in formulating and promulgating a law as well as the individual's understanding of the law in the context in which he acts. The authors attempt to resolve the contradiction between espousing relativism (no moral system is superior to another), on the one hand, and advocating a particular moral system (contextualism), on the other, by explaining that they are advocating "procedural contextualism" rather than "a guide to evaluating the moral behavior of those being studied." But is this distinction a workable one? How would a contextualist evaluate the moral behavior of a jurist who refused to consider the context of a crime in meting out "justice" to the criminal? And even if contextualism followed the unusual practice of urging its own adoption without criticizing the behavior of those who rejected it, what would be the rationale for making the case for contextualism in the first place—if not the belief that it represents a more reasonable

and just approach to crime and punishment than noncontextualist approaches?

This line of questioning plainly points to the conclusion that any form of social-moral advocacy or intervention on the part of social science requires a commitment to a moral hierarchy, the higher levels of which are superior in an objective or rational sense rather than in a purely subjective or arbitrary sense. One cannot urge a social-legal system to change so as to consider the full contextual range of factors that affect a human act, and simultaneously argue that one moral system is as good as another. One cannot demand equal treatment of those who kill by manufacturing dangerous aircraft and those who murder in the street, and say that all value systems are relative or arbitrary. One cannot urge television networks to present prosocial models rather than violent or prejudiced behavior unless there is some standard by which one kind of conduct is objectively more moral than the other. One cannot ask parents to rear their children in such a way as to foster altruism and compassion, and bystanders to intervene to help persons in distress, without some criteria for judging these moral tendencies to be better than cruelty or indifference. And clearly one cannot deplore a subject's submission to an experimenter's command to give painful shock to an innocent person unless one defines a morality of obedience as being inferior, in some nonarbitrary way, to a morality of respect for persons that is independent of social authority. Total relativity in the realm of moral judgment, either for an individual or a social science, logically leads to total neutrality in the realm of social action.

Granted that one cannot engage in social intervention without some criteria for distinguishing good from evil, can a scientist at least *study* moral development from a value-neutral standpoint? Clearly, no. The scientist who says that "morality" is what the rat does when it learns the "right" way to run a maze, and the scientist who says that "moral" is whatever the society chooses it to be, are both stating philosophical, not empirical, definitions of morality—definitions which inevitably affect how one studies and defines moral development. It is not epistemologically neutral, as Kohlberg (1971a) cogently points out, to say that all values are relative to culture. Nor is it scientifically impartial, since it prejudges the facts by assuming that there are *no* culturally universal criteria that can be used in judging the maturity of individual and cultural variations in morality. Neither, of course, is Kohlberg's theory philosophically neutral; it is highly doubtful that Kohlberg would have "discovered" his six stages of moral reasoning if he had not begun with the assumption that universal criteria for judging the moral do exist and that development can be defined as successively better approximations of a universal principle such as treating all persons justly. Obviously, the proof of the philosophical pudding must be in the eating—in the empirical demonstration that people do in fact develop toward the ideal form of the good as the theory has philosophically defined it. Kohlberg's theory would be in deep trouble, for example, if people were found to "progress" developmentally from a belief that right means impartially considering every man's claim to a conviction that right means whatever is best for me. The difference between philosophy and science is that the latter must ground its ideas in what the data show.

Deciding that moral philosophizing is indispensable and inevitable both in moral research and social intervention does not, however, make matters simpler in either domain. In Chapter 18, for example, Lockwood points out just how complex is the application of moral principles to the concrete solution of a social problem such as bussing; the principle does not prescribe what must be done, but only what must be considered. Moreover, a commitment to defining philosophical moral criteria prior to investigation of moral development does not tell the researcher *what* principles or criteria to use to guide his inquiry, or guarantee that his definition of the moral will be psychologically complete. I once attended a weeklong workshop, conducted by Kohlberg and his colleagues (Kohlberg et al., 1972). It touched on many aspects of his theory and research and included a session dealing with possible points of contact between Erikson and Kohlberg. A female associate of the latter said that from the perspective of women, Kohlberg's moral Stages 5 and 6 presently center on the issues of justice, equality, and rights—"the old rationalist, enlightenment values"— rather than on the issues of responsibility and obligation. The latter, she suggested, are likely to be more central values in the lives of women and could modify the definition of the moral stages and, by implication, the scoring of women's protocols if such issues were given greater consideration. Simpson (1974), in a critique of Kohlberg's work titled "Moral Development Research: A Case Study of Scientific Cultural Bias," argues that he draws his moral principles solely from Western philosophers (Kant, Mill, Ross, Rawls, Dewey) and that "an adequate explanation of the concept of morality throughout humanity implies the examination of its meaning in the *non*-Western world as well" (p. 84).

Dissatisfaction with how Kohlberg defines the highest stages of morality is presumably also part of the reason why in Chapter 8 psychiatrist Gilligan claims that there is a more mature stage of personal functioning "beyond morality," namely, a "love ethic" through which mutual need satisfaction arises out of psychological understanding of self and others rather than interpersonal sacrifice out of "moral obligation." Kohlberg might argue that Gilligan's "love" is really another name for justice, which also seeks to resolve competing claims (conflicting needs) in a way that respects the legitimate desires of all parties. In defining a love-ethic stage as different from a moral stage of development, Gilligan faces his own problems—explaining, for example, the meaning of Camus' well-known statement in the face of the French-Algerian war, "I should like to be able to love my country and still love justice." The idea that one can love a moral principle as well as individual people—or love people by living out a moral principle—is a challenge to any theory that would separate love and morality. Martin Luther King, Jr., to take another example, preached both universal love and universal justice. King fused these two principles into the belief that in order to respect a person and give him his due as a human being, you had to love him, even if he did you violence.

King's death at the hands of violence returns us to the heart of the issue: A psychology of moral development must be able to hierarchically order the morality of a martyr for justice and the morality of his assassin. To be able to construct a moral hierarchy is required for any kind of social intervention, which is ethically justifiable only on the grounds that the resulting social change moves people toward a rationally higher level of moral functioning. To delimit explicit moral criteria is also necessary both to conceive and to study moral development, since development, whether psychological or biological, is by definition movement *toward* something, toward some endpoint which represents a demonstrably higher, more integrated form of functioning.

What, if Anything, Is Universal in Moral Development and What Is Relative to the Culture or the Person?

No issue has stirred more heated debate in the ranks of social scientists engaged in the study of values than Kohlberg's statement that all cultures and subcultures employ the same basic moral concepts (e.g., love, respect, liberty, authority) and that all in-

dividuals, regardless of culture, go through the same stages of reasoning about these concepts. This progression is, furthermore, posited to be in the same order—varying only in how quickly and how far people move through the stage sequence. In defense of this controversial position, Kohlberg has written at length about the relevant philosophical issues (see especially his paper "From Is to Ought," 1971a), analyzing the sources of social scientists' resistance to a theory of moral universals; he has also marshaled empirical evidence from six different cultures, both Eastern and Western, which he believes supports his cross-cultural claims (1969b). Like Piaget's postulation of invariant logical stages (Piaget & Inhelder, 1969), Kohlberg's assertion of universal moral stages rests squarely on a critical theoretical construct: the distinction between *structure*, held to be universal and to follow the laws of development, and *content*, held to vary with specific patterns of experience and to follow the laws of learning (Kohlberg, 1969b). Content tells us *what* a person believes, which is obviously dependent upon culturally variable experiences, whereas structure tells us how a person *thinks about* the content of his beliefs, which reasoning, so the theory goes, is universal.

A study by Turiel (1974) sheds light on the structure–content distinction and suggests why it may be a necessary construct in the study of moral growth. To a sample of boys and girls from the sixth, ninth, and twelfth grades, Turiel administered two different measures of moral thought: (1) a moral knowledge test, comprised of items such as those previously used by Hartshorne and May (1928) describing various transgressions and requiring the subject to rate the degree of wrongness of an act on a five-point scale; and (2) a moral judgment interview requiring, in standard Kohlberg fashion, that the subject solve moral dilemmas and explain his or her reasoning. The two measures yielded opposite outcomes: Whereas stage of moral reasoning increased with age, as would be expected, scores on the moral knowledge test significantly *decreased* with age. Turiel (1974) interpreted the latter finding as indicating that as the structure of the child's moral thinking develops through an age-related stage progression, he changes his interpretation of the *content* of his social environment, such as social definitions of the rightness or wrongness of particular acts. Kohlberg (1964) points out that content-based measures in the behavioral realm (e.g., resistance to temptation), like the content-oriented moral knowledge tests used in Turiel's study, do not produce clear or consistent developmental increases. And yet adolescents and adults are obviously morally different from young children. Hence the need for a structural approach, using basic philosophical moral categories to define universal trends in moral development, just as Piaget used basic philosophical categories of knowing—for example, space, time, causality, and number—to analyze universal trends in cognitive development.

The impact of structuralism on the study of both moral and cognitive growth has been dramatic. In addition to generating an impressive number of empirical efforts within its own tradition (e.g., Kohlberg, Chap. 2), Kohlberg's theory of moral stages has in some way been taken into account by almost all other theories of moral development, as this volume attests. A cross-cultural theory such as Garbarino and Bronfenbrenner's in Chapter 4, for example, represents a change from an entirely cultural-relative typology (Bronfenbrenner, 1962a) to a theoretical synthesis that includes a culturally invariant system of moral levels as well as concepts for incorporating variability in cultural content.

Though the influence of structuralism is indisputable, the debate about its claims rages on. The argument generally centers on one or more of four issues: (1) empirical evidence for the universal existence and invariant order of the moral stages; (2) the impact of content (culture) on moral func-

tioning apart from stage structure; (3) the interactions between content and structure, and (4) the problem of deciding just what is structure and what is content in a person's moral thinking.

The cross-cultural evidence for Kohlberg's universal stage sequence has been challenged by Simpson (1974) on a number of points: (1) insufficiency in scope (Kohlberg, 1969b, has published data on development in Taiwan, Great Britain, Mexico, Yucatan, Turkey, and the United States, and has collected unpublished data on several other countries); (2) faulty data gathering with moral dilemma and verbal interview techniques that demand analytical modes of thought and language not valued by or developed in many cultures; (3) use of value categories such as "property rights" and "value of life" for scoring protocols that may not reflect the categories of the culture under study; and (4) inability of the theory to account for findings obtained, such as regression to earlier stages or the absence of any postconventional reasoning in some groups. While Kohlberg would have to concede the difficulty of adapting an assessment device to varied cultures so as to eliminate all performance factors but level of structural moral thought, he could raise at least two questions in his own defense: (1) Can one logically test the universality of moral stages, defined in terms of value categories, without using the same value categories from one culture to another? (2) Can one logically require that all groups everywhere must demonstrate all levels in the moral hierarchy in order to establish its universality, especially in view of the fact that the theory does not expect the higher stages to occur under sociocultural conditions that are deficient in role-taking opportunities (Kohlberg, Chap. 2)? If one were to require that every culture manifest the highest levels in order to validate a theory of universal stages, then one would also have to require that the highest levels be reached in every subculture, and—to carry the argument to the extreme—in every individual. Clearly this is not a workable test of the validity of a high-level moral stage, any more than it would be a workable test of the validity of a high-level logical stage such as Piaget's formal operations. Cultural differences in level of attainment should not rule a stage theory out of court any more than differences among individuals should.

The second issue in the structure–content argument pertains to the importance of moral content in its own right in understanding people's moral feelings and behavior. British psychologist Derek Wright (1971) suggests that "it is not unreasonable to suppose that *why* a person thinks an action is wrong is much less important than *that* he thinks it wrong" (p. 173). Wright points out that moral ideology—defined as the "total complex of a person's beliefs about what is right or wrong"—"can command much proselytizing zeal and vociferous defence" (p. 175). Moral anger also underlines the importance and the variability of belief-system content; "people specialize in the kinds of behavior that spark off their fiercest indignation" (p. 195). Most people, for example, may be at Kohlberg's conventional structural level, but not all would share the intense feeling of one of Wright's subjects who said, "I think of sexual intercourse before marriage as disgusting and think that people should treat intercourse after marriage with respect instead of wasting their whole lives by one cheap act" (p. 186). The affective loading of the content of an individual's moral belief system can have a strong influence on how he responds to the behavior of others; it therefore needs to be considered in addition to how the person reasons about the content of his beliefs.

Positive values can have an equally powerful effect on the style and purpose of moral life. In the wake of popular structural accounts of moral development, scales of values such as Allport and Vernon's (Allport, Vernon, & Lindzey, 1960) now receive little attention, despite the fact

that they have been shown to be related to basic life patterns. Similarly, Morris (1956) found "five primary values"[2] espoused to markedly different degrees by individuals depending upon the subjects' culture, sex, and period of life.

Alston (1971) argues that in dismissing time-honored character traits as a content-laden "bag of virtues," Kohlberg has thrown out a very necessary moral concept, namely, *habit*. Habits—regularities in the way people behave or respond to situations, described by terms such as cooperative, sociable, domineering, conscientious, sympathetic, and polite—are in Alston's view necessary to describe moral personality completely, and are actually parallel in concept to the "habits of mind" represented by Kohlberg's stages of moral reasoning. "Not all of what we need to know about a person to fully understand his moral character is culturally invariant," Alston (1971) asserts; "morality is content as well as form, and we need to know both" (p. 283).

The force of culture or content in governing moral life is obvious from Gilligan's sharply drawn picture of shame cultures and guilt cultures in Chapter 8. He conceives of these two differently oriented moralities as forming developmentally distinct levels; but within these levels there is vast variation. Not every shame-oriented culture displays the extreme fear of ridicule and savage aggression of the Kwakiutl Indians, and few guilt-oriented societies are characterized by the total self-renunciation and pacifism of the Hutterites. Such differences in content-defined moral value dispositions color virtually every aspect of the human relationships and goal-oriented activity of these cultures, yet they pass completely through the structural sieve.

So do salient differences between individuals. Carini (1968) has argued that the Piagetian tradition of studying the changing structure of knowledge has provided us with an extremely valuable theory of epistemological development but may have actually worked against the formulation of an adequate theory of psychological development. To understand total human development, she writes, psychology must look closely and longitudinally at the tone and texture of individual lives; this, she feels, is necessary in order to document "the themes and expressions that identify the person as an historical being, one continuous with himself in his origins, and yet transformed through the unique set of occurrences that constitute his life space" (Carini, 1968, p. 58). As an example of the need for this kind of approach in the moral realm (as opposed to a purely structural perspective), consider the possibility that Martin Luther King, Jr.—frequently cited by Kohlberg as a great moral leader exemplifying Stage 6 justice—and a recluse moral philosopher would be indistinguishable on Kohlberg's moral reasoning scale. And yet there is a dramatic difference between their lives and their impact on the moral lives of others. Structuralists, by placing moral stage in the broader context of ego development (Kohlberg, Chap. 2), seem to be recognizing that the content of a person's beliefs and life experience is indispensible to constructing a profile of the total moral personality.

A final point about the independent effect of content on moral functioning is that marked shifts in moral attitudes or behavior may occur without any corresponding structural change. Observation suggests that many American youths moved from the dominant middle-class culture to the hippie counterculture without actually leaving behind conformist moral reasoning. Similarly, society or government may reverse position on a major social policy for reasons (e.g., self-interest) that are structurally equivalent to those behind the original policy, as may well have been the case in the American abandonment of the Vietnam war. Of course, one can argue that such changes or differences in "moral content," whether in group or individual behavior, are not really *moral* changes,

since one kind of content cannot be defined as better than another on a hierarchical moral scale. Yet content of the sort discussed has an undeniably important role in the total scheme of human functioning and therefore deserves the attention of those who would study moral development and behavior.

Examination of the *interaction* between content and structure in moral functioning throws both into greater relief and offers a way of conceptually integrating these two distinct kinds of influences. Usually, the structure of thought is conceived as the "filter" that determines the meaning and impact of content. In Chapter 3 Aronfreed asserts that "cognitive change will be a critical determinant of how the child receives his social experience." Similarly, Kohlberg's theory holds that the individual's susceptibility to "content influences" varies with his developmental stage, susceptibility being greatest at the conventional level where the person's "principles" lead him to look to the group for moral definition of the situation. It is hardly surprising, from this perspective, that situations have the "enormous impact" that has been demonstrated again and again in the research literature and in the present volume (see Aronfreed, Chap. 3; Mischel & Mischel, Chap. 5; Burton, Chap. 10; Rosenhan, Moore, & Underwood, Chap. 13; Huston & Korte, Chap. 15), since most people function at a conventional level of moral reasoning that is by definition situationally influenced (Kohlberg & Turiel, 1971). The higher structural stages are by no means immune to the influence of content, however, especially when that influence has deep cultural roots. Kohlberg (1971a) points out that "Socrates was more accepting of slavery than was Lincoln, who was more accepting of it than King" (p. 178). A more contemporary example of how content can retard horizontal generalization of a moral stage is found in the complaint of the wife who charges that her husband, comfortable with culture-supported role discrepancies, is a liberal about everything but relations between the sexes.

Content may also overwhelm structure. The cross-cultural research on Piaget's moral judgment dimension of immanent justice, such as that cited by Lickona in Chapter 12, shows that a culture's adult belief system can bring about an apparent return to an earlier level of childish judgment. This is similar to what happens when adult social influence causes children to abandon at least temporarily a developmentally more advanced, intention-centered standard of moral responsibility in favor of a standard that focuses on material consequences (Bandura & McDonald, 1963). These changes parallel culturally induced "reversals" in the logical realm, such as the conversion among 11- and 12-year-old boys in the preliterate Atayal culture from a subjective concept of the dream as a thought, to the culture's belief that dreams are real experiences in which ghosts take the soul from the body to far places (Kohlberg, 1969b). Regardless of whether such changes represent genuine structural regression or a cultural "overlay" that obscures still-present structure, it is clear that in these cases content determines functioning.

Probably much more common than "regression" are instances in which the content of experience causes structural arrest. Simpson (1974) speculates that it may be cultural beliefs and values "not at all likely to be counteracted by the developmental process" that cause a ghetto child or Turnbull's primitive mountain people (1972) to remain at preconventional moral levels. The same kind of content-determined arrest, Simpson suggests, may occur in the moral development of women. They are more likely than men to remain at the conventional moral level perhaps because of cultural conditioning: The culture sends them the strong and unremitting message that a woman's role is to be nice and meet the expectations of others rather than to deal with the larger moral issues, such as justice and equality in the social realm. Similarly, one could argue that women who shed the shackles of conventional thought have heard and heeded the liberating message (content) that they are as good as any man. Cognitive-developmental accounts of moral development, in seeking to explain individual and group differences in moral level attained, have characteristically focused on differences in opportunities for involvement in "structural" processes such as role taking and participation in social institutions. While the evidence for the impact of these process factors is convincing (Kohlberg, Chap. 2, 1969b; Saltzstein, Chap. 14), social content may deserve more of the credit and more of the blame for rate of moral development than has been supposed.

Content also affects *what* structures are operationalized in behavior as well as how. As Wright (1971) points out, "though the same basic moral principles can be found in all the great ethical systems, opinions will always vary within a society as to the emphasis that should be given to different principles and the ways they should be applied" (p. 175). Along the same lines, Simpson (1974) maintains that there are great differences across class and culture in how abstract concepts like "justice" and "equality" are put into practice. "Working class Americans define equality as economic but not social, while upper middle-class Americans tend to conceptualize it as social, not economic" (Lipset, 1959). *Enacted* meanings of a moral principle, Simpson concludes, may be far more variable and culture-determined than their *expressed* meanings.

Exactly what is structure and what is content? is a reasonable question at this point and one which poses a continuing challenge to a structural analysis of morality. The problem is that one man's structure is another man's content. Mischel and Mischel (Chap. 5), for example, suggest that a large part of what cognitive-developmentalists consider structural changes in moral reasoning may instead be a shift to a different "style" of verbal justification for which the individual expects to be reinforced by his new social reference group. Pressing the same point, Simpson (1974) maintains that moral autonomy can be "the result of group values and training" and that principled moral reasoners "can probably even identify the groups in which they learned to reason abstractly about morality and to employ the kind of *terminology* which admits them to elevated ethical status" on Kohlberg's scale (p. 94, italics added).

For more than a decade, of course, Kohlberg (Chap. 2, 1964, 1969b) and his colleagues (e.g., Turiel, 1969) have advanced evidence which they believe shows that moral reasoning "reflects the internal patterning of social experience" rather than simply "verbal learning" (Kohlberg, 1964, p. 404). Nonstructuralists who have trouble distinguishing between the products of "internal patterning" and "verbal learning" can take solace from the fact that structuralists wrestle with the same problem. Kohlberg's new scoring system (Chap. 2) is an effort to do a better job of separating structure from content so that the theoretically expected invariant stage sequence can be observed. Achieving a sharper differentiation between the two is hardly a matter of hair splitting; based on the old aspect scoring system, which Kohlberg says confused the Stage 3 "Archie Bunker law-and-order" content with the Stage 4 social system–structural perspective, Holstein (1973) found developmental irregularities such as a reversal in some subjects from Stage 4 to Stage 3 and used these results to challenge the universality of Kohlberg's moral stage sequence. Critics of Kohlberg argue that he cannot keep changing the scoring system, while Kohlberg (Chap. 2) defends this kind of methodological refinement as built into the process of validating a structural developmental theory. The debate goes on.[3]

Regardless of how the issues defining the structure-versus-content argument are resolved, they provide theorists and researchers with a useful source of questions about moral development. Fundamentally, the effort to unravel the influences of structure and content in moral development, to identify what is universal and what is not, is an attempt to define and explain both constancies and variability in morality. This same search for order in the data and understanding of the "disorder" or variability appears in the form of another enduring issue: the question of consistency within and across the major domains of moral functioning—namely, thought, emotion, and behavior.

Are People Consistent in Their Moral Judgments, Feelings, and Behavior? Is Morality General or Situation-Specific?

James Gustafson (1970) in his essay "Education for Moral Responsibility" writes that " 'character' marks 'the sort of man' one is, the persistency of identity that makes us expect some consistency in a person's moral judgments, attitudes, and actions"; he then asks what kinds of educational experiences might foster "these more persistent characteristics of moral selfhood."[4] Gustafson, like the man on the street, believes that most people despite some variability are reasonably predictable in their moral lives, that they have a core of consistency that makes it possible both to speak about something like "character" and to think about how to aid in its development.

How does the concept of character or moral consistency fare in the face of the accumulated data of nearly a half-century's research on moral judgment, conduct, and feelings? Not very well, according to one line of reasoning and research that has its roots in Hartshorne and May's monumental character education inquiry (1928). These researchers carefully studied the behavior of 11,000 children who were given opportunities to lie, cheat, or steal in activities as varied as classroom work, home duties, party games, athletic contests. Although subsequent analyses of Hartshorne and May's results have found evidence of a modest general factor in moral conduct (see Burton, Chap. 10), the inconsistency of children was striking; it was impossible to predict, for example, whether a child who cheated on an arithmetic test would also cheat on a spelling test. A huge and ever-expanding body of research, much of it reviewed in these pages, has replicated Hartshorne and May's basic finding: Variations in the situation produce variations in moral behavior.

Findings of specificity rather than generality of morality have not been limited to the behavioral realm. Confronting the fact that their subjects' scores on tests of moral knowledge and opinion varied widely depending on whether the test was taken at a children's club, at home, in the classroom, or in Sunday school, Hartshorne May, and Shuttleworth (1930) concluded that "a child does not have a uniform generalized code of morals but varies his opinions to suit the situation in which he finds himself" (pp. 107–108). Even research on Piagetian moral judgments (Lickona, Chap. 12), emphasizing moral understanding rather than simple knowledge of cultural definitions of right and wrong, has failed to reveal anything like a consistent mode of moral thought stable across different content areas. Finally, in the affective realm, specificity also appears to be the rule. Typical is Allinsmith's conclusion (1960), based on his study of boys' completions of stories depicting immoral actions, that it is necessary to speak of many different situation-specific "guilts," rather than of "guilt" as a consistent response of the individual's conscience to varied transgressions.

Moreover, the preceding evidence of specificity pertains to moral functioning *within* a particular area such as behavior, judgment, or affect, where consistency should be easier to find than it would be *across* the three different dimensions of morality. The search for "dynamic consistency" (M. L. Hoffman, 1963a)—the tendency for a person who holds a particular moral standard to act according to it and to feel guilty when he does not—has produced even more meager results, as noted by Mischel and Mischel (Chap. 5) and Burton (Chap. 10). Social-learning theorists Mischel and Mischel have found all of this variability not in the least surprising; they state:

Since most social behaviors lead to positive consequences in some situations but not in other contexts, highly discriminative specific expectancies tend to be developed, and the relatively low correlations typically found among a person's response patterns across situations become understandable. . . . Rather than acquiring a homogeneous conscience, people develop subtler discriminations that depend on many moderating variables . . . and encompass diverse components [including] moral judgments, voluntary delay-of-reward, resistance-to-temptation, self-reactions following transgression, self-evaluative and self-reinforcing patterns, and many other syndromes, each of which includes further rather discrete subprocesses that tend to be only modestly and complexly interrelated, and that may be idiosyncratically organized within each individual.

This conception of moral development calls to mind Roger Brown's analysis (1965) that moralization involves at least four different kinds of learning—cognitive learning of moral concepts, reinforcement-shaped response acquisition, imitation, and classical conditioning—which are differentially important for the different dimensions of morality; hence unevenness in moral functioning should be expected. In Chapter 10 Burton concludes from his review of the literature on honesty and dishonesty that the search for generality should be redefined more realistically as an effort to identify stable functional relations between antecedent and consequent variables in moral behavior.

In spite of this compelling array of argument and evidence, the notion of generality in morality is alive and well, evidenced by the fact that in this volume most theoretical accounts of moral functioning use some kind of typology or system of developmental levels, which are essentially consistency constructs. To talk about a stage or level is to imply a "structural whole" (Kohlberg, 1969b), or underlying organization that causes the individual to respond in a similar way to different tasks or situations. Mischel and Mischel (Chap. 5) advance the interesting hypothesis that the insistence on broad consistency reflects a human need for a certain kind of self-image and a capacity for using cognitive processes such as selective perception and elimination of discrepancy to preserve such an image. Is consistency no more than a self-serving illusion? What points have been raised in defense of its viability and necessity as a construct in moral theory?

1. In the first place, there are the data. Hartshorne, May, and Shuttleworth, for example, because they found a correlation among their behavioral tests no matter how they varied their technique, were "quite ready to recognize the existence of some common factors which tend to make individuals differ from one another on any test or group of tests" (1930, p. 385).

2. Stage or level theories are able to account for the variability in behavior that exists in terms of "stage mix" (Turiel, 1969). In moral reasoning development, for example, a common profile is dominance of one stage of thinking, with lower percentages of reasoning at stages above and below (Kohlberg, 1971a; Rest, Chap. 11). Variation in functioning would therefore be expected, since the person has several developmental levels available from which to draw.

3. Empirical consistency both within and across the three dimensions appears to be a function of the methodology used to measure the dimensions in question. When, for example, Kohlberg's moral dilemmas are used rather than Piaget's stories, greater stage unity is found (Kohlberg, 1969b). When M. L. Hoffman (1970a) eliminated fear-of-detection responses to projective stories (included by Allinsmith,

1960, in his category of "guilt reactions") and scored as "guilt" only responses that involved an internalized moral standard, he found "highly significant and positive" relations for boys on three different guilt indices. When Burton (1963) eliminated from Hartshorne and May's results data from tests which proved to be unreliable, a picture of greater consistency emerged. When moral reasoning à la Kohlberg, rather than simple agreement with value statements, is correlated with position on a public policy issue, prediction improves considerably (Lockwood, Chap. 18). And according to Rest's report in Chapter 11, when objective versions of Kohlberg's moral judgment assessment are used as an alternative to interview methods, the strength of correlation with independent measures of moral comprehension and social-political attitudes varies as a function of whether rating, ranking, or stage-typing indices of moral judgment are employed.

An example of the importance of operational definition in assessing cross-dimensional consistency is the finding that prediction from moral judgment to behavior improves substantially when a structural stage diagnosis of judgment is used rather than a content-based Hartshorne and May type of moral knowledge measure. Kohlberg and his colleagues (Huston & Korte, Chap. 15; Kohlberg, 1969b; Lockwood, Chap. 18) have found theoretically consistent results between position on the moral stage scale and a variety of behaviors including honesty, civil disobedience, refusal to inflict pain on another, and bystander intervention, although theoretically unexpected findings have turned up in other studies (Burton, Chap. 10). In assessing moral consistency, then, methodology matters.

4. Consistency must be defined in theoretical rather than in purely behavioral terms—which is to say that it must be defined from the subject's point of view, and that the psychologist therefore needs a conception of the subject's point of view. The child who cheats on one occasion be-

cause he thinks he can get away with it but is "honest" at another time because the risk of cheating is too great, is being perfectly consistent with his preconventional moral principles. So is the Stage 3 individual who is honest when cheating would incur social shame but dishonest when other nice people are cheating (Kohlberg, 1969a). In fact, to be consistent with Stage 3 or 4 conventional moral principles, it is *necessary* to be "inconsistent"—to vary one's behavior to conform to the changing situational definition of the right thing to do. At Stage 5, prediction of behavioral choice in a resistance-to-temptation situation is easier, since cheating is difficult to reconcile with postconventional considerations of honoring a social contract to be honest and maintaining equality with other test-takers. In other situations, however, the choice for a Stage 5 person is less clear-cut—as when two principled values such as social contract and respect for the rights of others are in conflict. To walk out on the Milgram experiment, for example, indicates respect for the rights of the person being shocked but severing of participation according to instructions in the social contract with the experimenter. As Kohlberg (1969b, 1971) has pointed out, moral judgment is a better predictor of behavioral decision when it defines concrete rights and duties in a socially unambiguous situation. At Stage 6, where definition of moral obligation is clearest, prediction is best. However, as Richard Peters (1970) observes, sensitivity to the aspects of a situation that are made morally relevant by a principle "does not preclude adaptability due to differences in situations, especially if there is more than one principle which makes different factors in a situation morally important" (p. 36).

What is clear is that consistency of moral action must be defined psychologically in terms of the person's rationale for his behavior and cannot validly be equated with behavioral predictability, although much research has made this equation. A person may behave consistently with his principles even if we cannot predict his course of action and even if his moral choice varies from one situation to another. Such a redefinition of consistency has obvious implications for research on this issue; it suggests that data on behavior have little moral meaning without some assessment of its cognitive-motivational basis.

5. Clear continuities in moral behavior are more likely to emerge from a longer developmental look at the course of people's lives than from one-situation experiments. Longitudinal studies of aging (Palmore, 1970), for example, have revealed markedly fewer psychological and social changes than had been indicated by earlier cross-sectional studies. Nothing like Kohlberg's seventeen-year study (Chap. 2, 1969b) of the growth of moral reasoning in a sample of boys has ever been attempted in the realm of moral behavior. If such an investigation were undertaken, would distinctive behavior patterns (e.g., looking out only for one's own interest, seeking social approval, enforcing rules on others, placing fairness above other considerations) emerge as landmark achievements, each corresponding to the attainment of a different developmental stage of reasoning? As children grow in capacity for abstraction and generalization across diverse situations, will they manifest greater behavioral consistency and increasing integration of behavior with other aspects of morality? M. L. Hoffman (1963a) and Burton (Chap. 10) find some evidence for such a developmental trend from existing cross-sectional research, and Hartshorne and May recognized that even at younger age levels there were "integrated" (behaviorally consistent) children as well as "non-integrated" (situationally more variable) children. Finally, at the postconventional moral level, which only 25 percent of American adults now achieve (Kohlberg & Turiel, 1971), would the study of broad life patterns reveal moral consistency of the kind that appears to characterize moral leaders like King and Gandhi, and modern-

day Good Samaritans (Huston & Korte, Chap. 15)?

Naturalistic developmental research may contain some surprises regarding the consistency issue. It may be—to use Rosenhan, Moore, and Underwood's metaphor in Chapter 13—that when the winds of situational pressure are blowing strong we are not the masters of our moral ships as we think. But it could also be that situationally induced variations in behavior are only momentary departures from a course of moral conduct which the person charts and holds to over the long run, when the moral seas are calm. Longitudinal study may also reveal that some persons are able to control situations in a way that supports their own best moral selves, that makes it "easier to be good." Other persons, however, may exercise little control over or input into the situations that impinge on them on a day-to-day basis, thereby heightening their susceptibility to influence by external forces. In any case, the natural environment, whether internally or externally controlled, is probably much more stable than the great diversity of experimental situations whose powerful effects have furnished the basis for conclusions about the variability of moral behavior. Of course, even if greater generality is the phenomenon under natural conditions, it remains disturbing that changes in the situational context can radically alter moral response.

In attempting to illuminate the nature of moral behavior, different theories have begun with different kinds of questions. Social-learning theory and situation-centered social psychology have tended to ask what causes discriminativeness or variability in morality. By contrast, developmental theories have asked how we can account for the wholeness of human functioning. Starting with different questions, the different approaches arrive, not surprisingly, at different emphases regarding the generality–specificity issue. But the one approach needs the other: However valid a concept of stages or generality, it must be

sensitive to the great many factors other than an individual's moral philosophy which influence and cause variations in moral behavior. Whether for reasons of egoistic motives, anxiety, behavioral incompetence, or simply a failure of will, people often do not live up to their principles. In one study of honesty (Kohlberg, 1969b), for example, 20 percent of the "principled" subjects cheated, and in Milgram's study (1963) 2 of the 6 subjects who scored at Stage 6 nevertheless obeyed to the last, giving the highest intensity of electrical shock possible.[5] "To bring conduct under the dominion of morality," Roger Brown (1965) has written, "is a great task; it is the struggle for character" (p. 414).

What Is the Role of Affect in Moral Functioning and Development?

Emotion is often considered in terms of its effect on situational moral behavior rather than in terms of its role in development. When viewed situationally, emotion is generally seen as an irrational force that causes people to be less than their best moral selves. William Sloan Coffin, Jr. (1973), for example, reflecting on the men involved in Watergate, observed that "the rational mind is no match for an irrational will that needs to place popularity and power above truth." From a Piagetian viewpoint, too, strong emotion can be disruptive, interfering with operational thinking by causing the person to "center" on one aspect of a situation, frequently his own viewpoint, to the exclusion of other relevant considerations and points of view. The emphasis on the negative effects of emotion, however, has more recently been balanced by research showing, for example, that "the warm glow of success" or "the reparative flush of failure" can lead to an increase in prosocial behaviors such as helping or sharing (Rosenhan, Moore, & Underwood, Chap. 13). Richard Peters

(1970) has written positively of the "rational passions," arguing that "the usual contrast between reason and feeling is misconceived":

Strength of character is so often represented in negative terms as saying no to temptation, as standing firm, as being impervious to social pressure. . . . Rational people are able to do this only if they are passionately devoted to fairness, freedom, and the pursuit of truth and if they have a genuine respect for others and are intensely concerned if they suffer.[6]

Strong emotion, then, as "the passionate side of the life of reason," can be a force for stability and high moral conduct rather than an agent of moral downfall.

The affect of guilt provides another illustration of the ambivalence with which emotion has been regarded by the psychology of morality. Gilligan (Chap. 8) reflects the psychoanalytic tradition of viewing guilt as a necessary but immature and ultimately debilitating influence in moral functioning. Leading to rigidity and compulsiveness, guilt lacks the spontaneity and generosity of love, and ends up denying the legitimate needs of the self. Alston (1971), by contrast, sees "the anticipation of guilt—and the desire to avoid it"—as playing "a major and perhaps essential role in the transition from thought to action" (p. 280). Aronfreed (Chap. 3) agrees, warning that psychology is "in danger of overlooking the affective learning that is required to translate knowledge into social behavior." Allport (1955) maintains that there is a constructive guilt which motivates renewed effort to live up to one's moral ideals:

Whenever I make a self-referred value judgment—as if to say, "This is in keeping with my self-image, that is not"—then I feel a sense of obligation that has no trace of fear in it. . . . Guilt is a sense of violated value, a disgust at falling short of one's ideal self-image (pp. 72, 74).

To have moral integrity in Allport's terms is to have an emotionally compelling sense of oneself; it is respect for oneself that

precludes certain actions. Thomas More, in *A Man for All Seasons*, tries to convey this first to his friend the Duke of Norfolk, and then to his daughter Meg, both of whom implore him to save his life and swear to the oath declaring Henry VIII the head of the Church in England (Bolt, 1960).

(*To Norfolk*) I will not give in because I oppose it—*I* do—not my pride, not my spleen, nor any other of my appetites but *I* do—*I*! (p. 123)

(*To his daughter*) When a man takes an oath, Meg, he's holding his own self in his own hands. Like water. And if he opens his fingers *then*—he needn't hope to find himself again (p. 140).

This sense of self, to return to another theme, can be a basic source of consistency in moral conduct. The absence of this moral selfhood at lower moral levels is a plausible explanation of why such an astounding number of people so readily cheat when given the opportunity (Burton, Chap. 10). When the sense of self is strong and integrated, one identifies with one's own actions; they are the self extended. Not so when the sense of self is weak, enabling one to cheat or lie or walk away from it. The capacity for mature guilt, in this analysis, builds on personal identity, which is obviously bound up with both knowing and feeling.

Increasingly, theorizing about the place of affect in morality focuses not simply on its impact on present behavior but also on its larger role in long-term development. Speaking from this perspective, Kohlberg (Chap. 2, 1971a) states that the "moral sentiments"—fear, shame, and guilt—are not separate from cognition but spring from the person's underlying stage organization just as moral judgments do. "Guilt as dread of self-condemnation is the final step in a series of differentiations, which, like all differentiations in development, are cognitive in nature" (Kohlberg, 1971a, p. 189). Moreover, in Kohlberg's scheme (1971a) the effect of emotion on behavior cannot be predicted apart from a knowledge of the person's stage of moral reasoning:

Two adolescents, thinking of stealing, may have the same feeling of anxiety in the pit of their stomachs. One adolescent (stage 2) interprets the feeling as "being chicken" and ignores it. The other (stage 4) interprets the feeling as "the warning of my conscience" and decides accordingly. The difference in reaction is one in cognitive-structural aspects of moral judgment, not in emotional "dynamics" as such (p. 190).

The difference is a real one, Kohlberg (1969b) maintains: "intensive fear of punishment does not relate to resistance to temptation, whereas self-critical guilt does" (p. 392). In Milgram's study (1963) the moral stage of a subject predicted whether he continued giving shock to the learner or quit; a projective measure of sympathy did not (Kohlberg, 1969b).

If moral stage mediates the effect of emotion, does emotion influence the development of moral stage? Bettelheim (1970) speaks directly of the impact of need satisfaction on learning of any kind:

Nor can the ego support learning when the demands of the id overwhelm us because they are not satisfied. An empty stomach that clamors for food, a rotting tooth that hurts, a body abused by lack of rest, a mind that worries what violence awaits on the streets or at home, all these will swamp the ego as immediate pressures and prevent learning, because an ego overwhelmed by an unsatisfied id is much too weak to do its work.[7]

Bettelheim's basic point is independent of the psychoanalytic metaphors. In developing the theme that moral functioning is rooted in total personality, Simpson hypothesizes in Chapter 9 that "individuals who remain motivated by unfulfilled psychological needs may not be *able* to function at higher levels of moral development"; satisfaction of a given need stage in Maslow's hierarchy may be a prerequisite for attainment of the corresponding moral stage. Selman's clinical case studies

(Chap. 17) of two boys with severe problems in social relationships strongly suggest that affective egocentrism and low self-esteem were both cause and effect of their retarded social-moral growth. Gilligan's graphic account (Chap. 8) of the Kwakiutl Indians as people obsessed by the fear of ridicule and insult, who would "vie with each other in committing atrocities," reflects the extreme moral effects of intense shame. His statement that shame is an emotion "much more important [than guilt] in the actual moral experience of most people" suggests that fears of humiliation, loss of face, and rejection may frequently operate as an affective impediment to moral maturity. M. L. Hoffman (Chap. 7), after reviewing research showing a positive relation between emotional security and altruistic behavior, concludes that "egoistic need deprivation very likely leads to a state of preoccupation with the self—with one's own needs, hopes, and fears," whereas a state of well-being may facilitate moral development by "leaving the person more open and responsive to the needs of others." Need fulfillment and a strong conscience appear to go hand in hand.

While moral stages may be conceived in Kohlberg's terms as interpreting and channeling affect, and affect viewed as either blocking or facilitating the development of mature moral stages, it is also useful to conceive of the cognitive-moral and affective processes as interpenetrating each other. In Chapter 7 M. L. Hoffman takes a giant stride in developing this concept of interpenetration by elaborating stages in the developing integration of the cognitive sense of the other and affective response to another's distress. In this analysis, empathy, sympathy, and guilt are seen as different levels of synthesis of cognition and affect, levels which given rise to progressively farther-reaching forms of the altruistic motive.

Consideration of how thought and feeling act upon each other in moral functioning and development leads directly to the next persistent question in the effort to separate the many strands of human morality.

What Is the Relationship between Intelligence, Moral Judgment, and Behavior?

On one issue there is little theoretical dispute: Intelligence relates strongly to moral judgment and behavior (see Kohlberg, Chap. 2; Aronfreed, Chap. 3; Mischel & Mischel, Chap. 5; Lickona, Chap. 12; Selman, Chap. 17), as it does to a great many other dimensions of human functioning. The disagreement about the role of intelligence in morality turns on the issue of how much impact intelligence has, and whether high intellectual capacity ensures high moral development.

Mischel and Mischel (Chap. 5) survey a variety of studies showing a clear relation between cognitive competence and general adequacy of social functioning. Maturity on Piagetian moral judgments is positively correlated with IQ (Lickona, Chap. 12); and IQ and dishonest behavior have been found to be negatively related (Hartshorne & May, 1928). On the basis of such data, Aronfreed (1968c) and Mischel and Mischel (Chap. 5) accent "the role of sheer cognitive power in the operation of conscience" and question whether children "comparable in general cognitive capacity" (assessed by techniques more sensitive to the specific operations of their thought processes than the standard IQ test) would show "any significant variation in principles of conscience."

Is conscience no more than a matter of intelligence? Behavioral evidence that something else is involved is suggested by Burton's review in Chapter 10 of studies showing, for example, that the relation between IQ and honesty declines or disappears when the context is nonacademic (such as a stealing situation) or when the risk of getting caught is low. Turning to the realm of judgment, one finds that while

high-IQ children do better than low-IQ subjects on most Piaget tests of moral judgment, for some dimensions the reverse is true (Lickona, Chap. 12). Cognitive-developmental theorists such as Kohlberg (Chap. 2) and Selman (Chap. 17) have offered a way of clarifying the intelligence–morality relation: A given stage of cognitive development is a necessary but not sufficient condition for the parallel moral stage (with role-taking cognition operating as a requisite intermediate level). The relevant data are generally supportive: 93 percent of all 5- to 7-year-olds who passed a moral reasoning task at Kohlberg's Stage 2 (which involves primitive social reciprocity) passed a corresponding task of logical reciprocity, whereas 52 percent of the children who passed the logical task did not pass the moral test (Kohlberg & DeVries, 1969). The necessary but not sufficient relationship appears to hold at the higher levels as well: All adolescents and adults who score at Stages 5 or 6 are capable of formal reasoning on Piaget's pendulum and correlation problems, but many persons who are formal-operational on these logical problems fail to show any moral reasoning at the highest, postconventional stages (Kuhn, Langer, & Kohlberg, in preparation).

The research, then, appears to confirm a common intuition: Being smart and being moral are not the same. "Cognitive power" may be needed for principled moral thought, but it is not enough. History is full of examples of how human intelligence can be turned to great evil, the understanding of which stands as the next critical challenge to a science of morality.

How Does One Account for Evil in the World? What are the Sources of Extreme Individual Differences in Moral Behavior?

An adequate psychology of morality needs to be able to account for evil in the world and in individuals. Explaining the extremes of moral behavior is perhaps the most humbling task facing any moral theory. Simplistic notions of morality as mere conformity are clearly inadequate. As Wright (1971) has observed, "The moral differences between a Nazi concentration camp commandant and St. Francis of Assisi are not satisfactorily encompassed in the statement that the former broke the rules and the latter kept them" (p. 21).

To inflict pain, injury, or death on others seems to require the absence of any feeling for the victim; from this perspective, individuals who commit evil deeds seem "more deficient in compassion and empathy than in moral reasoning" (Mischel & Mischel, Chap. 5). Observation seems to support this interpretation. The psychopath, as described by Eysenck in Chapter 6, is characteristically "cruel" and "unfeeling," "callous" and "hedonistic," with "an incapacity for love." It seems plausible that the "natural" developmental integration of cognitive awareness of others and an affective response to their distress (M. L. Hoffman, Chap. 7) is, for whatever reasons, only partial and weak in many persons. The fact that evil appears to be more easily committed at a distance is consistent with the empathy hypothesis; Geis and Monahan's account in Chapter 20 of high-level aircraft company executives approving the manufacture of dangerous planes provides an example of men who could murder comfortably at least partly because they never saw the victims of their decisions. Rosenhan, Moore, and Underwood report (Chap. 13) that in Milgram's experiment (1963) the frequency of shocking the learner dropped from 70 percent when the victim was in another room to 25 percent when the subject had to hold the learner's hand. This finding lends further support to the notion that evil is most readily carried out when it is done impersonally, with little involvement with the victim.

A failure of empathy, however, does not seem to be the whole story. Many of Milgram's subjects (1963) have been de-

scribed as trembling, sweating profusely, and even biting through their lips as they steadily increased the voltage to the learner; in experiments on bystander intervention, subjects who ignore the desperate plight of another are often the most distressed by the experience of witnessing the emergency (Rosenhan, Moore, & Underwood, Chap. 13). And while distance from the victim may facilitate evil, it is useful to remember that when they obeyed the order to shoot, the soldiers at My Lai were face-to-face with the villagers. Empathy may be necessary for moral action, but, like intelligence, it is not enough. The human capacity to externalize responsibility for one's actions or inactions operates as a tremendous counterforce to empathy and may even preclude an empathic response. Louis Fieser, the inventor of napalm, stated, "It's not my business to deal with the political or moral questions" ("Napalm Inventor," 1967, p. 8).

Evil on a massive scale strains human comprehension even more. Morris Abram (1971), a former United States representative in the United Nations Human Rights Commission, writes that "the outrages perpetrated in South Asia" are part of a "century of massacre":

Beginning with the pogroms in Russia and the genocide of the Armenians, the century has witnessed the killings and deportations of World War I, the Stalin ravages of the Kulaks, the Japanese pillage of China, and the unparalleled massacres by Hitler. . . . The British retirement from India was the occasion for slaughter. The Indonesian revolution in the 1960's was accompanied by at least a half-million deaths inflicted by the most unspeakable means. Less than three years ago, the Ibos were decimated by sword, gun, and noose. Now, again, the Indian subcontinent is wracked with death . . . (Abram, 1971, p. 9).

It is difficult to make sense out of horrors of such magnitude without recourse to a phenomenon such as behavioral contagion. The power of models to shape human behavior has been documented beyond dispute (Mischel & Mischel, Chap. 5; Burton, Chap. 10; Rosenhan, Moore, & Underwood, Chap. 13; Liebert & Poulos, Chap. 16). Under social conditions of intense conflict, stress, or frenzy, the potential for an epidemic "spread" of modeled aggression appears to be greatly magnified. Even under normal social conditions, the phenomenon of behavior spread can be appalling, as, for example, when the televised news report of teen-agers setting fire to sleeping derelicts led to an immediate rash of such incidents.

Man's capacity for inhumanity may also be energized by characteristics of a social situation which are "inherently pathological," as was demonstrated when normally prosocial college students became "extremely antisocial" after being assigned the role of guards in a weeklong simulated prison situation (Mischel & Mischel, Chap. 5). The intrinsically pathological conditions of a concentration camp, in inextricable combination with modeled cruelty, personality dispositions, and social sanction for genocide, may account for the widespread barbarities inflicted on Jewish prisoners by the Nazis who ran the death camps—cruelties which made death in the ovens a merciful alternative (Shenker, 1974, p. 39).

Evil on a large scale must be traced to its origins in individuals, and so the search for understanding turns ultimately from the situation to the person. The commission of evil, Simpson (Chap. 9) states, appears to stem from a personality that believes "that evil is likely to be done him," that "the world is an unsafe, rejecting, hateful place over which he has little control." Gilligan's identification in Chapter 8 of shame and pride as a source of hostility and aggression affirms the idea that evil emanates from the affective organization of personality. Kohlberg's explanation of evil, on the other hand, emphasizes its cognitive basis; in rejecting conventional Stage 4 moral reasoning, some persons do not move directly to principled Stage 5 but "drop out" of the moral system— either temporarily, as did a portion of

Kohlberg's longitudinal sample (Kohlberg & Kramer, 1969), or permanently. Hitler and Stalin are examples of people who developed stable amoral ideologies "beyond good and evil"; Hitler in *Mein Kampf* (1943) says simply that morality is meaningless.

A description of Herman Goering (McCord & McCord, 1956), a major figure in Hitler's Germany, provides a chilling portrait of an individual possessed of an absolute contempt for morality:

Attracted by Hitler's militancy, Goering was swept into the Nazi party. He moved from honor to honor as president of the Reichstag, head of Nazi industry, and chief of the Luftwaffe. His objective was expressed in a Reichstag speech: "I am not here to exercise justice, but to wipe out and exterminate!" . . . Gilbert [chief psychologist of the Nuremberg trials], who came to know Goering during the trial, noticed a singular lack of guilt. After seeing a documentary film of mutilated bodies from a concentration camp, Goering commented only: "It was such a good afternoon . . . and then they showed that awful film, and it just spoiled everything."
Before ending his life with poison, Goering left this message for the West: "You Americans are making a stupid mistake with your talk of democracy and morality . . . you can take your morality and your repentance and your democracy and stick it up!" (pp. 30–31).

The problem with viewing Goering simply as having exchanged Stage 4 law and order for amorality sometime during adolescence or adulthood is that his "sadistic brutality" was evident even as a child, when, for example, he made "vicious attacks on his sisters" and on another occasion "bashed his mother in the face with both fists" (McCord & McCord, 1956, pp. 30–31). McCord and McCord also tell of a 10-year-old boy at the Wiltwyck reformatory school in New York who had shown "extreme aggressiveness and impulsivity" since 3½ years of age: "In public school, Paul attacked several children, set fire to the teacher, and ravaged the classroom.

. . . At the [Wiltwyck] home, Paul set fire to the furniture and curtains [and] horrified the other children by killing goldfish with pins and pulling out their intestines" (pp. 130–131). Paul, like many psychopathic individuals, had been severely rejected and brutally beaten by his parents since earliest childhood—data that link the capacity for cruelty with the experience of being treated cruelly during formative years. H. J. Eysenck (Chap. 6), however, maintains that many psychopaths "come from perfectly normal homes" and makes the case for a genetic interpretation of psychopathic behavior. The psychopath who is violent and destructive tends to show a pattern of low cortical arousal and consequent poor conditionability and high sensation-seeking, combined with high "psychoticism," a "personality trait predisposing a person to a particular kind of mental breakdown under suitable stress." Though environmentalism in some form continues to dominate current psychological theorizing about morality, Eysenck's work forces us to consider seriously whether there may be, at least for some persons, a biology of evil.

The extremes of personal goodness are perhaps even more obscure in their origins and motivating force than is extreme evil. Little is written about moral greatness. When psychology knows more about the Martin Luther King, Jrs., and the Eleanor Roosevelts, it will know more about how to develop morality in average men and women. It seems clear that the best way to prevent evil in the world is to promote the development of goodness.

What Optimizes Moral Development and Behavior?

All other questions about moral development culminate in a single concern: What can be done, on the basis of what is known, to develop morally mature persons and to maximize the likelihood that they will behave on their highest moral level?

Traditionally, the focus of this question has been childrearing. The best way to bring up children, of course, depends on one's theoretical point of view, as the contents of this volume make clear. H. J. Eysenck (Chap. 6), equating conscience with learned inhibitions, stresses the importance of proper conditioning procedures, combined with drugs to enhance conditionability in individuals who have low cortical arousal, and recommends that all children be tested for their conditionability (H. J. Eysenck, 1970b). The notion that moral development can be built on a base of anxiety conditioning has currency in other theories as well. Operating within a psychoanalytic framework, Bettelheim (1970) states unequivocally that people will not develop mature morality "without first having been subject as children to a stringent morality based on fear and trembling" (p. 87). Aronfreed (Chap. 3), a cognitive learning theorist, writes that even at the level of complex moral principles, the attachment of anxiety to the "internal cognitive monitor" is probably needed to motivate moral conduct. Burton (Chap. 10), pointing out that punishment as a method of behavior control is used the world over far more than positive reinforcement, agrees with Aronfreed that it is a necessary part of socialization, but concedes that a Skinnerian strategy of total positive reinforcement has never really been tested. Burton cites studies showing that punishing a little is more effective than punishing a lot and that when appropriate reasoning is introduced, parents need use only mild and delayed punishment to inhibit deviation. Intense punishment can actually increase deviation by raising anxiety to a level that intefers with discriminating right from wrong. Finally, Burton's review of the literature reveals that punishment works best in a context of love—not at all surprising when one recalls the previously discussed indications that security and a strong ego provide the affective underpinnings of prosocial behavior.

On the other side of the punishment issue, Saltzstein (Chap. 14) documents the aversive effects of negative forms of control, including love withdrawal, on the development of a morality of consideration for others. This morality is in contrast, he finds, to a moral order of unthinking conformity to rules, for which authoritarianism appears to be an effective antecedent. Saltzstein's chapter suggests that a behavioristic approach to conscience is no more than that: It may train certain behaviors, but it will not necessarily foster the development of spontaneous altruism or independent morality. M. L. Hoffman, dealing with the growth of sympathy and altruism in Chapter 7, sounds the same note: Punishment often arouses resentment and anxiety, focuses the child's attention on negative consequences to himself rather than on the needs of others, fails to give the child the experience of helping others, and provides a punitive rather than an altruistic parental model. Cognitive-developmental theory, broadly defined to include both Hoffman and Kohlberg, tends to take a more long-range, preventive approach to moral behavior, urging parents to maximize children's "role-taking opportunities" and their chances to become sensitive to the feelings and attitudes of others. From this perspective, peer interaction as emphasized by Piaget (Lickona, Chap. 12) becomes an important source of moral growth. Kohlberg's point in Chapter 2 that role taking goes on in all social interaction and communication situations implies that simply increasing the amount of reciprocal communication that occurs among people is likely to enhance moral development, as is also suggested by Holstein's finding (1973) that parental encouragement of dialogue about value issues is a good predictor of moral stage advance in children. That wise adults also make at least occasional use of their authority, however, is suggested by the finding that parents of children with a "humanistic conscience" (Saltzstein, Chap. 14) relied largely on other-oriented cognitive instruction; signifi-

cantly, they also discriminatively employed power assertion, more so than parents of children who were less oriented toward humanistic concerns. Apparently, a spoonful of medicine helps the reasoning go down.

The areas of agreement among theories of what constitutes good socialization are broader than the differences. Parents, it is agreed, should be reasonably consistent in what they approve and disapprove, and should act in accord with the precepts they preach (e.g., Burton, Chap. 10). There is a consensus that reasoning, either alone or in combination with other methods, helps to develop desired moral conduct, though (as Burton cautions) parents need to guard against talking their children to death and thereby decreasing the effectiveness of offering rationales. Moreover, the appropriate amount of "cognitive structuring" used to influence a child varies as a function of his level of cognitive development. Social-learning and cognitive-developmental approaches alike recognize that socialization techniques need to be consonant with, rather than counter to, the natural base of development "to capitalize on the formal properties of children's thinking" (Aronfreed, Chap. 3). Put another way, the content of the moral lessons parents provide should mesh with the current structure of the child's mind. That the more common parental pitfall may be underestimating rather than overestimating their children's cognitive capacity is suggested by a recent incident involving my 6½-year-old son (who has experienced an occasional swat on the seat but not for some time). After a display of bad table manners and a verbal reprimand from his parents, he spontaneously got up from his chair, walked over to his mother, turned around, bent down and calmly said, "Well, I deserve to be punished—here's the target, hit the bull's-eye." Children seem to develop detachment from physical punishment at an early age, perhaps as a way of maintaining their dignity; and when a young child dispassionately invites a whack on the bottom as a proper consequence for his misdeeds, that ought to tell us that punishment may not be too powerful a deterrent and not too sophisticated a means of advancing children to higher levels of moral understanding.

Another point of general agreement among observers of moral development is that children need to be taught how to be good as well as how not to be bad. Parental reasoning plus concrete suggestions for reparation appear to be most effective in developing consideration for others (Saltzstein, Chap. 14). Liebert and Poulos (Chap. 16) offer persuasive evidence that television, as a critical part of the socialization milieu, can model many prosocial behaviors as effectively as it now perpetrates prejudice and violence. Frequent and varied models of fair and cooperative behavior, whether on TV, in the home, or at school, may also support moral development by contributing to what Kohlberg calls the "moral atmosphere" of a group or institution. Moreover, modeling can contribute substantially to *moral competence,* by demonstrating specific ways to help others in particular situations—a technique that has been used quite successfully even with preschool youngsters (Yarrow, Scott, & Waxler, 1973). Many bystanders who do not come to the aid of persons in distress may fail to act largely because they feel incompetent to intervene effectively (Huston & Korte, Chap. 15).

Cognitive-developmentalists, as well as behaviorists, need to "catch the child being good." They need to explore the motivation underlying positive behavior with the aim of assisting the child in generalizing his highest level of moral reasoning to a broad range of actions (Kohlberg & Turiel, 1971). Such an approach to encouraging moral reflection is similar in some ways to Burton's recommendation (Chap. 10) of "training in consistency" by helping children to learn to perceive a variety of honesty situations as belonging to a similar class of moral problems to which common moral judgments apply. The effort to move

adults as well as children closer to the ideal of integrated moral functioning should also seek to eliminate social conditions that reward inconsistency, as, for example, when a politician is paid off privately for favors to corporate interests and simultaneously praised for his public stand on behalf of the consumer (Mischel & Mischel, Chap. 5).

A socialization concept that emerges as a major point of theoretical convergence is the idea of optimal conflict or tension, although different theories perceive its value differently. Social-learning theory (e.g., Burton, Chap. 10) sees a moderate level of anxiety as an optimally motivating state for learning new moral behaviors and performing already acquired ones. M. L. Hoffman's developmental theory (Chap. 7) of empathy, sympathy, and guilt views "the normal run of distress experiences" in childhood as providing a necessary affective base for altruism, and regards social conflict situations as important in developing children's sense of commonality with others and their feelings that differences can be worked out. Structural theories such as Kohlberg's and Piaget's see the experience of cognitive conflict—the arousing of internal contradictions in a person's own reasoning or his confrontation with optimally discrepant reasoning of others (one stage above his own)—as stimulating cognitive reorganization and consequent movement toward the next developmental stage. (One implication of this structural view of cognitive growth is that education ought to deal head-on with clashing viewpoints on social issues rather than systematically avoid them.) The concept of "optimal incongruity" in social-moral experience gets its most elaborate exposition in Chapter 4, where Garbarino and Bronfenbrenner advocate sociocultural pluralism as the environment most likely to develop a principled, independent conscience. In addition to emphasizing affective attachment in early childhood as an essential prerequisite to further social-moral growth, the authors of this theory stress that the differing pulls of multiple social agents, forcing the person to construct his or her own morality, must be cognitively and affectively manageable *within an integrated social structure*—one which is a delicate balance of diversity and consensus. Too little or two much social integration can arrest or reverse the developmental process.

Garbarino and Bronfenbrenner's documentation (Chap. 4) of the impact of the larger sociocultural context on individual moral functioning lays bare the serious inadequacy of focusing only on childrearing in determining techniques to foster morality. Essentially the same theme runs through other chapters. Kohlberg's contrast (Chap. 2) of the kibbutz with orphanage and prison environments throws light on the importance of the total moral climate of a social setting. Selman's description (Chap. 17) of effective summer camp "therapy" with a boy from a chaotic home illustrates the wisdom of altering the environmental context to support personal developmental change. Burton (Chap. 10) points out that for delinquent- and prisoner-training programs to have a lasting impact, poverty and the conditions of the ghetto must be simultaneously changed. Mancuso and Sarbin's essay (Chap. 19) on morality and the law suggests that a different system of jurisprudence, one which is scrupulously fair and context-sensitive in meting out justice, could set a different

moral tone in the society that should make itself felt in the lives of individuals. So should reform of the kind urged by Geis and Monahan (Chap. 20), who would establish Ralph Nader's vision of a "just social order [in which] responsibility [for social harm] shall lie where the power of decision rests," whether with an individual criminal or a large corporation. Finally, Huston and Korte (Chap. 15) give an account of laws that support Good Samaritanism, and community organizations that forestall violent crime and help people to aid the victim when crime occurs. These authors offer clear examples of how social conditions can be arranged to maximize the likelihood that persons will contribute to rather than detract from each other's welfare.

Conceivably, as Chapter 13 (Rosenhan, Moore, & Underwood) concludes, in a world or society or school or home where situational supports for moral behavior were consistently and strongly provided, many more people would develop the kind of principled moral system that no longer requires external supports. It has been wisely said that we need to create a world in which it is easier to be good. The problem with societal and individual efforts to optimize moral development, to paraphrase Chesterton, is not that they have been tried and found wanting, but that they have never been truly tried.

PART 2

THEORETICAL PERSPECTIVES ON MORAL DEVELOPMENT AND BEHAVIOR

CHAPTER 2

Moral Stages and Moralization

THE COGNITIVE-DEVELOPMENTAL APPROACH

Lawrence Kohlberg[1]

In this chapter we shall present an overview of the cognitive-developmental theory of moralization as elaborated in our studies of moral stages. We shall first present a theoretical description of the six moral stages, followed by an account of the development of our methods for identifying or scoring stage. Having presented a picture of what moral development is and how to assess it, we shall go on to present the theory of moralization which can best account for this picture of moral development, and to contrast this theory with approaches which see moral development as a result of socialization or social learning.

In a sense, this chapter represents an updating of earlier presentations of our theory of moral development stages (Kohlberg, 1969b). In this chapter, however, there is no attempt to review research comprehensively, as research reviews have appeared earlier (Kohlberg, 1964, 1969b) and are forthcoming (Kohlberg, in prep.). The philosophic assumptions and implications of our stages are also treated only briefly, having been thoroughly discussed elsewhere (Kohlberg, 1971a).

The Place of Moral Judgment in the Total Personality

To understand moral stage, it is helpful to locate it in a sequence of development of personality. We know that individuals pass through the moral stages one step at a time as they progress from the bottom (Stage 1) toward the top (Stage 6). There are also other stages that individuals must go through, perhaps the most basic of which are the stages of logical reasoning or intelligence studied by Piaget (1967). After the child learns to speak, there are three major developmental stages of reasoning: the intuitive, the concrete operational, and the formal operational. At around age 7, the child enters the stage of concrete logical thought; he can then make logical inferences, classify things, and handle quantitative relations about concrete things. In adolescence, many but not all individuals enter the stage of formal operations, at which level they can reason abstractly. Formal operational thinking can consider all possibilities, consider the relations between elements in a system, form hypotheses, deduce implications from the hypotheses, and test them against reality. Many adolescents and adults only partially attain the stage of formal operations; they consider all the actual relations of one thing to another at the same time, but do not consider all possibilities and do not form abstract hypotheses.

In general, almost no adolescents and adults will still be entirely at the stage of concrete operations, many will be at the stage of partial formal operations, and most will be at the highest stage of formal operations (Kuhn, Kohlberg, Langer, & Haan, in press). Since moral reasoning clearly is reasoning, advanced moral reasoning depends upon advanced logical reasoning. There is a parallelism between an individual's logical stage and his moral stage. A person whose logical stage is only concrete operational is limited to the preconventional moral stages, Stages 1 and 2. A person whose logical stage is only "low" formal operational is limited to the conventional moral stages (Stages 3 and 4). While logical development is a necessary condition for moral development, it is not sufficient. Many individuals are at a higher logical stage than the parallel moral stage, but essentially none are at a higher moral stage than their logical stage (Colby & Kohlberg, in prep.).

Next, after stages of logical development, come stages of social perception or social perspective or role taking (see Selman, Chap. 17). We partially describe these stages when we define the moral stages. These role-taking stages describe the level at which the person sees other people, interprets their thoughts and feelings, and sees their role or place in society. These stages are very closely related to moral stages, but are more general, since they do not deal just with fairness and with choices of right and wrong. To make a judgment of fairness at a certain level is more difficult than to simply see the world at that level. So, just as for logic, development of a stage's social perception precedes, or is easier than, development of the parallel stage of moral judgment. Just as there is a vertical sequence of steps in movement up from moral Stage 1 to moral Stage 2 to moral Stage 3, so there is a horizontal sequence of steps in movement from logic to social perception to moral judgment. First, a person attains a logical stage, say, partial formal operations, which allows him to see "systems" in the world, to see a set of related variables as a system. Next he attains a level of social perception or role taking, where he sees other people understanding one another in terms of the place of each in the system. Finally, he attains Stage 4 of moral judgment, where the welfare and order of the total social system or society is the reference point for judging "fair" or "right." We have found that individuals who move upward in our moral education programs already have the logical capacity, and often the social perception capacity, for the higher moral stage to which they move (Colby & Kohlberg, in prep.).

There is one final step in this horizontal sequence: moral behavior. To act in a morally high way requires a high stage of moral reasoning. One cannot follow moral principles (Stages 5 and 6) if one does not understand or believe in them. One can, however, reason in terms of such principles and not live up to them. A variety of factors determines whether a particular person will live up to his stage of moral reasoning in a particular situation, though moral stage is a good predictor of action in various experimental and naturalistic settings (Kohlberg, 1969b).

In summary, moral stage is related to cognitive advance and to moral behavior, but our identification of moral stage must be based on moral reasoning alone.

Theoretical Description of the Moral Stages

The six moral stages are grouped into three major levels: *preconventional level* (Stages 1 and 2), *conventional level* (Stages 3 and

4), and *postconventional level* (Stages 5 and 6).

To understand the stages, it is best to start by understanding the three moral levels. The preconventional moral level is the level of most children under 9, some adolescents, and many adolescent and adult criminal offenders. The conventional level is the level of most adolescents and adults in our society and in other societies. The postconventional level is reached by a minority of adults and is usually reached only after the age of 20. The term "conventional" means conforming to and upholding the rules and expectations and conventions of society or authority just because they are society's rules, expectations, or conventions. The individual at the preconventional level has not yet come to really understand and uphold conventional or societal rules and expectations. Someone at the postconventional level understands and basically accepts society's rules, but acceptance of society's rules is based on formulating and accepting the general moral principles that underlie these rules. These principles in some cases come into conflict with society's rules, in which case the postconventional individual judges by principle rather than by convention.

One way of understanding the three levels is to think of them as three different types of relationships between the *self* and *society's rules and expectations*. From this point of view, *Level I* is a *preconventional* person, for whom rules and social expectations are something external to the self; *Level II* is a *conventional* person, in whom the self is identified with or has internalized the rules and expectations of others, especially those of authorities; and *Level III* is a *postconventional* person, who has differentiated his self from the rules and expectations of others and defines his values in terms of self-chosen principles.

Within each of the three moral levels, there are two stages. The second stage is a more advanced and organized form of the general perspective of each major level. Table 2.1 defines the six moral stages in

terms of (1) what is right, (2) the reason for upholding the right, and (3) the social perspective behind each stage, a central concept to which our definition of moral reasoning now turns.

SOCIAL PERSPECTIVES OF THE THREE MORAL LEVELS

In order to characterize the development of moral reasoning structurally, we seek a single unifying construct that will generate the major structural features of each stage. In Chapter 17 Selman offers a point of departure in the search for such a unifying construct. He has defined levels of role taking which parallel our moral stages and which form a cognitive-structural hierarchy. Selman defines role taking primarily in terms of the way the individual differentiates his perspective from other perspectives, and the way in which he relates these perspectives to one another. From our point of view, however, there is a more general structural construct which underlies *both* role taking and moral judgment. This is the concept of *sociomoral perspective*, which refers to the point of view the individual takes in defining both social facts and sociomoral values, or oughts. Corresponding to the three major levels of moral judgment, we postulate the three major levels of social perspective as follows:

Moral Judgment	Social Perspective
I. Preconventional	Concrete individual perspective
II. Conventional	Member-of-society perspective
III. Postconventional, or principled	Prior-to-society perspective

Let us illustrate the meaning of social perspective in terms of the unity it provides for the various ideas and concerns of the moral level. The conventional level, for example, is different from the preconventional in that it uses the following reasons: (1) concern about social approval;

TABLE 2.1 The Six Moral Stages

Content of Stage

Level and Stage	What Is Right	Reasons for Doing Right	Social Perspective of Stage
LEVEL I—PRECONVENTIONAL Stage 1—Heteronomous Morality	To avoid breaking rules backed by punishment, obedience for its own sake, and avoiding physical damage to persons and property.	Avoidance of punishment, and the superior power of authorities.	*Egocentric point of view. Doesn't consider the interests of others or recognize that they differ from the actor's; doesn't relate two points of view. Actions are considered physically rather than in terms of psychological interests of others. Confusion of authority's perspective with one's own.*
Stage 2—Individualism, Instrumental Purpose, and Exchange	Following rules only when it is to someone's immediate interest; acting to meet one's own interests and needs and letting others do the same. Right is also what's fair, what's an equal exchange, a deal, an agreement.	To serve one's own needs or interests in a world where you have to recognize that other people have their interests, too.	*Concrete individualistic perspective. Aware that everybody has his own interest to pursue and these conflict, so that right is relative (in the concrete individualistic sense).*
LEVEL II—CONVENTIONAL Stage 3—Mutual Interpersonal Expectations, Relationships, and Interpersonal Conformity	Living up to what is expected by people close to you or what people generally expect of people in your role as son, brother, friend, etc. "Being good" is important and means having good motives, showing concern about others. It also means keeping mutual relationships, such as trust, loyalty, respect and gratitude.	The need to be a good person in your own eyes and those of others. Your caring for others. Belief in the Golden Rule. Desire to maintain rules and authority which support stereotypical good behavior.	*Perspective of the individual in relationships with other individuals. Aware of shared feelings, agreements, and expectations which take primacy over individual interests. Relates points of view through the concrete Golden Rule, putting yourself in the other guy's shoes. Does not yet consider generalized system perspective.*

Stage 4—Social System and Conscience	Fulfilling the actual duties to which you have agreed. Laws are to be upheld except in extreme cases where they conflict with other fixed social duties. Right is also contributing to society, the group, or institution.	To keep the institution going as a whole, to avoid the breakdown in the system "if everyone did it," or the imperative of conscience to meet one's defined obligations (Easily confused with Stage 3 belief in rules and authority; see text.)	*Differentiates societal point of view from interpersonal agreement or motives.* Takes the point of view of the system that defines roles and rules. Considers individual relations in terms of place in the system.
LEVEL III—POST-CONVENTIONAL, or PRINCIPLED Stage 5—Social Contract or Utility and Individual **Rights**	Being aware that people hold a variety of values and opinions, that most values and rules are relative to your group. These relative rules should usually be upheld, however, in the interest of impartiality and because they are the social contract. Some nonrelative values and rights like *life* and *liberty*, however, must be upheld in any society and regardless of majority opinion.	A sense of obligation to law because of one's social contract to make and abide by laws for the welfare of all and for the protection of all people's rights. A feeling of contractual commitment, freely entered upon, to family, friendship, trust, and work obligations. Concern that laws and duties be based on rational calculation of overall utility, "the greatest good for the greatest number."	*Prior-to-society perspective.* Perspective of a rational individual aware of values and rights prior to social attachments and contracts. Integrates perspectives by formal mechanisms of agreement, contract, objective impartiality, and due process. Considers moral and legal points of view; recognizes that they sometimes conflict and finds it difficult to integrate them.
Stage 6—Universal Ethical Principles	Following self-chosen ethical principles. Particular laws or social agreements are usually valid because they rest on such principles. When laws violate these principles, one acts in accordance with the principle. Principles are universal principles of justice: the equality of human rights and respect for the dignity of human beings as individual persons.	The belief as a rational person in the validity of universal moral principles, and a sense of personal commitment to them.	*Perspective of a moral point of view* from which social arrangements derive. Perspective is that of any rational individual recognizing the nature of morality or the fact that persons are ends in themselves and must be treated as such.

(2) concern about loyalty to persons, groups, and authority; and (3) concern about the welfare of others and society. We need to ask, What underlies these characteristics of reasoning and holds them together? What fundamentally defines and unifies the characteristics of the conventional level is its *social perspective*, a shared viewpoint of the participants in a relationship or a group. The conventional individual subordinates the needs of the single individual to the viewpoint and needs of the group or the shared relationship. To illustrate the conventional social perspective, here is 17-year-old Joe's response to the following question:

Why shouldn't you steal from a store?
It's a matter of law. It's one of our rules that we're trying to help protect everyone, protect property, not just to protect a store. It's something that's needed in our society. If we didn't have these laws, people would steal, they wouldn't have to work for a living and our whole society would get out of kilter.

Joe is concerned about *keeping the law*, and his reason for being concerned is *the good of society as a whole*. Clearly, he is speaking as a member of society. It's one of *our* rules that *we're making* to protect everyone in *our* society." This concern for the good of society arises from his taking the point of view of "us members of society," which goes beyond the point of view of Joe as a concrete, individual self.

Let us contrast this *conventional member-of-society perspective* with the *preconventional concrete individual perspective*. The latter point of view is that of the individual actor in the situation thinking about his interests and those of other individuals he may care about. Seven years earlier, at age 10, Joe illustrated the concrete individual perspective in response to the same question:

Why shouldn't you steal from a store?
It's not good to steal from the store. It's

against the law. Someone could see you and call the police.

Being "against the law," then, means something very different at the two levels. At Level II, the law is made by and for "everyone," as Joes indicates at age 17. At Level I, it is just something enforced by the police and, accordingly, the reason for obeying the law is to avoid punishment. This reason derives from the limits of a Level I perspective, the perspective of an individual considering his own interests and those of other isolated individuals.

Let us now consider the perspective of the *postconventional level*. It is like the preconventional perspective in that it returns to the standpoint of the individual rather than taking the point of view of "us members of society." The individual point of view taken at the postconventional level, however, can be universal; it is that of *any rational moral individual*. Aware of the member-of-society perspective, the postconventional person questions and redefines it in terms of an individual moral perspective, so that social obligations are defined in ways that can be justified to any moral individual. An individual's commitment to basic morality or moral principles is seen as preceding, or being necessary for, his taking society's perspective or accepting society's laws and values. Society's laws and values, in turn, should be ones which any reasonable person could commit himself to—whatever his place in society and whatever society he belongs to. The postconventional perspective, then, is *prior to society*; it is the perspective of an *individual who has made the moral commitments or holds the standards on which a good or just society must be based*. This is a perspective by which (1) a particular society or set of social practices may be judged and (2) a person may rationally commit himself to a society.

An example is Joe, our longitudinal subject, interviewed at age 24:

Why shouldn't someone steal from a store?
It's violating another person's rights, in this case to property.

Does the law enter in?
Well, the law in most cases is based on what is morally right so it's not a separate subject, it's a consideration.

What does "morality" or "morally right" mean to you?
Recognizing the rights of other individuals, first to life and then to do as he pleases as long as it doesn't interefere with somebody else's rights.

The wrongness of stealing is that it violates the moral rights of individuals, which are prior to law and society. Property rights follow from more universal human rights (such as freedoms which do not interefere with the like freedom of others). The demands of law and society derive from universal moral rights, rather than vice versa.

It should be noted that reference to the words *rights* or *morally right* or *conscience* does not necessarily distinguish conventional from postconventional morality. Orienting to the morally right thing, or following conscience as against following the law, need not indicate the postconventional perspective of the rational moral individual. The terms "morality" and "conscience" may be used to refer to group rules and values which conflict with civil laws or with the rules of the majority group. To a Jehovah's Witness, who has gone to jail for "conscience," conscience may mean God's law as interpreted by his religious sect or group rather than the standpoint of any individual oriented to universal moral principles or values. To count as postconventional, such ideas or terms must be used in a way that makes it clear that they have a foundation for a rational or moral individual who has not yet committed himself to any group or society or its morality. "Trust," for example, is a basic value at both the conventional and the postconventional levels. At the conventional level, trustworthiness is something you expect of others in your society. Joe expresses this as follows at age 17:

Why should a promise be kept, anyway?
Friendship is based on trust. If you can't trust a person, there's little grounds to deal with him. You should try to be as reliable as possible because people remember you by this, you're more respected if you can be depended upon.

At this conventional level, Joe views trust as a truster, as well as someone who could break a trust. He sees that the individual needs to be trustworthy not only to secure respect and to maintain social relationships with others, but also because as a member of society he expects trust of others in general.

At the postconventional level, the individual takes a further step. He does not automatically assume that he is in a society in which he needs the friendship and respect of other individuals. Instead he considers why any society or social relationship presupposes trust, and why the individual, if he is to contract into society, must be trustworthy. At age 24, Joe is postconventional in his explanation of why a promise should be kept:

I think human relationships in general are based on trust, on believing in other individuals. If you have no way of believing in someone else, you can't deal with anyone else and it becomes every man for himself. Everything you do in a day's time is related to somebody else and if you can't deal on a fair basis, you have chaos.

We have defined a postconventional moral perspective in terms of the individual's reasons *why* something is right or wrong. We need to illustrate this perspective as it enters into making an actual decision or defining *what is right*. The postconventional person is aware of the moral point of view that each individual in a moral conflict situation ought to adopt. Rather than defining expectations and obligations from the standpoint of societal roles, as someone at the conventional level would, the postconventional individual holds that persons in these roles should orient to a "moral point of view." While the postconventional moral viewpoint does also recognize fixed legal-social obligations, recognition of moral obligations may take priority when the moral and legal viewpoints conflict.

At age 24 Joe reflects the postconventional moral point of view as a decision-making perspective in response to Heinz's dilemma about stealing a drug to save his wife:

It is the husband's duty to save his wife. The fact that her life is in danger transcends every other standard you might use to judge his action. Life is more important than property.

Suppose it were a friend, not his wife?
I don't think that would be much different from a moral point of view. It's still a human being in danger.

Suppose it were a stranger?
To be consistent, yes, from a moral standpoint.

What is this moral standpoint?
I think every individual has a right to live and if there is a way of saving an individual, he should be saved.

Should the judge punish the husband?
Usually the moral and the legal standpoints coincide. Here they conflict. The judge should weigh the moral standpoint more heavily but preserve the legal law in punishing Heinz lightly.

SOCIAL PERSPECTIVES OF THE SIX STAGES

This section will explain the social perspective differences involved in each moral stage within each of the three levels. It will attempt to show how the second stage in each level completes the development of the social perspective entered at the first stage of the level.

We will start with the easiest pair of stages to explain in this way—Stages 3 and 4, comprising the conventional level. In the preceding section we quoted the "isolated individual" perspective of Stages 1 and 2 and contrasted it with Joe's full-fledged member-of-society perspective at age 17, a perspective which is Stage 4. Joe's statements about the importance of trust in dealing with others clearly reflect the perspective of someone taking the point of view of the social system. The social perspective at Stage 3 is less aware of society's point of view, or of the good of the whole of society. As an example of Stage 3, let us consider Andy's response to a dilemma about whether to tell your father about a brother's disobedience after the brother has confided in you.

He should think of his brother, but it's more important to be a good son. Your father has done so much for you. I'd have a conscience if I didn't tell, more than to my brother, because my father couldn't trust me. My brother would understand; our father has done so much for him, too.

Andy's perspective is not based on a social system. It is rather one in which he has two relationships: one to his brother, one to his father. His father as authority and helper comes first. Andy expects his brother to share this perspective, but as someone else centered on their father. There is no reference to the organization of the family in general. Being a good son is said to be more important not because it is a more important role in the eyes of, or in terms of, society as a whole or even in terms of the family as a system. The Stage 3 member-of-a-group perspective is that of the average good person, not that of society or an institution as a whole. The Stage 3 perspective sees things from the point of view of shared relationships between two or more individuals—relations of caring, trust, respect, and so on—rather than from the viewpoint of institutional wholes. In summary, whereas the Stage 4 member-of-society perspective is a "system" perspective, the Stage 3 perspective is that of a participant in a shared relationship or shared group.

Let us turn to the preconventional level. Whereas Stage 1 involves only the concrete individual's point of view, Stage 2 is aware of a number of other individuals, each having other points of view. At Stage 2, in serving my interests I anticipate the other guy's reaction, negative or positive, and he anticipates mine. Unless we make a deal, each will put his own point of view first. If we make a deal, each of us will do something for the other.

An example of the shift from Stage 1 to Stage 2 is shown by the following change in another subject's response between age 10 and age 13 to a question about whether an older brother should tell his father about his younger brother's misdeed, revealed in confidence. At 10, the subject gives a Stage 1 answer:

In one way it was right to tell because his father might beat him up. In another way it's wrong because his brother will beat him up if he tells.

At age 13, he has moved to Stage 2:

The brother should not tell or he'll get his brother in trouble. If he wants his brother to keep quiet for him sometime, he'd better not squeal now.

In the second response, there is an extension of concern to the brother's welfare as it affects the subject's own interests through anticipated exchange. There is a much clearer picture of the brother's point of view and its relationship to his own.

Turning to the postconventional level, a typical Stage 5 orientation distinguishes between a moral point of view and a legal point of view, but finds it difficult to define a moral perspective independent of the perspective behind contractual-legal rights. Joe, an advanced Stage 5, says with regard to Heinz's dilemma of whether to steal the drug to save his wife:

Usually the moral and the legal standpoints coincide. Here they conflict. The judge should weigh the moral standpoint more. . . .

For Joe, the moral point of view is not yet something prior to the legal point of view. Both law and morality for Joe derive from individual rights and values, and both are more or less on an equal plane. At Stage 6, obligation is defined in terms of universal ethical principles of justice. Here is a Stage 6 response to Heinz's dilemma:

It is wrong legally but right morally. Systems of law are valid only insofar as they reflect the sort of moral law all rational people can accept. One must consider the personal justice involved, which is the root of the social contract. The ground of creating a society is individual justice, the right of every person to an equal consideration of his claims in every situation, not just those which can be codified in law. Personal justice means, "Treat each person as an end, not a means."

This response indicates a very clear awareness of a moral point of view based on a principle ("Treat each person as an end, not a means") which is more basic than, and from which one can derive, the sociolegal point of view.

Four Moral Orientations and the Shift toward Greater Equilibrium within Stages

In discussing social perspectives we have not differentiated *perception* of social fact (role taking) from *prescription* of the right or good (moral judgment). What are the distinctive features of stages of moral judgment as opposed to social perspective in general?

To define the distinctively moral, we now turn to the moral categories analyzed by moral philosophy. These include "modal" categories (such as rights, duties, the morally approvable, responsibility) and "element" categories (such as welfare, liberty, equality, reciprocity, rules and social order). In typologizing moral philosophic theories, it is customary to analyze the primary moral categories of the theory from which the other categories derive. There are four possible groups of primary categories called *moral* orientations. Found at each of our moral stages, they define four kinds of decisional strategies, each focusing on one of four universal elements in any social situation. These orientations and elements are as follows:

1. *Normative order*: Orientation to prescribed rules and roles of the social or moral order. The basic considerations in decision making center on the element of *rules*.
2. *Utility consequences*: Orientation to the good or bad *welfare consequences* of action in the situation for others and/or the self.
3. *Justice or fairness*: Orientation to *relations* of liberty, equality, reciprocity, and contract between persons.
4. *Ideal-self*: Orientation to an image of actor as a *good self*, or as someone with conscience, and to his motives or virtue (relatively independent of approval consequences from others).

In defining the distinctively moral, some writers stress the concept of rule and respect for rules (Kant, Durkheim, Piaget). Others identify morality with a consideration of welfare consequences to others (Mill, Dewey). Still others identify morality with an idealized moral self (Bradley, Royce, Baldwin). Finally, some (Rawls, and myself) identify morality with justice. In fact, individual persons may use any one or all of these moral orientations. As an example, we have the following orientations to the property issue at Stage 3:

Why shouldn't you steal from a store, anyway?

1. *Normative order*: It's always wrong to steal. If you start breaking rules of stealing, everything would go to pieces.

2. *Utilitarian*: You're hurting other people. The storeowner has a family to support.
3. *Justice*: The storeowner worked hard for his money and you didn't. Why should you have it and not him?
4. *Ideal-self*: A person who isn't honest isn't worth much. Stealing and cheating are both the same, they are both dishonesty.

While all orientations may be used by an individual, we claim that the most essential structure of morality is a justice structure. Moral situations are ones of conflict of perspectives or interest; justice principles are concepts for resolving these conflicts, for giving each his due. In one sense, justice can refer to all four orientations. Sustaining law and order may be seen as justice (normative order), and maximizing the welfare of the group may be seen as justice (utility consequences). In the end, however, the core of justice is the *distribution of rights and duties regulated by concepts of equality and reciprocity*. Justice recognized as a "balance" or equilibrium corresponds to the structural moving equilibrium described by Piaget on logic (1967). Justice is the normative logic, the equilibration, of social actions and relations.

A person's sense of justice is what is most distinctively and fundamentally moral. One can act morally and question all rules, one may act morally and question the greater good, but one cannot act morally and question the need for justice.

What are the actual developmental findings regarding the four moral orientations? And do they support our theory's assertion of the primacy of justice? A partial answer comes from our longitudinal data. For this purpose, we group the normative order and utilitarian orientations as interpenetrating to form Type A at each stage. Type B focuses on the interpenetration of the justice orientation with an ideal-self orientation. Type A makes judgments more descriptively and predictively, in terms of the given "out there." Type B makes judgments more prescriptively, in terms of what ought to be, of what is internally accepted by the self. A Type B orientation presupposes both awareness of rules and a judgment of their fairness.

Our longitudinal data indeed support the notion that the two types are relatively clear substages. The B substage is more mature than the A substage in the sense that a 3A may move to 3B, but a 3B can never move to 3A (though he may move to 4A). Individuals can skip the B substage, that is, move from 3A to 4A; but if they change substage, it is always from A to B. In a sense, then, the B substage is a consolidation or equilibration of the social perspective first elaborated at the A substage. B's are more balanced in perspective. A 3A decides in terms of "What does a good husband do? What does a wife expect?" A 3B decides in terms of "What does a husband who is a partner in a good mutual relationship do? What does each spouse expect of the other?" Both sides of the equation are balanced; this is fairness. At 4A, the subject decides in terms of the questions. "What does the system demand?" At 4B the subject asks, "What does the individual in the system demand as well as the system, and what is a solution that strikes a balance?" Thus, a 4B upholds a system, but it is a "democratic" system with individual rights.

Because of this balance, B's are more prescriptive or internal, centering more on their judgments of what ought to be. They are also more universalistic, that is, more willing to carry the boundaries of value categories, like the value of life, to their logical conclusion. As an example, a Stage 3 subject responded to Heinz's drug-stealing dilemma by giving a standard A response, "A good husband would love his wife enough to do it." Asked whether a friend would steal a drug for a friend, he said, "No, a friend isn't that close that he has to risk stealing." He then added, "But when I think about it, that doesn't seem fair, his friend has just as much right to live as his wife."

Here we see a tendency, based on an orientation to justice, to universalize obligation to life and to distinguish it from role stereotypes. In summary, the full de-

velopment and consolidation of moral judgment at each stage is defined by the categories and structures of justice, although stage development occurs in all four moral orientations.

Methodology in Assessing Moral Judgment Development

THE ASPECT-SCORING SYSTEM

In our original formulation (Kohlberg, 1958, 1969b), the moral stages were defined in terms of twenty-five "aspects," grouped, in turn, under the following major sets: rules, conscience, welfare of others, self's welfare, sense of duty, role taking, punitive justice, positive justice, and motives. Each higher stage had a more internalized and autonomous idea of moral rules, a greater concern about the welfare of others, a broader conception of fairness, and so on.

Our first attempt to identify an individual's moral stage from his interview protocol used "aspect scoring." This was done with two methods: sentence scoring and story rating. Sentence scoring used a manual listing prototypical sentences on each aspect in each moral dilemma. Every statement of a subject was scored by aspect and stage; and these statements were then converted into percentages, generating a profile of stage usage for each subject.

The second method of aspect scoring was story rating. Here the subject's total response to a story was assigned a stage in terms of that stage's overall definition on each aspect. Stage mixtures were handled by intuitively weighting a dominant and a minor stage of response. An example of a story-rating manual illustrating Stage 1 reasoning on seven aspects is presented in Table 2.2, which refers to the classic example of Heinz's dilemma:

In Europe, a woman was near death from a rare form of cancer. There was one drug that the doctors thought might save her, a form of radium that a druggist in the same town had recently discovered. The druggist was charging $2,000, ten times what the drug cost him to make. The sick woman's husband, Heinz, went to everyone he knew to borrow the money, but he could only get together about half of what [the drug] cost. He told the druggist that his wife was dying and asked him to sell it cheaper or let him pay later. But the druggist said, "No." So Heinz got desperate and broke into the man's store to steal the drug for his wife.

Should the husband have done that? Why?

To illustrate the aspect-scoring procedure, we present an interview on the dilemma about Heinz and his dying wife, broken down into three statements and scored as Stage 1 by reference to Table 2.2.

Table 2.2   Aspect Scoring: Story Rating Manual with Prototypical Stage 1 Statements on Drug-Stealing Dilemma

---

Stage 1

1. *Rules:* Thinks Heinz should not steal the drug, since it is bad to steal whatever the motive; it's against external law and is a violation of the superior power of the police.
2. *Conscience:* Concern about the wrongness of stealing is in terms of fear of punishment.
3. *Altruism:* Thinks about his own welfare, not that of other people, like his wife.
4. *Duty:* Duty is only what he has to do, a husband doesn't have to steal for his wife.
5. *Self-interest:* Yields to power and punishment where rational self-interest would say to stick up for himself or to try to get away with it.
6. *Role Taking:* Since Stage 1 doesn't see things from other people's point of view, and doesn't expect them to see things from his, he expects punishment for stealing, no matter why he did what he did.
7. *Justice:* Justice in punishment is simply retribution for committing a crime, for breaking the law.

Statement 1

Should Heinz have done that?
He shouldn't do it.

Why?
Because then he'd be a thief if they caught him and put him in jail.

In terms of Table 2.2, this statement reveals the following Stage 1 moral conceptions:

1. *Rules:* It's bad to steal or break rules whatever the reason, "he'd be a thief," it's a violation of law and police.
2. *Conscience:* It's wrong because it leads to punishment.

Statement 2

Is it a husband's duty to steal?
I don't think so.

This statement indicates the following Stage 1 thinking:

3. *Altruism:* Doesn't focus on the welfare of others, such as one's wife.
4. *Duty:* Obligation is limited to what one has to do because of superior power, not obligation to other people as such.

Statement 3

If you were dying of cancer but were strong enough, would you steal the drug to save your own life?
No, because even if you did have time to take the drug, the police would put you in jail and you would die there anyway.

This statement indicates the following:

5. *Self-interest:* In thinking about his own welfare, he is not rational and does not stand up for himself or try to get away with a violation where it would be sensible to, because he believes he cannot escape the power and punishment system.

The limits of aspect scoring. In a sense, aspect scoring by story is still the easiest introduction to the stages, and yields sufficient interjudge agreement (.89). This method turned out, however, to contain too much extraneous content to yield a measure or classification meeting the invariant sequence postulate of stage theory. This failure appeared in our original analysis of twelve-year longitudinal data gathered every three years on fifty males aged 10 to 26 (Kohlberg & Kramer, 1969; Kramer, 1968). The most outstanding inversion of sequence was an apparent shift from a Stage 4 society orientation to a Stage 2 relativistic hedonism in some subjects who became "liberated" and "relativized" in their college years. Based on the fact that these subjects eventually moved on to Stage 5 principled thinking, we eventually concluded that this relativistic egoism was a transitional phase, a "Stage 4½"—a no-man's-land between rejection of conventional morality and the formulation of nonconventional or universal moral principles. The social perspective of the 4½ was clearly different from that of naive Stage 2. The 4½ questioned society and viewed himself and the rules from an "outside-of-society" perspective, whereas the Stage 2 saw things as a concrete individual relating to other individuals through concrete reciprocity, exchange, and utilities (Kohlberg, in prep.; Turiel, in press).

A second inversion of sequence was found in a small proportion of individuals who "regressed" from Stage 4 to Stage 3, or skipped from Stage 3 to Stage 5. These inversions, in turn, could be seen as due to an inadequate definition of Stage 4, a definition which equated "law-and-order" ideas (content) with taking a social system perspective (stage structure). As a result, we redefined as Stage 3 any law-and-order thinking which did not display a social system perspective (for example, an Archie Bunker concept of law and order).

These changes in conceptions of the stages reflected a growing clarity regarding the distinction between structure and content which led us to abandon aspect scoring. Our aspect scoring was based not on "structure," but on certain statistical or probabilistic associations between structure and content. For example, a social system perspective tends to yield moral judgments whose content is law and order. One can, however, have much of this content at Stage 3 without the social system perspective, or one can have the social system perspective without this content.

Accordingly, we decided to generate a new, more structural scoring method, which we call "issue scoring."

INTUITIVE ISSUE SCORING

In order to develop a more structural scoring system, the first step was to standardize or analyze types of content used at every stage. These types of content, called issues or values, represent *what* the individual is valuing, judging, or appealing to rather than his *mode of reasoning* about that issue. To analyze stage differences, we must first make sure each stage is reasoning about or from the same values. We had attempted to do this with the aspects, but they were a mixture of formal or structural characteristics of judgment (for example, motives versus consequences and sense of duty) and direct issues or value content (for example, law and rules). Accordingly, we developed the following list of issues, values, or moral institutions found in every society and culture:

1. Laws and rules
2. Conscience
3. Personal roles of affection
4. Authority
5. Civil rights
6. Contract, trust, and justice in exchange
7. Punishment and justice
8. The value of life
9. Property rights and values
10. Truth
11. Sex and sexual love

The new content issues each embody several different moral aspects. For example, thinking about the issue of contract and trust involves formal aspects of altruism, duty, rules, role taking, fairness, and so on.

Our classification of content in terms of issues also gave rise to a new unit to be rated. This unit is all the ideas a person uses concerning an issue in a story. The old system had rated each separate idea separately (sentence scoring) or else rated the story as a whole (story rating). But the sentence unit had proven too small for structural classification, while the story unit had proven too large for analytic, as opposed to ideal, typological scoring.

Having decided on issues, we then defined stage thinking on each issue. An example is the conception of life issue as worked out for Heinz's dilemma about stealing the drug (Table 2.3). To illustrate the use of this issue in scoring, here are excerpts from an interview with Tommy, a 10-year-old boy who spontaneously focuses on the life issue.

His wife was sick and if she didn't get the drug quickly, she might die. Maybe his wife is an important person and runs a store and the man buys stuff from her and can't get it any other place. The police would blame the owner that he didn't save the wife.

Does it matter whether the wife is important or not?
If someone important is in a plane and is allergic to heights and the stewardess won't

---

TABLE 2.3   Issue Scoring Stages in Heinz's Dilemma

Stage	*What is life's value in the situation?*	*Why is life valuable?*
Stage 1	Wife's life has no clear value here to husband or others when it conflicts with law and property. Does not see that husband would value his wife's life over stealing.	Does not give a reason and does not indicate understanding that life is worth more than property.
Stage 2	It is its immediate value to the husband and to the wife, herself. Assumes the husband would think his wife's life is worth stealing for, but he isn't obligated to if he doesn't like her enough. Life's value to a person other than its possessor depends on relationship; you wouldn't steal to save the life of a mere friend or acquaintance.	Each person wants to live more than anything else. You can replace property, not life.
Stage 3	Life's value is its value to any good, caring, person like the husband. The husband should care enough to risk stealing (even if he does not steal), and a friend should care enough to save the life of a friend or another person.	People should care for other people and their lives. You're not good or human if you don't. People have much more feeling for life than for anything material.
Stage 4	Even though he may think it wrong to steal, he understands the general value or *sacredness* of human life or the rule to preserve life. Sacredness means all other values can't be compared with the value of life. The value of life is general; human life is valuable no matter what your relationship to the person is, though this doesn't obligate you to steal.	Life is valuable because God created it and made it sacred. Or life is valuable because it is basic to society; it is a basic right of people.
Stage 5	He recognizes that in this situation the wife's *right to life* comes before the druggist's right to property. There is some obligation to steal for anyone dying; everyone has a right to live and to be saved.	Everyone or society logically and morally must place each person's individual right to life before other rights such as the right to property.

give him medicine because she's only got enough for one and she's got a sick friend in back, they should put the stewardess in a lady's jail because she didn't help the important one.

Is it better to save the life of one important person or a lot of unimportant people? All the people that aren't important, because one man just has one house, maybe a lot of furniture, but a whole bunch of people have an awful lot of furniture and some of these poor people might have a lot of money and it doesn't look it.

Is Tommy's response Stage 1, Stage 2, or Stage 3 in terms of "Why is life valuable?" Tommy does not seem to fit Stage 1 in Table 2.3, since his response indicates that the wife's life does have a value justifying stealing. His response is Stage 1, however, because Tommy does not clearly recognize that life is more valuable to an individual than property. He says the lives of a lot of people who aren't important are worth more than the life of one important person because all the ordinary people together have more furniture or property. This is Stage 1 thinking, not Stage 2, because the value of life depends on a vague status of being important, not on the husband's or wife's interests or needs.

STANDARDIZED ISSUE SCORING

The procedure just discussed is called *intuitive issue scoring* and is theoretically the most valid method of scoring, since it is instrument free, that is, applicable to any moral dilemma. It is adequately reliable (90 percent interrater agreement) in the hands of thoroughly trained or experienced scorers. Reliable intuitive scoring, however, cannot be learned without personal teaching and supervised experience. It also is too intuitive to provide satisfactory test-construction characteristics of item difficulty, item independence, written versus oral interviews, and so on. We are therefore now developing a manual for

standardized issue scoring (Kohlberg, Colby, Speicher-Dubin, & Lieberman, 1975). This manual is based on a standardized interview which probes only two issues on each of three stories. The standard form, Form A, contains three stories covering six issues as follows:

Story I: Heinz steals the drug
Issues: Life, punishment

Story II: The father breaks a promise to his son
Issues: Contract, personal relationship

Story III: One man cons, another steals
Issues: Property and conscience

There is a second form for retest purposes, Form B, with different stories covering the same issues.

The manual for standardized issue scoring presents criterion concepts defining each stage on each issue for each story. A *criterion concept* is the reasoning pattern that is most distinctive of a given stage. Theoretically, such reasoning follows from the structural definition of the stage. Empirically, the criterion concept is actually used by a substantial number of subjects at that stage (as defined by their global score) and not at other stages.

In the old sentence-scoring interview, sentences were matched to "prototypical" sentences of each stage in a manual. In some sense the new system returns to this procedure, but with controls. The first control is for the presence of the response in terms of the content or issue of response. The new system eliminates the problem of whether a criterion concept at a given stage is not expressed because the subject does not have a stage structure for that concept, or whether it is not expressed because the content (or issue) of response has not been elicited by the interview. The second control distinguishes between matching to a verbal sentence and matching to a criterion concept. On the unit-of-response side, this implies that the unit of interpretation is bigger than the sentence.

It also implies that the stage structure of the criterion concept is clarified or distinguished from particular examples or exemplars.

The methodology of establishing standardized scoring is like Loevinger's methodology (Loevinger & Wessler, 1970) for scoring ego stage in that criterion items are defined by reference to their use by individuals who have been intuitively staged. The difference, however, is that the criterion concepts are not the result of sheer empirical item analysis; rather they must logically fit the theoretical stage description.

In our opinion, this standardized scoring system goes as far toward standardization as is possible while maintaining theoretical validity. We define "validity" as true measurement of development, that is, of longitudinal invariant sequence. A more common notion of test validation is prediction from a test to some criterion external to the test of which the test is presumed to be an indicator. Using the latter notion, some people assume that a moral judgment test should be validated by predicting "moral behavior." In this sense, Hartshorne and May's tests (1928–1930) of "moral knowledge" fail to be valid, since they do not predict well to morally conforming behavior in ratings or experiments. We have argued that moral stage development predicts maturity of moral behavior better than Hartshorne and May's measures; but we have also argued that moral behavior is not a proper external criterion for "validating" a moral judgment test. From the point of view of cognitive-developmental theory, the relationship of the development of judgment to action is something to be studied and theoretically conceptualized; the issue is not one of "validating" a judgment test by a quantitative correlation with behavior.

Using the concept of external criterion validation, others have thought that a test of moral development should be validated

by its relationship to *age*, a key meaning of the term "development." While our measure of moral judgment maturity does correlate with chronological age in adolescents aged 10 to 18 ($r = +.71$), such a correlation is not "validating." Many adults are morally immature, so that a test which maximized correlation with age would ecologically relate to age but have little relation to *moral development*. The validity criterion of moral judgment development is construct validity, not prediction to an external criterion. *Construct validity* here means the fit of data obtained by means of the test to primary components of its theoretical definition. The primary theoretical definition of structural moral development is that of an organization passing through invariant sequential stages. The structural stage method meets this criterion in that longitudinal data so rated display invariant steplike change (Selman, Byrne, & Kohlberg, in prep.). The criterion for validity for our new standard moral-reasoning test is congruence with, or prediction to, structural scoring.

The construct validity of a moral development measure also has a philosophical or ethical dimension as well as a psychological dimension, that is, the requirement that a higher moral stage be a philosophically more adequate way of reasoning about moral dilemmas than a lower stage. This is a judgment about ways of thinking, not a grading of the moral worth of the individual. We claim (Kohlberg, 1971a) that each higher stage of reasoning is a more adequate way of resolving moral problems judged by moral-philosophic criteria. This claim is, again, made for structural scoring stages; a "standardized" test may be said to be valid insofar as it correlates with, or predicts to, structural stage.

An alternative approach to standardizing measurement of moral development is set forth in Rest's presentation of his Defining-Issues test (Chap. 11). Rest relies primarily on the more usual approach to empirical test construction and validation. Test construction is by empirical item analysis. The test is conceived as assessing a continuous variable of moral maturity rather than discrete qualitative stages. Test validation is primarily defined by correlations with various criteria such as age, having studied moral philosophy, and so on. Rest, like my colleagues and myself, is interested in construct validity, not simply prediction to an external criterion. His conception of construct validity, however, is the notion of moderate-to-high correlaions with other tests or variables expected to be associated with the test or variable in question. Instead, our conception of construct validity implies assignment of individuals to stages in such a way that the criterion of sequential movement is met. In our opinion, Rest's approach does provide a rough estimate of an individual's moral maturity level, as suggested by his reported correlation of .68 between his measure and an issue scoring of moral dilemma interviews.

We believe Rest's method is useful for exploratory examination of the correlates of moral maturity, but not for testing theoretical propositions derived from the cognitive-developmental theory of moral stages. Choice of various methods, then, must weigh facility of data gathering and analysis against relatively error-free tests of structural theory.

In What Sense Are the Stages "True"?

In claiming that our stages are "true," we mean first that stage definitions are rigidly constrained by the empirical criterion of the stage concept. Many possible stages may be conceptualized, but only one set of stages can be manifested as a longitudinal invariant sequence. The claim we make is that anyone who interviewed children about moral dilemmas and who followed them longitudinally in time would come

to our six stages and no others. A second empirical criterion is that of the "structured whole," that is, individuals should be consistently at a stage unless they are in transition to the next stage (when they are considered in mixed stages). The fact that almost all individuals manifest more than 50 percent of responses at a single stage with the rest at adjacent stages supports this criterion.

Second, in claiming that the stages are "true," we mean that the conceptual structure of the stage is not contingent on a specific psychological theory. They are, rather, matters of adequate logical analysis. By this we mean the following:

1. The ideas used to define the stages are the subjects', not ours. The logical connections among ideas define a given stage. The logical analysis of the connections in a child's thinking is itself theoretically neutral. It is not contingent on a psychological theory any more than is a philosopher's analysis of the logical connections in Aristotle's thinking.

2. The fact that a later stage includes and presupposes the prior stage is, again, a matter of logical analysis, not psychological theory.

3. The claim that a given child's ideas *cohere* in a stagelike way is a matter of logical analysis of internal connections between the various ideas held by the stage.

In short, the correctness of the stages as a description of moral development is a matter of empirical observation and of the analysis of the logical connections in children's ideas, not a matter of social science theory.

While *the stages themselves are not a theory*, as descriptions of moral development they do have definite and radical implications for a social science *theory of moralization*. Accordingly, we shall now (1) elaborate a cognitive-developmental theory of moralization which can explain the facts of sequential moral development and (2) contrast it with socialization theories of moralization.

Types of Moralization Theory:
Cognitive-Developmental,
Socialization, and
Psychoanalytic Theories

A discussion of a cognitive-developmental moral theory immediately suggests the work of Piaget (1932). Piaget's concepts, however, may best be considered as only one example of the cognitive-developmental approach to morality represented in various ways by J. M. Baldwin (1906), Bull (1969), J. Dewey and J. H. Tufts (1932), Harvey, Hunt, & Schroeder (1961), Hobhouse (1906), Kohlberg (1964), McDougall (1908), and G. H. Mead (1934). The most obvious characteristic of cognitive-developmental theories is their use of some type of stage concept, of some notion of age-linked sequential reorganizations in the development of moral attitudes. Other common assumptions of cognitive-developmental theories are:

1. Moral development has a basic cognitive-structural or moral judgmental component.
2. The basic motivation for morality is a generalized motivation for acceptance, competence, self-esteem, or self-realization, rather than for meeting biological needs and reducing anxiety or fear.
3. Major aspects of moral development are culturally universal, because all cultures have common sources of social interaction, role taking, and social conflict, which require moral integration.
4. Basic moral norms and principles are structures arising through experiences of social interaction, rather than through internalization of rules that exist as external structures; moral stages are not defined by internalized rules, but by structures of interaction between the self and others.
5. Environmental influences in moral development are defined by the general quality and extent of cognitive and social stimulation throughout the child's development, rather than by specific experiences with parents or experiences of discipline, punishment, and reward.

These assumptions contrast sharply with those of "socialization," or "social-learning," theories of morality. The work of Aronfreed (1968c), Bandura and Walters (1959), Berkowitz (1964), Hoffman (1970a), Miller and Swanson (1960), Sears, Rau, and Alpert (1965), and Whiting and Child (1953) may be included under this general rubric. The social-learning theories assume that:

1. Moral development is growth of behavioral and affective conformity to moral rules rather than cognitive-structural change.
2. The basic motivation for morality at every point of moral development is rooted in biological needs or the pursuit of social reward and avoidance of social punishment.
3. Moral development or morality is culturally relative.
4. Basic moral norms are the internalization of external cultural rules.
5. Environmental influences on normal moral development are defined by quantitative variations in strength of reward, punishment, prohibitions, and modeling of conforming behavior by parents and other socializing agents.

Research based on classical Freudian theory can also be included under the socialization rubric. While the classical Freudian psychoanalytic theory of moral development (Flugel, 1955) cannot be equated with social-learning theories of moralization, it shares with these theories the assumption that moralization is a process of internalization of cultural or parental norms. Further, while Freudian theory (like cognitive-developmental theory) postulates stages, these classical Freudian stages are libidinal-instinctual rather than moral, and morality (as expressed by the superego) is conceived as formed and fixed early in development through internalization of parental norms. As a result, systematic research based on Freudian moral theory has ignored stage components of moral development and has focused on "internalization" aspects of the theory (Kohlberg, 1963b).

A forthcoming book (Kohlberg, in prep.) reports on forty studies which represent an accumulation of replicated findings firmly consistent with a cognitive-developmental theory of moralization, and quite inexplicable from the view of socialization theories. The next section elaborates the cognitive-developmental view of how the social environment stimulates moral stage development.

How Does Cognitive-Developmental Theory Characterize Environmental Stimulation of Moral Development?

Moral development depends upon stimulation defined in cognitive-structural terms, but this stimulation must also be social, the kind that comes from social interaction and from moral decision-making, moral dialogue, and moral interaction. "Pure cognitive" stimulation is a necessary background for moral development, but does not directly engender moral development. As noted earlier, we have found that attainment of a moral stage requires cognitive development, but cognitive development will not directly lead to moral development. On the other hand, an absence of cognitive stimulation necessary for developing formal logical reasoning may be important in explaining ceilings on moral level. In a Turkish village, for example, full formal operational reasoning appeared to be extremely rare (if the Piagetian techniques for intellectual assessment can be considered usable in that setting). Accordingly, one would not expect that principled (Stage 5 or 6) moral reasoning, which requires formal thinking as a base, could develop in that cultural context.

Of more importance than factors related to stimulation of cognitive stage are factors of general social experience and stimulation, which we call *role-taking opportunities*. What differentiates social experience from interaction with things is

the fact that social experience involves role taking: taking the attitude of others, becoming aware of their thoughts and feelings, putting oneself in their place. When the emotional side of role taking is stressed, it is typically termed "empathy" (or "sympathy"). The term "role taking," coined by G. H. Mead (1934), is preferable, however, because (1) it emphasizes the cognitive as well as the affective side, (2) it involves an organized structural relationship between self and others, (3) it emphasizes that the process involves understanding and relating to all the roles in the society of which one is a part, and (4) it emphasizes that role taking goes on in *all* social interactions and communication situations, not merely in ones that arouse emotions of sympathy or empathy.

Although moral judgments entail role taking—putting oneself in the place of the various people involved in a moral conflict—attainment of a given role-taking stage, as indicated earlier, is a necessary but not a sufficient condition for moral development. As an example, the role-taking advance necessary for Stage 2 moral reasoning is awareness that each person in a situation can or does consider the intention or point of view of every other individual in the situation. A child may attain this role-taking level and still hold the Stage 1 notion that right or justice is adherence to fixed rules which must be automatically followed. But if the child is to see rightness or justice as a balance or exchange between the interests of individual actors (Stage 2), he must have reached the requisite level of role taking. Role-taking level, then, is a bridge between logical or cognitive level and moral level; it is one's level of social cognition.

In understanding the effects of social environment on moral development, then, we must consider that environment's provision of role-taking opportunities to the child. Variations in role-taking opportunities exist in terms of the child's relation to his family, his peer group, his school, and his social status vis-à-vis the larger economic and political structure of the society.

With regard to the family, the disposition of parents to allow or encourage dialogue on value issues is one of the clearest determinants of moral stage advance in children (Holstein, 1968). Such an exchange of viewpoints and attitudes is part of what we term "role-taking opportunities." With regard to peer groups, children high in peer participation are more advanced in moral stage than are those who are low. With regard to status in the larger society, socioeconomic status is correlated with moral development in various cultures (Kohlberg, in prep.). This, we believe, is due to the fact that middle-class children have more opportunity to take the point of view of the more distant, impersonal, and influential roles in society's basic institutions (law, economy, government, economics) than do lower-class children. In general, the higher an individual child's participation in a social group or institution, the more opportunities he has to take the social perspectives of others. From this point of view, extensive participation in any particular group is not essential to moral development but participation in some group is. Not only is participation necessary, but mutuality of role taking is also necessary. If, for instance, adults do not consider the child's point of view, the child may not communicate or take the adult's point of view.

To illustrate environments at opposite extremes in role-taking opportunities, we may cite an American orphanage and an Israeli kibbutz. Of all environments we have studied, the American orphanage had children at the lowest level, Stages 1 and 2, even through adolescence (Thrower, in prep.). Of all environments studied, an Israeli kibbutz had children at the highest level, with adolescents mainly at Stage 4 and with a considerable percentage at Stage 5 (Bar-Yam, Reimer, & Kohlberg, in prep.) Both orphanage and kibbutz environments involved low interaction with

parents, but were dramatically different in other ways. The American orphanages not only lacked parental interaction but involved very little communication and role taking between staff adults and children. Relations among the children themselves were fragmentary, with very little communication and no stimulation or supervision of peer interaction by the staff. That the deprivation of role-taking opportunities caused a retardation in role taking as well as in moral judgment was suggested by the fact that the orphanage adolescents failed a role-taking task passed by almost all children of their chronological and mental age. In contrast, children in the kibbutz engaged in intense peer interaction supervised by a group leader who was concerned about bringing the young people into the kibbutz community as active dedicated participants. Discussing, reasoning, communicating feelings, and making group decisions were central everyday activities.

Obviously, the kibbutz differed as a moral environment from the orphanage in other ways as well. Beyond provision of role-taking opportunities by groups and institutions, how do we define the *moral atmosphere* of a group or institution? We have said that the core of the specifically moral component of moral judgment is a sense of justice. While role taking defines the conflicting points of view taken in a moral situation, the "principles" for resolving conflicting points of view at each moral stage are principles of justice, of giving each his due. The core of the moral atmosphere of an institution or environment, then, is its justice structure, "the way in which social institutions distribute fundamental rights and duties and determine the division of advantages from social cooperation" (Rawls, 1971, p. 7).

It appears from our research that a group or institution tends to be perceived as being at a certain moral stage by its participants. Our empirical work on this has been primarily based on the perception by inmates of the atmospheres of various prisons in which they were incarcerated (Kohlberg, Scharf, & Hickey, 1972). While for reasons of comprehension inmates cannot perceive an institution as being at a higher level than their own stage, they can perceive it as being at a lower stage. Thus, Stage 3 inmates perceived one reformatory as Stage 1, another as Stage 2, and a third as Stage 3. An example of a Stage 3 prisoner's perception of staff in the Stage 3 institution is, "They are pretty nice and they show interest. I get the feeling that they care a little more than most people do." An example of a Stage 3 inmate's perception of staff as being Stage 2 in the Stage 2 institution is, "If a guy messes up in a certain way or doesn't brown-nose as much as he should, the counselor won't do a job for him. It's all favoritism. If you go out of your way for a guy, he will go out of his way for you."

Even more extreme perceptions of the subjects' world or institution as being low stage were shown in the orphanage study. With regard to parents, here is a 15-year-old boy's response:

Why should a promise be kept?
They aren't. My mother called up and says, "I will be up in two weeks," then I don't see her for eight months. That really kills you, something like that.

On the moral judgment test this boy was beginning to show some Stage 3 concern about affection, promises, and so on; but his world was one in which such things meant nothing. This boy's mother is Stage 2, but the orphanage environment presents no higher-stage moral world. While the nuns who direct this particular orphanage are personally conventionally moral, their moral ideology translates into a justice structure perceived as Stage 1 by this boy. He says:

It really breaks your heart to tell the truth because sometimes you get in trouble for it. I was playing and I swung a rock and

hit a car. It was an accident, but I told the sister. I got punished for it.

Obviously, prisons and orphanages are exceptional in representing monolithic or homogeneous lower-stage environments. It is plausible in general, however, that the moral atmosphere of environments is more than the sum of the individual moral judgments and actions of its members. It is also plausible that participation in institutions that have the potential of being seen as at a higher stage than the child's own is a basic determinant of moral development.

A notion that a higher-stage environment stimulates moral development is an obvious extension of experimental findings by Turiel (1966) and Rest and Kohlberg (in prep.) that adolescents tend to assimilate moral reasoning from the next stage above their own, while they reject reasoning below their own. The concept of exposure to a higher stage need not be limited to a stage of reasoning, however; it may also include exposures to moral action and to institutional arrangements. What the moral atmosphere studies we have quoted show is that individuals respond to a composite of moral reasoning, moral action, and institutionalized rules as a relatively unified whole in relation to their own moral stage.

Using the notion that creation of a higher-stage institutional atmosphere will lead to moral change, Hickey, Scharf, and Kohlberg (in prep.) developed a "just community" in a women's prison involving democratic self-government through community decisions as well as small-group moral discussion. This program led to an upward change in moral reasoning as well as to later changes in life-style and behavior.

In addition to the role-taking opportunities and the perceived moral level provided by an institution, a third factor stressed by cognitive-developmental theory is cognitive-moral conflict. Structural theory stresses that movement to the next stage occurs through reflective reorganization arising from sensed contradictions in one's current stage structure. Experiences of cognitive conflict can occur either through exposure to decision situations that arouse internal contradictions in one's moral reasoning structure, or through exposure to the moral reasoning of significant others which is discrepant in content or structure from one's own reasoning. This principle is central to the moral discussion program that we have implemented in schools (Blatt & Kohlberg, 1975; Colby 1972). While peer-group moral discussion of dilemmas leads to moral stage change through exposure to the next stage of reasoning, discussion without such exposure also leads to moral change. Colby (1972) found, for example, that a program of moral discussion led to some development of Stage 5 thinking on a posttest in a group of conventional level students who had shown no Stage 5 reasoning on the pretest.

Real-life situations and choices vary dramatically in their potential for moral-cognitive conflict of a personal nature. This conclusion comes from our longitudinal data on the movement of individuals from conventional to principled morality (Kohlberg, in prep.). One factor that appears to have precipitated the beginning of this shift was the college moratorium experience of responsibility and independence from authority together with exposure to openly conflicting and relativistic values and standards. The conflict involved here was between the subject's own conventional morality, and a world with potentials for action that did not fit conventional morality. Some of our other subjects changed in more dramatic moral situations which aroused conflict about the adequacy of conventional morality. One subject, for example, moved from conventional to principled thinking while serving as an officer in Vietnam, apparently because of awareness of the conflict between law-and-order "Army morality" and the more universal rights of the Vietnamese.

Moral Development and Ego Development

As we move from general characteristics of environments to the more individual life experiences that seem to promote moral change, a cognitive-developmental theory begins to seem limited and abstract. At this point, one begins to draw upon theories such as Erikson's (1963), which present age-typical emotional experiences as they relate to a developing personality or self. It then becomes useful to look at the individual's ego level as well as his moral stage. In this sense, ego-development theories represent possible extensions of cognitive-developmental theory as it moves into the study of individual lives and life histories. There is a broad unity to the development of social perception and social values which deserves the name "ego development." This unity is perhaps better conceived as a matter of levels than of structural stages, since the unity of ego levels is not that of logical or moral stage structures. The requirements for consistency in logic and morals are much tighter than those for consistency in personality, which is a psychological, not a logical, unity. Furthermore, there are relatively clear criteria of increased adequacy in logical and moral hierarchies, but not in ego levels.

Because moral stages have a tighter unitary structure, it would be a mistake to view them as simply reflections of broader ego levels. Writers such as Peck and Havighurst (1960) and Loevinger and Wessler (1970) have nevertheless treated moral development as part of more general stages of ego or character development—indeed, as a bench mark for such development. If ego development is seen as the successive restructuring of the relationship between the self and standards, it is natural for ego-development theorists to use changes in the moral domain as bench marks. Similar restructurings are assumed to hold in the relations of the self to values in other areas such as work achievement, sociability, art, politics, religion, and so on.

We hold, however, that there is a unity and consistency to moral structures, that the unique characteristics of moral structures are defined by formalistic moral philosophy, and that to treat moral development as simply a facet of ego (or of cognitive) development is to miss many of its special problems and features. We believe that

1. Cognitive development or structures are more general than, and are embodied in, both self or ego structures and in moral judgment.
2. Generalized ego structures (modes of perceiving self and social relations) are more general than, and are embodied in, moral structures.
3. Cognitive development is a necessary but not sufficient condition for ego development.
4. Certain features of ego development are a necessary but not sufficient condition for development of moral structures.
5. The higher the moral stage, the more distinct it is from the parallel ego stage.

While these propositions suggest a high correlation between measures of ego development and measures of moral development, such a correlation does not imply that moral development can be defined simply as a division or area of ego development. Moral structures distinct from ego structures can be found, however, only if moral stages are first defined in ways more specific than the ways used to characterize ego development. If this specification is not made in the initial definition of moral development, one is bound to find moral development to be simply an aspect of ego development, as Peck and Havighurst (1960) and Loevinger and Wessler (1970) have. Loevinger's inability to differentiate moral items from nonmoral items in her measure of ego development simply demonstrates that her criteria of moral development were not more specific than her general criteria of ego development.

In summary, a broad psychological cognitive-developmental theory of moralization is an ego-developmental theory. Furthermore, in understanding moral functioning, one must place the individual's moral stage within the broader context of his ego level. To see moral stages as simply reflections of ego level, however, is to lose the ability to theoretically define and empirically find order in the specifically moral domain of the human personality.

CHAPTER 3

Moral Development from the Standpoint of a General Psychological Theory

Justin Aronfreed

Introduction

It is characteristic of anything really complex about the human condition that it offers a severe test of both the power and the breadth of a psychological theory. As in the case of any other science, each theoretical perspective in psychology is necessarily built on a limited realm of observation and experiment. And different perspectives vary in the degree to which they focus on observations that are basic or general enough to be extended to other realms. Of course, any robust psychological theory wants to demonstrate its vigor on aspects of human behavior other than those for which it was specifically designed. But the pressure of social reality seems to offer an especially strong temptation for a point of view to expand in splendid isolation when the domain of expansion is special or essential to human affairs. There the tendency often is to overextend concepts which should have been used more modestly, or else to succumb to the most obvious surface features of human action and thought, without sufficient regard for the more fundamental analysis that is required to advance knowledge. Among the social and philosophical issues that exercise a fatal attraction on psychological theory, it is doubtful whether any has been more seductive than the question of man's status as a moral creature. I will try in this brief essay to outline some of the ways in which the problem of understanding moral development illuminates the larger problems of a general psychological construction of the child (and the adult).

Psychoanalytic theory may fairly be considered the first fully psychological theory of moral development. Like other theorists among philosophers as early as Augustine, S. Freud (1927; 1936; Chap. 8) tried to distinguish between the functions of knowledge and feeling in the operation of an internalized conscience. Freud's conception of the superego was also sensitive to the massive behavioral expressions of conscience, which often appeared not to require rational thought or even voluntary decision. However, the direction taken by psychoanalytic theory was not well suited to a more integrative account of the affective, cognitive, and behavioral ingredients of the child's acquisition of conscience.

The ideological force of the theory, with its emphasis at first on "instincts" and later on an inner emotional life, tends to separate if from whatever empirical and conceptual progress has been made within other paradigms of psychological science. It is particularly difficult to find meeting points between psychoanalytic theory and more contemporary knowledge of the processes of learning and development in children. Our current paradigms tend toward a more refined picture of the child's plasticity in transactions between his predispositions and his experience of the external world.

Behavioristic theories of learning have also been elaborated into a strong point of view about the origins of social conduct. The earliest extensions of these theories were little more than extrapolations from the patterns of learning displayed by animals (Holt, 1931; N. E. Miller & Dollard, 1941; Thorndike, 1911). However, later versions escalated their observational base to human social behavior and its antecedents in childrearing (Mowrer, 1960, chap. 3; Sears, Maccoby, & Levin, 1957, chap. 10; J. W. M. Whiting & Child, 1953, chap. 11). They also went well beyond an account of the immediate effects of external rewards and punishments, in an attempt to explain how internalized monitors of conduct could become independent of direct social reinforcement. These later versions even have a discernible second generation, which has used experimental paradigms of children's "social learning" to argue that the internalization of conscience can be understood as the shaping of the child's behavior by such processes as imitative modeling and self-generation of reinforcing events (Bandura & Walters, 1963; Kanfer & Phillips, 1970; Mischel, 1966).

Although these learning-theoretical approaches generally assume that their mechanisms of learning will cope with the transmission of values from socializing agents to children, they do not specify any developmental analysis of either the cognitive or affective dimensions of values.

Social-learning theories, even in their most sophisticated extensions, restrict values to the role of an inferred cognitive mediator of overt behavior. They do not really address the question of how values gain control over the child's actions. And since these theories also do not examine the nature of representational thought, they can hardly be expected to illuminate the contribution that moral judgment makes to the development of conscience.

The conceptual tradition that concerns itself most specifically with moral judgment has been the qualitative description of the substance and structure of different types of thinking about the rules governing human interactions. Durkheim (1961) may have been the first to offer, early in the twentieth century, a thoroughly psychological as well as sociological treatment of moral thought in this tradition. His analysis of the child's internalization of normative values deserves more attention than it has received from psychologists who are interested in the most highly developed forms of human cognition. The distinctions that Durkheim made among different orientations to moral rules were based primarily on an implicit notion of changes in the child's perspective on the relationship between himself and others. But the later expressions of this tradition placed the varieties of moral thought explicitly in a framework of sequential stages of cognitive development, which were conceived of as qualitatively distinct structures.

Piaget's investigations (1932; Lickona, Chap. 12) of children's conceptions of rules of conduct led him to the view that there are two major stages in the development of moral thought (after an initial stage in which the very young child shows only certain stereotypes of concrete action). Piaget characterized the first stage as a moral heteronomy of absolute and rigid judgments oriented toward multiple sources of external authority. The second stage he described as a more autonomous and relativistic subscription to principles obtained through social contract. Kohlberg (1969b, 1971b) has advanced a far more systematic and elaborate classification of sequential stages of moral development, which he describes in Chapter 2. Based on respondents' rationales for choices of acts in hypothetical story-situations, his system distinguishes six stages of moral thought, which reduce in turn to the three essential types of *preconventional, conventional,* and *principled.*

In contrast to the focus of "social-learning" theories on the internalized control of the overt behavioral surface of conduct, cognitive theories of moral development are based on verbal indices of changes in the thinking processes which underlie the child's choices among alternative actions. It is especially clear in Kohlberg's system that the developmental stages of moral judgment differ not only in the substance of their axioms of legitimacy or justification, but also in the type and power of the reasoning applied to the axioms. Developmental-cognitive approaches to the acquisition of conscience provide a welcome antidote to a behavioristic paradigm in which an act is regarded as "moral" by virtue of its conformity to an external norm. Since representational thought is far richer in structure and potential variety than are the mere acts of conduct which can be subjected to normative definitions of conformity or deviance, it follows that the moral status of an act cannot be determined without knowing the categories and operations of value through which it has been processed.

At the same time, stages of moral thought are markedly deficient as a complete account of the development of the child's conscience. Although their systematic exposition is sometimes set forth under the claim of affective or motivational as well as cognitive criteria, their essential base of evidence in fact reduces to different types of reasoning. But knowledge is not equivalent to action. And the richest cognitive map of the child's moral domain does not specify the affective mechanisms that are required in order for reasoning to control behavior. The power of affective components in the internalization of conscience is well demonstrated in the great repertoires of human conduct which are molded by the rewards and punishments of socialization, yet come to be independently maintained in a automatized or stereotyped manner. Common observation as well as introspection can raise some very serious questions about whether any significant amount of moral decision-making enters into the internalized control of conduct for most human beings (despite the fact that various states of moral knowledge may be available to them). Moreover, even when the control of conduct takes place through evaluative cognition, it may more typically rest on representational thought that is not structured in truly moral categories. Accordingly, the conception of the child as a miniaturized moral philosopher leaves something to be desired when one takes a larger psychological view of the full range of manifestations of conscience.

There is the further consideration that most of the relevant evidence for moral stages is not in the form of longitudinal succession within the individual, but consists rather of increments and declines of specific stages over cross-sectional groups of respondents of different ages, together with a high incidence of mixed but adjacent stages within the prescribed order (Kohlberg, 1963a; Kohlberg & Kramer, 1969). The interpretation of the evidence therefore tends to drain into an oversimplified typology of character, in which a premium is placed on the stages regarded as "higher" or more "mature." Aside from the sheer cognitive power that is obviously required for a respondent's formulation of the higher stages, the reasons offered for such a system of classification do not go persuasively beyond a commitment to a philosophical position. And in such an evolutionary framework, it is sometimes difficult to distinguish natural philosophy from moral philosophy. The difficulty is not resolved by demonstrations that the different stages have some correlation with variations in the actual behavior of respondents in situations of apparent moral conflict (Kohlberg, 1969b). It is easy enough to find a behavioral situation that divides the value categories of one stage from those of another. Adding behavioral components to character portraits cannot be a substitute for theoretical and empirical analysis of the nature of the bonds between thought and action.

An Illustrative Experiment

I have offered elsewhere (Aronfreed, 1968c) some detailed experimental and conceptual analyses of the socialization process and its transformation into the internalized control of conduct. These analyses aim at both the affective and cognitive mechanisms that underlie the child's acquisition and maintenance of conscience. The mechanisms are required to account not only for the internalized residues of the child's direct experience of reward and punishment, but also for the enduring behavioral and representational products of imitation, of empathic or vicarious learning, and of other transmission processes which rest on the observation of social models. For our purpose here, which is to illustrate how an understanding of the development of conscience needs a more fundamental psychological base, it will be sufficient to describe briefly one line of work. This work examines the effectiveness of punishment learning in producing internalized suppression of the child's punished behavior. Although punishment learning is usually seen as bearing upon only one aspect of conscience, its analysis can be made to include many of the central issues in a general account of moral development.

The choice of punishment learning as an illustration may serve also to dilute a long-standing and uncritical ideological conviction that children do not learn well in its dominion. It is in fact doubtful that socialization ever takes place without those inherently aversive events which a child must perceive as contingent on his own actions and intended by others to suppress his behavior. When punishment is defined broadly enough to include rejection, disapproval, and other kinds of "psychological" discipline—and not just the more obvious physical or verbal attacks—it can be clearly seen to be an inevitable part of childrearing. The pervasiveness of punishment, rather than the question of its social desirability, is a proper starting point for scientific investigation.

The experiment I shall outline here is given only in the most basic features of its methods and results. It is conducted with boys and girls ranging roughly from 8 to 10 years of age. And the results are the same for both sexes. The details of experimental method, and the numerous variations of conditions and parameters, have been extensively described elsewhere (Aronfreed, 1968a).

The experiment begins with a training period in which the individual child is presented, over a series of ten successive trials, with different pairs of very small toy replicas of real and familiar common objects. Although the toys vary from one trial to another, one of the toys in each pair is always highly attractive, while the other is relatively unattractive and nondescript. In each trial the child is asked to pick up the toy that he wants to tell about, to hold it briefly in his hand, and then to tell something about the toy when requested to do so. Somewhere within this sequence of behavioral components, the child is punished during any trial on which he chooses the attractive toy. The punishment consists of verbal disapproval ("*No!*") and deprivation of candy by the experimental agent of socialization, without any further explanation (other than that implied in the original instructions, which simply warn the child that some choices are not permitted, without specifying which ones).

The timing of the punishment with respect to the onset and termination of a transgression sequence varies in four steps, which represent distinct experimental training conditions. But the timing remains consistent over trials for the subjects within any one of these conditions. In contrast, the subject is always permitted to choose and tell about an unattractive toy without punishment. Although the children invariably begin with choices of the attractive toys, they learn very quickly in this type of training. Almost all of them begin to choose the unattractive toy after only one or two punishments. And they continue to do so throughout the trials.

The really interesting observation occurs during a common test for internalization, which directly follows all four of the different training conditions. The child is left alone on a carefully prepared pretext, under conditions which free him of any apparent risk of surveillance. Again he is confronted with a pair of small toys. The attractive toy is a minute glass, in which salt descends from an upper to a lower chamber (it is extremely difficult for children to resist the urge to handle this object). And the unattractive toy is more nondescript than ever.

It is now possible to see the internalized power of the behavioral suppression that punishment has induced during training. The strength of the suppression, as indexed by covert monitors of the occurrence and latency of a transgression, is highly predictable from the four training variations in the timing of punishment. For example, after the training condition in which punishment is introduced quite early in the sequential components of the act of transgression (while the child is still reaching), the majority of children never touch the attractive toy during the test for internalization. Other children in this condition succumb to temptation only after a long period of resistance. But for virtually all children who have been punished *during* training at the latest point in the act of transgression (after telling about the toy), handling of the attractive toy usually begins almost immediately when the experimental agent leaves the room. Intermediate values in the timing of punishment during training also produce reliably distinct strengths of suppression during the test for internalization.

After the experimental session is over, the children are questioned about their choices of toys during both training and test. Almost none of them can verbalize anything that even approaches an evaluative standard. In trying to account for their actions, they refer uniformly only to the danger of external punishment (in the presence of the agent). This result can hardly be surprising when we consider its parallels in the socialization process in natural settings. Many of the initially dominant behavioral dispositions of very young and even preverbal children can be effectively suppressed only by the aversive outcomes transmitted in the reactions of their parents. And even when parental reactions are not so explicit as to fit the ordinary meaning of punishment, they may be aversive enough that the child's behavior continues to be suppressed in the parents' absence. Yet it is often quite clear that children at this early age do not have a standard of judgment capable of differentiating punished actions from unpunished alternatives—particularly in view of the complexity of the distinctions to be made not only among actions, but also among their situational determinants and possible consequences, in the definition of a transgression. One need only observe the infant who can just crawl as he reaches for an electrical outlet, yet refrains from touching it because of a few past experiences with the reactions of other people (even though no one is now visibly present). It is sobering also to consider that essentially the same experimental effect on internalized suppression can be obtained with dogs (Solomon, Turner, & Lessac, 1968).

Of course, the experiment described was not designed to produce an internalized suppression that would last over a long period of time, without the benefit of any further external reinforcement. The long-term maintenance of internalized control based on punishment will often require a distribution of the child's experience over a far greater period of time, along with many opportunities to probe surveillance and response from his social environment. What the experiment does reveal is something about the basic mechanisms of (Pavlovian) conditioning through which punishment begins to induce control of conduct in the absence of external monitors. The experiment is in fact designed to support the inference that punishment attaches anxiety to certain *internal* monitors, which are correlated with the occurrence of transgressions, and that these internal monitors then become capable of exercising some affective control over the child's behavior.

What is the nature of these internal monitors which come to govern the child's conduct? The critical experimental finding is that punishment is most effective when it is used early in the onset of transgression. This finding confirms an expectation that the internalized strength of suppression will be determined by the magnitude of anxiety that has been conditioned specifically to internal *precursors* of a transgression. The precursors of a punished act. may consist, for example, of behavioral cues which are produced by the child's own motoric orienting actions. But they may also take the far more interesting form of cognitive processes which range from the simplest representational images to the most complex evaluative structures (such as moral principles). If anxiety can be attached to such monitors, and if these monitors can assume a temporal position in which they precede a punished act, it becomes possible to see how suppression of the incipient act may be later motivated even when there is no longer an objective danger of punishment. During the socialization process, un-

punished alternatives to the punished act will conversely acquire some intrinsic value for reduction or inhibition of anxiety.

An Apparent Paradox

A fairly simple experiment confronts us, then, with something of a paradox in its apparent relevance to the development of conscience. It demonstrates the child's internalization of control over conduct, without our having provided any verbal evaluation or even categorical representation of his transgression. The demonstration thus confirms the obvious: Human beings are highly conditionable animals, whose social habits often assume an autonomy and permanence unburdened by any evaluative thought processes. At the same time, we have every reason to suppose that the substance of thought can enter powerfully into a child's internalized control over his own behavior. The mere presence of a mental representation of action, as a monitor for some independence of social reaction, would be only a first step toward cognitive control. It need not imply that the child also has an evaluative structure in which to place the representation. But children do acquire categories of value, moral and otherwise; and these categories can develop into internalized structures which are sensitive to large realms of social experience.

Just as it is clear that many behavioral manifestations of an internalized conscience do not require moral judgment, it is likewise clear that moral values can sometimes be significant determinants of conduct. Values cannot be regarded as merely a form of knowledge or reflection that has a passive relationship to conduct. We are left with the question of how it is possible for *both* conditioning *and* moral knowledge to contribute to the organization of conduct—and to its at least partial independence of the individual's expectation of social reward or punishment. An attempt to answer this question will allow us to begin to see the generality of the theory required for an account of the acquisition of conscience.

I want to suggest that one requirement of an answer to the question posed above is the recognition that moral judgment turns out to be a rather specialized capacity, as soon as one tries to set any interesting criteria as to when a value may be called moral. Although moral judgment may bear upon some choices of conduct for most human beings, it may actually represent a very small part of the total range of cognitive and affective resources through which socialization induces the child's internalized control over his conduct. I have emphasized at first the kind of internalization process that proceeds without the benefit of evaluative thought. But even the organized structures of value that the child acquires—though they may permit him to evaluate his actions with great independence of external control—can be built around many concepts other than moral ones. The larger issue, then, is how the child's representational capacities enter into the internalization process. And the question of how moral judgment enters is a derivative one. Of course, we know very little about the acquisition processes through which the cognitive competence of children develops. And we know even less about how this competence interlocks with social experience to produce internalized structures of value.

The power of cognitive mediation of internalized control over conduct—even when it takes the form of the simplest verbal representations—can be illustrated with the results of some further variations of the punishment-training experiment described earlier. The method used in the additional variations is exactly the same as that used in the original experimental conditions (Aronfreed, 1968a), except for the following modifications:

During the training trials of all of the new variations, punishment is delayed until six seconds after the child's completion of a transgression (choosing and picking up the attractive rather than the unattractive toy). This interval of delay of punishment was the third of the four timing variations used in the original experiment. In the absence of any verbalized reasons for the occurrence of punishment, the delay had produced a relatively ineffective suppression during the test for internalization that immediately followed the training. In comparison, the use of punishment as soon as a child reached for an attractive toy during training had made the children very resistant even to any handling of the attractive toy when they were later left alone. Now the experimental agent of socialization introduces, into the delayed-punishment condition, a verbalized cognitive structure which the child can use to represent certain properties of the transgression. During the initial instructions, and together with each occurrence of punishment, the agent states that certain toys are "*hard to tell about*" and are therefore "*only for older boys (girls).*" The agent's verbalization is preceded by the verbal disapproval ("*No!*") and coterminous with the deprivation of candy, so that it will be interwoven with components of punishment.

It will be observed that the agent injects a cognitive structure of ease versus difficulty into the child's choice of which toy to tell about. But this structure does not specify any particular category of toy. Nor is it especially rational or appropriate (and purposely so) for a distinction between attractive and unattractive toys. Nevertheless, the verbal provision of this structure during punishment training induces more effective suppression of handling of the attractive toy during the test for internalization. Children who are exposed to this form of training show more prolonged internalized suppression than was shown by children who were trained without cognitive structure (but under the same delay of punishment) in the original experiment. And most of the children who are given cognitive structure are able to verbalize the standard of ease versus difficulty, when they are asked after the experiment to explain their predominant choices of unattractive toys during training.

Another training variation injects the same cognitive structure of ease versus difficulty into the child's choice within each pair of toys. But it focuses the agent's explanation of punishment on the child's *intention*. Each time that a transgression occurs, the agent coordinates punishment with a statement that the child had *"wanted"* to pick up a toy that was *"hard to tell about."* This focus on intention produces a very effective suppression during the test for internalization, in spite of the fact that punishment is substantially delayed. Children trained under this cognitive focus on intention show a strength of internalized suppression which is fully comparable to that shown by children who were punished during training immediately upon reaching for an attractive toy (under the original condition of no provision of cognitive structure). A great many of these intention-trained children never handle the forbidden toy during the test for internalization. The remainder do so only quite late in the ten-minute test period.

Most readers will find the results of these experimental variations perfectly consonant with their expectations: Children should show better internalized control of their conduct when their transgressions are defined by verbal explanation, and particularly when the explanation sensitizes them to their own intentions. Presumably the provision of verbal structure in socialization gives the child a richer cognitive representation of the nature and conditions of transgression. But how does this cognitive representation—even when it includes a dimension along which a transgression may be evaluated (as in the case of the experimental treatment)—come to be able to actually control the child's behavior? Why does it not merely remain transfixed in representational thought? The experimental results begin to suggest, I think, that representational thought assumes its

power over conduct because of the affective loadings which become attached to the representations themselves.

When internalization is based on punishment training, we would expect an aversive affective state to be "conditioned" to those cognitive representations of the child which are initially contiguous with the occurrence of punishment. Correspondingly, a reduction or inhibition of this affective state would become attached to the representations that are contiguous with avoidance of an anticipated or uncertain punishment. The aversive state may be experienced with different qualities—for example, fear, shame, or guilt—depending on the cognitive structure in which it is housed (Aronfreed, 1968c, chap. 9). But here we may continue to think of the aversive state as anxiety, with respect to its generalized motivational properties.

If the child's cognitive representations of actions were as immobile as the proprioceptive cues inherent in the actions themselves, then the anxiety attached by punishment to these representations would also be locked to the precise points at which the punishment had occurred for previous transgressions. Thus internalized anxiety might be mobilized only at a point well past the completion of a transgression. However, the child's representation of an act is undoubtedly far more mobile than are the behavioral cues in the overt initiation and commitment of the act. Cognitive representation can be induced by verbal socialization long after the actual occurrence of a transgression; and yet such representation may also later assume an anticipatory relationship to the same transgression. Accordingly, the child's evaluation of a punished act can come to activate anxiety at the point of an incipient transgression, even though evaluative standards may have been transmitted by others only in conjunction with punishment that originally occurred after transgressions already had been committed. And the anxiety can serve to motivate suppression of the incipient transgression, without the continued support of external surveillance or threat of punishment.

The fact that a verbal medium of socialization makes the precise timing of a child's punishment less critical, in yielding an effective internalized suppression of transgression, is entirely in accord with what we find in the natural setting of the home. If the internalized behavioral consequences of parental punishment were dependent only on Pavlovian mechanisms for the conditioning of anxiety directly to the child's overt acts, the punishment could hardly make much contribution to the later suppression of an incipient transgression. It is rather unusual for parents to have the opportunity to react to a child's potential transgression before it is committed. Yet their punishment is generally quite effective, even though it occurs almost always after the completion of a transgression—and could therefore not attach much anxiety directly to the behavioral precursors of the transgression. We can attribute this effectiveness to the representational medium that is structured by the verbalization of parents. The adequacy of this medium for evaluative cognition will vary greatly, of course, across different agents of socialization. But even its more primitive forms will provide a representation to which some anxiety can be attached, and which is mobile with respect to the point of onset or anticipation of a subsequent transgression.

The results of some other variations of experimental conditions, beyond those already described, provide further confirmation of the importance of an attachment of affective value to whatever representations the child is expected to use for his own evaluation and control of transgressions. For example, after training that consistently separated the point of punishment on each trial from the point at which the experimental agent verbalized a cognitive structure (of ease versus difficulty in telling about toys), the strength of suppression was much weaker on the internalization test, in which the agent was absent,

than it had been after the training conditions where punishment was always contiguous with the agent's verbalization. Similar effects were obtained with the introduction into training of still other variations that provided a cognitive focus on the child's intentions in choosing an attractive toy (as described earlier). When the precise temporal location of punishment was varied for different groups of children over the several behavioral components of a transgression—for example, reaching for an attractive toy, picking it up, or then telling about it—the strength of internalized suppression following training was far greater if punishment immediately coincided with the behavioral component that the agent always identified verbally as the prohibited aim of the child's intention.

These findings clearly indicate that the power which verbal representation gives to the child's internalized control is a function of contiguity in time between social transmission of the representation and other correlated events which have a significant affective value for the child (in this case, punishment and punishment avoidance). We are again compelled to infer that the attachment of changes of affective state to representation is what gives the child's evaluative cognition its control over conduct.

Affective Mediation of Cognitive Control

The conception of the affective and cognitive mechanisms of internalization that I have advanced thus far is not peculiar to the child's aversive experience of transgression and punishment. It appears to be equally applicable to experimental and theoretical analyses of the socialization of altruism and sympathy (Aronfreed, 1970), of self-criticism (Aronfreed, 1964), and more generally of internalized choices of conduct based on reward (Aronfreed, 1968c, chap. 5). Nevertheless, it may not be accidental to the very nature of socialization that the clearest picture of the child's acquisition of internalized control has emerged from empirical studies of the effects of punishment on his initially predominant behavioral dispositions (see also, for example, Parke & Walters, 1967; Walters, Parke, & Cane, 1965).

Insofar as the experiments described include the role of cognitive representation in the socialization process, they are very short indeed of the general theoretical requirements for an understanding of moral development. They do not tell us what, for example, are the properties of a cognitive structure (much less a moral structure). They do not reveal how such a structure organizes the categories of value in which potential acts of conduct can be classified. And they certainly do not resolve the question of how such categories are transmitted in the first place. Of course, we would need to know a great deal more about the development of children's conceptual thinking (than we now do), in terms of basic acquisition and storage processes, in order to project either experiments or theories to the realm of moral judgment. But what the analysis does provide is some appreciation of the pervasiveness of internalized affective states in the control of conduct, together with the implication that the child's representational monitors of his own conduct must also work through affective pathways.

These conclusions do not mean merely that conscience consists of thoughts and feelings. The evidence shows specifically that a moderate amount of verbalization of standards to the child, particularly when it focuses on his intentions, will yield much more effective internalized control than might be expected if the control depended on the coincidence between overt action and punishment. And, secondly, there are very strong indications that the representations transmitted by verbalization must, in order to be effective, be given an affective value by a fairly precise association with the punishment.

The emphasis here on the importance of affective mechanisms in the child's internalized control of conduct is in no way intended to underplay the significance of moral cognition. The reasons for conduct, and not only its behavioral conformity, are critical ingredients of the individual's social experience. But there has been so much recent (and justifiable) investment in the child's capacity to represent the world in thought, and to form complex rules and concepts, that we are in some danger of overlooking the affective learning which is also required to translate knowledge into social behavior. And the most general kind of interest in the socialization process must recognize that societies do not transmit only knowledge. They also transmit motivations to compel action.

Repetition does not dull our astonishment at the resources of moral perception that young children can verbalize in social situations that they know well. These resources sometimes include an understanding not only of the consequences of their actions, but also of their obligations to particular other people, and even of the relevance of their intentions—when these components are being considered with respect to their own concrete actions, rather than from the perspective of the more hypothetical and abstract situations that Piaget (1932) and others have posed to them. Only the more naive among us would also be surprised to observe that these cognitive resources of children (and of adults as well) are often not realized in their actual conduct. The discrepancies between knowledge and action simply reflect once again that the affectivity generated by a child's evaluation of potential alternative acts may be insufficient to direct the choices known to have the greater valuation on a moral dimension. Further increments of socially rewarding or aversive experience may be necessary to attach a greater magnitude of affect to the child's categories for the moral status of these choices.

However, though it may be useful for theoretical analysis, separating the cognitive and affective components of an evaluative representation has a certain artificiality. The child's classification of an act (under the constraints of its context) within a judgmental category is a cognitive coding. This classification is not sufficient to define the *value* of the act. A workable definition of what we might wish to mean by values would surely specify some inherent affective components as well as a cognitive substance. The nature and intensity of these affective components is what we should expect to be critical in permitting values to exercise control over the child's behavior. Obviously the affective mediation between thought and action will be complex and highly variable across different situations and different areas of conduct. It is therefore perfectly sensible that many investigators have uncovered less than startling consistency when they have tried simply to correlate overt behavioral indices of the child's conduct with various verbalized expressions of his conscience (Hartshorne & May, 1928; M. L. Hoffman, 1970a; Kohlberg, 1969b; Terman et al., 1925).

I once attended a conference on moral education at which I was much surprised by the interactions between philosophers and psychologists on the question of how to teach moral decision-making to children (Aronfreed, 1971). One of the arguments advanced was that moral reasoning ought to be used to overcome the "emotional prejudices" implanted by early experiences in the home. A counterargument, from the perspective advanced in this chapter, would be that moral education must build upon the strong affective dispositions acquired in early experience —that affective values are, as it were, the ultimate axiomatic base upon which moral principles can engage the child's conduct among and toward others. If the wrong emotions (by whatever criterion) have been attached to certain actions during childhood, then affective reeducation and not just moral reeducation will be required. The consequences of aggression, the fidelity of words to actions, and the distribution

and possession of objects of value are observable events around which socialization takes place every day in a child's life. There are a massive number of opportunities for the child to experience these events in affective media which are pleasurable or aversive—though these media are often far more subtle than explicit rewards and punishments. Both the affective and cognitive residues of these early experiences will yield fundamental dispositions for which later moral principles can only be an elaboration rather than a replacement.

The priority of the most basic affective and cognitive ingredients of early socialization is apparent in the few points of agreement among the findings of numerous studies that have attempted to assess the relationship between the disciplinary practices of parents and various indices of their children's internalized control of conduct (Allinsmith, 1960; Aronfreed, 1961; Bandura & Walters, 1959; Burton, Maccoby, & Allinsmith, 1961; M. L. Hoffman & Saltzstein, 1967; MacKinnon, 1938; Sears, Maccoby, & Levin, 1957, chaps. 7, 10; Sears, Whiting, Nowlis, & Sears, 1953; J. W. M. Whiting & Child, 1953, chap. 11). The findings are clearest in respect to the child's internalization of reactions to his own committed transgressions. But they also apply to the child's internalized dispositions to suppress the occurrence of transgressions.

What emerges from these studies is that children show more effective internalization when their parents use what are often termed "psychological" forms of discipline. I have suggested that these disciplinary habits be called *induction* because they inscribe a pattern of learning that induces internalized monitors of the child's anxiety in response to an anticipated or committed transgression (Aronfreed, 1961; Saltzstein, Chap. 14). One key component of this category of discipline is simply the parent's use of explanation or reasoning. But a second and somewhat independent component, which indicates the importance of affective context, is the parent's focus on withdrawal of affection (and its restoration for the child's termination or correction of prohibited behavior). The power of this affective component would obviously depend on the establishment of the parent's affection as a base of value. And it is interesting to note that many studies have reported evidence of weak internalization among children whose parents are unusually lacking in nurturance toward them (Bandura & Walters, 1959; Bronfenbrenner, 1961; J. McCord, McCord, & Howard, 1963; W. McCord, McCord, & Howard, 1961; Sears, Maccoby, & Levin, 1957, chap. 10; J. W. M. Whiting & Child, 1953, chap. 11).

In placing such a heavy burden on affective mechanisms in the development of conscience, I am not implying that we know very much about the properties of specific affective states or about how these properties can be differentiated in their control of the child's behavior. A specification of the varieties of emotion or affectivity would be another requirement for a more general theory of moral development. Affect is used here as a construct with which to make some theoretical sense out of both common observation and experimental analysis of the phenomena of conscience. We have recognized the obvious distinction between aversive and pleasurable affective states. We have seen the explanatory value of the ease of conditionability of changes of affective state to cognitive representation as well as to overt action. And we have shown that the attribution of motivating and reinforcing properties to affective states can be used as part of an account of the child's internalization of control over conduct. What we have not done is to go beyond these rather primitive properties into the cognitive structures or housings which give different affective states their specific features of qualitative experience—although an attempt to begin such an analysis has been made elsewhere (Aronfreed, 1968c, chap. 9).

Further Requirements: Cognitive Transactions

I have as yet given little attention to one other requirement of a more general theory of the psychological processes in moral development: an understanding of the forms of social experience, and of the mechanisms of transition, which produce different qualitative organizations or "stages" of moral judgment. Such an understanding will depend, of course, on our broader state of knowledge of the development of children's thought and language. Any conception of a developmental sequence of types of reasoning based on moral values must be derived from a larger conception of changes in the cognitive resources with which the child codes or processes his social experience, in the categories with which he represents that experience, and in the operations or transformations of thought which he is able to impose on those categories.

The study of basic phenomena in cognitive development has become a heavy and rewarding contemporary investment of developmental psychologists. Readers who are not as familiar with it as they might wish can consult the latest edition of *Carmichael's Manual of Child Psychology* (Mussen, 1970). But it is clear that the conceptual and empirical state of the science is only beginning to touch upon the mechanisms of change which mediate transitions between different levels of cognitive capacity in the child. And it is quite certain that the study of moral judgment has not yet moved beyond the description of qualitatively distinct expressions of thought in children of different ages.

A psychological theory that addresses moral values (or any other kind of value system) must be concerned with cognitive and affective dispositions of considerable breadth and stability. An individual's values are rarely constructed around a few very specific or isolated acts of conduct, or around a highly limited set of external social contexts. A system of values will ordinarily give representation to complex interrelationships among a wide spectrum of alternative actions, the conditions under which the actions can occur, and the possible outcomes of the actions. That children do acquire the cognitive structures which are the substrate for a value system, and that such structures can mediate the highly differentiated behavioral controls of which human beings are capable, are remarkable accomplishments in the light of what current theories of learning seem able to digest.

One reason for the absence of a theory of how children acquire values is the lack of an intellectually engaging psychological conception of the nature of values. I pointed out earlier that values are not merely cognitive schemas. They must carry affective loadings of varying quality and magnitude in order to add *value* to their representational power to control behavior. But there is also a very considerable problem in formulating the cognitive properties of values. For heuristic purposes here we might treat a system of values as being, in its representational aspects, a hierarchical system of categories for classification of social actions (or objects), in which some criterial markers are subordinated to the priority of others. The structure of such a categorical system would be inherent in the relationships among the categories, in the presence of critical dimensions along which events could be multiply ordered, and in other fixed properties of the classification scheme. The different operations of thought which could be imposed on this representational base would then constitute the evaluative processes of moral judgment.

The most widely cited investigations of children's moral judgment have not yet concerned themselves with the basic cognitive processes underlying the acquisition and functioning of values. These studies are still engaged in the descriptive assessment of developmental stages in the criteria which the child applies to the evaluation of conduct. Although Piaget (1932) did include some evidence of children's conceptions of rules in an actual game of marbles, these descriptive studies generally elicit the child's verbalized evaluation of an action, together with his explanation or justification, in a hypothetically posed situation. Among children in Western societies at least, the results of this method of inquiry commonly disclose an ordered sequence in the evaluative structures of conscience. The structures are distinguished from one another in part by the child's criteria of value, in part by the qualitative organization of his thinking, and in part by the type of reasoning he applies. And the order in which the different moral conceptions are acquired appears to be reliably correlated with developmental time, even though they are not consistently fixed to specific ages.

In general, the developmental changes in children's expressions of moral thought may be characterized as transitions along a continuum moving from an externalized to an internalized orientation toward the resolution of problems of conduct. Piaget's description (1932) of these changes is well known (see Lickona, Chap. 12). It has often been replicated by other investigators, though sometimes with only partial or uncertain confirmation. Kohlberg's system (1963a, 1971b) of classification probes more deeply and broadly into the child's thinking, produces a larger mass of verbal data, and is based on a somewhat more integrative view of the child's criteria of value across a number of different kinds of situations of moral conflict. Kohlberg's observations in Chapter 2 suggest that the child's first organized pattern of moral thought focuses on rewards or punishments, and is followed by an intermediate (and very common) type of thought which justifies choices of conduct by reference to the maintenance of authority or to the conventional requirements of social approval. Finally, Kohlberg notes that the most advanced type of moral thinking employs more abstract principles of justice which are oriented toward the welfare of others in a "social contract," or toward the categorical intuition of whether an action is right or wrong.

Because these shifts in children's moral conceptions seem to have an invariant developmental sequence, both Piaget and Kohlberg have been tempted to assume that they represent a succession of developmentally preprogrammed cognitive stages—with the corollary (not too well suppressed) assumption that social experience serves mainly as a generalized and not highly determinant nutriment or catalyst. Among the difficulties attached to this view is its neglect of the nature of the learning that might give rise to the transformations of thought. There appears to be little interest in going beyond the speculation that changes in the child's moral thought arise from an interaction between his intrinsic dispositions toward cognitive growth and the expansion in the variety of his potential social roles. In this evolutionary perspective, moral judgment moves from lower to higher stages in a natural order. And if the sequence fails to reach its final stage, we are left with the problem of whether we should infer an "unnatural" or socially undesirable source of developmental arrest.

The conception that the child carries an intrinsically ordered incipient program of moral development, which unfolds under the stimulation of social experience, confronts a number of problems of evidence from other sources. We can only briefly summarize these problems here (a more thorough exposition can be found in Aronfreed, 1968c, chap. 10). To begin with, middle-class and working-class children in Western societies are often found to differ in the speed and extent of their developmental shifts in moral thought. The amount of change with advancing age among working-class children is sometimes so small as to seem trivial when compared with the very substantial and long-term differences between the two social classes. These class differences persist to some degree, interestingly enough, even when the

effect of intelligence is statistically removed through the conventional standardized indices.

Secondly, children drawn from non-Western societies sometimes do not show, as they become older, the same decline of an externalized orientation of moral judgment. In some cross-cultural studies, a more highly internalized orientation toward the evaluation of conduct never does develop; rather, an externalized orientation appears to be the terminal point of acculturation. A third problem is the finding by some investigators that young adults in our own society can show a great variety of moral orientations. Their differences in moral perspective are correlated with their subscription to certain religious, political, or other ideologies. Such differences are not sensibly ordered on a developmental continuum. Finally, we must take account of the radical changes of values which occasionally take place among adults under the stress of very unusual experiences—for example, in prisoner-of-war or concentration camps. These changes may either parallel or reverse those which occur in developmental time during childhood.

In addition to the evidence cited above, the findings of a number of studies indicate that children's verbalizations of moral thinking undergo significant shifts under the impact of brief exposures to the social influence of alternative models. All of the evidence points to one conclusion: that although the child's structures of moral value may be successively reorganized around different rules or principles in the course of development, he nevertheless remains able to draw on more than one type of evaluative structure. Since the different structures appear to be able to displace one another to some extent (even after some have been subordinated to others over developmental time), it would seem that none of them is actually lost as a result of cognitive development. Of course, one would very much like to know just what kinds of cognitive mechanisms would permit one type of moral value to predominate over others, and yet allow others to become more salient under specified conditions. But common observation must make it obvious that these phenomena exist. Because fully developed adults can apply more than one criterion to the evaluation of conduct, many social situations will induce them to think and react in ways that are beneath their maximal capacity for moral reasoning (or sometimes in ways that are beneath any reasoning at all).

The question of whether stages of moral development can be illuminated by closer analysis of underlying cognitive processes remains to be addressed. It can be best illustrated by an incident of which I am inordinately fond: A 7-year-old girl showed herself to be quite capable of gross physical violence toward her younger brother, even though her intended action was arrested at the last moment by her awareness of my presence. When the incident came up casually in a later conversation, she also showed a clear capacity to expose her intended action to a moral examination. Not only did she spontaneously express her understanding of an obligation not to hurt her brother, but she also verbalized her own disapproval of having wanted to react so strongly to a petty affront. What she said might be taken as evidence of only the beginnings of moral perception. But it can hardly be doubted that she had a moral principle of conduct at her command.

The young lady who is the heroine of this incident will certainly acquire more abstract cognitive structures as she grows older. And she will therefore attain correspondingly more complex moral rules, which integrate many different features of an act and its consequences. She will also become more complex in her language and in her operations of thought on the physical world. Greater abstraction and complexity are in the very nature of development. And it may well be that the substance of moral values is only one of many representational systems on which cognitive development simultaneously works its transformations. We might then consider the possibility that the thinking of young children already shows most of the fundamental properties of moral judgment. The fundament of their moral conceptions may well be the product of rather specific, though almost universal, forms of social experience. And the subsequent stages through which their moral thought moves may reflect successive impositions upon this substantive moral base—impositions that represent advances in the power of reasoning, and in the abstraction and organization of criteria.

To make the argument above even more explicit, I am suggesting that the basic cognitive and affective substance of moral value is formed fairly early in the socialization process, and that it remains relatively stable thereafter. But it does become subordinated to increasingly differentiated structures and increasingly powerful operations of thought. This distinction between substance and form may be useful in understanding whatever cross-cultural regularities may exist in moral development. The fundamental substantive dimensions of moral value may well vary from one society to another. Yet there may also be some uniformities in the forms or structures which children's cognitive operators allow them to impose sequentially on any categorical substance. Of course, these same operators could also be imposed on many other systems of representation which the child obtains from his transactions with the social and physical world, quite irrespective of any moral content. Thus, one would expect an analysis of the transformations of the child's thought in the moral domain to uncover much the same pattern as can be seen in his conceptions of time, space, or physical quantity. Indeed, there is now some initial evidence of just such parallelism (Kohlberg, in press). The implication is clear: The stages that can be discerned in moral development are subsidiary to more general shifts in the child's cognitive power. And these structural changes are not in themselves intrinsically moral; their moral status resides only in the substantive base of values upon which they operate.

There are a number of limitations, then, on the heuristic value of the conception of moral development as moving through a universal sequence of stages. The first qualification is that a number of different evaluative structures, varying in their power and complexity, are apparently available to the conscience of the ordinary person. The transformations between stages therefore either are reversible or else leave preceding stages functionally intact. Furthermore, it is distinctly possible that any universality in the acquisition of conscience is to be found in changes of cognitive capacity rather than in changes of the basic substance of moral values. The children of any society may acquire an increasingly abstracted and internalized moral orientation (up to the point of support from whatever cognitive devices the society provides). Many members of Western societies may be motivated to use their cognitive capacities to arrive at principled values of self-direction which go beyond the more obvious kinds of external constraints. In other societies, however, elaborate and abstract principles of conduct may be constructed around values which take a much more externalized perspective on human relationships; an excellent example can be found in Erikson's description (1950) of the moral focus of Yurok society on values of cleanliness and economic exchange.

These limitations are boundary conditions which must be honored by any conception of the development of moral thought. They are perfectly consistent with the view that the child's moral cognition does undergo structural and qualitative transformations. And they do not contradict evidence that the attainment of some rules of moral value may be prerequisite to the attainment of others. But we need to recognize that the boundary conditions present large problems for a conception of discontinuous stages of moral judgment. What we now know about moral judgment and conduct might be better contained by the view that they evolve from continuities in the interaction between the child's cognitive capacity and his social experience. Cognitive change in itself will be a critical determinant of how the child receives his social experience. An external program of socialization will not induce more complex or autonomous moral principles in a child who does not have the requisite cognitive capacity. Conversely, cognitive development is too general a phenomenon to account specifically for the substance of moral values. An understanding of how conscience is acquired will therefore depend on a knowledge of how concrete experiences of socialization both induce and capitalize on the structural changes in children's thinking.

CHAPTER 4

The Socialization of Moral Judgment and Behavior in Cross-Cultural Perspective

James Garbarino and Urie Bronfenbrenner

Introduction

Cultural variations in moral judgment and behavior have posed a knotty theoretical problem for the student of human development. Cross-cultural studies of morality have typically remarked on the complexity and diversity of values to be found across time and space (Ferguson, 1958; Robertson, 1947; Sidgwick, 1960). One commentator has been led to conclude that "There is scarcely one norm or standard of good conduct that, in another time and place, does not serve to mark bad conduct" (Melden, 1967, p. 7). One possible exception to this conclusion is the universality of the incest taboo (Murdock, 1949), although even here we find variation in the scope and applicability of the moral prohibition. In general, it does appear that the substance of morality—that is, the actual rules of ethical conduct, the values and mores that govern behavior—is deeply embedded in specific cultural patterns (Benedict, 1934).

When, however, we probe deeper and look cross-culturally at the abstract principles of morality—at justice, for example

—a more consistent pattern begins to emerge. Along the same lines, anthropologists point to the *structural function* of values, which tends to be more stable than their content. In this view, the most sophisticated and most primitive cultures attend to the same basic human needs. As a result values can be analyzed in terms of their common functional purposes, and in such terms are seen to be equivalent despite gross differences in specific content (Goodman, 1967).

The cognitively oriented "stage" theories of Piaget (1932; see also Lickona, Chap. 12) and Kohlberg (Chap. 2, 1969) have added an important dimension of coherence to the study of moral development, but are not readily amenable to the study of cultural variation, given their emphasis on essentially acultural invariant sequences. Contrasting with the cognitively oriented stage theories are conceptions employing a nonhierarchical "typology" (for example, Bronfenbrenner, 1962a). While such approaches are amenable to the study of cross-cultural variation (since moral "type" is conceived as varying with culture), they have not been able to deal adequately with observed moral hierarchies in either developmental or cognitive terms. Moreover, typology approaches have failed to specify the operational mechanisms by which broad sociocultural influences make their impact on individual socialization.

The purpose of this chapter is to attempt to overcome these inadequacies in the study of cultural variations in moral judgment and behavior. In pursuit of this goal we propose first a model of moral development which accommodates both the "stage" and "type" approaches. Second, we advance a model of socialization capable of handling our view of moral development. We then relate our socialization and moral development model to a cross-cultural perspective, using historical cases to illustrate the relation of large-scale social events and organization to individual social and personality development—particularly moral development. Finally, in order to provide a preliminary empirical test of our hypothesis, we propose an operational mechanism at the sociocultural level to account for cultural differences in moral judgment and behavior.

An Integrative Model of Moral Development and Socialization

The impetus to organize morality in terms of structural schema has been a strong one. It is present in nearly all considerations of moral judgment and behavior, be they by philosophers or psychologists. We have pointed out that two major emphases in modern psychological approaches to moral development have been the stage and type analyses represented by Kohlberg (1969b) and Bronfenbrenner (1962a), respectively. Kohlberg's theory (see Chapter 2) postulates six hierarchical developmental stages of moral reasoning which are held to be inextricably tied to cognitive development, invariant in order, and generated by the interplay of maturation and general environmental experience.

In contrast to Kohlberg's stage approach, Bronfenbrenner's analysis (1962a) describes five types of moral judgment and behavior:

1. *self-oriented*: in which the individual is motivated primarily by impulses of self-gratification without regard for the desires or expectations of others, except as objects of manipulation;
2. *authority-oriented*: in which the individual accepts parental strictures and values as immutable and generalizes this orientation to include moral standards imposed by other adults and authority figures;
3. *peer-oriented*: in which the individual is an adaptive conformist who goes along with the peer group—which is largely autonomous of adult authority and ultimately of all social authority—and in which behavior is guided by momentary shifts in group opinion and interest;
4. *collective-oriented*: in which the individual is committed to a set of enduring group goals which take precedence over individual desires, obligations, and interpersonal relationships;
5. *objectively oriented*: in which the individual's values are functionally autonomous—that is, having arisen through social interaction but are no longer dependent, on a day-to-day basis, upon social agents for their meaning and application—and in which the individual responds to situations on the basis of principles rather than on the basis of orientations toward social agents.

This social-psychological scheme, however, lacks a developmental dimension. The process through which a person or a group arrives at one or another orientation is not specified and remains unclear. Nor is it clear whether one type emerges from another, or whether there is a typical sequence of types in development.

This paper attempts a reconciliation of the two major models—the stage and type approaches—through a formulation that incorporates both developmental and social components. Thus, our conception complements Kohlberg's approach. While his view emphasizes the common features of social environments and institutions across and within cultures, ours focuses on the differences. It represents an attempt to place Bronfenbrenner's earlier type analysis in a model that includes a logical and developmental hierarchy. In short, we propose a *socialization* model for moral development. Like the Piagetian-Kohlbergian model, this formulation envisages a series of hierarchical stages. But our formulation views the hierarchy not as the product of universally immanent motivational forces, but as the result of an interaction between maturing capacities and motivations of the child, on the one hand, and *particular* characteristics of his sociocultural milieu, on the other.

In general, we envision three developmental levels, the order of which would be the same for all persons and cultures. At the bottom is an essentially amoral pattern in which some primary hedonic orientation is the organizing principle. This is clearly an ethic of self-interest, of pleasure–pain dichotomies, of manipulation and instrumentalities governed by no end other than self-satisfaction. In terms of the two approaches considered above, this level roughly corresponds to Kohlberg's *premoral* Stage 0 (Kohlberg & Selman, 1972; Selman, Chap. 17) and to Bronfenbrenner's self-oriented type. Such an individual is "unsocialized"; he is in a sense outside the human community normatively, behaviorally, and psychologically. This level may be thought of as developmentally "normal" only in very early childhood. As we shall see below, the first development of attachment to social agents moves the child toward a Level 2 form of moral behavior. For Level 1, premoral behavior to occur in an older child or adult is in principle pathological, both for the individual and his society. Below we consider instances of such pathogenic conditions.

The second level is constituted by patterns of morality having as their dominant characteristic allegiance and orientation to some system of social agents. This is a level in which the individual's moral judgment and behavior are given direction by individuals or groups that are salient for his affective and social needs. If we are to think in terms of Kohlberg's stages, Level 2 corresponds roughly to Stages 1 to 4. In Bronfenbrenner's type analysis, Level 2 includes the authority orientation, peer orientation, and collective orientation.

Within Level 2 we see the following possible relations among the authority, peer, and collective orientations. First, it is conceivable that there is one hierarchical sequence of orientations through which persons proceed, in which case it would be appropriate to assess the relative position of individuals in the hierarchy of stages. Second, and more likely from our point of view, there may be within Level 2 alternative sequences of particular orientations both within and across cultures. Within the same social system, for example, some individuals may develop first an authority and then a peer orientation, while for others the reverse may be true. A third possibility is that multiple orientations are not arranged as a sequence, but exist simultaneously. In any case, it should be stressed that, in principle, the combinations are as numerous as the social orders which can be observed cross-culturally or hypothesized to exist. For example, Western societies may be in the process of evolving new social structures which may lead to new moral socialization patterns. Similarly, the socialization patterns of the "new China" may give rise to new progressions of moral orientations. Particular forms of moral orientation, in our view, are as malleable as overall human development, though we see the three broad structural levels of moral development as being sequentially constant. Variation will occur in the specific moral posture or orientation the individual manifests within a given level.[1]

The third major moral level has the "highest" logical and developmental pattern. At this level, values, principles, and ideas rather than social agents are the directing forces. The individual applies standards of ethical conduct in a primarily intellective fashion, largely independently of psychosocial factors. In Kohlberg's terms, this is the morality of principles, of contract and conscience (Stages 5 and 6). In Bronfenbrenner's type approach, this is the objective orientation. The critical question becomes one of determining the cultural conditions conducive to movement from the first to the second and from the second to the third levels. Each upward movement, however, presents different psychosocial questions. That is, whereas Level 2 forms of morality are expected to develop in almost everyone, (barring massive disruption of socialization processes), attainment of Level 3 morality is conceived as occurring only under a relatively restricted set of social conditions. Specifically, attainment of Level 3 morality requires a setting in which an individual is provided opportunities, security, and social support for the development of abstract thinking and speculation as a consequence of partially competing and overlapping social allegiances. That is, there must be relative freedom and security to develop an intellectual resolution of competing social loyalities dissonant enough to promote a measure of tension, but not so incompatible as to be overwhelming. We shall deal in more detail with these conditions below. At this point, let it suffice to say that such a configuration of social conditions does not occur in every culture, either at the group or individual level, and hence is not a given either of social systems in general or of the conditions of life for particular persons.

Cultural Factors Influencing Moral Socialization

We turn next to a consideration of the cultural factors affecting socialization with an eye to assessing cultural variations in moral development as defined by the three-level moral hierarchy described above.

Our model suggests the following questions: What socialization contingencies are involved in bringing about developmental movement from Level 1 to Level 2? What socialization factors determine which type or types of moral orientation will occur within Level 2? What patterns of socialization lead to development of Level 3? Under what conditions, if any, does "regression" from a higher to a lower level occur?

In our view, developmental movement from Level 1 to Level 2 is based on and stimulated by *attachment*, the primary socialization of the organism to "belong" to and with social agents. This is the process by which the individual organism becomes an acculturated person. Without this development of affective and cognitive orientation to other people, the motivation to incorporate a system of morality defined and directed by social agents may well not arise. This view is supported by research indicating that patterns of interaction and responsiveness during early infancy are associated with early obedience to adult prohibitions (Stayton, Hogan, & Ainsworth, 1971). Furthermore, studies of the long-term consequences of early social neglect indicate a pattern of psychopathology which may be characterized as amoral (Bowlby, 1946). Ordinarily this development of attachment is initially directed toward the parents, but comes to be oriented toward other social agents as a function of the patterns of social interaction that obtain in early and middle childhood. This process of social *redirection* or transference leads us to our second question: What determines the particular type of moral orientation within Level 2?

After the task of primary socialization has been accomplished, the child, in most settings, first develops an adult- or authority-oriented morality. It seems that the patterns of child care surrounding the infant determine whether this or some other orientation arises. For example, A. Freud and Dann (1951) report a case in which a small group of children developed a peer orientation in earliest childhood as a result of having been without the care of adults on a regular and enduring basis. These children, growing up together in Nazi concentration camps without permanent parents, apparently did not develop an adult orientation during this period. It was not until after the children were put into a setting of strong adult presence and influence—as a rehabilitative measure after liberation from the concentration camps—that they began to orient to adults. Similarly, Soviet child care arrangements result in a very early collective orientation (Bronfenbrenner, 1970a, 1970b), though they are built upon and exist concurrently with strong maternal attachment.

The specific nature of the child's moral orientation within Level 2, however, can change. The adult orientation is first in the sense that in most cultural settings —as a result of the patterns of child care implied by the "universality" of the family (Murdock, 1949)—attachment to specific adults is the initial form of social orientation. This orientation is, however, specific to the care-giving adults, and it remains an open question whether the child's allegiance will be generalized to a comprehensive adult orientation or to some other form. In settings in which the adults continue to exert a dominant role in the social life of the child, it may be expected that the authority orientation will endure and develop. This is development in the sense that it represents a systematic extension of allegiance from the care-giving adults to adults in general, and then to institutions and figures of authority in general. In such a progression, Kohlberg's description (1969b) of successive stages may prove useful as a way of representing cognitively more sophisticated features of this expanding allegiance to authority.

In settings in which adults abrogate their interactive and directive role, peers may be expected to fill the vacuum, and peer orientation arises. In settings in which adults deliberately transfer their authority to groups organized around socially sanctioned values and goals, it may be expected that the collective orientation will dominate. In each case, it should be noted, the motivational basis of the orientation is the primary socialization, the involvement with the human community founded on the strength of the attachment in infancy. The crucial events, then, center on the direction in which that primary attachment is turned by the culturally determined patterns of childhood socialization.

Development of the third level— orientation to principle rather than to control by social agents—is predicated upon a social structure characterized by multiple social agents to whom the child is attached and who are "pulling" him in *somewhat* different directions. The consequences of intensely contradictory pulls, by contrast, have generally been thought to be pathological. Bateson (1956), for example, has termed the latter situation a "double bind" in which the individual is "damned if he does and damned if he doesn't"—a condition that can lead to schizophrenia if it persists. In our view, however, when environmental contradictions are moderate, the development of moral judgment is enhanced. In such circumstances, the individual cannot merely conform. Rather, he must choose, reconcile oppositions, and overcome contradictions; in short, he must make independent judgments. For such a resolution to occur, the conflict must be cognitively and affectively manageable. This requires, in addition to the presence of supporting but differentiated agents in the near environment of the family and peer group, that the social structure itself must be integrated. In other words, it is important that the competing social forces share a common commitment to the social and political order, some stake in the "public peace." Almond and Verba (1963) have discussed such a setting of sociopolitical "diversity within consensus," and the politically disintegrative consequences of too much diversity and insufficient consensus. These consequences, in Almond and Verba's analysis, include apathy, alienation, and absolutism.

When the delicate balance of diversity and consensus is attained, the individual may be expected to develop an orientation to principles—to abstract values no longer tied to particular social agents—which he can then apply to concrete situations. By contrast, for the person operating at Level 2, orientation to the social agent is paramount. The kind of social structure capable of generating a Level 3 morality, as we have indicated, is a balance of competing forces. Neither monolithic nor anomic, it is best characterized as pluralistic.

By *pluralistic* we mean a setting in which social agents and entities represent somewhat different expectations, sanctions, and rewards for members of the society. These differences generate intergroup conflict which is largely regulated by a set of "ground rules" (such as a constitution) and a common commitment to integrative principles or goals (such as a religious ethic). A monolithic setting, in contrast, is one in which all social agents and entities are organized around a single set of goals or principles. Conversely, an *anomic* setting is one in which there is almost no integration; social agents and entities are either absent or represent a multiplicity of divergent forces without any normative or institutional coherence.

Pluralism would apply to various aspects of the socialization process, both within the family—for example, two parents versus one, extended family versus nuclear—and to relations between the family and other socializing systems such as peer group, school, neighborhood, community, world of work, and civic and political organizations. Such pluralism might also be expected to vary within cultures as a function of social class—that is, as a function of socioeconomic factors affecting the individual's opportunities for exposure to multiple allegiances, to diverse cultural experiences, and to different points of view in education.

Evidence consistent with the formulation that pluralism facilitates moral development comes from several sources. First, Bronfenbrenner (1961, 1970) and his associates have found that families in which the parents both have strong and differentiated identities and family roles tend to have children who rate highest on teacher ratings for such dimensions as responsibility, autonomy, independence of judgment, and interpersonal adjustment. Children from families in which one parent dominates or in which neither parent exerts a strong influence are characterized by relatively low ratings on the same dimensions.

Similarly, Bronfenbrenner (1970a, 1970b) found differences between Soviet adolescents exposed to a single socialization setting (boarding school students) and those exposed to multiple settings (day school students) in the degree to which their moral judgments oriented toward adult authority. The students exposed to the monolithic social setting expressed more authority-oriented moral judgments than those exposed to the pluralistic setting. The latter students, living at home, were not oriented to a single focus but were forced to find a balance between competing social agents and agencies—in this case, school peers versus parents.

Studies by Baumrind (1967, 1971; Baumrind & Black, 1967) provide another source of evidence for the pluralistic hypothesis. Baumrind's work has revealed a pattern among families with young children which she designates as *authoritative*. This pattern stands in contradistinction to the *permissive*, on the one hand, and the *authoritarian*, on the other. Each of these two latter types is characterized by the dominance of one participant in the child-parent relationship. In the permissive case it is the child who is dominant, whereas in the authoritarian it is the parent. In the authoritative case, however, there is a reciprocal, *interactive*, relationship in which forces exerted by the parent and the child are in a state of creative tension. From our theoretical perspective, Baumrind's authoritarian and permissive patterns correspond to the monolithic and anomic orientations. Baumrind's finding that the authoritative pattern is associated with the highest levels of competence, responsibility, and other developmentally important characteristics (assessed observationally and through teacher reports) is consistent with our hypothesized relation between pluralism and moral development.

An additional, and somewhat indirect, source of support for the pluralistic model comes from the theories of Hunt (1965) and White (1963) and from the empirical findings of Kagan (1971), which suggest that an intrinsic *incongruity mechanism* is the directing motivational factor in much of human development. This incongruity mechanism is held to thrive on *optimal discrepancy*. According to Kagan, informational inputs that are so undifferentiated as to be "boring" or so highly differentiated as to be "confusing and indistinguishable" do not activate the motivational and exploratory cognitive processes associated with the incongruity mechanism. The optimal input pattern is one which is moderately complex and differentiated, which can be matched with an internal standard to assess its incongruity with established schema. Kagan reports data in support of this theoretical orientation. Hunt (1965) goes so far as to propose a relation between this incongruity mechanism and the classical conceptions of human rationality provided by Aristotle, St. Thomas Aquinas, and Locke. He further suggests a relationship between the incongruity mechanism and rationality, on the one hand, and theories of political pluralism, on the other. This implies that a pluralistic setting corresponds to a state of optimal discrepancy and is cognitively enhancing, unlike the unstimulating monolithic setting and the confusing anomic setting. Furthermore, given the functional relationship between cognitive development and social-moral development (for example, see Kohlberg, 1967; Lee, 1971), it seems plausible that the pluralistic setting would result in the highest level of moral development. As Hunt suggests, one can postulate that human rationality inheres in the incongruity mechanism and that the development of such an inherent rationality, particularly as represented in morality, is facilitated by pluralistic settings.

Turning to the question of regression from higher to lower levels, a shift from Level 2 to Level 1 might be expected to occur when primary agents of socialization are removed or cease to function, so that there is no one who offers the individual either resistance or support. Regression from Level 3 to Level 2 would be expected to occur coincidentally with a collapse of the pluralistic pattern—either through a disintegration of the social commitment holding together the competing elements of the system, or a totalistic integration of the separate elements into a monolithic entity. It should be noted that, in our view, the individual operating at Level 3 can continue to function despite the breakdown of the supporting conditions, *at least for a period of time*. This affords a measure of stability to the moral socialization system, a kind of positive cultural lag. The critical point to be made is that if the supporting pluralism deteriorates, the long-term result will be a reduction in Level 3 throughout the social system. A case in point is provided by Bettelheim's description (1943) of the moral breakdown of prisoners in concentration camps and their adoption of their jailers' attitudes, actions, and attire.

In summary, the accomplishment of primary socialization requires a setting in which sustained interaction between child and parent can establish the primary attachment necessary for socially oriented motivation. This initial motivation is then expanded through social interaction with others to become a comprehensive orientation toward a specific social agent—Level 2. This orientation can in turn lead to a series of multiple social allegiances which require the individual to develop an autonomous set of principles as guides for action. If the pattern of multiple competing allegiances occurs, development of an objective orientation can result. Maintenance of this Level 3 morality for the society as a whole depends on the degree to which a condition of pluralism is maintained, as opposed to either a monolithic-totalitarian or anomic-chaotic context.

TABLE 4.1   A Model for Studying the Relationship of Sociopsychological Pluralism to Moral Development

Developmental Level	Moral Socialization Outcome	Critical Pluralistic Variables
Infancy	Establishment of attachment, i.e., primary socialization.	Care-giving patterns, both behavioral and normative, contribute to progressively more complex systems of reciprocal infant-adult interaction.
Early Childhood	Expansion of primary attachment relationships into ever-widening circles.	*Structure of child-other interaction:* Progressive expansion of patterns of association from primary caregiver–infant dyads to larger social systems consistent with the "optimal discrepancy model." Initial pluralistic social settings with several different persons serving as objects for the child's attention and affiliation and as sources of demands. Initial ability to respond to differential influences through "objective cognitive response orientation."
Later Childhood	Development of relationships to social collectivities, particularly peer groups and children's institutions.	Development of *multiple* associations rather than complete immersion in one collectivity.
Adolescence	Resolution of relationships to social collectivities so as to achieve both objective-principled moral orientation, and social identity cementing individual-system relationships of allegiance and commitment.	Integration of individual into adult roles and experiences. Relative congruence between goals and values of peer groups and adult institutions; neither "cultural warfare" of peer group against adult social structures nor domination of peer groups by adult authority. Provision of pathways to adult activities which are consonant with previous socialization experiences.
Adulthood	Maintenance of creative tension between social identity and moral objective-principled orientation.	Systems of social support for alternative patterns of access to economic and social resources. Feedback to parental childrearing which supports encouragement of identity and diversity (i.e., neither authoritarian nor permissive, but authoritative childrearing). Pluralism for adults to encourage pluralism for children.

Table 4.1 provides a schematic description of a socialization system capable of generating Level 3 moral development as a general phenomenon. The table shows the moral socialization outcomes and critical variables at each stage of the life cycle. Thus it describes the circumstances leading to development of Level 2 from

Level 1 (during infancy and early childhood) and the subsequent attainment of Level 3 (in later childhood, adolescence, and adulthood). Moreover, Table 4.1 indicates that environmental pluralism—which implies involvement in varied and increasingly complex social interactions and settings—is critically important for social-moral development throughout the developmental range, not just between Level 2 and Level 3.

Historical Instances of the Moral Socialization Model

To illustrate the workings of the socialization model described above, we now turn our attention to several historical examples at the cultural and social structural levels. These examples are intended to illustrate the following aspects of the model.

1. Sociocultural breakdown can result in massive instances of behavior at Level 1 of our morality hierarchy, both through nonsocialization of young children and through regression from Level 2 to Level 1.

2. Human intervention can result in a "recovery" of individuals who have regressed to Level 1 or shifted to a less socially desirable orientation within Level 2. Restructuring the socialization environment of the individual can alter as well as create the orientation toward social agents.

3. Disrupting the institutional pluralism of a social system for a long enough time will result in regression of individuals' moral functioning from Level 3 to the various types within Level 2. Redirection of the society's institutional life along totalitarian lines, for example, can be accomplished in a relatively short time. Resistance to such redirection is strong in individuals and groups as a function of their commitment to alternative social allegiances.

Historically, there have been circumstances of social disruption so extreme that the natural processes of socialization, the "ties that bind," have broken down. Such a breakdown occurred, for example, in the social upheaval and civil strife which filled the decade from 1919 to 1929 in the Soviet Union. There appeared a large number of unattached and uncared-for children and adolescents. These children, referred to as "*bezprizorniye*" (literally, "without looking after") were abandoned and homeless victims of the social chaos. Their numbers—reaching, according to some estimates, as high as *nine million* in 1922 (Geiger, 1968)—reflected the pervasiveness of the social disruption, since many were the victims of abandonment by desperate, confused, and besieged adults. The moral behavior of these children and adolescents is described by one student of the period as follows: "Not only did the homeless children present a pitiful spectacle, become diseased and die, but they gradually became a public menace, roaming the streets in gangs and committing every crime and violent act" (Geiger, 1968, p. 74).

These were children unattached to the adult human community physically as well as psychologically. Over time, they apparently developed a vicious form of peer orientation. The rehabilitative strategy and tactics developed to deal with the *bezprizorniye* by the Soviet educator and psychologist Makarenko (1955) reflect one of the few consciously conceived efforts to deal with the task of primary socialization and large-scale redirection of an antisocietal peer orientation. Makarenko perceived the necessity of establishing a psychological commitment to, and dependence upon, the social structure of the human community—first through the children's collective, then through the larger community, and finally through a total integration of the individual into the overall social structure. Upon this foundation of social identification were to be based all the higher aspects of socialization, particularly moral judgment and behavior. In the specific historical circumstances in which Makarenko worked, the net result was the development of a well-disciplined and highly responsible group of children and adolescents. In the long run, Makarenko's strategy became a system of socialization and education currently applied throughout the Soviet Union to produce children and adolescents who are so highly socialized and integrated into the collective identity that their behavior and attitudes are overdetermined by social authority (Bronfenbrenner, 1970a, 1970b).

A second example of disruption and social identity is to be found in Israel. One of the more important aspects of the Israeli experience has been the integration of Jews from diverse ethnic, racial, and geographic origins into the common culture of the new state of Israel. This process has achieved success, although there have been many difficulties and integration has sometimes been marginal. The Jews of Morocco provide an example of a difficult integration experience. While resident in their indigenous culture and locale, the Moroccan Jews constituted a reasonably stable and responsible group. When they moved to Israel, either because of commitment to Zionist principles or as the result of political expulsion, severe disruption occurred in many cases. The process of translocation and the status difficulties that they experienced in Israel were accompanied by some forms of moral breakdown such as juvenile delinquency (Willner, 1969). Increased levels of juvenile delinquency and community and personal disorganization appear to be a common consequence of social dislocation and disruption.

A less extreme but nonetheless serious breakdown of the human ecology—with attendant problems of social disorganization, alienation, and impaired moral socialization—may be observed in the growing estrangement of adults and children from each other in Western industrial societies. A review by Bronfenbrenner (1962a) indicated a decrease in all spheres of interaction between parents and children. Similar conclusions are drawn in a series of cross-cultural studies (Bronfenbrenner, 1970a, 1970b; Devereux, Bronfenbrenner,

& Rogers, 1969; Devereux, Bronfenbrenner, & Suci, 1962). Evidence points to a pattern in which the age-segregated peer group increasingly moves into the vacuum left by the retreating adults. A study by Condry and Siman (1968) has revealed that at every age and grade level, children today show greater dependency on peers than they did a decade ago. The same investigators have found, consistent with our own thesis, that susceptibility to peer-group influence is higher among children from homes in which one or both parents are frequently absent. The absence of salient adults appears to lead to greater domination by peers and presumably greater orientation to the peer group as a source of moral direction—and is associated with such antisocial behavior as lying, teasing other children, "playing hookey," and "doing something illegal." Bronfenbrenner (1973) points to this pattern of peer orientation as the origin of ever-increasing rates of juvenile delinquency.

Architectural and community planning can also contribute to the isolation of children from social agents who are diverse in age and background. In a comparison of the "old town" versus the "new town," West German investigators found that children in the new "model" communities felt cut off from life and hostile to adults, whereas children in the old cities had a more integrated social identity and were more positive about adults (Bronfenbrenner, 1973). The new towns, which are essentially "bedroom communities," may clearly be expected to disturb the condition of social pluralism posited as necessary for enhanced moral socialization.

What appears to be essential in moral development is a process by which social and personal identity form the foundation upon which moral behavior is built. But our account of the long-term results of Makarenko's integrative program (1955) of socialization suggests that the relationship between identity and morality is not a simple one. If, as clearly seems to be the case, too little integration of the individual into the social collectivity undermines the psychosocial foundation upon which moral judgment and behavior are based, what about the opposite extreme? Is there a point at which total social integration becomes as morally destructive to the individual as social disarray?

Turning once again to history, we see Hitler's Germany as a case in point. The aim of Nazification was to align institutional and personal life with service to the state. Every aspect of the public and private life of the people was to be integrated into a comprehensive ideological master plan. The result was an amalgamation of moral orientations into a single overarching submission to authority. In this way the countervailing forces of other Level 2 orientations and Level 3 morality were effectively neutralized. It should be noted that this example underscores the importance of a pluralist setting above and beyond its impact on the individual's moral socialization. That is, a pluralist system is needed to generate higher-order moral systems in order to allow societal diversities to coexist harmoniously (assuming elements of the system do not seek to destroy the pluralist diversity). In the case of Nazi Germany, the deterioration of moral judgment throughout the society has become legendary, and leaves an image of a people caught in a totalitarian moral debacle (Shirer, 1960).

Consideration of those who retained their moral identity in the midst of such terror and who continue to assert their ethical values through moral judgment and behavior will return us to the major thesis of this discussion. Over and over, the accounts of "resisters" to Nazism—whether Jews in the concentration camps who refused to allow themselves to be dehumanized and morally denuded (Bettelheim, 1943) or clergymen who continued to judge and oppose (Bonhoeffer, 1953)—reveal some alternative or competing allegiance, some identity not under the sway of Nazi totalitarianism. Even in the case of the army leaders who attempted to assassinate Hitler we find a pattern of alternative allegiance, for it appears their action was based on loyalty to the Officer Corps and its tradition, and on a desire to preserve it from destruction (Shirer, 1960). Social pluralism safeguards mature and independent moral judgment and behavior by providing countervailing social forces which preserve and foster Level 3 moral development. Once again we are brought back to our central theme: *Morally mature and independent judgment and behavior are facilitated by a pluralistic, as opposed to a monolithic or anomic, sociopsychological human ecology.*

An Empirical Illustration

We will finally undertake a preliminary empirical test of our hypothesis with data available from a continuing program of cross-cultural research being conducted at Cornell University.

First, however, we may review our basic concepts. A pluralistic setting is one in which social agents and entities represent somewhat different expectations, sanctions, and rewards for members of the society. These differences generate intergroup and interindividual conflict which is largely regulated by a set of "ground rules" and a common commitment to integrative principles and/or goals. A monolithic setting, on the other hand, is one in which all social agents and entities are organized around an identity of goals and principles. Conversely, an anomic setting is one in which there is almost no integration; social agents and entities are either absent or represent a multiplicity of divergent forces having no normative or institutional coherence.

In terms of our typology, the Soviet Union of the 1920s was an anomic setting, whereas Germany under the Nazis was a monolithic setting. Identification of such historical examples is relatively easy. Systematic analysis of the factors contributing to a pluralistic setting, on the other hand, is very difficult. On the political level, the task has engaged the efforts of political philosophers and social scientists, and has proven to be an extremely thorny problem (Garbarino, 1968).

Because of the systematic interdependence of the sociocultural structure and moral development, we would expect to find a strong relationship between cultural indices of sociopolitical pluralism and a measure of individual pluralism, that is, the extent to which individuals have competing allegiances to different social agents in considering moral questions. Moral pluralism is viewed as the condition out of which Level 3 arises. In other words, to the extent that moral pluralism arises out of sociopolitical pluralism in a particular setting, we may expect persons in that setting to develop Level 3 moral judgment and behavior. Our preliminary test of this general hypothesis involves a comparison of an index of sociopolitical pluralism and the results of an independent series of investigations of the moral judgment of 12-year-old children in thirteen societies.

The technique for assessing moral judgment is the Moral Dilemma Test (Bronfenbrenner, 1970), in which children are asked to respond to a series of thirty hypothetical conflict situations such as the following:

The Lost Test: You and your friends accidentally find a sheet of paper which the teacher must have lost. On this sheet are the questions and answers for a quiz that you are going to have tomorrow. Some of the kids suggest that you do not say anything to the teacher about it, so that all of you can get better marks. What would you really do? Suppose your friends decide to go ahead. Would you go along with them or refuse?

Refuse to go along with my friends

absolutely certain	fairly certain	I guess so

Go along with my friends

I guess so	fairly certain	absolutely certain

Other items in the Moral Dilemma Test deal with such situations as going to a

movie recommended by friends but disapproved by parents, neglecting homework to join friends, standing guard while friends put a rubber snake in the teacher's desk, leaving a sick friend to go to a movie with the gang, joining friends in pilfering fruit from an orchard with a no-trespassing sign, wearing styles of clothing approved by peers but not by parents, and running away after accidentally breaking a window while playing ball. These items were developed through a series of interviews and pretests in which parents, teachers, and schoolchildren were asked to indicate the kinds of behaviors about which adults and children disagreed. The items chosen were those which in a factor analysis had the highest loadings on a general factor of adult-approved versus adult-disapproved behavior, and the lowest loadings on factors specific to a particular situation. Each response was scored on a scale from -2.5 to $+2.5$, a negative value being assigned to the behavior urged by age-mates. Three equivalent forms of the instrument were administered, and the mean of the three was used in this analysis. Thus on the Moral Dilemma Test a child can obtain a score ranging from -25 to $+25$ (for 10 items), with 0 representing equal division between behavior urged by peers and adults (Bronfenbrenner, 1970a, 1970b).

Consequently, a high positive score indicates a high orientation toward conformity to adult social authority, whereas a high negative score indicates a high level of conformity and orientation toward peers. A score close to zero indicates a kind of "moral pluralism," that is, adult and peer authority in competition. (We would not expect highly peer-oriented scores, given that the subjects are all enrolled in schools, are preadolescent, and take the test in the school setting.)

Our index of sociopolitical pluralism is taken from a cross-national analysis of sociopolitical indices conducted by Vincent (1971). Vincent performed a factor analysis of 91 variables using the universe of 129 nation states as observations. The result was 19 factors. The factor accounting for the largest proportion of the total variance, 21.1 percent, was labeled "underdeveloped." The second orthogonal factor, and the one in which we are interested, accounted for 14.9 percent of the total variance and was labeled "democracy." For the purposes of our analysis, however, we shall term this latter factor *pluralism,* an interpretation which seems justified by an inspection of the variables that correlate highly with this factor. Table 4.2 lists these variables.

TABLE 4.2   Variables Highly Loaded on Pluralism Factor

1. Effective constitutional limitations (.96)
2. Current electoral system competitive (.89)
3. Current regime is representative (.86)
4. Freedom of group opposition (.86)
5. Considerable horizontal power distribution (.85)
6. Effective current legislature (.85)
7. Weak executive (.83)
8. Police not politically significant (.80)
9. Free speech (.78)
10. Considerable interest group aggregation by legislature (.80)
11. Limited interest articulation by institutional groups (.71)
12. Nonelitist political leadership (.69)
13. Military neutral in political affairs (.67)
14. Non-communist (.61)
15. Infrequent interest articulation by anomic groups (.52)
16. Bicameral legislature (.43)
17. Votes with West in United Nations (.40)
18. Low political inculturation (.39)
19. Power vertically distributed (.35)

Source: After Vincent (1971; p. 270).

Our hypothesis relating pluralism to moral judgment may thus be tested by assessing the relationship between the score of a country on the pluralism factor and the scores of its children on the moral dilemma experiment described above. A high positive score on the pluralism factor indicates a high level of sociopolitical pluralism; a high negative score indicates a low level of such pluralism. We would

therefore predict that there will be a strong *negative* relation between the pluralism score and the moral dilemma score; *high* political pluralism scores should be associated with low moral dilemma scores, that is, scores relatively close to zero and indicative of a pluralistic rather than a monolithic moral orientation. Table 4.3 reports the sets of scores for the thirteen countries in the Cornell study. For the thirteen countries the correlation between the pluralism scores and the moral dilemma scores is $-.89$. *This indicates that the greater the sociopolitical pluralism, the less authority-oriented the children, or conversely, the greater the moral pluralism.* (Inspection of the data reveals, however, that this correlation is primarily due to the dichotomous break between "East" and "West," there being little relationship between political pluralism and children's moral dilemma scores *within* these two major sociopolitical typologies.)

While the empirical test described above supports our major thesis, it leaves a number of questions unanswered. First, what are the dynamics relating pluralism

TABLE 4.3   Pluralism Factor Scores and Moral Dilemma Scores

Country	Pluralism Factor Score[a]	Moral Dilemma Score[b]
United States	1.25	2.22
West Germany	1.18	2.83
Switzerland	1.13	−2.09
Netherlands	1.11	1.18
Sweden	1.08	.41
Japan	1.05	3.75
United Kingdom	.94	2.63
Israel	.83	1.50
Canada	.78	4.32
U.S.S.R.	−1.63	13.52
Czechoslovakia	−1.73	9.46
Hungary	−1.79	14.06
Poland	−1.83	6.14

[a] Range of -2.11 to $+1.25$; minus indicates nonpluralistic, plus indicates pluralistic.
[b] Average of three administrations.

at the level of the sociopolitical ecology of institutions to pluralism at the level of the sociopsychological ecology of the child and his family? Our expectation is that the processes and relationships hypothesized in Table 4.1 point to an explanation of these dynamics. We might also explore the impact of political change on adults' childrearing patterns in times of drastic alteration such as in Germany under Nazification and again in the postwar period under de-Nazification. Such an investigation might shed some light on the impact of political climate on teachers, parents, and other socializing agents. It might also suggest the importance of adults' belonging to formal organizations as a stabilizing influence on their moral judgment and behavior and hence on the socialization of their children.

Second, what are the factors accounting for individual differences within a particular society both in terms of the degree to which particular individuals encounter a pluralistic sociopsychological ecology and the degree to which individuals are able to use such ecologies to enhance their own moral development? We must be alert to factors that affect the individual's ability to profit from diversity. That there is variation in this capacity is suggested by investigations of the ability to profit from situations involving choice (Condry, 1971), of the socialization of feelings of control over one's environment (Rotter, 1966), and of the ability to handle cognitive complexity and dissonance (Festinger, 1957).

Factors such as the size of educational institutions have been shown to have an important effect upon the number and diversity of an adolescent's nonacademic activities (Barker & Gump, 1966). Involvement in such activities has in turn been shown to relate to the student's sense of responsibility to the school and to his classmates, and to the kind of "satisfactions" he experiences as a function of participation (Barker & Gump, 1966). Analogous research is needed to assess the impact of participation in multiple institutional and cultural settings upon the moral judgment and behavior of parents and children, as well as on the childrearing practices of parents, teachers, and other socializing agents.

Finally, although we can begin to analyze the effects of monolithic settings upon moral judgment and behavior, little can be said about anomic settings. We have indicated evidence that suggests pockets of anomie exist in Western industrial societies as a function of the abdication of interactive and directive roles by adults, but it is difficult to study such a phenomenon at the level of the entire culture—presumably because a social system cannot tolerate such a state for very long. We must turn to historical events such as those that gave rise to the *bezprizorniye* in order to examine the relation of anomic social settings to moral development. Once we have a firmer grasp of the conditions under which anomic and monolithic settings arise, we may be better able to specify operationally the conditions necessary to generate and sustain sociocultural diversity and, consequently, moral pluralism.

CHAPTER 5

A Cognitive Social-Learning Approach to Morality and Self-Regulation[1]

Walter Mischel and Harriet N. Mischel

Introduction

In this chapter we will consider some of the main constructs of a cognitive social-learning position (Mischel, 1973) and examine how they apply to the psychological analysis of moral judgments, moral (prosocial) conduct, and self-regulation.

Parts of this discussion will focus on the *processes* through which moral and self-regulatory patterns are acquired, evoked, maintained, and modified (e.g., Bandura, 1969; Mischel, 1968). An adequate approach to complex human behavior also requires attention to the psychological products within the individual of cognitive development and social learning experiences. Therefore we will also consider some of the *person variables* that are the consequences of the individual's social and biological history and that in turn mediate how new experiences influence subsequent behavior. Such person variables and their interaction with conditions are crucial for an understanding of how behavior becomes organized and patterned within individuals, as well as how certain

developmental sequences tend to become normative for the social community. Consequently, the present discussion will include the role of such person variables, and of person-situation interactions, in a cognitive social-learning view of morality and self-regulation.

Human beings not only generate behaviors but also categorize, evaluate, and judge them. Thus a comprehensive psychological analysis of "morality" must consider *judgments* about moral behavior as well as the determinants of moral *behavior* itself. To adequately discuss moral judgment and behavior it will also be necessary to deal with the topic of self-regulation. Moral judgment, moral conduct, and self-regulation at first glance may seem to be separate topics, but from the present perspective a comprehensive psychological approach to any one of them requires considering the others. Moral judgment, moral conduct, and self-regulation all involve man's efforts to deal with good and bad, right and wrong. Moral judgment concerns the *evaluation* of good–bad (right–wrong) and of what one "ought to do"; moral conduct and self-regulation concern the processes and behaviors relevant to the *achievement* of the good and the avoidance of the bad and thus of realizing (or falling short of) one's moral ideals.

In a psychological analysis of morality it is also necessary to distinguish two components: the individual's *competence* (capacity) to generate prosocial behaviors, and the motivational (incentive) variables for their *performance* in particular situations. This difference between competence and performance mirrors the basic distinction made between acquisition (learning) and performance in social learning formulations (e.g., Bandura, 1969; Mischel, 1968, 1971). Acquisition or learning depends mainly on cognitive-sensory processes (although it may be facilitated by incentive or reinforcement conditions). The products of acquisition are a person's competencies, that is, the repertoire of what the individual *can* do, and encompass what he knows, and the skills, rules, and cognitive capacities which he has acquired and which permit him to generate (construct) behaviors (Mischel, 1973). In contrast, performance depends on motivational variables and incentive conditions, as will be discussed in later sections.

In sum, a comprehensive psychological approach to morality needs to include the individual's conceptions of what he "should" do (his moral judgments, good–bad evaluations) as well as the moral conduct and self-regulatory behaviors required to achieve moral ideals. The present analysis will include all three of these topics. It will also distinguish the determinants of the individual's competence for moral judgment and conduct from the motivational (performance) variables that influence whether or not he enacts and achieves the behaviors of which he is capable in particular situations.

In the present paper we will consider, first, the topic of moral competence. Thereafter conditions relevant to the performance of moral conduct and the achievement of self-regulation will be discussed. Finally we will deal with some basic issues in the organization and inter-relations of moral judgment, moral conduct, and self-regulation.

Moral Competence

In the course of development, and by means of both direct and observational learning, each person acquires information about the world and his relationship to it. As a result of cognitive maturation and continuous social learning, the individual acquires an increasingly large potential for generating organized behavior. The existence and importance of observational (cognitive) learning have been demonstrated clearly (Bandura, 1969a; Campbell, 1961), but it is less certain how to construe what is acquired. The phenomena include such diverse learnings as the structure (or construction) of the physical world (Piaget, 1954); the social rules, conventions, and principles that guide conduct (Aronfreed, 1968c; Kohlberg, 1969b); and the personal constructs generated about self and others (G. Kelly, 1955). These acquisitions have been discussed by some psychologists in terms of information processing and information integration (e.g., N. H. Anderson, 1972; Bandura, 1971a; Rumelhart, Lindsay, & Norman, 1971), and by others in terms of schemata and cognitive templates (e.g., Aronfreed, 1968c), while still others have invoked a series of discrete, sequential developmental stages, each characterized by distinctive cognitive structures (Kohlberg, 1969b).

THE CONCEPT OF COGNITIVE AND BEHAVIORAL CONSTRUCTION COMPETENCIES

The concept of *cognitive and behavioral construction competencies* encompasses the great variety of man's psychological acquisitions and refers to the diverse cognitions and behaviors that the individual is capable of constructing. The term *constructions* emphasizes the constructive fashion in which information appears to be retrieved (Neisser, 1967) and the active organization through which it seems to be categorized and transformed in the course of its processing (Bower, 1970; Mandler, 1967, 1968). There is little doubt that instead of mimicking models or emitting unedited copies of earlier observations, every person constructs (generates) his renditions of "reality" in a highly selective fashion. Research on modeling effects, for example, has consistently indicated that the products of observational learning involve novel organization of information by the observer and rule-governed performances, rather than mirroring of observed responses (Bandura, 1971c; Mischel & Grusec, 1966). The concept of construction competencies is intended to emphasize the person's *cognitive activities* (the operations and transformations that he performs on information), rather than the finite cognitions and responses that he "has" in a more passive, static, sense.

Each individual acquires the capacity to construct a great range of potential behaviors—moral, immoral, and amoral; and different individuals acquire different behavior construction capabilities in different degrees. Obviously there are enormous differences between people in the range and quality of the cognitive and behavioral patterns that they can generate in any domain. To assess an individual's potential for the construction of a particular behavior, incentives can be offered for the most complete, adequate performance that he can achieve on tasks sampling the behavior of interest. The assessment conditions for this purpose are identical to those in achievement testing (Wallace, 1966). The same tactics can be employed to assess what subjects "know" (i.e., the cognitive constructions they can generate, for example, about principles of justice and ethical conduct) and what they are capable of doing (as in the achievement of particular patterns of

moral conduct, such as helpfulness toward others and resistance to temptations). To assess what they had acquired from observing a model, children were later offered attractive incentives contingent upon their reproducing the model's behavior (Bandura, 1965b; Grusec & Mischel, 1966). The data indicated that the children had acquired a great deal of information by observing the model and were capable of reconstructing this knowledge in detail, but only when they were given appropriate incentives for doing so.

CORRELATES OF COGNITIVE COMPETENCE

In spite of their long neglect by traditional personality theories, cognitive-intellective competencies are highly relevant to understanding most of the phenomena of personality in general and of prosocial behavior in particular. This relevance is reflected in the important, persistent contributions of indices of intelligence to the obtained networks of personality correlations (Campbell & Fiske, 1959; Mischel, 1968). Cognitive competencies (as tested by mental age and IQ tests) tend to be among the very best predictors of "honesty" in conduct (Hartshorne & May, 1928) and of later social and interpersonal adjustment (J. Anderson, 1960). Brighter, more competent, people presumably experience more success (interpersonally and through work achievements) and hence are more positively assessed by themselves and by others on the evaluative good–bad dimension so ubiquitous in trait ratings (Vernon, 1964). As noted elsewhere (Mischel, 1973), competence and achievement also may be reflected in the substantial "first factor" pervasively obtained on such tests as the MMPI (J. Block, 1965), often interpreted as connoting "adjustment" at the positive end and maladaptive character structure at the negative end. Cognitive achievements and intellective potential, as measured by mental age or IQ tests, are being given a central role in current cognitive-developmental theories (Kohlberg, 1969b) and appear to be important aspects of such concepts as *moral maturity*, *ego strength*, and *ego development*. Finally, indices that are strongly correlated with cognitive-intellective competence—such as age and the demographic variables of socioeconomic level and education—also tend to be among the best predictors of the adequacy of social functioning (Robins, 1972).

The importance of "sheer cognitive power in the operation of conscience" (Aronfreed, 1968c, p. 265) is also supported by studies that have found intelligence to be significantly correlated with the complexity of the information that children can deal with in their judgments of conduct (e.g., Kellmer Pringle & Edwards, 1964; Whiteman & Kosier, 1964). For example, the child's increasing capacity for verbal complexity seems to be a crucial determinant of age-related changes in the ability to utilize the principle of intentionality in the appraisal of other people's conduct (Breznitz & Kugelmass, 1967). Thus there is a triad of associations: Indices of the growth of conscience tend to be correlated with independent measures of the child's intelligence as well as with his age (Abel, 1941; R. C. Johnson, 1962; Kohlberg, 1964; MacRae, 1954).

Many age-related changes in conceptual styles and cognitive competencies have been identified and often have been interpreted to reflect fixed maturational sequences of cognitive development (e.g., Baldwin, 1967; Piaget 1926b). But a growing body of empirical evidence also suggests that these age-related cognitive patterns are modifiable when subjects are exposed to relevant cognitive and social-learning experiences designed to alter them (Bandura & Harris, 1966; Odom, Liebert, & Hill, 1968; Carroll, Rosenthal, & Brysh, 1969; T. L. Rosenthal & Whitebook, 1970; T. L. Rosenthal, Zimmerman, & Durning, 1970; Siegler, Liebert, & Liebert, 1973). These studies suggest that such cognitive skills as linguistic construction and conceptual organization of a set of stimuli are amenable to change through observational learning and reward procedures. Cognitive competencies specifically relevant to moral reasoning and conduct also have been shown to be modifiable in the same manner (Bandura & McDonald, 1963; Cowan et al., 1969; Prentice, 1972). Thus widespread age-related changes in both cognitive competencies and preferred cognitive styles may reflect age-correlated alterations in the social-learning variables salient at different points in development (to be discussed in later sections) as well as maturational changes in cognitive capacities—perhaps in almost inextricable interactions.

MATURITY IN MORAL REASONING

As noted before, judgments of right–wrong comprise an important aspect of morality. An evaluative dimension consistently emerges when people rate each other's traits and attributes (or assess themselves), as well as when they rate meanings of words and events. On the semantic differential, for example, a primary evaluative (good–bad) factor accounted for about half to three-quarters of the extractable variance (Osgood, Suci, & Tannenbaum, 1957). The same evaluative factor also was found pervasively in trait ratings of persons (e.g., Mulaik, 1964; Vernon, 1964). There is little doubt that good–bad evaluations are a basic ingredient of human judgment, but there is much less agreement about the nature and determinants of such judgments, especially with regard to morality.

Most challenging and controversial is the view that moral judgment, and specifically moral reasoning, involves the child's passage through a series of successive stages characterized by increasing degrees of maturity in the mode of organizing the social and moral order (Piaget, 1932; Kohlberg, 1963a, 1969b).[2] To help test this contention, Kohlberg (1958, 1969b) has provided an increasingly popular measure of maturity in moral reasoning. On this test the subject is confronted with a set of conflict-inducing moral dilemmas, and his answers are scored for their level of "moral maturity." This measure and the theorizing related to it have become increasingly influential in conceptions of morality (as the contents of the present volume attest).

Unfortunately, the Kohlberg measure of maturity in reasoning about moral dilemmas does not permit one to separate the type of moral reasoning of which the respondent is capable from the moral reasoning which he favors (or which he prefers to use). To separate *competence* in moral reasoning from *performance* (or preference) it would be necessary for the test to encourage all subjects to display the "best" (highest, most mature) moral reasoning that they are capable of generating. This could be achieved by offering incentives for maximum performance (as on other achievement tests). Without such a procedure one cannot determine whether a subject's performance reflects the most mature moral reasoning that he *can* generate or the degree to which he uses (prefers) different types of moral reasoning in the dilemmas sampled or (as most likely occurs) some indeterminate mix of both. One cannot be sure from the test, for example, whether a "Stage 3" subject who displays a dominant "good boy" orientation does not know more abstract principles which go beyond approval seeking, or whether he may "have" such concepts but prefer not to verbalize them when reasoning about moral dilemmas.[3]

Since subjects often use moral reasoning at levels judged to be above their current stage, it would be implausible to view their assigned stage as an index of their current maximal competence. As Kohlberg (1969b, p. 387, fig. 6.4) reports, on the average somewhat less than 50 percent of a subject's moral judgments fit a single stage, the remainder being dis-

tributed in the form of a normal curve encompassing the stages both above and below the modal one. Similarly, Bandura and McDonald (1963, p. 280) found that children at all ages (from 5 to 11 years) "exhibited discriminative repertoires of moral judgment" (i.e., used reasoning at various stages). Among college students "not one of the subjects studied employed moral reasoning that was exclusively rated at any single level of development" (Fishkin, Keniston, & MacKinnon, 1973, p. 114). To the extent that a subject uses *any* moral judgments at levels higher than the level he is assigned to by his modal score, one must conclude that he is capable of constructing such judgments but normatively prefers not to make them. Thus the assigned stage of "maturity" in moral judgment may be seen to reflect *preferred* modes of justifying moral conduct, and not necessarily to indicate the subject's cognitive limits. Moreover, the heterogeneity across situations of both moral reasoning and moral conduct which may be displayed by an individual assigned to any given stage requires explanation. From the present perspective, such intraindividual differences, as well as differences between individuals, may be understood in terms of each person's unique social-learning history and experiences; they reflect the interaction of the products of cognitive development and social learning with the specifics of the immediate psychological situation in which behavior is generated.

Some Determinants of Moral Conduct and Self-Regulation

The individual who knows how to behave competently in prosocial, constructive, ways is *capable* of such behaviors, but whether or not he enacts them at any given time (or chooses less virtuous courses of action) depends on specific motivational and performance considerations in the psychological situation. So far we have considered what the individual is capable of doing, that is, his competencies and abilities. But the person who is capable of the most virtuous moral conduct may also be capable of aggressive and morally despicable action. To go from competence and potential behaviors to actual performance, from construction capacity to the construction of behavior in specific situations, requires attention to the determinants of performance. In this regard, the variables of greatest interest are the person's expectancies and subjective values.

EXPECTED RESPONSE CONSEQUENCES

It often helps to know what an individual can do, but to predict specific behavior in a particular situation one must consider the individual's specific expectancies about the consequences of different behavioral possibilities in that situation (e.g., Mischel & Staub, 1965). The subject's own behavior-outcome expectancies guide his selection of behaviors from among the enormous number which he is capable of constructing within any situation.

In part, expectancies about environmental contingencies may be based on direct experience (e.g., Rotter, 1954, 1972). Yet behavior-outcome expectations depend not only on the outcomes one has obtained for similar behavior in similar situations but also on the consequences one has observed occurring to other people. Information about the outcomes of other people's behavior may provide valuable information about the probable consequences to oneself for trying similar behavior.

After one has observed that other people ("models") obtain positive consequences for a response pattern, one tends to act more readily in similar ways. For instance, if a child sees other children receive encouragement and praise for, let us say, helpfulness and generosity at play, his own tendency to behave altruistically in similar situations will increase. Conversely, when social models are punished

for their behavior (e.g., for aggressing), observers tend to become more inhibited about displaying similar behavior (Bandura, Ross, & Ross, 1963a). However, when incentives are later offered for imitating the aggressive model, children who had initially seen the model punished give evidence of as much imitation learning as children who had seen the model unpunished or rewarded (Bandura, 1965b). It may be concluded that the children in all conditions had learned the model's behavior equally well; the observation of different consequences, however, had inhibited or facilitated their later performance of the behavior.

Modeling cues and vicarious response consequences have been shown to influence performance measures of both moral reasoning (Bandura & McDonald, 1963; Cowan et al., 1969; Prentice, 1972) and prosocial behavior (Bryan & Test, 1967; Rosenhan, Moore, & Underwood, Chap. 13; Staub, 1973). In the present view, these effects were probably mediated by alterations in the observers' expectancies regarding the desirability (consequences) of their displaying behavior similar to the behaviors that they saw modeled and rewarded. Even reactions to frustration, which often tend to be aggressive, are likely to become prosocial and cooperative when the positive consequences for such constructive behaviors are enhanced and made salient. For example, when domineering, hyperaggressive children were exposed to modeling situations that depicted positive consequences for cooperativeness in response to interpersonal conflicts, their own behavior became increasingly cooperative even in a follow-up assessment one month later (Chittenden, 1942). Bandura (1973) has documented in detail the often subtle and complex ways in which anticipated response consequences may facilitate antisocial aggressive behavior or lead to prosocial alternatives.

Although laboratory studies provide the most conclusive demonstrations of the close links between the occurrence of behavior and expected consequences, naturalistic observations serve to further document the social implications. Consider, for example, the collective modeling of airline hijackings (Bandura, 1973). While air piracy was unknown in the United States until 1961, successful hijackings of Cuban airliners to Miami were followed by a wave of hijackings, reaching a crest of eighty-seven airplane piracies in 1969. The phenomenon was given fresh impetus by news of a hijacker who successfully parachuted from an airliner with a large sum of extorted money, but hijackings in the United States finally seemed to end when new security procedures greatly reduced the likelihood of success.

In sum, one does not have to enact particular behaviors in order to learn their consequences; modeling cues and vicarious as well as direct consequences of performances influence subsequent behavior. One does not have to be arrested for embezzling to learn some of its consequences; one does not have to be searched personally to learn of airport security arrangements and the penalty for concealed weapons; nor does one have to rescue a drowning child to discover the positive consequences of such an act. Information that alters the person's anticipations of the probable outcomes to which a behavior will lead also changes the probability that he will engage in the behavior. Modeling cues (both live and symbolic) provide an extremely effective way of changing an observer's behavior-outcome expectancies, and thus enhancing or inhibiting the behaviors involved.

Modeling cues and vicarious response consequences may have powerful effects on performance, but not all models are equally effective for all people. The attributes of the observer (e.g., Bandura & Walters, 1963; Turiel, 1966) and of the model (e.g., prestige, status, power, similarity to the observer), as well as the model's relationship with the observer (e.g., nurturance and warmth), will affect the likelihood that the modeled behavior will be influential

(Grusec & Mischel, 1966; Mischel & Liebert, 1967). For example, children tend to adopt the performance standards displayed by adult models who are rewarding and powerful, but tend to reject the same standards when they are modeled by adults who are low in those attributes (Mischel & Grusec, 1966). Similarly, children with nurturant caretakers who had modeled helpfulness in both live and symbolic distress situations were later themselves more helpful and consistently altruistic (Yarrow, Scott, & Waxler, 1973). These experimental findings are congruent with naturalistic and field studies reporting some correlations between the affection and nurturance of the parents and the prosocial behavior (e.g., "consideration") of their children (M. L. Hoffman & Salzstein, 1967) and suggest that parental nurturance tends to be conducive to children's prosocial behavior especially when it is combined with judicious control (see Staub, 1973).

"Direct training" for prosocial behavior may encompass a wide variety of experiences such as role playing, role exchange, and reasoning to encourage responsibility, empathy, and consideration for others (Staub, 1973). Experiences of this type presumably help to sensitize the individual to the consequences of his behavior for other people and not merely for himself. Not surprisingly, concern for others seems to be learned most effectively when more than moral exhortations are involved. Cross-cultural research suggests that children's altruistic–egoistic tendencies may depend most strongly on the degree to which the children are actually involved in the maintenance of the family's welfare. Children tended to be more altruistic in their behavior when the culture required them to assume more interpersonal obligations and responsibilities, such as caring for younger siblings and animals (J. W. M. Whiting & B. Whiting, 1969). Increasing responsibilty for the welfare of others tended to generate increasing altruism. In the present view, the assignment of such responsibilities and their successful execution serve to generate enduring expectancies regarding the positive consequences of mutually helpful behaviors, and hence tend to increase their likelihood. Just as aggression tends to feed on aggression (Berkowitz, 1973b), so does a person's future prosocial behavior thrive on his past prosocial behavior.

Opportunities to practice prosocial behavior and to observe or experience its positive consequences facilitate the future occurrence of similar behavior, but it is also easy to use "rewards" unwisely in socialization. A major purpose of socialization is to wean the individual from external controls and rewards so that his behavior becomes increasingly guided and supported by intrinsic gratifications, that is, satisfactions closely connected with the prosocial activity itself. Therefore it is essential to use incentives judiciously and only to the extent necessary to initiate and sustain desired prosocial behavior.

SUBJECTIVE VALUES

Even when different people share similar expectancies, they may choose different patterns of behavior because of differences in the *subjective values* of the outcomes that they expect (Mischel, 1973; Rotter, 1954). For example, given that all persons expect approval from peers to depend on verbalization of particular value judgments, there may be differences in the frequency of such verbalizations due to differences in the perceived value of obtaining peer approval. Similarly, while approval from peers for a particular behavior pattern in a particular situation may be more important for one individual than parental approval, these values may be reversed for a second person and irrelevant for a third.

The subjective (perceived) value for the individual of particular classes of events (his stimulus preferences and aversions) is an important determinant of behavioral choices. *Subjective value* refers to stimuli that have acquired the power to induce positive or negative emotional states

in the person and to function as incentives or reinforcers for his behavior. The subjective value of any stimulus pattern may be acquired and modified through instructions and observational experiences as well as through direct experiences (Bandura, 1969a) and obviously may change substantially in the course of development. The highest subjective values of a 40-year-old may have little appeal for his young child, and vice versa.

The *affective value* (valence) of any stimulus depends on the exact conditions— in the person and in the situation—in which it occurs. The many variables known to affect the emotional meaning and valence of a stimulus include its context, sequencing, and patterning (Helson, 1964); social comparison processes (Festinger, 1954); and the cognitive labels the person assigns to his own emotional arousal state (Schachter & Singer, 1962).

Even when subjective values for particular activities are shared, individuals may differ in how they tolerate (and respond to) deviations from these values either in their own behavior or in the conduct of others. For example, to the surprise of many sociologists, members of the lower class (gang and nongang) and of the middle class, both black and white, were found to endorse similar values "in principle"; but individuals from these different subcultures differed in the degree to which they tolerated behavioral deviations from the prosocial norms that they all abstractly endorsed (Gordon et al., 1963). Such differences in tolerance are presumed to be partly a function of differences in people's self-regulatory systems. These systems are discussed next.

SELF-REGULATORY SYSTEMS

Tests of moral maturity (i.e., moral reasoning) focus on how the individual solves hypothetical moral dilemmas in story situations, but the successful realization of moral choices in real life often depends on the faithful execution of long-term commitments that demand high levels of self-control. Moral conduct requires the individual to adhere behaviorally to reciprocal commitments and obligations even (or especially) under extremely difficult conditions, and not merely to endorse them in principle. Such prolonged self-control sequences involve more than abstract problem solving and right–wrong decision making; they hinge on the individual's ability to regulate his own behavior in the face of strong temptations and situational pressures for long periods and without the aid of any obvious external rewards and supports. As noted at the start of this chapter, self-control is an important aspect of morality, for without it moral ideals cannot be realized. Indeed, some philosophers suggest that *all* virtues are forms of self-control (Von Wright, 1963, chap. 7). To go from moral thought to moral conduct requires self-regulation.

Although behavior is controlled to a considerable degree by externally administered consequences for actions, each person also regulates his own behavior by self-imposed goals (standards) and self-produced consequences. Even when there are no external constraints and social monitors, individuals set standards for themselves and criticize or commend their own behavior depending on how well it fits their expectations and standards. The notion of self-imposed standards has figured in Rotter's "minimal goal" construct (1954) and more recently in conceptions of self-reinforcing functions (Bandura, 1971c; Kanfer, 1971; Kanfer & Marston, 1963; Mischel, 1968, 1973).

A fundamental quality of self-regulatory systems is the subject's adoption of *contingency rules*, which guide his behavior in the absence of and sometimes in spite of immediate external situational pressures. Such rules specify the kinds of behavior appropriate (expected) under particular conditions, the performance criteria (standards, goals) that the behavior must achieve, and the consequences of achieving or failing to reach these standards. Different individuals may differ, of course, in each component of self-regulation, depending on their unique earlier histories or their more recent experiences (e.g., situational information).

Research on goal setting and self-reinforcement has demonstrated some of the components in self-regulation (e.g., Bandura & Perloff, 1967; Bandura & Whalen, 1966; Mischel & Liebert, 1966). These studies reveal that even young children will not indulge in freely available immediate gratifications; instead they follow rules that regulate conditions under which they may reinforce themselves. Far from being hedonistic, children, like adults, make demands of themselves and impose complex and often stringent contingencies upon their own behavior. These self-imposed criteria are grounded in the observed standards displayed by salient models, as well as in the individual's direct socialization history (e.g., Bandura & Walters, 1963; Mischel & Liebert, 1966).

When modeling cues and direct tuition for a pattern of standards are congruent they tend to facilitate each other, and when they conflict (as often occurs in life) the observer's behavior is affected jointly by both sources (e.g., Mischel & Liebert, 1966; Rosenhan & White, 1967). Thus an observer is most likely to adopt modeled standards for behavior when the standards used by the model for himself are consistent with the standards used by the model to train the child. When there is a discrepancy between what is practiced and what is preached, observers are more likely to adopt the least stringent standards available for behavior. Mischel and Liebert (1966), for example, found that when models imposed stringent standards for behavior upon children and displayed similarly rigorous standards in their own self-evaluation, all children subsequently adopted these high standards. But when the models permitted and encouraged lenient standards in the children, the youngsters were uniformly lenient with themselves, even when the models had been stringent in their own standards.

After the individual has set his standards (terminal goals) for conduct in a particular situation, the route toward their realization may be long and difficult. In that case, progress may be mediated extensively by covert symbolic activities, such as praise and self-instructions, as the individual reaches subgoals en route. When reinforcing and noxious stimuli are imagined, their behavioral consequences may be the same as when such stimuli are presented externally (e.g., Cautela, 1971). These covert activities serve to maintain goal-directed work until the performance reaches or exceeds the person's terminal standards (e.g., Meichenbaum, 1971). Progress toward goal attainment also may be aided by self-generated distractions and cognitive operations through which the person can transform the aversive self-control situation into one that he can master effectively (e.g., Mischel, Ebbesen, & Zeiss, 1972; Mischel & Moore, 1973; Mischel, Moore, & Zeiss, 1973). When important goals are attained, positive self-appraisal and self-reinforcement tend to occur, whereas the individual may indulge in psychological self-lacerations and self-condemnation if he fails to reach significant self-imposed standards.

People can readily perform *cognitive transformations* on stimuli (Mischel, 1974), focusing on selected aspects of the objective stimulus; such selected attention, interpretation, and categorization may substantially influence how any stimulus affects their behavior (see also Geer, Davison, & Gatchel, 1970; Schachter, 1964). The significant role of cognitive transformations in self-regulation is demonstrated in research on the determinants of how long preschool children will actually sit still alone in a chair waiting for a preferred but delayed outcome before they signal with a bell to terminate the waiting period and settle for a less preferred but immediately available gratification (Mischel, 1974; Mischel, Ebbesen, & Zeiss,

1972). The results reveal that the same child who may terminate his waiting in less than half a minute on one occasion may be capable of waiting for long periods on another occasion a few weeks earlier or later, if cognitive and attentional conditions are conducive to delay.

Studies on cognitive transformations during delay have also helped to clarify the role of attention in self-control. As early as 1890, William James noted a relationship between attention and self-control, and contended that attentional processes are the crux of the self-control phenomena usually subsumed under the label "will" (or since James's time under the concept "ego strength"). In James's words (1890), "Attention with effort is all that any case of volition implies. The essential achievement of will is to attend to a difficult object" (p. 549). Beginning with the research of Hartshorne and May (1928) some correlations have been found between indices of moral behavior and measures of attention or resistance to distraction on mental tests (Grim, Kohlberg, & White, 1968). Such correlations have led to the suggestion that a person's ability to resist temptation may be facilitated by how well he attends to a task. Yielding to temptation in most experimental paradigms hinges on the subject's becoming distracted from the main task to which he is supposed to be attending. In such paradigms a subject's ability to focus attention *on* the task and to resist distraction may automatically make it easier for him to resist such temptations as cheating, as Grim, Kohlberg, and White (1968) have noted.

Findings on the role of attention during delay of gratification, however, reveal another relationship: *Not* attending to the goal (potential reward) was what facilitated self-control most dramatically (Mischel, Ebbesen, & Zeiss, 1972). More detailed analyses of attentional mechanisms during delay of gratification showed that the crucial variable is not *whether* the subject attends to the goal objects while delaying, but *how* he focuses on them (Mischel, 1974). It was found that through instructions the child can cognitively transform the reward objects that face him during the delay period in ways to either permit or prevent effective delay of gratification. For example, if the child is left during the waiting period with the actual reward objects (pretzels or marshmallows) in front of him, it becomes difficult for him to wait for more than a few moments. But through instructions he can cognitively transform the reward objects in ways that permit him to wait for long periods (Mischel & Baker, 1975). If he cognitively transforms the stimulus to focus on its nonarousing qualities, for example, by thinking about the pretzel sticks as little brown logs, or by thinking about the marshmallows as round white clouds or as cotton balls, he may be able to wait for long time periods. Conversely, if the child has been instructed to focus cognitively on the consummatory (arousing, motivating) qualities of the reward objects, such as the pretzel's crunchy, salty taste or the chewy, sweet, soft taste of the marshmallows, he tends to be able to wait only a short time (Mischel, 1974). By knowing the relevant rules of cognitive transformation and utilizing them during self-control efforts, individuals may be able to attain considerable self-mastery in pursuit of their goals, even in the face of strong countervailing situational pressures.

Affective states also influence the person's self-control and self-reactions. After positive (as compared to negative) experiences, individuals become much more benign toward both themselves and others. After success experiences or positive mood inductions, for example, there is greater selective attention to positive information about the self (Mischel, Ebbesen, & Zeiss, 1973), greater noncontingent self-gratification (Mischel, Coates, & Raskoff, 1968; Moore, Underwood, & Rosenhan, 1972), and greater generosity (Isen, Horn, & Rosenhan, 1973).

The organization of self-regulatory behaviors also requires attention to the individual's priority rules for determining the sequencing of behavior and stop rules for the termination of a particular sequence of behavior. Like other complex human actions, prosocial, morally relevant behaviors depend on the execution of lengthy interlocking sequences of thought and behavior. The concept of plans as hierarchical processes that control the order in which an organism performs a sequence of operations (G. A. Miller, Galanter, & Pribram, 1960) seems applicable. Introspectively, we do seem to generate plans. And once a plan is formed and adopted (to marry, to divorce, to report suspicions about another's immoral act to authorities, to resist the draft, to join a protest movement), a whole series of subroutines follows. While the concept of plans is intuitively plausible, it has not yet led to the necessary personality-oriented cognitive research. Helpful first steps toward the study of plans are the concepts of behavioral intentions (Dulany, 1962), intention statements and contracts (Kanfer et al., 1974). Self-instructions and intention statements are likely to be important aspects of the individual's plans and the hierarchical organization of his self-regulatory behavior.

In sum, a comprehensive approach to prosocial behavior must take account of the individual's self-regulatory systems. These systems include (1) the rules that specify goals or performance standards in particular situations; (2) the consequences of achieving or failing to achieve those criteria; (3) the self-instructions and cognitive stimulus transformations required to achieve the self-control necessary for goal attainment; and (4) the organizing rules (plans) for the sequencing and termination of complex behavioral patterns in the absence of external supports and in the presence of external hindrances.

AGE-RELATED CHANGES

In the present view, age-related changes in the individual's moral judgments and his prosocial and self-regulatory patterns reflect correlated changes in the interaction between his growing cognitive and behavioral competencies and the social-learning variables salient at different points in his experience. Early in the child's life, the consequences for moral and immoral behavior tend to be defined and presented in a concrete, tangible, immediate fashion. When a mother is socializing her toddler not to hurt his siblings, she is likely to say such things as "Don't! That's not nice! If you do that again I'll have to (specific threat)." Or she might praise good behavior with, "Now Johnny's being a good boy; nice Johnny." She is certainly unlikely to express abstract rules about general moral principles to her barely verbal child.

The young child's moral understanding comes to reflect the regime of personal constraints, of punishments and approvals, of rules and conventions, which are modeled and upheld by parents, peers, and other significant persons at different points in his development. Similarly, the child's changing prosocial conduct reflects the changes in his expectancies, subjective values, and self-regulatory systems caused partly by his changing competencies and experiences. The specific shifts in these socialization patterns with age and developmental progress during early childhood probably have considerable similarity to the first few moral stages conceptualized by Kohlberg (1969b). For example, the most primitive phases of moral reasoning (in their orientation to retaliation for wrong doing and to the assessment of transgressions in terms of their objective magnitude) tend to mirror the practices to which the child is exposed earliest in the socialization process.

The young child does not have good control over his own behavior and tends to interpret both positive and negative outcomes as the result of factors outside himself (Mischel, Mailer, & Zeiss, 1973). Moreover, the magnitude of the young child's transgressions is often unintended and unanticipated, as when a poke at a milk bottle produces a spill that badly upsets an adult. Not surprisingly, at this point in socialization the youngster learns that the damaging consequences of an act, rather than its motivations, signal the probable occurrence and magnitude of punishment. But with the growth of cognitive and behavioral competence, the child learns to hold himself increasingly responsible for his own behavior. He becomes more sensitive to the fact that cues about intentions, often conveyed verbally ("I didn't mean it!"), determine the response consequences for an act. While a parent may punish the older child's transgression if it seems voluntary, punishment is less likely and less severe if the act is judged to be accidental. Expectancies about behavior-outcome relations gradually become moderated by a host of social cues, including those for inferring the intentions motivating behavior (i.e., its perceived causes). Over time a person's reactions to a physical blow from another will depend on whether it was perceived as accidental or deliberate. Similarly, whether praise and attention will have a positive effect on the recipient or will generate suspicion (and a rebuff) depends on whether the behaviors are perceived as sincere or as ingratiating (Jones, 1964).

The relations between socialization practices and the child's age and cognitive competencies are not arbitrary; they probably reflect a continuous interaction of the child's increasing cognitive competencies with the priorities and practices of socializing agents. It is essential for a mother to prevent young Johnny from injuring his sibling, even when she does not have the time, and Johnny does not have the capacity, to reason about the moral bases of this constraint; therefore she must rely on specific admonitions and punishments. Later in socialization, when the child's cognitive and verbal skills expand, the justification for right and wrong courses of action tends to be increasingly based on rules—first of an arbitrary authority-oriented type but gradually of a more abstract and reasoned nature.

Consider, for example, the differences in how a 12-year-old delinquent from a lower socioeconomic-class family and a professor in an Ivy League college might handle moral dilemmas in ways that result in the delinquent's being assigned to Stage 2 or 3 of Kohlberg's scale of moral maturity, while the professor is likely to reach higher levels. To understand the differences between these two people it is necessary to take account of the differences in their cognitive and verbal skills as well as in the ways in which moral issues and conduct are represented and treated in their respective experiences. In part, the delinquent youngster and the professor differ in the cognitive and linguistic maturity with which they can conceptualize and articulate "reasons." That is likely to be the case regardless of whether the issues about which they are asked to reason are moral dilemmas or morally irrelevant—for example, esthetic judgments about why they prefer particular paintings, books, movies, or music. When justifying either his moral reasoning or his esthetic preferences (or any other choice, morally relevant or not) the professor is likely to deal in "higher" abstractions (e.g., about justice, about beauty), to invoke more generalized rules (e.g., about reciprocity in ethics, about harmony in esthetics) than will the twelve-year-old. The latter is likely to be not only more concrete but also more self-centered and peer-centered in his explanations.

Some of the differences between the juvenile delinquent and the professor reflect their different cognitive capacities; but it is also essential to consider the enormous differences in the consequences which they expect and value for different courses of action and for different verbalizations, and their different self-regulatory systems. For example, both the delinquent and the professor may be partly motivated by expected consequences such as the approval of their relevant peer group and their own self-esteem. But such a sense of approval and self-esteem may require strict conformity to the group's conventions for the delinquent; for the professor it may be

contingent on adherence to reciprocity, consistency, and appeals to abstract universal principles. For the professor, moral reasoning oriented explicitly toward approval from others and adherence to conventional authority is unlikely to be rewarding, unlikely to be valued, and thus unlikely to be used. His moral reasoning will probably be structured and justified in far more impersonal, "unselfish," abstract terms, with generalizations about universal principles (which would produce a much higher moral maturity score). But while the particular consequences to which the professor and the delinquent are especially alert may be different, and while they may justify their choices at different levels of abstraction and verbal sophistication, both will be guided by a concern with the external and self-administered outcomes expected from the available alternatives.

In sum, in the present view, age-related changes in the style and content of moral reasoning and conduct reflect changes in the individual's cognitive and verbal capacities (e.g., the ability to deal with abstract concepts) in interaction with the social-learning variables salient for him at different points in the life cycle. The specific manner in which socialization variables interact with the individual's cognitive capacities in different ways at different points in the development of prosocial behavior has been documented elsewhere (see Aronfreed, 1968c). To the degree that the development of cognitive competencies follows a sequential course (e.g., in the direction of greater verbal and abstract concept-formation skills), some universality may also be found in the age-related sequence of indices of morality across cultures. But while moral judgments may generally move from a focus on immediate consequences to more temporally distant concerns, and from concrete justifications to more abstract general rules and principles, their content will depend on the culture in which the individual develops. The increasing cognitive and verbal competencies of the child follow an age-related sequence which in turn is reflected in age-related changes in moral reasoning. But it would not be parsimonious to believe that the latter reflects more than the growth of cognitive competencies interacting with socialization practices.

While there is considerable controversy about the possible existence and specific content of any "universal" hierarchy of moral judgment (Alston, 1971; Aronfreed, 1968c; Kohlberg, 1971a), there is widespread agreement about what is *not* an index of high levels of moral maturity. Specifically, even when the outcome of an act is judged as "good" by an evaluator, the actor is less likely to be judged as having "high moral maturity" when he seems to be motivated by obvious immediate, tangible gratifications, rather than altruistic concerns. In the course of development the perceived subjective intent (motivation) attributed to the actor replaces the objective outcome of the behavior as a main determinant of evaluative moral judgments (Weiner & Peter, 1973).

Psychological theorists, just like laymen, also base judgments about the goodness of an act on the actor's inferred intentions, not merely on its outcome. When it is easy to identify the specific situational incentives or pressures that seem to motivate behavior, there is no reason to credit the performer with moral maturity, with advanced ego development, or with altruistic motivations. For example, to help another person either in order to get an apparent reward for oneself, or because one is under duress to give aid is generally not considered an act of moral virtue or maturity. Behavior that is obviously related to immediate rewarding or punishing consequences for the actor can be easily explained without recourse to any internal moral or ego regulators. But when there are no obvious justifications for an act, the popular explanation changes quickly. Why does a child refrain from attractive pleasures even in the absence of external constraints? Why does one berate oneself for enacting, or even fantasizing, behaviors that others cannot detect? Why does one aid another even when doing so is painful and costly to oneself? Why does one share one's bounty with others even when not pressured to be so generous? These are the kinds of questions that have led to the construction of mediating systems as explanations. These questions also point to some of the conditions under which behaviors are more likely to be judged as moral, good, and "self-controlled"—conditions in which the outcomes of a behavior are evaluated as good but the motivation for the action does not seem adequately explained by immediate incentives and constraints in the actor's situation.

A tendency to judge either "selfishly" or "situationally" motivated behaviors as less moral, or indeed premoral, is seen in the writings of cognitively oriented developmental psychologists. Consider, for example, Kohlberg's (1958, 1969b) stages of moral maturity (levels of moral reasoning). Such stage conceptions of moral maturation suggest that in the lowest maturity levels behavior (or its evaluation) is governed by immediate consequences to the self such as fear of retaliation, punishment, or detection. At intermediate levels the conduct and assessment of behavior are said to depend on conformity to external rules and expected benefits to the self versus disapproval from others and from conventional authorities. At the higher levels of maturity, however, behavior is said to become governed by less selfish, less concrete, more abstract considerations. For Kohlberg (1969b), the highest stages of moral development involve a contractual legalistic orientation (Stage 5) and a conscience or principles orientation (Stage 6) "involving appeal to logical universality [and to] conscience as a directing agent and to mutual respect and trust" (p. 376).

But from the present perspective, even the noblest altruism supported by the "highest" levels of moral reasoning still depends on expected consequences, although the consequences are often temporally distant, are not in the immediate external environment, are not easily identified, and reside in the actor himself rather than in social agents. The young child's behavior may be governed primarily by expected immediate concrete consequences for himself, but with greater maturity the evaluation and reinforcement of behavior become increasingly autonomous of external rewards and punishments and include more temporally distant and abstract considerations and self-reaction on the part of the actor. But such autonomy does not imply that the behavior no longer depends on expected consequences; it does suggest that these consequences increasingly hinge on self-evaluations and self-administered outcomes contingent upon one's achieving or violating one's own standards and on more abstract, temporally distant response consequences (as the foregoing section on self-regulation indicated). An individual who says, for example, that a particular action is wrong because it "violates universal standards of justice" or "goes against my conscience" is still considering the consequences of the act, but is evaluating them in more abstract terms, which go beyond immediate, concrete, externally administered outcomes for himself and which encompass a long time span (see Rachlin, 1973).

The Organization of Moral Conduct and Self-Regulation

Traditional personality-oriented approaches to the study of prosocial and self-regulatory behaviors have searched for generalized dimensions on which individual differences in stable, consistent cross-situationally attributes could be discovered. For this purpose, measures of individual differences on dimensions of impulsivity, self-control, moral thought, and conduct were constructed and their networks of correlates elaborated by empirical studies. The basic intention of this traditional approach was to discover consistent cross-situational individual differences in generalized dispositions to behave in prosocial ways. Proponents of this approach asked such questions as, "Is the individual whose moral attitudes seem immature also likely to show consistently less self-control, greater impulsivity, less altruism, less resistance to temptation?" In accord with common sense, they assumed the answer would be clearly affirmative and sought empirical support for their intuitions. The search for consistent individual differences in moral character structure became a major effort of both trait and psychodynamic approaches to morality for many decades. In this section we will examine briefly the results and implications of these efforts as they bear on the organization of self-control, moral conduct, and moral judgment within individuals.

THE SEARCH FOR CONSISTENCIES

Correlational work on "ego strength" in general, and delay of gratification in particular, as a dimension of individual differences is illustrative of both the strategies and the findings of the dispositional approach to the organization of self-regulation and morality.

On the basis of extensive correlational research including cross-cultural studies, two contrasting patterns of delay versus impulsivity have been conceptualized as extreme poles (e.g., Mischel, 1966, 1974). The person who predominantly chooses larger delayed rewards or goals for which he must either wait or work represents one pole on this dimension. This individual is more likely to be oriented toward the future (Klineberg, 1968) and to plan carefully for distant goals. He is also likely to be brighter and more mature; to have a high level of aspiration, high scores on ego-control measures, high achievement motivation; to be more trusting and socially responsible; and to show less uncontrolled impulsivity and delinquency (e.g., Mischel,

1962, 1966, 1971, 1974; Mischel & Gilligan, 1964). This extreme pattern resembles what has been labeled the "Puritan character structure." This pattern tends to be found most often in middle and upper (in contrast to lower) socioeconomic classes, and in highly achievement-oriented ("Protestant ethic") cultures. This pattern of high ego strength is also related to a relatively high level of competence marked by higher intelligence, more mature cognitive development, and a greater capacity for sustained attention (Grim, Kohlberg, & White, 1968).

At the opposite pole is the individual who predominantly prefers immediate gratification and rejects the option of waiting or working for larger delayed goals and future satisfactions at the cost of immediate pleasures. Correlated with this orientation is a greater concern with the immediate present than with the future, and greater impulsivity. Socioculturally, this pattern is correlated with membership in the lower socioeconomic classes, with membership in cultures in which achievement orientation is low, and with indices of lesser social and cognitive competence. Clinically, persons diagnosed as "delinquents" and "psychopaths" are often characterized by an immediate reward choice pattern.

A dimension of gratification patterns such as this one also has some obvious similarity to a continuum that ranges from ego overcontrol to ego undercontrol which has been emerging from independent work by other investigators, especially the research of Jack Block and Jeanne Block (e.g., 1972; Block & Martin, 1955). While such dimensions are of descriptive value, it is important to recognize that self-control patterns tend to be highly discriminative and idiosyncratically organized within individuals (Mischel, 1973, 1974).

The extensive patterns of correlations obtained with measures of self-control have provided evidence not only for convergent validity but also for discriminant validity, which is equally important in the present theoretical view. To illustrate, Trinidadian lower-class blacks often preferred immediately available, albeit smaller, gratifications in choices offered by a white promise-maker (Mischel, 1958, 1961c). In their past experiences promises of future rewards from whites had often been broken, and they had participated in a culture in which immediate gratification was modeled and rewarded extensively (Mischel, 1961a, 1961b). The same people nevertheless saved money, planned elaborately, and were willing to give up competing immediate gratifications in order to plan ahead for many future outcomes (such as annual feasts, religious events, and carnival celebrations) whose preparation and realization were under their own control, making it plain that any generalizations about their cross-situational "impulsivity" are not justified.

It was also found that responses to questionnaires dealing with attitudes and hypothetical matters may correlate with answers on other questionnaires, but are less likely to predict nonquestionnaire behavior (Mischel, 1962). Children in one study were asked about whether they would postpone immediate smaller rewards for the sake of larger delayed outcomes in hypothetical situations (e.g., "If your father gave you a choice between a cheap new bicycle now or a fancy racing bike next month, which would you take?"). Their answers were related to their verbal responses on other questionnaires dealing with trust and a variety of verbally expressed attitudes. But what they said was not related to what they did in real delay-of-reward choices that went beyond questionnaires—for example, actual choices between things like cheap toys now or more attractive objects later (Mischel, 1962). Preferences for delayed rewards in choice situations also are unrelated to the standards children set for evaluating and rewarding their own behavior (Mischel & Masters, 1966), and to their choice of immediate, as opposed to delayed, unavoidable punishments of different magnitudes (Mischel & Grusec, 1967).

Similarly, measures eliciting direct nonverbal behavior may relate strongly to other behavioral indices in the same domain, but not strongly to questionnaires. Thus real behavioral choices between smaller but immediately available gratifications, as opposed to larger but delayed rewards, correlated significantly with such behavioral indices as resistance to temptation, but not with self-reports on questionnaires (Mischel, 1962, 1966, 1968). These findings further underline the "specificity," or discriminativeness, of behavior and the fact that close links between attitudinal and hypothetical measures, on the one hand, and behavioral ones, on the other, cannot be assumed and in fact generally are tenuous (Abelson, 1972; Mischel, 1968, 1973, 1974).

The relatively great discriminativeness and specificity that characterized research findings on self-regulation in much of the delay-of-gratification data are congruent with results from many studies of prosocial conduct found in other lines of research. Traditional trait approaches to prosocial behavior and moral conduct also have hypothesized global personality dispositions, such as "honesty" and "empathy," as generalized determinants of the individual's prosocial behaviors across diverse situations. In the last few decades empirical research on self-control and moral behavior has tended to concentrate on three areas: moral judgment and verbal standards of right and wrong (Kohlberg, 1963a); resistance to temptation in the absence of external constraint (e.g., Aronfreed & Reber, 1965; Grinder, 1962; Mackinnon, 1938; Mischel & Gilligan, 1964); and posttransgression indices of remorse and guilt (Allinsmith, 1960; Aronfreed, 1964; Sears, Maccoby, & Levin, 1957; J. W. M. Whiting, 1959). Empirical research shows these three areas of moral behavior to be either completely independent or at best only minimally interrelated (Becker, 1964; M. L. Hoffman, 1963a; Kohlberg, 1963a).

Specificity within each area also tends

to be the rule. For example, an extensive survey of all types of reactions to transgression revealed no predictable relationship among specific types of reaction (Aronfreed, 1961). In the same vein, Sears and his co-workers (1965) did not find consistent associations among various reactions to transgression. As a third example, in a study with teen-age boys, Allinsmith (1960) inferred moral feelings from the youngsters' projective story completions of descriptions of various immoral actions. The findings led Allinsmith to conclude that a person with a truly generalized conscience is a statistical rarity. Similarly, R. C. Johnson (1962) found that moral judgments across situations tend to be highly specific and even discrepant in many cases, as MacRae (1954) had noted earlier. Given these data on the discriminativeness of prosocial behavior, it is understandable that a comprehensive review indicates the "search for general [personality] correlates of prosocial behavior is . . . short-sighted" (Gergen, Gergen, & Meter, 1972, p. 105). Instead of broad links between global dispositions and diverse prosocial behaviors, the relations involve highly complex and specific interactions which cannot be adequately understood without carefully delineating the particular situation as well as the particular person variable (e.g., Staub, 1974).[4]

The discriminativeness of morality suggested by correlational findings is paralleled by results from experimental studies. For example, there is no reason to expect the changes produced by specific modeling influences to generalize widely across many contexts unless situational supports are provided to facilitate such generalization. This point is evident in a study by Prentice (1972) which demonstrated that the modeling of intentionality both by live and symbolic modeling cues was highly effective in increasing subjects' sensitivity to intentions, but had no effect on another dimension of moral judgment ("moral relativism") and no effect on antisocial behavior (postexperimental delinquent offenses). The lack of generalization from modeling of intentionality to either moral relativism or moral conduct is not surprising in view of probable differences in the specific variables influencing both of these behaviors.

Similarly, a series of studies reported by Bryan and Walbek (1970b) has indicated the discriminativeness of modeling effects on prosocial behavior. Verbal modeling of generosity (that is, statements endorsing generosity) increased children's verbal advocacy of generosity, but had no effect on their subsequent generous behavior. Conversely, modeled demonstrations of actual sharing had no effect on children's verbal endorsements of either selfishness or generosity. The children's verbal advocacy of generosity was found to be virtually unrelated to their behavioral generosity.

RELATIONS BETWEEN MORAL REASONING AND BEHAVIOR

Kohlberg (1969b), alert to the issue of the discriminativeness of prosocial behavior, provided some evidence for a relationship between level of moral reasoning and moral conduct. A close analysis of the magnitude of these associations, however, shows that they do not justify claims for a strong link. The previously noted high degree of heterogeneity in type of moral reasoning within any given subject raises questions about the internal consistency of moral reasoning across situations and hence about the upper limits of external validity for Kohlberg's measure. In fact, the predictive validity from moral reasoning to moral behavior does not appear to be better than the modest, albeit often statistically significant, personality coefficients (averaging .30) typically found in correlational personality research linking measures across diverse response modes (Mischel, 1968).

A representative example is the study by Schwartz, Feldman, Brown and Heingartner (1969) cited by Kohlberg (1971a)

as evidence for the moral reasoning–moral behavior link. These investigators correlated level of moral thought with two measures of moral behavior: helpfulness and cheating. The relationship with helpfulness was not significant for the sample as a whole. On the cheating measure, of eighteen subjects classified high in moral thought, 17 percent cheated, whereas 53 percent of those low on this dimension cheated. This relationship between cheating and moral level reached statistical significance at the .05 level of probability by means of a one-tailed chi square test. In the same study, an almost equally strong relationship was found between the subject's need for achievement and cheating, and a higher association was found between the need for affiliation and helpfulness ($p < .01$).

The moral reasoning measure seems to predict incorrectly the moral behavior of about half the subjects at the lower stages of moral maturity. Consequently, it is hard to justify the claim of a strong link between moral judgment and action. Correlations of the type obtained so far suggest that, overall, knowledge of individuals' moral reasoning would permit one to predict no more than about 10 percent of the variance in their moral behavior. This degree of predictive accuracy is not better than that found in efforts to predict moral behavior from other individual difference variables (Mischel & Gilligan, 1964), and hence does not support the unique or incremental value of moral reasoning for the prediction of moral behavior. It seems likely that predictive accuracy from moral reasoning to moral behavior would be better for selected subsamples such as the relatively small number of individuals identified as reaching the highest levels of moral maturity, and this does seem to be the case (Staub, 1974), although the sample sizes tend to be too small to permit firm conclusions. On the other hand, the value of moral reasoning for predicting moral behavior undoubtedly would be even less if one partialed out the role of intelligence, socioeconomic level, and age—all of which affect both moral reasoning and moral behavior (Kohlberg, 1969b). To adequately assess the discriminative value of moral reasoning in predicting moral behavior, one would want to compare predictions from moral maturity scores with those achieved from measures of IQ, socioeconomic level, and age in the same sample. One must recall that Hartshorne and May (1928) found IQ to be correlated .344 with honesty—a correlation approximately as large as the average consistency of honest behavior itself.

Kohlberg (1958) did one of the rare studies in this domain which tried to partial out the role of IQ and age. In his study of boys aged 10 to 16 he found a correlation of .46 between maturity of moral judgment and teachers' ratings of the boys' consciences. Since both moral maturity scores and conscience ratings were correlated with both IQ and age, a partial correlation was computed to control for mental age. The resulting coefficient was .31—a figure not discriminable from the average "personality coefficient" found throughout the domain of personality research.[5] This result is even more modest when one considers that in the study of morality, just as in other content areas, correlations tend to be spuriously high when based on trait ratings (as in Kohlberg, 1958) rather than on behavioral tests. Correlations from such trait ratings tend to be inflated by the variety of biases and distorting stereotypes discussed previously (D'Andrade, 1970; Mischel, 1968).

Recognition of the limits of moral-reasoning measures for the prediction of moral conduct should not detract from the interest in the development of moral judgments. How people reason about the solution of moral dilemmas is a fascinating phenomenon, and age-related changes in this activity are especially informative. But it should be apparent that an understanding of moral reasoning does not obviate the need to understand the many other aspects and determinants of moral (and immoral) behavior. Alston (1971) a philosopher, commenting on Kohlberg's position, puts it this way:

there is no reason to think that [Kohlberg's moral stages (1971a)] will do the whole job. In fact, there is every reason to think that it will not. So long as there is any significant discrepancy between the moral judgment a person makes about a situation (or would make if the question arose) and what he actually does, there will be a need, in describing persons, for an account of what they are likely to do as well as what they are likely to think. And Kohlberg has given us no reason to suppose that there is no such significant discrepancy (p. 283).

In most content domains, different measures of ideology, beliefs, and attitudes tend to be more closely related to each other than to noncognitive indices of behavior in the same content area (Mischel, 1968, 1969). This also seems to hold in the domain of morality, in which indices of moral ideology tend to relate well to other measures of social and political beliefs. For example, it is reassuring (but not particularly surprising) to find that a student responding to Kohlberg's moral dilemmas test with reasons involving principles of equality, the universality of all moral formulations, and concern with the issue of justice (thereby earning a Stage 6 score) would be unlikely to agree with a sexist slogan such as one that denigrates the political role of women on the conservatism scale of an ideology measure (Fishkin, Kenniston, & Mackinnon, 1973). Similarly unsurprising, the same study found that individuals who dominantly justify their moral decisions in terms of law and order are less likely to endorse such slogans as *Kill the pigs, Property is theft,* and *Turn on, tune in, and drop out.* Such internal consistencies in belief statements were demonstrated by high correlations between moral reasoning emphasizing law and order and a conservative opposition to radical violence on an ideology scale. These data provide further support for the well-established conclusion that there is substantial consistency in answers to measures of political and social ideology (e.g., the classical F-scale research on political and social conservatism in beliefs and attitudes). But while cognitive measures of beliefs and values may be both internally consistent and temporally enduring (E.L. Kelly, 1955), the link between attitudes and behavior may be tenuous (Abelson, 1972; Festinger, 1964).

IMPLICATIONS

In sum, data on the discriminativeness of self-control and moral behavior provide little support for belief in a unitary intrapsychic moral agency like the superego or for a unitary trait entity of conscience or honesty (Mischel, 1968, 1971). Rather than acquiring a homogeneous conscience which determines uniformly all aspects of their self-control, people develop subtler discriminations which depend on many moderating variables, involve complex interactions, and encompass diverse components (Mischel, 1973, 1974). These components include moral judgments, voluntary delay of reward, resistance to temptation, self-reactions following transgression, and self-evaluative and self-reinforcing patterns, each of which includes rather discrete subprocesses which tend to be only modestly and complexly interrelated, and which may be idiosyncratically organized within each individual (Mischel, 1974). In light of the multiplicity and complexity of the determinants of the diverse components of choice behavior in general, and of "ego strength" and prosocial behaviors more specifically, it becomes understandable that gross, overall, appraisals of a person's status on any single dimension of individual differences tend to have limited utility. For example, to predict an individual's altruistic behavior accurately one may have to know his age, his sex, the experimenter's sex, the expected consequences of altruism in that situation,

the models to whom the subject has been exposed recently, and the subject's immediately prior experience—to list only a few of the many variables which may be relevant.

This does not mean that predictions cannot be made with some accuracy from subject variables to relevant self-control and prosocial behaviors, but it does imply stringent limits on the range and level of relationships that can reasonably be expected. A representative example comes from a recent attempt to relate individual differences in young children's expectancies about "locus of control" to their behavior in theoretically relevant situations (Mischel, Zeiss, & Zeiss, 1974). To investigate these interactions, the Stanford Preschool Internal–External Scale (SPIES) was developed as a measure of expectancies about whether events occur as a consequence of the child's own action ("internal control") or as a consequence of external forces ("external control"). Expectancies about locus of control were measured separately for positive and negative events so that scores would reflect expectancies for degree of internal control of positive events $(I+)$, of negative events $(I-)$, and a sum of these two (total I). Individual differences in $I+$, $I-$, and total I were then correlated with the children's ability to delay gratification under diverse working and waiting conditions.

The results provided highly specific but theoretically meaningful patterns of relationships. To illustrate, relationships between total I and overall delay behavior were negligible, and $I+$ was unrelated to $I-$. As expected, $I+$ (but not $I-$) was found to be related to persistence in three separate situations where instrumental activity would result in a *positive* outcome; $I-$ (but not $I+$) was related to persistence when instrumental activity could prevent the occurrence of a *negative* outcome. The total findings showed that individual differences in children's beliefs about their ability to control outcomes are partial determinants of their goal-directed behavior; but the relationships depend on extremely specific moderating conditions, with regard to both the type of behavior and the type of belief. If such moderating conditions had not been taken into account, and if all indices of "delay behavior" had been combined regardless of their positive or negative valence, the actual role of the relevant individual differences would have been totally obscured.

Given such results (reviewed in Mischel, 1968), the present orientation to self-regulation emphasizes the relative specificity of the components of self-control behavior and hence the importance of the specific cognitive and situational variables that influence them and interact with person variables (Mischel, 1973, 1974). Consequently it is necessary to be increasingly sensitive to the role of situational variables, and to the need to study experimentally the specific mechanisms that influence self-regulation and prosocial conduct (see Rosenhan, Moore, & Underwood, Chap. 13, and Staub, 1974).

The significance of the psychological situation for prosocial behavior has been vividly demonstrated in a simulated prison study (Haney, Banks, & Zimbardo, 1973). College student volunteers were carefully selected, on the basis of extensive interviewing and diagnostic testing, to have exemplary backgrounds and no antisocial tendencies. Nevertheless, less than one week after being exposed to what the authors refer to as the inherently pathological characteristics of the realistically simulated prison situation itself, all subjects assigned the role of guards were exhibiting extreme antisocial behavior. The authors concluded that few of the "guards' " reactions could be attributed to individual differences on generalized dimensions (such as, empathy, rigid adherence to conventional values, Machiavellianism) existing before the subjects begin to play their assigned roles. The potency of the situation undoubtedly left some lasting effects, particularly in the realm of beliefs as evidenced by the subjects'

postexperimental statements—for example, "I learned that people can easily forget that others are human" (Haney, Banks, & Zimbardo, 1973, p. 88). But it is also most likely that once the prison experiment was over, the "guards" gave up their new affrontive and harassing behavior and all subjects soon started to respond in terms of the current context of their lives.

THE INTERPRETATION OF CONSISTENCY AND DISCRIMINATIVENESS

Affect, attitude, cognition, and behavior are not inevitably linked in any specific or uniform manner. Whether or not they will be correlated depends on whether or not they lead to common or differential consequences. Thus the correlation between the expression of aggressive attitudes or beliefs and hurtful actions will be low when one is allowed but the other is firmly prohibited (Bandura, 1973). Similarly, if moral judgments, prosocial beliefs, and prosocial actions are each influenced by different contingencies in particular situations, they should not be expected to covary. If the same public official is rewarded privately for his special attention to corporate interests, but receives enthusiastic praise and votes for his public utterances on behalf of the consumer, conditions are ripe for discrepant behavior. Indeed, so-called moral dilemmas may be viewed as the result of discrepancies in behavior-outcome contingencies across response modes or situations. People may often be indignant about what they view as a moral outrage, condemn it in principle, experience sincere emotional upset about it, and nevertheless remain uninfluenced in their own conduct.

Since most social behaviors lead to positive consequences in some situations but not in others, highly discriminative specific expectancies tend to be developed and the relatively low correlations typically found among a person's response pattern across situations become understandable (Mischel, 1968). Expectancies also will not become generalized across response modes when the consequences for similar content expressed in different response modes are sharply different, as they are in most life circumstances. Therefore, expectancies tend to become relatively specific, rather than broadly generalized. Although a person's expectancies (and hence performances) tend to be highly discriminative, there certainly is some generalization, but their patterning in the individual tends to be idiosyncratically organized.

From the viewpoint of the traditional personality paradigm, the "specificity" and "inconsistency" found in behavior are construed as a problem that is usually blamed on methodological flaws and inadequate tests. In that light, the specificity of the relations between social behavior and conditions traditionally has been interpreted as reflecting the inadequacies of the measures, poor sampling, and the limitations of the particular clinical judges or raters. These and many other similar methodological problems undoubtedly are sources of error and seriously limit the degree of consistency which can be observed (J. Block, 1968; Emmerich, 1969). But from the present perspective, the specificity so often obtained in studies of noncognitive personality dimensions accurately reflect man's impressive discriminative facility and the inadequacy of the assumption of global dispositions—not merely distortions of measurement (Mischel, 1968). Indeed, as previously noted (Mischel, 1973), the term "discriminative facility" seems to fit the data better than "specificity" and avoids the unfortunate negative semantic connotations of "specificity" when applied to persons (e.g., the implications of inconsistency, insincerity, fickleness, unreliability; see also Gergen, 1968).

An emphasis on the discriminativeness of behavior and its close links to the conditions in which it occurs also leads to a different interpretation of data on the age-related sequence of moral judgment.

Moral judgments which do not fit clearly into a fixed, progressive developmental sequence have been interpreted as representing regressive behavior (Kohlberg & Kramer, 1969) or the disequilibrium of stage transitions (Turiel, 1973). For example, a longitudinal study of moral judgments by Kohlberg and Kramer (1969) reported that a small percentage of subjects who had been assessed primarily at Stage 4 during late high school showed a good deal of Stage 2 thinking during their college years. These same subjects reached Stage 5 by the time they were in their early twenties. Kohlberg and Kramer interpret this interruption in stage progression as a temporary regression caused by the pressures of college life. Turiel (1973), on the other hand, suggests that responses reflecting the conflict and disequilibrium of transition may be incorrectly categorized as regressive because they resemble earlier stages in content. He argues that transitional reasoning has the structure of later stages, thus invoking the phenotypic–genotypic distinction often called in to explain discrepant or anomolous behaviors (Mischel, 1969). But a finding like the one that college students give moral reasons scorable at a lower stage than those they gave in high school can also be seen as reflecting not a regression from an invariant sequence, but a discriminative responsivity to changing models, reference groups, values, and personal contingencies in the individual's changing life-style. The college students in this case may be seen as responding to the relativism encouraged and modeled in a liberal academic atmosphere, rather than either as regressing or as experiencing disequilibrium in their progress through a series of predetermined stages.

ENCODING STRATEGIES AND THE CONSTRUCTION OF CONSISTENCY

Like the psychologist, the layman also groups events into categories and organizes them actively into meaningful units. He encodes and categorizes events rather than describing his experience with operational definitions. Observers readily tend to group information about persons in dispositional categories, such as *honest, intolerant, freaky, do-gooder* (Jeffery & Mischel, 1972). Recognition of the existence of sharp discriminativeness in behavior must be coupled with the realization that people easily construct consistent impressions about their own and others' generalized characteristics. People invoke traits and other dispositions as ways of describing and explaining their experience and themselves, just as professional psychologists do, and tend to go easily beyond the analysis of specific behaviors to the attribution of generalized dispositions. Hopefully the investigations of personal construct systems (e.g., Argyle & Little, 1972), of implicit personality theories (e.g., Hamilton, 1971; Schneider, 1973), and of self-concepts (e.g., Gergen, 1968) will clarify an important set of still inadequately understood person variables.

In the process of grouping personality information about the self and others the subject tends to jump quickly from the observation of discrete acts to the inference of global internalized dispositions (Heider, 1958). While behavior may often be highly situation-specific, it also seems true that in daily life people tend to construe each other as if each were highly consistent, and they construct consistent personalities for each other even on the basis of relatively inconsistent behavioral fragments. Thus perceived unity often exists in the face of behavioral discriminativeness. It is remarkable how each of us usually manages to reconcile his seemingly diverse behaviors into one subjectively consistent whole. The same individual who cheats on one occasion but not on another, who lies in one context but is truthful in another, who steals at one time but helps a friend generously and unselfishly at another, may still readily construe himself as basically honest and moral. People show impressive ingenuity in their ability to transform their seemingly discrepant behaviors into unified wholes (Mischel, 1969).

How can we understand the discriminativeness of behavior in light of the equally compelling impression of basic consistency in ourselves and in the people we know? Many complex factors are probably involved (Jones & Nisbett, 1971; Kahneman & Tversky, 1973; Mischel, 1968, 1969); but part of the answer to this question may be that people tend to reduce cognitive inconsistencies (Festinger, 1957) and, in general, to simplify information so that they can deal with it.

Cognitive consistency also tends to be enhanced by selective attention and coding processes which filter new information in a manner that permits it to be integrated with existing cognitive structures (Norman, 1969). Cognitive processes that facilitate the construction and maintenance of perceived consistency have been elaborated elsewhere (D'Andrade, 1970; Hayden & Mischel, 1972; Mischel, 1968, 1969). After information has been integrated with existing cognitive structures and becomes part of long-term memory, it remains enduringly available and exerts further stabilizing effects. For example, the individual's subjective conception of his own identity and continuity presumably rests heavily on his ability to remember (construct) subjectively similar behaviors on his part over long periods and across many situations. That is, the person can abstract the common elements of his behavior over time and across settings, thereby focusing on his more stable attributes.

In the construction and attribution of dispositional consistencies, observers tend to be self-enhancing. Consider, for example, the attribution of the causes for behavior to internal causes (the person's dispositions) versus external causes (situations). Two studies investigated the attribution of internality (locus of internal–external control) for positive and negative events by children of various ages and by college students (Mischel, Mailer, & Zeiss, 1973). Subjects were asked to make internal versus external attributions for the same positive and negative events occurring to the self, to a liked other, and to a disliked other. Attributions tended to be consistently self-enhancing, with more credit given to the self for positive events and less for negative events (compared especially to a disliked other).

JUSTIFICATION PROCESSES AND HAZARDS

The discriminativeness of prosocial behavior, and its idiosyncratic organization within each person, has important social implications. It should alert us to the fact that the same individual who espouses high moral principles may engage in harmful aggressive actions against others who violate his conceptions of justice. Pascal's comment that "Evil is never done so thoroughly or so well as when it is done with a good conscience" is supported by the many historical and contemporary incidents in which the individuals who committed evil deeds seemed more deficient in compassion and empathy than in moral reasoning (Keniston, 1970).

History is replete with atrocities that were justified by invoking the highest principles and that were perpetrated upon victims who were equally convinced of their own moral principles. In the name of justice, of the common welfare, of universal ethics, and of God, millions of people have been killed and whole cultures destroyed. In recent history, concepts of universal right, equality, freedom, and social equity have been used to justify every variety of murder including genocide. Presidential assassinations, airplane hijackings, and massacres of Olympic athletes have been committed for allegedly selfless motives of highest morality and principle. The supreme moral self-sacrifices of the Japanese suicide pilots in World War II were perceived as moral outrages by others who did not share their perspective.

People tend to be facile about justifying their own diverse actions and commitments—no matter how reprehensible these acts may seem to others. A wide variety of self-deceptive mechanisms may be used to facilitate and excuse the most horrendous acts. Invocation of higher principles, dehumanization of victims, diffusion and displacement of responsibility, blame attribution, and the adoption of inhumane codes for self-reinforcement all may serve to maintain extraordinarily cruel aggressions (Bandura, 1973).

The extremely complex relations among diverse aspects of prosocial behavior within the same person, and the specific interactions between human conduct and the psychological conditions in which it occurs, prevent global generalizations about the overall nature and causes of moral—and immoral—actions. It is tempting but misleading to categorize people into the cross-situationally moral versus the broadly immoral. A world of good guys versus bad guys—as in the Western films in which the cowboys' white or black hats permit easy identification of the virtuous and the villainous—is seductive. More sophisticated social science versions of stratification systems which categorize people in terms of their overall level of morality, unless carefully moderated, can lead to an elitism that is empirically unjustified as well as socially hazardous. While it may be useful for some purposes to label and assess people's status on our dimensions of character and moral value, perhaps the greatest challenge to social science will be to discover the optimal conditions that can help each person realize himself in the ways he construes as best within the great range of capacities open to him.

CHAPTER 6

The Biology of Morality

H. J. Eysenck

Introduction

The study of morality must begin by asking the right question. The usual problem posed, that of evil, is not the real problem at all. It is pointless to ask why people behave in a selfish, aggressive, immoral manner; such behavior is clearly reinforcing in that it gives the person or organism acting in such a fashion immediate satisfaction. Furthermore, such behavior is demonstrated by animals and young children without any need of teaching; it is "natural" in a real and obvious sense. The proper question is rather the opposite one: How does it come about that people (and animals) do not always act in an immoral, antisocial, or asocial manner? How can we account for "good" behavior, that is, behavior which at first sight at least goes counter to the interests of the person concerned?

The answer often given is that socialized behavior is enforced on us by the existence of laws, and the sanction of police and prison. But this answer is clearly not sufficient, even though it contains some elements of truth. The force of law is necessary, but not sufficient, to account for socialized behavior. Many actions are outside the scope of legal sanction, and yet are performed in a socialized manner. Even when we look at criminal activities, law enforcement comes into contact with only a small fraction of these. The majority of crimes are never brought to the attention of the police. Of those which are, only a minority are ever brought home to the perpetrator, and even then he often gets away with a caution. The chances of "getting away with it" are probably between 90 and 99 in 100; in other words, the odds are overwhelmingly in favor of the criminal. On a rational calculus, crime probably does pay; yet most of us do not indulge in serious crime. If this were not so, civilized society would be impossible to maintain; we would need more policemen than private citizens to maintain law and order—and who would maintain law and order among all the policemen? Even among thieves, we are told, there must be honor; how does this come about? Clearly the appeal to the force of the law accounts for only a portion of socialized conduct; for the major part we must look for another explanatory principle. Religion gives us the word *conscience* to explain such conduct; an "inner light" guides our behavior in the direction of morality. But religion fails to tell us just how this miracle is accomplished, and even if the answer were revealed, divine guidance would not be a scientific explanation.

Psychologists often talk about the "internalization" of external (usually parental) rules and precepts. This may serve as a verbal explanation of "conscience," but unless we can independently and experimentally examine this process of internalization, it cannot tell us much about the phenomenon in question. What precisely goes on when rules and precepts are internalized? What are the mechanisms used? Why does this process work in some children and not in others, even when to all appearances circumstances are very similar?

A Conditioning Theory of Conscience

My own explanation links the acquisition of a "conscience" with the conditioning of anxiety. In terms of this hypothesis, *conscience is a conditioned reflex.* Consider the young child's behavior; he will frequently do things that his parents, teachers, and peers regard as *bad*, *naughty*, or *wicked*. Swift punishment usually follows such actions: a slap, being sent to his room, going without supper, writing five hundred lines, being laughed at, or some other unpleasant consequence. Now here we have a perfect conditioning paradigm. The naughty action is the conditioned stimulus, like Pavlov's bell to which the dog became conditioned. The "punishment" is the unconditioned stimulus, like the food Pavlov presented to his dog after the bell sounded. And the unconditioned response is the pain experienced as a consequence of the punishment, just as in Pavlov's experiment salivation was the unconditioned response. We would expect

that anxiety (conditioned fear) would gradually become the conditioned response to carrying out or even contemplating the naughty action, and that this immediate negatively reinforcing consequence would discourage both contemplation and execution of the action in question. This conditioned anxiety is experienced by the child as "conscience." The acquisition of this "conscience" is, of course, facilitated by labeling, as is its generalization over different types of actions. By calling a variety of actions bad, evil, or naughty, we encourage the child to identify them all in one category, and to react in the future with anxiety to everything thus labeled. This, very briefly and not altogether adequately, is my account of the growth of "conscience." The supporting evidence is discussed in detail in my book *Crime and Personality* (H. J. Eysenck, 1964/1970a).

The advantages of this account of conscience are twofold. In the first place, it makes use of well-established principles based on detailed laboratory experiments; it does not invoke divine guidance or ad hoc concepts. In the second place, it leads to testable deductions. We shall be concerned next with these deductions. Let us here note merely one implication of the scheme set out above. If good conduct results from proper conditioning, then bad behavior and immorality can result from two separate causes (both of which could be acting simultaneously). The first set of causes might be identified as *social factors*. Conditioning of the kind required for socialization will not take place if parents, teachers, and peers fail to provide the requisite unconditioned stimuli; and it will not take place if they provide unconditioned stimuli in response to the wrong conditioned stimuli. Perhaps the very multiplicity of social agents will ensure that some conditioning does take place. A child's parents may be found wanting, but his teachers may play their role, or else the child's peers may set upon him if he is found to steal, lie, or otherwise misbehave. But the lack of adequate social conditioning is clearly an important consideration in the formation of bad behavior, and the laissez-faire doctrines introduced by Freudian fears of repression are likely to have lessened the impact of proper conditioning procedures.

The second set of causes of immoral behavior might be identified as *biological factors*. Pavlov showed that there are enormous differences in conditionability among dogs. Some would need only two or three trials, while others would barely condition after two hundred or three hundred. Similar differences can be found in humans. Some people are very difficult to condition, while others condition with great ease. These individual differences are very important, and they form the basis of my account of moral behavior. In dealing with these biological factors I shall, for the sake of exposition, disregard the social factors mentioned above. I am doing this not because social factors are unimportant, but because little research has been done on them, and also because other authors in this book will be dealing with them. In reading my account, readers should always bear in mind the usual scientific caution of *ceteris paribus*.

Conditioning and Personality

The concept of conditionability provides us with a link between criminality, psychopathy, and general immorality, on the one hand, and personality, on the other. To make clear the nature of this connection, we must first state briefly, and again rather dogmatically, the conception of personality employed here. Descriptively, there is much agreement that two major dimensions of personality account for a good deal of the individual differences which are observed among people. These two major dimensions (or types) are given various names by different authors, but will be referred to here as *extraversion–introversion* (*E*) and *neuroticism–stability* (*N*) (H. J. Eysenck & Eysenck, 1969).

Extraverts are typically sociable, impulsive, talkative, carefree, and dominant, while introverts are the opposite. Not everyone is totally an extravert or an introvert, of course; these traits are distributed in the rough shape of the normal probability curve, with most people somewhere in the middle (ambivert) zone. High neuroticism is evidenced by anxiety, worries, sleeplessness, touchiness, restlessness, and other emotional disturbances; with stability being characterized by the opposite qualities. These two dimensions are independent of each other, as shown in Figure 6.1; they are also independent of intelligence. There is strong evidence that heredity plays a powerful part in determining a person's position in this two-dimensional framework (H. J. Eysenck, 1967), and this genetic predisposition interacts with environmental pressure to produce the phenotype, that is, the observable personality.

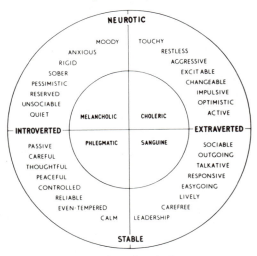

Figure 6.1 Two-dimensional factor pattern showing main dimensions of personality.

This two-dimensional account of personality does not embrace everything that is known about personality, or everything that remains to be known. It is relevant to our discussion for the simple reason that criminals and others whose conduct is "immoral" are found in the high *E*–high *N* quadrant, that is, are found to share high neuroticism and high extraversion. (Neurotics were predicted, and have been found, to fall into the high *N*–low *E* quadrant, that is, to share high neuroticism and high introversion). These findings have been documented elsewhere (H. J. Eysenck, 1970a) in considerable detail; we will return to them later. Here let me just quote one example of the work that has been done to substantiate the theory. Burt (1965) studied 763 children and followed them over a thirty-year period. These children had been rated by their teachers with respect to *E* and *N*; 15 percent and 18 percent, respectively, later became habitual offenders or neurotics. Of those who became offenders, 63 percent had been rated as high on *N*, and 54 percent had been rated high on *E*; only 3 percent had been rated high on introversion. Of those who became neurotics, 59 percent had been rated high on *N*, and 44 percent high on introversion; only 1 percent had been rated high on *E*. The relationship is far from perfect, but when we consider the many chance factors that confuse lawful connections, and the unreliability attending teachers' ratings, then we may appreciate that there is indeed a link between personality, crime, and neurosis very much as predicted.

What led to the prediction? The writer has put forward a theory of personality, and supported it with much evidence from laboratory research, which may be used to forge the link between these various concepts. Put very briefly, this theory says that behaviors associated with *E* and *N* are mediated by certain physiological-anatomical structures, as shown in Figure 6.2. Differences in *N* are mediated by the autonomic nervous system, which is known to subserve emotional expression and whose functioning is governed and coordinated by the visceral brain (VB). If this system is overactive—reacting too quickly and too strongly to emotional stimuli, and failing to cease acting upon withdrawal of the

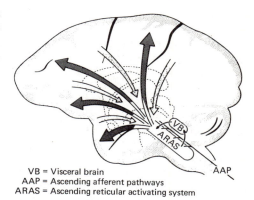

VB = Visceral brain
AAP = Ascending afferent pathways
ARAS = Ascending reticular activating system

Figure 6.2   Diagrammatic representation of physiological basis for two main dimensions of personality.

stimuli in question—then we are dealing with a person predisposed to high degrees of neuroticism or emotionality. Low *N* subjects, on the other hand, react slowly and weakly, with cessation of reaction immediately after the stimulus is withdrawn. This, then, is the biological basis of *N*. The biological basis of *E* is centered on the arousal system, and in particular on the ascending reticular activating system (ARAS). This system maintains tonus in the cortex, alerting it to deal with incoming stimuli. These stimuli activate the reticular system through collateral neurons, and the reticular system in turn activates the cortex to enable it to deal with the incoming information. High degrees of arousal are posited to be associated with introversion, low degrees of arousal with extraversion. In other words, introverts are characterized by a strongly dominant cortex, extraverts by a much less dominant cortex.

It is important to grasp very clearly the implications of this theory, as at first sight the relation may seem to be the wrong way round. The behavior of the extravert is uninhibited, but his cortex is in a state of *disarousal*, or inhibition. Conversely, the cortex of the introvert is in a state of *disinhibition*, or arousal, but his conduct is inhibited. This is so because the main function of the cortex is to inhibit the activities of lower centers; thus a highly aroused cortex inhibits behavior. Alcohol furnishes a good example. It inhibits the cortex, and thus disinhibits behavior, making people more extraverted. So much for the general theory; details and experimental support are given elsewhere (H. J. Eysenck, 1967).

How do we connect these inherited differences in the physiological-anatomical structures of the brain, and the various types of behavior which cause us to label a person extravert or introvert, neurotic or stable? In the case of N there is no difficulty. It is the direct experience of high degrees of excitation of the autonomic system which the individual labels fear or anxiety or worry. But in the case of cortical arousal and extraversion, the connection is less direct. We can indeed introspect and feel degrees of arousal or drowsiness, but only if these states are extreme. The usual run of differences encountered during the course of the day is probably not introspectible at all, or at best only with great difficulty. In any case, these experiences are not themselves motivating, as experiences of autonomic excitation are. Strong sympathetic stimulation—with its attendant quick and strong heartbeat, cessation of digestion, drying up of the mouth, and many other unpleasant consequences—is itself negatively reinforcing, and thus provides motivation for action.

How, then, is cortical arousal linked with behavior? One direct line is through conditioning. Pavlov showed that conditioning is directly dependent on cortical arousal, and experiments with human subjects have since verified this point abundantly. If introverts do indeed live in a general state of higher cortical arousal than do extraverts, then we would expect introverts to condition more quickly; this was the burden of an earlier version of my theory (H. J. Eysenck, 1957). We could go on from there to argue that the failure of extraverts to condition is instrumental

in their tending toward criminality, just as the ease with which introverts form conditioned anxiety responses is responsible for their liability to neurotic disorders. In both cases N would be conceived as a drive that multiplies with the particular habits (criminal or neurotic) that are being established, making these habits much stronger than would be the case in low N subjects. There is evidence that N fulfills precisely this function (H. J. Eysenck, 1970a). The link is clear and direct, but is the theory true?

There are by now almost one hundred studies of the hypothetical relation between E and conditioning, using various types of conditioned response (for example, eye blink to puff of air, galvanic skin response to shock). These experiments do not always support the hypothesis. The reason for the failure is quite simple. The theory I put forward indicates clearly that the predicted relation is dependent on certain parameters, and that improper choice of parameter values will lead to zero correlations, or even to a reversal of the expected relationships. Among the parameters explicitly mentioned were strength of the unconditioned response (weak responses being favorable to introverts), conditioned stimulus–unconditioned stimulus interval (short intervals being favorable to introverts), and partial versus complete reinforcement (partial reinforcement being favorable to introverts). Most of the studies unfavorable to the theory used wrong parameter values, and hence are irrelevant. H. J. Eysenck and Levey (1967) have reported an experiment on eyelid conditioning in which they systematically varied all three parameters; Figures 6.3 and 6.4 report the results. It will be seen that under conditions which the theory predicts as favorable to introverts, introverts condition very much better, while under the reverse conditions extraverts condition somewhat better.[1]

Other criticisms made of the notion of "conditionability" are that (1) it implies that different types of conditioning should

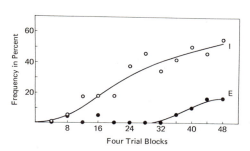

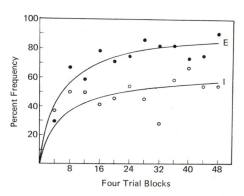

Figure 6.3 Eye-blink conditioning of intro-verted and extraverted subjects under unfavorable conditions.

Figure 6.4 Eye-blink conditioning of intro-verted and extraverted subjects under favorable conditions.

intercorrelate, which on the whole they do not; and (2) aversive conditioning has usually been sampled, and appetitive conditioning might not follow the same laws. The reason for the failure of differ-ent types of conditioning to intercorrelate is, as noted, the disregard of experimenters for the proper choice of parameter values; unless these are properly chosen, no corre-lations can be expected. There is now in existence a study that refutes both of the above criticisms by demonstrating a healthy correlation between an appetitive and an aversive form of conditioning (Barr & McConaghy, 1972). While this whole field is still very much in a state of ferment, the available evidence supports the general theory, with respect to both the personality-conditioning correlation and the import-ance of parameter values.[2]

Sensation Seeking

The conditioning link is not the only one that connects arousal patterns in the cortex with certain types of conduct; there are many others (H. J. Eysenck, 1967). In religious terms, immoral conduct is mediated through two concepts. *Con-science* warns us against such conduct, and may succeed in preventing us from indulging in it; but we would never have

occasion to contemplate the desirability of behaving in such a fashion were it not for *temptation*. Lack of cortical arousal can generate its own kinds of temptation. Moralists have often pointed out that the devil finds work for idle hands. A state of boredom, which motivates the individual to seek sensations of various kinds, is closely allied to a state of cortical dis-arousal. I have posited an optimal level of cortical disarousal to which each individual aspires. When there is too little arousal, the individual is bored, and seeks to in-crease arousal; when there is too much, the individual is overextended, and seeks to decrease arousal (H. J. Eysenck, 1963). This notion of sensation seeking has been taken up and extended by Zuckerman, Kolin, Price, and Zorb (1964), who have constructed a special "sensation-seeking scale" to measure this hypothetical quality. Farley and Farley (1967, 1970) have demonstrated that this scale correlates quite well with extraversion—particularly with impulsivity rather than sociability—and there is also evidence that criminals score more highly on this scale (Zucker-man, 1972). Along this line of argument, we might account for the greater sexual delinquency of extraverts, their liking for constant change (work, sexual partners, homes, etc.), and also their preference for strong sensory input ("bright lights and loud music"). The well-documented greater susceptibility of extraverts to drugs (they drink more, smoke more, and take more soft and hard drugs than do introverts) might also be a consequence of low cortical arousal.

Thus extraverts have a greater built-in susceptibility to temptation, because of their low level of cortical arousal. Their needs are greater than those of introverts; and the pursuit of these needs is likely to bring extraverts into conflict with society —although not necessarily with the law. Many of the sexual practices of the extravert, as compared with those of the introvert, are considered "perverted" but not criminal (H. J. Eysenck, 1971); and although their attitudes in this field are asocial or antisocial, they do not fall foul of the law. However, a liking for wine, women, and song, though at first innocent, may easily lead to other less innocent activities, just as drug taking may often lead to more serious crimes, through a need to obtain money for drugs. There is clearly a continuum here. Whether the extravert will go so far along this continuum that he comes into conflict with the law depends on many factors in his environment, his luck, and so on. What seems to be clear is that sensation-seeking tendencies in the extravert expose him to temptations the introvert does not encounter—or at least not to anything like the same extent. The very dangers inherent in antisocial conduct may act as an incentive to the low-arousal extravert!

We now have a model linking extraversion, through failure to condition and through sensation seeking, with antisocial and asocial conduct. This model has received much support from studies linking extraversion with criminality. The observed correlations are not nearly as strong as one might wish (Passingham, 1972), and it might be useful to look at the reasons for this comparative failure. In the first place, criminals are far from being a homogeneous group. Murderers are notoriously different from thieves, and in fact have been found to be introverted rather than extraverted (S. B. G. Eysenck & Eysenck, 1970). Sex criminals differ from other types of criminal; the violent differ from the inadequate; and so on. It is clearly foolhardy to try to generalize about such a heterogeneous group, and it is surprising that positive results are possible at all.

In the second place, the theory states that it is in the high N–high E quadrant that an undue proportion of criminals should be located. This hypothesis cannot be adequately tested by using one dimension at a time, as has usually been done. Burgess (1972) has shown that even with data where there are no significant differences on E between criminals and controls, highly significant differences can be found in the proportions which fall into the quadrant in question.[3] A third possible reason for the lower than expected correlation between extraversion and criminality is that extraversion is a concept which rests essentially on the intercorrelations among a number of more restricted traits such as sociability, impulsivity, and optimism. The possibility exists that the correlation between E and criminality depends more on some of these traits than on others. It has been shown several times, for example, that impulsivity is far more important than sociability in this context (H. J. Eysenck & Eysenck, 1970; S. B. G. Eysenck & Eysenck, 1971). The finding that sociability is less important might be due to inherent difficulties in the questionnaire study of incarcerated prisoners, difficulties which arise particularly strongly in relation to sociability. Questions relating to partygoing or social intercourse may be rather meaningless to prisoners cooped up in isolation. It is unlikely, however, that this possibility would account fully for the greater significance of impulsivity in the correlation between E and criminality. Levey (1972) has shown that the correlation between E and eye-blink conditioning similarly depends far more on impulsivity than on sociability. Isolating the critical components of extraversion is an important task for future study. (Levey has also shown that the differences in conditioning between introverts and extroverts are much larger with high N subjects than with low N subjects; this clearly links up with the previously cited Burgess quadrant studies, 1972.) When all these cautions are borne in mind, the relation between theory and fact becomes reasonably close.

Psychopathy and Cortical Arousal

In spite of this relatively good correspondence between theory and data, there are sound reasons for looking for alternative ways of testing the theory. The main reason is the very gross fashion in which *criminality* measures *immorality*. Clearly a large measure of error is involved here. Some activities are criminal today but may not be tomorrow. Homosexuality was a crime in England a few years ago, but is not a crime now. Moreover, the criminals we test are not a random sample of all criminals, but only of those who got caught, and there may be marked differences between those who are and those who are not caught. Even among the criminals we study, there are great variations in immorality. Large numbers are criminal to their fingertips—evil, immoral beasts who prey on society and use almost all their talents and strength to harm others. Large numbers are also dull and inadequate— people who have no wish to harm anyone, but who simply cannot get by in our complex society and become criminals *faute de mieux*, as it were. Such men will throw a brick through a shop window on a cold winter's night, and then wait for the police to run them in; this is their only way of securing a warm bed and some food. Clearly our theory does not apply to such prisoners, who are often introverted and solitary, and lack basic social skills. Prisoners are too heterogeneous a conglomerate to make a really satisfactory experimental group—even if the so-called control group could be guaranteed to consist of "good" men. But, of course, the latter situation is far from likely. Quite a high proportion of any random control group is made up of former or future prisoners, or at least of criminals who may never be found out.

Are alternative groups of subjects better suited to a proper testing of our theory? The answer is probably yes. A better comparison group would be *psychopaths* or *sociopaths*, defined in the *Diagnostic and Statistical Manual of Mental Disorders* of the American Psychiatric Association (1968) as "chronically antisocial individuals who are always in trouble, profiting neither from experience nor punishment, and maintaining no real loyalties to any person, group, or code. They are frequently callous and hedonistic, showing marked emotional immaturity, with lack of responsibility, lack of judgment, and an ability to rationalize their behavior so that it appears warranted, reasonable, and justified." In addition, a detailed and widely accepted description of such individuals has been given by Cleckley (1964), who lists characteristics such as superficial charm; unreliability; untruthfulness and insincerity; lack of remorse or shame; antisocial behavior without good cause; poor judgment and failure to learn from experience; pathological egocentricity and incapacity for love; unresponsiveness in general personal relations; impersonal, trivial, and poorly integrated sex life; and lack of any real life plan. Individuals of this kind may or may not be criminals, and criminals may or may not be psychopaths. There is much overlap, but nothing like identity. Psychopaths are probably much closer to our target group, and our theory in principle applies with much more force to psychopaths than it does to a random assortment of criminals. The difficulty with using psychopaths as the target group, of course, lies in the inevitable subjectivity of diagnosis, and the marked differences in judgment among psychiatrists who perform the diagnosis. Although the imprisonment of men judged criminal may reflect police or court error, diagnostic difficulties with prisoners could be said to be less than with psychopaths. Under the circumstances, we may perhaps say that both prisoners and psychopaths have advantages and disadvantages as target groups for experimental studies, and both may be used with advantage provided that we keep in mind the necessary qualifications when interpreting the results.

Frequently the psychopath as described above is called *primary* in contradistinction to another type of person labeled *neurotic*, or *secondary psychopath*. As Karpman (1961) points out, many antisocial and aggressive acts are committed by people who suffer from severe emotional disturbances, unbearable frustrations, and inner conflicts. Their aggressive or antisocial behavior is believed to be the consequence of these more basic emotional problems. R. D. Hare (1970) has reviewed several studies which give support to the primary–secondary distinction.

We may now restate our hypothesis in a form that permits it to be tested in relation to psychopaths. We would predict that psychopaths will show extraverted personality traits, will be characterized by low cortical arousal, and will perform on laboratory experiments relevant to arousal in such a way as to conform to the pattern of low arousal; for example, they will condition poorly. On such tests, in other words, psychopaths as compared with controls will perform very much as extraverts compared with introverts. All these predictions are eminently testable, and many experiments have been performed in this context. I shall review a representative number; for a full account, R. D. Hare's book (1970) should be consulted.

Direct evidence of low cortical arousal in psychopaths must depend on EEG studies of brain-wave formation. Several such studies agree that psychopaths usually have abnormal brain waves, with an undue preponderance of slow-wave activity. One possible interpretation is that this finding is indicative of lower cortical arousal, although our understanding of the

electrical activity of the brain is not such that we can consider this conclusion certain. There is some similarity here between psychopaths and extraverts, in that the latter are characterized by low alpha frequency and high alpha amplitude (Gale, Coles, & Blaydon, 1969; Savage, 1964).

Fox and Lippert (1963), R. D. Hare (1970), and Lippert and Sentner (1966) have shown that psychopaths have less spontaneous electrodermal activity than controls; this is in agreement with the hypothesis of less cortical arousal. Crider and Lunn (1970) have similarly shown that extraverts show less spontaneous activity in the galvanic skin response (G. S. R.). Rose (1964) found two-flash thresholds to be higher for psychopaths than for controls; this is an indication of lower arousal among psychopaths. Extraverts quite generally have higher sensory thresholds (H. J. Eysenck, 1967); this seems closely related to Rose's finding, if not an exact replicate. Psychopaths, too, have higher sensory thresholds (R. D. Hare, 1968; Schoenherr, 1964).

Vigilance is a direct consequence of arousal, and extraverts and psychopaths should perform more poorly on tasks requiring vigilance than introverts and controls. The evidence regarding extraverts has been reviewed by Stroh (1971), and seems to be in accord with this prediction. Orris (1967) found that psychopaths performed less well than control criminals. Along a different line, preference for novel and complex stimulation should theoretically be higher in psychopaths (Skrzypek, 1969) and extraverts (H. J. Eysenck & Levey, 1965); results seem to bear this out.

We have already discussed the poor conditioning of extraverts. With respect to psychopaths, there is also evidence to suggest poor conditioning on eye-blink (J. G. Miller, 1964) and eye-blink discriminant conditioning (Warren & Grant, 1955), as well as on GSR conditioning (R. D. Hare, 1965a; Lykken, 1955). The results from psychopaths might have been more impressive had experimenters paid more attention to suitable choice of parameter values. As they stand, the data are more suggestive than definitive.

In line with these studies, some rather complex avoidance-learning experiments found psychopaths to be inferior in acquiring conditioned fear responses (Lykken, 1955; Schachter & Latané, 1964; Schoenherr, 1964; Schmauk, 1968). In these experiments the subjects had to learn to thread a path through a maze by manipulating certain levers, and also had to learn to avoid shock associated with some of the levers. Psychopaths learned the maze as well as controls, but they failed to learn to avoid punishment by shock. R. D. Hare (1965c) has argued from results of this type that psychopaths should be characterized by "short-range hedonism," and performed an interesting experiment in which numbers from 1 to 12 were exhibited in turn, with shock accompanying number 8. Electrodermal responses anticipating shock were taken, and these responses were found not only to be weaker in psychopaths but also to be less anticipated. It is interesting to note that Broadbent (1958) has similarly argued that extraverts have less "time-spanning" ability than introverts. Lippert and Sentner (1966) and Schalling and Levander (1964) have reported results similar to Hare's.

R. D. Hare (1970) reports a number of studies on psychopaths in which verbal conditioning was used with inconclusive results. Much the same is true of work with extraverts; some investigators find differences in the expected direction, others do not. The reason lies quite probably in the neglect of an important parameter, namely, *awareness*. An unpublished study from our laboratory found that subjects who are unaware of the contingencies involved in verbal conditioning (for example, that the experimenter says "Good" in order to reinforce a given response) show the expected superiority of introverts over extraverts. When subjects are aware of the contingencies, however, extraverts show better performance. This pattern is very much as expected. Under conditions of awareness, extraverts are more eager to please; this is part of their sociability. Under conditions of nonawareness, however, such social factors are eliminated and conditioning depends much more on cortical arousal. It is suggested, therefore, that in future work on verbal conditioning with psychopaths, the parameter of awareness be strictly controlled. Without such control it is unlikely that worthwhile results can be obtained.

We may with advantage summarize the outcome of our discussions so far. I have suggested that basic to antisocial conduct is a failure to form conditioned responses, which are the building material for a proper "conscience." This failure in turn is attributed to a genetically low level of cortical arousal. Both low arousal and poor conditioning are suggested to be causally related to a whole gamut of personality traits, correlating together and usually referred to as extraversion. Antisocial conduct becomes aggravated when extraversion is coupled with neuroticism. N acts as a drive to amplify whatever habits have been formed in the individual's past; and in the case of extraverts these habits are hedonistic, asocial, and selfish.

There is a large literature to support, with varying degrees of strength, deductions from these hypotheses. For the most part, target populations have been chosen to represent individuals characterized as antisocial; the two most widely used groups are prisoners and psychopaths (diagnosed psychiatrically and/or in terms of questionnaire responses). Experimental difficulties are associated with both target groups, but the theory would not be worth retaining if positive results could not be obtained with groups so clearly deviant as these. In the majority of cases, results have been favorable to some such theory as that put forward, although there are still many anomalies, and the differentiation achieved between deviants and controls is far from perfect. It seems likely that many of the difficulties experienced have resulted from the imperfections of the experimental groups, rather than from a failure of the theory. Whether this likelihood is fact or bias, however, can be ascertained only by future experiment.

Psychopathy and Social Factors

The theory as outlined is based on the premise that the differences between criminal-psychopathic groups and control groups are largely due to biological and genetic factors. This view is opposed by many psychiatrists and psychologists who look for social causes. It seems clear to me that both types of cause are implicated, but a discussion of some of the evidence adduced by environmentalists may be useful in ascertaining whether our conclusion requires a reconsideration.

Most of the environmental evidence is related to factors in the upbringing of the child. Thus Gregory (1958) and Greer (1964) reported a high incidence of parental loss in psychopathic individuals; and Craft, Stephenson, and Granger (1964) showed that the more severe the disorder, the more likely is the presence of parental deprivation. It is important to note, however, that such differences seem to be due to parental loss by separation. Moreover, separation from the father seems much more important than separation from the mother (Oltman & Friedman, 1967). The child might have inherited the genes largely responsible for his father's psychopathic conduct and grown up like him not for the environmental reasons given, but because of the action of heredity pure and simple (or possibly in combination with environmental factors). The evidence is clearly not sufficient to enable us to make a decision, but we may note that (1) many children of separated parents grow up into perfectly normal individuals; (2) many psychopaths come from perfectly normal homes; thus Cleckley (1964) comments that "during all my years of experience with hundreds of psychopaths . . . no type of parent or of parental influence, overt or subtle, has been regularly demonstrable." What is actually responsible for this difference in reaction to similar circumstances?

Bell (1968) has advocated another hypothesis, namely, that the behavior of the parents may be a reaction to the psychopathy of the child. Thus the finding that excessive use of punishment is related to psychopathic tendencies might be interpreted not as punishment causing psychopathy, but as psychopathic behavior inviting excessive punishment. Similarly, as Wiggins (1968) has noted, the frequent finding that inconsistency of parental behavior is related to psychopathy may be simply a result of parental puzzlement, rather than a causal factor of pathology. What all this amounts to, of course, is very simply that this type of data, although interesting, is correlational and hence not capable of throwing much light on causal connections. All or some or none of the theories canvassed might be true, and it certainly would not be admissible to use them either in support of or against a genetic interpretation of psychopathic behavior and its origins.

Primary and Secondary Psychopathy

Before beginning a more detailed discussion of the distinction between primary and secondary psychopathy, we must consider an extension of the general theory presented so far. We have made use of two major personality variables, E and N, in our attempts to account for psychopathic behavior, but this account has certain weaknesses. In the first place, while the theory may explain the type of psychopathy often referred to as *secondary*, which is explicitly linked with neurotic predisposition or even manifest disorder, it does not seem to account for *primary* psychopathy, which by definition is free of neurotic contamination. In the second place, the theory does not properly account for some of the behavior patterns of the primary psychopath, such as the violent, aggressive, and destructive tendencies that make him such a compelling contrast to the secondary psychopath.

Even though we may continue to regard high extraversion (particularly the traits of impulsivity and sensation seeking) as essential in all psychopathy, clearly an alternative additive to N must be found to account for primary psychopathy. It has been suggested (H. J. Eysenck, 1970a) that the missing additive is psychoticism (P), a third major dimension of personality first suggested and empirically researched by H. J. Eysenck (1952a, 1952b) and H. J. Eysenck, Granger, and Brenglemann (1957). This factor bears the same relation to psychosis as neuroticism does to neurosis. In other words, it is conceived as a widely distributed personality trait predisposing a person to a particular kind of mental breakdown under suitable stress. The precise nature of this factor in normal populations, as well as in psychotics and criminals, has been studied in a series of papers (H. J. Eysenck & Eysenck, 1968; S. B. G. Eysenck & Eysenck, 1968, 1969a, 1969b, 1972a; Verma & Eysenck, 1973), and evidence regarding its genetic determination has been offered (H. J. Eysenck, 1972a).

Questionnaire items with high loadings on psychoticism suggest that persons with high scores on this variable are somewhat odd—unsociable, hostile, unemotional, unfeeling, and cruel. It is suggested that whereas $E \times N$ identifies the secondary psychopath, $E \times P$ identifies the primary psychopath—although one qualification must be added to this statement. As pointed out before, we do not conceive of these diagnostic categories as qualitatively different "diseases," but consider them as points in a dimensional framework (H. J. Eysenck, 1970b). Thus psychopaths are not conceived of as *either* primary *or* secondary, but as located somewhere in the octant high E–high N–high P of the three-dimensional E, P, N, structure. Typical primary psychopaths would be high on E and P, with average N, while typical secondary psychopaths would be high on E and N, with average P. However, not all, or even the majority, of psychopaths would be typical in this sense. In view of the independence of these dimensions, a person might be high on E, P, and N, or high on E and middling on P and N; indeed, all possible combinations might be found. This seems to be a much more realistic picture of what we encounter when we study "immoral" people; the categorical, diagnostic approach is arid and rigid to an extent that falsifies reality. Most psychiatrists have realized the drawback of diagnosis and have tended in recent years to play it down more and more. The well-known lack of reliability in most diagnostic systems is further indication that they do not fit reality very well (H. J. Eysenck, 1968).

The question must now be faced of why we postulate a connection between psychoticism and the performance of antisocial acts. The evidence is twofold. In the first place, there is direct evidence that prisoners score exceptionally high on questionnaire measures of P (H. J. Eysenck & Eysenck, 1971; S. B. G. Eysenck & Eysenck, 1970, 1971). Indeed, the sores on P of prisoners are no lower than those of psychotics (H. J. Eysenck, 1970a). These data support our hypothesis, but they do not explain why the hypothesis was put forward. The second set of evidence does. It has frequently been observed that psychotics (mainly schizophrenics) have an undue number of children who are psychotic, and also an equal or greater number of criminals, psychopaths, or generally antisocial offspring whose behavior closely resembles that described above as typical of high P scorers. In other words, there seems to exist a genetic connection between psychotic disorders, on the one hand, and criminal and psychopathic behavior, on the other.

I will here list only a few of the studies relevant to my point. Ödegard (1963) reported that relatives of psychotic probands were classified as psychopaths, criminals, and alcoholics in 10 percent of all cases. As Planansky (1966b) points out, "The psychopathic personalities are the most persistently reported group among close relatives of schizophrenics, and certain forms of these vaguely defined disorders appear to be not only structurally but also developmentally connected with schizophrenic psychosis." Planansky (1966a) also traces the history of this association from Kahlbaum (1890) through Kraepelin (1913) to Schafer (1951) and Delay, Deniker, and Green (1957), and summarizes the empirical literature by saying "that there is an abundance of reports concerning incidence of schizoid psychopathic personality in families of schizophrenic probands."

These studies have generally started with the psychotic proband (Essen-Möller, 1946; Planansky, 1966c), but of equal interest are studies starting at the other end, using psychopathic probands (Meggendorfer, 1921; Riedel, 1937; but see also Stumpfl, 1936). These investigations have dealt with so-called schizoid-psychopathic personalities. However, there is also a considerable agglomeration of nonschizoid-psychopathic personalities in relatives of schizophrenics (Medow, 1914; Rüdin, 1916). The most important research in this field is Heston's study (1966) of children of schizophrenic mothers. These children had been removed immediately after birth and raised by foster parents. Out of the 47 children, 9 were later diagnosed as sociopathic personalities with antisocial behavior of an impulsive kind, and had long police records. Of the total sample 4 children developed schizophrenia and 20 developed other behavioral abnormalities. These findings demonstrate that the incidence of psychotic and nonpsychotic abnormalities is high in the progeny of schizophrenics, under conditions in which direct environmental determination has been ruled out. The data, then, are very much in accord with our two hypotheses of the close relation of a general factor of psychoticism with inherited predisposition to psychopathic or criminal behavior.

The evidence adduced so far is, of course, not conclusive. Complex theories which try to account for even more complex human behavior patterns have to be tested in many different ways before we can feel any great confidence in their adequacy. The theory here discussed rather briefly has not been in existence long enough to generate the vast amount of supporting evidence required. There is, however, supporting evidence besides that already mentioned. In an unpublished factorial study of personality dimensions and various different types of criminal behavior, it was found that P loaded on the same factor as crimes of violence and sex crimes, while N loaded on crimes of "breaking and entering." Clearly a very important task for future research will be the detailed investigation of specific types of criminal or psychopathic activity, with particular reference to personality factors. The stress hitherto accorded overall gross comparisons between criminal and noncriminal, or psychopathic and nonpsychopathic, behavior is not likely to add much more to our knowledge. Of much interest, too, are follow-up studies. One such unpublished study of Borstal boys (juvenile offenders in special open prisons) over a period of three years found that recidivism correlated with E, P, and N. Within-prison conduct, too, may be of interest; misbehavior in prison, for example, correlates with E.

Many possibilities, therefore, exist for extending our knowledge of the relationship between personality and antisocial behavior. Predictions derived from the theory I have outlined can be made and tested. Until many such tests have been carried out and proved successful, however, the theory can claim only limited acceptance.

Drug Effects on
Antisocial Behavior

One area, however, provides us with a strictly experimental test of some of our hypotheses, particularly those linking cortical arousal with moral behavior. While arousal levels are probably largely genetically determined, it is possible to change them chemically. Drugs have been used since time immemorial to produce precisely such changes. In particular, drugs such as alcohol and the barbiturates *depress* the level of cortical arousal and thus have an extraverting effect. Stimulant drugs such as amphetamine or caffeine *increase* the level of cortical arousal, and thus have an introverting effect (H. J. Eysenck, 1963). One would expect that the administration of stimulant drugs would produce noticeable changes in the direction of more socialized behavior in criminals and psychopaths, although these changes would presumably disappear once the drug was withdrawn. The literature on the extraverting and introverting effects, respectively, of depressant and stimulant drugs has been reviewed elsewhere (H. J. Eysenck, 1967), and the results strongly support the theory. Of particular interest are the differences produced by these drugs in conditioning: Stimulant drugs increase conditioning, depressant drugs reduce it.

Do the direct effects of drug administration on behavior (Wender, 1971) also agree with the theory's prediction? Several experiments have been conducted, largely with behavior-disordered children and juvenile delinquents. Treatment consisted of medication with one of the stimulant drugs, usually amphetamine. Observations were made of the behavior of the subjects over a period of weeks. There were no particular attempts to alter their moral behavior and no attempts at psychotherapy. There was an astonishing, almost immediate, improvement in the behavior of the patients. They became much more amenable to discipline and much more socialized in their pattern of activities and often ceased to show behavior problems. Usually the improvement ceased when the drug treatment was stopped, but sometimes the improvement continued well beyond this point and seemed to become an enduring characteristic of the individual's behavior.

One typical study was carried out by two American psychiatrists, Cutts and Jasper (1949), who investigated 12 behavior-problem children. When given benzedrine, a stimulant, half of these children showed marked improvements in behavior. When the children were given phenobarbital, a depressant, their behavior became definitely worse in 9 out of 12 cases. A similar study has been described by Lindsley and Henry (1942), who studied 13 behavior-problem children of average intelligence with a mean age of 10½ years. The behavior of the children was rated in the ward, the playground, and the schoolroom, with particular focus on the problem behavior for which they had been referred. After a base line was established during an initial control period when no drugs were given, the children were administered benzedrine over a week, and were again rated during this time. During the following week, each subject received phenobarbital, a depressant drug expected to exacerbate their symptoms. Finally, after an interval of two weeks, the children were again rated under conditions of no drugs, this constituting the terminal control. The authors report that "Phenobarbital resulted in an exacerbation of the symptoms. . . . Under benzedrine medication all subjects show better than 10 per cent improvement in their behavior scores over those of the initial control periods; 9 subjects show better than 50 per cent improvement." The results are shown in Figure 6.5 (below). In view of the short periods of medication, they seem remarkable.

In another study, Bradley and Bowen (1941) investigated the effects of amphetamine on 100 behavior-problem children. Of these, they found that 54 became more "subdued." As an example,

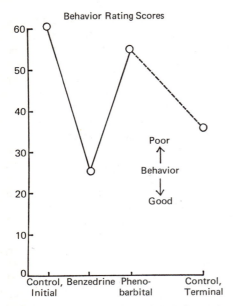

Figure 6.5   Effects of administration of a stimulant drug (benzedrine) and a depressant drug (phenobarbital) on the behavior of 13 behavior-problem children. (Redrawn from Lindsley & Henry, 1942.)

they cite the case of John, a 10-year-old boy who was admitted to the hospital because of hyperactivity, destructive behavior, poor school progress, and failure to mingle satisfactorily with older children. He teased his companions incessantly, quarreled with them, pushed them, and took their toys. His overactivity had been noted since early childhood, but the social problems which it caused worsened when he entered school. Although he was under psychotherapeutic treatment for fifteen months, he was overactive, irritable, noisy and disturbing in the ward, the playground, and the classroom, where he made little progress. He demanded a great deal of attention in school, and worked acceptably only when the teacher left the room. He was restless and distractible in all activities. At mealtimes, he stuffed food in his mouth, laughed and talked noisily, and constantly teased the other children. He gave no evidence of profiting from suggestion or

training. When amphetamine was started, however, there was immediately a definite change in his behavior. On the ward he was much quieter, and none of his usual hyperactivity was noted. He was prompt for meals and school, and became pleasant and congenial with children and adults. He cooperated well in all matters of routine; no longer restless, he applied himself to daily tasks. In the classroom he accomplished a great deal every day and showed excellent initiative.[4]

While these effects of administering drugs to antisocial persons are in line with the prediction, not enough work has been done to allow us any certainty about the particular manner in which the drugs operate. It is unlikely that much conditioning is involved, particularly as the effects seem to be noticeable and quite strong almost from the beginning. Perhaps we are on safer ground in assuming that the drugs operate to reduce impulsivity and sensation-seeking behavior. This interpretation would be consistent with the fact that drug treatments do not have very strong lasting effect (Eisenberg et al., 1963). I have suggested that treatment of criminals should combine a proper course of conditioning with the administration of amphetamine (H. J. Eysenck, 1964/1970a), but this suggestion has not to my knowledge been taken up. Such a program could provide a crucial test of my theory.

Some work has been done on the conditioning of socialized responses in criminals and delinquents without the use of drugs. I have given an extended discussion of this elsewhere (Eysenck, 1972b). Most of this work has used principles of operant conditioning, in particular the so-called token economy. In this method, the subject can obtain tokens which are exchangeable for small privileges, such as fifteen minutes of TV-viewing time, or cigarettes or specially liked foods. The principle on which these tokens are doled out is obedience to a specified set of items of "good" socialized behavior (Ayllon & Azrin, 1968). This procedure was originally introduced into penal treatment by the great innovator Alexander Maconochie almost a hundred years ago. Its revival is too recent, however, to have permitted time for proper follow-up studies, which are vital to ascertaining whether the remarkable short-term effects will endure.

Conclusion

What can we say in conclusion? If we identify "moral" conduct as freely willed and responsible decision-making behavior in accordance with philosophical premises, then the contents of this chapter will hardly seem relevant to a discussion of morality. Indeed, one might say that such a definition of moral conduct would rule out any kind of scientific investigation, and would in addition postulate a meaningless and improbable mentalism that goes counter to all modern biology has to teach us. If we concern ourselves rather with types of behavior to which terms such as *antisocial*, *criminal*, or *immoral* can be applied with a fair degree of consensus, then I think we may say that a number of facts indicate that biological factors play an important part in the genesis of such behavior, and in the causation of individual differences relevant to it.

In particular, there appears to be an important connection between moral behavior and strong cortical arousal. Introverts are found to show such arousal more frequently and more strongly than extraverts, and are also more likely to behave in socially approved ways. Furthermore, there is genetic evidence to show that introverts are more likely to be affected by environmental factors, presumably through conditioning (Jinks & Fulker, 1970). The lesser conditionability of extraverts, especially when associated with some degree of mental abnormality, is likely to lead them into paths of immorality. When E is associated prominently with N, we have the picture of the secondary psychopath. When E is associated prominently with P,

we have the picture of the primary psychopath. These clinical diagnoses are, of course, Platonic ideas closely approached only by a small number of typical cases, but they draw attention to combinations of personality traits which can be measured, and on which research can be undertaken with advantage.

I have suggested that there are two main lines along which the genetically determined cortical arousal level may be linked with the prosocial or antisocial behavior of the individual. My argument is that moral behavior is mediated through the individual's "conscience" and that this conscience is acquired through a process of conditioning. Conditioning in turn is dependent upon the level of cortical arousal. I have also maintained that impulsive, sensation-seeking, behavior is motivated at least in part by low levels of cortical arousal. The combination of these two factors, sensation seeking and poor conditioning, provides the biological background for psychopathic and criminal behavior.

This chapter has pointed out several times that these genotypic factors must interact in complex ways with environmental influences in order to produce the phenotype that is the subject of our empirical investigations; an extended treatment of these environmental factors has perforce been excluded. Similarly, there are many additional factors which for reasons of space have been treated very briefly; clearly our discussion is only an outline of a theory. Nevertheless, this theory does generate a large number of testable predictions; and, insofar as these have been tested, they have been verified in a satisfactory number of instances. It should also be noted that the theory provides suggestions for the rehabilitation of criminals, and quite generally for the improvement of the socialization process in children and adolescents as well as in adults. Future work along these lines should provide the evidence on which to base a more definite decision about the adequacy of this theory.

CHAPTER 7

Empathy, Role Taking, Guilt, and Development of Altruistic Motives[1]

Martin L. Hoffman

Introduction: Evidence of Altruism in Animals and Humans

Western psychology has evolved along lines seemingly antithetical to giving consideration for others a central place in the overall view of personality. The doctrinaire view, present in both psychoanalysis and behaviorism, has been that altruistic behavior can always be explained ultimately in terms of instrumental self-serving motives in the actor. The assumption of this chapter, by contrast, is that man is innately capable of both egoistic and altruistic motivation, and our aim here is to propose a theory of how the latter may develop in the individual. First, we will take a brief look at the relevant research literature—animal and human—to see if it is at all supportive of the idea that altruistic behavior may be based on other than selfish motives.

The evidence for altruism in animals is scanty, anecdotal, and often subject to alternative interpretations (See the recent controversy between D. L. Krebs, 1970a, 1971; and Hebb, 1971). Several of the detailed descriptive reports in the literature,

however, do seem to provide reasonably good evidence for altruistic rescue behavior. In one study, the experimenter inflicted pain on a chimpanzee, which then screamed, whereupon her cagemate began alternatively to pull her to safety and to attack the experimenter (Nissen & Crawford, 1936). A week later when the experimenter reappeared and the previously harmed animal approached him, the cagemate tried strenuously to pull her away and continued to do so for the brief period that the experimenter remained. Similarly, porpoises aid wounded members by raising them to the surface of the water for air (Hebb & Thompson, 1954).

In the human research, *altruism* has been implicitly defined as any purposive action on behalf of someone else which involves a net cost to the actor. Two types of altruistic behavior have been studied: (1) rescue, or helping another in distress; and (2) sharing, or making an anonymous donation to someone in need. The research in general presents a less bleak picture than that depicted in the social commentary following reports of bystander unresponsiveness in emergencies. In the studies reported thus far, anywhere from a sizable minority to all of the subjects (observers) have been found to help the victim when the observer was the only bystander. Among the more dramatic findings are the following: Darley and Latané (1968) found that 85 percent of their subjects attempted to help someone whom they thought was having an epileptic fit, and 90 percent of those helping acted within sixty seconds; all of Clark and Word's subjects (1972) rushed to help a man they heard fall and cry out in pain (average reaction time was nine seconds); and Schwartz (1970b) found that 59 percent of his subjects were willing to donate blood marrow to a stranger described as desperately in need, though warned in advance that a general anesthetic and a day in the hospital would be required and that they would feel sore for several days afterwards.

The findings with children are less dramatic but consistent. Murphy (1937) reports that the nursery school children she observed who had the necessary coping skills typically offered help to other children in distress. Using more structured observations of normal and retarded children in two age groups (3- to 5-year-olds and 8- to 10-year-olds), Severy and Davis (1971) found that 35 to 57 percent of the opportunities to help others were taken by the children. These figures are consistent with those obtained by Staub (1970a, 1971a, 1971b; Rosenhan, Moore, & Underwood, Chap. 13) in a more controlled laboratory setting. This consistency is particularly interesting in view of the restraint often shown by young children in laboratory studies.

There is also evidence that helping others is not associated with deprived need states in the actor, an association that would be expected if helping were a primarily egoistic need-satisfying act. Thus Murphy (1937) reports that though some of the nursery school children's helpful acts seemed calculated to win adult approval, many obviously were not (for example, shoving an attacker away from the victim, showing intense concern for the victim and being oblivious to others about him). Murphy also reports that the children who seemed most concerned about others in distress were among the more popular and emotionally secure members of the group. Jeanne Block (personal communication, 1972) reports a similar positive relation between helping behavior and such personal attributes as emotional security and self-confidence. Similarly, Staub and Sherk (1970) obtained a negative correlation between making charitable donations and the need for social approval in children. Finally, several studies (reviewed by Rosenhan, Moore, & Underwood Chap. 13) report evidence that situationally induced feelings of well-being, rather than deprivation, contribute to helping behavior.

It thus appears that helping and sharing, though often viewed as effective means of gaining rewards such as social approval, do not characterize the very people who have the greatest need for these rewards; nor are these helping behaviors associated with the arousal of egoistic needs in the situation. This makes sense when we realize that egoistic need deprivation very likely leads to a state of preoccupation with the self—with one's own needs, hopes, and fears. Such concern for the self should be expected to interfere with the individual's inclination to help others, rather than contribute to it. A state of well-being and need fulfillment, on the other hand, may very well facilitate prosocial behavior because it reduces pressures toward egoistic self-concern, leaving the person more open and responsive to the needs of others.

That people will help others when their own needs are not salient, indeed when they are in a state of well-being rather than want, lends credence to the view that an altruistic motive system separate from the egoistic may exist within the individual. The remainder of this chapter will be taken up with a theoretical account of the development of the altruistic motive. The scheme which will be presented rests ultimately on the human capacity to experience the inner state of others who are not in the same situation. This analysis attempts to pull together what is known about the individual's affective response to another person's distress (empathy, sympathy, guilt), on the one hand, and cognitive development and role taking, on the other.

Affective Response to Another's Distress

Empathy refers to the involuntary, at times forceful, experiencing of another person's emotional state. It is elicited either by expressive cues which directly reflect the other's feelings or by other cues which convey the affective impact of external events on him.

The tendency to respond empathically to another in distress has long been noted in children and adults. Murphy (1937, p. 295) in her classic study described numerous instances of empathic responses in nursery school children and concluded that "experiencing distress when another is in distress seems primitive, naive, reasonably universal"—as natural a response as anger is to threats to the self (and, as with anger, only the specific form of empathy is due to learning). N. D. Feshbach and Roe (1968) found that 4- to 7-year-old children typically gave empathic responses to a series of slide sequences depicting other children in different affective situations. College students respond affectively, as indicated by physiological measures, when observing another person being administered electric shock or heat, or failing in a task (Berger, 1962; Craig & Weinstein, 1965; Stotland, 1969; Tomes, 1964; R. F. Weiss, Boyer, Lombardo, & Stich, 1973). Clore and Jeffery (1972) found that watching someone in a wheel chair for an hour produced feelings of empathy and diminished potency in the observer.

The various explanations for empathic distress boil down to two basic classical conditioning paradigms. One paradigm views empathy as developing early in infancy with the bodily transfer of tension from the caretaker to the child. A second, more general, paradigm holds that the unpleasant affect accompanying one's own painful past experiences is evoked by another person's distress cues which resemble the stimuli associated with the observer's own experiences. A simple example is the child who cuts himself, feels the pain, and cries. Later on, he sees another child cut himself and cry. The sight of the blood, the sound of the cry, or any other distress cue from the other child associated with the observer's own prior experience of pain can now elicit the unpleasant affect that was initially a part of that experience.[2] Because the process involved in the second paradigm is neither confined to early infancy nor limited to distress originating in physically communicated tensions, it opens up the possibility of a multiplicity of distress experiences with which the child can empathize.

EMPATHY AND ALTRUISM

The possible contribution of empathy to altruism has long been noted in the literature. In the 1920s Stern (1924) suggested that empathy contributes to such acts as attempting to comfort, help, or avenge a distressed person. Isaacs (1933) similarly viewed empathy as one root of reciprocity, the ability to take turns, and to cooperate through active sharing. And Anna Freud (1937), in discussing altruistic "surrender," saw the individual as projecting his own needs to others and then gaining vicarious gratification from his efforts to satisfy these needs. More recently it has been suggested that the parent's use of induction (discipline techniques that point out the harmful consequences of the child's act for others) contributes to moral development partly because it arouses empathy for the victim of the child's actions (M. L. Hoffman, 1963b, 1970, in press; M. L. Hoffman & Saltzstein, 1960, 1967; Saltzstein, Chap. 14). Aronfreed and Paskal (1965, 1966) have proposed a two-stage theory of empathy and altruism: Empathic distress results from observing another's distress in close temporal association with one's own experience of distress; the altruistic act is then acquired by observing another person's altruistic act in conjunction with the reduction of one's own empathic distress.

Most of these writers have stressed the affective and reinforcing properties of empathy, to the relative neglect of the cognitive. Since cognitive processes help determine how even the simplest emotion is experienced, the same must be true for a complex emotional experience such as empathy. It seems likely, for example, that the actor experiences not only the feelings but also some of the perceptions, thoughts, and wishes of the other person, as well as images of his own past distress and the actions of others who helped relieve it (these images may serve as cues to what might be done to help the other in the immediate situation). These cognitions may have obvious ramifications for altruistic motivation and action. More fundamentally, since it is a response to cues about the affective state of others, empathy must depend to a great extent on the actor's cognitive development, especially his level of self–other differentiation. We now turn to an examination of self–other differentiation, after which we will attempt to combine this differentiation with empathy to account for the development of altruistic motives.

Development of a Sense of the Other

The literature bearing on development of a sense of the other can be organized around three topics: attainment of object permanence in infancy; role taking, espe-cially in early childhood; and identity in later childhood and adolescence. Since our aim is a developmental synthesis of empathy and the sense of the other, we must estimate, within the limits of available data, the age at which each of these capabilities exists.

OBJECT PERMANENCE

To have a sense of the other means at the very least to be aware of the other's existence as a separate entity from the self. That the young infant lacks such awareness is indicated by Piaget's studies (1954) of object displacement. If, for example, a desired object is hidden behind a screen before the infant's eyes, he will before 6 months of age lose interest in it, as though it no longer existed. After that age he will typically remove the screen to obtain the hidden object. Not until 18 months, however, will the infant go after an object that has been *invisibly* displaced (i.e., first hidden in front of the child in a container, which is then hidden behind a screen and brought out empty after the object has been removed from it in the hidden place). From this pattern of behavior, Piaget and others infer that it is not until about 1½ years of age that the child shows true "object permanence," that is, a stable sense of the separate existence of physical objects even when they are outside his immediate perceptual field.

"Permanence" with respect to persons, more important for our purposes, appears to develop before object permanence (Fraiberg, 1969). The existence of stranger anxiety (Spitz, 1950) as early as 7 months suggests that at this age the child can carry an internal image of a preferred person, such as his mother, although a similar stimulus (e.g., another human face) is probably necessary to evoke the anxiety. S. M. Bell (1970) tested the child's ability to retrieve (1) a toy and (2) his actual mother when both had been visibly and invisibly displaced; Bell concluded that person permanence preceded object permanence by several months in most subjects. Early in the second year of life, then, the child has a sense of his mother—and perhaps other persons whom he values and interacts with frequently—as separate physical entities.

ROLE TAKING

Having attained a sense of the separate existence of persons, the child still has a highly limited sense of the other. He is bound up in his own point of view, which he regards as absolute: The world exists as he perceives it. According to Piaget (1932), it is not until about 7 or 8 years of age that this egocentrism begins to give way to the recognition that others have their own perspective. The research by and large supports Piaget's view. Its emphasis, however, has been heavily cognitive, dealing with the other person's perceptions and thoughts rather than with the other's affections and emotions. Furthermore, the tasks used often require the subject to utilize cognitive skills that may facilitate role taking at times, but not be critical to it. The result, as we shall see, may be an overestimation of the age at which the child becomes capable of role taking.

Consider first the studies of "perceptual role taking" (Flavell, 1968; Lovell, 1959; Piaget & Inhelder, 1956; Selman, 1971b). The procedures used in these studies are variants of the classic one devised by Piaget in which the child is seated facing a scale model of three mountains and tested for his ability to predict how the model would look to another child seated at various positions around it. In this type of task, the presence of the other person is incidental; the child could just as well be alone and asked what he would see if he were located elsewhere in the room. In other words, the skill tested bears on the child's conception of space and his competence in spatial relations—more specifically, the ability to imagine how things would look from different vantage points.[3] This ability is not necessary for assessing another's inner state except when such an assessment is dependent on visual stimuli to which the other, but not the observer, is exposed. In short, the tasks in the studies of spatial perspective shifting involve a cognitive skill which may contribute to role taking under certain conditions, but is not an essential part of it.

In other role-taking studies the subject is asked to communicate a message to someone whose perspective is deficient in some respect; the receiver is, for example, much younger than the subject or handicapped by being blindfolded (Chandler & Greenspan, 1972; Flavell, 1968). In a representative study by Flavell (1968), the child is shown an ordered series of seven pictures which tell a story in comic-strip fashion. After the child has narrated the story, the experimenter removes three of the pictures, leaving a four-picture sequence that illustrates a very different story. A second experimenter then enters the room, and the subject is told that this person has never seen the pictures before. The subject's task is to predict the story he thinks the newcomer will tell on the basis of having seen only the set of four pictures. One could attribute the failure of younger children on this task to their inability to keep the details of both stories separately in mind rather than to their inability to shed their own previously formed perspective and adopt the other person's fresh and naive one. The picture-sequence task thus appears to be primarily a cognitive one; and, as with the spatial tasks described previously, the subject can give the correct response without actually attending to the other person and making inferences about his perspective.

There is a small body of research dealing directly with the ability to infer another person's emotions in different situations. Borke (1971), for example, told 3- to 8-year-old children stories in which the main character might be perceived as happy, sad, afraid, or angry. Based on her finding that even the youngest children could correctly differentiate between happy and unhappy responses in the story characters, Borke concluded that children as young as 3 years of age are able to adopt the point of view of another, and consequently cannot be described as egocentric. Borke's conclusion may be questioned in light of an earlier study by Burns and Cavey (1957) which found that 3- and 4-year-old children who were shown pictures in which a child's facial expression was incongruent with the situation tended to overlook the incongruity and to respond in terms of how they would feel in the situation. This finding suggests that young children cannot assess another's emotional state when it differs from their own, although the measure Burns and Cavey used may have been too cognitively demanding to provide a true test of this ability.

To summarize, the dominant focus of the role-taking research has been on the cognitive aspects of the other person's perspective, and the tasks used typically put a premium on cognitive and verbal skills. When cognitive or verbal operations beyond the child's capacity are required, his actual role-taking capability may be masked. It follows that to estimate how early in life the child can take another's role requires evidence from studies employing measures that are minimally complex cognitively; thus far only Selman's measure (1971b) comes even close to this ideal. Selman's subjects were given a simple concept-sorting task and asked to predict what choices would be made on a similar task by another child from whom one of the test items had been hidden. Nearly all 6-year-old subjects could perform the task, while younger subjects did poorly. The question may be asked, however, whether younger children would show evidence of role taking in tasks requiring even less cognitive processing—for example, where the child already has the information necessary for assessing the other person's thoughts and feelings in the situation and is maximally motivated. To provide a tentative answer, we must draw on anecdotal evidence in natural settings familiar to the child.

Although Flavell concludes from his research that the budding awareness of perspective differences does not occur until about age 6, he gives several anecdotal examples of cognitive role taking in 4- and 5-year-olds. An incident which I observed involved a still younger child. Marcy, aged 20 months, was in the playroom of her home and wanted a toy that her sister Sara was playing with. She asked Sara for it, but Sara refused vehemently. Marcy then paused, as if reflecting on what to do, and then began rocking Sara's favorite rocking horse (which Sara never allowed anyone to touch), yelling "Nice horsey! Nice horsey!" and keeping her eyes on Sara all the time. Sara came running angrily, whereupon Marcy immediately ran around Sara directly to the toy and grabbed it. Without analyzing the full complexity of Marcy's behavior, one can infer from her actions that she had deliberately lured her sister away from the toy. Though not yet 2 years of age, Marcy was capable of being aware of another person's inner states that were different from her own. While her behavior was Machiavellian rather than altruistic, this child demonstrated that she could take another's role. Yet had she been a subject in the experiments discussed previously, it is doubtful that she could have understood the instructions, much less performed the designated role-taking response.

The final example is in some respects less dramatic and depicts a cognitively less demanding behavior, but the child was only 15 months old and the context is more germane to our altruistic concerns. The boy, Michael, was struggling with his friend, Paul, over a toy. Paul started to cry. Michael appeared concerned and let go of the toy so that Paul would have it, but Paul kept crying. Michael paused, then gave his teddy bear to Paul, but the crying continued. Michael paused again, then ran to the next room, returned with

Paul's security blanket, and offered it to Paul, who then stopped crying. Several aspects of this incident deserve comment. First, it does seem clear that Michael assumed that his own teddy, which often comforts him, would also comfort his friend. Second, its failure to do this served as corrective feedback, which led Michael to consider alternatives. Third, in considering the processes underlying Michael's final, successful act, three possibilities stand out: (1) he was simply imitating an effective instrumental act observed in the past; that is, he had observed Paul being comforted with the blanket. This can be tentatively ruled out, since Michael's parents could not recall his ever having such an opportunity. (2) In trying to think of what to do, he remembered seeing another child being soothed by a blanket, and this reminded him of Paul's blanket—a more complex response than might first appear, since Paul's blanket was out of Michael's perceptual field at the time. (3) Michael, as young as he was, could somehow reason by analogy that Paul would be comforted by something that he loved in the same way that Michael loved his own teddy.

I favor the last interpretation, although it does postulate a complex response for a young child. Regardless of which, if any, of the three explanations is correct, the incident suggests that a child not yet 1½ years of age may be able, with the help of a very general form of corrective feedback[4] (Paul's continuing to cry when offered Michael's teddy), to assess another's specific needs that differ from his own. The same conclusion may be drawn from a strikingly similar incident recently reported by Borke (1972). This age is a far cry from the 5 or 6 years suggested by the laboratory research—a discrepancy too large to be explained strictly in terms of Michael's precocity.

In conclusion, it appears that just as person permanence may precede object permanence by several months, certain forms of role taking in familiar and highly motivating natural settings may precede the more complex forms investigated in the laboratory by several years. The child who can take the role of a familiar person at home may behave egocentrically in complex role-taking tasks in the laboratory because he cannot utilize the available cues regarding the inner states of others and must therefore rely on his own perspective. In other words, the rudiments of role-taking competence may be present before the child is 2 years old (not long after he has attained person permanence), although role-taking performance varies with the cognitive and verbal complexity of the particular task.

AWARENESS OF IDENTITY

The sense of the other as having his own personal identity, that is, his own life circumstances and inner states beyond the immediate situation, has been largely ignored in the literature. The conception closest to it is Erikson's concept (1950) of ego identity, which pertains to the individual's own sense of sameness through time. Erikson's view is supported by the likelihood that at some point the child develops the cognitive capacity to integrate his own discrete inner experiences over time, and to form a conception of himself as having different feelings and thoughts in different situations, but still remaining the same continuous person with one past, present, and anticipated future.

Research by Kohlberg (1966) suggests when this awareness of identity develops. He asked 4- to 8-year-old children if a pictured girl who wanted to be a boy could be one if she played boys' games or if she wore boys' haircuts or clothes. Kohlberg (1966) found that "by age 6 to 7, most children were quite certain that a girl could not be a boy regardless of changes in appearance or behavior" (p. 95)—in contrast to younger children, who were often thrown off by physical appearances and thought that girls could become boys by altering their appearance. This finding suggests that the child has a sense of stabilization and continuity regarding gender by about 6 or 7 years of age.

The findings on racial identity are similar. Proshansky (1966), after reviewing the research literature, concluded that a firm sense of one's racial identity does not appear to be established until about 7 or 8 years of age. Finally, Guardo and Bohan (1971), in a developmental study of self-identity in middle-class white children, found that 6- and 7-year-olds recognize their identity as humans and as males or females mainly in terms of their names, physical appearance, and behaviors—a finding that is consistent with the results for gender and racial identity. These children's sense of self-continuity from the past and into the future was still hazy, however. It was not until 8 or 9 years of age that more covert and personalized differences in feelings and attitudes made a contribution to these subjects' sense of identity—although even then most felt that their names, physical characteristics, and behaviors were the essential anchorage points of identity.

Sometime between 6 and 9 years, then, the child's conception of his own continuing identity appears to begin. This emerging sense of identity may be presumed to result by early adolescence in a broadening of his view of others. Once he has the cognitive capacity to see that his own life has coherence and continuity despite the fact that he reacts differently in different situations, the individual should soon be able to do the same with regard to others. He can then not only take the role of others and assess their reactions in particular situations but also generalize from these interactions and construct a concept of others' general life experiences. In sum, his awareness that others are coordinate with himself expands to include the notion that they, like himself, have their own identity as persons, which goes beyond the immediate situa-

tion. His perspective on others and his interpretation of their response in the immediate situation are thereby dramatically altered.

Development of Altruistic Motives: A Theory of Synthesis

The foregoing analyses of empathy and a sense of the other provide needed background for the following theory of altruistic motivation, which is essentially a developmental account of the synthesis of these affective and cognitive capacities.

EMPATHIC DISTRESS

Developmentally first is empathic distress. As discussed previously, this kind of empathy is very likely a conditioned affective response based on the similarity between distress cues from someone else in the immediate situation and elements of one's own actual distress experiences in the past. The neural capacity necessary for such a response is minimal, since both classical and operant conditioning are known to be possible in the early weeks of life (e.g., Kessen, Haith, & Salapatek, 1970). It follows that the infant is capable of empathic distress long before he has developed a sense of self or a sense of the other.

As a result of this lack of self–other differentiation, the child for at least most of the first year is presumably unclear as to who is experiencing any distress that he witnesses, and he will often behave as though he were experiencing it. That is, he sees the other's distress cues, and they automatically evoke an upset state in him. This global empathic distress includes unpleasant feelings which he wishes would terminate, and perhaps also images of his own and others' acts that would relieve or comfort him because they have comforted him in the past. He may then seek comfort for his own distress. This was recently illustrated by an 11-month-old child of a student of mine. On seeing another child fall and cry, she first stared at the victim, appeared as though she were about to cry herself, and then put her thumb in her mouth and buried her head in her mother's lap—her typical response after *she* has hurt herself and needs comforting.

This is obviously a very primitive response. We use the word *empathy* to describe it, but the child does not really put himself in the other's place and try to imagine what he is feeling. The child's response is rather a conditioned, passive, involuntary one based on the pull of surface cues associated with elements of his own past. If there is action, its dominant motivation is hedonistic—to eliminate discomfort in the self. Nevertheless, empathic distress is basic in the early development of altruistic motivation precisely because its occurrence shows that we may involuntarily and forcefully experience others' emotional states rather than only the emotional states pertinent and appropriate to our own situation—that we are built in such a way that distress will often be contingent not on our own, but on someone else's painful experience.

SYMPATHETIC DISTRESS

A major change in the child's reaction to distress occurs when he becomes capable of distinguishing between himself and others. When confronted with another person in pain, he still experiences empathic distress, but because of this new cognitive capacity he will now know that the other person, not himself, is in actual pain. The recognition that the other is actually experiencing the distress transforms the empathy *with* the victim, a parallel affective response, into sympathetic concern *for* the victim, a more reciprocal response. This is not to deny that the response may continue to have a purely empathic component, or that the child may also fear that the undesired event will happen to him. The important thing, however, is that

the quasi-hedonistic motive to alleviate the child's own distress ("I want to get rid of my distress") gives way, at least in part, to the more prosocial motive to alleviate the other's distress ("I want to get rid of his distress"); and this prosocial motive is a new addition to the child's repertoire. The transformation of empathic into sympathetic distress occurs in three stages, which are tied to the three levels of cognitive apprehension of the other: permanence, role taking, and identity. The three stages of sympathetic distress—each stage defined in terms of the synthesis of empathic distress and a cognitive level—will now be descibed. Following this an attempt will be made to probe more deeply into the transition between empathic and sympathetic distress.

Empathic distress and person permanence. At the level of person permanence the child has acquired a sense of the other only as a physical entity. He knows that the other is the victim, and his empathic reaction is transformed by this knowledge into a genuine concern for the other. But he cannot yet distinguish between his own and the other's inner states (thoughts, perceptions, needs). Without thinking about it, he automatically assumes that the other's states are identical to his own. Consequently, although he can sense the other's distress, he does not understand what caused it nor does he know what the other's needs are in the situation (except when they happen to coincide with his own). This lack of understanding is often evidenced in the child's efforts to help, which consist chiefly of giving the other what he himself finds most comforting. In the example cited earlier, Michael's initial attempt to placate his friend is a case in point. I have also heard a description of a 13-month-old child who brought his own mother to comfort a crying friend, even though the latter's mother was equally available, and of another child the same age who offered his beloved doll to comfort an adult who looked sad. (At this age the child's helping behavior may sometimes be quite transitory, and the next moment he may strike the person he was just comforting.)

This first level of sympathetic distress is in some ways as primitive as the empathic distress described earlier—a passive, involuntary, and sometimes grossly inaccurate and transitory response to cues perceptually similar to those associated with the child's own past distress. It is a significant advance, however, since for the first time the child experiences a desire to help the other, though his effort to do so may be misguided because of his cognitive limitations. This motive to help is aroused by the awareness of someone in distress, although its qualitative aspects—including the conception of the nature and intensity of the other's distress and the type of action needed to relieve it—will depend on the child's level of cognitive development.

Empathic distress and role taking. At the second developmental level of sympathetic distress, the child has begun to acquire a sense of others not only as physical entities but also as sources of feelings and thoughts in their own right. That is, he is no longer certain that the real world and his perception of it are the same thing. He has begun to realize that others may have inner states that differ from his own, as well as different perspectives based on their own needs and interpretations of events, although he may be uncertain what their perspectives actually are. This advance, as mentioned in the discussion of role taking, is very likely the result of the child's cognitive development combined with experiences in which his expectations that others have identical inner states are disconfirmed by corrective feedback from them.

The awareness that the other has inner states independent of his own has profound effects on the nature of the child's response to distress. Though the affective distress aroused in him remains essentially the same, and though he may continue to project his own feelings on the victim as in the past, these reactions are now only part of a more conscious orientation to the other's state. The child is, moreover, aware of the guesswork involved and therefore uses other inputs besides his own empathic distress in formulating an idea of the other's needs and feelings—inputs such as specific information about which acts will alleviate the other's distress and which will not. Initially he may engage in trial and error based on his own past experience and then, like Michael in the example discussed earlier, alter his behavior in response to corrective feedback in the situation. Eventually the trial and error and reality testing take place internally, and external feedback is no longer needed except perhaps in new and complex situations.

For the first time in our developmental account, then, the child begins to make an active effort to put himself in the other's place, although he remains aware of the tentative and hypothetical nature of the inference he makes. He has now achieved genuine role-taking. His motivation to relieve the other person's distress is far less egocentric than before and it is based to a far greater degree on a veridical assessment of the other's needs. As a result, his attempts to help are more sophisticated and appropriate.

Empathic distress and identity. Despite this obvious progress, the child's response at the second level of sympathetic distress is still confined to the other's distress in the immediate situation. This deficiency is overcome at the third level, owing to a significant new input: the child's emerging conception of others, as well as of himself, as continuous persons with their own histories and identities. By the time he has reached the preadolescent years, the child is presumably fully aware that others react with feelings of pleasure and pain, not only in immediate situations but also within the context of their larger pattern of life experiences. He continues to react to others' momentary distress, but feels worse when he knows it is chronic. He may also imagine their repeated experiences of distress, even when these are not reflected in the immediate situation. In sum, being aware that others have inner states and a separate existence beyond the immediate situation enables the individual to respond not only to their transitory, situation-specific, distress but also to what he imagines to be their general condition. (The transitory and the general are ordinarily consonant, but when they conflict the individual's response will be determined by the latter, since it is the more inclusive, and hence more compelling, index of the other's welfare. An exception to this rule is when the cues of the transitory are far more salient than those of the general.)

This third level of sympathetic distress, then, consists of the synthesis of empathic distress and a mental representation of the other's *general* plight—that is, his typical day-to-day level of distress or deprivation, the opportunities available or denied to him, his future prospects, and the like. If this representation of the other falls short of what the observer conceives to be a minimally acceptable standard of well-being (and if the observer's own life circumstances place himself above this standard), this third level of the sympathetic distress response will typically be evoked, regardless of the other's apparent momentary state.

To summarize thus far, the individual who progresses through these three stages may reach the point of being capable of a high level of sympathetic response to another person in distress. He can process all levels of information—including that gained through his own empathic reaction, immediate situational cues, and general knowledge about the other's life. He can act out in his own mind the emotions and experiences suggested by these sources of information, and introspect on all of this. He may thus gain an understanding of the

circumstances, feelings, and wishes of the other, have feelings of concern for him, and wish to help—while all the time maintaining the sense that the other is a separate person from himself.

With further cognitive development the person may acquire the capacity to comprehend the plight not only of an individual but also of an entire group or class of people to whom he is exposed, such as those who are economically impoverished, politically oppressed, socially outcast, victimized by war, or mentally retarded. Since the observer is part of a different group, his own distress experiences may not be quite like those of the less fortunate group. All distress experiences have much in common, however; and by this stage the individual has the capacity to generalize from one distress experience to another. It may therefore be assumed that most people have the cognitive and affective requisites for a generalized empathic distress (although the salience of others' misfortune may be necessary to activate this capacity). Possible exceptions are people whose socialization has rendered them incapable of empathy, or whose status in life has permitted only the most superficial contact with less fortunate people (consider Marie Antoinette's apocryphal "Let them eat cake" in response to the peasants' clamoring for bread). In any case, the synthesis of empathic distress and the perceived plight of an unfortunate group results in the developmentally most advanced form of sympathetic distress.[5]

TRANSFORMATION OF EMPATHIC DISTRESS INTO SYMPATHETIC DISTRESS

A key assumption in this theoretical account is that with the development of a sense of the other, the child's self-oriented empathic distress is transformed into a true sympathetic concern for the other. The question may be asked, Why doesn't the child, once he realizes that the other is not actually in distress, simply feel relieved and ignore the other's plight? The answer requires a closer look at the transition between empathic and sympathetic distress.

As discussed previously, the child at first does not differentiate himself from others, and when he observes someone in distress he feels it is his own distress. He has unpleasant feelings that he wishes would terminate, and he may also imagine acts by others that will relieve or comfort him, perhaps because these acts have done so in the past. Since the young child experiences a global empathic distress which fuses his own feelings with his impressions of another, it seems reasonable to assume that his undifferentiated unpleasant feelings, wishes, and images would be subsequently transferred to both the separate "self" and the "other" which emerge from the global self later in development. That is, the properties of the whole become the properties of its emerging parts. As a consequence, the child's initial concern to relieve his own empathic distress becomes in part a sympathetic concern to relieve the distress of the other.

Second, the process of self–other differentiation is gradual and very likely subject to occasional regression, for example, when the child is fatigued or under tension. This means that in the early stages of differentiation he is only vaguely and momentarily aware of the other as distinct from the self. He must therefore go through a period of responding to another's distress by feeling as though his dimly perceived self and the dimly perceived other are somehow simultaneously—or perhaps alternately—in distress. That is, the self and the other slip in and out of focus as the person whose distress the child wishes to have terminated. Consider a colleague's child whose typical response to his own distress beginning late in his first year was to suck his thumb with one hand and pull his ear with the other. At 12 months, on seeing a sad look on his father's face, the child proceeded to look sad himself and to suck his thumb while pulling

his father's ear! An early period of subjectively overlapping concern such as this, in which the self and the other are experienced as "sharing" the distress, would seem to provide a further basis for a positive orientation toward the emerging other. The gradual nature of self–other differentiation is therefore important, because it gives the child the experience of simultaneously wanting to terminate the emerging other's distress as well as his own—thus providing a link between the initially hedonistic empathic distress response and the earliest trace of sympathetic distress. If the sense of the other were attained suddenly, the child would lack this experience; when he discovers that the pain is someone else's, he might simply react with relief (or even blame the other for his own empathic distress).

Though the child now responds with sympathetic distress, he is still egocentric; and his concern for the other may be due partly to his assumption that the other's inner states are the same as his own. When the child develops role-taking capabilities, the question that introduced this section may be reformulated as follows: Why should the child continue to be positively oriented toward others once he discovers that they are the sources of their own inner states? The reason I would advance is that in the course of discovering that others have their own internal reactions to situations, the child finds that although their reactions at times may differ from his, the differences are typically outweighed by the similarities. The role-taking literature, to be sure, stresses development of the capacity to grasp another's perspective when it differs from one's own. This is done only to make clear the nature of the child's progress away from egocentrism, however. In real life, when the child takes the perspective of others, he is apt to find that it is usually like his own except for minor variations. In the case discussed earlier, though Michael found out that he and his friend would want different comforting objects in the same situation, the basic feeling that he initially projected to his friend was shown by the final outcome to be veridical. That is, his assumption that his friend's basic emotional needs would be the same as his own was confirmed. Thus while moving away from the automatic, egocentric, assumption that the other's inner states are identical to his own, the child discovers both that others react as persons in their own right, and that their responses are often very similar to his own. The realization that his feelings resemble those experienced independently by others in similar situations must inevitably contribute to a sense of "oneness," which preserves and may even enhance the child's developing motivation to alleviate others' distress.

To summarize, there are three significant aspects of the child's early response to another's distress. These may account for the seemingly paradoxical notion that self–other differentiation, which might be expected to create a barrier between persons, and empathic distress, which is partially hedonistic, combine to produce the developmental basis for a motive to help others. Two of these aspects are manifest in the earliest stages of self–other differentiation: (1) the transfer of the unpleasant affect associated with the initial global "self" to its emerging separate parts (self and other) and (2) the subjective experience of "sharing" distress, which is due to the gradual attainment of a sense of the other and gives the child the experience of wishing the other's distress to end. The third aspect of the child's early response to another's distress, a growing awareness of the similarity between his own and the other's independent affective response to situations, occurs during the shift away from egocentrism.[6] When we add the fact that all children have the same basic nervous system, an increasing capacity for stimulus generalization on the basis of both conceptual and perceptual similarities, and many experiences in common during the long period of socialization, it would appear that the human potential for a sense of oneness, empathy, and sympathy may well be enormous. The developmental synthesis of empathic distress and the cognitive sense of the other, postulated here, may thus be a fundamental fact of life for most individuals.

It should be noted that by *synthesis* we do not mean an instantaneous occurrence, but a reciprocal process in which the empathic and the cognitive enhance one another. Thus the empathically produced cues within the observer serve as one source of cognitive information about the other's state. The cognitive understanding of the other's state, on the other hand, may trigger, intensify, or give broader meaning to the observer's empathic response. Which of the two, cognitive or empathic, initiates the process of synthesis is presumably a function of personal style and the nature of the situation. Where there is close contact between observer and victim, the empathic response may be aroused prior to full comprehension of the victim's plight. In other situations, such as seeing a stranger drowning, cognitive comprehension may precede empathic distress.

THE ROLE OF COGNITIVE MEDIATION

Besides the central role that cognitive development plays in the transformation of empathic distress into the different forms of sympathetic distress, it also has an obvious mediational function throughout. The child's response initially is dependent on the physical similarity between cues of the other's distress and those associated with his own past distress. That is, he can respond only to visible types of distress such as cries over falls, cuts, bruises, and lost possessions. Further cognitive development enables him to respond on the basis of inferred as well as perceptual similarities, and verbal as well as physical expressions of distress—thus opening the door to a host of psychologically more subtle types of empathic distress such as those resulting from another's feelings of rejection and disappointment or his state of being unfulfilled. A growing capacity for cognitive mediation also enables the child to make inferences about another's distress on the basis of information about the other's life conditions, even when these differ from his own and the other person is not physically present. That is, knowing only the other's life condition may be sufficient for grasping his perspective and responding sympathetically. Finally, cognitive growth may eventually help the individual attain a generalized concept of distress experience which enables him to respond sympathetically to types of distress that he has not experienced himself.

The Relation between Motives and Altruistic Action

The focus of this chapter is on motives; a full treatment of the relation between motives and action is beyond its scope. This topic cannot be ignored, however, since the importance of motives ultimately lies in their influence on behavior. The assumption implicit in our formulation is that motives do relate to action—that both empathic and sympathetic distress predispose the individual to act, though only in the latter case does he feel himself to be acting on the other's behalf. Developmentally, this means that as the child acquires coping skills, he will tend to use them in the service of these motives. At first, he simply enacts behaviors that have alleviated his own distress in the past, as exemplified in our earlier illustrations of empathic distress and the lowest level of sympathetic distress. Eventually he experiences doubt about the appropriateness of these acts for the other person; role taking and higher levels of cognitive processing begin to intervene between the motives and the act; and the child's response becomes more veridical in terms of

the victim's needs. Presumably there is also some feedback or reinforcement process throughout, whereby acts that successfully alleviate the other's distress are retained and repeated in the future. The corrective feedback which often follows unsuccessful, inappropriate acts may lead to trial and error or the operation of higher-level cognitive processes which in turn result in appropriate acts.

To date, there is only modest empirical support for the key point in this formulation—that sympathetic distress predisposes the person to act altruistically. In the intensive nursery school observations by Bridges (1931) and Murphy (1937), the younger children usually reacted to another in distress with a worried, anxious look but did nothing, presumably because of fear or lack of necessary skills. Had they been in the familiar surroundings of the home, however, these subjects might have responded more actively, as the 20-month-old son of a colleague did when a visiting friend, about to leave, burst into tears complaining that her parents were not home (they were away for two weeks). His immediate reaction was to look sad, but then he offered her his beloved teddy bear to take home. His parents immediately reminded him that he would miss the teddy if he gave it away, but he insisted—as if his sympathetic distress were greater than the anticipated unpleasantness of not having the teddy. His insistence may be indicative of the strong motivational potential of sympathetic distress.

In any event, Murphy (1937) found that for older children sympathetic distress was usually accompanied by an overt helpful act. The laboratory studies by N. D. Feshbach and Roe (1968) and Staub (1970a) also suggest that preschool and older children typically react to another child's distress with both sympathy and attempts to help. Finally, several other studies cited earlier, when considered as a group, provide evidence for a similar association between altruistic motivation and behavior in adults. Witnessing another person being shocked or failing in a task typically results in both an affective reaction, as measured physiologically, and an overt attempt to help (Berger, 1962; Craig & Weinstein, 1965; D. L. Krebs, 1970b; Stotland, 1969; Tomes, 1964; R. F. Weiss et al., 1973). In a similar study, DiLollo and Berger (1965) found that exposure to the pain cues of a victim in a simulated shock experiment resulted in a decrease in reaction time for a button-pushing response. Though this was not a helping response, the finding supports the idea that the individual's affective response to another's distress is accompanied by an overt response tendency.

It would appear, then, that sympathetic distress is accompanied by tendencies toward helpful action. Whether it motivates or is merely associated with the action is uncertain, although there is some evidence in one of Murphy's empirical generalizations (1937) that it may motivate: "As verbal and physical techniques develop to the point where the child can cope with a large portion of the varied situations to which he is exposed, an active response (to help) occurs and there is less likelihood of prolonged affective response" (p. 300). Thus when the child overtly helps the other, the affective portion of his sympathetic distress diminishes; when he does not help, the affect is prolonged. This applies both developmentally (more action and less affect with age) and within the same child at a given age. Latané and Darley (1968) found something similar with adults: Subjects who helped a person who seemed to be having an epileptic fit showed less emotion afterwards than those who did not help. These findings are all consistent with the notion that sympathetic distress predisposes the person to act; acting reduces the sympathetic distress, whereas inaction does not."[7]

Though sympathetic distress may predispose the child to act altruistically, it does not guarantee that he will act. Whether the child acts depends on other things besides the strength and developmental level of the altruistic motive. Action is more likely when the appropriate thing to do is obvious and within the person's repertoire, and less likely when there is little that he can do. The costs to the observer and the strength of competing motives aroused in him by the situation must also be taken into account. In an individualistic society such as ours, for example, altruistic motives may often be overridden by more powerful egoistic motives. Our society, moreover, often sends out mixed messages about altruism. Though encouraged by our traditional religions, for example, altruism is often suspect, regarded as serving the actor's egoistic needs to feel superior to the other, or viewed as an invasion of the other's privacy or a sign of insensitivity to his need to help himself. Finally, as noted by M. L. Hoffman (1970a) and Staub (1970a), American children are often socialized to behave altruistically and to follow the rules; but in some situations following the rules will interfere with altruistic action. In such a society altruistic motives may well have a reliable effect on behavior only in situations in which one encounters someone in distress and is not preoccupied with himself or subject to conflicting social norms.

Pending clarification in future research, I would suggest the following formulation of the relationship between altruistic motives and action. Distress cues from another person trigger the altruistic motive-and-response system. That is, the observer experiences sympathetic distress and his initial tendency is to act. If he does not act—because of situational counterpressures, competing motives, lack of necessary skills, or whatever other reasons—he will typically either continue to experience sympathetic distress or to cognitively restructure the situation to justify his own inaction, for example, by derogating the victim or otherwise convincing himself that the victim wanted or deserved what he got.

Guilt and Reparative Altruism

Thus far nothing has been said about what happens when the observer sees himself as the cause of the other's distress. Blaming oneself becomes possible once one has acquired the cognitive capacity to recognize the consequences of his action for others and to be aware that he has choice and control over his own behavior.[8] The combination of sympathetic distress with an awareness of being the cause of another's distress may be called *guilt*, since it has both the affectively unpleasant and cognitive self-blaming components of the guilt experience.

Personal or true guilt may be experienced directly as the result of commission (things the person did) or omission (things the person did not do which might have helped the other). This type of guilt, which has been found to relate to parental discipline (M. L. Hoffman, 1970a; M. L. Hoffman & Saltzstein, 1960, 1967), differs from the psychoanalytic conception of guilt. The latter is based not so much on the actual harm done to others as on the transformation of anxiety over loss of parental love into self-blame, and the direction of unsuccessfully repressed hostile impulses toward the self (see J. Gilligan, Chap. 8). Actually, little is known about the development of the guilt response. Though Murphy (1937) reports numerous instances of sympathetic distress in preschool children, she found few examples of guilt or reparative behavior. Harming others usually occurred in the context of a fight or argument, and the victim was typically helped by a bystander rather than the aggressor. In the few instances of accidental harm, however, the responsible child was sympathetic or made some spontaneous attempt at reparation. A boy on a swing who knocked a girl down, for example, gave her a long ride on the swing afterwards, pushing her gently all the while. Such instances suggest that young children are capable of an immediate awareness and reaction to the harmful effects of their own behavior. There is also indirect evidence that their reaction may extend beyond the immediate situation: Children exposed to parental discipline which pointed to the harmful effects of their behavior were generally considerate of their nursery school peers (M. L. Hoffman, 1963b).[9]

Most of the 10- to 12-year-old subjects in our moral development research (M. L. Hoffman, in press; M. L. Hoffman & Saltzstein, 1967), some of which is unpublished, gave guilt responses to projective story completion items in which the transgression committed by the central figure was an act of commission (cheating, accidentally harming another) or omission (not helping a small child who later suffered as a result). In most cases the guilt feelings described by our subjects were followed immediately by the attribution to the story character of some sort of reparative behavior, which functioned to reduce his guilt. When reparation was precluded by the story conditions (it was too late for anything to be done), the guilt response was typically prolonged. (This pattern is similar to Murphy's finding, 1937, that sympathetic distress typically leads to action that diminishes the actor's affect, but if there is no action the affect is prolonged.) The central figures in the story were also often portrayed by our subjects as resolving to become less selfish and more considerate of others in the future. This suggests that one mechanism by which guilt may contribute to altruistic behavior is to trigger a process of self-examination and restructuring of values which may help strengthen one's altruistic motives.

Experimental evidence that guilt contributes to altruism has been obtained in a number of studies in which adults who were led to believe they had harmed someone showed a heightened willingness to help others. They did this by engaging in various altruistic deeds such as volunteering to participate in a research project

(Freedman, Wallington, & Bless, 1967), contributing to a charitable fund (J. W. Regan, 1971), and spontaneously offering to help a passerby whose grocery bag had broken (D. T. Regan, Williams, & Sparling, 1972). These studies are limited, since they showed only short-run effects (the altruistic deed immediately followed the guilt induction), and the subjects were all college students. Together with the story completion data for children, however, these studies support the view that guilt may result in a generalized motive for altruistic action beyond immediate reparation to the victim.

The fact that 10-year-olds in the M. L. Hoffman study (in press) show evidence of guilt over inaction is worthy of note. The central figure in the story completion items has really done nothing wrong but just happened to be present when someone needed help, and children are not often taught to feel bad over such inaction. I would suggest that the guilt the subjects projected was due to their sympathetic distress response to the victim, in combination with an awareness of what the central figure (with whom they identified) might have done to help were it not for his selfishness. Guilt over inaction thus appears to have much in common with sympathetic distress—the difference being that the observer is aware of something he could have done. Guilt over inaction is also very likely more advanced developmentally than guilt over the actual commission of an act, since the former requires the capacity to visualize something that might have been done but was not.

EXISTENTIAL GUILT

The human capacity for experiencing guilt even when no wrong has been done is illustrated still more dramatically in other situations. The well-known phenomenon of survivor guilt in natural disasters and in war is a case in point. A recent example is the Navy pilot whose right arm had been partially crippled by shrapnel, who said on being released after two years as a Vietnam war prisoner, "Getting released, you feel a tremendous amount of guilt. You developed a relationship with the other prisoners . . . and they're still there and you're going away" (*Newsweek*, 1972, p. 27).

This remark suggests that despite a person's own plight, he may feel guilty if he feels he is far better off than others. This possibility contrasts interestingly with "social comparison processes" (e.g., Festinger, 1954; Masters, 1972b), which focus on self–other comparisons in a competitive context, for example, the enhancement of one's self-esteem that may result from outperforming others. Keniston (1968) very neatly captures the essence of guilt over being relatively advantaged when he describes his sample of affluent young social activists of the mid-1960s as stressing "their shock upon realizing that their own good fortune was not shared . . . and their indignation when they 'really' understood that the benefits they had experienced had not been extended to others" (pp. 131–132). One of Keniston's respondents, in discussing some poor Mexican children he had known years earlier, vividly described his realization of relative advantage in a way that suggests its possible role in altruistic action.

. . . I was the one that lived in a place where there were fans and no flies, and they lived with the flies. And I was clearly destined for something, and they were destined for nothing. . . . Well, I sort of made a pact with these people that when I got to be powerful I might change some things. And I think I pursued that pact pretty consistently for a long time (p. 50).

I call this reaction existential guilt to distinguish it from true guilt, since the person has done nothing wrong but feels culpable because of circumstances of life beyond his control.

Existential guilt may take on some of the qualities of true guilt, however. The activist youth in Keniston's sample, for example, appears to have concluded that his privileged position makes it possible for him to do something to alleviate the condition of the less fortunate, and that if he does nothing he becomes personally responsible for helping perpetuate the conditions he deplores. For some individuals existential guilt may shade still further into a sense of individual complicity or true personal guilt, should they come to view the other's plight as due to the action of people with whom they identify, for example, parents or members of their social class.

Another example of existential guilt shading into true guilt comes from the response given by a Congressional intern to the question, Why are so many middle-class youth turned off by the very system which gave them so many advantages and opportunities?

They feel guilty because while they are enjoying this highest standard of living, American Indians are starving and black ghettoes are overrun by rats. . . . This goes on while they eat steak every day. Their sense of moral indignation can't stand this; and they realize that the blame rests on the shoulders of their class (*New Republic*, Nov. 28, 1970, p. 11).

The statements and actions of some of the white radicals of the 1960s suggest that existential guilt may at times be a far more potent motivating force than the simpler type of true personal guilt discussed earlier. Existential guilt may require continued activity in the service of alleviating human suffering rather than merely a discrete act of restitution in order to afford one a continuing sense of self-worth.[10] It also seems likely, as with true guilt, that the person who does nothing will continue to feel guilty, or will cognitively restructure the situation so as to justify himself or to deny his own relative advantage ("The other has other pleasures and enjoys living the way he does"; "He is a bad person and brought his misfortune on himself"; "I worked hard for what I have").

Another alternative may be to reduce the relative advantage by renouncing one's privileges or in other ways "identifying with the lowly." This alternative may take on the character of pure self-punishment and cease to be altruism. Indeed, for some individuals existential guilt may be an obstacle to the development of personal competence, achievement, and success. A recent study of achievement and fear-of-success motives (L. W. Hoffman, 1974) provides a possible illustration of this phenomenon. Horner's projective story cue (1968), "John finds himself at the top of his medical school class," drew the following response from a male college student: "John is perplexed upon hearing the news. He's mad that everything is so assured. Resents the fact that he's hereditarily good and others are not." If this response really does reflect guilt over competence and is representative, it might mean that existential guilt is contributing to the erosion of the competitive, individualistic ethic in the affluent highly educated group in which this ethic has traditionally been foremost.[11]

GUILT AND SYMPATHETIC DISTRESS

Though guilt and sympathetic distress differ, the preceding analysis suggests that these affective states at times overlap and enhance one another. Developmentally, guilt probably also relates to the levels of sympathetic distress discussed earlier. Thus at the second level (synthesis of empathy and role taking), the child will experience sympathetic distress when he is not responsible for the other's plight. When he is responsible for the other's distress, however, his sympathetic distress will be transformed into guilt feelings. With further cognitive development, this transformation can result from the awareness of not helping when one might reasonably have been expected to help. Eventually, with the capability of foreseeing the consequences of action and inaction, anticipatory guilt also becomes a possibility. From then on sympathetic distress may always be accompanied by some guilt, except when the situation clearly rules out the possibility of helpful action. In line with this analysis,

83 percent of the subjects in the Schwartz study (1970b) who volunteered to contribute blood marrow said afterwards that they would have felt guilty or self-critical if they had not volunteered.

Similarly, at the highest level of sympathetic distress, if the focus of concern shifts from the other's general plight to the discrepancy between it and the observer's relatively advantaged state (in the absence of moral justification), sympathetic distress may be transformed into existential guilt. Since this comparison requires "decentering," in Piaget's sense of cognitively processing two aspects of an event simultaneously, existential guilt may be developmentally more advanced than sympathetic distress. Furthermore, once the capacity for this dual self–other perspective is attained, there is no reason to believe it will be abandoned in subsequent observations of unfortunate people. Existential guilt may then become part of all future experiences of sympathetic distress.

To summarize, (1) sympathetic distress is both a necessary developmental prerequisite and a continuing part of the guilt response; (2) guilt is the synthesis of sympathetic distress and of the awareness of one's blame or relative advantage; (3) once the capacity for guilt over inaction and relative advantage is attained, guilt may be part of all subsequent responses to another's distress in situations where one thinks that he might have helped the other or that he is relatively advantaged without justification. Guilt may therefore be important in any theoretical account of altruism which stresses sympathetic distress.

Implications for Socialization: Several Hypotheses

The theory presented here, that altruistic motives develop out of the synthesis of empathic distress and the child's increasingly sophisticated cognitive sense of the other, is essentially a theory of a naturally evolving process. Under normal conditions of growing up everyone acquires the capacity for sympathetic distress, assuming he is sufficiently secure emotionally to be open to the needs of others. The child's socialization experiences may nevertheless play an important role by strengthening or weakening the child's natural empathic tendencies, shaping his developing attitudes toward others, and placing more or less stress on competing motives which may neutralize the altruistic. Though peripheral to this chapter, three hypotheses about socialization that derive directly from the theory will be briefly presented in the hope that they will stimulate needed research. They are:

1. Sensitivity to the needs and feelings of others may be fostered by allowing the child to have the normal run of distress experiences, rather than shielding him from them, so as to provide a broad base for empathic and sympathetic distress in the early years.

2. Providing the child with opportunities for role taking and for giving help and responsible care to others—these with corrective feedback when he is unable to interpret available cues—should foster both sympathetic distress and awareness of the other's perspective, as well as the integration of the two.

3. Encouraging the child to imagine himself in the other's place, and pointing out the similarities as well as differences between him and others, may also make a significant contribution to the development of altruism.

Another hypothesis is that development of altruistic motives is enhanced when the child is exposed for a long time to loved models (parents) who behave altruistically and communicate their own thoughts and feelings as well as the presumed inner states of the persons they are helping. A special case is the model of consideration displayed by the parent in relation to the child (for example, the willingness, within limits, to accept inconvenience for the sake of the child and in other ways show consideration for his needs).[12] To make altruism salient in the child's life, the model should also communicate a general and deep concern with the moral and ethical dimensions of life within the family and outside it (for example, in handling such issues as playing with unpopular children). Parents should make it clear that desired behavior in any situation can be deduced from broad principles concerning human kindness and consideration.

Since encounters with another in distress often involve conflict between the needs of the actor and the other, the child's prior experience in conflict situations, especially with peers, must play an important role in the development of altruistic motives. Does he emerge from these situations with little understanding of the other's point of view and the feeling that differences between him and the other are irreconcilable; or does he emerge with greater understanding of the other as an entity like himself having similar feelings and needs, and with the recognition that differences can be worked out mutually? The outcome of a child's conflict experience depends in part on how the conflicts are handled by parents and other socialization agents (Hoffman, 1975).

Socialization can also foster personality characteristics which may be important in certain situations in converting a disposition to help into action. Courage and autonomy, for example, may be crucial when altruism requires taking the initiative in the absence of group support (London, 1970). Children may also be trained in specific ways of aiding others in non–conflict situations by appeals to motives such as mastery and autonomy ("Big boys help others") or by pointing out positive consequences of the child's acts for the recipient ("Now he feels good"). Finally, direct reinforcement of altruistic behavior may make a positive contribution, although total reliance on this approach would presumably have the effect of making subsequent altruistic action dependent on the continuation of reinforcement.

Future research has the vital task of determining the combinations of experiences that will develop a person who both feels compassion for his fellow human beings and acts upon it.

CHAPTER 8

Beyond Morality:

PSYCHOANALYTIC REFLECTIONS ON SHAME, GUILT, AND LOVE

James Gilligan

Introduction: The Inadequacy of the Moral Perspective

Morality is dead. It killed itself; the self-criticism moral philosophy subjected itself to over the past two centuries (Hume, 1739; Kant, 1787, 1788/1952; Nietzsche, 1886/1927a, 1887/1927b; Wittgenstein, 1921) left it no honest choice but to recognize that the only knowledge possible is of scientific facts, not of moral values.

It was with the psychoanalytic investigation of neurosis that the study of morality first passed from philosophic to scientific scrutiny. It became possible through psychoanalysis to study moral experience (affects, reasoning, and behavior) empirically, as a phenomenon of human psychology; more importantly, the replacement of moralistic value judgments and condemnations with psychological understanding represented the transition to a new and higher stage of human cognitive development in the sphere of what philosophers call practical, as opposed to speculative, reason.

This historical development, and its implications for our understanding of the cognitive bases of morality, has been largely obscured by the fact that until now the psychoanalytic theory of the affective sources of morality has been seriously incomplete, since it has centered almost exclusively on the endpoint or highest stage of moral development, namely, guilt and the morality derived from that affect. It has largely ignored the precursor of guilt, namely, the affect of shame, an emotion that is much more important in the actual moral experience of most people. By *shame* I mean the feelings of inferiority, humiliation, embarrassment, inadequacy, incompetence, weakness, dishonor, disgrace, "loss of face"; the feeling of being vulnerable to, or actually experiencing, ridicule, contempt, insult, derision, scorn, rejection, or other "narcissistic wounds"; the feeling of not being able to "take care of" oneself. Jealousy and envy are members of this same family of feelings. By *guilt* I mean the feeling of having committed a sin, a crime, an evil, or an injustice; the feeling of culpability; the feeling of obligation; the feeling of being dangerous or harmful to others; and the feeling of needing expiation and deserving punishment. While a number of psychoanalysts since Sigmund Freud have written about the psychology of shame and guilt, and a number of others have written about the psychology of morality, none has explicitly attempted to integrate concepts of shame and guilt into a psychoanalytic theory of moral experience. This chapter is a brief summary of my attempt to do that; it represents both an expansion of a portion of earlier work (J. Gilligan, 1965) and a précis of parts of a forthcoming book (J. Gilligan, in prep.).

I am presenting a psychoanalytic theory of moral experience which sees morality as a force antagonistic to life and to love, a force causing illness and death—neurosis and psychosis, homicide and suicide. I see morality as a necessary but immature stage of affective and cognitive development, so that fixation at the moral stage represents developmental retardation, or immaturity, and regression to it represents psychopathology, or neurosis.

Moral beliefs and value judgments are simply the cognitive counterparts of the painful affects that underlie all morality and all neurosis, namely, shame and guilt. That is, moral judgments are motivated by shame and guilt and in turn reinforce these feelings. Shame and guilt are forms of psychic pain that are as necessary to the personality—as symptoms of illness, trauma, or danger—as physical pain is to the body. They clearly have their adaptive utility, as does physical pain. Nevertheless, like the physical defense mechanisms of the body, the mental defenses that shame and guilt motivate can be as maladaptive as the forces that initially brought them into being. People are not always protected by their symptoms and defenses, they also die from them: The pneumonia patient drowns in his own secretions; the hypermoral, depressed patient dies from the suicide motivated by his guilt feelings. The goal of a preventive and social psychiatry, like the goal of preventive medicine, can only be to reduce all forms of illness, as well as their painful symptoms, to the lowest possible level. From the standpoint of

affects, emotional health requires maturation beyond the stages of affective development at which morality in the form of shame and guilt is dominant to the stage at which morality is unnecessary, because it has been replaced by the capacity for active love of self and others.

I will use the term *morality*, then, to refer to action and thought motivated by a sense of compulsion or obligation rather than by love (spontaneous inclination or wish), and by a negative wish to avoid painful feelings (shame or guilt) rather than by a positive wish to express feelings of love. That is, by morality I mean specifically the *motivating* of behavior by the *moral emotions* of shame or guilt, and the *cognitive structuring* of social relations in terms of *moral ideas* ("ought" and "should") rather than in terms of scientific ideas (psychological understanding).

As a cognitive structure, psychoanalysis performs the same function at the scientific stage of cognitive development that morality did at the philosophic and earlier stages. This function is *providing an intellectual framework that enables one to think and act and reach conclusions and make decisions* about such universal and unavoidable questions as *how to live* and *what to do*, especially with regard to interpersonal relations. Psychoanalysis goes about this not as ethics does, by *telling* people (or inducing them to tell themselves) what they *should* do, but by *asking* them what they *want* to do. Only the psychological question is answerable, and hence meaningful. Moreover, only when people are doing what they want to do, rather than what they "should" do, can they act out of love rather than out of fear (compulsion and constraint, shame and guilt). And since the first and universal answer to the question of what one wants to do is, necessarily, "To live," the psychological question reduces to, How can people live together? What forces enhance and promote and protect life, and what forces oppose it? Not, What forces are good or evil? It is to these psychological and sociological questions that I will turn in the next section of this chapter; and the reader will not be surprised that among the most potent pathogenic, life-destroying forces we will discover are the different forms of morality.

Shame and Guilt in Culture

The idea that shame and guilt motivate opposite moral values and behavior can be illustrated and confirmed by examining anthropological studies of shame and guilt cultures. Anthropologists have used the term *shame culture* to refer to societies in which the source of moral sanctions and authority is perceived to reside in other people, in their ridicule, criticism, or contempt; in contrast, *guilt cultures* rely on an internalized conscience and its resultant conviction of sin and absolute standards of morality (Benedict, 1946, pp. 222–223).

The consensus among anthropologists is that the major moral sanction in practically all "primitive" cultures and in most Oriental ones is not guilt but shame; in fact, an internalized sense of guilt or sin seems to be confined largely to the Judeo-Christian tradition, though individuals in mixed shame-and-guilt cultures, such as the United States, can also be very sensitive to shame (Kroeber, 1948, p. 294; Piers & Singer, 1953, p. 45). I will speak of a *pure* (as opposed to *mixed*) shame culture as one in which the predominant moral sanction is shame only, not guilt; and of an *extreme* (as opposed to *mild*) shame culture as one in which experiences of shame are relatively frequent and intense.

For an example of a pure and extreme shame culture we can turn to the Kwakiutl Indians of Vancouver Island, as described by Ruth Benedict (1934/1958):

Behavior . . . was dominated at every point by the need to demonstrate the greatness of the individual and the inferiority of his rivals. It was carried out with uncensored self-glorification and with gibes and insults poured upon the opponents. . . . The Kwakiutl stressed equally the fear of ridicule, and the interpretation of experience in terms of insults. They recognized only one gamut of emotion, that which swings between victory and shame (p. 198).

Benedict points out that the Kwakiutl pursuit of self-glorification reached such grandiose extremes that it would be diagnosed in our culture as megalomania.

The Hutterites, a Protestant sect descended from an antiworldly Reformation offshoot called Anabaptism, exemplify a pure and extreme guilt culture. They are now scattered throughout the northern Middle West and southern Canada in about ninety colonies or communal farms, where they consciously attempt to adhere strictly and literally to the ethic of the New Testament. Kaplan and Plaut (1956) describe them in this way:

Religion is the major cohesive force in this folk culture. The Hutterites consider themselves to . . . live the only true form of Christianity, one which entails communal sharing of property and cooperative production and distribution of goods. The values of brotherliness, self-renunciation and passivity in the face of aggression are emphasized. The Hutterites speak often of their past martyrs and of their willingness to suffer for their faith at the present time (p. 12).

Eaton and Weil (1955) point out that along with the Hutterites' stress on religion and duty to God and society, "there is a tendency in their entire thinking to orient members to internalize their aggressive drives. Children and adults alike are taught to look for guilt within themselves rather than in others" (p. 86). Thus Eaton and Weil conclude that the Hutterites' strongly held religious faith is "responsible for the high frequency of guilt feelings" (p. 217) and that "it clearly is aggressive impulses that seem to cause the most guilt in Hutterite society" (p. 80).

Pure and extreme shame cultures place a positive value on aggressiveness toward others (war, murder, torture, and theft), and a negative value on aggression directed toward the self. The Kwakiutl, for example, engaged in headhunting, cannibalism, burning slaves alive, and undiscriminating, merciless war and murder against even totally innocent, unsuspecting, hospitable, sleeping friends, neighbors, relatives, or hosts—men, women, and children. They would "vie with each other in committing atrocities" (Boas, 1938, p. 685); their warriors "were taught to be cruel and treacherous" (Boas, n.d.). Furthermore, it seems clear that the motive for this aggressiveness was the desire to minimize or wipe out feelings of shame, humiliation, and "loss of face," and to maximize feelings of pride and social prestige; and aggressive behavior was a recognized and honored way of doing this (Codere, 1950, p. 99). The sense of shame is the fear of ridicule, and the most direct way to stop others from laughing at oneself is to make them cry.

Guilt cultures, by contrast, condemn aggression toward others, though they place a positive value on aggression directed toward the self. According to Eaton and Weil (1955, p. 141) there has not been a single case of murder, assault, or rape among the Hutterites since their arrival in America in the 1870s. Not only is physical aggressiveness banned, but even its verbal expression: "No fighting or verbal abuse is permitted. It is expected that a Hutterite man will not get angry, swear, or lose his temper" (Kaplan & Plaut, 1956, pp. 19–20). This is all the more remarkable when it is realized that the Hutterites have been constant victims of severe persecution by their neighbors everywhere they have lived. In Europe, "ghastly atrocities . . . during several periods brought the sect close to physical extinction" (Kaplan & Plaut, 1956, p. 12); nevertheless, as Kaplan and Plaut note, their martyrs are looked up to as models of saintly behavior. The Hutterites are strict, absolute pacifists, which is why emigration to this country was their only alternative to complete extinction, and since coming here many have been punished and even imprisoned for

their pacifism. They internalize their own aggressiveness in the form of feelings of guilt and sin; frequent and severe depressions; actively provoking or passively submitting to martyrdom and persecution ("moral masochism"); shaming themselves through publicly confessing their sins; punishing themselves as penance; and occasional suicides.

Shame and Guilt in History

While the Kwakiutl and many others provide examples of shame cultures, only the study of the Western tradition provides us with the opportunity to observe the developmental transition from a shame to a guilt culture within one society. Dodds (1957) has documented this transition in Greek history from an earlier shame culture, the society depicted in the *Iliad*, to a later guilt culture, classical Athens at the time of the tragedians and philosophers. Speaking of "the uninhibited boasting in which Homeric man indulges," Dodds says that

Homeric man's highest good is not the enjoyment of a quiet conscience, but the enjoyment of *tīmē*, public esteem [honor]. . . . And the strongest moral force which Homeric man knows is not the fear of god, but respect for public opinion, *aidōs* [shame or sense of shame, sense of honor]. In such a society, anything which exposes a man to the contempt or ridicule of his fellows, which causes him to "lose face," is felt as unbearable (pp. 17–18).

By the time the Greeks became a guilt culture, however, they worried not about experiencing too little pride and prestige, but too much—overweening pride or arrogance—for which they used the term *hubris*. Far from being the highest good, pride by this time was the "prime evil," as Theognis called it; the *hamartia*, or "tragic flaw," for which, in Aristotle's analysis, Sophocles' Oedipus punished himself. In the earlier Homeric shame culture's version of the Oedipus myth, however, Oedipus continued to reign in Thebes, neither punishing himself nor feeling guilty, and was eventually buried with royal honors (Dodds, 1957, pp. 36, 55)!

For the fullest development of the sense of guilt, however, we must turn from the Greeks to the Jews, for "the record amount of guilt consciousness" was brought into the world, as Nietzsche (1887/1927b) put it, by "the appearance of the Christian god" (p. 709). The greater intensity of guilt in Christian, as compared with Greek, culture is indicated by the growth in guilt-affective tone of the word *hamartia*, from "tragic flaw," the usual translation of Aristotle's meaning, to "sin," the *New Testament* meaning of the word. And long before S. Freud (1919) explained masochism as the turning of sadism against the self under the influence of guilt, scholars as different as Gibbon (1787) and Nietzsche (1887/1927b), among others, pointed out that the tortures which the early Christians imposed on themselves surpassed anything even the most cruel and ingenious tyrants could possibly have subjected them to, and demonstrated that phenomena such as martyrdom and penance were motivated not by love, but by hate directed against the self—that is, guilt (the sense of sin).

What Nietzsche called Christ's "transvaluation of values" is precisely the reversal of moral values from those held by a shame culture to those held by a guilt culture. Just as in Greece—where Socrates initiated and came to symbolize a similar moral reversal—public esteem and pride came to be valued negatively by the Christian guilt culture. It proclaimed that "the last shall be first," that is, those with least public esteem shall be valued most highly. And, as Dante, Aquinas, and Chaucer conveyed, Pride became the deadliest of the Seven Deadly Sins. Nietzsche called the Christian ethic "slave-morality," since it valued slaves and the qualities necessary to be slaves most highly, and contrasted it with the earlier, pagan "master-morality,"

which valued social status, pride, and power most highly.

However, with the emperor Constantine's conversion in 313 A.D., Christianity became the religion of the masters, not just the slaves; and the motives for becoming a Christian changed accordingly. Thus in 313 Christianity changed from a relatively pure and extreme guilt culture to a mixed shame-and-guilt culture, capable of inspiring extremes not only of masochism, as formerly, but also of sadism; of martyrdom *and* murder, saintliness *and* savagery, piety *and* power, Christ *and* Torquemada. The earlier self-sacrificing guilt culture of Christianity survived, or was revived, in only a few atypical pockets of extreme religious fervor, such as some monastic communities and sects such as the Hutterites.

Shame and Guilt in Personality

In the closing pages of *Civilization and Its Discontents* (1930), S. Freud referred to the intensification of guilt feelings as "the most important problem in the development of civilization," and stated that "the price we pay for our advance in civilization is a loss of happiness through the heightening of the sense of guilt" (p. 134). He felt that the hypertrophy of guilt was probably inevitable if civilization and, indeed, the human race, were to survive. For "the greatest hindrance to civilization," he thought, was the "inclination of human beings to be aggressive towards one another" (p. 142). And Freud theorized that beyond certain limits, the only way people could solve the problem aggression posed for their very existence was by learning to introject their aggression, which then became an unconscious sense of guilt manifesting itself as a need for punishment. S. Freud (1930) saw guilt feelings as the cause of ethics ("out of their sense of guilt" the Jews "created the overstrict commandments of their priestly religion,"

p. 127), and ethics as "a therapeutic attempt . . . an endeavour to achieve, by means of a command of the superego, something which has so far not been achieved by means of any other cultural activities" (p. 142). But the attempt to solve the problem of aggression by means of ethics is doomed to failure, Freud felt, because aggression is an instinct which must be directed toward oneself or others.

Freud had to overestimate the extent to which aggression is instinctive, because he had no theory of shame for understanding the extent to which aggression is *defensive*, the extent to which aggression is motivated by shame as a defense against opposite instinctual drives, namely, passive, dependent libidinal needs, including homosexual ones, to be loved and taken care of. Or, to conceptualize instinctual drives more consistently with current ethological and psychophysiological research, we could say that while aggressive impulses and behavior patterns are certainly programmed into the very anatomy and biochemistry of the central and autonomic nervous systems, they are more of an inborn potential that can be "released" by the appropriate "triggers" or stimuli than they are rigid, unvarying quanta of "aggressive energy." They can therefore, within certain as yet unknown biological limits, be increased or decreased by varying the stimuli from the social environment; and among these stimuli, shaming is one of the most important and least studied triggers that release our preexisting potential for aggression.

Another difference between Freud's view and my own is that whereas he saw shame and guilt as more or less parallel in their effects on behavior, I see them, with Piers (Piers & Singer, 1953), as dynamic opposites or antagonists. The differences between shame cultures and guilt cultures, cited above, illustrate the profoundly different effects these two emotions have on behavior.

The first developmental statement about shame and guilt on which there is some general psychoanalytic agreement is that the development of the capacity to experience shame precedes that of the capacity to experience guilt; that shame corresponds to an earlier and more primitive stage of psychic development than guilt does (Alexander, 1933, 1938; Erikson, 1950; Piers & Singer, 1953). On the other hand, both shame and guilt have been found by many psychoanalysts to be associated with all three stages of psychosexual development: oral (Piers & Singer, 1953), anal (Erikson, 1950), and phallic (Fenichel, 1945; Reich, 1933).

One way to integrate these observations is to view each of the three psychosexual stages as having two phases (Abraham, 1928): an earlier one associated with shame and a later one associated with guilt. The oral stage, for example, can be conceptualized as an earlier passive–receptive suckling phase, followed, when teething begins, by a sadistic-cannibalistic biting phase. We can postulate that shame arises as the motive of defense against the passive libidinal needs of the first phase of each of the three stages: oral-suckling, anal-erotic, and phallic-urethral. Guilt, in this formulation, arises as the motive of defense against the active, aggressive drives associated with the second phase of each of the three stages: oral-biting-cannibalistic-sadistic, anal-sadistic, and phallic-competitive. These distinctions may now be illustrated with examples from my own clinical practice.

1. *Schizophrenia* is a condition in which the ego is overwhelmed by *oral shame* resulting from an underlying wish for passive oral gratification. For example, one unmarried chronic undifferentiated schizophrenic woman in her late twenties said she thought "the highest form of love is the giving of a mother's milk." The most gratifying part of lovemaking to her was sucking on her lesbian lover's nipples and imagining they were her mother's. She lived at home without working, so in a

psychosocial as well as a psychosexual sense she "sucked on" her mother, who was herself alcoholic and emotionally depriving. During one acute psychotic episode she thought she was God and attempted to kill her mother. Both the delusion and the homicide attempt may be seen as desperate attempts to ward off shame. She substituted for her shame-provoking realistic image of herself as passive and dependent a fantasied image of herself as omnipotent and self-sufficient, in which she could take pride; the homicide attempt substituted active-aggressive behavior for the passive-dependent (oral suckling) behavior which caused her shame.

2. In *psychotic depressions*, the ego is overwhelmed by *oral guilt* resulting from underlying oral-sadistic-biting-cannibalistic impulses. For example, soon after one woman's psychotic depression lifted she elaborated a fantasy about a cannibalistic child who ate his playmates and killed his mother. When she was not depressed, she liked to bite her husband, often severely, when making love. She also punished herself for her oral sadism by turning it into oral masochism: She nearly starved herself to death; and the sexual act she found most gratifying (and from which she reached orgasm) was manipulating her nipples with pins, causing pain and bleeding, while she imagined that a sadistic starving Nazi general was getting milk from them by biting them. In other words, she punished herself by doing to her own nipples what she wanted to do to her mother's. Her psychosexual fixation, like the schizophrenic's, was a paradigm or metaphor of her psychosocial mode of relating to others, in that she voraciously and insatiably "gobbled up" the time, energy, patience, and love of everyone who would give it to her (including her mother, who seemed to give as endlessly as a martyr), until she "bled them dry." Unlike the schizophrenic patient, however, this psychotic's underlying impulse was aggressive rather than dependent, so that she felt guilt

rather than shame and attempted to kill herself rather than her mother.

3. In *paranoia* the ego is overwhelmed by *anal shame* caused by underlying passive anal-erotic (homosexual) wishes. For example, one woman had a chronic paranoid delusion that her sister was plotting to commit "anal lesbian rape" on her, that is, to assault her anus sexually with her finger or an enema tube. This delusion developed after the death of the patient's mother, who gave the patient enemas as a child. After her mother's death she felt extremely dependent on, and abandoned by, both her mother and her sister. She warded off the shame caused by her passive homosexual wishes by projecting them onto her sister, and also by reversing them into active-aggressive impulses: On one occasion she threw a hammer at her sister and nearly fractured her skull.

4. *Obsessive-compulsive neurosis* results from defenses, motivated by guilt, against anal-sadistic impulses. An obsessional male scientist, for example, was full of barely controlled rage, of anal-sadistic impulses to "shit all over" his colleagues and rivals, which caused him to feel so guilty that he developed constipation (both literal and figurative—i.e., procrastination, passive aggressiveness) and anal masochism. He had a block against finishing his doctoral dissertation and noticed that whenever he was able to overcome it and start writing, he first had to defecate. When his rigid obsessive defenses began to yield to therapy, he experienced several episodes of loss of anal sphincter control. He used to masturbate by inserting a toothbrush, bristles first, into his anus. This was exquisitely painful, but it was the only way he could feel intense sexual sensation. His regression to anal sexuality was itself an attempt to ward off the phallic guilt he felt after his mother divorced his father and then started behaving seductively toward him.

5. *Hysteria, sociopathy, sexual sadism, phallic narcissism,* and *pseudo-hypersexuality* (the "Don Juan" syndrome,

"nymphomania") are a related group of disorders caused by *phallic shame* resulting from an underlying early phallic-urethral wish to be passively loved, gratified, and admired sexually, including homosexually —but not to love and gratify others in return. This represents a wish to hold on to the passive-dependent position of childhood in respect to sexuality, the sense of "narcissistic entitlement," and results in feelings of sexual immaturity and inadequacy. For example, a hysterical woman with multiple conversion and dissociative symptoms was massively ashamed of her body, especially her genitals. She demanded constant reassurances from her many lovers that she was really beautiful and sexually exciting, but could never believe them when they told her she was attractive. She also had repeated unsatisfactory homosexual experiences, each of which served to reassure her—but not for long—that she was not a lesbian after all. She wanted to be loved, but not to love in return; in fact, she would be sadistic toward any man who loved her. Her passive-dependent need for narcissistic reassurances about her sexual attractiveness and adequacy, which dated back to feeling unloved by her father, were as endless as her feelings of genital shame and inferiority.

Another patient, a sociopathic male inmate of a state prison who had been repeatedly incarcerated for assault and battery, armed robbery, and attempted homicide finally acknowledged that when he was out of prison, he got so tired of being hungry and cold and sleeping in parked cars that he began wishing to be back in prison (which he soon arranged). At least there he was provided with three meals, a warm bed, and people who cared enough about him to make sure he was there at night. He had suffered chronically most of his life from enuresis, a condition which he was intensely ashamed. In prison he had had occasional homosexual experiences and was ashamed of them, too. What he wanted from women was to be

taken care of, but not to have to take care of them in any way. So the tough, sadistic, pseudo-hypermasculine behavior that got him into prison was a face-saving way of meeting passive-dependent needs, including homosexual ones, to be loved and taken care of, which he was too ashamed of to admit openly or to gratify in any less disguised way. Behind the defensive mask of aggressiveness and arrogance was a frightened, helpless, dependent little boy whose childhood need to be taken care of still remained because it had never been adequately met by anyone.

6. *Masochism* and at least some forms of defensive *homosexuality* are caused by guilt over phallic-sadistic-competitive impulses. For example, a young woman was able to reach orgasm with men only when they beat her with a belt; she was orgastic without pain only with women. When she was just entering puberty, she had felt guilty because she felt her father openly preferred her to her sister. She complained about this to him and repeatedly provoked him to punish her, which he finally did by beating her with a belt. In short, she felt so guilty about her defeat of her rival in an incestuous triangle that she could permit herself sexual pleasure only when it was accompanied by pain; the only time she did not feel this guilt was when she withdrew from heterosexual competition altogether and regressed to a relatively more innocent, though shame-provoking, lesbianism.

Shame and Guilt in Morality: Shame Ethics versus Guilt Ethics

DIFFERENCES BETWEEN SHAME ETHICS AND GUILT ETHICS

We can now advance a psychoanalytic theory of moral experience by developing the concepts of shame ethics and guilt ethics. By a *shame ethic* I mean a value system in which the most negatively valued experience is shame (humiliation), and in which the highest good is the opposite of shame, namely, pride. A *guilt ethic* is a diametrically opposite value system in which the worst evil is pride, and the highest good is humility (self-humiliation). A second difference is that what is conscious for the one is unconscious for the other. Thus, behind the conscious humility of the guilt ethic is unconscious pride, and behind the conscious arrogance and pride of the shame ethic is unconscious shame. Nietzsche (1886/1927a) understood the unconscious pride behind the conscious humility of guilt ethics, for example, when he wrote, "He who despises himself, nevertheless esteems himself thereby, as a despiser" (p. 453).

The example from history that most closely corresponds to what I mean by a guilt ethic is the moral value system enunciated by Christ; the best historical illustration of a shame ethic is the moral philosophy of Nietzsche. Speaking of Judeo-Christian ethics, S. Freud (1939) commented that "these ethical ideas cannot . . . disavow their origin from the sense of guilt felt on account of a suppressed hostility to God" (p. 134). He explained a central ethical commandment of Christ, for example, as due to guilt: "The true masochist always turns his cheek whenever he has a chance of receiving a blow" (S. Freud, 1924, p. 165).

Nietzsche's distinction between "master-morality" and "slave-morality" (1886/1927a; the following quotations are taken from p. 260) corresponds in all essentials to my distinction between shame ethics and guilt ethics, respectively. "Pride in oneself" belongs to "noble morality," he said, as does "contempt for . . . those who humble themselves, the doglike people who allow themselves to be maltreated." The noble man "honours whatever he recognizes in himself; such morality is self-glorification." Christianity he saw as "the one immortal blot of shame upon the escutcheon of humanity." However, while Nietzsche had the profoundest insight into the psychology of Christian morality before Freud

(he saw clearly that it was caused by guilt, and that the guilt in turn was caused by hostility) he failed almost completely to analyze or understand the unconscious psychological roots of his own "master-morality."

The most fundamental difference between shame ethics and guilt ethics has to do with the opposite moral valuations they make of love and hate toward oneself and others. Shame ethics place a positive value, and guilt ethics a negative value, on love of one's self—pride, egoism, narcissism. Guilt ethics value, and shame ethics devalue, love for others—altruism, sympathy, compassion (the latter two terms mean literally "suffer with," and suffering with others, of course, appeals to the guilt-ridden masochist's wish for punishment). Shame ethics value and guilt ethics devalue hatred and aggression toward others—sadism, homicide, war. Guilt ethics value and shame ethics devalue hatred and aggression toward oneself—penance, masochism, suicide, martyrdom. These relationships are summarized in Table 8.1.

MORAL DEVELOPMENT AS THE TRANSITION FROM SHAME ETHICS TO GUILT ETHICS

The most important empirical work that bears on the hypotheses I am presenting about shame and guilt ethics has been done by Piaget (1932) and Kohlberg (Chap. 2). Piaget's theory, like my own, finds evidence of two moralities. The developmentally earlier of Piaget's moral stages is *heteronomous*, when moral sanctions are perceived as coming from outside the self; the later stage is *autonomous*, when moral sanctions are perceived as being self-determined. I assume that it is reasonably clear why I would identify the first as a shame ethic and the second as a guilt ethic; the perceived source of moral sanctions alone defines them in that way. In addition, the belief at the heteronomous stage that one is subject to moral sanctions imposed by others who have more power

TABLE 8.1   Positive (+) and Negative (−) Values Placed on the Giving of Love and Hate, Pleasure and Pain, and Life and Death, toward Oneself and Others, by Shame Ethics and Guilt Ethics, Together with the Resulting Attitudes and Behaviors

	Shame Ethics	*Guilt Ethics*
	Love, Pleasure, Life	
Toward Self	(+) Egoism—pride, narcissism, boasting, megalomania, self-aggrandizement, sense of "narcissistic entitlement," selfishness. Hedonism. Self-reliance.	(−) Humility—self-humiliation, self-effacement, selflessness. Asceticism. Self-neglect.
Toward Others	(−) Contempt—lack of love toward others, rejection, abandonment, and neglect of others. Indifference toward the pleasure of others, as in rape.	(+) Altruism—nurturance, philanthropy, charity, sense of responsibility and obligation toward others, rescue fantasies, need to be a messiah or Good Samaritan.
	Hate, Pain, Death	
Toward Self	(−) Avoidance of punishment—feeling of innocence. Self-defense.	(+) Wish for punishment—feelings of guilt and sinfulness; self-punishment through penance, suicide; punishment from others, through masochism, martyrdom. Self-sacrifice.
Toward Others	(+) Hostility toward others. Sadism. Homicide. War.	(−) Nonviolence. Tenderness. Pacifism.

is tantamount to seeing oneself as passive rather than active, dependent rather than independent, weak rather than powerful—in short, the self-image that causes shame. The opposite of all these qualities is true of Piaget's internalized autonomous morality.

Kohlberg's studies (Chap. 2) of the development of moral reasoning also indicate the existence of two types of moral motives, invoked by his subjects in justifying judgments about moral dilemmas: (1) the motive to avoid sanctions that are perceived as coming from *others* (what I am calling shame); and (2) the motive to avoid sanctions that are perceived as coming from the *self* (guilt). "Stage 1 value assumptions [for example, the most primitive ones] are externalized from the motivational point of view" (Kohlberg, 1963a, p. 20). In succeeding stages, "motivation for rule obedience or moral action . . . represents successive degrees of internali-

zation of moral sanctions" (Kohlberg, 1968c, p. 489). In my terms, his stages range from a Nietzschean "will to power" shame ethic (Stage 1), in which the goal is to be on the side with the most power through "conformity to power-figures," to a guilt ethic (Stage 6), in which the motive is to "avoid self-condemnation" (Kohlberg, 1963a, p. 20) from one's own conscience (guilt). The intervening stages represent variations of a shame ethic, as they are motivated by concern with sanctions coming from others, combined with increasing sensitivity to guilt as one goes up the developmental ladder. The middle stages, in other words, are mixed shame-and-guilt ethics which are transitional between the relatively pure and extreme shame ethic of Stage 1 and the guilt ethic of Stage 6. At Stage 2, for example, the individual is motivated to conform "to obtain rewards from others"; at Stage 3, to "avoid disapproval and dislike by others"; at Stage 4, to "avoid censure by legitimate authorities and resultant guilt" (in my terms, of course, shame, since both the censure and moral authority at Stage 4 are still largely external to the self); and at Stage 5, to maintain respect from the community and avoid disrespect (shame). Thus, Kohlberg's data are in agreement with my own conclusions in showing that (1) *the motive for morality is to avoid either shame or guilt, not to express active love;* (2) *the developmental trend is from an earlier, shame-motivated morality to a later, guilt-motivated one.*

Kohlberg summarizes much of the research on the relationship between guilt and the development of moral reasoning with the conclusion that projective measures of internal guilt show the same general age trends and social correlates as shown by measures of maturity of moral judgment (Kohlberg, 1968c, p. 493).

To analyze more specifically the relationship between shame and guilt ethics and Kohlberg's stages, let us remember that a shame ethic aims to *maximize* self-love or pride and hatred and cruelty toward others, and to *minimize* love of others (altruism, romantic love) and the receiving of anger or punishment. Thus, it is typical of a shame ethic to be motivated, as Stage 1 morality is, by the desire to avoid punishment. Being punished by others is humiliating, and while punishment and humiliation relieve guilt, they only intensify shame. It is also consistent with a shame ethic that Stage 1 subjects would wish to maximize their own power, since that increases their prestige and pride.

Eichmann, for example, whose moral judgments from the Jerusalem trial transcript Kohlberg (1969b) scored mostly at Stage 1, exemplifies all the characteristics of a shame ethic:

1. *Maximization of anger toward others:* "If we had killed all the Jews, I would say, 'Good, we have destroyed an enemy' "— the speaker was, in fact, a mass murderer.
2. *Minimization of anger toward self:* Ab-

sence of self-blame and wish to avoid punishment from others—"I regret nothing"; "I am neither a murderer nor a mass murderer"; "It would be pointless to blame me"; "we carried on a proper war."
3. *Minimization of love for others:* Indifference, contempt—". . . the people who were loaded on these trains meant nothing to me."
4. *Maximization of self-love:* Maximization of pride through identification with and conformity to power figures—"[Hitler's] success alone proves to me that I should subordinate myself to this man."

The same considerations may be seen to apply, *mutatis mutandis*, to Kohlberg's next three stages—all of which wish to maximize gratification, approval, or respect from others and to minimize disapproval or censure from them.

When we come to principled morality, however, especially Stage 6, we have to make a Copernican revolution. Here the motive is to avoid disapproval from the *self*, not from others; and the way one does this is precisely the opposite from the way one avoids disapproval or punishment from others. In fact, clinical experience suggests that the way to avoid self-disapproval and self-punishment (guilt) may be precisely *by* receiving punishment and disapproval from others. And that is what the historical (and/or mythical) experience of such Stage 6 exemplars as Socrates and Christ would seem to suggest. They lived the principles of a guilt ethic:

1. *Maximization of anger toward self:* Socrates committed suicide, though he could easily have avoided it; Christ predicted and exposed himself to his own martyrdom; both refused either to defend themselves or to allow their disciples to.
2. *Minimization of anger toward others:* Both practiced nonviolence and forgiveness toward their persecutors, "turned the other cheek," and refused to let their followers be violent, punitive, or vengeful.
3. *Maximization of love for others:* Both expressed and acted on attitudes of concern, compassion, and love both for those they

were trying to help and for their enemies; both put their love of others, and of the community at large, ahead of self-love.

4. *Minimization of love for self:* Both expressed conscious attitudes of humility—Socrates said, "All I know is that I know nothing," and subordinated his self-interest and survival to what he saw as the overriding needs of the *polis;* Christ identified with the poor, humble, and powerless rather than with the arrogant and powerful.

It is important to note that behind the conscious arrogance of Eichmann lay an image of himself as actually being mediocre and insignificant ("I was merely a little cog in the machinery", "I am a man of average character", "I subordinated myself to [Hitler]"). And behind the conscious intellectual humility of Socrates lay the implicit awareness of his vast intellectual superiority over his interlocutors; in fact, this superiority may well have been one of the characteristics which most infuriated them and which Socrates was able to use to provoke them to martyr him—since despite all his humility and avowals of ignorance, he made intellectual fools of them, humiliated and shamed them. Behind Christ's humility—his conscious identification with the poor and humble and powerless—lay an easily discernible pride amounting to a kind of megalomania; he believed he was the Son of God!

Since only a small fraction (10 to 15 percent) of adults mature to Kohlberg's highest stage of moral development, in the cognitive sense, it might be assumed that an even smaller number mature beyond that to what I am calling the scientific (psychological) stage. And if this is so, is most of humanity limited to being motivated by shame and guilt, with their attendant neuroses, rather than being capable of what I am calling active love?

I would say that the answer is yes, and that the history of man's inhumanity to man (including himself) is the surest proof of it. Nevertheless, not everyone is inhuman to everyone all the time, and it is important to point out that there are cultures with little shame or guilt: A culture may be "immature" (less highly developed, both cognitively and affectively) without being "sick" (i.e., plagued by behavior patterns that threaten its own or others' survival). Neurosis is *relative* immaturity, such as the attempt to solve the problems and survive the stresses of an advanced stage of development with the solutions of a more immature stage, the failure to develop the (affective, cognitive, and behavioral) capacities that are needed to solve the problems one currently faces. Until now the human species may not have needed to utilize its most mature cognitive and affective capacities (love and psychological understanding) in order to survive. Now, however, our maturation to the scientific stage of cognitive development in the sphere of speculative reason (physics, chemistry, biology) poses problems of such magnitude (nuclear and chemical warfare, overpopulation) that the continued survival of the human species is more doubtful than assured. In this situation, nothing threatens humanity more than the continued survival of the psychological anachronism called morality. And yet, paradoxically, nothing threatens humanity more than the accomplished central fact of the modern world, namely, the death of morality. In this situation nothing is more urgently needed than the development of the more mature affective and cognitive capacities, love and psychological understanding. We cannot solve the problems of a scientific age with the solutions of a philosophic one.

Conclusion: Beyond Morality to Love

What, then, does psychoanalysis have to contribute to our understanding of morality? One way to answer that question would be to ask what a psychoanalyst might say to Heinz, the protagonist of one of Kohlberg's moral dilemmas (see Chap. 2), if Heinz came and asked what he should do—steal the drug or let his wife die? The analyst, I suggest, would ask Heinz what his hang-up over the issue of "should" was all about, and he would wonder if Heinz were not asking himself what he "should" do (an unanswerable, and therefore meaningless, question) as a way to avoid asking himself a question that is emotionally more threatening but cognitively more relevant, namely, "What do I *want* to do, and *why* do I want to do it?" The analyst, in other words, would wonder what defensive purpose, what rationalization, all this moralizing was serving; what unacceptable wish it was attempting to hide. And the analyst would be much more concerned with attempting to understand, and to help Heinz understand, what forces were motivating him to make the choices he was making. To the psychoanalyst the preoccupation with intrinsically unanswerable moral questions and dilemmas is a symptom of neurotic resistance against the much more difficult task of attaining self-knowledge.

Shapiro (1965) illustrates this resistance in his discussion of the cognitive style of obsessive-compulsive neurosis. When obsessional neurotics are confronted by the necessity for a decision, they

typically attempt to reach a solution by invoking some rule, principle, or external requirement which might . . . provide a "right" answer. [If they can find such a principle] the necessity for a decision disappears as such; that is, it becomes transformed into the purely technical problem of applying the correct principle. . . . In an effort to find such requirements and principles, the obsessional neurotic will invoke morality, "logic," social custom and propriety, the rules of "normal" behavior (especially if he is a psychiatric patient), and so on. In short, he will try to figure out what he "should" do (Shapiro, 1965, pp. 46–48).

Such persons try to deal with decision making as if it were simply a technical problem—the search for the "right" answer. But, of course, there is no right answer in interpersonal relations, in the sense

that there is a right answer to a technical problem. "The decision, as much as he shrinks from the fact, comes to a choice, a preference" (Shapiro, 1965, p. 48). Why does he shrink from that fact? Because "the act of decision, which, by its nature, pivots around wants . . . can only be extremely discomforting" to the person who wants to remain unconscious of his wishes because he suffers from neurotic feelings of guilt or shame" (Shapiro, 1965, p. 46).

The goal of Heinz's psychoanalysis, correspondingly, would be to enable him to understand himself and his feelings and wishes; to grow beyond the passing of moral value judgments and to make his choices on the basis of an honest acknowledgment of what he wants to do, coupled with a realistic assessment of the price he may have to pay for any given choice. In practice this does not lead to a regression to a moral egoism which needlessly sacrifices other people's wishes to those of the self; instead it leads *beyond* a moral altruism which needlessly sacrifices the wishes of the self to those of others.

In other words, psychoanalytic insight does not lead to criminality, to the creation of Eichmanns or Iagos. On the contrary, the Eichmanns and Iagos of this world do what they do precisely because they are too ashamed to admit what they really want, which is to be loved and taken care of, and therefore they attempt to conceal their passive-dependent libidinal needs behind a defensive mask of exaggeratedly active-aggressive behavior. Iago, for example, felt shamed by Othello on several counts: He had been passed over for promotion and therefore was treated like an inferior; he had jealous suspicions that Othello was sleeping with his wife, and so on. What Iago really wanted was to be loved and respected rather than shamed and humiliated. Similarly, the prison inmate whose case I described committed violent crimes as a face-saving way of getting himself into prison, where he knew he would be taken care of. If, however, the potential criminal can acknowledge and find more successful ways to gratify his underlying wishes, his defensive need for criminality disappears. In other words, the psychology of criminality (or immorality) can be understood in terms of the psychology of shame.

The same considerations apply to the active-aggressive drives that underlie guilt. Nobody, for example, is more narcissistic and orally sadistic than a deeply depressed, guilt-ridden, person; the only reason the guilt in depression exists is because of the underlying sadism. However, that sadism itself is caused or at least intensified by shame; that is, it results from the frustration of a shame-induced, infantile, unrealistic, and insatiable sense of narcissistic entitlement. In other words, *intense shame always lies behind intense guilt; shame feeds the anger that feeds the guilt. If shame, like the guilt and unfulfilled narcissistic wishes, can be openly and honestly acknowledged and more successful ways found to gratify or outgrow, and hence renounce, the underlying wishes, the need for both morality and immorality will disappear.*

The fundamental distinction between moral and psychological thought is that morality structures interpersonal relations so as to set up moral dilemmas or mutually exclusive choice situations (in which one person can be helped only if another is hurt), even where such dilemmas are not forced on the self by objective circumstances, whereas psychology works constantly to transcend the dichotomy between egoism and altruism, shame ethics and guilt ethics, by finding ways to structure relationships not only in thought but in reality, so that the individual can meet other people's needs through meeting his own.

We can see this more clearly the moment we begin analyzing any real situation, as opposed to hypothetical moral dilemmas. Let us consider, for example, the trial of Socrates, and then a clinical illustration. Socrates, as described in the *Apol-*

ogy and *Crito*, structured his relationships with others in moral terms—that is, in terms that made it appear that he must either destroy himself or the state (the law), but that both could not survive. And yet this interpretation is clearly not an even remotely realistic reading of the situation Socrates was actually in. It is abundantly clear that he could have saved himself, without destroying either his integrity or the state (he did not have the *power* to destroy the state!) in a variety of different ways before, during, and after his trial. He could have left Athens instead of being condemned to death and also after being condemned, although even that stark choice (between death and exile) was a last resort which he could have avoided had he not been such a moral masochist. And Socrates' notion that if he escaped from jail, he would destroy the laws and the state (see *Crito*) represents the overestimation of one's own destructive power (together with the unconscious pride that accompanies such a notion) with which we are familiar in guilt-ridden persons. In fact, his idea would have been called a delusion of guilt if he had escaped and then thought that by doing so he had destroyed either the state or the law.

In other words, morality creates the very dilemmas it claims to be able to resolve; and it does not resolve these dilemmas, for it structures them so that they are intrinsically insoluble, in the sense that *somebody* (oneself or others) ends up being hurt or destroyed. A person who is reasoning morally creates these dilemmas either by misperceiving situations, so that he sees dilemmas as existing where they do not, or by manipulating people so that dilemmas do come to exist in the manner of self-fulfilling prophecies, or most commonly, by doing both, as Socrates did. Because morality is forever saying that one must either hurt oneself in order to help others (guilt ethic), or hurt others in order to help oneself (shame ethic), it tends to create situations in which that stark either/or choice becomes increasingly necessary, even if it could have been avoided earlier. A psychotherapeutic approach, on the other hand, is always directed toward the *resolution* of conflicts, the *transcending* of dilemmas, and the *solving* of problems.

Perhaps I can make this clearer by describing what I see as the difference between a moral relationship and a love relationship. A *moral relationship* is one in which there is a conflict between egoism and altruism. Morality claims to resolve this conflict: shame ethics by prescribing egoism; guilt ethics by prescribing altruism. Neither is a true resolution of the conflict, because both end in the sacrifice of oneself or another.

A *love relationship* is one in which the conflict between egoism and altruism has been transcended, because through meeting one's own needs one meets another's, and vice versa. The paradigm of this is sexual love, in which it is through the very actions by which one receives pleasure that he gives it as well. But the same principle applies in all love relationships, in parent-child love, to take one example. A clinical case may serve to illustrate this. A mother sought therapy because she was severely depressed and suicidal.

Prior to that time, she had felt an almost limitless obligation to "give" to her children, so that she had not set reasonable limits on their behavior, or disciplined them in any effective way, with the result that they were engaging in behavior that was really dangerous to them, and were behaving toward her in ways that made it impossible for her to enjoy living with them. It was obvious that her need to discipline them and make reasonable demands on them corresponded to their need to have her help them control their potentially dangerous impulses and learn how to live with other people. Her self-sacrificing, altruistic behavior not only had not met her needs, but had not met theirs either. It was only when she could see this that she could begin the process of transforming her relationship with them from one of guilt-motivated morality to one of love.

If mental and emotional health and maturity mean anything, they seem to me to mean the ability to structure one's relationships with others in such a way that it is through meeting one's own needs that one meets others' needs as well. And this can be accomplished only through love, not through morality.

CHAPTER 9

A Holistic Approach to Moral Development and Behavior

Elizabeth Léonie Simpson

A Holistic Theory
of Moral Development

In Chapter 2, Kohlberg argues that the structure or formal properties of moral thought provide the most adequate means of describing moral growth. This chapter proposes a transformation of Kohlberg's cognitive-developmental theory into what might be called a *holistic* one, which is, to put it awkwardly, a cognitive-affective-conative developmental theory because it tries to give equal deference to three aspects of human personality: thought, emotion, and motivation. Within this theoretical variant, moral development is seen as a substantial aspect of ego development; and ego, as Loevinger (1966) has written, is conceived not as "one interesting personality trait among many, but as the master trait" (p. 195), second only to intelligence in accounting for human variability.

Moral maturity, then, is not simply the attainment of principled autonomy, but in its most advanced form implies the achievement of an integrated identity. In making choices, the morally mature person might well be guided by Rollo May's three moral questions (1969):

Does the proposed way of acting make for the *integration* of the individual as a totality? Does it—at least potentially—make for the expansion of *interpersonal* meaning in his life? . . . Would this way of acting, if adopted by other people (in principle, all of mankind), make for an increase of interpersonal meaning? (p. 158).

It seems to me that the advent and utilization of moral reasoning represent a complex biosocial process that is profoundly involved with the emotional, as well as the intellectual, growth of the individual. In one sense, of course, it has always been possible to integrate emotional aspects of personality into Piaget's studies (1932) and Kohlberg's work, since, regardless of the perceived locus of the source of moral authority, the maturing individual learns to associate anxiety with his own deviance, and moral indignation with the deviance of others (see MacRae, 1954, for example, and such investigators of guilt as M. L. Hoffman, 1970b, and Rawlings, 1970a). But emotion and motivation are implicated in morality in other ways. For example, the structure that Kohlberg posits seems intimately related to universal conative structures such as the one described by

Maslow (1954) in his well-known hierarchy of human needs. If this is the case, then individuals who remain motivated by unfulfilled psychological needs may not be *able* to function at higher levels of moral development, regardless of their stage of cognitive development. These needs may be isolated as an important mediating factor which shapes the effects of environmental conflict on moral reasoning and behavior.

MASLOW'S HIERARCHY OF NEEDS

Maslow (1954, 1962) describes four fundamental psychic needs of man: (1) *survival*, (2) *security*, (3) *belongingness* or *affiliation*, and (4) *esteem* (further differentiated into "esteem from others," or status within the group, and "self-esteem," based on the individual's sense of competence or mastery). To state Maslow's theory in oversimplified terms, as each of these prepotent needs is gratified, the individual moves to a higher motivational level. The individual's perception of his needs, rather than their objective reality (except insofar as that reality affects the individual's perception), is what defines them. When the satisfaction of these basic needs can be taken for granted, the person is freed to utilize his abilities to the fullest, that is, to actualize his potential as a human being. The needs which then motivate him are growth-producing rather than deficiency-compensating.

KOHLBERG'S MORAL REASONING TYPOLOGY

Kohlberg's cognitive scheme of moral development describes a structure of morality in which the acquisition of new modes of thought is dependent upon the reorganization and displacement of preceding modes through a self-constructive process of organism-environment interactions. Three levels succeed one another in developmental sequence: the *preconventional*, the *conventional*, and the *postconventional*. The first two levels are grounded in external authority, and the third is based

on internal principles. The three levels, in turn, each have two stages, which have been elaborated by Kohlberg in Chapter 2.[1] Although the stages are ordered in a given sequence, they are not age-specific. One may find, for instance, examples of Stage 1 thinking (goodness or fairness for the sake of escaping punishment from external authorities) even among adults. Aeschylus was expressing Stage 1 thinking when he wrote these lines in the *Oresteia*:

Cast not from your walls
All high authority; for where no fear
Awful remains, what mortal will be just?

Kohlberg claims that the stages he has delineated are universal—that all peoples go through the same stages in the same order —although not all achieve the ultimate goal of moral maturity. That different cultural groups may be *defined* out of this achievement and Kohlberg's paradigm— with its prize of principled reasoning biased in favor of industrial Western man— has been suggested by a recent analysis of Kohlberg's writings and scoring manuals (Simpson, 1974).

THEORETICAL CONGRUENCE BETWEEN KOHLBERG AND MASLOW

Like Maslow, Kohlberg refers to the types he has delineated as an invariant developmental sequence, and related research has supported his claim (Turiel, 1966, 1969). Like Maslow, he holds that at any particular time most people operate primarily at a single level and that higher-level functioning replaces, rather than accrues to, lower states. Other parallels exist between the two typologies; Table 9-1 shows a well-defined congruence between Kohlberg's description (1963a) of the motivational aspects of moral development, that is, the motives mentioned by subjects in justifying moral action at each of the stages, and the typology of motives identified from Maslow's clinical studies and further supported by Aronoff (1967), Knutson (1972), and Simpson (1971a).

TABLE 9.1   Parallels between Motivational Aspects of Kohlberg's and Maslow's Theories

Kohlberg: Stages of Motives for Moral Action	Maslow: Hierarchy of Needs
1. Fear of punishment by another	1. Physiological needs
2. Desire to manipulate goods and obtain rewards from another	2. Security needs
3. Anticipation of approval or disapproval by others	3. Belongingness or affiliation needs
4. Anticipation of censure by legitimate authorities, followed by guilt feelings	4. Need for esteem from others
5. Concern about respect of equals and of the community	5. Need for self-esteem from sense of competence
6. Concern about self-condemnation	6. Need for self-actualization

Kohlberg's Stages 1 and 2 are congruent with Maslow's two lower levels of need. Doing good is first seen as a way to survive, a way to avoid damaging punishment from external forces with power and authority. Later, at Level 2, goodness becomes a means of controlling the contingent rewards provided by outside agents. This control is sought by the individual who feels that he lives in a basically insecure and untrustworthy world. At Stages 3 and 4, conventional morality, persons choose ways of behaving that will be approved by members of their group or by the legitimate authorities who sanction the existing traditional rules, norms, and laws. Conventional-level reasoning derives from the dominant need to belong, to be accepted as a legitimate member of a stable group or groups. At the level of postconventional reasoning, the individual seeks more from the community group than simple affiliation; he wants to receive a good name and positive approval, from the esteem of those with whom a social contract has been made and honored. Finally at the highest stage, the individual is motivated by his need for a sense of inner competence or mastery, and he reasons at the universal principled level. To violate his principled moral reasoning would conflict with his *own* image of how he should behave, rather than with the expectations of someone else. The self-actualizing person, impelled by the need to utilize his highest capacities, will reason at the autonomous, principled level because he defines moral competence in that way.

RELATED AND NEEDED RESEARCH

The hierarchy of moral reasoning has been related to various other developmental sequences—for example, to levels of political development (Lockwood, Chap. 18; 1970), and to sexual aspects of moral reasoning (C. F. Gilligan, Kohlberg, Lerner, & Belenky, 1971), for instance. Van den Daele (1968) has found correlations with levels of ego development, and Sullivan, McCullough, and Stager (1970) have found low but suggestive relationships between the moral stages, Loevinger's ego-development stages (1966), and Harvey, Hunt, and Schroder's levels (1969) of conceptual complexity.

Nowhere, however, has the relationship between emotional development and cognitive development in the moral domain been explored empirically, although, as I have shown here, one can reasonably infer an association between the developmental stages of Maslow's hierarchy of basic needs and the levels of moral reasoning conceptualized by Kohlberg. Nowhere, indeed, has the question been seriously examined why older individuals fixate at a low level of moralization, rather than developing to moral maturity. (As with other types of cognitive development, the general assumption has been made that later environmental stimulation can increase growth only in a limited way because individual plasticity tends to decrease with age. See, for example, Ausubel, 1958.) Nor have the conditions of developmental regression of moral functioning been explored empirically. These are areas in which the hypothesized relationship between psychic deprivation and moral development may have considerable importance.

If the individual remains fixated at a particular moral level, would consistent gratification of his central needs, so that he moves to the next motivational level, facilitate his continuing moral growth? If he regresses to a lower level than his norm, can that moral retreat be associated with changed inner and/or external environmental circumstances? For example, is a man who has lost his job, his health, or his wife—or any other victim of social or physical catastrophe—the same man morally that he was previously? Although motivational or need level remains generally constant for most people, situational factors must enter into the maintenance or failure of maintenance of that level. And if need gratification is related to stage of moral development in some causal way, facilitating the first should also affect the second.

Further indications of the affective-cognitive association in moral development may be found in Kohlberg's cross-cultural studies of children in Taiwan, Turkey, Yucatan, and Mexico, as well as in his cross-social class studies within the United States (1968a, 1971b). In village, peasant, and tribal communities, Kohlberg did not find the two highest stages of autonomous and principled development. The absence of these stages may be culturally determined—but not simply, as Edel (1968) suggests, because these cultures lack the emphasis on individual rights, democracy, and individual conscience which has characterized Western European culture in the last two centuries. It is also likely that preindustrial and traditional societies do not provide their members with means for gratifying the basic psychic needs that would allow the development of motivation toward personal growth and the values of equality and justice, which are the core of autonomous moral judgment. Evidence for this formulation may be found in Kohlberg's report (1968a) that children of low socioeconomic status are slower than higher-status children in passing through his stages of moral development, as well as less likely to achieve the highest levels. Evidence supporting this analysis also appears in research indicating that delinquents do not show expected age-developmental changes in moral reasoning (Selman, 1974). Although neither Kohlberg nor Selman infer the following relationship, from my revised version of the cognitive-developmental theory it can be reasoned simply that lower-socioeconomic-status children and delinquents have been less able to satisfy the psychic needs that must be met before higher moral development can occur.

Viewed from the perspective of personal emotional history, the commission of evil also appears to be rooted in total personality, not simply in limited powers of reasoning. He who does evil is someone who has been convinced by experience that evil is likely to be done him, or who believes deeply that it has already been done him—that the world is an unsafe, rejecting, hateful place over which he has little or no control. If he believes that he has humane principles, he manages to exclude from the category of humanity the classes of persons to whom he does not wish to apply them—those who are in out-groups and foreigners, either culturally, racially, or ideologically. Careful reasoning alone will not make a human moral.

Reasons can also be a shelter, as we all know, especially when they are developed after the fact and are applied to our own behavior or to that of someone in whom we have an ego investment. In any case, reasons are inseparable from the personality of the reasoner, whether they apply to his own behavior or that of others. They are grounded not in the situation in which decisions are made, but in the reasoner's psychic definition of past experience, and that psychic definition frequently crosses all boundaries of rationality. Passionate irrationality in the name of impassioned reason occurs in the market, the classroom, and in science, as well as elsewhere, and often unconsciously.[2]

Moral Competence and Irrationality

According to Kohlberg (1969b, 1971b), the basic dimensions of the social environment which facilitate the development of moral reasoning are *role-taking opportunities*—opportunities to participate in what is socially new and cognitively challenging to the individual. Hence, in rural or preindustrial societies where social structure and roles are relatively simple and stable, the life experience of the child may be less conducive to the formation of higher cognitive-moral structures. Turiel (1966) has pointed out that structural change occurs when the individual confronts reasoning just one level above his own on the developmental scale. But, as Maccoby (1968) has written, the exact conditions which stimulate or retard movement through the stages have not yet been fully spelled out.

It is my hypothesis that there are at least two major requisites to moral progress, apart from role-taking opportunities or direct exposure to specific levels of moral reasoning. One requisite is the gratification of basic psychic needs. A second, derivative, condition is the cultivation of *imagination*—the use of the power to create—which increases the sense of environmental mastery and self-esteem.

Kohlberg (1968a) has suggested that the person who understands justice and how to reason about it in accordance with particular principles is most likely to behave justly. But rationality by itself is not necessarily the progenitor of positive social relationships. In his own eyes, authoritarian 'enry 'iggins was a reasonable man.

In the eyes of much of the nation, so was Lieutenant Calley. In some cases at least, irrationality may be more useful socially. Schuman and Harding (1964), for example, found in a series of studies of prejudice in Boston that "irrational" respondents tended to be more favorable to minorities than did "rational" ones (see also Scott, 1958). While linked to cognitive development, altruism is also firmly associated with nonrational positive affect such as sympathy or empathy (B. S. Moore, Underwood, & Rosenhan, 1973), feelings of success, or good feelings arising from a variety of circumstances (Rosenhan, 1972; Rosenhan, Moore, & Underwood, Chap. 13). Sustained commitment to prosocial causes, observed in a naturalistic context, seems to be based on affect, not cognition (Rosenhan, 1970, 1972). (See Wispé, 1972, for a variety of discussions about the origins, forms, and correlates of prosocial behavior.)

Elsewhere (Simpson, 1971b) I have described in detail the way in which the utilization of nonrational processes may foster the development of the sense of competence and self-esteem which, in turn, becomes the basis for intellectual, social, and moral growth. Therapists, for example, have used many creative processes, to the benefit of their clients: working with paints, crayons, or clay, body movement, guided fantasy, or simply unfettered verbal communication. Vich and Rhyne (1967) describe how the use of art can bring about changes in the individual's self-concept and interpersonal concepts.

Further support for an important relationship between imagination and generalized moral development is found in work by Kohlberg and two of his collaborators (Rest, Turiel, & Kohlberg, 1969), who found that children tend to prefer levels of moral thinking that are above their own stage of development. Since these researchers also found that the children did not *comprehend* what they preferred if it was more than one stage above their own —that is, they could neither repeat the reasoning accurately nor explain it—the choices they expressed seem clearly to be based on imaginative reaching rather than on reasoning.

Although McClelland's work (1953) on the need for achievement (in which individuals are taught to fantasize about doing things well and in which the images are then tied to reality) is a notable exception (see also Kolb, 1965), the fantasy life of the learner as a force for competence is typically overlooked in our objective, sense-based, fact-oriented society. There has been good reason for this: Freedom is often a seduction, and so it may be for some aspects of free-floating imagination. Unlimited and undefined, imagery can drift into the reverie of an endless, confusing, quicksand trap. But fantasy bottomed and bounded may reveal us to ourselves and others to us as well.

How deeply irrational processes are embedded in our rational life and in developing biosocial cognitive skills is well-described in Flavell's studies (1968) of role taking in children between 8 and 10 years of age. Imagination plays an integral part in the cognitive reorganization of these children and indeed is used instrumentally in the application of new modes of thinking to the solution of interpersonal problems. According to Flavell, children develop the capacity to imagine themselves in the place of another through a biosocial maturational process. By age 10 they are also beginning to understand that role taking functions reciprocally and that another can take their point of view at the same time that they are taking the other's—a more complicated process. Thus, children at this stage of development can not only imagine what someone else will do in a given situation but can also realize that the other is capable of taking into account what *they* are likely to do, think, and feel; they realize that empathy can be one-sided, two-sided, or a transactional process.

Although he does not use the term "imagination," Kohlberg (1967b) himself

theorizes that higher levels of moral reasoning require imaginative thinking, since he finds that some form of formal operational thought, the ability to abstract, is a developmental prerequisite for even conventional moral judgment. He describes the characteristics of conventional morality (usually achieved between the ages of 9 and 13) as moral stereotyping, empathic moral definition, sensitivity to and self-guidance by anticipated approval or disapproval of others, and identification with authority and its goals. All of these characteristics require the capacity to imagine —to project oneself into the being of others—to empathize. Selman (1974) has also demonstrated that empathy and role taking are prerequisite to Stage 3 moral reasoning.

In their national study of public reactions to Calley's trial, Kelman and Lawrence (1972) give a vivid example of the use of empathy in decision making at the conventional level. Those who disapproved of the trial because they believed it was unfair to hold Calley individually responsible for My Lai identified with him as a "little man," a "simple soldier" of relatively little education and low socioeconomic status who was doing "what normal people would and should have done": accepting "the authorities' definition of the situation and its requirements" (p. 209). That minimum imaginative skill is required to attain conventional morality suggests that the capacity to generate freer images and relationships among them would assist the child to reach principled and autonomous moral levels. It is also entirely possible that the rigid identification with role models which prevents the individual from moving upward to principled autonomy is a common failure of an imagination which has snapped shut, trapping the model and the roletaker. Permanent identification is such an extreme form of empathy that it implies negation of empathy.

The deficiency of conventional morality is its inability to let a role *go*, especially when the role is invested with authority. I am he simply because I can enter his experience; I am myself because I can withdraw from it. I can also withdraw in fantasy from aspects of *myself*, and there are times when this is developmentally necessary or helpful. Throughout the lifespan of both sexes there are transitions whose locks would provide easier passages with the use of anticipatory imagination, such as practice in the claim and release of roles such as parent, child, student, friend, or worker (cf. Erikson's life stages, 1968).

Imagination can provide a tentative morality as well, which, like anticipatory socialization, allows the individual to assume a point of view and a set of values before he actually acquires them, so that he may taste, test, and explore them without inappropriate or permanent commitment. Sometimes imagination gets locked into roles which never existed or which existed only in the past. Fantasy provided mythical races in National Socialist Germany, the *Deutsche Volk*, and in Enoch Powell's twentieth-century England. Mythic imagination endowed the affluent Buddhist kingdoms of Ceylon, Burma, and Thailand with false inscriptions which glorify, rather than record, the past; American history textbooks have done the same thing. In these cases, as in permanent identification with others, imagination has failed, for, as Harvey Cox (1969) has said, fantasy's job is to operate a "dialectic between the real and the possible" (p. 60).

Imagination as Ethicogenic

Imagination is ethicogenic in the sense that it helps to form both the conceptual and the behavioral boundaries of the moral universe. It is implicated in moral behavior in many ways, including its role as a substitute for action. As David Bakan (1969) has recognized, the thinking of evil is not evil. Evil is action, and fantasy may serve

as a safe outlet for antisocial feeling, in lieu of behavior. Contrived or imposed imagination is not at all the same thing. Pornography, for example, ultimately may be seen as immoral not only because it is frequently sadistic but also because, like other bad art, it depicts life as forced-choice categories, and human relations as extremes without subtlety. Pornography may be condemned on ethical grounds because it destroys imagination, the capacity to fantasize for oneself, and hence to choose one's thoughts instead of certain types of behavior.[3]

Creative imagination is also a factor underlying the conceptual development and change of the norms, laws, and principles that define moral behavior. In the beginning, rules and laws were probably the work of creative ethicists, as is their redefinition today. Like all social change, the evolution of law and concepts of good and evil displays the force of human imagination. From time to time, the failure of that imagination to make necessary redefinitions and inventions has been spectacular and fatal. Rubenstein (1968), for example, explains the failure of German Jews to recognize the nature of their peril under Hitler and to resist it as a failure in imagination. During their long history of persecution since the Roman destruction of the temple in 70 A.D., the Jews had developed an adaptive pattern of submission which had guaranteed group, if not individual, survival. This way of behaving had served them well in dealing with limited evil. At the crucial moment, however, they were unable to redefine the twentieth-century evil they were experiencing as genocide. What had been adaptive became maladaptive.

Biological man may be, as Hogan (1973) suggests, a rule-formulating, rule-following animal; but human culture and individual personalities have thoroughly shaped the nature of these rules. Moral systems expressed in principles, rules, and laws are a creative invention as much as any other human product. According to Gheselin (1963),

. . . a creative product is distinguishable from all others by the presence in it of a configuration which is intrinsically new. . . . The escape from the closed world of configurations is accomplished neither by drifting nor by willful propulsion. . . . The creative mind is drawn out of it by desire for an order that does not exist, for some distribution of its energies which no configuration is available to determine . . . (pp. 360–364).

Wherever such ordering has taken place, fundamental changes have shaped the process of morality and the rules that express it, in including the limits and ends of the sanctions which support those rules.

A brief glance at the history of law suggests a parallel between individual moral development and cultural moral development through such ethico-social inventions as law. Inner ethical development corresponds isomorphically to social-ethical development. Historically, the individual or group refrained from immoral behavior because of fear of consequences from external sources, such as God or other mortals whose primitive views of justice might require multiple vengeance, retaliation far greater than the specific evil done, disproportionate repayment by the evildoer, or compensation or punishment of whole groups or clans.

Law began in the history of Western religion with a conception of the Father-God as the source of order, reason, form, and law in both physical and moral realms. His authority was based on that notion that, as the creator of all things, he brought cosmos out of chaos. His authority was capricious and absolute, as the story of Abraham in the Old Testament shows. God ordered Abraham to sacrifice his son, Isaac, and, in obedience to God's command, Abraham prepared to do so. In human terms, Abraham's intent was murder. Kierkegaard (1941), in *Fear and Trembling*, describes this situation as the conflict between ethical values and obedience to authority, which Abraham re-

solved in favor of authority. There is, Kierkegaard believes, a "suspension of the ethical" in such a situation. Abraham acted in instrumental response to the law as he saw it, to the powerful external authority capable of devastating punishment for wrongdoing or disobedience.

A later conception of the law and authority, corresponding to the stage of preconventional instrumental reciprocity in individual moral development, was the *lex talionis*. Today this form of measure-for-measure justice is frequently used as an example of primitive, even barbaric, law. When it originated, however, it represented a moral advance, superseding a tradition of justice as multiple punishment, the avenging of one person's crime against his entire clan. Against the background of these archaic punitive practices, the talion principle can be seen as a positive social invention.

In both cultural and individual developmental terms, the next evolutionary step, corresponding to conventional morality and authoritarian law, expressed the need for an enduring and stable social order. Authority is external to the individual and inherent in the law, which is seen as static or even eternal. Law regulates the life of the individual for the sake of maintaining the group, and punishment is directed to preventing harm to society. Law creates guilt, and with guilt, conscience—a new form of punishment for harm done—is born. Law viewed from this perspective represents a type of ethical enslavement in which the individual is not able to alter his moral stance adaptively. Unquestioning legal and moral conformity, like other conventional modes of thought and behavior, inevitably elicits some sacrifice of imagination, openness, originality, and individuality.

For security's sake, conventional morality must be rigidly defended against all comers; and to maintain the conventional, moral outrage is directed at those who have alternative perceptions of the ethical or legal. Awareness that one's own freedom has been restricted creates an encroaching resentment of the freedom of others. A tragic example of how such resentment operates comes from the accounts (Bettelheim, 1960) of the hopeless Nazi captives who, knowing they were scheduled to die, refused to attempt to escape and informed on those who did try. Those who resign themselves to being cheated of their lives or their creative autonomy are determined that others must be cheated, too. (For a compelling and thoughtful description of the phenomenon of moral outrage and its effects, see Wren-Lewis, 1966).

Movement toward the present historically (and toward ego maturity developmentally) has been marked by the emergence of the social contract. This form of law binds by agreement, and creates a balance of interests and values protected by a system of rules consciously and mutually agreed upon. Law here is defined, as is morality, by its responsiveness to the social needs of the group and by the consciousness of individuals who see law as a flexible tool, a product of human creativity.

The steps up the ethico-legal ladder can be summed up as moving from the fear of vengeance—of evil as chaos, one might say—to the love of both order and change, the abolishment of fear, and the remaking of the law in a new range of feeling. At the highest, historically most recent, levels (where the fundamental needs of people are to some degree supplied by the society), slavish obedience to the law yields to a faith comparable to the basic trust described by Erikson (1968), which in its most mature and competent form sees the law as a democratic contract and the universal principles upon which it is based as derived from a particular positive model of man.

Man's creative imagination, using the law as an adaptive mechanism, has unfolded this progression and continues to shape it. Today we may be on the edge of redefinition once again: Law as the historical preventative of harm may be converted into law as the facilitator or requirer of good. Law, in the future, may be used as an encouragement to prosocial behavior by structuring reward systems to induce desired behavior (Kaplan, 1972, p. 225; Huston & Korte, Chap. 15). This might be done, for example, by mandating public rewards for actions benefiting the group rather than the self.

Imagination in the Service of Individuation

Before *Sesame Street*, the only widespread serious use to which fantasy had been put in American culture was in the marketing of products. Yet, turned to the service of ethical development, imagination could permit us to rip open those predefined barbed enclosures of culture and situation which restrict our perception and our wholeness. Imagination invests meaning and saliency in persons and events. In Shaw's *St. Joan*, an elderly priest blames the repetition of evil in generation after generation on the failure of imagination; he himself had to actually *see* the young girl burned to realize the enormity of the act. He asks, "Must then a Christ perish in torment in every age to save those that have no imagination?"

Comparing Job's status with that of the Jews under Hitler, Rubenstein (1968) graphically describes the failure of German social imagination to see the Jewish victim as human:

Hideously afflicted, Job sat on his dung heap. No matter how terrible his condition became, he was at all times recognized as a person by both God and man. At Auschwitz, the Jew did not sit upon the dung heap. He became less than the dung heap. . . . No "Thou" was addressed to the Auschwitz Jew by either God or man. The Jew became a non-person in the deepest sense. Neither his life nor his death mattered. There was no question because there was no Job. Job went up in smoke. His question went with him (pp. xvi–xvii).

The increase in explicit sex and violence in the American media (see Liebert & Poulos, Chap. 16) could easily be interpreted as a symptom of atrophying fantasy once used in the service of the ethical. Indeed, evidence is all around us that this process is under way, even among preschoolers to whom pictures and dioramas of people in various kinds of distress are more salient than are live humans in the same predicaments (Yarrow, Scott, & Waxler, 1973). The situation is aggravated by the fact that in contemporary Western civilization the irrational processes that clinicians have found most useful as access routes to the person are systematically being denied.

Where acceptance of inner sources of knowledge is taken for granted, imagination can be an artful and powerful tool for cognitive development, not simply because of its generalized integrative function described earlier but because it forces each person to see through his own eyes and his own perceptions. Fantasy is an individual act, even where its modes and content are those of a specific cultural inheritance. Fantasy can be encouraged or inhibited from afar, but cannot be produced externally. There are collective dreams and wishes, myths and legends; but these are group imagination—shared products of a cultural heritage—and not the person's own.

The joke about the impossibility of finding *one* right-winger in a roomful of people expresses an important truth: Collective morality may be destructive to individual morality, for it leads to the loss of personal integrity, to individual exculpation through the foisting of blame onto others. Imagination, inward and self-generated, may be one means of avoiding the cultural legitimization of evil. It may be a means of endlessly examining the moral premises upon which cultural systems are built, so that we become the active constructors of a fair world personally defined and, indeed, participants in our own socialization. The individuation of adulthood and maturity which separates

one from collective standards is not rebellion, but the acceptance of individual responsibility—a responsibility which includes a profound and lasting search for alternatives to harmful and limiting behavior.

Imagination is not ornamental; it is structural. Rather, it is, as Willard Waller wrote long ago, the extension of a cognitive task already begun. How outrageous that we do not automatically develop that task as the examination of the ethical positions and processes which may occur among human beings! For more than a decade now, imagination—labeled creative thinking—has been systematically utilized in problem-solving techniques in school and industry. Such techniques include the use of remote associations, metaphors, and analogies (M. S. Allen, 1962; DeMille, 1967; W. J. J. Gordon, 1961; Osborn, 1963; Parnes & Harding, 1962). Why shouldn't imagination also be utilized, deliberately and purposefully in the moral sphere? The creative unconscious is the ally of the conscious, cognitive mind, and not its enemy in the battle to recognize evil and destructiveness and to deal appropriately with them.

Conclusions and Implications

Like Hogan (1973)—and in contrast to Piaget and Kohlberg—I believe that morality is fundamentally irrational—that is, that differences in even such obviously cognitive phenomena as moral reasoning and judgment derive from essential personological structures. Moral reasoning and behavior are a function of the *person*, and not simply of his capacity to think logically or to learn concepts and norms. When Odysseus refused Calypso's offer of immortality on the condition that he remain with her, his action flowed from a much more powerful fount than socialization to conventional standards. He was responding as a whole human being to the lucid horror of moral seduction, to the loss of his autonomy.

I see personality development as a whole—and not cognitive development alone—as the basis of morality. And, if my premise is correct, I am asking whether principled moralization can take place at all where survival or other low-level needs act as primary motivators. This is an empirical question, not simply a theoretical one; and, to my knowledge, it has only been very tentatively explored. Building on past research that relates the needs of the individual to the attitudes, values, and beliefs he holds (e.g., Katz, 1960; M. B. Smith, Bruner, & White, 1956), I studied 50 upper-middle-class secondary school students to determine whether emotional factors were correlates of Kohlberg's preconventional, conventional, and principled levels of moral judgment (Simpson, 1972). In the only significant findings, the needs for belongingness and esteem for others (social esteem) were negatively associated with principled reasoning; and the need for self-esteem in the sense of competence was positively associated with principled reasoning. While these findings appear to support my conception of the integrated nature of moral development, they should be taken with a large grain of salt because of the lack of reliability of Kohlberg's instrument. (Independent scorer agreement was impossible to achieve at a respectable level; scores were finally assigned consensually). Further testing of my hypothesis awaits more careful and sophisticated instrumentation. Cognitive openness, as measured by the Dogmatism Scale (Rokeach, 1960), has already been associated with the gratification of psychic needs (Knutson, 1972; Simpson, 1971a, 1971b). If my theory is valid, then imagination, too, should be found to be related to principled moral reasoning.

If the development of principled morality in society does not take place automatically, and we seriously believe that such reasoning is important, then we must consider strategies for systematically developing it. We need to experiment with the manipulation of need variables during the formal socialization process, together with the direct teaching of values and the opportunity to explore roles and sample ethical dilemmas not only through observation but also through imaginative and sober trial, withdrawal, and tentative retrial. Elsewhere (Simpson, 1971a) I have discussed the effects of structural changes in institutionalized education on the satisfaction of deficiency needs and the probable outcomes of such reforms for the development of democratic values. Hunt (1971), too, has been explicit about the types of learning environments prescribed to foster growth at particular stages of conceptual development or interpersonal maturity. Although varied, each of these prescribed environments contains an implicit affective component of respect and acceptance for the child, which could be expected to supply some of the psychic needs for security, affiliation, and self-esteem described by Maslow.

Curriculum in the narrow sense of what is actually taught in the classroom can, and does in some recent approaches to social study, provide for the examination of personal and cultural values through a variety of cognitively based methods. Some of these methods involve value clarification (and a spurious neutral approach); some attempt to teach logic, including a low-level cost-accounting approach to morality in which the child is essentially asked what's in it for him or anyone else. Others entail discussion structured by questions or role playing. In all, however, value analysis is the central method—although Oliver and Bane (1971), in an important discussion of changes needed to create a mutually trusting environment in the schools, have come close to advocating intuition, imagination, and personal emotions as facilitating the analysis of values. Our curricula need more spaces for imagination in every sphere—from mathematics to sewing—and especially in areas where social meanings are being taught. We need more exercises in empathy —not the analytic, dissection-at-a-distance kind (like studying culture at a distance, this is risky business), but the global, multiple-entry, experiencing kind which depends for its success on wholesale imagining.

It seems to me that now is the time to state clearly that proper educational goals should go beyond the processes of reasoning, analyzing, or reflecting on moral stands and value conflicts in our mundane lives. In their behavioral forms, our goals should include the definable end states of approach, openness, and acceptance under conditions of equality, justice, and freedom for our fellow humans. The enactment of these goals depends upon emotional, as well as intellectual, education; and I believe that in performing this task education will draw increasingly upon the vast repertoires of clinical therapies designed for use with normals. The proliferating network of curricula in emotional (affective, confluent, psychological, humanistic, call-it-what-you-will) education is symptomatic of our broadened perception. Education in this creative mode will draw on the untapped human resources of the schools to help meet the student's basic needs. It will commit itself to the view that internal demands have as much or more to do with ethical life as do external ones. Creating the ethicogenic situation depends upon heeding these inner demands and utilizing all the psychic instrumentalities available to the whole, creative human being.

Development in general occurs when challenges requiring new adaptive responses confront the individual who has been freed from the necessity of maintaining unconscious defensive devices (Langer, 1969). Securing this freedom must be the prior task—not to heal the sick, but to make competent and masterful the healthy through the use of all of his resources and not simply his analytic mind. The need for a defining framework of reason and the overwhelming attribution of decision making to rational processes can themselves be products of defensive repression. They may be a means of coping with a fearful world. Paradoxically, emotion plays its part in the choice of stripped-down rationality; sweet reason is based in sourness, acerbity, the pain of lack, and the too readily available, potentially destructive mechanisms for the avoidance of that pain. Whether life's challenges stimulate or defeat the individual depends upon his past experience and the satisfaction of his basic emotional needs. Then he is able to respond with growth—to break out of his old, tight cocoon and burst into bright, new colors.

To conclude, then, perhaps one may regard moral development as one area of human competence, one expression of the need to function and to function well. How well we spend our lives depends upon many factors, but as Ricoeur (1967) has written, "One lives only that which one imagines . . . life is a symbol, an image, before being experienced and lived" (p. 278). Morality is not the *imposing* of order and law upon a chaotic universe, but the *living* of that order and existing within it. This process is the creation of reality, the generation of an imaginative moral self-fulfilling prophecy.

PART 3

RESEARCH

CHAPTER 10

Honesty and Dishonesty

Roger V. Burton

Introduction

Philosophers and social theorists in every period of recorded history have devoted much discussion to moral conduct, not only to what it is but also to how parents and teachers might encourage or unintentionally interfere with its development in the young. When socially acceptable ethical systems are codified, the various facets of honesty tend to be explicitly stated, for example, "Thou shalt not bear false witness" and "Thou shalt not steal." There is probably a consensus that if everyone abided by these Commandments, the world would be better for it. Yet the very simplicity and specificity of these explicit proscriptions provide grist for the moral philosopher's mill. After weighing all the factors that place a particular act within a larger social context, the simple, direct proscription of the biblical Commandment, "Thou shalt not bear false witness," is transformed into the more sophisticated, mature form: "It is wrong to lie in most circumstances; but sometimes it is neither right nor wrong, and under some conditions it would be immoral not to lie."

What seemed simple at first clearly becomes quite complicated when specific instances of conduct are to be labeled as good or bad.

In spite of the tremendous attention directed to the complexities of moral conduct throughout the ages, there has been little empirical investigation of the several theories of ethical behavior until relatively recently. This chapter reviews the empirical research on honesty, with the purpose of arriving at some conclusions about the factors that influence moral conduct and how these influences operate. Broadly speaking, investigators have focused on three facets of honesty: the behavioral, judgmental, and affective. We shall first consider the generality–specificity issue for the behavioral realm and follow this with a look at the extent to which behavior is consistent with other facets of honesty such as moral judgment and affective reactions to transgression. Studies exploring the correlates of honest conduct are reviewed for the robustness of their results. A consideration of environmental inputs in the development of honesty leads to a discussion of socializing and childrearing techniques. Finally, this writer speculates on the research required to provide the empirical data necessary for establishing firm psychological generalizations leading to greater understanding of the development of honesty.

Generality of Honest and Dishonest Conduct

There were a number of empirical studies of honesty in the early 1900s, but the most thorough program of research was conducted by Hartshorne and May (1928; Hartshorne, May, & Maller, 1929; Hartshorne, May, & Shuttleworth, 1930). These investigators were struck by the lack of empirical evidence on actual conduct. Accordingly, the definition of honesty for Hartshorne and May's research program was intrinsically linked to overt behavior. To qualify as an acceptable test, the situation had to tempt the child to do something for personal gain which he would not want others to know about. The crucial part of their definition of honesty was the element of *active deception*: an effort to deceive and/or an attempt to conceal one's behavior. They devised thirty-three different tests to measure three types of deceit: cheating, lying, and stealing. With these data, they were able to consider the degree of generality in the individual behavior of children: To what extent can an individual be considered to have the "trait" of honesty? Basing their conclusion primarily on analyses of correlations between the different tests of deceit, they enunciated the *doctrine of specificity*: There is little evidence that a general trait of honesty exists within individuals. Their interpretation stemmed from the fact that the correlations tended to be low among the tests, and that the magnitude of a particular correlation was inversely related to the extent of the differences between the two test situations or types of deception involved; that is, the greater the difference between the tests, the smaller the correla-

tion. Hartshorne and May's interpretation (1928) of these data was "that neither deceit nor its opposite, 'honesty,' are unified character traits, but rather specific functions of life situations. Most children will deceive in certain situations and not in others. Lying, cheating, and stealing as measured by the test situations used in these studies are only very loosely related" (p. 411).

To appreciate the meaning of the doctrine of specificity, we must consider carefully the trait theory that Hartshorne and May rejected. They defined a character trait as "an inner entity operating independently of the situation in which the individual is placed" (1928, p. 385). The model of personality traits for which Hartshorne and May found no support was clearly an extreme position regarding individual consistency. This trait model required any test of honesty to correlate highly with any other test of honesty and to be an excellent predictor of the individual's behavior under all conditions.

Hartshorne and May's assessments of generality–specificity were based on the average degree of overlap among tests tapping different situations and different forms of deceptions. However, when the different tests were applied in the *same situational context*, such as a schoolroom, and the *form* of deception was the same, such as copying on a test, then the average intercorrelation among all the different tests of honesty in the various situations was .23; the average correlation among all the classroom cheating tests (including the academic achievement, speed, and coordination tests) was .46; and the average among the academic achievement tests was .68. The relation between any one test and the summed score based on all other tests was .53.[1] This last correlation indicates the tendency for the score from a particular cheating test to overlap with a broader-based assessment of the individual child's cheating proclivity. Although the magnitude of this .53 correlation is too low for individual prediction, it indicates that a summary score based on an adequate sampling of honesty measures can nevertheless be adequate as a general index of honesty for statistical comparisons of groups. Hartshorne and May obviously agreed with this conclusion, since many of their analyses of different groups, such as different classrooms and very deceitful versus very honest groups, used an overall score of honesty obtained by summing the standardized scores of the individual tests.

A full reading of Hartshorne and May's report (1928) reveals, therefore, that it would be wrong to cite them as having demonstrated that there was no generality or individual consistency of moral conduct, that acts of resisting temptation were completely situationally determined with nothing attributable to individual differences in the subjects. They state, "We are quite ready to recognize the existence of some common factors which tend to make individuals differ from one another on any test or on any group of tests" (p. 385). In their later studies (1930), Hartshorne, May, and Shuttleworth also noted that they obtained small but consistently positive and significant correlations among the different moral conduct areas of honesty, service, charity, cooperation, persistence, inhibition, and moral knowledge: "The 23 tests used in securing our total character scores, for example, intercorrelate .30 on the average" (1930; p. 364).

Soon after the third and final volume of the *Studies in the Nature of Character* was published (Hartshorne, May, & Shuttleworth, 1930), other investigators expressed concern that the authors' conclusion of specificity could be exaggerated or that the model of trait theory they had rejected was too extreme. One of the first to withdraw from the conclusion that there was no consistency in behavior was J. P. Maller (1934), a co-author of the second volume (Hartshorne, May & Maller, 1929). Using Spearman's tetrad difference technique, Maller demonstrated that individual behavior was influenced not only by specific factors but also by a common factor, which he called "delay of gratification," found throughout the intercorrelations of the character tests of honesty, cooperation, inhibition, and persistence as reported in the third volume (Hartshorne, May, & Shuttleworth, 1930).

From data gathered in Romania in the late 1930s, Barbu (1951) reported finding strong evidence of a behavioral honesty factor in the correlations of nine behavioral tests and one questionnaire measure with a sample of 250 14-year-old boys. In another factor-analytic study, Brogden (1940) isolated an honesty factor empirically defined primarily by behavioral tests of cheating and by contributions of two paper-and-pencil tests.

This author (Burton, 1963) analyzed the original intercorrelations of the Hartshorne and May data (1928) with multivariate methods in order to reconsider the interpretation of the doctrine of specificity. To increase the stability of these analyses, tests without demonstrated reliabilities of at least .70 were eliminated. Both principal component and Guttman simplex analyses provided evidence of a single general factor. This factor was interpreted as demonstrating that there are individual differences along a *broad* dimension of resistance to temptation.

My own conclusion was similar to that of Hartshorne and May. It differed, however, by suggesting that certain social-learning conditions could contribute to differential degrees of generality–specificity within an individual; this approach rejects both the extreme trait model, demonstrated by Hartshorne and May to be without foundation, and also the extreme specificity conclusion that there is no internal or individual predisposition to be honest or to deviate. My social-learning model suggested the learning experiences that might lead some individuals to be relatively consistent in their honesty or dishonesty and others to be relatively inconsistent. The differences in consistency would be contingent on the learning conditions found to influence the narrowness or broadness of the generalization gradients, that is, the breadth of transfer of what is learned in one situation to a different setting. The model also suggests how behavior exhibited at one time might be modified, how children who show little consistency might be trained to be more consistently honest—that is, to perceive a greater variety of honesty situations as belonging to a similar class of moral conflicts.

Further studies have supported the conclusion that there is some generality in honest conduct. Sears, Rau, and Alpert (1965) found that, even with 4-year-old children, behavioral tests of resistance to temptation produced primarily positive correlations. Nelsen, Grinder, and Mutterer (1969), using six behavioral tests on 11- and 12-year-olds, explored the generality–specificity issue with both factor analysis and analysis of variance methods. Through factor analysis, they extracted nearly the same percentage of common variance (35 to 40 percent) for a general factor as the author (Burton, 1963) found in his reanalysis of the original Hartshorne and May (1928) data.

Hetherington and Feldman (1964) and Heilman, Hodgson, and Hornstein (1972), studying college students, also found evidence supporting consistency in moral behavior across situations. In the Hetherington and Feldman study (1964), 59 percent of the students cheated on one of the three regular course examinations. Half the students cheated on the objective and essay-type tests; but only 22 percent cheated on the oral exam, where they had to look at the text being used for the test when the examiner left the room. It is striking that 24 percent of the cheaters cheated in all three test situations, and 64 percent more cheated on two of the tests. Therefore, only 12 percent of the cheating students (or 6 to 7 percent of all the students) were single-situation cheaters. Such consistency, however, may have been due to the fact that all of the tests were academic examinations in the same course.

Heilman, Hodgson, & Hornstein (1972) produced more impressive evidence of consistency. They isolated "the uninvolved," a group of students who committed both sins of omission and commission. These students both avoided reporting their involvement in doing harm to another and cheated more than other groups in scoring their own "intellectual" ability to recall blocks of words flashed onto a screen.

The implication of these studies is that a small but consistently manifested honesty factor distinguishes individuals. But, as Hartshorne and May (1928) stated, one must be cautious when using "honesty" as a personality trait; the data clearly indicate that the conditions of each test situation greatly affect the individual's behavior in spite of any generalized predilection to resist temptation.

Consistency across Different Facets of Honesty

The final volume of *Studies in the Nature of Character* (Hartshorne, May, & Shuttleworth, 1930) explored the degree to which moral conduct related to other assessments of the child's moral functioning. Verbal measures of the child's moral knowledge and commitment in response to moral dilemmas were shown to relate positively to moral conduct, but the magnitude of association was low, especially when individual tests were correlated. When a summary score of all tests of honesty was correlated with a summary score of moral knowledge tests, however, the correlation approached .40 (corrected to .46). Teachers' ratings of honesty also correlated .35 with actual conduct.

Subsequent studies have produced extremely variable evidence of the relationship between verbally obtained measures of morality and actual conduct. Kohlberg (1965) reports "an ambiguous" positive relationship between cheating and moral judgment in sixth-graders, and also a tendency for adults with a principled moral orientation (Stages 5 and 6 in the Kohlberg moral judgment test) to refuse to continue to administer high levels of shock in a Milgram (1963) obedience study. However, the relationship between moral judgment and obedience was not monotonically related. In contrast, Podd (1972) reported no relationship between Kohlberg's moral judgment test and the level of shock administered to a peer in the Milgram obedience test. R. L. Krebs (1967) found a slight positive relation between Kohlberg's scale of moral judgment and honest conduct if the moral judgment measure had been obtained prior to the conduct test. However, when moral judgment was rated from an interview following the temptation test, there was a somewhat stronger tendency for judgment to relate *negatively* to honesty.

Schwartz, Feldman, Brown, and Heingartner (1969), testing college students, also report a relationship between moral judgment and actual honest behavior. The magnitude of the correlation was about .38 as a phi coefficient and approached a significant level. Nelsen, Grinder, and Biaggio (1969) found little support among raw correlations for a relationship between honesty and moral judgments in young boys; but the moral judgment and conduct test together defined the major factor in a factor analysis of all the morality measures. For girls, however, the cognitive measures defined a factor independent of the conduct measure. Nakasato and Aoyama (1972) found no relationship between legal conduct and changes in their delinquents' judgments regarding intentionality. The marked increase in the subjects' moral judgments on intentionality after a nine-month period was independent of the number and severity of their delinquent offenses during this period.

Dermine (1969) found that schoolgirls who valued honesty more than intelligence tended to cheat less on an "intelligence test" than those with the contrary ranking. However, when the test was not presented

as a measure of intelligence, the association between value and behavior disappeared. A link between value and behavior was demonstrated by C. F. Gilligan (1963), who found a positive relation between boys' ranking of "honesty" as their most valued self-concept and the honesty of their behavior in an achievement game.

The evidence indicates that there is certainly not a strong relationship between overt behavior and verbal measures such as moral judgment, moral knowledge, and values, although the relationships reported tend to be positive. The small magnitude of overlap, however, suggests that the primary determinants of verbal responses to moral dilemmas may well be different from the major determinants of overt behavior in specific situations. The slight increase in the relation between moral orientation scores and conduct scores with age indicates that people become more integrated as they reach adult status.

The association between overt behavior and ratings of moral conduct by peers and teachers tends to be similarly low. Like Hartshorne and May (1928), who found a positive relationship between teachers' ratings and actual conduct (average $r = .35$), Grim, Kohlberg, and White (1968) found positive correlations between ratings of conduct by peers and teachers, and subjects' actual conduct (.11 to .26). Although the latter correlations were not statistically significant, the rating measures found by Grim and his colleagues did load high on a behavioral honesty factor for sixth-grade children. The relationship for first-graders was essentially zero and did not load on the behavioral factor of honesty.[2] Data from a study by the author (Burton, 1960) also indicated that teachers' ratings of the honesty of 4- and 5-year-old children were unrelated to the subjects' honesty in a game.

Walsh (1969), however, found that teachers' ratings of children's compliance with school norms were different for different types of honest children. Teachers tended to rate correctly the group of children who cheated, and the group who did not cheat and manifested little temptation conflict (showing instead rigid control). In contrast, a third group of children who did not cheat but were active and showed natural curiosity toward the forbidden toys were rated by the teachers as possessing least self-control. The activity and curiosity of the children seemed to spread inappropriately to the moral realm, causing the teachers to perceive these active children as having low self-control. A similar process of judgmental bias was shown by Dion (1972), who found that undergraduate women predicted the honesty of 7-year-old children on the basis of their physical attractiveness in a photograph. Mussen, Rutherford, Harris, and Keasey (1970) used peer ratings of who would be most likely to be honest in tests and similar situations, and found positive correlations between the ratings and actual conduct for both 12-year-old boys and girls (.29 and .27, respectively). Leveque and Walker (1970) found that teacher ratings of the honesty of 16-year-old students in geometry classes of three different schools correlated with the subjects' actual honesty during a geometry achievement test (total $r = .38$ with the three samples producing r's from .25 to .42). These data suggest that ratings of teachers and peers have some validity, but the percentage of variance in common with actual conduct is too small to justify considering ratings as a substitute measure for overt conduct. Furthermore, the consistency with which ratings (especially from teachers) correlate with grades, IQ, and social class—all of which correlate with honesty—suggests the possibility that the rating-honesty association results from a "halo" bias.

Honesty measured behaviorally has also been correlated with projective measures. This author (Burton, 1971) has demonstrated that responses to incomplete stories of deviation and temptation cannot justifiably be used to infer general "conscience strength." The assumption, based mainly on psychoanalytic theory, has been that projective responses portraying infrequent parental punishment for a deviation combined with frequent reparation and confession by the child would reflect high conscience development and be positively related to honesty. The findings for 4-year-old children, however, were that confession was unrelated to resistance to temptation, and that reparation and punishment related to honesty in nearly the opposite direction expected. After the behavioral temptation test, cheaters produced more responses of parental reparation of damage portrayed in the deviation story and few punishment responses compared with their responses to a matched set of stories administered prior to the temptation test. In contrast, honest children increased their frequency of portraying punishment, both parental and self-administered, and decreased their frequency of depicting parental fixing of the damage. These changes in verbal responses fit well predictions from cognitive dissonance theory (Festinger & Freedman, 1964) that cognitive restructuring makes expressed attitudes and values consonant with the moral conduct in the temptation situation. The findings also conform to predictions from the social-learning position (Solomon, 1960; Solomon, Turner, & Lessac, 1968; J. W. M. Whiting, 1954) that a child is deterred from cheating by anxiety aroused during temptation. This anxiety, having been acquired through previous association with parental punishment in similar temptation situations, is manifested by an increase in children's fantasies of punishment for deviation after they have been honest in the test. The interpretation for the cheaters is that the increase in reparation represents a response learned to avoid parental disciplinary action and consequently also results in a decrease in responses depicting parental punishment.

Other studies also show that the moral measures obtained from projective stories (both doll play and written story completions) show little correspondence with actual behavior (Medinnus, 1966b;

Ross, 1962; Sears, Rau, & Alpert, 1965; Stein, 1967; Wurtz, 1959). There is some suggestion (Burton, 1971; A. H. Stein, 1967) of a slight correspondence between actual behavior and projective responses when the stories closely parallel the behavioral test situation. However, the very small relationships indicate that even if larger samples produced statistically significant associations, behavioral and projective tests would still be measuring mostly different things.

The absence of a relationship between behavioral honesty and behavioral confession noted for the 4-year-old children in Burton's study (1971) holds for older subjects also. For example, Hartshorne and May (1928) compared three groups of children classified as consistently honest, consistently dishonest, and "confessors." It was found that the "confessors"—children who cheated and then confessed—were the most handicapped in the three broad areas measured: family relations, socioeconomic and cultural status, and personal status (IQ, maladjustment, and deportment). Confession among these children was clearly not an indication of advanced moral development.

Brodsky and Jacobson (1970) found that among college students 10 percent cheated on a test, and only 12 percent admitted their act. For a group of prisoners, the percentages were 17 percent and 34 percent, respectively. However, only half of the confessed cheaters in the college sample and 27 percent in the prison sample were observed to have actually cheated! In both samples, confession of cheating and cheating behavior apparently touched different dimensions of morality. Fischer (1970) found that only 6 of 86 cheaters admitted cheating in an anonymous questionnaire; and even after being told that cheating had been measured and that half the students had cheated, only 25 of the 86 would anonymously acknowledge deception. Self-reports and confession of cheating, then, should be considered as minimal estimates of cheating. Analyses comparing confessed "cheaters" and "noncheaters" will include many cheaters in the noncheater group and some confessed "cheaters" who did not deviate, at least as cheating was operationally defined, in the cheater group.

This review of research bearing on the generality question does not support attempts to generalize from a single measure of moral behavior to all measures of that mode, such as from following rules in a beanbag game to honest conduct in other temptation conflicts involving achievement. To extend generalizations across different facets of morality, by assuming, for example, that a finding for moral judgment may apply to moral conduct also, is even less warranted by the evidence. It may be, nonetheless, that certain functional relations pertaining to the influence of group norms, models, or childrearing practices are stable across different moral conduct measures. Attention is now turned to this aspect of the generality or consistency question: To what extent are there consistent functional relations between situational conditions and their influence on the performance of honest conduct?

Situational and Personal Correlates of Honest Conduct

AGE

The notion that children grow smarter as they grow older is one of the bases for developmental tests of moral judgment, and the evidence has confirmed the expectation of age-related increases in complexity of moral thought. The data for specific tests of overt moral conduct, however, provide little evidence of a continuing development of honesty with age. Hartshorne and May (1928) actually found a slight positive relation between age and the summed score of cheating ($r = .14$), which they attributed mainly to greater cheating among older children on the speed tests on which they simply had greater ability to cheat. When ability was partialled out, the correlation was reduced essentially to zero. Feldman and Feldman (1967) also found age to be related to greater cheating on an academic test for secondary school students, but only for boys. The relation was attributable to the increased cheating among the twelfth-grade males who planned to attend college and were highly motivated to perform well on achievement tests.

More in line with our general expectations are the results of the analysis of integration of moral conduct by Hartshorne, May, and Shuttleworth (1930). They found a positive correlation between age and a behavioral consistency score, with older children becoming more consistently honest *or* dishonest and younger children performing in a less integrated way, that is, demonstrating more variability across the different tests.

Subsequent studies have tended to find some slight evidence of increasing honesty with age. G. Moore and Stephens (1971), in a longitudinal study, reported that honesty (not cheating on a test and turning in "lost" property and money) increased with age in both normals and retardates. Tattling about someone else's deviations—an apparent conflict between honesty to the experimenter and loyalty to a peer—decreased with age for both retardates and normals. When mental age was controlled, the retardates tended to be as moral as the normals in their conduct on these measures. Honesty has also been found to relate positively with age in elementary school children on ray-gun games, fictitious achievement claims, and peeping tests (Grinder, 1964; Kanfer, 1966; Kanfer and Duerfeldt, 1968; Medinnus, 1966a).

In general these correlations tend to be low and to control very small amounts of variance. The correlation between age and honesty seems to be due to other variables that correlate with increasing age, such as an awareness of risk, ability to perform the task without the need to cheat, and greater understanding of the moral infraction itself. It may also be that a test that is tempting to a small child is no longer tempting to an older child, so that holding a test constant serves to decrease the temptation for older subjects. However, when one looks at the 50- to 80-percent range of cheaters on college examinations, it is clear that if the honesty test has relevance for the subjects, cheating continues at a high rate regardless of age.

Still, if the measure is not simply cheating on a particular task, but consistency across moral conduct measures, as Hartshorne and May employed in their behavioral studies, there will be an increase in integration with age. Henshel (1971; Dermine, 1969) found age to be related positively to integration between valued honesty and actual honest conduct. This kind of consistency measure seems appropriate for comparison with the developmental aspects of moral judgment measures used by Piaget (1932) and Kohlberg (1964). If such an integration measure is used, then conduct may also demonstrate the characteristics demanded of a developmental measure.

INTELLIGENCE, ACADEMIC ABILITY, AND ACHIEVEMENT

A commonly accepted finding in moral conduct studies is that intelligence and academic ability are positively correlated with honesty. Hartshorne and May (1928) established a relationship between IQ and cheating of approximately $-.50$ which increased to $-.60$ when age was controlled. Subsequent studies have found the same general relationship (Canning, 1956; Hetherington & Feldman, 1964; Howells, 1938; Johnson & Gormly, 1972; Kanfer & Duerfeldt, 1968; Nelsen, Grinder, & Biaggio, 1969; Parr, 1936).

This relation between ability and honesty has been shown, however, to depend on the type of test used. Hartshorne and May (1928) noted, for example, that when the task involved a routinized mechanical or perceptual motor skill, such as crossing out letters or matching letters to numbers, and when the subject had no standard for judging the adequacy of his performance, cheating was positively correlated with the ability to perform the task. They also found that IQ and school grades were unrelated to cheating in the party and stealing tests—temptation situations not associated with previous experiences of success or failure. The relationship of honesty to IQ, therefore, was essentially limited to academic-type tests in which previous experience of failure in similar school situations led low-IQ and low-achieving subjects to cheat. Cheating for these children had become a means of accomplishing what seemed unattainable by honest routes. For tests with which the intelligent child had not had a previous history of successful achievement, level of IQ was unrelated to cheating, since many high-IQ children cheated as much or more than the lower-IQ children. Evidence from Johnson and Gormly (1972) also indicates that when risk is decreased, the relation between honesty and IQ is reduced. This finding suggests that the correlation between honesty and IQ depends, at least partly, on the degree to which intelligence permits the child to weigh the possibility of being discovered for his deviation. This finding does not demonstrate that greater honesty accompanies greater intellectual ability. For children of all intellectual abilities, then, under the appropriate conditions cheating can serve as a means of avoiding failure.

SEX DIFFERENCES

Girls are generally thought to be more obedient than boys (Meyer & Thompson, 1956; Terman & Tyler, 1946). R. L. Krebs (1969) found that sixth-grade girls were perceived by their teachers as being more moral than boys on scales of trustworthiness, obedience, and respect for others' rights. Furthermore, Roskens and Dizney (1966) found more self-reported cheating

for males than for females in college students—a finding that reinforces the stereotypes of sex differences in honesty and obedience.

When one turns to empirical evidence of sex differences in observed behavioral honesty, there is less consistent support for the stereotypes. R. L. Krebs (1969) found no consistent sex differences in behavioral honesty for the same sixth-grade class in which girls had been rated by their teachers as more honest than boys. The middle-class girls cheated slightly more than boys, and the working-class girls cheated less than boys on a ray-gun game; but both sexes cheated equally on two other tests.

Hartshorne and May (1928) explored sex differences across many ages and across their many tests. They found that girls tended to cheat more than boys on most of their tests, although the investigators tended to discount these sex differences as due to differential motivation aroused by the tests. The fact that girls cheated more in the athletic contests, however, tends to fly in the face of the interpretation that boys were less motivated to demonstrate skill on the tests than the girls. Hartshorne and May (1928) also found that girls cheated significantly more at all ages on the lying test, a self-report questionnaire of obedience to the generally accepted moral code. Burton (1971) also found 4-year-old girls cheating more than boys in a beanbag game. Women college students cheated more than men on a modified version of the WAIS symbol test (Jacobson, Berger, & Millham, 1970) and lied more than men about having cheated (Canning, 1956).

A review of other behavioral studies of honesty suggests, however, that the more frequently reported sex difference in deception reinforces the stereotypical perception that boys cheat more than girls (Feldman & Feldman, 1967; Hetherington & Feldman, 1964; Parke, 1967; Sears, Rau, & Alpert, 1965; Stephens, Miller, & McLaughlin, 1969; Walsh, 1967; Weinberger, 1961; Worell & Worell, 1971).

However, even in these studies there are interactions that qualify the generality of the sex differences. For example, Feldman and Feldman (1967) found no differences for 12-year-olds; but among 17- and 18-year-olds, boys cheated more than girls. As already noted, this age-related sex difference seems connected to differential sex-role expectations that boys will go on to college to prepare for occupational success. Just the opposite age trends, however, were reported in the longitudinal study of Stephens, Miller, and McLaughlin (1969). They found sex differences in children of 6 to 10 years (boys cheated more than girls); but this sex difference in honesty decreased with age, until in late adolescence (14 to 18 years) there was no difference. The conclusion from these findings is that there are no reliable overall sex differences in honesty. The differences found are contingent on other factors that interact with the sex of the subject, such as the motivation elicited by the tests and the age of the subjects.

NORMS, GROUP CODES

One of the major determinants of honesty and dishonesty found by Hartshorne and May (1928) was the group code. Even with the smallest social unit, such as siblings, there was a correlation among the cheating scores of that group's members. The total cheating scores of siblings in their sample correlated even higher (.47) than did the siblings' scores on IQ tests (.12 to .35). The relationship between close friends' cheating was also positive and varied directly with the physical proximity of the friends in their school. For example, the deception of close friends sitting next to one another correlated up to .73. It was also found that when class groups were studied over time, their cheating scores became more homogeneous, indicating that a group code was being more firmly established. Prediction of average honesty in a classroom from the average classroom moral knowledge (or vice versa), then, is far more reliable than the prediction for individuals within the classroom. To illustrate, correlations increased from .29 for individual scores to .84 for classroom means in one school; and in another school the comparable correlations were .27 and .76. These analyses clearly demonstrate the influence of group norms on diverse measures of moral conduct.

Studies based on self-report measures also substantiate the influence of norms on behavior. For example, fraternity or sorority membership is associated with greater self-reported cheating than nonmembership (Bonjean & McGee, 1965; Bowers, 1964; Harp & Taietz, 1966). Furthermore, the normative attitudes toward cheating in different schools or colleges or courses of study within a university are distinctly different. Roskens and Dizney (1966) found that business administration students (mainly men) were low in their concern about cheating, whereas education majors (mainly women) were high in concern about cheating. Course major and fraternity-sorority membership have been more strongly related to the self-report of cheating than personal background measures (Bonjean & McGee, 1965; Bowers, 1964) and are independent and additive in their relation to self-reported cheating (Harp & Taietz, 1966).

Additional normative measures related to self-reported cheating are the systems for controlling cheating used by the colleges (less cheating with internal control, the honor system, than with external control, proctors) and the reported norms both of the respondent himself and of his friends regarding deception in taking exams. Bowers (1964) demonstrated that the greater the disapproval of deviation by one's peers, the less the individual reported participation in deviation. A study by Knowlton and Hamerlynck (1967) indicated that observations of deception committed by friends and acquaintances, as well as by oneself, contribute to the establishment of normative standards for one's own conduct.

Studies measuring actual behavior support these findings regarding self-reports of deception. Sherrill, Horowitz, Friedman, and Salisbury (1970) found that cheaters tend to sit adjacent to one another rather than scatter randomly, and furthermore, that a student who sits near or next to cheaters is more likely to cheat on the next exam. Canning (1956) studied the effect of instituting an honor system on actual cheating. Prior to the introduction of the honor system, 81 percent of the students cheated on an examination. During the four-year period of establishing and revising the honor code, cheating was reduced to 41 percent of the students. In a follow-up study five years after the honor system began, only 30 percent of the students cheated. These data substantiate the finding of Bonjean and McGee (1965) that the inculcation of a normative standard of internal control based on the honor system is related to less cheating than a system in which proctors and external monitors are used to inhibit deception.

The relation between honesty and social class can also be interpreted as demonstrating the effect of the context of normative standards on moral conduct. Hartshorne and May (1928) found that various measures of class status related positively to honesty, the most consistent single measure across all types of cheating being the father's occupation (average, .41). Pearlin (1971; Pearlin, Yarrow, & Scarr, 1967) has demonstrated how parents' position in the social structure and parents' childbearing practices and aspirations for children can interact to affect deceptive behavior. High parental pressures to succeed (assessed in a questionnaire) related to actual deception when the parent and child interacted on a cheating test, and this relation was especially prominent when the family was of low economic status and the parent expressed high educational aspirations for the child.

An especially effective way to *change* the norms for conduct is to provide the subject with standards of performance set by others. Hartshorne and May (1928), for example, found that informing the subject about how well other students did increased cheating if this information produced an unfavorable discrepancy with his own score; adding the information that the test performance contributed to the course grade increased cheating even more. Taylor and Lewit (1966) found in a strength test with delinquent boys that cheating increased as the subjects were given information about the "superior" performance of a peer and as their own performance was made public (versus anonymous). J. P. Hill and Kochendorfer (1969) replicated the finding that knowledge of another's superior performance increases cheating. These findings suggest that the norms for moral conduct are not rigidly fixed and determined only by extended interaction with the group, but can be manipulated in the immediate situation. Perhaps this flexibility of norms is most clearly demonstrated by modeling experiments.

MODELING EXPERIMENTS

Modeling experiments clearly demonstrate that dishonest models can increase deception in children, but less clearly indicate that honest models can increase honest conduct. In a study by A. H. Stein (1967), a deviant adult model increased deviation among children assigned a boring job, but nondeviant models had little influence. Ross (1971) similarly found that a deviant model (a same-sex peer in this study) increased "stealing" (94 percent of the children) and that a nondeviant peer had a positive effect, producing less stealing (19 percent) than in the no-model group (41 percent). Rosenkoetter (1973) found similar effects, though of lesser magnitude. Although statistical significance of the prosocial effects for the Ross and Rosenkoetter studies is low ($p < .07$ and $< .10$, respectively), these studies indicate that modeling effects can have a positive influence.

Wolf and Cheyne (1972) have extended this experiment to compare live behavioral, televised behavioral, and live verbal models, and to include assessments of the effects after a month. Immediately after the model treatments, the conforming models significantly increased resistance to temptation (playing with a prohibited toy), and the deviant models significantly increased deviation. The effect of the deviant models, especially the live and televised behavioral models, continued to be significant on the follow-up test one month later. The effects of the conforming models, however, were quite different. Children who had observed the live conforming behavioral model continued to resist playing with the prohibited toy, but the children who had observed either the televised behavioral or the live verbal models were significantly less resistant to the temptation than a no-model control group. For these children, it was as if the original televised or verbal prohibition had enhanced the forbidden toy's attractiveness. The use of same-age peers by both Ross (1971) and Wolf and Cheyne (1972) has demonstrated that modeling effects that disinhibit antisocial behavior are not simply procedural influences of adult models condoning prohibited behavior, as has been suggested by some investigators (e.g., W. Weiss, 1968).

In a study where cheating consisted of not reporting that one had received a grade higher than deserved, McQueen (1957) found that 96 percent of college students cheated. This behavior was dramatically reduced by having a confederate student immediately report an overscoring (only 42 percent then cheated) and was further reduced by having the instructor praise the confederate for his honesty (only 14 percent then failed to report

overscores). In this real-life situation, the positive model clearly influenced behavior in the direction of increased honesty.

Support for a cumulative modeling effect on prosocial, as well as antisocial behavior, was provided by the finding of Hartshorne and May (1928) that the model of honesty (or dishonesty) provided by parents increases the consistency of honesty (or dishonesty) in their child.

RISK

Motivational variables such as fear of failure are affected by the risk involved in a deception. Hartshorne and May (1928), for example, found that within any mode or type of cheating situation, degree of risk was directly related to the inhibition of deception.

Many subsequent studies have confirmed this functional effect of risk. Canning (1956) found that cheating was less when subjects were given an ink pen to use than when they were given an erasable pencil. Howells (1938) used two highly concealed techniques for measuring cheating. The test that elicited more suspicion, as indicated in a subsequent questionnaire, produced significantly lesser amounts of cheating. Atkins and Atkins (1936) found that cheating increased with less risk of having the deviance observed: Students who had to turn around to look at test answers on the blackboard cheated less than students seated directly facing the board. These researchers also found that cheaters took more chances in trying to guess answers.

INCENTIVE

A common-sense notion about temptation is that there should be a greater motivation to deviate if there is more to gain. Using two cheating tests with two types of incentives manipulated, Mills (1958) found that more cheating was elicited by the high incentive of tangible prizes as compared with the low incentive of having the names of successful performers read aloud in class. However, offering fifty cents (low incentive) versus five dollars (high incentive) had no effect on cheating behavior among the students. The monetary incentive was either irrelevant or appeared to be unreasonable or "fishy" to the subjects. By contrast, five-dollar versus fifty-cent levels of incentive were effective with prisoners in the Brodsky and Jacobson (1970) study, but again, had no influence on the honesty of college students. Nakasato and Aoyama (1970) found that when extensive cheating was required to obtain a badge attesting to shooting skill more cheating was elicited among delinquents than among high school students.

High importance placed on performance in a vocabulary test increased cheating in sixth-graders, who cheated less when the test was presented as unimportant (Vitro, 1969). An interesting field study of altruistic honesty by Merritt and Fowler (1948) used a technique of dropping addressed and stamped envelopes. When the envelope contained a sheet of paper folded like a letter, most people mailed it (85 percent); but when a fifty-cent piece appeared to be enclosed, only 54 percent of the letters were returned, some obviously resealed. In this low-risk situation, the incentive of money clearly increased deviation.

There is some indication (Burton, 1960) that the age of the child as well as the type of test has much to do with the effect that external incentives will have on cheating. With a beanbag game test, attractive prizes were required to obtain about a 50 percent dichotomy between cheating and no cheating with middle-class white children of 4 years. But when 5-year-olds were tested in this same game, the external incentives became superfluous: The percentages of cheaters remained quite constant whether or not a prize was offered. The incentive to score was adequate to elicit deviations among the 5-year-

olds, whereas the 4-year-olds required external prizes to arouse enough temptation to violate the rules.

Incentive, then, seems to have an effect if it is matched to the interest of the subjects and does not arouse suspicion. It may also be shown that the differences in incentives interact with the degree of risk involved, so that deception increases with a low incentive only if the risk is quite clearly negligible; with risk held constant, incentive is directly related to the tendency to deceive.

FEAR OF FAILURE AND NEED TO SUCCEED

As noted above, knowledge of others' performance scores increases cheating. This method of manipulating norms may also increase the motive to avoid a feeling of failure, especially if one's relatively poor performance should become public (J. P. Hill & Kochendorfer, 1969; Taylor & Lewit, 1966).

C. F. Gilligan (1963) found that test anxiety, assumed to assess fear of failure, correlated strongly with cheating by sixth-grade boys in an achievement game. This finding was corroborated by Shelton and Hill (1969) for 15- to 16-year-old boys and girls in a word construction test. Both of these studies indicate that the relation of fear of failure to cheating interacts with other motives also. C. F. Gilligan (1963) found that the combination of high achievement motivation and high fear of failure produced the largest number of deviators, whereas the combination of high achievement motivation with low fear of failure was related to the least amount of deception.

A recent study by Burton and Goldberg (n.d.) demonstrates how fear of failure and need to succeed can be directly inculcated by parents and inadvertently elicit dishonesty in children. A comparison of the behavior of children when tested alone and when tested with their mothers present clearly showed that the mothers' presence delayed the onset of cheating and reduced the amount. Nevertheless, more children eventually cheated in their mothers' presence than had cheated when alone. Analyses of the mother-child interactions showed that maternal pressures on the child to achieve success overcame the initial inhibitory influence of her presence and led to the child's cheating.

The possibility of a relationship between one's self-esteem and reactions to fear of failure has been investigated in several studies. David (1967) employed an ego-strength scale, developed to predict successful response to psychotherapy, and found rather surprisingly that ego-strength scores of college women correlated with cheating ($r = .49$), a finding opposite to expectations based on Kohlberg's hypothesis (1964) that ego strength should relate positively to honesty. There was no relation for men. Similarly, the study by Jacobson, Berger, and Millham (1970) found that women with high scores on a self-satisfaction test—which measured the difference between their level of aspiration and expectancy of success scores (similar to a measure of self-esteem)—tended to cheat more than women with low self-satisfaction scores. Again, there was no relation for men.

The picture begins to lose focus with data from other studies. For example, Eisen (1972) found self-esteem unrelated to honesty for 11- to 12-year-old girls, but there was a positive correlation for boys ($r = .40$). In contrast, Mussen and his colleagues (1970) reported that measures of self-esteem for 11- to 12-year-old boys related positively to cheating. For girls, however, the relation was opposite to these previous findings and supported the Kohlberg hypothesis that self-esteem relates positively to honesty. A positive relationship between self-esteem and honesty for females was also indicated in an experimental study by Aronson and Mettee (1968). These authors manipulated the self-esteem of women college students by giving them false feedback about their personality profiles. The women in the lowered self-esteem group cheated more than those in either the control group or the raised self-esteem group.

A comparative study of high school students in Georgia, Quebec, and Scotland found that students in all three societies perceived the major cause of cheating in schools to be fear of failure (Schab, 1971). Similarly, in a study by C. P. Smith, Ryan, and Diggins (1972), college subjects reported that competition for grades is the major cause for academic cheating in college. It seems clear that people are aware of a connection between fear of failure (anxiety) and cheating.

DELAY OF GRATIFICATION

Maller (1934) labeled the general factor extracted from Hartshorne and May's measures of character a *delay of gratification* dimension. This motivational concept seems to apply to many of the tests of honesty; and yet, as our review has indicated, it appears to be only one of many motivational determinants of honest conduct. Mischel and Gilligan (1964) directly tested the relationship between cheating and delay of gratification in a ray-gun game with sixth-grade boys. Preference for a delayed, larger reward, as opposed to an immediate, smaller reward, was associated with greater resistance to temptation and also to a smaller amount of cheating in the boys who did yield. The implication was that "impulse control" was the underlying dimension shared by both the measures of delay of gratification and of resistance to temptation. A study by Brock and Del-Giudice (1963) found that second- through eighth-graders who resisted the temptation to take money were more oriented to concepts of time, such as *yesterday, last month, next week*, than were children who stole money. The stealers evidenced a "now" orientation: They were unlikely to use temporal concepts in telling stories, and the actual time span covered by their stories was very limited.

The evidence by Nakasato and Aoyama (1970) that delinquents tend to deviate early in a game, compared with normal pupils, provides some validation that inability to delay gratification is related to lower self-control. Johnson and Gormly (1972), however, found no direct relation between delay of gratification and honesty. Yet delay of gratification was related to a network of other measures, such as achievement motivation, course grades, and belief in internal control over one's own academic achievement. This suggests that the delay-of-reward and honesty indexes both reflect an underlying dimension of self-control, but may not always be significantly correlated with each other.

This review of situational and personal determinants of honesty provides evidence of the variability of moral behavior. But there is a counterbalancing picture of consistency. Functional relations between moral conduct and certain experimental treatments—such as the manipulation of norms, risk, incentive, or modeling —and the functional relations between conduct and some motivational measures —such as knowledge of others' performance and fear of failure—are consistently produced. Many different measures of honesty have been used, and various measures of these independent variables have also been employed; yet the consistency of the functional relationships is impressive. We see, therefore, that an assessment of the generality of honesty based only on the extent of intercorrelations among measures of honest conduct would have been incomplete.

With this consideration before us, let us turn from situational determinants of already learned behaviors to the effects of different socialization paradigms that may contribute to the development of honesty, that is, factors influencing the acquisition of moral conduct.

The Socialization of Honesty

This chapter began with a discussion of the development of conscience in children as a central part of the socialization process. We now look at the studies that most directly explore socialization techniques.

WARMTH

The psychoanalytically derived hypothesis that a warm mother-child relationship is a necessary condition for high conscience development has led to many studies assessing this relationship. Reviewers of this literature generally agree that the evidence supports the conclusion of a positive relationship between the warmth of the mother and conscience development in the child (Yarrow, Campbell, & Burton, 1968). However, most of the data contributing to this conclusion come from interview studies, many of which involve measures obtained from the same source: the warmth assessments and the measures of the child's conscience both come from either the parent or the child. The rearing measures also entail recall of treatments at earlier periods, a procedure whose validity is suspect (Burton, 1970; Yarrow, Campbell, & Burton, 1968). Furthermore, the measures of the child's conscience have emphasized reactions following deviation (i.e., guilt) rather than resistance to temptation or actual moral conduct in the temptation situation. As shall be seen, studies based on independent measures of childrearing antecedents and child behavior show far less consistency in revealing a relation between parental warmth and honesty.

In a study of 4-year-olds (Burton, Maccoby, & Allinsmith, 1961), the interview measure of maternal warmth developed by Sears, Maccoby, and Levin (1957) was found to be related to behavioral cheating for girls, but there was a tendency toward a positive relationship between warmth and honesty for boys.

Grinder (1962) found no relation between cheating in a ray-gun game at age 12 and the maternal interview measures of warmth (Sears, Maccoby, & Levin, 1957) obtained when the children were 6 years old. Sears, Rau, and Alpert (1965) discovered little consistent relationship between parental warmth and honest conduct. The father's hostility was positively related to honesty, but so was the father's affectional demonstrativeness for boys. For girls, measures reflecting paternal warmth were negatively related to honesty. Maternal warmth was unrelated to honest conduct for either boys or girls. Mussen and his colleagues (1970) used a card-sorting measure in a maternal interview for assessing mother-child warmth. This measure related to cheating for boys and to honesty for girls, exactly the opposite of what Burton, Maccoby, and Allinsmith (1961) found. There is, then, no consistency to be found in the relationship between warmth as measured through a maternal interview and behavioral honesty assessed in a temptation test.

Warmth has also been assessed by observational ratings. Hartshorne and May (1928) did home observations on a relatively small subsample of their children and found that the warmth of both parents was significantly related to the child's honesty. It was interesting, however, that the children who evidenced one aspect of conscience, confession, were the children from the *least warm* family environment. In the previously cited interview studies, warmth and guilt were positively correlated; but in Hartshorne and May's study (1928), based on *behavioral* observations, warmth and guilt were negatively associated. The cross-cultural research of J. W. M. Whiting and Child (1953) found neither a positive nor a negative relation between warmth and guilt.

The study by Burton and Goldberg (n.d.) demonstrates that the relation between warmth and honesty depends on how warmth is manipulated as a reinforcer

in shaping honest or deceptive behavior. In this study, children were tested for honesty in following the rules of a game. A week later, mothers, not knowing the child was to play by specified rules, were asked to be with their child while he replayed the game. In this achievement-oriented situation, an index of all observed expressions of maternal warmth correlated positively with the child's cheating. However, further analyses showed that cheating related exclusively to the mother's use of warmth contingent with the child's successful performance, whereas noncontingent warmth was unrelated to honesty.

For further analyses, the study assumed that the mother's long-term affectional relationship was reflected by the noncontingent warmth observed during the experiment. If one grants this assumption, the findings can be taken as demonstrating that noncontingent warmth—that is, warmth as a general context of the mother-child relationship—may markedly affect the impact of the mother's immediate warmth on the child's honesty, especially in boys. Contingent warmth in a low-warmth context related strongly to the boys' cheating, but in a high-warmth context a slight tendency in the opposite direction was found. Contingent warmth tended to relate positively with sons' honesty. Techniques involving withdrawal of love (e.g., criticism of the child's performance) in a high-warmth context related to cheating, but they related with honesty in a low-warmth context. Finally, direct pressures for achievement related to cheating when the level of warmth was high, but such pressures were ineffective in a low-warmth context.

These results indicate that warmth does not invariably lead to honesty, but is an effective reinforcer used by the parent to shape the child's behavior to conform to the values the parent sees as appropriate to the situation. In an achievement context, where success conflicts with honesty, warmth may be used inadvertently by the parent to shape deception. For research purposes it may be more profitable to conceptualize warmth in a long-term relationship as a resource dispensed at a stabilized rate. If dispensed at a high frequency, warmth may have to be withheld to be effective as a contingent reinforcer. If warmth is already being given at a low rate, no further withdrawal is necessary.

PUNISHMENT

A basic goal of socialization is to teach children that their immediate wishes cannot always be satisfied. It is clear when one considers the socialization of children the world over that negative sanctions are used far more to inculcate standards for behavior than are positive reinforcements (J. W. M. Whiting, 1959).

The major theoretical explorations of the effects of punishment have come primarily from laboratory studies with animals. The independent variables studied most have been the timing, intensity, consistency, and frequency of the punishment, the previous establishment of the response to be punished by positive or negative reinforcement, and the general context preceding and following the punishment. Since the 1960s, conclusions from these experiments with animals have been tested in experiments with children. Studies of human subjects have explored the additional independent variables of the cognitive context in which the punishment occurs and the direct versus vicarious experience of punishment. The most recent reviews of these studies have been by Aronfreed (1968c) and Parke (1970). The present discussion of punishment will consider the factors of intensity, response alternatives, and interactions with reasoning. (See Aronfreed, 1968c, chap. 5, for a discussion of timing.)

Intensity. As Church (1963) has noted in his review, the intensity of a punishment can have quite different effects on behavior depending on the history of punishment and the context in which it has previously occurred. If punishment begins at a very low level of intensity and gradually increases, it becomes a discriminative stimulus for the occurrence of a response, rather than a suppressor. If a low to moderate level of punishment is maintained and frequently administered, the organism adapts to it, rendering it less effective in suppressing behavior. If a particular punishment is administered for a response that had been learned to avoid this same punishment, the response seems to be strengthened rather than suppressed. However, a new type of punishment administered for the same response will suppress it (Carlsmith, 1961).

For obvious social and ethical reasons, there has been a paucity of research on varied intensity of punishment for humans, but some studies using different intensities have explored in humans the parallel effects that have been found with animal subjects (Aronfreed & Leff, 1963; Cheyne, 1971, 1972; Cheyne & Walters, 1969; Leff, 1969; Parke, 1969; Parke & Walters, 1967). In these studies, punishment intensity varied by different levels of tone or noise such as 65 decibels versus 96 decibels of tone (Parke & Walters, 1967), or 50 decibels versus 88 decibels of noise (Parke, 1969). The differential levels of intensity were always combined with at least the verbal rebuke, "No!" It would have been useful for some of these experiments to vary only the physical punishment rather than always combining it with some verbal component, even if the verbal comment seemed very mild. Although intensity, like timing and other variables of punishment, involves complex interactions, the general function is for the intensity of punishment to monotonically increase the suppression of a response.

The sensitive parent must realize that the long-term context determines the effectiveness of a stimulus as a punisher. The general rule is that the initial level of punishment should be high enough to be effective for inhibiting the behavior. However, if parents are careful to reserve punishment for actions that they consider really important to suppress, very mild intensities tend to be adequate for children.

Response alternatives. The suppression of certain behavior is only part of the process of socializing children. Theory and evidence clearly indicate the desirability of providing an acceptable alternative response in a resistance-to-temptation situation (Aronfreed, 1968c; Benton, 1966; Solomon, 1964; J. W. M. Whiting & Mowrer, 1943). The combination of punishment for the forbidden response and reinforcement for a desired act that is incompatible with the transgression is the most effective paradigm for shaping moral conduct.

Furthermore, various procedures for punishing deviation can lead to qualitatively different forms of anxiety (Benton, 1966; Cheyne, 1971; Grusec & Ezrin, 1972; Ross, 1971; Solomon, Turner, & Lessac, 1968; Walters & Cheyne, 1966). If an acceptable, alternative response is available during the temptation period, or a punishment-terminating response is available following the deviation, the initial association of punishment-aroused anxiety with the prohibited response leads to the desired socialization. If the opposite conditions prevail—that is, if the desired, prosocial behavior is difficult to learn and punishment appears to be beyond the individual's control—the result is a generally debilitating and restrictive state of anxiety. This state can lead to the inhibition of all behavior in the situation or to fixated actions.

An extended time perspective is necessary in considering the training of honest behavior, especially since much dishonesty involves its own immediate reward. When attempting to modify dishonesty, socializing agents can be quite conscious of punishing the undesirable behavior and providing positive reinforcement for the mutually exclusive honest act. But with some progress, the agent may overlook occasions for giving positive reinforcement. Inadvertently, conditions for extinguishing the honest response may occur. If the level of punishment intensity is very low, the dishonesty previously shown may reappear. If the dishonest behavior is highly rewarding, it will now be more difficult to suppress in order to reinstate the positive reinforcement for the alternative response. Therefore, parents and teachers who want to use minimally aversive punishment need to maintain their awareness of and reactions to the child's honest prosocial behavior.

Cognitive structure and reasoning. A major distinction between the research on animals and on humans is that with people, the cognitive context contributes significantly to the experimental effects. Sears, Maccoby, and Levin (1957) noted that the use of reasoning permits the parent to generalize from the specific instance in which the child is being trained to other instances in which the same orientation would apply. A cognitive generalization gradient was also considered a major factor contributing to generality of honesty in the social learning model proposed by the author (Burton, 1963). The moral discriminations that the child must learn are made easier with the addition of verbal information.

An experiment by Kanfer and Duerfeldt (1968), however, showed that *labeling* alone does not effectively decrease cheating if there is a strong motivation to achieve the gain. Apparently cognitive structure can increase honesty only when conditioned emotional responses previously associated with punishment also enter into the suppression of the prohibited response. Where it does not increase their sense of risk, labeling has apparently little impact on suppressing deviation in very young children. There was some indication in this experiment that labeling alone did make a difference in increasing compliance in older children. In adolescent boys, aversive punishment and a rationale were equally effective and were not additive in their effects (LaVoie, 1973). However, when the child's socialization history (in which these labels are likely to have been associated with direct punishment) is taken into account (Burton, Maccoby, & Allinsmith, 1961; Yarrow, Campbell, & Burton, 1968), there is a strong suggestion that reasoning alone may be effective with older children only because it remains associated with an emotional response of anxiety in an obedience situation.

In almost all of the experimental studies, the variables of timing, intensity, and cognitive structure were tested on only two levels. Despite this limited exploration of the variables, investigators have concluded that the relationships between the independent variables and the suppression of prohibited behavior are linear. In a rare exception, Cheyne (1972) reported a parametric study in which cognitive structure varied on three levels. Suppression of the prohibited response was directly related to the levels of concrete information provided to specify a rationale for the child's not performing the response. The evidence further indicated that the effect depended on the child's ability to understand the cognitive support provided. Kindergarten children gained very little when a normative statement was added to a simple rule statement. However, third-grade children showed a consistent linear effect, with increasing suppression accompanying the more elaborate cognitive structure.

Field experiments support the laboratory results regarding provision of clear and relevant cognitive structure. Atkins and Atkins (1936) showed that cheating among education students decreased from a mean of 3.45 changes of answers in a class test when achievement pressure was high, to .25 when the test immediately followed a discussion of how to prevent pupils' cheating on the type of test being taken. A more recent study by Fischer (1970) demonstrated similar effects for elementary school children.

PUNISHMENT AND REASONING COMBINED

It is increasingly rare, as the child becomes more mobile, for a parent to be present when the child is about to perform a deviation or has just performed one. This fact makes the principles of immediate (versus delayed) punishment of less practical use as children get older. Furthermore, parental reluctance to use intensely aversive forms of punishment renders the findings on high-intensity punishment essentially irrelevant from the standpoint of childrearing. When cognitive structure is introduced, however, there is evidence that the parents need use only mild and delayed punishment to inhibit deviation.

A study with special relevance for childrearing was conducted by Andres and Walters (1970). This study demonstrated that re-creating a deviation by one of three methods—videotape, the experimenter's verbal description, or the child's performance—and punishing the deviation when it occurred in the re-created version was an effective deterrent to subsequent deviation. Delayed punishment without any attempt to re-create the temptation situation was ineffective. What this study clearly demonstrates is the important principle that the stimulus conditions in which a deviation has occurred can be verbally reinstated, at least to some degree, allowing punishment to be administered in the re-created account at the point most effective for inhibiting subsequent deviation.

By clarifying what is required and forbidden in the situation, cognitive structure can also modify the effects of the motivational level aroused by punishment. Data provided by Aronfreed and Leff (1963) nicely fit with the Yerkes-Dodson (1908) hypothesis that there is an optimal level of motivation for learning a discrimination of a given level of complexity. On a simple discrimination, 42 percent of the children subjected to high-intensity punishment deviated during a test, whereas 75 percent of the children subjected to low-intensity punishment deviated; with a complex discrimination, 72 percent of the children deviated in the high-punishment condition, whereas 42 percent deviated in the low-punishment condition. These data indicate that high arousal of affect in a complex moral dilemma could serve to increase rather than suppress prohibited behavior.

Some evidence suggests that reasoning may cancel and possibly reverse the general effects of timing and intensity of punishment. That is, high-intensity punishment administered early in the response sequence may produce less suppression of a prohibited response than a low intensity of delayed punishment if the same level of reasoning accompanies both punishment conditions (Cheyne, 1971; Cheyne & Walters, 1969; Parke, 1969; Parke & Walters, 1967). Delayed punishment of low intensity seems to increase the child's attention to the reasoning given by the agent. Changes in heart rate produced by early and intense punishment suggested that heightened emotional reactions interfere with the child's discrimination of the disapproved behavior from the acceptable response (Cheyne, 1971; Cheyne, Goyeche, & Walters, 1969).

Provision of cognitive structure generally supplies the child with verbal labels which he may then use for "self-instruction" during resistance-to-temptation situations. For examples, studies by O'Leary (1968; Monahan & O'Leary, 1971) demonstrate that children instructed to label their own behavior as *Right* and *Wrong* or as *Yes, I should do this* and *No, I shouldn't do that*, suppress prohibited behavior more than uninstructed children.

A recent field study by Greenglass (1972) indicates the need to test these conclusions regarding the provision of cognitive structure and reasoning in natural situations. In her study, the quality of maternal communication was scored from observations of mother-child interactions during decision-making tasks. These measures were then related to the 9- to 10-year-old child's performance in a temptation test. Honesty was positively associated with restrictive and authoritative maternal patterns of communication and negatively related to the use of reasoning! Furthermore, honesty in girls was related to their perception that their parents exerted strong control over their behavior. These data certainly contradict the expectations based on the findings of the experimental studies on cognitive structure and reasoning, as well as the findings suggesting that moral conduct is related to the individual's perception of his behavior as self-determined rather than externally controlled (e.g., Aronfreed, 1963; Lepper, 1973; White, 1972). Clearly, the importance of observation-based findings so contrary to the conclusions drawn from controlled experiments requires the replication of these naturalistic data.

CONSISTENCY OF SCHEDULES OF DISCIPLINE

In child development literature *consistency* in childrearing is considered desirable and means that parents should always evaluate the same acts of their children as being good or bad. A recent study by Stouwie (1971) confirms this interpretation. Children subjected to consistently prohibitive instructions by two adult experimenters were the most resistant to temptation, whereas children subjected to consistently permissive instructions were the most deviant. When one adult was permissive and the other was prohibitive, the children were in-between the two consistent groups and differed significantly from both of them. Clearly, when one parent interprets a response as a deviation and the other parent sees it as insignificant and morally irrelevant, the discrimination of proper conduct is made difficult for the child. The child's task would be even more confusing were the same parent to sometimes punish, sometimes ignore, and sometimes reward the same action. The combination of being rewarded and punished for the same behavior has been shown to produce the most persistent deviance when the behavior is subjected to extinction (both reward and punishment are stopped) or when punishment continues and all reward ends (Deur & Parke, 1968, 1970). Studies of delinquents and their parents indicate that just such inconsistent or capricious discipline is associated with socially undesirable behavior.

Consideration of the experimental literature, however, indicates that *a certain kind* of inconsistency in the use of disciplinary techniques is desirable for producing internalized self-control (Burton, 1968). But *inconsistency* here means that the parents do not *always* punish the deviation or register approval of (reinforce) honesty, and that they do not *always* employ the same technique of punishment or reward for the same act. Evidence supporting this hypothesis has been provided in a study by Leff (1969). Intermittently punished children (i.e., those punished only half of the time and in an unpredictable sequence) suppressed a deviant response the same as children who had received twice as many punishments under continuous conditions. These data demonstrate that intermittent schedules are both as effective as continuous schedules and certainly more humane.

Conclusions and Directions for Research

The generality of moral conduct was the first issue of this review. Consistency across different measures of honesty or any other personality concept must be considered by any empirical investigator who implies that findings are relevant beyond the operational definitions of a particular study. One always hopes to draw conclusions from data with the broadest possible context, extending the findings to persons beyond the immediate sample and also to other instances of behavior connoted by the label honesty. However, the evidence indicates only a modest level of generality among different measures of honest conduct, and even less generality across behavioral, judgmental, and affective dimensions of honesty. Thus, to employ a single or small number of measures to classify an individual as more or less honest or moral is simply not supported by empirical evidence.

In studying factors affecting the acquisition and performance of honest conduct, the proper focus is the functional relation between the antecedent and the consequent variables (e.g., between the timing of discipline for an unacceptable act and the subsequent resistance to temptation involving the same act). Generalization in this context involves the assumption that another measure of behavioral honesty will demonstrate the same functional relation—*all other things being held constant.* Our review of the studies on the effects of situational determinants on honest conduct has provided a more optimistic picture of consistency than was found for the assessment based only on alternative measures of behavioral honesty, and certainly stronger support than was obtained from searching for generality across different modes of morality. Findings have been stable across studies with different measures and samples of subjects, although the findings have frequently involved rather complex, contingent interactions. For example, the relation between age and honesty was slight and unreliable when honesty was measured by summing individual test scores; but when honesty was assessed by consistency across many different measures of behavior, the association between age and honest conduct was noticeably stronger. Similarly, stable relations were found between various measures of honesty and other situational factors such as risk, norms for behavioral tests, and the effect of contingent punishment on suppression of deviation.

Even though the functional relations between honesty measures and environmental factors are more robust than for other measures of generality, the conditions affecting these functional relations must also be explored. We have seen how a general relation can be modified by an additional variable. The association between risk and cheating holds only for persons with some fear of failure, and the relation between timing of punishment and suppression of deviation applies only to conditions of low cognitive structure. Moreover, the generality of a functional relation has been shown to interact with the characteristics of the honesty test: Too much affective arousal either during the learning of a difficult discrimination between the honest and deviant choices or during a test of what has been learned can interfere with the directive control provided by cognitive mediation. In order to clarify the kind of interaction that occurs, designs that replicate the simpler relations previously established are needed.

Experimental studies of socialization also need to extend the parametric variations of independent variables. For the most part, studies have involved two levels of each variable. The differences found between these two levels and in the interactions between variables may well demonstrate linear functions. However, the many examples of contingency relations in studies of complex human behavior strongly indicate that all of the findings currently available will not remain simple linear associations.

Some of the studies reviewed here suggest, in line with Skinner's advocacy of positive reinforcement (1953), that punishment in natural socialization is superfluous in eliciting moral conduct. This would be welcome information to parents who want to avoid subjecting their children and themselves to the unpleasant experience of aversive disciplinary practices. Yet this author agrees with Aronfreed (1968c) that consideration of theory and all available evidence indicates that affective components of low magnitude are adequate and necessary for cognitive structure to exert a directive control over overt behavior. Once a response that avoids pun-

ishment and its concomitant fear arousal has been learned well, performance can occur with little elicitation of the originally heightened affective components (Solomon & Wynne, 1954). This "anxiety conservation" seems especially plausible in view of the human capacity to employ verbal mediators to direct behavior; once established, the mediator appears to function independently of its emotional origins.

In spite of this evidence, research is still needed to answer the question, Is it possible to inculcate reliable moral conduct solely through positive reinforcement? Certainly we should explore more thoroughly the use of different types of positive reinforcement in shaping resistance to temptation. For example, it might be possible to produce reliable moral conduct by using intermittent schedules and by providing much more reinforcement for a desirable response than is gained by a deviant response. Even if unsuccessful, such research could demonstrate the minimum amount of punishment necessary for inculcating self-control in temptation situations. Clinical literature (cf. Mowrer, 1950) shows that punitive training for conscience development can have deleterious effects which are studiously to be avoided. To minimize and, whenever possible, to eliminate punishment is, therefore, not only more humane but also functionally desirable.

A continuous interplay between laboratory and field studies is also needed to prevent and correct inappropriate extensions of experimental findings. For example, it is concluded from laboratory findings that suppression of undesirable behavior by punishment permits reinforcement of mutually exclusive, alternative responses that the socializing agent wants to inculcate in the child. In applying this principle, the parent may assume that scolding and bawling out the child is punishing and will suppress the undesirable act. Yet field observations of children with their parents and teachers have indicated that such seemingly punitive techniques can serve as positive reinforcers for the child's undesirable behavior (Scott, Burton, & Yarrow, 1967). When direct observations in the natural settings establish that certain stimuli are aversive or rewarding for a child, then the principles derived from the controlled laboratory experiments can be employed appropriately rather than misapplied.

Furthermore, the attempt to establish control and careful measurement in the natural setting can bring into focus variables not yet explored in the laboratory, but crucial in real life. Socialization theory and research often imply that parents, especially mothers, are the primary socialization agents, and, therefore, their actions deserve to be the major focus in socialization studies. Yet, as the child moves into the outside world, there is no assumption that the mother remains the primary agent. As Bandura (1971b) has noted, a social-learning position assumes quite the opposite. Siblings, peers, nonfamilial adults, and models—live, televised, and literary—also influence the child's development. With the addition of these socializing agents, conflicting values and standards are presented to the child. The inconsistencies are complex, the dissimilarities being not only between significant agents but within the agents, who may attempt to impose different standards on the child and on themselves. Again, this is an area where the controlled laboratory study and the natural, ecological study can feed one another. The current studies on inconsistent models will provide greater specification of the effects of such socializing agents.

The social-learning laboratory approach to morality has been challenged with not accounting adequately for how behavior as complex as moral conduct becomes "independent" of external control. The major focus of moral conduct studies is on how a person acts when he is not under surveillance. The evidence of the resistance-to-temptation paradigms indicates that the manipulation of external events does differentially affect internalized

behavior. It may be argued that the behavior becomes so dissociated from external control that there must be additional principles to account for its persistence or "functional autonomy." Yet these reservations seem dissipated by the experimental evidence of the stubbornness of behavior produced through aperiodic schedules of reinforcement, especially if these intermittent schedules also involve rewards and punishments for the behavior. These experiments demonstrate that an action that persists despite the apparent absence of visible reinforcement may, nevertheless, be the result of a complex history of external reinforcement. Although the most dramatic example of this phenomenon is the pigeon who continues until death to peck a key at a high rate after the food dispenser has been shut off, the same principle would seem to apply even more to humans. The child's growing capacity for verbal coding which can facilitate the acquisition of self-reinforcing mediators increases the likelihood that intermittent schedules are operative in human development. Furthermore, the exploration of the environmental control of such persistent behavior provides optimistic hints of how undesirable persistent behavior may be modified.

Studies with sociological and cross-cultural points of view provide perspective for the principles of controlled experiments. The laboratory data demonstrate how individual behavior can be shaped, made relatively persistent, and generalized to many situations. These studies also demonstrate that moral conduct is subject to current, situational conditions. Consideration of this evidence in a sociological and cross-cultural context clearly indicates that the best way to decrease deviance is to arrange the total environment so as to reduce temptation. For example, the pressures for competitive success could be lessened in school situations. Development of such competitiveness may be good for maximizing profit in middle-class business, but an overemphasis on obtaining success and avoiding failure can conflict with moral conduct in many real-life situations and lead to "white-collar" or "corporate" crime; perhaps most painfully exposed in the immoral conduct of those who participated in Watergate activities.

Even more importantly, the studies employing broad social variables, such as class and family structure, indicate how factors outside the experimenter's control can frustrate attempts to engineer long-term changes in individual behavior. The behavior of an individual can be dramatically modified in a controlled environment, such as a jail or halfway house; but upon release, the individual's behavior typically reverts to what it was prior to training and complies with the reinforcing contingencies of the subject's natural environment. The evidence and theoretical principles of social learning predict just such "flexibility," or responsiveness to environmental contingencies. Obviously, applications of social-learning principles to ameliorate special problems are doomed to failure in the long run if limited to settings other than natural conditions. For delinquent- and prison-training programs to have a lasting impact, poverty and ghetto conditions must also be simultaneously changed. Thus, principles of social learning must be seen in their broadest context—as environmental contingencies that impinge on the individual whether they are under his control or occur as a result of his position in the larger social structure.

Cross-cultural and field investigations also provide perspective on the kinds of measures used to explore the acquisition and performance of moral conduct. The experimental studies of self-control have utilized simple exercises that seem to be unambiguous tests of honesty. These measures reflect a particular social group's consensus of what is honest or dishonest conduct. A cross-cultural perspective, however, indicates that a behavior may be considered deviant in one social context and prosocial and altruistic in another. Within the competitive Anglo-American culture, letting another copy one's answers is cheating; but in Mexican and other cultures with noncompetitive values and early inculcation of the child's responsibility for others, helping someone with a problem would simply be required altruism (J. W. M. Whiting & Whiting, 1974).

The cross-cultural perspective on important aspects of moral conduct in our society is demonstrated in studies of crime. A strong and stable relationship has been found between delinquency and the deprived environment of the lower class in our society. Cross-cultural data demonstrate that an exclusive mother-child living arrangement—theoretically related to sex-identity conflict in males—is strongly correlated with theft and personal crime (Bacon, Child, & Barry, 1963; Burton & Whiting, 1961; B. B. Whiting, 1965). In lower-class, high-crime ghettos the frequency of father-absent households is high. Thus, the cross-cultural studies provide clues to the specific factors related to crime among those living in the deprived conditions of a ghetto.

Field studies are also needed to explore how to maintain the effectiveness of conditions demonstrated to control behavior in the experimental setting. For example, it is the experience of many parents that children do not attend to their instructions, to the cognitive structure the parents offer. Certainly, some children disregard their parents' demands more than those of a stranger (Landauer, Carlsmith, & Lepper, 1970). Do middle-class parents talk their children to death in attempts to provide rationales for discipline? Is it possible that reasoning loses its effectiveness more rapidly than other techniques?

In this review, studies using measures that could be termed "sins of omission" have been noticeably rare. Yet the frequency of such temptations in daily life should be recognized in research on honesty. Do the same relations hold for honesty requiring some positive action as for honesty based on the inhibition of negative action?

There is a manifest need for further

development of observational methods and analytic procedures to apply to interactional data in natural settings. Although it is generally recognized that the behavior of the socializing agent is influenced by the child as well as conversely (Sears, 1951), few studies have analyzed data according to interactional sequences. Reliable and wieldy procedures would permit more precise exploration of many difficult questions such as the sources of omnipresent, though highly variable, sex differences. Data are needed on differential treatment of children from infancy onward so that we may understand why reactions to experimental treatments or situational conditions vary as a function of factors such as sex, class, and ethnicity. In the absence of reliably quantified observational measures, interpretations now hinge on the investigator's personal predilections regarding the contributions of nature and nurture.

CHAPTER 11

New Approaches in the Assessment of Moral Judgment

James R. Rest

Introduction

Empirical investigation in any area typically begins by sketching out the grand ideas, and then undertaking the first round of studies in the hope of producing meaningful data trends. If encouraging results are obtained, then the viability of the research area depends upon continuing reexamination and refinement of the theory and methods of investigation, a process whereby the original promise of an approach is progressively actualized in terms of precision and practicality of methodology and generalizability of findings.

In 1966 Pittel and Mendelsohn reviewed efforts from the turn of the century to the early 1960s in conceptualizing and measuring moral values. In the dozens of approaches they examined, they discerned no substantial cumulative progress. They concluded that an important improvement in the field would be for researchers to focus more on investigating moral values as subjective phenomena in their own right rather than simply as verbal predictors of moral behavior. In the past ten years the outstanding development in the study of subjective moral values has been work initiated and inspired by Lawrence Kohlberg (1958, 1964, 1969b, 1971a, 1972). Kohlberg's work can be seen as a continuation of Piaget's work in moral judgment (1932); it extends and refines Piaget's basic notions of the development of moral judgment and introduces new methods of study. Many important findings and ideas have come from Kohlbergian research, yet virtually all of them have been based on the methods of assessment devised by Kohlberg in his 1958 dissertation or on slightly modified versions of them. The aim of this chapter is to reconsider these methods of assessment—to examine their underlying logic and assumptions; to evaluate methodological decisions made by Piaget and Kohlberg and suggest other options now available; and to consider problems in existing methods in terms of what complications need to be dealt with in a more adequate methodology of research in moral judgment.

Procedures for Gathering
Data on Moral Judgment

THE USE OF HYPOTHETICAL STORIES

Piaget and Kohlberg gather data by asking subjects to respond to hypothetical stories. These stories raise moral judgment issues and ask subjects to explain and justify their views. Piaget characteristically employs a story pair, in which both stories are similar except in one aspect.[1] In a typical Piaget item, for instance, one story depicts a boy who walks into the dining room, and accidently knocks over a tray of cups hidden by the door, breaking fifteen cups (1932, p. 122). The other story of the pair depicts a boy who is trying to sneak some jam out of the cupboard and knocks over and breaks one cup. The subject is asked first to judge which boy is naughtier, the one in the first story or the one in the second story, and then to explain his judgment and answer follow-up probe questions, such as "If you were the daddy, which one would you punish most?" These stories about the broken cups are designed to find out whether the child bases his moral judgment on the amount of physical damage done (a purely objective notion of responsibility) or on the intentions of the actors (a subjective notion of responsibility).

Kohlberg employs a single story, raising a dilemma in which an actor has two choices of action. One of Kohlberg's stories (Chap. 2; 1969b) depicts the dilemma of Heinz, a man whose wife is dying of cancer and needs a drug that the town druggist will sell only at an exorbitant price. Subjects are asked to tell whether it would be right for Heinz to steal the drug from the druggist, and to justify their answers. Subjects' responses are then classified by trained judges according to whether the answer is oriented toward avoidance of punishment and deference to authority (Stage 1), toward prudent and purely self-centered concerns (Stage 2), toward a husband's natural love and affection for his wife (Stage 3), toward the necessity of unwavering adherence to society's system of rules in order to prevent social chaos (Stage 4), and so on.

Piaget's use of stories is a more focused data-gathering procedure than Kohlberg's. A set of contrasting Piaget stories is designed to highlight one aspect of moral judgment, and questioning is aimed at eliciting information for a specific scoring decision (e.g., whether the subject judges in terms of objective responsibility or subjective responsibility). The subject is essentially in a forced-choice situation, where he must choose which boy was naughtier. Some researchers (Cowan, Langer, Heavenrich, & Nathanson, 1969) have been concerned that an individual's choice in a Piagetian interview may not be a valid measure of his reasoning processes, because a subject might oblige an interviewer by choosing one of the boys without really understanding the stories' contrast. However, when researchers have compared choice data with the explanations that subjects give in justification of their choice, the two sources of data are very closely related. The correlation between choices and explanations was .87 in the study by Cowan et al. (1969), and a similar relationship was found by Bandura and McDonald (1963).

Kohlberg's method of data gathering is much more open-ended than Piaget's, and the method of characterizing a subject's thought much more complex. In response to Kohlberg's multifaceted stories, a subject may choose to discuss any of a number of aspects; in the Heinz story, for instance, he may talk about the druggist's property rights, the husband-wife relationship, law, or punishment. Whereas Piaget anticipates in his stories what scoring decisions a judge will have to make, Kohlberg does not set up his dilemmas with a specific scoring characteristic in mind. In one of the most frequently used forms of Kohlberg's scoring system (cf. 1969b, p. 376), a subject's response is characterized in terms of a two-dimensional scoring grid of 25 aspects and 6 stages (125 scoring possibilities). Obviously, a system which requires the scorer to classify a response into one or more of 125 categories is more complicated than a system demanding only a simple dichotomous decision (Piaget's method). The difficulty in categorizing the free responses of subjects to Kohlberg's stories will be attested to by anyone trying to use the scoring system. The problem is often that the information about the subject's thinking is not decisive or complete enough for a scorer to decide clearly into which of the categories the response should be classified. When the subject has not given sufficient cues to apply a scoring guide, or when the subject's responses do not seem to fit very well into any of the scoring categories, there is not much a scorer can do but guess.

On the other hand, an advantage of Kohlberg's open-ended method of data gathering has been that it has led to the postulation of many new developmental characteristics of moral judgment beyond those brought to light by Piaget (cf. Kohlberg, 1964). On the basis of responses to Kohlberg's stories, dozens of new distinctions and thought patterns have been suggested as markers of development. Furthermore, since Kohlberg's stories are more complex and since he has gathered interviews from older subjects than Piaget's, Kohlberg has had information on which to postulate more advanced developments than those embodied in Piaget's scheme. Whereas the upper end of Piaget's portrayal of moral judgment development was attained by 12- and 13-year-old adolescents, Kohlberg's portrayal of the most advanced forms of development depicts how moral philosophers make moral judgments. Thus the decrease in specificity of scoring characteristics and in focused data-gathering procedures in Kohlberg's system compared to Piaget's is balanced by an increase in scope. One possible line of future work will be to design stories and probe questions which will yield more complete and decisive information for a scorer to use in applying Kohlberg's scoring categories to interview material.[2]

A final contrast between Kohlberg's method and Piaget's pertains to the relation between a subject's choice in a story situation and the type of justification he gives for it. Whereas there appears to be a close relationship between the two in Piaget's tasks, there is not this kind of correlation in Kohlberg's tasks. Kohlberg (1958) reported that the course of action chosen by a subject from two dilemma alternatives (e.g., should Heinz steal the drug or not?) does not correlate very well with the type of reasoning used to support his decision. Researchers, therefore, should be warned about assuming, as some studies have (LeFurgy & Woloshin, 1969), that choice data from Kohlbergian stories are a useful measure of moral judgment.

JUDGING ANOTHER'S MORAL JUDGMENTS

Using prototypic statements. In considering the various ways that moral judgment data can be collected, we should note that when subjects are reacting to hypothetical stories and neutral probe questions, they are reporting their own spontaneous views on the problem. The subject's own thinking is deliberately sought; Piaget and Kohlberg caution the interviewer not to interject thinking different from the subject's spontaneous views. Important as this kind of moral judging is, it is not the only important kind of moral judgment.

People also make judgments about the moral judgments of others. When a person is faced with a moral dilemma, he often seeks the advice of others rather than acting on his own immediate solution to the dilemma. In taking or not taking another's advice we are making judgments about their judgments. In public debate over moral-political issues, we are hardly ever aware of a dilemma without also hearing someone's moral judgment of it. Democratic political process involves our reacting to the judgments of candidates for office and presumably voting for candidates whose judgments we approve. And quite often one's own views on a matter come to be defined in terms of agreeing or disagreeing with the positions of certain advocates.

Several studies (e.g., J. Carroll, 1974; Rest, 1973; Rest, Cooper, Coder, Masanz, & Anderson, 1974; Rest, Turiel, & Kohlberg, 1969) have asked subjects to make judgments about other moral judgments. This method involves writing statements which exemplify various ways of thinking about a moral issue—that is, statements which prototype a moral judgment stage— and then asking the subject to react to the statements instead of asking him to give his own views directly. Below are a few examples of prototypic statements written in the context of the Heinz story:

The druggist can do what he wants and Heinz can do what he wants to do. It's up to each individual to do what he wants with what he has. But if Heinz decides to risk jail to save his wife, it's his life he's risking; he can do what he wants with it (Stage 2).

Stealing is bad, but Heinz isn't doing wrong in trying to save his wife. He is only doing something that is natural for a good husband to do. You can't blame him for doing something out of love for his wife (Stage 3).

It is a natural thing for Heinz to want to save his wife, but it's still always wrong to steal. You have to follow the rules regardless of how you feel or regardless of the special circumstances. Even if his wife is dying, it's still his duty as a citizen to obey the law. No one else is allowed to steal, why should he be? If everyone starts breaking the law in a jam, there'd be no civilization, just crime and violence (Stage 4).

In this method, of course, the researcher must already have developmental characteristics in mind and must be able to represent these characteristics in prototypic statements which communicate the idea to other readers. Hence the use of prototypic statements is not appropriate for searching for *new* characteristics of thinking (the

free-response method of Kohlberg is better for that), and it cannot automatically be assumed that a statement designed to exemplify some distinctive characteristic of moral judgment (e.g., a Stage 2 idea) does clearly convey that idea. The chief advantages of the method, however, are that it allows us to focus the subject's attention on specific moral judgments and to systematically inventory a subject's reactions to a standardized set of stimuli statements. In contrast, in the free-response, spontaneous interview method of data collection a subject may wander from point to point and even forget to mention some ideas that had earlier come to mind; different interviews are not comparable if subjects do not happen to touch on the same points each time; and if interviewers use their "clinical sense" to probe interesting comments by subjects, then each interview situation may not involve the same stimuli. The use of a standard set of prototypic statements can minimize these problems.

Different tasks for data gathering. Several studies (e.g., Rest, 1973; Rest, Turiel, & Kohlberg, 1969) have asked subjects to perform various tasks with a set of prototypic statements:

1. *Preference measure:* Subjects are asked to rate each statement on a Likert-type scale or in terms of how much the subject likes the statement or how forceful or persuasive he finds its arguments.
2. *Comprehension-recapitulation measure:* Subjects are asked to paraphrase or recapitulate the statement or demonstrate understanding of the statement by drawing out its implications.
3. *Comprehension-by-matching measure:* Subjects are asked to read a statement and then select from four other statements the one that comes closest in meaning to the original statement.
4. *Recall measure:* Subjects are asked to read statements, and then at a later time reproduce them.

There are other tasks as well that could be performed with a set of prototypic statements in collection of moral judgment data. One could, for example, present a statement that conveys a point of view as it applies to one story and ask a subject to apply that point of view to another story; or one could present a number of statements purportedly made by other persons, with several examples of each stage included, and ask a subject to group together the statements that most probably came from the same person.

Differences in task requirements. Does it make any difference what data collection procedure is employed—whether moral judgment is assessed by preference measures or comprehension measures or spontaneous reactions to a story? It certainly does. First, note that the comprehension and recall tasks are capacity or ability measures. Rather than asking a subject to indicate his own value judgment, the comprehension and recall tasks ask a subject to demonstrate that he *can* think in a certain way, apart from whether he personally endorses it. On the other hand, in giving spontaneous reactions to a story the subject is not reporting all the thoughts possible for him, but only a selection of these possibilities. On the preference task a subject does not have to demonstrate understanding of a statement, but only has to indicate how well he likes it, for reasons unspecified.

Second, several studies (Rest, 1973; Rest, Turiel, & Kohlberg, 1969) indicate that the spontaneous production, comprehension, and preference tasks are assessing different levels of acquisition of an idea; a person can recognize and discriminate and thus prefer an idea before he can paraphrase it or before he can spontaneously produce the idea in response to a story dilemma. Hence researchers who use tasks of different difficulty for collecting moral judgment data are likely to locate the same subject at different stages. The Rest (1973) study has indicated that many subjects fully *comprehend* statements at higher stages than the predominant stage

which they spontaneously *use* on the Kohlberg free-response interview and, furthermore, that most subjects *prefer* statements at stages higher than the stage used or the stage comprehended. The developmental hierarchy, in ascending order of "difficulty," thus appears to be preference, comprehension, and spontaneous use. The interpretation offered for this finding is as follows: In reacting spontaneously to a hypothetical story (Kohlberg's free-response interview) a subject has to interpret the problem and construct a solution from scratch—that is, he must identify the relevant features, imagine the consequences of various courses of action, and integrate all of these considerations into a coherent justification of one course of action. In the comprehension task, statements are provided and the story and solutions already structured for the subject; all he has to do is to follow the points that the statement is making and discuss them in equivalent form. Consequently, many subjects who are not quite able to put a solution together at a high stage in the free-response, spontaneous-production task are able to follow the ideas as they are spelled out in the comprehension task statements and thus show understanding at a higher level than their stage of spontaneous production. Similarly, the preference task is even easier, for here not even the discussion of equivalent ideas is required. If a subject consistently prefers high-stage statements over lower-stage statements, one may suppose that the subject has some discrimination of higher-stage thinking, and that the preference task is furnishing the earliest signs of his acquisition of new ideas. According to this line of reasoning, the different tasks (spontaneous production, comprehension, and preference) manifest the acquisition of new ideas at different points of consolidation.

The conclusion that different moral judgment tasks tap different levels of acquisition is corroborated by a study by Breznitz and Kugelmass (1967). They studied the use of intentionality (considering the motives of an actor when judging his responsibility for an action) on tasks ranging from a test of ability to evaluate acts according to intentions without being able to specify the criteria, to a test of ability to justify the criteria of intentionality in competition with other criteria. The latter tasks required an increasingly abstract and verbally articulated level of intentionality for a subject to be credited with "having" the concept of intentionality, and the researchers found a cumulative pattern of the use of intentionality—that is, the subjects able to meet the criterion in difficult tasks could also meet the criterion on less difficult tasks, but not vice versa.

The contention that different tasks assess different levels of a competence is not new in psychology. In memory experiments, for example, subjects regularly score higher on recognition measures than on recall measures (R. Davis, Sutherland, & Judd, 1961). Children can recognize a triangle or a square before they can draw one (Piaget & Inhelder, 1956); the same is true for diagonals (Olson, 1968). Children comprehend grammatical features in sentences that they cannot generate (Fraser, Bellugi, & Brown, 1963) and identify phonemic contrasts that they cannot produce (Jacobsen & Halle, 1956). Similarly, Flavell (1971) has identified different levels of role-taking operations. These research findings imply that it is ambiguous in moral judgment assessment to say merely that a subject *has* or *does not have* a particular concept (such as intentionality) or that a subject is *at* a certain stage, without also specifying the task employed in data collection. A really complete description of a subject's location in a developmental sequence would assess the subject's stage—or stages—by a spectrum of tasks.

This line of argument also has practical implications. A person's conversation may reveal much less than he can comprehend or appreciate. A politician, for instance, who only gives back to his constituency the reasoning or level of thinking that he hears from them may be short-changing his constituents by underestimating what they can appreciate; he should recognize that a behavior such as voting does not require the production of a rationale, but only the expression of a preference. To take another example, a teacher who tries to meet students "at their level" should know the students' level of comprehension, not just their level of production. Vygotsky (1962) has pointed out that a child who comprehends something even though he does not produce it is more apt to be ready for upward movement than the child who comprehends only at his own level of production. Vygotsky (1962) tells of his experience in aptitude testing:

Having found that the mental age of two children was, let us say, eight, we gave each of them harder problems than he could manage on his own and provided some slight assistance: the first step in a solution, a leading question, or some other form of help. We discovered that one child could, in cooperation, solve problems designed for twelve year-olds, while the other could not go beyond problems intended for nine year-olds. The discrepancy between a child's actual mental age and the level he reaches in solving problems with assistance indicates the zone is four for the first child and one for the second. Experience has shown that the child with the larger zone of proximal development will do much better in school (p. 103).

Therefore, a subject's readiness for change may be indicated by the advance of his preference or comprehension beyond his level of production. Subjects may be frozen at some developmental stage because their comprehension and preference levels are the same as their level of production.

DEFINING ISSUES AS A DATA SOURCE—OBJECTIVE TESTING

So far we have discussed the use of prototypic statements as an alternative method of data collection to the spontaneous production of moral judgments employed by Piaget and Kohlberg. Note that prototypic statements present a line of reasoning in support of some action or conclusion. But people are influenced not only by the conclusions that another person advises but also by the way that another person defines the problem. When asking for advice, we often seek another's judgment not only on what ought to be done but also on how the other "sees" the problem—how he analyzes the issues involved and what he regards as the crucial issues. In public policy matters much attention often centers on defining the "crucial issue" involved in a problem situation. Consider, for example, one of the major social-moral problems of our time, variously referred to as the *busing issue, states' rights, racial prejudice,* and *equal opportunity.* The definition of the crucial issue that one accepts in thinking about this social problem is a very important moral judgment and of interest in its own right.

Developmental stages of moral judgment, defined as successive transformations in the way people view the mutual responsibilities in social relationships (Rest & Kohlberg, in prep., b), have distinctive ways of defining a given social-moral dilemma and of evaluating the crucial issues in it. I and my colleagues (Rest et al., 1974) have constructed the Defining Issues Test (DIT), which attempts to assess what people see as crucial moral issues in a situation by presenting subjects with a moral dilemma and a list of definitions of the major issues involved. In the case of Heinz's dilemma of whether to steal the drug, for example, subjects have been asked (Rest et al., 1974) to consider such issues as "whether or not a community's laws are going to be upheld," "Isn't it only natural for a loving husband to care so much for his wife that he'd steal?" "Is Heinz willing to risk getting shot as a burglar or going to jail for the chance that stealing the drug might help?" and "What values are going to be the basis for governing human interactions?" For each of six stories, subjects evaluate a set of twelve

issues and are asked to rate how important each issue is in deciding what ought to be done (*most importance, much, some, little, no*) and to rank their choices of the four most important issues. Since each issue statement represents a moral judgment stage, a subject's choices of the most important issues over a number of moral dilemmas are taken as a measure of his grasp of different stages of moral reasoning.

The method of rating and ranking issues on the DIT, while somewhat similar to the preference measure mentioned before, represents an improvement over assessment by preference. In previous research using the preference technique (Rest, 1973), there was little discrimination among subjects in preference for prototypic statements; almost all preferred Stage 6 statements. Another problem with the preference measure was that the statements typifying stage characteristics were so long it was difficult to know what cues the subjects were responding to, and whether they were really only agreeing with the statement's conclusion rather than its reasoning. In an effort to avoid this problem, the DIT focuses the judgment task more by using much shorter stimulus statements, constructed in the following manner.

1. The underlying stage structure of each issue statement is emphasized so that higher-stage statements appear stark and abstract and do not lend themselves to being interpreted as fancier ways of stating a lower-stage idea. Instead of a statement such as "The value of life is more important than property," we have the statement "What values are going to be the basis for governing how people act toward each other?" The first statement can appeal to subjects at many stages, whereas the second one does not, presumably because it expresses the issue in terms of a question that does not argue for a specific conclusion to the moral dilemma under consideration.

2. Among items representing the stages are nonsense items which use high-

sounding phrases (e.g., "What is the value of death prior to society's perspective on personal values?"). Such distractor items give a check on the tendency of subjects to choose on the basis of complex, abstruse verbiage rather than on the basis of meaning.

3. Care is taken to match issues from various stages on word length, complexity of syntax, and use of technical or unusual terms.

4. In each set of considerations several items of a stage are presented so that if one example of a stage's orientation is not suitable to a particular subject, he will still have other examples of that orientation to choose from. Through these precautions, the DIT issue statements have eliminated some of the shortcomings of the earlier preference measures and have succeeded in discriminating subjects at different levels of development (Rest et al., 1974).

The DIT is one of several recent attempts (see also Buchanan & Thompson, 1973; J. Carroll, 1974; Costanzo, Coie, Grument, & Farnill, 1973) to assess moral judgment by an objective format—that is, by using completely standardized stimuli and test conditions and by having the subject respond in terms of ratings or rankings instead of in the free-response mode. One might question whether such a structured format completely defeats the purpose of cognitive development assessment. If the purpose is to map an individual's subjective structuring tendencies, then would not an objective test thwart this intent?

In dealing with this question, it is helpful to consider the two basic options in moral judgment assessment: (1) having the subject talk or write about his moral thinking in a free-response mode and then having a scorer use some standardized system to classify the response, (2) presenting the subject with a set of standardized alternatives representing the scoring categories and having the subject rate or rank them. The essential difference is that in the first case the scorer judges how the sub-

ject's thinking fits the categories, whereas in the second case the subject in effect decides the fit by indicating the statements that are closest to his own judgment. When research is at the groundbreaking stage, the open-ended method has the advantage of allowing the subject to express his thinking freely and the researcher to inductively formulate scoring categories after the subject has provided the necessary raw material. In order to find out what people actually think without prejudging the case, the free-response method is an essential first step. Research using this kind of interviewing made it possible subsequently to construct the DIT items and to formulate clearly the stage characteristics on which the items are keyed (Rest & Kohlberg, in prep.). Generally, items of an objective test of moral judgment should be based on actual recurrent types of responses given in the free-response mode. However, after recurrent response types have been identified and a scoring system has been devised, and when the purpose of data collection is no longer to explore new scoring characteristics but to provide assessments of moral judgment development, then the advantages of the free-response method are diminished.

In conclusion, information about a person's moral judgment can be elicited by asking a subject to do any of several different tasks: solve hypothetical moral dilemmas, indicate a preference among moral judgment statements, or rank the most important issues in a dilemma. The various data-gathering procedures have different properties: Some are largely a measure of capacity, whereas others focus on personal values; some seem to tap the early phases of acquisition of an idea, whereas others tap later phases; and some are relatively standardized and highly structured, whereas others are open-ended and unstructured. Much research remains to be done in comparing these different data-gathering procedures, but it is clear now that a complete picture of a person's moral judgment cannot come from just one type of information. Moreover, the choice of data-gathering procedures should suit the specific aims of a study. If the researcher is trying to discover new scoring characteristics, for example, then the open-ended, spontaneous production interview is appropriate; if he is interested in cognitive capacities, then a comprehension measure is suitable; if he is interested in relating moral judgment to voting patterns, then a structured test of preference or the Defining Issues Test would be the most appropriate measure.

Identifying Cognitive Structures in Moral Judgments

For a moment let us disregard the complication in assessing moral judgment that derives from the fact that different methods of data collection tap different aspects of moral judgment. Let us also disregard the problem of gathering sufficient information from a subject so that his response can be decisively allocated to one or another data categories. Let us assume that we have settled upon some task for the subject (e.g., responding to dilemma stories and justifying a course of action), that we know exactly what stage characteristics and scoring decisions are involved,[3] and that our information-gathering procedure gathers sufficient material from a subject, so that we can unambiguously classify his response. Then it might seem that moral judgment assessment would be straightforward. Unfortunately there are additional complications.

The notion of *cognitive structure* in moral judgment implies that if we look at a subject's judgments over several moral situations, we can discern an underlying pattern—that is, that a certain general perspective or organizational pattern or basic problem-solving strategy characterizes a person's responses. Without any generality or consistency, the postulation of cognitive structure would be gratuitous. On the other hand, if people were completely consistent, a researcher could determine a subject's cognitive structure simply by sampling one instance of moral judging in response to virtually any moral problem. The truth seems to be that people are only partially consistent in the way they make moral judgments from situation to situation, from testing to testing.

INCONSISTENCY BECAUSE OF TEST STIMULI CHARACTERISTICS

Several studies have shown partial consistency in moral judgment and have suggested possible reasons for inconsistencies. Medinnus (1959) administered two Piaget-type stories to subjects, each story being designed to tap the same moral judgment characteristic. He found that children seemed more advanced on one story than on the other, and he suggested that the discrepancy may have been due to differences in the explicitness of relevant story cues and to differences in the familiarity of children with the different incidents depicted. Magowan and Lee (1970) systematically investigated the effects of giving children Piaget-type stories describing familiar or unfamiliar settings and found that greater familiarity was strongly associated with more advanced moral judgments. Similarly, Liebermann (1971) found that some stage responses were more likely with some of Kohlberg's stories than with others, that is, that the story partially determines the stage of the response.

Performance discrepancies such as these may occur, even though different test situations have been designed to tap the same cognitive structure. In a recent discussion of performance on cognitive-developmental tests, Flavell and Wohlwill (1969) have pointed out that response variability may stem from differences in factors such as "stimulus materials and their familiarity, the manner of presentation of the relevant information and the amount of irrelevant information from which it has to be abstracted, the sheer magnitude of the information load placed on the child in dealing with the problem, and the role played by memory and sequential processing of information" (p. 99). It is not easy to know beforehand what factors in a story or test situation will make that story harder or easier for a given subject. If the stimulus material differs from story to story, however, something will probably cause variability in the subjects' level of moral judgment. Therefore, two implications for moral judgment assessment seem clear. (1) A single story or a single test situation cannot be assumed to represent the general moral judgment level of a subject. This finding casts doubt on the conclusions of studies that have used only one item to assess moral level (Abel, 1941; Dennis, 1943; Havighurst & Neugarten, 1955). (2) Whenever comparisons are made among subjects, the same set of test stimuli should be employed under standardized conditions. If somewhat different stories are used or if subjects are interviewed with different probe questions or under different test conditions, then differences in scores cannot be unambiguously attributed to developmental differences among subjects. This suggests that researchers who use a free-response method of data collection, such as Kohlberg's, may be introducing discrepancies in stage scores not caused by developmental differences. Standardizing test formats is one way of correcting this problem; another way is to identify through research the test stimuli that affect cognitive structure assessments and to quantify the degree to which each factor affects stage scores.

SUBJECT INCONSISTENCY AND THE QUANTITATIVE–QUALITATIVE ISSUE

So far we have discussed response inconsistencies caused by differences in test stimuli or test conditions. In addition, subjects themselves may vacillate in responding, this having nothing to do with changes in test stimuli. Flavell and Wohlwill (1969,

p. 100) point out that cognitive-developmental research suggests that subjects are particularly likely to be inconsistent in responding even to the same stimuli when they are in transitional periods of acquiring a new cognitive structure. It is in the transitional phase that responses are unstable and confused, and the process of reaching the next developmental stage seems to be gradual rather than abrupt. Therefore if we wish to characterize a subject's point of development, the use of only qualitative descriptions ("subject is in Stage 2," "subject is in Stage 3") is artificial because it disregards the gradual nature of acquisition. Flavell and Wohlwill suggest that the manifestation of a given stage of responding in a specific stimulus condition ought to be thought of in terms of a continuum of probability of occurrence ranging from zero to 1.0.

Factors such as subject vacillation, inconsistencies in response because of test stimuli characteristics, and discrepancies in manifested stage level because of different information-gathering procedures give us many reasons to question the appropriateness of the present practice of designating the moral judgment of subjects in terms of stage types. Currently, we have a strange situation in moral judgment assessment. Stage theory has emphasized qualitative differences in moral judgment. To many people this focus seems to require researchers to adopt as the goal of assessment the classification of subjects into types or stages. Logically, this conclusion does not necessarily follow; and research to date indicates that the question "What stage is a subject?" requires a more complicated answer than may be immediately anticipated. Rarely if ever does a subject respond 100 percent at one stage. Bandura and McDonald (1963) helped focus attention on this fact in regard to Piaget's moral judgment stages. For Kohlberg's six stages, research (Kohlberg, 1969b, p. 387) shows that not even a majority of a subject's responses are on the average at his predominant stage—only 47 percent are. Also, studies of change (e.g., Bandura & Mc-Donald, 1963; Kohlberg & Kramer, 1969; Turiel, 1966) clearly indicate that developmental advance is not abrupt movement from all one type one day to all another type another day. Moreover, the usual procedure in Kohlberg's research for classifying subjects into stage types is to look at the subject's *quantitative* distribution of responses and to designate the type with *most* responses as the subject's own stage. Often the subject's predominant type is only a few percentage points above his second most-used type. Perhaps we should rephrase the assessment question from "What stage is a subject?" to "What are the probabilities of occurrence of each stage type for a subject?" This latter approach would retain the qualitative differences in types of response, but would treat each response type as also being on a quantitative continuum of probability of occurrence. Instead of talking about, say, a Stage 4 subject, we could talk about a subject with a 30 percent probability of a Stage 4 response on such and such a task, a 15 percent probability of a Stage 3 response, and so on. We can acknowledge qualitatively different types of responses and at the same time recognize that the best way to represent a subject's cognitive structure may not be to designate him as a type.

Locating a Subject in a Developmental Sequence

The discussion thus far has cited a number of complications involved in accurately assessing a subject's moral judgment. If a researcher were to take all these factors seriously, he would test a subject by several data-gathering procedures (e.g., comprehension, preference) which employed diverse but standardized test contents (e.g., a number of stories), and which would report for each data-gathering procedure the percentages of usage of each stage. With so many bits of data for each subject, how does the researcher locate a

subject in a developmental sequence? The cognitive-developmental approach is premised on the notion that a Stage 1 type of response lays the foundation and is a prerequisite for Stage 2, which in turn lays the foundation for Stage 3, and so on. If we assert that it is inappropriate to designate subjects as being "in a stage," then how do we represent where a subject is in his development?

HYPOTHETICAL TYPES OF RELATIONSHIPS AMONG SEQUENTIAL STAGES

How to locate a subject developmentally depends on the nature of the developmental sequence. To date researchers have not clearly recognized that even if one stage in a linear sequence is in some sense a prerequisite for the next, there are still many other ways in which sequential stages may be interrelated. First, let us assume the simplest situation (which we know is actually not the case): We are studying many subjects longitudinally and our method of assessment enables us to unambiguously identify responses as stage types (see Figure 11.1). Let us further assume that at the youngest age of testing, all subjects produce all Stage 1 responses; then at a second testing at a later age each subject in this longitudinal sample gives a mix of

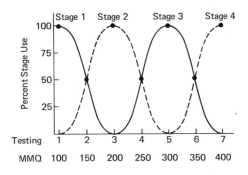

Figure 11.1. Hypothetical interrelationships of moral judgment stages assuming successive and 100 percent prevalence of each stage at equal intervals, mix of only adjacent stages at transition phases, and symmetrical curves.

Stage 1 responses and Stage 2 responses; then at the next testing each subject gives all Stage 2 responses; then a mix of Stage 2 and Stage 3; then all Stage 3; and so on. Figure 11.1 depicts this simple case in terms of four curves representing the relative prevalence of each of four successive stages. Note that each stage peaks at 100 percent at different points in time, that only adjacent stages mix, and that each stage rises and falls in equal intervals.

Given the conditions of Figure 11.1, a subject's point of development could be located by the two methods used by Kohlbergian researchers: classifying a subject according to (1) his predominant stage or (2) in terms of Kohlberg's Moral Maturity Quotient (MMQ). A subject at testing 1 would be a Stage 1 subject. The MMQ is a weighted average computed in this way: Take the percentage of Stage 1 usage and multiply it by 1; take the percentage of Stage 2 usage and multiply by 2; take the percentage of Stage 3 usage and multiply by 3; and so on; then add the six products together. In the situation in Figure 11.1, a subject might be 100 percent Stage 2, in which case his MMQ would be 200. Or if he were 90 percent Stage 2 and 10 percent Stage 3, his MMQ would be $(90 \times 2) + (10 \times 3)$, or 210. Using such a weighted average to locate a subject in the sequence would be justifiable, since each stage increases and decreases in equal amounts at equal intervals in the hypothetical sequence shown in Figure 11.1. Furthermore, it would make sense to talk of subjects going through the stages "step by step," since each stage has a unique time of ascendency and 100 percent prevalence.

Now let us consider Figure 11.2. In this case, our hypothetical longitudinal subjects at testing 1 are on the average producing 75 percent Stage 1 responses, 20 percent Stage 2 responses, and 5 percent Stage 3 responses; then when the subjects are tested a second time, they produce on the average 20 percent Stage 1 responses, 55 percent Stage 2 responses, 20 percent Stage 3 responses, 5 percent Stage 4 responses, and so on. In other words Figure

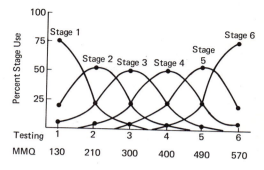

Figure 11.2. Hypothetical interrelationships of moral judgment stages assuming symmetrical curves and successive but not 100 percent prevalence of each stage at equal intervals.

11.2 depicts subjects as always showing stage mixture (as the research indicates; see Turiel, 1969). The mixtures are not only directly adjacent (e.g., Stages 1 and 2, 2 and 3, 3 and 4) but also nonadjacent (e.g., Stages 1 and 3 at the same testing). Designating the subjects in Figure 11.2 at testing 3 as "Stage 3 subjects" does make some sense, in that Stage 3 is predominant and the prevalence of Stage 3 is an identifiable point in the sequence. But it does not mean what "a Stage 3 subject" means in Figure 11.1, in which all the subject's responses are Stage 3 at testing 3. In this second scheme, moreover, there are problems in attempting to locate subjects in terms of a weighted average (MMQ), even though the stages do peak at equal intervals. It can be seen in Figure 11.2 that curves which are not completely symmetrical tend to attenuate values at either end of the continuum (e.g., the MMQ at testing 1 is 130 instead of 100). In the Figure 11.2 situation it is less clear than in Figure 11.1 that "subjects move through the sequence step by step," since developmental change from testing to testing is more a matter of shifts in percentage of usage of a number of stages. Nevertheless, there is no difficulty in determining whether subjects are more or less advanced at testing 3 or testing 4; the more use of higher stages, the more advanced the subject. In Figure 11.2 this rule for determining developmental advance could be used to compare the moral progress of any two subjects for any testing and to unambiguously decide which subject was more advanced.

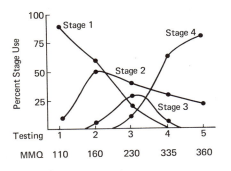

Figure 11.3. Hypothetical interrelationships of moral judgment stages assuming only a linear order in the acquisition of stages.

Now consider Figure 11.3. Figure 11.3 satisfies (as do Figures 11.1 and 11.2) the cognitive-developmental assumption of a linear order in the acquisition of response types. Stage 1 predominates before other response types occur to any extent; then Stage 2 sharply increases, followed by sharp increases in Stage 3, Stage 4, and so on. If there were logical or theoretical reasons for supposing that Stage 2 is a prerequisite for Stage 3, and Stage 3 for Stage 4, data such as are presented in Figure 11.3 could be used as empirical support. Yet the curves of Figure 11.3 do not conform to several assumptions made in Figures 11.2 and 11.1, namely, that the developmental curves of stage prevalence are symmetrical, or that each stage type has a period of prevalence, or that stage increase and decrease occurs at equal intervals, or that stage overlap is symmetrical. For the sake of illustrating the condition in which these assumptions are not met, we have drawn the hypothetical curves of Figure 11.3, but many other curves could have illustrated this condition as

well. The main point is that Figures 11.1 and 11.2 make assumptions about developmental sequences which are not necessary to developmental theory and which are not supported by research.

INADEQUACIES OF USUAL TYPES OF MORAL STAGE INDICES

How could a researcher locate a subject in a developmental sequence such as that depicted in Figure 11.3? Stage typing a subject would certainly be inappropriate. Such a procedure would overlook Stage 3 as a developmental marker (since Stage 3 is never predominant); it would also fail to differentiate between testings 4 and 5; and it would designate subjects as Stage 2 when Stage 2 was actually on the decrease. Although a Moral Maturity Quotient can always be calculated, this index is really a jumble of numbers when applied to a sequence such as the one in Figure 11.3. Weighted averaging as is used in the MMQ is a dubious procedure if the stages are not acquired at equal intervals, and if the acquisition and outgrowing of a stage are not symmetrical for each stage.

NEW TYPES OF STAGE INDICES

A continuous index based on a single response type. Although the two usual methods of locating a subject in a developmental sequence are inappropriate if research does not support their assumptions, there are available several alternative methods that do not make these assumptions. A researcher may be particularly interested in the development of one type of response, such as Stage 4 usage. In that case, one would simply look at the amount of usage of that stage and disregard the other response types. In Figure 11.3 focusing attention on only Stage 4 would not be a bad way of representing development in general, since the amount of Stage 4 usage fairly well indexes overall changes at each testing, except changes between testings 1 and 2.

In research using the DIT (Rest et

al., 1974) the procedure of indexing development by focusing on only one response type, principled morality, has been useful. Recall that in the DIT a subject reads twelve varied statements defining the crucial issue of a hypothetical moral dilemma and ranks his choice of the four most important issues. Since some of the issue statements define the dilemma according to a principled moral perspective, Kohlberg's Stages 5 and 6 (see Kohlberg, Chap. 2; Rest & Kohlberg, in prep., b, for a recent discussion of principled moral thinking), a score of principled moral thinking (hereafter, P) can be computed for each subject based on the extent to which he ranks the principled statements across the six dilemma situations in first, second, third, or fourth place. (Of course, such a score can be computed for other stages too, reflecting the extent to which a subject ranks the items representing those stages as most important across the six dilemmas.) The P score is a continuous variable, that is, it is acquired gradually and does not have an all-or-nothing probability of occurrence. Figure 11.4 shows some actual cross-sectional data collected from four different student groups (junior

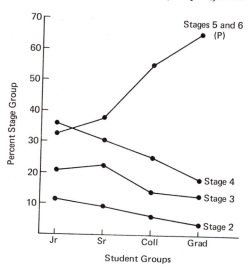

Figure 11.4.   Stage endorsement by different student groups (cross-sectional sample) on the DIT (rank P).

high school, senior high, college, and graduate students in the seminary or in doctoral programs in political science or moral philosophy). Their P scores as well as scores for Stage 2, 3, and 4 items reflect how the different groups ranked the issue statements. For the limited age range used in this study, an older range than typically studied, indexing development using only one response type as a continuous variable was quite satisfactory (as will be explained in the next section).

Indexing by exceptional usage. Another way of indexing development without the assumptions of Figures 11.1 and 11.2 is to stage-type subjects in terms of exceptional use of a stage rather than predominant use of a stage. If we refer again to Figure 11.3, we see that subjects at testing 3 were using more of Stage 3 than at any other testing—in other words, these subjects were exceptional in their use of Stage 3. Similarly, at testing 2, subjects were using more Stage 2 than at any other testing, even though Stage 2 was not the predominant stage used at testing 2. Accordingly, we might designate subjects at testing 2 as exceptionally high in Stage 2, even though Stage 1 was still prevalent.

In research using the DIT, exceptional stage usage was employed to classify subjects into types. Subjects in junior high school, senior high, college, and graduate school constituted the sample. For each response type (Stage 2, 3, 4, 4½, 5A, 5B, and 6)[4] average percent of endorsement and standard deviations were computed for the whole sample. Then all stage-type scores were converted to standardized z scores (the total sample average Stage 2 score was subtracted from a subject's score on Stage 2, and then divided by the standard deviation, thus yielding a Stage 2 standardized score; and similarly for scores on other stages). Each subject then had a set of standardized scores, which was inspected for exceptionally high z scores on any stage. For illustrative purposes, consider the following standardized scores for two hypothetical subjects:

TABLE 11.1   Standardized Stage Scores on Two Hypothetical Subjects

	Standardized Scores						
Subject	Stage 2	3	4	4½	5A	5B	6
1	−0.1	−0.2	+1.25	0.0	−0.3	−0.8	−1.3
2	−0.3	+0.1	−0.1	−0.3	+1.3	+0.4	+0.7

Table 11.1 shows that subject 1 has an exceptionally high Stage 4 and that subject 2 has an exceptionally high Stage 5A score. A standardized score of +1.0 can be set as a cutoff point; a subject with a score this high or higher on any stage would be classified as "belonging to" that stage grouping. (Thus, subject 1 is in the Stage 4 grouping, and subject 2 in the Stage 5A grouping.) If more than one score is above +1.0, then the highest score is used to classify the subject. If a subject has no standardized score on any stage above +1.0, then that subject is classified as a "mixed type." By this procedure 160 subjects in the Rest study were classified, about 75 percent of the subjects having at least one stage of exceptionally high usage that allowed them to be classified into stage groupings.

An advantage of this method is that it does not assume that each response type is predominant at some point in development; it requires only that some subjects use more of a type of response than other subjects and uses this difference to locate a subject in a developmental sequence. Another advantage of this technique arises in connection with the fact (Liebermann, 1971) that Kohlberg-type moral dilemma stories do not equally elicit the several moral stages. One story, for example, may elicit a disproportionately large number of stage 3 responses from all subjects, resulting in an inflated number of subjects whose predominant stage is Stage 3. However, if the classification is not done by predominant stage but by grouping subjects by their stage of exceptional use (relative to a standard group), then such story bias is not a problem. If the stories are eliciting Stage 3 responses from all subjects, then the overall average of Stage 3 will be high and only subjects who go well beyond the average will be classified in the Stage 3 exceptionally high group.

Indexing by highest stage of substantial usage. With Figure 11.3 again in mind, another question can be raised: What part of the growth curve of a stage is most important? The indices mentioned so far have paid most attention to the peaks in the curves—the points at which usage of a particular stage is predominant or exceptionally high. However, researchers may discover when correlating moral judgment to other measures or predicting long-range development, that it is most important to note when stage usage starts to rise substantially. In other words, the peaks of the curves may not be as important developmental markers as the ascending slopes.

In one study (Rest, 1973) note was taken of the most advanced stage in Kohlberg's sequence, at which a subject produced at least 20 percent of his responses. Assume, for example, that the stage usage of three subjects is distributed as in Table 11.2:

TABLE 11.2   Stage Usage in Three Hypothetical Subjects

	Percent Usage					
Subject	Stage 1	2	3	4	5	6
1	5	5	40	45	5	0
2	10	40	30	20	0	0
3	0	10	20	30	25	15

In this example, subject 1's highest stage of substantial usage (at least 20 percent) is Stage 4; subject 2's highest stage of substantial usage is also Stage 4 (even though his predominant stage is 2); and subject 3's highest stage of substantial usage is Stage 5. A provocative finding of the Rest (1969) study was that more meaningful relationships with other measures (e.g., comprehension and IQ) resulted when the index used was the highest stage of substantial usage rather than the predominant stage. The implications of this finding, if confirmed by further research, will be momentous, for it suggests that the moral judgment research done since 1958 using Kohlberg's method of stage typing by predominant stage usage should have been indexing development instead by the highest stage of substantial usage! This one study is far from conclusive, but it calls for further research on the comparative usefulness of various kinds of developmental indices.

Indexing by rejection of low stages. In a recent dissertation by J. Carroll (1974), still another part of the stage curve has been looked at: the declining side of the curve, when a subject gives up or rejects a stage. The rationale for this approach comes from previous research (Rest, 1973) suggesting that subjects' preferences for high-level moral statements are likely to be confused and vacillating because these preferred statements are typically at the upper limits of a subject's understanding, whereas statements at stages below a subject's current stage are likely to be clearly understood and consistently rejected. Accordingly, Carroll's research has investigated rejection of statements at low stages by different age groups and has found that older subjects are clearly more consistent than younger subjects in rejecting low stages. Presumably, the more stages at the low end that a subject consistently rejects, the further advanced he is and the more discerning his judgment. Hopefully, this research will help chart the downward slope of the developmental curves.[5]

Validating a Measure of Moral Judgment

The gist of the discussion thus far has been to point out problems and complications in the usual methods of moral judgment assessment and to suggest possible options in data-gathering procedures, test formats, and ways of indexing development. The question then arises, Are any of the options any good? Putting the question slightly differently, How does one go about judging the usefulness of any assessment method and of comparing the usefulness of different methods?

Since moral judgment is a psychological construct purporting to represent different organizations of thinking, the validity of a moral judgment measure cannot be established simply by correlating the measure with some external behavior. The purpose of moral judgment assessment is not simply to collect verbal statements in order to predict observable behavior, but rather to use verbal information as indicators of inner thought patterns and processes. A moral judgment measure may turn out to have striking relationships with some observed behavior, but the validation of a moral judgment measure is not based simply on this correlation. The referent of the measure is something inside the head, as in the case with other psychological constructs such as intelligence and need achievement. The validation of such constructs is based on indirect evidence or "construct validation" (Cronbach & Meehl, 1955) in which the theoretical implications of the construct are tested. Validating a measure of moral judgment therefore is a multifaceted procedure and a matter of determining the degree to which a measure produces data trends conforming to a set of theoretical expectations.

An example of validation research (Coder, 1975; Cooper, 1972; Panowitsch,

1975; Rest et al., 1974) comes from our recent work at the University of Minnesota. The validating criteria for the moral judgment measures employed in our studies were

1. Test-retest stability
2. Age trends
3. Correlation with comprehension of moral-political concepts
4. Correlation with attitudes and political stances on current controversial issues
5. Correlation with existing moral judgment measures (Kohlberg's)
6. Increases in moral judgment test scores after experiences which theoretically should accelerate the development of higher-stage judgment.

A major goal of this research has been to explore various methods of measuring moral judgment and to determine which method generates data that optimally fit the validating criteria. In researching the DIT, we became aware of many options in constructing a measure of moral judgment—whether to use ratings or rankings of statements, for example, and whether to represent a subject's development in terms of stage typing (i.e., allocating a subject to one stage) or in terms of a point on a continuum. A decision on which kinds of scaling and measurement choices to utilize is not determined by developmental theory (as are the validating criteria or types of developmental sequences). Operationalizing a construct involves many intermediate decisions which can be tested for soundness only by trying out the options and looking to see which set of decisions in constructing a measure optimizes the fit between moral judgment data and validating criteria. The following account of DIT research exemplifies a process of systematically checking out assessment options.

Our discussion will briefly consider each of the validating criteria in turn and the findings on three DIT indices. There are actually dozens of possible indices of moral judgment which can be constructed from DIT data (see Cooper, 1972, for discussion of many of these), but the three indices presented here are representative of major families of indices. The first index uses rating data and the second, ranking data; and both of these indices locate subjects developmentally in terms of a continuous dimension—namely, the degree of importance that subjects attribute to principled moral considerations in making a moral decision. The third index is also based on ranking data but stage-types subjects, locating them developmentally in terms of the stage they use to an exceptionally high extent. Hereafter, these three indices will be designated "DIT (rate P)," "DIT (rank P)," and "DIT (stage type)," respectively.

TEST-RETEST STABILITY

One of the first properties of an index that we checked was its stability over a short period of time (two weeks). Estimates of stability came from a group of twenty-eight ninth-graders. The test-retest Pearson product–moment correlation for the DIT (rate P) was .62; for the DIT (rank P) it was .81. The Spearman rank correlation of the DIT (stage type) on test-retest was .30; the average correlation of the individual stage standardized scores was .44. Therefore, on the first criterion, the DIT (rank P) was the superior index.

AGE TRENDS

Age trend data has been the chief validating criterion for Piaget and Kohlberg in their postulation of stages of moral judgment. If we assume that chronological age is at least a rough index of development, then the higher one's age, the greater should be his usage of more advanced stages. The DIT was administered to junior high school subjects (grade 9), to senior high students (grade 12), to college juniors and seniors, and to graduate stu-

TABLE 11.3   Student Group Differences on Three DIT Indices

Index	Student Group			
	Jr. high	Sr. high	College	Graduate
DIT (rate P)	25.2[a]	27.9	32.3	36.3
DIT (rank P)	32.7[b]	37.4	54.9	65.1
DIT (stage type)				
Stage 2	32.5[c]	15.0	5.0	2.5
3	7.5	22.5	2.5	10.0
4	20.0	15.0	7.5	2.5
4½	7.5	17.5	12.5	10.0
5A	2.5	2.5	17.5	15.0
5B	2.5	2.5	17.5	15.0
6	0.0	7.5	17.5	22.5
Mixed type	27.5[d]	17.5	20.0	22.5

[a] Average P scores of each academic group. The scores are computed for each subject on the basis of how high the subject rated items exemplifying principled morality (Stages 5 and 6). The higher the score, the more importance a subject attributed to principled moral considerations.

[b] Average P scores, based on ranks instead of ratings. Otherwise, interpretation is same as in preceding footnote a.

[c] Percentages of students at each stage in each academic group. In other words, 32.5 percent of the junior high school subjects had exceptionally high Stage 2 scores (relative to the other subjects in the study) and were classified as exceptionally high Stage 2 subjects.

[d] Percentage of subjects who did not endorse any stage's items more than one standard deviation above the mean for the entire sample.

dents (seminarians and doctoral students in moral philosophy and political science). Table 11.3 shows how DIT scores differentiated the student groups (Total $n = 160$).

All three DIT indices show age trends of increased use of higher moral stages by the more educationally advanced groups. (One-way analysis of variance of the rank-P index gives highly statistically significant differences among the groups). The Pearson product-moment correlation of age with DIT (rate P) was .66, and with DIT (rank P) was .62. The Spearman rank-order correlation of DIT (stage types) with age was only .51 (even after elimination of mixed types, whose inclusion would have lowered the correlation even more).[6] Again, it appears that stage-typing the subjects yields a less clear data trend than other methods. Similar age trends were found in another student sample ranging from junior high to graduate students (see Rest et al., 1974, for further data and discussion of age trends).

CORRELATION WITH MORAL COMPREHENSION

Do subjects pick higher-stage issue statements because they appreciate their greater adequacy as conceptual frameworks? Or do subjects select such statements without understanding them, responding perhaps to their high-sounding language? Correlating the DIT with an independent measure of comprehension indicates whether understanding accompanies preference for high-stage issue statements.

The comprehension test (Rest, 1972) employed in the DIT studies first asked a subject to read a paragraph, then to read four statements, and finally to choose which of the four statements most closely recapitulated the main idea of the paragraph. Here is an example:

Obeying the law is not as important as obeying your conscience. A person must decide for himself what he feels is right and good, and hold himself to those ideals, or else he is being untrue to himself. One's conscience often demands more of a person than the law. In Heinz's case, if the law is different from what Heinz thinks is right, he should still live up to the values that he believes in.

(a) As long as Heinz feels he's right, he can do as he pleases. Your own conscience is more important than the law.
(b) Heinz should do what he feels is right and break the law because he loves his wife and that is more important than the law.
(c) A person must act according to the set of standards he has chosen for himself throughout his life even if these standards conflict with the law.
(d) A person must guide his behavior according to the values he was taught to believe are right. Your conscience tells you whether or not something is right and good.

Fifteen sets of paragraphs and statements were used, each designed to test comprehension of social-moral concepts such as social contract, legitimate authority, due process of law, and conscience as an internal standard. Subjects who usually picked the answer keyed as the correct recapitulation were scored as having high comprehension. As corroboration of our a priori key, the graduate doctoral students in political science and moral philosophy most often agreed with the key and had higher comprehension scores than subjects in the junior high, senior high, college, or seminarian groups.

Comprehension correlated with DIT (rate P) at .59, with DIT (rank P) at .63, but with DIT (stage type) at only .32.[7] And so, again, the stage-type index bore the weakest relationship to a validating criterion. The high correlation between comprehension and the DIT (rank P) was replicated with another student sample (.67, Rest et al., 1974) and also with an adult sample (.52, Coder, 1975). Further corroborating evidence that high scores on the DIT reflect greater cognitive capacity comes from its positive association with IQ-type measures: The DIT correlates in the .30's and .40's with the Differential Abilities Test and the Iowa Test of Basic Skills

for ninth-graders (Cooper, 1972), and .42 with the IQ Quick Test for adults (Coder, 1975).

The correlation between comprehension and the DIT (rank P) was further examined by controlling for age (taking only the ninth-graders) and also statistically partialling out their mutual correlations with the Differential Abilities test, the Iowa Test for Basic Skills, father's education, and father's occupation. The partial correlation between comprehension and DIT remained highly significant (in the .50s) even after attenuation by partialling out the other variables.

CORRELATION WITH SOCIAL-POLITICAL ATTITUDES

There are two reasons for seeking correlations of DIT with social or political attitudes. One is to seek evidence that moral judgment is not just a value-neutral intellectualizing skill or style, but one that relates to value commitments as well as to purely cognitive capacities. The DIT is expected to correlate with certain value positions required by a high-stage perspective, but which may seem paradoxical from a lower-stage perspective. In other words, moral judgment is expected to correlate with the attitude tests whose items correspond to stage characteristics.[8] In our studies, two attitude tests were used. The first, the Law and Order Test, is comprised of fifteen controversial public policy issues such as the following:

Under present laws it is possible for someone to escape punishment on the grounds of legal technicalities even though the person may have confessed to performing the crime. Are you in favor of a tougher policy for treating criminals? (check one)

_____ strongly agree with tougher policy
_____ mildly agree
_____ mixed agreement and disagreement
_____ mildly disagree
_____ strongly disagree

Items were written regarding wire tapping, civil disobedience, youth protest, and so on. Responses which advocated giving excessive powers to authorities or supporting the existing social system at the disproportionate expense of civil rights or individual welfare were keyed as law and order (Rest et al., 1974). The second attitude measure, the libertarian democracy test, was one of several scales devised by Patrick (1971) for use in studying democratic political orientation and was composed of items such as the following: "If a person wanted to make a speech in this city favoring Communism, he should be allowed to speak." The subject is asked to indicate his endorsement on a five-point scale ranging from "strongly agree" to "strongly disagree," and by his responses presumably reflect his support of civil liberties under unfavorable circumstances. Both the Law-and-Order and the libertarian scales were chosen because on theoretical grounds their items seemed to be sensitive to the important division between the law-and-order orientation of Kohlberg's Stage 4 and the principled morality of Stages 5 and 6.

A second reason for seeking evidence of an association between the DIT and attitude measures is the desire to relate responses to hypothetical situations to responses to actual current value controversies. The DIT and the comprehension test employ hypothetical dilemmas which are quite distant from the actual decision making of subjects in day-to-day situations. The question naturally arises, What does this have to do with real life? Researchers who are interested in relating moral judgment to public behavior that has some effect on the flow of real-life events have already sought correlations of moral judgment with behavioral measures such as cheating on school exams or on games, obeying an authority, and helping a person in distress (Kohlberg, 1969b; in prep.). Usually a statistically significant relationship is found, but of only moderate magnitude (r's in the .30s and .40s). It seems to us that another arena of real-life behavior is more closely related to moral

judgment tests, namely, taking a stance on a value issue—whether speaking out publicly, voting in an election, or discussing the issue with co-workers and friends. As people participate in moral discussions and publicly support and defend certain sides of an issue, they are making public moral judgments that have influencing effects on others. Too often moral judgment researchers have overlooked this kind of behavior, perhaps because it is most notable in age groups older than those typically studied, or because verbal behavior seems less "real" than other actions. Although we did not actually observe people in public meetings making speeches or in voting booths in an actual election, our own studies (Rest et al., 1974) collected information concerning actual issues of the day in a fashion somewhat like that of a Gallup poll.

The correlations of all three DIT indices were highly statistically significant as the table below shows. Similar correlations were found in other samples (Coder, 1975; Rest et al., 1974).

TABLE 11.4   Correlations of DIT Indices with Attitudes

	Law-and-Order Attitude	Libertarian, Democratic Attitude
DIT (rank P)	−.59	.62
DIT (rate P)	−.59	.59
DIT (stage type)	−.40	.42

The way people select the most important issues of hypothetical moral dilemmas seems, therefore, to be highly associated with their stances on certain current public policy issues.

FURTHER VALIDITY STUDIES

Comparison among the three DIT indices on the validating criteria shows that the DIT (rank P) index was about the same as the DIT (rate P) index except for the test-retest stability, in which the rank index had a decided advantage. Since the rank index was also consistently superior to the stage-type index, we have chosen as a general rule to represent DIT data in terms of the rank index. Three other studies have been done with the DIT (rank P) index.

1. The DIT was correlated with Kohlberg's measure of moral stage on forty-seven subjects, ranging from junior high age through adulthood (see Rest et al., 1974). The correlation was .68, not high enough to regard the two tests as equivalent. At the same time the correlation is, to our knowledge, the highest one between Kohlberg's measure and any other moral judgment variable on a sample of this size. The research necessary to delineate further the relationships between the DIT and Kohlberg's scales may have to wait until both are developed into a more finished form.

2. The DIT was administered at the course's start and end to a college ethics class and a logic class. If the DIT is selectively sensitive to gains in *moral* thinking in contrast to gains simply in complexity of thinking in general, then we would expect higher gains on the DIT in the ethics class—both because of the influence of the ethics class itself and of the possible greater interest in ethics of students who chose that class instead of logic. In dissertation research by Panowitsch (1975), both classes were comparable on the DIT pretest; on the posttest twelve weeks later the ethics class showed statistically significant gains in contrast to the logic class.

3. The susceptibility of the DIT to faking was investigated by McGeorge (1973), who administered the DIT twice to several groups, all of which took the test under standard conditions, after which different groups were asked to take it faking "good," "bad," and so on. McGeorge found that subjects could depress their scores by faking bad, but could not increase their scores by faking good.

Additional studies on the DIT are under way—studies on its sensitivity to longitudinal change and interventional change, and its correlations with other attitude and personality measures. To date the validity of the DIT seems to compare well with that of other measures of moral judgment, while at the same time the DIT appears less time-consuming and less vulnerable to certain biases of interviewing and scoring.

Conclusion

Regardless of the final evaluation of the DIT as an assessment device, a general process for developing assessment methods has been exemplified in this chapter. It involves envisioning alternatives in data-gathering procedures and in indexing development, and systematically checking the options by putting them in competition with each other to see which optimally fits a set of validating criteria. The grand ideas of a research approach can be only as powerful and useful as the methodology employed in their operationalization. In moral judgment research, the time has come to pay more attention to alternative assessment procedures if we are serious about improving the state of the art.

CHAPTER 12

Research on Piaget's Theory of Moral Development

Thomas Lickona

Piaget's Theory of Moral Judgment Development

In *The Moral Judgment of the Child* (1932) Piaget relates a conversation he had with a 7-year-old boy, Stor, about playing marbles:

Stor tells us that children played at marbles before Noah's ark. "How did they play?— *Like we played*." . . . Stor invents a new game in the shape of a triangle. . . . "Is it as fair a game as the [other game] you showed me?—*No.*—Why?—*Because it isn't a square.* —And if everyone played that way, even the big children, would it be fair?—*No.*—Why not? *Because it isn't a square*" (p. 60).

Stor, interviewed here for his thinking about the rules of a game, was one of scores of Swiss children that Piaget and his Genevan associates queried a half-century ago in a pioneering effort to discover how children reason about rules and transgressions, right and wrong. The book on moral judgment (Piaget, 1932) which resulted from that effort has since stimulated a spate of studies on children's moral thinking and helped to establish the cognitive-

developmental approach (see Kohlberg, Chap. 2, 1969b) as a major theoretical framework for conceptualizing the moral growth of the child as well as related facets of social development, such as the capacity for friendship and love (Lickona, 1974). This approach views all children as moving through a series of stages or patterns of thought which are qualitatively different from each other, constructed by the individual through his own active experience, and the same in sequence for all persons and all cultures.

Piaget began his search for stages in moral development with the notion that the core of morality is twofold, based on (1) respect for the rules of the social order, and (2) a sense of justice—a concept of the rights of persons that stems from considerations of equality, social contract, and reciprocity in human relations. In order to identify the nature of change in these two broad facets of morality, Piaget used the flexible "clinical interview" technique to try to strike beneath the surface content of children's statements at the underlying structure or qualitative aspects of their spontaneous moral reasoning. He typically began his interviews by reading the child a story or pair of stories about transgressions or some other moral events involving children, and then proceeded to probe the child's thinking about whatever dimension of moral thought the stories were designed to elicit. For example, the child might be asked to explain who was naughtier—a well-meaning boy who accidentally gave wrong directions to a man who then got lost, or a boy who deliberately gave wrong directions to a man who found his way anyhow. In this fashion, Piaget questioned 5- to 13-year-old children[1] about various moral matters such as where rules come from, whether a rule can be changed, what a fair punishment is, what defines a lie, how rewards should be distributed, why it's wrong to cheat, and whether it's ever right to disobey an adult.

Through these conversations with children, Piaget identified what he believed to be two major stages of moral development. The developmentally earlier stage he alternately called *heteronomous morality, moral realism*, or a *morality of constraint*; the later stage he called a *morality of cooperation*. These two stages differ on nine dimensions—the left pole defining constraint, the right cooperation. These dimensions are:

1. Absolutism of moral perspective, as opposed to awareness of differing viewpoints
2. Conception of rules as unchangeable, as opposed to a view of rules as flexible
3. Belief in inevitable punishment, "immanent justice," for wrongdoing, as opposed to a naturalistic conception of punishment
4. "Objective responsibility" in judging blame, as opposed to consideration of the actor's intentions
5. Definition of moral wrongness in terms of what is forbidden or punished, as opposed to what violates the spirit of cooperation
6. Belief in arbitrary or expiatory punishment, as opposed to belief in restitution or reciprocity-based punishment
7. Approval of authority's punishment of peer aggression, as opposed to approval

of eye-for-an-eye retaliation by the victim
8. Approval of arbitrary, unequal distribution of goods or rewards by authority, as opposed to insistence on equal distribution
9. Definition of duty as obedience to authority, as opposed to allegiance to the principle of equality or concern for the welfare of others (adapted from Kohlberg, 1968b).

Piaget believes that the young child's morality of constraint is the product of two interacting factors: cognitive immaturity and unilateral emotional respect for adults. The first is the more fundamental source; Piaget sees moral realism as one expression of a generally immature cognitive organization which is both egocentric and "realistic." In this view, egocentrism, the child's broad failure to distinguish between aspects of the self and aspects of the external world, prevents him from taking the viewpoint of others in social situations. Realism, a consequence of egocentrism, refers to the child's confusion of subjective and objective aspects of experience. In the moral realm this confusion causes him to externalize moral rules and treat them as immutable absolutes, rather than as flexible instruments of human purposes and values.

Manifestation of the contrasting moralities of constraint and cooperation typically coexist in the same child, Piaget (1932) observed; he concludes that the two moral stages are best conceived as overlapping thought processes, the more mature of which "gradually succeeds in dominating the first" (p. 133). The child's progress to cooperative morality is a process of developing the *capacity* to function at the higher level. A morally mature child can, but does not necessarily, apply the principles of autonomous cooperation in his moral judgment.

Piaget (1932) holds that all children make the transition from a morality of constraint to a morality of cooperation, unless their development is retarded by deprivation of opportunities for reciprocal social interaction. Piaget (1932) maintains that under conditions of mutual respect and equality in social interchange, the developing mind cannot help coming to regard the principle of cooperation as "an immanent condition of social relationships" (p. 198). At this advanced level of development, morality is seen not as the will of authority, but as a system of modifiable rules expressing common rights and obligations among equals, a system essential to the intact functioning of any social unit.

The Validity of Piagetian Moral Judgments as Developmental Dimensions

MORAL DIMENSIONS RELATED TO THE DEVELOPMENT OF COGNITIVE DIFFERENTIATION

In defining moral development in terms of general cognitive growth as well as in terms of an emotional shift in orientation of respect, Piaget identifies four moral judgment dimensions which bear a clear relation to his conception of overall cognitive development as a process of progressive differentiation between the subjective and external aspects of experience. These dimensions (defined by their immature poles) are (1) absolutism of moral perspective, (2) concept of rules as unchangeable, (3) belief in immanent justice, and (4) evaluation of responsibility in terms of consequences. What does the research show regarding these four judgmental dimensions?

Absolutism of moral perspective versus awareness of different viewpoints. Several studies (e.g., Pinard & Laurendeau, 1970) have replicated Piaget's finding (Piaget & Inhelder, 1956) that the child under 6 years of age is egocentric in his perceptions of the physical world, believing, for example, that someone standing opposite him has the same view of a model mountain that he has. This kind of egocentrism, Piaget says, also prevails in the moral thinking of young children, who believe that there is only one viewpoint, held by everyone, on whether an act is right or wrong.

Absolutism of moral perspective (Dimension 1) and its developmental decline were demonstrated clearly in the responses of different-aged children who were told or read a story about a lazy schoolboy named Frank (E. Lerner, 1937b). Frank's teacher, to make him work harder, had forbidden his classmates to help him or play with him; but a boy named Paul broke the teacher's rule and helped Frank anyway. The experimenter asked the children whether they thought the friendly classmate was right or wrong for helping, whether Paul himself thought he was right or wrong, what the lazy boy Frank thinks, what the teacher thinks, and so on. At age 6, most children said that everyone in the story would think the same as they did. By age 9, most children recognized that different characters would have different views of the situation.

Similarly, Feffer and Gourevitch (1960) found marked improvement with age on a test of role taking which requires a child to make up a story and retell it from the viewpoint of each of the characters. Older children were able to shift perspective and to coordinate successive retellings of the story with previous ones. Children also show increases with age in the ability to be self-critical (Kohlberg, 1963b), a trend consistent with the developing child's abandonment of an egocentric, single-perspective view of his experience.

Conception of rules as unchangeable versus conception of rules as flexible. Piaget maintains that the failure of egocentric thinking to distinguish in the natural arena between the psychological and the physical (for example, between dreams and real events) is paralleled by a confusion of these two realms in moral judgment. Thus, young children view moral rules as being permanent regularities, like physical laws (Dimension 2)—an attitude that becomes even more rigid, Piaget believes, because of the child's deep respect for the adult authority which created the rules.

Research by Epstein (1965) has confirmed Piaget's findings on rule rigidity during early childhood, but has not supported Piaget's analysis of the attitudinal underpinnings of this rigidity. Consistent with Piaget's hypothesis, Epstein found that only 25 percent of 4-year-olds believed that the rules of a game could be changed, and none believed a school rule or law could be changed, whereas by age 7, a majority of children said that it was possible to change all three types of rules. A closer look at Epstein's results, however, calls into question Piaget's interpretation that young children's inflexibility springs from a full consciousness of rules as the sacred creations of authority. Epstein found five steps between the ages of 4 and 7 in children's awareness and understanding of rules that formed a scale of difficulty such that a child who "passed" a given step had to also have passed all the earlier steps in the sequence. Almost all the youngest children (4 years) had not yet mastered the second step (can give an example of a prohibited or prescribed activity) or even the first (understands that certain activities are prohibited or required). How, then, can a young child orient to rules as fixed and unchangeable if he has not yet really developed a concept of a rule?

An answer to this puzzle is suggested by another five-step scale which Epstein (1965) identifies as describing the development between ages 4 and 7 of the child's thinking about the issue of changing rules. The five developmental steps are as follows:

1. The child can respond to a description of "changing a rule" as some kind of departure from established practice.

2. The child can distinguish between changing a rule and breaking a rule; and the child recognizes that changing a rule is better than breaking it.

3. The child states that it is possible for a child in a game or the children and the teacher in a class to change a rule.

4. The child discriminates between some rule changes which would be "fair" and some which would not be, because they would be harmful or discriminatory.

5. The child has some sense of the necessity of majority consent for rule change in a game or the law, and for the teacher's consideration of the children's viewpoint and rights in changing classroom rules.

What Epstein's findings suggest is that "insofar as the young child does claim that the rule is unchangeable, it is largely because he does not distinguish between changing and breaking a rule" (Kohlberg, 1968b, p. 122). If, however, the children had a conception of rule change as distinct from rule breaking—as most of the 5-year-olds in Epstein's bright laboratory school sample did—then they were quite likely to say that the rules of a game *could* be changed. Jacqueline, aged 5 was typical.

Can you ever change a rule in this game?
Some times we give them a hint of which color it is.
Are they fair rules when you change them?
My mother lets me change the rules if I want.
What about your friends?
My friends let me do it. Sometimes they change rules.
Are they good rules when they change them?
I think so (quoted in Kohlberg, 1968b, p. 124).

Jacqueline said, however, that a classroom rule couldn't be changed by children ("It's not allowed"), nor could a law ("The police won't let you"). But "grown-ups," she said, "can change the real, real rules." Teachers can change the rules in the classroom, except the ones the principal makes, "because the principal would throw them out of the school."

Epstein's interviews (1965) indicate, then, that a child's judgment of a rule's changeability depends on his perception of where the power lies. Once he has grasped that changing a rule is different from violating it (Step 2 in the scale), he is ready to understand that the rules of a game among equals can be changed (Step 3). This flexibility is not immediately generalized, however; subordinates in an authority structure are not allowed to change rules. This analysis of immature thinking about rules differs from Piaget's interpretation (1932) that young children believe that "rules are sacred and unchangeable because they partake of parental or divine authority" (p. 48). The young child's reasoning appears from Epstein's research to be determined less by reverential respect than by his assessment of who's in charge.

The rule rigidity that Piaget observed in young Swiss children, illustrated by the interview with Stor at the beginning of this chapter, may have been due to their having not yet reached Step 2 in the rule comprehension scale: knowing the difference between changing and breaking a rule. In another manifestation of poor cognitive differentiation, some of Epstein's subjects (1965) seemed unable even to distinguish breaking a rule from breaking a physical object. In general, then, Epstein's interviews show Piaget to be correct in identifying cognitive immaturity as a source of the young child's inflexibility about rules and in identifying increasing flexibility toward rules as a developmental change in the child's conception of the social-moral order.

Belief in immanent justice versus naturalistic concept of justice. Another moral judgment dimension with a clear cognitive component is the child's belief about consequences for wrongdoing (Dimension 3). Because the young child does not distinguish between violating a social rule and

violating a physical law, Piaget (1932) reasons that the child expects the physical universe to aid in maintaining the moral order. Consequently, young children who are told a story about a boy who steals money and runs across an old wooden bridge say that the bridge will collapse because the boy stole, but would not collapse had he not stolen (Piaget, 1932). As another illustration of this view of justice, Piaget (1932) cites the reactions of children who look upon nightmares as punishments for the bad things they did during the day.

A substantial body of research, spanning several continents (Europe, Africa, and North America) and different social classes, has replicated Piaget's own finding that belief in automatic, or "immanent," justice exists early in development and gives way gradually to the belief that punishment for misdeeds in a social phenomenon, like the transgression itself, and therefore not necessarily inevitable (Caruso, 1943; Dennis, 1943; Grinder, 1964; Jahoda, 1958; R. C. Johnson, 1962; E. Lerner, 1937a; Liu, 1950; MacRae, 1954; Medinnus, 1959; Najarian-Svajian, 1966). The exceptions to this trend, however, have been cited (M. L. Hoffman, 1970b) as evidence against Piaget's claim that his stage sequences are universal. Curdin (1966), for example, found a curvilinear relation between age and immanent justice, with 8-year-olds being more mature than both younger and older children. Medinnus's finding (1959) of decreasing immanent justice with age for one story but increasing immanent justice for another story suggests that situation-specific factors may override general developmental tendencies in determining the child's judgment.

The power of culture to retard or even reverse Piagetian moral judgments has been brought into focus by Havighurst and Neugarten's study (1955) of ten American Indian groups. In four of these groups, the researchers found no age decline in belief in immanent justice, and in six groups they found *increases* to as high as 85 percent of 12- to 18-year-olds. Kohlberg (1968b), in reexamining these data, finds "some evidence (not clear-cut) for a natural childhood developmental trend toward naturalistic interpretation of misfortune, followed by an adolescent 'regression' to the adult cultural belief in immanent justice" (p. 87). Similarly, Curdin (1966) has explained his finding that immanent justice first declined and then rose in his sample of American boys by citing his subjects' growing awareness of their religion's fundamentalist belief that sin is always punished. Even if one maintains that the initial childhood tendency away from immanent justice is a universal feature of moral development, these studies underscore the point that development occurs in a particular sociocultural context, which over the long run may alter the "natural" or typical course of growth.

Personality as well as culture has been shown to affect the belief that retribution is inevitably visited upon the wrongdoer. Hart (1962), for example, discovered that men hospitalized for mental illness (but not women) held to a more primitive concept of justice on Piagetian stories than normal subjects; this finding suggests that regression to earlier levels on Piaget moral judgment dimensions may occur in adulthood and stem from idiosyncratic factors within the person as well as from external influences in the acculturation process.

Objective versus subjective concept of responsibility. How do young children evaluate the badness of what they believe to be a moral offense? Piaget (1932) has found that they judge actions in terms of observable physical aspects and consequences rather than in terms of the actor's intent (Dimension 4), presumably because they do not yet differentiate the subjective domain from things that are external and physical. A harmless but implausible exaggeration ("A little boy said he saw a dog

as big as a cow") is therefore considered a naughtier "lie" than a deliberate deceit that deviates less from probable reality ("A girl told her mother she got good grades in school when she didn't"). In assessing blame for negative material consequences, the young child judges as worse the person who has done more damage, regardless of motives. Around the age of 7, intentions become more important to the child than consequences; in Piaget's terms, the child's concept of responsibility becomes subjective rather than objective. The developmental trend toward increasing intentionality, found in different countries (Switzerland, Great Britain, Belgium, the United States, Taiwan, and Israel) and in different social classes, is perhaps the best documented of all Piaget's moral judgment dimensions (Armsby, 1971; Boehm, 1962; Boehm & Nass, 1962; Caruso, 1943; Cowan, Langer, Heavenrich, & Nathanson, 1969; Dworkin, 1966; Grinder, 1964; R. C. Johnson, 1962; Kohlberg, Havighurst, & Neugarten, 1967; R. L. Krebs, 1965; Kugelmass & Breznitz, 1967; Lerner, 1937a; Lickona, 1967, 1971; MacRae, 1954; Medinnus, 1962; Nass, 1964; Whiteman, 1964).

A refinement of the global objective-to-subjective shift described by Piaget comes from a study by R. L. Krebs (1965). Using picture stories with children 4 to 7, Krebs elucidated three substages in the transition from consequence-centered judgment to full subjective responsibility. The child progresses from (1) recognizing intentions when consequences are equal to (2) recognizing intentions when consequences are weighed against them ("Breaking one cup when you're stealing jam is worse than breaking eight cups while you're helping your mother") to (3) recognizing that intentions can make an act with bad consequences good ("Helping his mother was good even though he broke a lot of cups").

My own research (Lickona, 1971, 1973) has examined sensitivity to intentions in the realm of lying. First-graders from both middle- and lower-class backgrounds almost invariably were found to say that a plausible intentional deception was worse than an implausible unmalicious exaggeration—at an age when Piaget's Swiss children (1932) tended to say just the opposite. Thus a boy who told his father he had a headache in order to get out of helping to shovel snow was considered naughtier by my American first-graders than a boy who got so excited that he said a kneehigh snowfall was way over his head. Intentionality declined sharply, however, when innocent mistruths carried observable negative consequences. Only 51 percent of the time did children orient to intentions when they compared a boy who unsuccessfully tried to trick his sister by telling her the wrong time with a boy who unwittingly told his brother the wrong time, causing him to miss the bus. The results indicated that these two kinds of lying items formed an order of difficulty; all children who were intentional in judging honest misstatements with negative consequences were also intentional in judging harmless exaggerations, but not vice versa. A parallel relationship was found for lying items and items depicting material damage. About half of the children who showed intentionality on lying stories such as the one about telling the wrong time gave no intentional responses at all to damage stories about dropped cups or spilt paint. These findings provide another illustration of the interaction between the structural tendency of the child's thinking and the situation being considered. Moral judgment clearly is formed by both content and structure.

A major cross-cultural investigation of intentionality was carried out by Kohlberg, Havighurst, and Neugarten (1967). They asked members of thirteen different Indian and Atayal tribes who was worse— a child who broke five bowls by accident while carrying them for his mother or a child who broke one bowl while playing with it after having been told not to. In eleven groups, there was a clear trend toward intentionality; in one group the trend fell short of becoming the majority answer of late adolescents; in another, there was a regression toward a consequences orientation during the years 13 to 18. Even in these last two "deviant" tribal cultures, however, the change during the childhood years 6 to 11 was toward greater intentionality. This tendency provides evidence of a natural or universal trend in early development which is subsequently obscured by countervailing cultural forces. These data parallel the previously cited cultural departures from the typical developmental pattern for immanent justice.

A significant modification of Piaget's conception of intentionality is indicated in Kohlberg's longitudinal research (1968b) on the development of reasoning about moral responsibility. Beyond the "mature" intentionality depicted by Piaget is a level that Kohlberg characterizes as an orientation to categorical rules, in which the person judges an action by its conformity to a rule regardless of intentions or consequences: "Stealing is stealing, no matter what your motives, and obeying your mother is still obedience even if you break five cups in the process." Beyond this categorical level is another stage at which the individual recognizes that a good motive can modify disapproval of a transgression, but also believes that in general a good end does not justify a bad means: "I don't blame [Heinz] for stealing the drug to save his wife: I can see why he did it, but you can't have everyone stealing whenever they get desperate."

The fact that a categorical or literalistic orientation to rules appears late rather than early in the developmental sequence casts doubt on Piaget's belief that young children focus on the consequences of an act rather than on its spirit because they have a letter-of-the-law concern for rules. R. L. Krebs's study (1965) indicates that the reverse is true: Children are consequence-centered *until they* have a concept of respect for rules. He found that passing a test of "internality," which measured children's ability to judge the rightness of an act apart from whether it was rewarded or punished, was a prerequisite for passing Piaget's test of intentionality.

OTHER PIAGETIAN MORAL JUDGMENT DIMENSIONS

Studies of the five other Piagetian dimensions defined in the first section of this chapter—while not as extensive as research on the four dimensions just reviewed—permit at least tentative conclusions about whether these other dimensions define genuine developmental trends in moral thinking. Harrower (1934) and Medinnus (1962) have replicated Piaget's finding (1932) that as children grow older they focus less on punishment and prohibitions and more on trust and fairness in explaining why it is wrong to lie or cheat. (Dimension 5). Further evidence of the tendency toward greater independence from external sanctions in moral judgment comes from research in which subjects were required to evaluate situations where children were punished by an adult for doing something good or rewarded for doing something bad (R. L. Krebs, 1965; R. L. Krebs, Brener, & Kohlberg, 1967). By age 7 a majority of children could say, for example, that a boy did a good thing by obediently watching his baby brother, even though the boy got spanked when his mother returned.

The next four judgmental dimensions (6 to 9) are presented by Piaget as reflecting the developing child's increasing awareness of reciprocity as the organizing principle of social relations—an awareness that Piaget holds to be at the heart of the child's affective shift from unilateral respect for authority toward mutual respect among equals. One manifestation of this shift, Piaget believes, is the change which occurs in the child's concept of what is appropriate punishment (Dimension 6) for misdeeds such as lying, damaging another's property, refusing to help out, or betraying a peer. Several studies (Boehm,

1962; Boehm & Nass, 1962; Harrower, 1934; R. C. Johnson, 1962; MacRae, 1954) have found that from about age 7 on children increasingly reject arbitrary or expiatory punishments (such as spankings), which bear no intrinsic relation to the offense, in favor of reciprocity-based punishments, which do to the culprit as he did to others, allow the offender to suffer the natural adverse consequences of his offense, or require him to make active restitution. A cross-cultural investigation (Boehm, 1957), however, found that a majority of Swiss children, whose teachers and parents stress respect for authority, preferred adult-administered expiatory punishment for bloodying the nose of a classmate at an age when most American children opted for directly apologizing to the injured peer.

Piaget (1932) has also sought to tap orientation to reciprocity by asking children, "If anyone punches you, what should you do?" He found that children "maintain with a conviction that grows with their years [6 to 12] that it is strictly fair to give back the blows one has received" (p. 302)—a trend that is followed in adolescence by a realization that "there can be reciprocity only in well-doing" (Dimension 7). Durkin (1959a, 1959b, 1959c; 1961) was unable to replicate this developmental pattern for American children, finding instead that approval of nonretaliatory responses was dominant at all ages and that junior and senior high school children as well as elementary school children typically recommended telling an authority rather than dealing directly with a peer aggressor. R. L. Krebs (1965), measuring reciprocity orientation somewhat differently, found a clear increase between ages 4 and 7 in reciprocity-based explanations (for example, "You wouldn't like somebody to do that to you") of why it is bad to aggress against a peer.

Piaget's last two moral judgment dimensions (8 and 9) define reciprocity in terms of the child's allegiance to the principle of equality as opposed to unquestioning submission to authority. With development, Piaget (1932) found, children come to regard equal distribution of goods as more important than the need to punish wrongdoing (Dimension 8); thus, older children tend to say that a mother was unfair to give more cake to her obedient little girl than to her disobedient daughter. Finally, children are with age increasingly prone to place equality and the concern for the welfare of peers that arises from equal relations above obedience to adult authority (Dimension 9). Thus, older children are more likely than younger ones to say that a child should not obey a command to do work alone that should be shared by several children (Piaget, 1932), that a child should not submit to an adult's demand to tattle on a sibling or friend (MacRae, 1954; Piaget, 1932), and that a child is justified in stealing a bag of apples from a supermarket for a poor and hungry friend (Grinder, 1964). Boehm (1957) and Nass (1964) found that increasing age was also accompanied by a greater tendency to prefer advice on a problem from a talented peer rather than from an adult described as having no competence in the problem area. This last age trend appears to lack universality, however, since most Swiss children continue into adolescence to insist that teachers and parents always give the best advice—even in the face of evidence to the contrary (Boehm, 1957).

In a critique of Piaget's theory, Kohlberg (1968b) has argued that the judgment dimensions that emphasize "peer conformity versus adult conformity" lack the clear cognitive basis of other Piagetian moral judgments; hence the difficulty in replicating age trends. "There is nothing rational," Kohlberg (1968b) maintains, "about orientation toward peers as opposed to authority" (p. 92). Piaget was not, however, seeking to measure orientation toward peers so much as orientation toward reciprocity and equality as the basis for determining what is right and just. Inconsistencies in the research findings may be due

more to weaknesses in the judgmental dimensions which Piaget used to measure this changing orientation than to his theoretical conception of rational morality. As discussed in Chapter 2, Kohlberg's own research seems to show clearly that the concepts of reciprocity and equality stand at the rational center of mature moral thought.

Piaget's Moral Judgments as Stages: The Issue of Consistency

In defining moral development as a "process that is repeated for each new set of rules" (1932, p. 109), Piaget states that a child can be morally autonomous in his thinking about the rules of a game, but heteronomous in his thinking about lying or justice. Although Piaget's theory thereby rejects the notion of completely unitary stages, it calls for a certain consistency on the part of the child, since his various moral judgments are presumed to be the spontaneous products of a general cognitive and emotional disposition rather than learned responses acquired in separate situations. What is the evidence that the different facets of a child's moral thinking form a reasonably consistent pattern, that is, a "stage" of development?

Such a pattern of judgmental uniformity is hard to find in the existing data. Boehm and Nass (1962), in an investigation of children's thinking about lying, justice, authority, and responsibility, found that developmental differences for the *same* child from one type of story to the next were as great or greater than differences between age levels or between social-class groups. They concluded that "stage" of conscience development varies with the specific situation involved. R. C. Johnson's correlational study (1962) of 809 midwestern children in grades 5 through 11 found moderate consistency within a given area of judgment such as intentionality, but only low positive correlations (ranging from zero to .34) between different judgmental areas such as intentionality and belief in the efficacy of severe punishment. These results, providing only slender evidence of a general unifying factor in moral judgment, were essentially replicated by Harris (1970) in a study of 100 white and 100 black children in grades 4 to 6. Intercorrelations among five Piagetian judgmental dimensions ranged from .12 to .44, about the same as the modest correlations Hartshorne and May (1928) found among their various behavioral tests of honesty (see Burton, Chap. 10).

MacRae (1954) did a cluster analysis of Piagetian moral judgments, holding age constant. Rather than a single general factor, he found four relatively independent factors, which he identified as (1) sensitivity to intentions, (2) concept of punishment, (3) ability to take another's perspective, and (4) attitude toward deviating from the norms of authority. It makes no empirical sense, MacRae concluded, to treat questions dealing with these different aspects of moral development as measuring a single underlying stage such as "moral realism."

In the face of such data, one might speculate that inconsistencies in judgments about different areas of morality would sort themselves out with time. The research, however, uncovers no visible age trends toward greater consistency across different judgmental domains; the correlation between some pairs of Piaget dimensions has actually been found to decline between the ages of 11 and 17 (R. C. Johnson, 1962). Another way to try to make sense out of the data on the consistency issue would be to reconceptualize moral thought as reflecting a family of separate dimensions, each with its own developmental timetable. Correlational studies such as MacRae's and Johnson's have in fact found good consistency *within* judgmental areas such as justice concept, responsibility evaluations, and moral perspective taking. Likewise, Durkin's studies (1959a, 1959b) of Piaget justice concepts found that children, as they grow older, recommend nonretaliatory responses to social offenses with increasing regularity.

But even the existing evidence that children respond consistently within a particular area of judgment seems to pale by comparison with the mounting evidence of within-area variability. Lickona (1971) found only a low positive correlation (.25) between intentionality on stories contrasting different degrees of material damage and intentionality on stories contrasting deliberate lies with honest mistakes or exaggerations. Several other studies of intentionality have shown that varying the format (picture versus verbal stories, forced-choice versus open-ended) and the story content (simple versus complex situations, minor versus severe negative consequences) causes the level of judgment to fluctuate accordingly (Armsby, 1971; Caruso, 1943; Costanzo, Coie, Grument, & Farnill, 1973; R. L. Krebs, 1965). Armsby (1971), for example, found that 6-year-olds tend to judge in terms of motives if blame is to be assessed, but have difficulty judging in terms of motives when stories require comparison of positive rather than negative outcomes. Magowan and Lee (1970) demonstrated that stories assessing immanent justice tended to elicit high-level answers when the story was based on conditions familiar to the subject, and low-level responses when the story was based on situations taken from foreign cultures. Just the reverse was found in a study of beliefs of Navajo mountain children (aged 6 to 18 years) about the changeability of rules; they showed "immature" judgment for a situation close to home (rules of Navajo games could not be changed) and "mature" judgment for a more culturally remote situation (rules of American games could be changed) (Havighurst & Neugarten, 1955). There is obviously no simple rule of thumb for calculating the outcome of the complex interplay between culture and development (see also Lickona, Chap. 1).

In addition to lacking a strong foundation of empirical consistency, Piaget's moral judgments fail as stages by another criterion as well. As Kohlberg (1968b) points out, they do not, as Piaget's logical stages do (Piaget & Inhelder, 1969) specify a definite development going on in a delimited time period (for example, from age 5 to 8). A Piagetian dimension such as intentionality shows regular quantitative increases beginning at 5 to 6 years of age (Caruso, 1943; R. L. Krebs, 1965) and extending at least as late as 17 years (Kugelmass & Breznitz, 1967). If the individual's moral growth from ages 5 to 8 and his growth during adolescence can be characterized equally well in terms of increasing intentionality, then such a dimension cannot be considered part of a stage that defines a particular period of development.

It has been argued (Kohlberg, 1968b) that the problem with Piaget's theory of moral stages is not that stage patterns do not exist, but that Piaget's forced-choice stories (requiring the child, for example, to say which of two characters is naughtier) do not elicit the free, open-ended responses needed to get at the underlying thought structure that defines a stage. Because of the forced-choice methodology, Kohlberg (1969b) maintains, many of Piaget's dimensions "are really matters of content rather than cognitive form" (p. 375); that is, they describe *what* children believe, which is variable, rather than *how they reason* about moral beliefs, which is theoretically universal. Consequently, Piaget's dimensions do not show the properties, such as intercorrelation, which characterize components of "true structural stages." R. C. Johnson (1962) cites another problem with the classical Piagetian story items, namely, that their relatively low reliability of about .60 (children often change their minds about the same story) limits the size of the intercorrelations that can appear between different areas of judgment.

Whatever the reasons, the available research does not reveal a clear clustering of Piagetian moral judgments. This lack,

coupled with the gradual, drawn-out changes in these judgments, leads to the conclusion that the various features of heteronomous and autonomous morality are best viewed as relatively distinct developmental dimensions, showing steady age increases under most circumstances, rather than as closely knit stages of moral thought.

Field Research on Piaget's Theory of the Causation of Moral Judgment Development

In addition to documenting how children's moral thought changes as they grow older, much of Piaget's *The Moral Judgment of the Child* (1932) is an effort to explain *why* it changes. Piaget theorizes that three factors account for moral development: general intellectual growth, the experience of social equality with peers, and liberation from the coercive constraint of adult authority. But his own work does not attempt to test this explanation. A good deal of subsequent research, however, bears directly or indirectly on his theory of developmental change.

GENERAL COGNITIVE DEVELOPMENT AND MORAL JUDGMENT CHANGE

The validity of Piaget's argument that the child's level of moral development is anchored to his general level of cognitive functioning is suggested by a well-documented positive relationship between IQ and moral judgment maturity (Abel, 1941; Boehm, 1962; Durkin, 1959a; R. C. Johnson, 1962; MacRae, 1954). The contribution of intelligence to moral reasoning is also quite clearly demonstrated by R. L. Krebs's finding (1965) that moral judgment differences between kindergarten and first-grade children disappeared when children of the same mental age were compared. Similarly, Boehm (1967) found that retarded adolescents aged 16 to 21 scored at the same level as younger normal children of equivalent mental age on dimensions of intentionality and peer reciprocity.

Further evidence of the relation between cognitive and moral development comes from an interesting longitudinal study by Pringle and Gooch (1965) of children during the years 11 to 15. These investigators found that mental age rather than chronological age was the best predictor of response to the task, "Make a list of the most wicked things anyone could do." At 11 years of age, 100 percent of "bright" children mentioned murder, compared with 81 percent and 57 percent of the "average" and "dull" children, respectively. Many of the dull 11-year-olds were still at the level of listing trivial or exotic offenses such as "swearing," "smoking," "ripping someone's eyes out." By age 15 these same low-intelligence children had progressed to the point of listing offenses of a conventional-legal nature (such as stealing), while bright children by 15 had advanced to listing acts of personal or social injustice such as letting someone down, racial discrimination, or starting a war. Bright 15-year-olds mentioned acts of this latter category much more often than did their average or dull agemates, or than they themselves had when they were 11. Shifts in children's conceptions of evil appear from these data to be tied to changes in their general level of intellectual development.

Other research, however, suggests that it is not simply IQ or mental age which accounts for moral judgment maturity. Kohlberg (1968b) cites the example of a morally immature 9-year-old boy with an IQ of 128 who, in a fashion characteristic of younger children, defined moral wrongness in terms of whether the person got caught and punished by the police, and the value of life in terms of how much furniture a person owned. MacRae (1950) found that high-IQ children believed *more* strongly in immanent justice than low-IQ children, though the former were superior in terms of Piaget's hierarchy on measures of intentionality and attitude toward punishment.

The problem with conventional IQ measures in the context of Piaget's theory, however, is that they do not measure intellectual functioning as he defines it, and are therefore inadequate as a test of his notion that logical and moral progress go hand in hand. A better test would be to correlate Piagetian developmental measures of logical thinking with Piagetian moral judgment measures. Kohlberg (1968b) has done this, and reports positive correlations between consideration of a person's motives (subjective responsibility) and conception of a dream as a subjective event, between moral reciprocity (one good turn deserves another) and logical reciprocity (one physical change can compensate for another), and between maturity of moral judgment and physical conservation (something can remain the same in spite of apparent change), all with IQ controlled. Another investigation (Stuart, 1967) using a Piaget-based measure of cognitive development found that among 7- to 13-year-old children, "high decentraters" (facile at taking another's spatial and social perspective) were much more likely than "low decentraters" to show mature judgment on stories tapping intentionality, although the former group showed no superiority on immanent justice items. Lee (1971), in a study of 195 boys aged 5 to 17, found that as children mastered Piaget's concrete logical operations, they gave fewer authority-based moral judgments and more reciprocity-based responses. She also found that progress in adolescence to Piaget's highest intellectual stage, formal operational thinking, was predictive of the development of "societal, idealistic moral modes of conceptualization." Similarly, Kohlberg and Gilligan (1971) have reported evidence that the formal operational ability to consider many possibilities is prerequisite to the moral awareness of the multiplicity and relativity of values, and a recent study (Tomlinson-Keasey & Keasey, 1974) of logical problem-solving and moral reasoning in sixth-grade girls and college women found that only formal operational thinkers could reason at principled moral levels.

Since Piaget (1932) sees a connection between moral judgment and moral behavior—the function of the judgmental principle of cooperation being "to lead the child to the practice of reciprocity" (p. 71)—studies of moral behavior can also be used to evaluate his explanation of developmental change. Several investigations have suggested a link between declining cognitive egocentrism and increasing maturity of moral conduct. Rosenhan (1969a) reports "a large increment in the incidence of altruism from ages 6 to 7, much larger than that in the years that precede or follow those ages" (p. 9), and points out that this behavioral change occurs at the age when Piaget says the child is moving out of egocentrism toward the general capacity to experience the world from the viewpoint of another. Ugurel-Semin's study (1952) of sharing found a marked increase in children's generosity at about the same age, and a dominance of egocentric reactions in younger, more selfish subjects. Many of the youngest children believed that their partner did not want the extra nut in a pile of nine or were unable to see any way of dividing the odd number except to give the extra nut to themselves.

M. L. Hoffman and Saltzstein's study (1967) of childrearing disclosed that disciplinary techniques that reduced egocentrism by focusing the child's attention on the needs of others are associated with advanced moral development on a variety of behavioral and judgmental indices. Experimental evidence of the importance of perspective taking in cooperation comes from Chittenden's success (1942) in training initially domineering and self-centered children to anticipate and reconcile the reactions of doll characters in imaginary social conflict situations. Most 5-year-olds trained over several weeks subsequently showed a clear increase in cooperative preschool behavior.

EXPERIENCE OF SOCIAL EQUALITY WITH PEERS

The core of Piaget's theory (1932) of moral development is its emphasis on equalitarian peer interaction as the principal source of the awareness that the ethic of cooperation is the basis of harmonious social relationships. Investigators of Piaget's theory have translated this emphasis into the prediction that peer-group participation will be positively related to moral maturity.

The data on the peer participation hypothesis are mixed. On the negative side, Kugelmass and Breznitz (1967) found that Israeli kibbutz children, reared in a peer group with great emphasis on peer-group morality, were no more sensitive to the intentions of others than Israeli children reared in conventional family settings. R. L. Krebs (1965) found no differences in intentionality between popular 6-year-old children with reciprocal friendships and socially isolated children matched with their popular classmates for chronological and mental age. In a study of young adolescents, Porteus and Johnson (1965) found no relation between popularity ("He or she makes a good friend") and maturity on a moral measure combining Piaget items on intentionality, immanent justice, and severity of punishment. Dilling (1967) found a low, nonsignificant relationship between a sociometric measure of acceptance by peers and two variants of internalized conscience ("humanistic" and "conventional"), assessed in terms of attitude toward norm violations. Finally, E. Lerner (1937b) concluded from his research that peers can have a negative effect on even the older child's moral judgment, very much like the effect of adult constraint, when peer majority opinion runs counter to the principles of co-operation and fairness.

In contrast to this negative evidence, a variety of studies lend support to Piaget's theory that peer social interaction promotes moral development. Some of the findings, which are suggestive rather than conclusive, come from behavioral research. Ugurel-Semin's study (1952) of sharing found a negative relationship between selfish behavior and family size, the most selfish children coming from small families. Kibbutz children, while not superior on a specific judgmental dimension such as intentionality (for which only a "necessary minimum" of positive peer interaction may be required), display a marked and early sensitivity to the moral norms of their peer group, a strong sharing orientation, and a relative absence of such antisocial behaviors as stealing (Spiro, 1958). In a study of honesty, Einhorn (1971) has found a negative relation among 8-year-old children, but not among 5-year-olds, between cheating on a competitive task and the variables of peer-group cohesiveness and social experience (as inferred from sociometric data). Einhorn views this finding as confirming Piaget's theory that group ties and social interaction lead to moral autonomy at age 8, but not at age 5.

Judgmental data also support the peer participation hypothesis. Using Kohlberg's moral judgment interview, Keasey (1971) found that higher stages of moral reasoning were positively associated with social participation as measured by teacher and peer ratings of popularity and leadership and by self-reports of membership in social organizations. Performance on Piaget moral judgment tests, though unrelated to participation in scouting or Sunday school, has been found to be positively influenced by attendance at ungraded classrooms combining children of different ages, a condition which can be construed as an enrichment of the social environment (Whiteman, 1964). Especially intriguing is Nass's finding (1964) that a class of congenitally deaf children achieved independence of adult judgment on Piaget stories somewhat sooner than hearing children, and were far ahead of their hearing agemates in developing a concept of atonement in terms of peer reconciliation rather than adult punishment. A plausible interpretation is that greater peer solidarity of the deaf children, stemming from their common handicap and school experience, accelerated their progress on related moral dimensions. Equally interesting is the finding that deaf children were two years *behind* their hearing peers in learning to evaluate others according to their motives, awareness of which is presumably diminished by reduced verbal communication. Different judgmental dimensions such as intentionality and attitude toward punishment are apparently differently affected by the same experience. If this is so, then peer experiences, positive or negative, should not be expected to have a uniform effect on all areas of moral judgment development.

Combined data from two separate studies of childrearing by M. L. Hoffman (1960) and M. L. Hoffman and Saltzstein (1967) point to the importance of peer relations in moral development. In the earlier study, M. L. Hoffman (1960) found a strong association between a mother's use of coercive or punitive power assertion as a disciplinary technique and her child's adjustment with his peers in nursery school. Mothers high on power assertion had children who were themselves power-assertive with other children, hostile toward playmates, and resistant to peer influence. In the later study, M. L. Hoffman and Saltzstein (1967) found that seventh-grade children of power-assertive parents tended to be relatively retarded on measures of guilt, acceptance of responsibility, and internalization of moral principles. Quite possibly, the link between a mother's early coercive behavior and an older child's lagging moral development is the disruption of the positive peer relationships that Piaget regards as vital to moral growth. This interpretation gains credibility in the light of Dilling's finding (1967) that an external conscience orientation, characterized by fear of punishment as opposed to internalized values, was associated with low peer acceptance among fifth and sixth grade children.

The effects on moral judgment of institutionalization (a form of deprivation of social interaction) were examined in a study (Abel, 1941) comparing three groups of retarded girls aged 15 to 21 and matched for mental age. The first group lived in the community and attended a trade adjustment school, while the second group had been institutionalized for one year and the third for five years. On Piaget intentionality stories only 31 percent of the community-based group gave immature consequence-centered judgments, compared with 53 percent of the one-year institutionalized group and 63 percent of the five-year group. The differences were even greater on immanent justice stories. Kohlberg (1968b) interprets these findings as suggesting that marked social deprivation of a general sort does lead to retardation of Piaget moral judgments, even though reduced peer-group interaction (as in the case of sociometric isolates) does not. Reduced peer interaction *is* reflected, however, in Kohlberg's moral stages, with socially participating children being more advanced than peer isolates (Kohlberg, 1968b). This finding suggests that peer experience is important, but that Piagetian moral judgment dimensions are not adequately sensitive to variations in peer experience. As with the consistency issue discussed earlier, Piaget's general theoretical conception of moral development appears to be stronger than the methodology he used to measure it. Even with this limitation, though, the data seem to substantiate Piaget's notion that peer interchange plays a role in the development of mature moral thinking.

An important qualification of the discussion of peer interaction is that Piaget does not maintain that only a child's agemates can provide the experience of social equality necessary for moral develop-

ment. He simply observes that peers are typically the most common source of such experience for children. Piaget emphasizes, however, that an adult can choose to relinquish his unilateral authority and interact with the child on the basis of mutual trust and respect. Piaget (1932) states that if a parent gives the child "a feeling of equality by laying stress on one's own obligations and deficiencies" (p. 137) and "preaches by example rather than precept, he exercises an enormous influence" (p. 319) on the child's progress toward moral maturity. This affirmation of the value of nonauthoritarian childrearing is the bridge between Piaget's discussion of equalitarian peer interaction and his conception of a third source of moral growth, namely, increasing independence of the constraining effects of adult authority.

INDEPENDENCE OF ADULT CONSTRAINT

Increasing independence of adult constraint is conceived by Piaget to be both a cause and an effect of the child's growing allegiance to a mature morality of cooperation, just as the decline of cognitive egocentrism is seen as both cause and effect of increasing peer cooperation. Piaget does not convert this idea into specific predictions of behavior, but other researchers have derived two testable hypotheses from his discussion of independence:

1. The child's maturity of moral judgment should correlate positively with judgmental and behavioral independence of or flexibility toward authority-based norms.
2. Parental encouragement of independence by, for example, democratic childrearing practices should relate positively to maturity of moral thought in the child, while parental authoritarianism should relate negatively.

The first independence hypothesis finds some support in Abel's finding (1941) that institutionalized adolescent girls who were rebellious against authority and consequently continually punished scored much higher on an intentionality measure than passive, obedient girls, who were rarely punished. This finding suggests that the individual's *perception* of authority rather than his experience of constraint per se relates to moral judgment. Kohlberg (1963a) likewise found that a lack of deference to adult authority accompanied advance on his moral judgment scale to a reciprocity-oriented morality.

A surprisingly different pattern of associations, however, emerges from studies by Boehm (1962) and Boehm and Nass (1962), in which many children who were mature in their moral judgments about lying and responsibility nevertheless gave immature responses to stories requiring a choice between peer reciprocity and submission to adult authority. Moreover, Boehm discovered that while her middle-class children were clearly superior to lower-class subjects (with IQ controlled) on stories measuring intentionality, the reverse was true for stories measuring independence from adults. On the latter, lower-class children were significantly more advanced. This same pattern of social-class variation showed up in MacRae's investigation (1954) of Piaget's theory and undercuts earlier conclusions (Harrower, 1934; E. Lerner, 1937b) that the upper- or middle-class child, presumably enjoying greater parental permissiveness, is uniformly more advanced in moral thinking than his lower-class counterpart. The fact that middle-class children are superior on one dimension but inferior on another also points up again the impracticality of conceptualizing cognitive-moral development as a global advance with even progress on all fronts.

The second independence hypothesis, focusing on "democratic childrearing" as an antecedent of mature independent judgment, is supported by Boehm's previously mentioned finding (1957) that American children become peer-oriented and adult-independent considerably sooner than Swiss children, who are reportedly encour-

aged to regard adults as omnipotent and omniscient. R. C. Johnson (1962) has gone one step further than Boehm and actually measured parental attitudes on scales of *dominativeness, possessiveness,* and *ignoringness.* These attitudes correlated only infrequently with five Piaget moral judgment dimensions, but then usually in the theoretical direction; parents high on dominativeness, for example, had children who were rated immature on judgments about punishment. Interestingly, extreme ratings of parental attitudes on either end of the three scales related negatively to mature judgment, suggesting that the relationship between parental permissiveness and some aspects of moral development may be curvilinear.

A key study by MacRae (1954) dealt with both independence hypotheses and suggested a fruitful reformulation of the independence issue. He found that neither the extent of parental effort to control the child's behavior nor the child's compliance with parents' demands (an inverse behavioral measure of independence) correlated significantly with Piagetian measures of intentionality, punishment concept, or perspective shifting. MacRae did find, however, a significant negative correlation between the variables of parental control and childish compliance, on the one hand, and the child's willingness, on the other hand, to approve of acts violating norms of obedience or truth telling when those norms conflicted with other moral values such as loyalty. In MacRae's study (1954), children who were either less regulated by their parents or less compliant with existing regulations were more likely to approve norm violations.

One way to make sense out of Mac-Rae's findings would be to classify Piaget's moral judgment dimensions into two distinct categories: The first category includes dimensions such as perspective shifting and concepts about punishment and responsibility which do *not* involve definitions of what would be right and wrong for a child *to do.* Such cognitions appear from MacRae's study to be unrelated to the parent's authoritarianism or to the child's behavioral independence of the parent, and from Boehm's studies (1962; Boehm & Nass, 1962) to be unrelated to his judgmental independence of adults. The second category of judgments deal with what would be good and bad for a child to do—whether good behavior consists in accommodation to an adult-imposed morality or in following cooperative principles which may or may not conform to the conventions of authority.

The development of moral priorities in this second category of judgment is more "emotional" than the development of judgments in the first category. This greater emotionality arises because parental authority is quite capable of generating anxiety about judgments regarding rule deviations. This line of reasoning would anticipate MacRae's finding (1954) that highly controlling parents tend to have convention-bound children. This analysis also dovetails with M. L. Hoffman's finding (1960) that the children of parents who relied upon love withdrawal, an anxiety-arousing technique, internalized conventional moral rules quite readily but applied them much more rigidly than children of parents who relied more upon reasoning in dealing with their children's transgressions.

The above twofold classification of moral judgments makes it possible to deal with some research findings that have been troublesome for Piaget's theory. In the context of this scheme, for example, no problem is posed by Liu's finding (1950) that Chinese-American children, despite strong filial piety, are ahead of white American children in developing a subjective concept of responsibility. The Chinese child's criterion for assessing moral responsibility falls into the first category of judgments, which does not require him to be independent of adults.

To summarize, the first independence hypothesis predicts a positive relationship between the child's independence of au-

thority and his maturity of moral judgment. The research has supported the prediction for some measures of independence and some dimensions of moral judgment, but not for others. The second independence hypothesis predicts a negative correlation between parents' authoritarianism and the child's judgmental maturity. The research confirmed this prediction only for judgments about departures from conventional norms.

For all three hypothesized causes of moral change—cognitive development, experience of social equality, and increased independence of adult constraint—the research reviewed thus far has been correlational rather than experimental. The most that can be said on the basis of these naturalistic data is that the factors identified by Piaget as sources of moral growth have typically been found to correlate with mature judgment on one or another of his dimensions. The evidence is strongest for the role of cognitive development, mixed but generally supportive regarding the contribution of peer experience, and weakest with respect to the role of freedom from the constraining influence of adult authority. In search of further clarification of the nature of moral development, let us now turn to experimental investigations that have directly manipulated potential antecedents of moral judgment change.

Experimental Modifications of Piagetian Moral Judgments

Can the child's moral judgment on Piaget's dimensions be experimentally changed? An affirmative answer comes from six tests of the responsiveness of Piaget's moral judgments to a variety of experimental ingenuities (Bandura & McDonald, 1963; Cowan et al., 1969; Crowley, 1968; Dworkin, 1966; Lickona, 1967, 1971, 1973). These experimental efforts, however, have been narrowly focused; all of them have dealt with only one of the nine Piagetian dimensions: the child's attention to motives versus consequences in evaluating another's responsibility for an action (Dimension 4).

The very first investigation of this nature took the form of a challenge to Piaget from the rival, social-learning theory of moral development, which views moral judgments as modifiable products of observation learning rather than as manifestations of irreversible developmental tendencies. Bandura and McDonald (1963) demonstrated that 5- to 11-year-old children could be influenced to change their responsibility judgments in the direction of a model who gave responses that contradicted the child's pretest orientation. Initially intentional children and initially consequence-centered children both made a 30-percent shift in the opposite direction after hearing the experimenter reinforce an adult model for answers that were contrary to those of the subject. These changes held up during an intentionality posttest with no model present, and were cited as evidence that "the developmental sequence proposed by Piaget is by no means invariant . . . because the so-called developmental stages were readily altered" (Bandura & McDonald, 1963, pp. 207, 209). Following this frontal assault on Piaget's theory, the rationale, procedures, data analysis, and conclusions of Bandura and McDonald's investigation became the target of critical scrutiny by several writers (Cowan et al., 1969; Dworkin, 1966; Lickona, 1969; Turiel, 1966). Among other things, Bandura and McDonald were criticized for failing to report data on the reasons children gave for their judgments, and for inadequately assessing whether overt judgmental changes reflected merely short-term conformity or lasting change in moral orientation.

Using a design that attempted to correct the deficiencies of the Bandura and McDonald study, Cowan et al. (1969) found that lower-class subjects showed just as much model-induced change as had Bandura and McDonald's upper middle-class population. Cowan and his co-workers also found, however, that children who were "pure cases"—either 100 percent objective or subjective on the intentionality pretest—changed less during training than subjects with mixed pretest performances. Most significantly, these investigators found that on a second posttest two weeks after training, "trained-up" (initially objective) children showed even greater intentionality than they had on the immediate posttest. In distinct contrast, the "trained-down" (initially subjective) children began to return to their pretraining orientation toward intentions. This finding can be taken as evidence of a natural developmental direction (objective to subjective) which training-down had reversed only superficially and temporarily. LeFurgy and Woloshin (1969), employing Kohlberg-type dilemmas rather than Piagetian stories, likewise found that morally relativistic seventh- and eighth-graders trained downward returned gradually to their pre-experimental level over a 100-day period, whereas initially rigid subjects trained upward toward relativism maintained their large experimental gains.

Dworkin (1966) criticized Bandura and McDonald for confounding the variables of "modeling cues" and "cognitive information." He sought to separate these by devising an *imitation only* condition, (model simply names the naughtier of two story characters), a *cognitive information* condition (model also provides justification for naming response), and an *imitation plus reinforcement* condition (experimenter verbally reinforces the model and the child for desired naming response). He found that the cognitive information condition produced a 50 percent increase in intentional judgments, which was more than double the gains under the other two conditions and still in evidence four weeks later.

Crowley (1968), in the most intensive Piagetian moral judgment acceleration study thus far conducted, carried out small-group rather than individual training with first-graders in sessions that totaled three hours over a two-week period. He found that simply labeling for the child which story character was naughtier and giving prizes for intentional responses produced the same dramatic rise in intentionality, a stable 80 percent gain, as did labeling plus discussion of why the ill-intentioned character was worse. Crowley attributed the effectiveness of both his experimental conditions to their heightening the salience of intentions by using "simple" training stories which varied motives while holding damage constant. However, his simultaneous use of extrinsic rewards and corrective feedback, in addition to labeling, makes it impossible to isolate the contributions of the several training influences.

A training study of my own (Lickona, 1967) found that only 20 percent of initially objective children became subjective after having been cast in the role of the well-meaning offender in a hypothetical story about the subject and a friend. Most of these first- and third-graders who ignored motives in judging others did the very same thing when judging themselves. Intention-based responsibility judgments obviously require more than mere access to the viewpoint of the well-meaning offender, since these children remained consequence-oriented even though the subjective viewpoint of the "good child" in the story was their own.

Since none of the previous training studies directly investigated Piaget's ideas about why moral judgment changes, I attempted to put his hypotheses to an experimental test by providing judgmentally immature children (objective in their responsibility judgments) with the experiences presumed by Piaget to stimulate development (Lickona, 1971, 1973). These experiences were translated into three training conditions: (1) *decentering*, using stories with accompanying cartoon sequences (Figure 12.1) to help children differentiate motives from consequences and hold both in mind at once; (2) *peer interaction*, involving face-to-face debate between an objective subject and an al-

ready subjective peer in order to break down the former's egocentrism and increase sensitivity to another's viewpoint; and (3) *adult conflict*, exposing children to adults who repeatedly and assertively contradicted each other and themselves in their story judgments in order to reduce monolithic adult constraint on the child's moral thinking. A fourth, non-Piagetian condition, *didactic training*, was included as a theoretical foil, and consisted of simply telling the child straight out that a judgment based on intentions was right, and explaining why this was so.

All four experimental conditions generated substantial training-phase increases in intentional judgments among first- and second-grade subjects, and all but adult conflict gains were maintained during posttesting one month later (see Figure 12.2). Decentering training stimulated an overall 32 percent pretest-to-posttest increase, but over a third of the children in this group showed no change at all. Some even explicitly acknowledged the good intentions of a character while still convicting him of being the guiltier culprit—a finding that substantiates the suggestion of my earlier study (Lickona, 1967) that a subjective responsibility concept depends on the child's *valuing* intentions as well as being aware of them. The clash of viewpoints between objective and subjective children in the peer interaction condition was followed by a 60 percent gain in subjectivity for initially objective children, but no regression whatever for initially subjective children. The fact that change under this condition followed what Piaget sees as the natural direction of development suggests that downward training effects in previous studies were most likely no more than subjects' outward accommodation to the standard of authority (the adult model).

The results of adult conflict training were puzzling. Most children in this group increased their intentional responses during training, but gains were stable for only half of the subjects. Of the 16 children, 5 actually showed a net "loss" and gave sig-

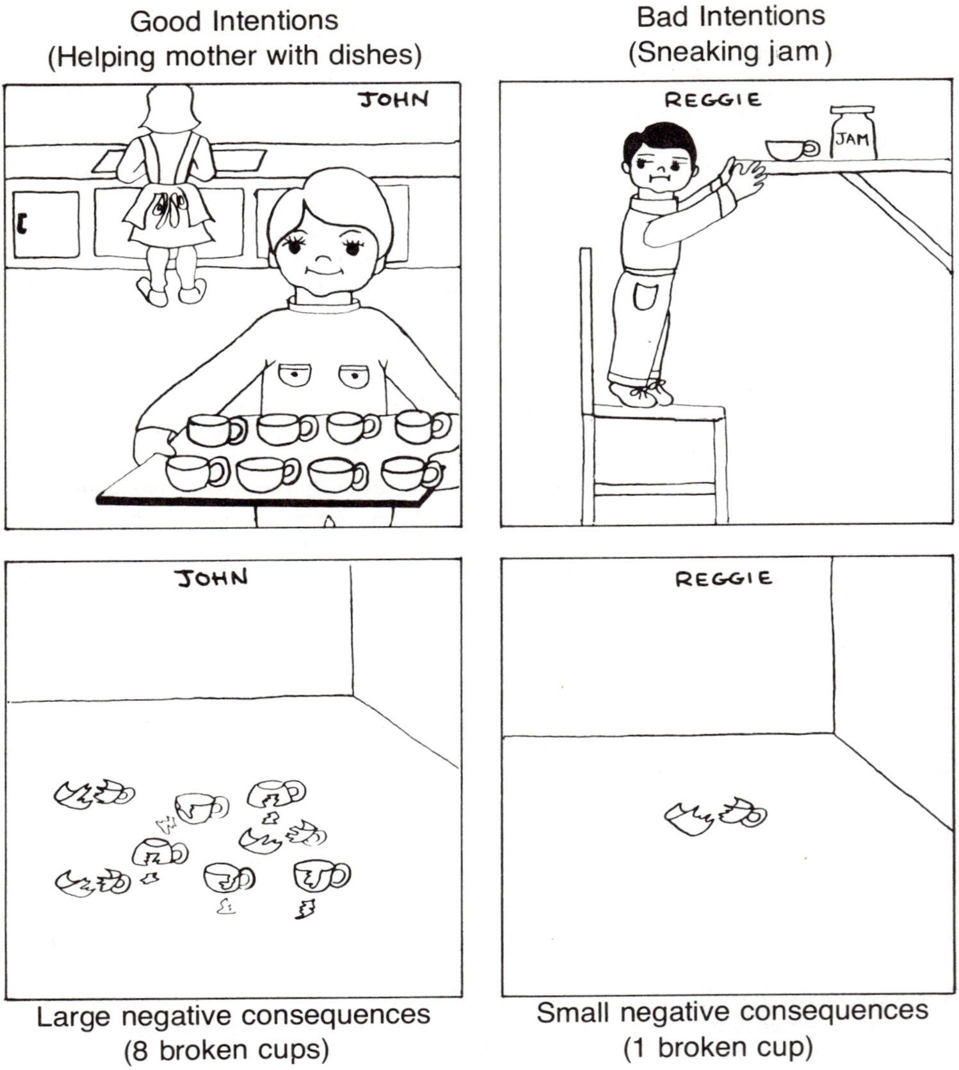
Good Intentions
(Helping mother with dishes)
Bad Intentions
(Sneaking jam)
JOHN
REGGIE
JAM
JOHN
REGGIE
Large negative consequences
(8 broken cups)
Small negative consequences
(1 broken cup)

Figure 12.1. Sketches used in intentionality training (Lickona, 1971) to promote decentering of attention to include both the intentions and damage of story characters (*drawings by Cheryl Lickona*).

nificantly fewer subjective responses on the posttest than they had given on the pretest. This regressive tendency appears to parallel Langer's finding (1969) that some children trained in "class inclusion" became more primitive in their classification behavior after being given an impossible problem designed to facilitate understanding that a whole class is greater than any of its component subclasses. Children seem to differ in their tolerance of the affective disequilibrium created by input the cannot readily assimilate to what they already know and understand.

The result in my study that is most difficult for Piaget's theory to assimilate is

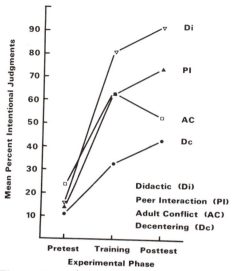

Figure 12.2. Pretest, training, and posttest percentages of intentional judgments on Piagetian responsibility stories for four experimental groups (Lickona, 1971).

the 76 percent gain under authoritative didactic training, which also produced the only significant generalization of trained intentionality to posttest stories about children's lies. These impressive gains could be interpreted as showing that Piaget underestimates the power of language to stimulate disequilibrium and cognitive reorganization in children. Kohnstamm (1970), for one, has taken Piaget to task for his "assumption that as soon as the adult starts speaking, the child stops his active handling and operational thinking and becomes a passive machine, waiting for the atomistic S-R connections to be stamped in" (p. 371). Or the didactic-training gains could be taken to mean that children simply learned what to say (content) but did not acquire a deeper grasp of reasons (structure), and that a didactic lesson in *objective* responsibility could easily reverse this surface learning. The latter interpretation implies that as a general procedure, all experimentally induced changes in moral judgment should be subjected to tests of

"resistance to extinction" such as those used to determine the durability of trained logical operations such as conservation (Smedslund, 1961).

On the whole, the moral judgment training research leaves one with the feeling that the sources of change that Piaget speaks about, such as peer interaction and broad cognitive growth, do not lend themselves to being telescoped into a brief experimental session. Even though Piagetian antecedents may be quite important over the course of development, they seem doomed to fare badly in short-term experiments when compared to straightforward modeling or didactic methods. Longitudinal training research, with varied and long-range follow-ups to test both permanence and generalization of change, is perhaps the only legitimate way to conduct an experimental test of a developmental theory.

Conclusion

At the end of this tour through the Piagetian moral judgment literature the reader may feel that—contrary to the honored axiom of scholarship—more research is not needed. His intuition is probably sound. All of the evidence may not be in, but there is enough from a generation of testing Piaget's theory to render a verdict on at least the broad outlines of his conception of moral judgment growth.

Moral judgment, as depicted by Piaget, is indisputably developmental; it changes with age and experience. Piaget has demonstrated that the young child, in his conscience as in his logic, cannot be viewed as an adult in miniature, lacking only an adequate dose of indoctrination. It is at the same time evident that children's moral judgments do not exist in a social or cultural vacuum; however spontaneous they may be in their origins, they are very much subject to direct and indirect social influence both in their rate of development and, at least for some judgmental dimensions, in the shape they take in adulthood. The available research also shows plainly that the child's moral thought, as it unfolds in Piagetian interviews, is not all of a piece but more of a patchwork of diverse parts.

The findings also suggest that while Piaget's analysis of the cognitive basis of moral judgment is well founded, his speculations about its affective side are on shaky ground. Young children do not, as their parents or teachers can wearily attest, stand in awe of the authority of adults or the rules they repeatedly set forth. When a preschool boy flushes the father doll down the toilet, as Kohlberg (1968b) observes, it is hard to view his action as consistent with a sense of heteronomous respect for the patriarchial father. Rather, the research (R. L. Krebs, Brener, & Kohlberg, 1967) indicates that loyalty to and genuine respect for personal authority, like respect for rules, is something that children must *develop* during the early school years (ages 4 to 7) and something that accompanies *advance*, not immaturity, on moral dimensions such as judging the rightness of an action apart from its external consequences. The child's early obedience orientation in moral thinking appears to be based less on respect for the moral status of adults than on simple recognition of their superior power.

Moral judgment also appears to mature more slowly than Piaget's theory leads us to believe. Using Piaget-type stories with 11- to 18-year-olds representing a variety of personality and subcultural types, Loughran (1967) concluded that "adolescents arrive at Piaget's level of mature autonomous judgment between 12 ture autonomous judgment between 12 and 17 years, not between 11 and 12 as Piaget says" (p. 89). Kohlberg's longitudinal research (see Chap. 2) has led to the postulation of three stages *beyond* the relatively simple "Golden Rule morality" that constitutes Piaget's highest, autonomous-cooperative stage—indicating that the latter is "yet far from the morality of mutual respect and social contract which is shared by both humanitarian liberals and bureaucratic constitutionalists" (Kohlberg, 1968b, p. 139). And if Kohlberg's authority-independent but still self-centered Stage 2 morality is a universal step in development, then Piaget also errs at the lower end of the moral ladder by omitting this intermediate second stage and presenting children as moving directly from a Stage 1 obedience orientation to a Stage 3 morality based on concern for the approval and welfare of others.

A comparison of Piaget's two-stage theory with Kohlberg's highly refined six-stage moral sequence makes it clear that an early, groundbreaking cognitive-developmental theory has been subsumed and supplanted by a later, more comprehensive theory in the same tradition. It is not surprising that moral judgment research tends increasingly to be done within Kohlberg's framework. Kohlberg and his colleagues are, however, continuing what Piaget largely began with his gentle inquisitions of Swiss children some forty years ago: the charting of developmental changes in thinking about moral issues, the search for sequential and universal stages, and the effort to understand how conceptions of morality are bound inextricably to the overall growth of the human mind.

CHAPTER 13

The Social Psychology of Moral Behavior[1]

D. L. Rosenhan, Bert S. Moore, and Bill Underwood

Introduction

To speak of the social psychology of moral behavior is to speak of issues that are at once obvious and yet difficult to accept. It is perfectly clear that we are not flowers in the garden of the Lord, entirely self-contained, entirely self-nourished by attitudes and values acquired in the past and regnant in the present. Rather, we are commonly, and often to our dismay, creatures of our environment. Our behaviors vary, often to a great extent, according to the environmental pressures that impinge upon us. And our moralities, to speak loosely, vary similarly.

Yet however difficult it is to accept the notion that some behavior is situationally determined, it is much more difficult to accept the application of that notion to moral behavior. Our views of human responsibility, indeed our notions of law (cf. Mancuso & Sarbin, Chap. 19), are nearly wholly predicated on the assumption that the individual, and he alone, is responsible for his behavior. True, exceptions to this rule are made when a person is very sick or crazy. But these exceptions seem to un- derscore the pervasiveness and power of the rule: One needs to be *in extremis* to be free of personal moral responsibility. Under most circumstances, personal responsibility for behavior is a basic premise. The ordinary situations in life are not seen as shaping one's moral view and behavior.

Yet the reverse seems to be the case. Common, "garden variety" situations appear to have enormous impact on moral behavior. Indeed, an analysis of the literature with a view to determining whether morality is more strongly influenced by personality (i.e., beliefs, values, attitudes, and dispositions) or situations leads us to conclude that the latter are far more powerful. Granted that a comparison between personality and situational influences may be premature, the implications of such a comparison are not to be underestimated.

The social-psychological influences on moral and prosocial behavior are numerous. The issues include general theoretical matters such as the relative influence of personal dispositions on behavior, as well as practical ones such as cue availability, authoritarian imperatives, momentary frustrations, and the role of external restraints.

Given the limitations of a single chapter, we have chosen to focus on a few issues that seem to us to be either highly significant as situational factors, or often overlooked. We have omitted significant areas such as resistance to temptation (cf. Burton, Chap. 10) and have dealt only briefly with the influence of models (cf. Mischel & Mischel, Chap. 5; Burton, Chap. 10; Liebert & Poulos, Chap. 16), which is treated extensively elsewhere in this volume.

One can approach this area by treating exemplars of situations or by examining processes. In the main, we have chosen to examine the social-psychological processes likely to affect behaviors across a variety of situations. Thus, we examine diffusion of responsibility, victim derogation, evaluation apprehension, and momentary moods as they appear to affect behavior. One exception to this method is our brief discussion of obedience, which may be both a situation and a process.

Obedience

Nowhere is the evidence for situational determinants of moral and prosocial behaviors more compelling than in regard to the capacity of people to inflict great harm on others. In the course of summarizing the findings of a series of vivid experiments on obedience, Milgram (1965) observes:

With numbing regularity good people were seen to knuckle under to the demands of authority and perform actions that were callous and severe. Men who in everyday life are responsible and decent were seduced by the trappings of authority, the control of their perceptions and the uncritical acceptance of the experimenter's definition of the situation, into performing harsh acts.

The results . . . raise the possibility that human nature, or, more specifically, the kind of character produced in American democratic society, cannot be counted on to insulate its citizens from brutality and inhumane treatment at the direction of malevolent authority. A substantial proportion of people do what they are told to do, irrespective of the content of the act and without limitations of conscience, so long as they perceive that the commands come from a legitimate authority (pp. 74–75).

Milgram's findings have disturbed observers for a variety of reasons, not the least of which is that they appear to constitute an enormous indictment of the people we know, perhaps ourselves included, and the personality theories that we believe. Recall Milgram's paradigm: In the name of a scientific experiment ostensibly concerned with examining the effects of punishment on learning, subjects are asked to teach paired associates to learners and to administer shock to these learners in increasingly severe dosages each time an error is made. The shock levels range from 15 to 450 volts, in steps of 15 volts. The voltages are designated numerically and by statements that read *slight shock, strong shock, extreme intensity shock, danger: severe shock*, and **XXX**. Despite the apparent clarity of the experimenter's communication and the evident implications of continuing to shock the learner, close to 70 percent of the subjects in the basic experiment (Milgram, 1963) obeyed the experimenter's command to continue the experiment throughout the entire series of 450 volts. Moreover, *no subject in the basic paradigm terminated the experiment prior to 300 volts.*

Milgram's description (1963) of the experiment makes it clear that subjects were *not* blasé about their performance: "Subjects were observed to sweat, tremble, stutter, bite their lips, frown, and dig their fingernails into their flesh. These were characteristic rather than exceptional responses to the experiment" (p. 375).

These experiments touch the heart of our conceptions of human nature and of personality. According to predictions solicited formally by Milgram (1963) and informally by many teachers of introductory and social psychology, most persons do not expect so many people to obey the experimenter and deliver such harsh pain. Even sophisticated clinical psychologists and psychiatrists estimated that fewer than 2 percent (whom they labeled psychopathic or otherwise disturbed) of subjects would administer the full complement of 450 volts. Moreover, efforts to uncover personality variables associated with obedience (Elms & Milgram, 1966) have been almost entirely unsuccessful. In an unpublished study, Rosenhan found that the variables most likely to be associated with obedience, such as aggressiveness, submission to authority, and anxiety (all measured by a variety of personality scales), were completely unrelated to behavioral obedience. Examination of the raw data revealed that the lack of relationship was not due to restriction of range in either the personality scales or in obedience. The personality differences that did emerge pointed to general personality processes rather than specific traits of, say, aggression, authoritarianism, or submissiveness. Thus, the tendency to be a "naysayer," that is, to be rather critical-minded and to possess high cognitive energy, was related to the capacity to defy authority and to disobey.

THE EFFECTS OF MODELS ON OBEDIENCE

Much research has shown that the presence of a model can serve to elicit either prosocial or antisocial behavior (Bandura & Walters, 1963). The same effects hold with regard to obedience. Milgram (1964) reports that the presence of disobedient models who exert group pressure can have a liberating effect on the subject instructed to give the shocks. The incidence of complete obedience among such subjects was much reduced when one confederate refused to continue after 150 volts, and another after 225.

Similar findings were obtained by Rosenhan (1969b) in a study that examined the effects of models without group pressure. In that study, subjects entered the experiment in time to see other teachers still participating. The subjects were told that the experimenters were running behind schedule, and were asked to wait their turn. They observed models (not real subjects) either obey the experimenter and continue to administer the full complement of shock to the victim, or disobey him. Disobedience took one of two forms: The model delegitimized the experimenter by questioning his credentials and good sense, or the model expressed enormous sympathy for the victim and consequently could not continue to administer shock.

The true subject observed these models. And as one might expect, disobedient models substantially reduced the subject's own proclivity to obey. Obedient models, however, had no effect, presumably because the base rate for obedience in this study (85 percent) was already very high.

THE EFFECTS OF PHYSICAL RELATIONSHIP TO THE VICTIM

In the experiments described thus far, the subject who administered the shock was in one room, while the victim was in another. To the extent that concrete evidence of anguish was obtained, that evidence came to the teacher aurally, through the screams of the victims. Milgram (1965) provides evidence that the extent of obedience varies according to the physical remoteness of the victim to the subject. Thus, when the subject is not in the same room as the victim, Milgram obtains obedience from close to 70 percent of his subjects. When, however, the subject must hold the victim's hand in the shock box, obedience drops to 25 percent. Thus, physical proximity to the victim—quite apart from other considerations—appears to have a profound situational impact on obedience.

The Impact of the Situation on Bystander Intervention

We turn now to another phenomenon in which situational factors apparently play an enormous role: bystander intervention. Huston and Korte provide a full discussion of bystander intervention in Chapter 15. We consider the matter briefly here because it is so obviously related to the social psychology of moral behavior.

Bystander intervention occupies a curious position on the dimensions of morality. Ordinarily, morality is judged by the presence of an act, not by its absence. Donating to charity is a moral act, but failing to donate is not commonly considered immoral. Cheating on a test is an immoral act, but refraining from cheating is not especially moral. But the act of intervening on behalf of a distressed person is considered a moral one, while the failure to intervene, if we are to believe the news media, is held by most people to be quite immoral. For example, the failure of bystanders to interevene in the wanton murder of Kitty Genovese in the mid-1960s, either directly or by alerting the police, was viewed as a moral failure and resulted in widespread public and editorial outrage toward the observers.

The Genovese incident produced a number of morbid sociological and social-psychological explanations of the bystanders' failure to act. Some editorials suggested that the incident reflected widespread alienation. Others noted the apathy, even hostility, generated by life in complex urban environments. Still others saw a failure to adhere to religious and moral teachings.

One problem with these explanations is that they apply equally well to the numerous acts of heroism that occur daily in our cities. Such global explanations of failure to intervene in emergencies simply explain too much; they explain failure to act when action has in fact occurred. Since intervention behavior varies, any adequate explanation must explain the variability. Dissatisfaction with the "reasons" that the media proposed prompted Darley and Latané (1968) to offer an alternative explanation.

Darley and Latané felt that the explanations for the failure to intervene were either too global ("the city") or too personal and specific ("those people"). Situational factors, they believed, govern the likelihood that people will intervene to help another in distress. They analyzed the characteristics of the emergency situation that made the intervention process particularly susceptible to social influence processes. Because emergencies are rare events which usually happen suddenly and unexpectedly, the definition of a situation as an emergency requiring personal action is often complicated by the social context in which the event occurs. How do we know that we are observing a real emergency, not a prank or a game or a movie being produced? Darley and Latané suggest that people fear making an inappropriate response in ambiguous situations to such a degree that they look to others for information regarding what is transpiring. How others interpret the situation will be a strong determinant of their own behavior.

To test this hypothesis, Latané and Rodin (1969) created a situation in which subjects heard a woman in the next room fall and cry out in apparent pain. These subjects were either alone or with a friend, a stranger, or a confederate. The ostensibly injured woman received least help when the subject was with a confederate who was unresponsive to the emergency, presumably because the confederate attitude maximized the subject's risk of being embarrassed by intervening. More help was given by the subject when he was with a stranger who provided more cues supporting an emergency definition of the situation than did the confederate, and who therefore presumably made intervention less embarrassing. Even more intervention occurred when the subject was with a friend; in this case the subject was presumed to have even less fear of embarrassment. Finally, of course, the most help (though not significantly more than in the friend condition) occurred when the subject was alone. Alone the subject had least reason to fear being embarrassed. A similar interpretation of these data can be made in terms of the informational cues from the subject's partner, which increasingly enabled the subject to define the situation as an emergency. The confederate, with his studied passivity, provided least information; the uncoached stranger somewhat more; and the friend even more, since friends tend to be more comfortable in defining these situations for each other.

DIFFUSION OF RESPONSIBILITY
IN EMERGENCY SITUATIONS

Intervention is not only a matter of situational definition; it depends also on the number of potential interveners. Even when there is agreement about what is happening, responsibility for intervention is diffused when there are multiple witnesses. The Genovese witnesses, feeling confident that they were not the only people aware of what was happening, also felt less personal responsibility to act. Some assumed that someone else was already doing what needed to be done.

To differentiate the process of diffusion of responsibility from the previously discussed problem of defining a situation as an emergency, Darley and Latané (1968) created a situation in which each subject was alone in a small room (thereby equalizing social cues) but varied the number of people who the subject thought were also overhearing the incident. Subjects were told that they would be members of either a two-, three-, or six-member discussion group. Each member of the group was supposedly in a separate cubicle, and the group members were to communicate via an intercom system. One of the participants, who previously had mentioned an epileptic condition, began to have a seizure while speaking over the intercom. The subject under study was thus in a situation in which he believed that either four, one, or no other bystanders were aware that the seizure victim needed help. The subject's speed of help decreased significantly as the number of other bystanders increased.

Staub (1969) has attempted to manipulate perceived responsibility quite directly in children. Children were brought individually to the experimental room and

were told in the responsibility condition that the experimenter had to leave for a few moments and that the child was in charge of things. Other children were simply told that the experimenter had to leave the room. While the experimenter was absent the child heard a crash from an adjoining room, followed by severe crying and sobbing. In the distress–help condition, the child also heard calls for help. Staub found that children who had responsibility focused on them were more likely to help than were those in the control conditions and even in the distress–help condition. While this finding does not establish that diffusion of responsibility is the only factor operating in emergency situations, it certainly indicates that such a process can be an important determinant of bystander intervention.

DEVELOPMENTAL STUDIES
OF EMERGENCY INTERVENTION

Staub (1970a) has reported a developmental study of bystander intervention that is relevant both to social comparison processes (aimed at avoiding embarrassment) and to the diffusion-of-responsibility hypothesis. Elementary school children were brought either alone or in same-sex pairs to a room where they were subsequently left for a brief period. During this period the sound of a falling chair, followed by the severe crying and moaning of a young girl, was heard in the next room. Staub found that the amount of help given the distressed child first increased and later decreased with the age of the helper. This initial increase, perhaps resulting from increased empathy for others or from increased competence to help, had been anticipated; but the decrease with age was a surprise. In questioning the children after returning to the room, Staub noted that many of the older children expressed fears of negative evaluation by the experimenter if they went into the adjoining room to offer help. Although anecdotal, this finding seems to indicate that during the elementary school years fear of negative evaluation by others may develop and become a significant factor in determining bystander intervention.

Staub's findings (1970a) also indicate that very young children are more likely to help when waiting with another than when waiting alone, quite the opposite of results obtained in several studies with adults (Latané & Rodin, 1969; Schwartz & Clausen, 1970). Older children were found not to differ in their willingness to help alone or with another. These results suggest that the process of diffusion of responsibility may not develop (or at least may not be as important as other opposing processes in determining bystander intervention) until late childhood. Staub speculates that this particular developmental trend is due in part to the fact that the presence of a peer may reduce fear and distress in the younger children, and in part to the fact that children become more concerned with peer evaluation as they grow older. The older children may therefore be inhibited by fears of appearing foolish before a peer. Thus it appears that we succeed quite early in convincing our children that outward appearances and evaluation by others are of the utmost importance. Using a similar paradigm, Staub (1971b) has further demonstrated that a warm, nurturant relationship between a child and the experimenter can increase the child's tendency to offer aid to a peer in distress during the experimenter's absence. Staub suggests that this increase may be due to a reduction in the child's fear of disapproval for inappropriate behavior.

Staub (1971a) has obtained other results which suggest that the fear of negative evaluation by others may either be situation-specific or age-specific (and overcome to some extent as the child matures). In this study, children and adults received no information or information that permitted or prohibited their going into an adjacent room in the experimenter's absence. In the permission group, children were told that they could play with some

games in the next room if they needed a break, while adults were told that they could go into the next room if they desired coffee. In the prohibition group, both children and adults were told not to go into the next room because they would disturb someone who was taking a test there. In all conditions, the experimenter then left the subject alone. After a short time, a crash, followed by sounds of distress, came from the next room. Staub found that more children helped in the permission group than in the no-information or prohibition groups, which did not differ significantly. Adults, however, were more likely to help in both permission and no-information groups than in the prohibition group, while the permission and no-information groups did not differ from each other.

These results suggest that children are unlikely to help unless they have definite reason to believe that they will not incur others' disapproval. Adults, on the other hand, are likely to help unless they receive information that suggests their action will be disapproved. This finding is rather encouraging, in that the results indicate that people become more likely to intervene in an ambiguous situation as they enter adulthood. The fact that such a trivial prohibition can inhibit aid in an apparent emergency, however, must be a matter of some concern. Indeed, this result leaves open the possibility that the fear of negative evaluation has not decreased at all, but perhaps only the tendency to expect negative evaluation in an ambiguous situation. It seems clear, at any rate, that the threat of other people's disapproval remains a powerful determiner of our behavior even as adults.

THE ROLE OF OVERT THREAT

Of course, threats other than the disapproval of others can also influence bystander intervention. H. Allen (1972) investigated the effect of overt threats. His study involved the use of a confederate who incorrectly answered a question that had been directed toward the subject. In order to manipulate the perceived threat to the subject if he corrected the misinformation, Allen had previously had the subject witness the confederate's physically threatening or sarcastic response to someone who stumbled over the confederate's feet while walking through a subway car. Control groups with no prior experience of the confederate's response were also utilized. Results indicated that the threat conditions produced less correction of misinformation by subjects than did control conditions, with the physical threat condition producing least helping.

The threatening confederate then left the subway car while the misinformed questioner and the subject remained, so that the subject had an opportunity to correct the misinformation in the absence of any threat. Interestingly, this correction was not made; total corrections remained less in the threat than in the control conditions. Either the subjects had attached a "threat value" to the situation which endured even after the source of the threat had been removed, or they were reluctant to make a delayed correction after having failed to make an immediate one. In any event, it seems that a threat made to the potential helper at his earliest opportunity to help can reduce his tendency to intervene not only at that time but even after the threat has disappeared.

CONCLUSION

Clearly, situational characteristics are powerful determinants of how we respond to the plight of others. The finding that the presence of others, the possibility of disapproval, and the awareness of physical threat can inhibit our helping each other in need calls strongly into question the facility with which we make judgments regarding the morality of those who fail to react to crisis in a socially sanctioned way. Darley and Latané's subjective impression (1968) was that the subjects who failed to intervene were often the most distressed by overhearing the emergency. To assume that apathy causes us to callously disregard the needs of our neighbors does not seem supported. Instead, it seems that our "morality" is a complex social phenomenon which is as determined by the characteristics of the situation in which we find ourselves as by our own personal characteristics.

Finally, despite the proliferation of studies on bystander intervention, there remains little we can say about the most interesting, and probably most important, case: the hero. The factors characterizing heroic action may eventually prove to be as situational as the factors characterizing failure to act. In any event, a common thread of prosocial concern, surely the basis for heroism, appears to exist in us despite our frequent failure to act upon it.

Derogation of Victims

M. J. Lerner (1970) raises a perplexing problem for issues in moral and prosocial behavior:

All of us know that there are great numbers of people in our midst whose lives are filled with suffering—pain, emotional anguish, deprivation of the body and spirit. Many people live under conditions of devastating poverty. Many others spend the greater part of their lives in mental hospitals with budgets barely adequate to provide minimal care, let alone the kind of treatment which could give them back their lives. And many children spend their most vulnerable and formative years in overcrowded and potentially crippling institutions.

The question that plagues the concerned observer is: why do we allow such suffering to continue? As a nation, we have the money and technology to virtually eliminate poverty and provide the kind of professional facilities and services which would dramatically enhance the life chances of the parentless child or the emotionally ill person. Yet we allow this suffering and deprivation to continue while we pursue comparatively frivolous, self-interested, and often quite expensive goals. . . . We seem not to care enough; perhaps we do not care at all. We are apparently callous, indifferent, and cynical about the suffering of others (p. 205).

How does one account for this societal callousness and disregard—especially when it appears to coexist with a deep and abiding societal concern for others? A possible answer may lie in the "just world hypothesis."

There is evidence from a variety of social-psychological sources that people experience a strong need to view the world as reasonable, consistent, and predictable (Festinger, 1957; Heider, 1958). We want the world to operate in a manner consistent with our experience, and we want ourselves to operate in a manner consistent with our beliefs. When there is inconsistency between some beliefs, or between our beliefs and our actions, we are motivated to reconstrue or reorder the events and/or beliefs in a more congruent manner. M. J. Lerner (1970) suggests that the need for consistency applies equally to the area of moral behavior. He speaks of a *just world hypothesis*, which he describes as a general tendency to see the world as operating in a consistent, just manner where the good are rewarded and the bad are punished. He and others (Berscheid & Walster, 1969; E. E. Jones & Davis, 1965) have suggested that the desire for consistency orders our world so that we can maintain self-perceptions as caring, concerned, individuals in the face of an unjust world.

Bramel (1969) has suggested that there are several ways in which this drive for consistency may manifest itself. Although Bramel is concerned with situations in which one person has directly injured another, the same processes seem applicable in any situation where there is a victim. In such circumstances, the person can (1) convince himself that the injury he has caused is very slight or nonexistent, (2) convince himself that he had no choice about how to act, (3) resolve to repair the damage he has done and thus believe that

he can undo the dissonant act, (4) convince himself that the injurious act has other consequences which are positive and beneficial, or (5) convince himself that the victim deserved to be punished. Situational factors undoubtedly have much to do with which of these options a person chooses.

The last method of reducing dissonance—derogating the victim—is especially interesting because of its heavy implications about our perceptions of others and our future actions toward them. It follows from the just world hypothesis that when people choose to harm others, and when they have no opportunity or inclination to make amends, they will be strongly inclined to derogate their victim. This was demonstrated in an interesting experiment by K. E. Davis and Jones (1960) in which subjects were asked to evaluate a person whose voice they had heard in another room. They were then either asked or directed to read a very negative evaluation of the person to the person himself. Those who freely chose to read the negative evaluation, when asked to do so, "derogated" their victim much more than those who were directed by the experimenter to read the same statement. Moreover, subjects who felt that they would not subsequently meet the victim derogated him much more than those who anticipated a subsequent meeting.

We do not, of course, always derogate victims. Indeed, Berscheid and Walster (1967) have demonstrated that when a harm-doer is able to make what he perceives to be adequate compensation, the likelihood that he will derogate diminishes considerably. Only when restitution is not seen as a viable means of restoring equity is derogation very likely to occur. In fact, this finding has important implications for childrearing and for society at large: We need to maximize the opportunities for restitution.

One does not need to be a direct harm-doer in order to derogate a victim. Merely observing an innocent victim is sufficient to call our notions of a just world into operation and to lead us to derogate. M. J. Lerner and Simmons (1966) had subjects observe a person in a learning experiment who was receiving electric shock. Subjects were led to believe that the victim had either finished her series of shock, still had half to go, or had volunteered to take more shock so that they could get course credit for participating in the experiment. Subjects who believed that the ordeal was over and that they would not have to witness further shock were most lavish in their ratings of the victim's likability and attractiveness. When they were led to believe that she was still in the middle of the learning experiment, they were more rejecting. And the subjects were most rejecting of the victim when told she had volunteered to continue in order that they could gain course credit. This rather surprising and counterintuitive finding is, however, consistent with the notion that in order to maintain their view of a just world, the subjects needed to consider the victim a damned fool for undergoing that kind of torture. Antagonism, rather than pity or gratitude, was aroused.

These views make the general neglect of the poor, the aged and infirm, and the mentally ill more comprehensible. In order to maintain their view of justice, many people seem to say of these victims that "if that's where they are, that's where they must deserve to be." Similarly, in *Sanctions for Evil* (Opton, 1971) a soldier is quoted as saying:

No one has any feeling for the Vietnamese. They're lost. The trouble is no one sees the Vietnamese as people. They're not people. Therefore, it doesn't matter what you do to them (p. 55).

Situationally Induced Affect

It may seem odd to describe affect in situational rather than personality terms, and we have no intention of removing affect entirely from the personality domain. But affect is quite commonly induced by situational cues and events. The death or illness of a friend, one's own successes and failures, some good luck, or the warm embrace of a friend—all of these events induce affective states. Indeed, the cognitive and situational contributions to the experience of affect have been well documented (Schachter & Singer, 1966). And these affective states seem quite powerful in their effects on moral and prosocial behavior (Rosenhan, 1972).

A large psychological and sociological literature (Berkowitz, 1962; Merton, 1957) relates frustration to aggression and social disorganization. Berkowitz and Connor (1966) have argued that goal frustration may lead a person to violate norms of social responsibility; and, conversely, goal attainment may make those who have recently succeeded more willing to assume the discomforts involved in living up to moral adjurations and sacrificing their own gains.

To examine this hypothesis Berkowitz and Connor (1966) offered subjects a bonus payment of one dollar if they could complete a crossword puzzle in two-and-a-half minutes. Subjects who won the dollar were subsequently more helpful to a supervisor who needed their assistance in making envelopes than were control subjects or subjects who failed to complete the puzzle. These findings led Berkowitz and Connor to believe that success generates a "glow of goodwill" which is accompanied by greater willingness to tolerate the increased psychological costs associated with helpfulness.

Isen (1970) induced success and failure by manipulating scores on a test alleged to measure creativity. She found that successful people were more willing to aid a confederate who was carrying (and dropping) a large load of books and papers than were those who had failed the test. Moreover, those who failed recalled less about the confederate and her actions than those who succeeded. The relationship between attention and affect was not significant enough statistically to prove that failure leads to reduction of attention, which in turn leads to a failure to help. Yet that relationship requires further investigation, since the number of subjects in Isen's study was quite small. Finally, Isen reported that successful people were more willing to initiate conversation with the confederate than were controls, who in turn initiated more conversations than subjects who had failed.

These findings with regard to situationally induced success and failure have now been replicated in a variety of situations and populations. Isen, Horn, and Rosenhan (1973) found that the helping behavior of children is influenced by success and failure in a way that depends on whether the child's task performance is public or private. When children are fairly certain that no one has observed their success or failure, those who have succeeded contribute more to charity than those who have failed. When, however, they feel that their success or failure is being observed by an adult, differences in charitability are entirely obliterated, with failing children contributing as much as those who have succeeded. These findings suggest that failure has differential effects if there is an opportunity to repair one's image in the eyes of the observer of the failure (cf. Schneider, 1969). When the failure is public, image repair will ensue. When failure is private, however, and no image repair is necessary, very little charitability occurs. We shall have more to say about this matter below.

Success and failure are obviously complex experiences that have implications for expectancy for future success (Feather, 1966), competence (Kazdin & Bryan, 1971; Midlarsky, 1968), aspiration (Locke, 1967), and a host of other variables. In order to exclude such variables as competence and expectancy, Isen and Levin (1972) induced positive affect by distributing cookies in a library to students who were studying there. These students were subsequently asked to help the experimenter in a study of creativity. As predicted, those who had received cookies helped more than those who had not. The same study revealed, however, that positive affect does not uniformly generate dispositions to be helpful. Students who received cookies and were subsequently asked to make noise, rattle papers, and otherwise distract other students from their work were significantly *less* helpful to the experimenter than were students who had not received cookies. Positive affect leads to compliance with a request for help only when the helpfulness is prosocial in its effects on others.

Aderman (1972) induced moods in male college students by asking them to read statements that progressed gradually from neutrality to either "elation" or "depression." Those who were elated were subsequently more willing to oblige an experimenter's request for a favor than those who were depressed. Elated subjects were similarly more willing to volunteer for a subsequent hot-room experiment.

B. S. Moore, Underwood, and Rosenhan (1973) paid children to participate in a hearing test. Then they induced affect by asking the children to reminisce about experiences that had made them happy or sad. The subjects were subsequently given an opportunity to contribute their earnings from the experiment anonymously to children who would not have an opportunity to participate in the experiment. Subjects who were happy contributed significantly more than controls, who contributed more than those who were sad.

The general evidence, then, is that positive affect promotes prosocial behavior. It may be useful to note in this regard that the effects of positive affect are not limited to kindness to others, but seem also to mobilize kindness to self. Masters (1972a), Masters and Peskay (1972), and Mischel, Coates, and Raskoff (1968) have shown that children who experience success engage in considerably more noncontingent self-gratification than do controls or those experiencing failure. And Underwood, Moore, and Rosenhan (1973) have demonstrated that positive affect contributes to the greater willingness of children to reward themselves. These results—combined with Isen and Levin's finding (1972) that positive affect may promote prosocial but not antisocial behaviors—suggested that positive moods evoke a disposition to do unto others as one would have others do unto him. In a further experiment, Rosenhan, Underwood, and Moore (1974) demonstrated that this possibility was indeed the case. Children were given the opportunity to do two things in the same experiment: to self-gratify by helping themselves to candy, and to contribute their experimental earnings to others. When they were experiencing positive affect the rank correlation between self- and other-gratification was .51.

NEGATIVE AFFECT

While the facilitating effects of positive affect on prosocial behavior seem clear and straightforward, the effects of negative affect seem more complex. We have already seen that when failure occurs privately, or when negative affect is evoked through reminiscence of unhappy experiences (again, private events), such affect retards charitability. But when the subject feels that his failure has been observed, he may be more inclined to be charitable in order to repair his tarnished image with the experimenter (Isen, Horn, & Rosenhan, 1973).

There is, in addition, a category of negative affect that seems likely to evoke positive behavior. This is the negative affect loosely described by the term *guilt*. Wallace and Sadalla (1966), for example, have found that persons who had been induced to break an expensive machine were subsequently more likely to volunteer for an experiment. Brock and Becker (1966) similarly found that those who had done a great deal of damage to a piece of equipment conformed more with an experimenter's request than those who had done minimal damage. Freedman, Wallington, and Bless (1967) found that subjects who lied to an experimenter were more willing to volunteer for a subsequent experiment than subjects who had not lied. These investigators also reported that people who accidentally upset someone's research data were more willing to volunteer for an experiment (but not with the person whose work had been upset!). Similar findings have been observed by Carlsmith and Gross (1969), Darlington and Macker (1966), J. W. Regan (1971) and, in a naturalistic setting, D. T. Regan, Williams, and Sparling (1972).

When guilt is not implicated, the findings for negative affect seem more straightforward. We have described some of the effects of negative affect, induced via reminiscence or through failure, on charitability and helpfulness. One additional finding may serve to illuminate the processes involved. Rosenhan, Underwood, and Moore (1974) in the experiment described in the preceding section, found a strong negative correlation (−.50) between self- and other-gratification under conditions of negative affect. Thus, the more one took for oneself, the *less* one was willing to give to others—quite the reverse of the findings for positive affect. These findings suggest that negative affect promotes sociophobia, the desire to avoid others and to husband one's resources for oneself. Positive affect, on the contrary, creates sociophilia, the tendency to move toward others and to consider their needs on a par with one's own.

Conclusions

This chapter has been a selective analysis of social-psychological processes that impinge on moral behavior and cognition. It is by no means exhaustive. Even for the issues that we have chosen to discuss, we have been narrowly discriminating, stressing interesting and relevant matters and overlooking others entirely.

What shall we make of these data? Their open meanings are clear enough: Social-psychological processes such as modeling and the presence of a victim powerfully influence altruistic and moral responses. Situational contingencies play an enormous role in determining whether a helpful or hurtful response will be forthcoming. In many of these situations, such as Milgram's obedience paradigm, the environmental contingencies are so powerful and seem to affect so many people that there is little room for individual differences. And in other situations where individual differences appear (i.e., where the response to the situational contingency is not overwhelmingly uniform), the source of these differences is not very clear. Perhaps personality differences, as they are commonly construed, account for the variations. But perhaps—and there is some evidence for this view—differences in cognition, attention, and perception (cf. Mischel, 1973) account for the variations. It is too early to decide which variables determine the differences; but it is not too early to say that situational or social-psychological variables are heavily implicated in moral and prosocial action and judgment.

The latent meanings of these findings are both troublesome in regard to ego-centered theories of personality, and optimistic in regard to the promotion of moral and prosocial behaviors. On one hand, the cumulative impact of these studies suggests that we are not the masters of our moral ships we believe we are. But, on the other hand, they suggest that situational factors can be arranged to maximize moral and prosocial behavior. Indeed, it is conceivable that in a world or society or school or home where situational supports for prosocial behavior were consistently and strongly provided, many more people would develop the kind of moral system that no longer requires external supports. Therein lies a potentially important role for personality, as it develops from and interacts with social-psychological forces.

CHAPTER 14

Social Influence and Moral Development

A PERSPECTIVE ON THE ROLE OF PARENTS AND PEERS[1]

Herbert D. Saltzstein

Studies of the socialization of morality are numerous and extremely heterogeneous in the measures of morality used and in the aspects of parental childrearing studied. The major focus of this chapter will be discipline—the way in which parents control and influence their children—but it will also examine the ways in which children influence their parents and each other.

Research on Discipline

Early studies (for example, J. W. M. Whiting & Child, 1953) usually divided discipline into techniques which are primarily material or physical (such as physical punishment or material deprivation) and those which are not. The "not" category has been variously labeled. Some investigators have simply termed it "psychological discipline." Others have focused on the degree to which affection and approval are manipulated, and have termed the technique "love withdrawal." A central hypothesis (for example, J. W. M. Whiting & Child, 1953) has been that love withdrawal by parents, in contrast to physical punishment, promotes various aspects of moral development.

A study by Sears, Maccoby, and Levin (1957) has often been cited in support of the love withdrawal hypothesis. These investigators operationally defined "conscience" as the mother's report that the child confessed or expressed guilt in some other way after having transgressed but before having been detected. They found that 42 percent of the children whose mothers were generally warm to their children and reported frequently using love withdrawal as a form of discipline, had a high conscience index, compared to 24 percent of the children whose mothers were warm but reported using love withdrawal infrequently. The relationship between love withdrawal and conscience, however, has not been consistently replicated. A more recent study (Yarrow, Campbell, & Burton, 1968), for example, using similar measures found no evidence of an association between "conscience" and love withdrawal under conditions of high or low warmth.

In the face of these inconsistent findings, Hoffman and Saltzstein (M. L. Hoffman, 1963b; M. L. Hoffman & Saltzstein, 1960, 1967) have suggested a different hypothesis: Induction, not love withdrawal, is the critical variable in conscience development. *Induction* primarily involves pointing out to a transgressor the consequences of his behavior for other persons (the parents themselves or some third party). This technique contrasts with *power assertion*, defined as physical punishment or any other exercise of physical or material power over the child (such as threatening loss of privileges and physically forcing the child to do or not do something), and with *love withdrawal*, defined as nonphysical expression of anger or withdrawal of love (such as the parent's telling the child that she doesn't love him or is angry with him, or her walking away in disgust).[2]

In their survey of seventh-graders, M. L. Hoffman and Saltzstein (1967) examined parents' and children's reports of both the mother and father's present discipline practices, and also asked the parents to indicate their practices when the child was about 5 years old. In addition, the study assessed several facets of conscience: severity of guilt as expressed in story completions, internality of moral judgments (that is, judgments of right and wrong independent of rewards and punishment), teacher's ratings of the child's acceptance of responsibility for wrongdoing, mother's report of the child's tendency to confess after transgressing, and peers' sociometric nominations of classmates they judged most considerate of other children. Controlling for intelligence and social class, Hoffman and Saltzstein (1967) found that higher scores on the various indices of morality generally were negatively associated with use of power assertion, positively associated with use of induction, and unassociated with use of love withdrawal. The same results were obtained regardless of whether the child, parent, teacher, or peers was the source of information for the moral index, or whether the mother or the child reported the mother's discipline. The authors

explained the "superiority" of induction over power assertion in terms of the nonaggressive model that induction provided, and the opportunity it afforded for learning and role taking.

In a subsequent unpublished study, M. L. Hoffman (1974) found that sociometric ratings of seventh-grade boys' consideration for others were positively associated with their mothers' peer-oriented induction (that is, their mothers' practice of pointing out the consequences of the child's action for peers) when such induction was coupled with a suggested reparation. Similarly, Shoffeitt (1971), using Kohlberg's scale (Chap. 2) found that adolescent boys' stage of moral reasoning was positively associated with parents' use of reasoning (a form of induction) and negatively associated with both parental power assertion and love withdrawal. When love withdrawal is separated from other-oriented techniques such as induction, then, more consistent relationships emerge.

The Relationship between Parental Discipline and Different Kinds of Moral Orientations

Just as understanding of the relation between childrearing and moral development may be advanced by distinguishing among different kinds of psychological discipline, distinctions among different kinds of morality may help us establish order in the socialization of morality.

While it is generally agreed that moral issues must immediately or ultimately have consequences for others, it is also clear that this concept of consequential morality only gradually becomes differentiated in development from conformity to moral rules for extrinsic reasons, such as consequences to the self, and from conformity to rules for the sake of conformity or deferring to authority (Piaget, 1932; Kohlberg, 1963a). Conformity to rules for extrinsic reasons, such as fear of punishment or hope of reward, has been typically treated as lack of or poorly developed morality, as in Kohlberg's preconventional level of morality. But what of a morality in which conformity to moral rules is neither directed to self-interest nor to the welfare of others, but to a blind deference to authority? In this section, we shall treat this deference as one kind of internalized morality, which we shall term *conventional*, or *conformist*, morality, to be distinguished from an internalized morality in which adherence to moral rules is based on concern for the direct or indirect welfare of others, termed *altruistic*, or *humanistic*, morality. While we understand that this distinction bears a complex relationship to age and development (see, for example, Kohlberg, 1969b), we shall begin by treating these two moral orientations as different though fully developed types of moralities, and consider research findings in terms of this distinction.

HONESTY VERSUS ALTRUISTIC MORALITY

A major study which begins with a distinction between two kinds of moral standards, honesty and altruism, was carried out by Mussen, Harris, Rutherford, and Keasey (1970). The subjects were 11- and 12-year-olds of at least normal intelligence, mostly from lower-middle-class families. Four types of moral measures were used, two of honesty and two of altruism. Each of these two categories was assessed by an overt behavioral measure in the laboratory and also by a sociometric measure. The overt behavioral measure of honesty was resistance to temptation (RTT) in a ray-gun test situation in which the subject was tempted to cheat in order to win a prize that he could not otherwise win; the overt behavioral measure of altruism was a variation of the prisoner's dilemma, a game in which two players have to choose between cooperating to their mutual advantage or seeking to maximize their individual gain at the expense of each other and with the risk of mutual loss. The sociometric measures of honesty

and altruism, based on ratings by peers, were factor-analyzed for each sex separately. For both sexes, the factor analysis revealed an honesty factor and an altruism factor. The study also included questions designed to measure the subject's self-concept and the mother's childrearing attitudes and practices, including discipline.

For boys, altruism, whether measured by the game situation or sociometrically, was negatively associated with mother's reported use of isolation, a kind of love withdrawal ($r = -.28$; $r = -.30$, respectively, both at a borderline level of significance). For girls, the sociometric measure of altruism was positively associated with mother's reported use of reasoning-explanation ($r = +.49$) and showing disappointment and shaming ($r = +.35$). Altruism, measured sociometrically, was also associated with a generally unpunitive and warm parent-child relationship and with high self-esteem in the child. The results for girls with the prisoner's dilemma measure of altruism were quite different, however, with high altruism (that is, cooperation to mutual advantage) associated with the mother's belief in the usefulness of scolding and criticism ($r = +.44$). Mussen et al. (1970) suggest that for girls, behavior in the prisoner's dilemma game may not reflect altruism or cooperation, but nonconformity or conformity to the experimenter's expectations that competition, a form of aggression, is appropriate in the game. Girls who do not employ competitive game strategies under these circumstances may be those who have strong inner restraints against expressing even sanctioned aggression, perhaps traceable to the mother's use of criticism and scolding.

Four other findings using behavioral measures generally support the position that morality as altruism or consideration is associated with parental use of induction. First, M. L. Hoffman (1963b) found that nursery school children's consideration for other children was positively associated with their parents' use of induction, but only when parents did not frequently use power assertion after an initial influence attempt had failed ($r = .75$, $p < .01$). The second investigation (Staub, 1971c) studied the effect of different role-playing procedures on the likelihood that kindergarten children would help another person in need. In the training situation the subject heard, or was told about, a child in physical distress, and either role-played the situation or was encouraged to suggest ways to help, or was given both kinds of training. In the posttraining test of transfer, the subject had the opportunity to share some candy with a "poor boy" and to help the experimenter retrieve paper clips which she had dropped. Following the role-playing training, girls were more apt than children given no training to help the child in distress, while boys given training were more likely than controls to share with the needy child. That is, the girls showed a direct effect of training, while boys showed a transfer effect. Induction surprisingly decreased the children's tendency to help the adult retrieve the paper clips, however. Third, in the already discussed M. L. Hoffman and Saltzstein (1967) study, sociometric ratings of girls' consideration for others were positively associated with mothers' reports of induction in regard to parents and induction in regard to peers. The one negative finding from this last study is the failure to obtain a relationship for boys between the sociometric ratings of consideration for others and parent- or peer-oriented induction. A fourth, unpublished, finding (M. L. Hoffman, 1974) supporting the association between boys' consideration and mothers' induction combined with suggestions for reparation has already been discussed.

The findings for honesty obtained by Mussen and his colleagues (1970) are quite different from the results for altruism. Girls' resistance to temptation in the laboratory was negatively associated with their mothers' belief in physical punishment ($r = -.32$) and in scolding ($r = -.33$) (both at the .10 level of significance) and with frequency of scolding as reported by the children ($r = -.29$). Girls' sociometric honesty scores also tended to relate negatively to their mothers' belief in scolding and threat of physical punishment, both correlations in the mid-30s and at borderline significance levels. For boys, the laboratory and sociometric measures of honesty were largely unrelated to specific discipline techniques. Over and above these specifics, however, was the general tendency for RTT to be associated with accepting, nonpunitive, and "democratic" attitudes by the mothers of *girls* (for example, "I am easygoing and relaxed with my child"; "I usually take into account my child's preference in making plans for the family"; "I let my child make many decisions for himself") and, by contrast, with generally restrictive and authoritarian attitudes by the mothers of *boys* (for example, "I believe in toilet training a child as soon as possible"; "I do not allow my child to get angry with me"; "I do not allow my child to question my decisions"). These correlations were of moderate strength, in the .30s and .40s, and some were of borderline significance, but the pattern is rather consistent within each sex. Furthermore, while RTT was correlated with high self-esteem for girls, it was, somewhat surprisingly, correlated with low self-esteem for boys.

The study raises a number of interpretive difficulties. For one thing, "scolding" is not defined and is therefore a psychologically ambiguous category. Scolding may include diverse parent behaviors: screaming and yelling abusive enough to constitute power assertion, verbal rejection tantamount to love withdrawal, or occasionally even induction. Thus, it is difficult to draw any firm conclusions about the relationship between a disciplinary technique such as scolding and honest behavior. A second interpretive puzzle is the sex difference in the findings for resistance to temptation; honesty in the laboratory was associated with a positive relationship with parents and high self-esteem for girls, but with the opposite for boys. Mussen and his co-workers (1970) suggest that RTT in the laboratory may be indicative of a lack of sex-role autonomy for boys. Since the child was asked to adhere to a rule that he was quite tempted to violate and that he could violate without *apparent* deleterious consequences for others, *in this experimental instance*, honesty may represent hyperconformity to adults.[3] If this possibility is true, then it is not so surprising that RTT in boys proved to be associated with a repressive and emotionally expressed authoritarian upbringing, and with an unrelaxed relationship with parents, peers, and self (e.g., M. L. Hoffman, 1953). In support of this line of reasoning is the finding that the item "I do not allow my child to get angry with me" is associated with RTT honesty for boys, but not for girls. Thus, to make sense out of these data it seems necessary to assume that RTT in the laboratory had different meanings for the boys and the girls.

The strength and statistical significance of the results obtained by Mussen and his co-workers (1970) were often weak to moderate for both honesty and altruism—findings not unusual in this area. Nevertheless, their study is important because it demonstrates that the correlates of morality as honesty (especially as resistance to temptation) and the correlates of morality as altruism (or consideration for others) are quite different. To sum up, the sociometric measure of morality as altruism was positively associated with reasoning and expression of disappointment for girls, and negatively associated, although weakly so, with love withdrawal for boys. Resistance to temptation was positively associated with scolding and an emotionally expressed parental authoritarianism for boys, and negatively associated with power assertion and scolding for girls.

CONVENTIONAL VERSUS HUMANISTIC MORALITY

In a study of seventh-grade middle-class boys and girls, M. L. Hoffman and Saltzstein offered a distinction between moral orientations analogous to the distinction between RTT and altruism. They differentiate between a morality in which conformity to the rules for its own sake is the primary moral standard, and a humanist morality in which consideration for human needs is the primary criterion (M. L. Hoffman, 1970b; M. L. Hoffman & Saltzstein, 1960). The distinction is based on two aspects of moral judgments: flexibility versus rigidity in applying moral rules (e.g., against stealing), and the moral value used to justify moral judgments. *Conventionals* were defined as children who, for example, judged stealing and lying as *always* wrong (even in extenuating circumstances when the act was to save a life or to spare someone's feelings) and who judged these acts to be wrong because they broke legal, religious, or social rules (e.g., "Stealing is wrong because it's against the law . . . breaks God's commandments"). *Humanists* were defined as children who flexibly applied moral rules (and, would approve or at least forgive stealing a drug to save a life) and who judged moral transgressions as wrong because of their consequences for human beings, either material (e.g., "How's the storekeeper going to feed his family if you steal from him?") or psychological (e.g., "Deceiving someone is wrong because you're breaking a trust with him."). Both the conventional and humanistic internalized groups were contrasted with a group of *externals*, children who focused on detection and punishment (e.g., "Stealing is wrong because you can get put in jail if you're caught") on at least one moral judgment item. These three groups were roughly matched for class background and intelligence.

As expected, the conventional and humanistic groups differed from the externals, but not from each other, in teacher ratings of acceptance of blame for wrongdoing, mother's report of confession, ratings of severity of guilt as expressed in completions of two stories in which an otherwise sympathetic protagonist of the same age and sex as the subject transgresses, and in use of detection or punishment to resolve the story plot. This pattern of results helped to confirm the assumption that the conventionals and humanists, in contrast to the externals, had internalized moral orientations.

The two internal groups differed from each other in terms of their emotional basis and functioning of conscience. The story completion data suggest that the humanists, compared to the conventionals, experienced or conceived of guilt in more conscious rather than unconscious forms and as part of the self rather than as alien to the self. The humanists also seemed better able to tolerate antisocial impulses and to integrate them with moral responses. These conclusions were inferred from the findings that (1) the humanists were more likely than the conventionals to express guilt in conscious form rather than in unconscious equivalents, such as fortuitous accidents, in completing a story involving disobedience to parents; and (2) the humanists were more apt to include feelings of pleasure along with or followed by guilt and remorse in completing a story involving cheating. A separate sentence completion test also suggested that the conventionals were more likely to have repressed aggression, especially toward their parents. For example, in completing sentences such as "The main thing about my father is . . . ," "Kids my age are often afraid that . . . ," "I could get real mad if . . . ," "Tests like this . . . ," the conventionals were more apt to express anxiety, to reveal aggression toward their parents, to erase an original response or fail to complete the sentence. These findings suggest that the consciences of the humanists and conventionals have different psychodynamics.

The discipline scores in this study of conscience types were based on paper-and-pencil questions administered to the children and on interviews with their mothers and fathers. Discipline questions were concerned with four specific hypothetical child behaviors: (1) failing to carry out a parental request, (2) talking back to a parent, (3) breaking something accidentally, and (4) failing in school. Information was obtained from the child by having him indicate the relative frequency with which each parent used particular kinds of discipline; the child did this by selecting from alternative parental responses in the four given hypothetical situations; responses included, for example, "the mother hits the child"; "says, 'Wait 'till your father comes home' "; "takes away a privilege"; "gives you an angry look and walks away"; "says she won't talk to you or have anything to do with you unless you say you're sorry"; "says she's hurt or disappointed by what you said"; "says she'd do it herself but she's tired or not feeling well." In the interviews with mothers and fathers, the parent was administered the first two situations (child talking back and refusing a request) twice, once to respond as he or she would now discipline the child and once to respond as the parent would have disciplined the child when the child was about 5 years old. In addition, the parent was simply asked how he or she would respond in each of two situations: (1) the child at age 5, after being verbally provoked by a friend, destroys something that the friend has built; and (2) the child at 6 to 10 years of age makes fun of another child.

Mothers of conventionals and mothers of humanists were both found to use less power assertion and more induction than mothers of externals. Refined discipline categories were also used to compare the conventionals and humanists directly. Though the findings here were more scattered than for the internal–external comparisons, a pattern did emerge. The parents of the conventionals reported generally relying on love withdrawal and, surprisingly, parent-oriented induction (pointing out the consequences of the action for the parents), especially in the talking-back-to-parent situation, more than the parents of the humanists. In the refusal-of-parent's-request condition, the humanists' parents relied more than the conventionals' parents on reasoning and power assertion. Power assertion was resorted to in this situation when the child had flatly refused a request (to leave the TV set and do an errand) and probably primarily involved physical force (e.g., picking up the child) but not physical punishment. The parents of humanist boys had power assertion scores which were (on the average) lower than those of parents of externals, but higher than those of parents of conventional boys. The moral autonomy of the humanistic children may have derived from an intermediate level of discipline and control—an interpretation consistent with findings on preadolescents' autonomy by Devereux, Bronfenbrenner, and their co-workers (Devereux, 1970; Devereux, Bronfenbrenner, & Rodgers, 1969; Devereux, Bronfenbrenner, & Suci, 1962). The unexpectedly greater reliance by the conventionals' parents on pointing out consequences of children's actions for the parent is consistent with the idea that parent-oriented induction, while arousing empathy for another person, may also imply withdrawal of parental love. Furthermore, it should be noted that the parents of the conventionals were not higher on peer-oriented induction. Finally, the parents of the conventionals and the humanists were both higher than the parents of the externals on use of parent-oriented induction.[4]

Although in all these studies a causative relationship is only suggested by the data, the following hypothesis may be advanced: Frequent use of power assertion, especially physical punishment, retards the development of any kind of internal morality. Psychological techniques, especially pointing out the consequences of actions for others, facilitate the development of internal morality. Reasoning is conducive to the development of an altruistic or humanistic morality, that is, one based primarily on consideration for others. Love withdrawal is conducive to the development of a conformist or conventional morality, that is, one based on rigid conformity to rules for their own sake or in deference to authority. The influence of parent-oriented induction on the child's moral development, conformist or altruistic, is uncertain probably because the meaning of this parental behavior for the child is ambiguous. At certain times or for some children, the technique may primarily arouse empathy and encourage role taking, promoting the development of an altruistic morality; at other times or for other children, it may primarily arouse fear of loss of love, contributing to the development of a conformist morality.

The Problem of Causal Direction

THE NATURE OF THE PROBLEM AND POSSIBLE SOLUTIONS

In most of the studies cited so far, childrearing variables and measures of children's moral development have been correlated rather than manipulated experimentally. Unequivocal conclusions cannot be drawn about causal direction from correlational data. While it is certainly possible to conclude, for example, that parental use of power assertion inhibits the child's moral development, it is also possible to interpret the research to mean that a child's poor moral development elicits power assertion from the parent. As one prominent researcher in this area put it to this writer, parents could conclude, "When all else fails, hit the kid." The possibility that the child's capacities influence the parent's practices is implicit in some of the labels given to disciplinary techniques; the term "guilt induction," for example, implies that the child is capable of having guilt induced.

In a provocative review, Bell (1968) has suggested that some precursors of morality such as sociability and assertiveness may in part be inherited. Support for this viewpoint comes from studies of twins (e.g., Scarr, 1965) which show greater concordance on sociability measures between identical twins than between fraternal twins, and from observations of adult-child interactions which indicate that variability in the adults' responses to children is due to responses the children bring to a given situation (e.g., Yarrow, Waxler, & Scott, 1971). Of course, the variance caused by heredity and environment will change from one behavioral realm to another. Nevertheless, it is important to recognize that the child's genetic endowment and personality may exert a considerable influence on the parent's approach to childrearing.[5]

Two research strategies that may help to solve the problem of determining causation are available. The first strategy is the use of time-lag data, collected from children and from parents on several occasions in the course of development. Parental measures obtained at time n may be correlated with child measures at time $n + 1$, and child measures at time n correlated with parental measures at time $n + 1$. If the first correlation is stronger than, or at least as strong as, the second correlation, this would strongly suggest that the parent influenced the child, rather than vice versa. For example, if parental use of power assertion at the child's age 4 correlates strongly with the child's deviance at age 8, but the child's deviance at age 4 does not correlate with parental use of power assertion at age 8, we may suspect that the use of power assertion probably influenced the child's deviance more than the deviance elicited the parent's use of power assertion. To my knowledge, no studies of morality have systematically employed this design.

The second possible strategy is experimentation, in which a variable or a set of variables is manipulated and the consequent effects on another variable or set of variables are observed. Inferences as to causal direction then become less ambiguous than in correlational studies. But experimental research has its own shortcomings. The time span over which effects are studied is typically quite short, rarely exceeding two or three hours. Furthermore, the behaviors examined are usually of minor importance. Aggression against inanimate objects (e.g., Bandura, 1962), picking up a forbidden toy (e.g., Aronfreed, 1968c) and cheating in a noncompetitive game (e.g., Grinder, 1962) are typical of the experimental tests of morality, and it is questionable how much they reflect real-life morality. Experimental studies of altruism (e.g., Bryan & Walbek, 1970b) are not as open to this criticism, since the behavior studied in these experiments at least involves consequences for others.

Some studies have managed to implement experimental methods in a naturalistic setting such as a preschool nursery or kindergarten, where teachers can serve as the experimenters. They may be instructed to reinforce certain behaviors positively, or to treat certain children one way, say, warmly, and other children, or the same children on other occasions, coldly. Problems of control and of inferring causal direction may arise even in this kind of experiment, however. An investigation by Yarrow, Waxler, and Scott (1971) has shown that even when the experimenter-caretakers have been instructed to act nurturantly and nonnurturantly according to schedule, children still manage to influence them to behave otherwise. Yarrow, Waxler, and Scott infer the operation of this influence process from the considerable within-treatment variability in the experimenters' behavior and from within-condition correlations between children's behavior on one day and adults' behavior on subsequent days. Boys' bids for approval, for example, correlated with adults' negative contacts under some conditions.

THE RELATION BETWEEN THE CHILD'S SUSCEPTIBILITY TO SOCIAL INFLUENCE AND MORAL DEVELOPMENT

As already suggested, an alternative hypothesis may be drawn from the correlational studies of discipline and moral development: The child's level of moral development determines the kind of discipline the parents use. This hypothesis is buttressed by the observation that parents use different types of discipline for the same child at different ages. In particular, parental use of power assertion typically declines as the child grows older (M. L. Hoffman & Saltzstein, 1967).

Is there additional research evidence in support of the hypothesis that the moral development level of the child affects the kind of discipline the child will respond to and the parent will use?

Although the study of parental discipline has usually been considered separately from the general study of social influence, it seems obvious that a discipline encounter is a social influence interchange between parent and child. While such interchanges have special properties which differentiate them in part from other social influence encounters, such as those between children and teachers or between peers, they also have much in common. Thus, any evidence as to the general susceptibility of children to different kinds of social influence attempts should be relevant to children's responsiveness to different discipline practices.

Piaget (1932) informally reported that children at the immature, heteronomous stage of morality were more easily swayed during moral judgment interviews than those at the more mature, autonomous stage of morality. Fodor (1971) confirmed this conclusion by showing that children who yielded to the suggestions of the adult interviewer scored lower on Kohlberg's scale of moral stages than those who resisted such influence.

Clearly, the relationship between the child's moral level and his susceptibility to social influence is not a simple one. Moral issues are not the only factors bearing on the child's decision to conform or to remain independent. Furthermore, the relationship between morality and social influence behavior will depend on the kind of social influence being considered. Kelman (1958) identifies three types of attitude change (and, by implication, three types of change in response to social influence

attempts in general): compliance, identification, and internalization. These processes are defined in terms of the antecedent conditions which give rise to them and the consequent conditions which establish their limits. *Compliance* is motivated by the subject's desire to attain external rewards and to avoid external punishments, and is manifested only under surveillance by the influence agent; *identification* is motivated, consciously or unconsciously, by a desire to be like the influence agent and is manifested only where the relationship to the influence agent is salient; and *internalization* is motivated by the desire to be correct and internally consistent, ultimately with one's own values. In internalization, change is also manifested in private situations where the influence is neither physically nor symbolically present, and in attitudes different from, but related to, the attitude originally subjected to the influence attempt.

A fourth, and distinctly moral, kind of social influence behavior remains. This is *conformity to a group* because of a sense of obligation to the group growing out of the recognition of interdependence. Experimental evidence of this phenomenon has been provided by Deutsch and Gerard (1955) and Jackson and Saltzstein (1958), among others. These studies found that conformity to a bogus group judgment was greater when the group was being evaluated in terms of its performance rather than in terms of individual performance. That is, goal interdependence among persons increases their susceptibility to social influence. Furthermore, several of the adult female subjects in the Deutsch and Gerard study explicitly stated during the post-experimental interview that they had conformed because they felt an obligation to the group. These results suggest that conformity may be based on a sense of moral obligation which grows out of a recognition of interdependence.

There seems to be a rough parallel between these social influence processes and the major kinds of discipline: power assertion goes with compliance; love withdrawal and sometimes parent-oriented, and even peer-oriented, induction with identification; and the reasoning component of induction with internalization.

A second rough parallel exists between Kelman's social influence processes and Kohlberg's stages of moral development. Compliance seems related to Kohlberg's preconventional level, Stages 1 and 2. Identification finds a rough parallel in the conventional level, especially Stage 3. Internalization seems related to the later stage of the conventional level (Stage 4), and especially to the principled level, Stages 5 and 6.

In summary, the moral development of the child may determine the social influences to which he is susceptible, which in turn shape the kind of discipline the parents will use. Children at the preconventional level are primarily susceptible to social influence aimed at compliance, and they elicit various forms of power assertion from their parents; children in the early stage of the conventional level (Stage 3) are susceptible to social influence involving identification with individuals or groups, and they elicit love withdrawal and other emotionally threatening and psychologically coercive techniques from their parents. Children at the later stage of the conventional level (Stage 4) and at the principled level (Stages 5 and 6) are susceptible to social influence involving internalization, and they elicit reasoning and other principled appeals from their parents.[6]

This analysis leaves an important question unanswered. If not discipline, then what does account for the development of the child's moral reasoning? Role-taking opportunities—as provided by social participation in the family, peer groups, and other social settings—may be the essential factor that determines the rate at which moral thought progresses. The idea that role taking is the critical dynamic underlying moral development has been proposed by Piaget (1932), G. H. Mead (1934), and Kohlberg (Chap. 2, 1969b).

Empirical support for the importance of social participation may be found in studies of moral maturity and participation and sharing in family decisions (Holstein, 1968; Peck & Havighurst, 1960). Peck and Havighurst (1960), using ratings of various forms of participation in family decisions (family democracy) and their own measures of moral character, found that family democracy was associated with moral maturity, but only when combined with consistency and mutual trust. Kohlberg (1969b) has criticized this study on the grounds that the investigators confused premoral opportunism with moral autonomy. Holstein's study (1968), however, employed Kohlberg's own method of assessing moral development and found that higher levels of moral reasoning were associated with the extent to which the parent encouraged the child to participate in family discussions of hypothetical moral situations. Moreover, a number of studies have demonstrated a direct relationship between role taking and moral development (e.g., Lee, 1971; Selman, 1971a). A recent study by Gunsberg (1973) has even demonstrated that role-taking training may facilitate development from Kohlberg's Stage 1 toward Stage 2. Further work on role taking as a method of facilitating moral development is being carried out by the present writer (Saltzstein, 1975). Discipline, too, may be conceptualized in terms of role-taking opportunities (e.g., M. L. Hoffman & Saltzstein, 1967; Kohlberg, 1969b) and may contribute to moral development via the role-taking mechanism. Thus, the process of moral development is best conceived as circular: The moral development of the child determines his susceptibility to different discipline techniques, which affect his role-taking opportunities, which in turn determine his rate of moral development.

The parent can further facilitate the development of the child's moral thought by presenting him or her with moral reasoning one stage above the child's own stage. Turiel (1966) and Rest, Turiel, and

Kohlberg (1969) have shown that children tend to approve, understand, and adopt moral reasoning passages one stage above their own $(+ 1)$, but tend to reject those one stage below their own $(- 1)$, and approve but fail to understand moral reasoning two stages above their own $(+ 2)$, instead assimilating it to their own stage level. It is quite likely, for example, that one of the facilitative effects of discipline that has been termed "reasoning" rests on an appropriate level of verbal argument contained in such techniques. Such appeals to reason may include direct or indirect examples of $+ 1$ reasoning which not only effect an immediate change in the child's behavior but a long-term change in his moral thought as well.

Reasoning is usually treated as a unitary category. But reasoning techniques probably vary in their degree of abstractness, that is, the degree to which they emphasize concrete rules or abstract principles, and in the degree to which they encourage the taking of more extensive perspectives (roles) of a situation. The relationship of reasoning techniques to the child's moral level may depend on this degree of abstractness.

The above discussion suggests that the best match between parental discipline and the child's moral development level may not be an exact correspondence but a one-step difference between the moral thought expressed through the parent's discipline and the child's current moral reasoning level.

Peer Influence and Moral Development

In this section we shall extend the previous discussion concerning parent discipline and moral development to the question of direct exercise of peer influence. It has been argued that since the influence to which the child is susceptible depends partly on his level of moral development, the discipline the parent finds effective will change as the child grows older. When this idea is extrapolated to peer influences, the following two hypotheses are the result.

1. Adult influence should be most potent at the younger ages because of the child's compliance orientation, involving deference to power (Kohlberg's Stage 1, obedience orientation). Adult influence should decline with age, with peers becoming increasingly prepotent. At Kohlberg's Stage 2 (instrumental hedonism), for example, material reciprocity ("You scratch my back and I'll scratch yours") should be the guiding principle in deciding how to respond to social influence pressures. At Stage 3, the reciprocity is no longer material but emotional ("I'll do what you say because I like you and want you to like me"). Adults should again become influential as the child moves to Stage 4, where conformity to legitimate (traditionally accepted and institutionalized) authority becomes one's duty. Subsequently, the importance of the source of the influence, as contrasted with the message that the influence conveys, should decline as the adolescent approaches principled moral reasoning.

2. With development, group interdependence should increasingly become grounds for justifying conformity to the group. The sense of obligation to conform should grow with the increasingly sophisticated ability of the child to "take the role of the other," as documented by Flavell, Botkin, Fry, Wright, and Jarvis (1968); P. H. Miller, Kessel, and Flavell (1970); and Piaget (1926a, 1932). With increasing experience in role taking, reciprocity becomes abstract and universal instead of remaining concrete and bound to particular others.

Evidence relevant to these hypotheses has generally come from studies of social influence on nonmoral (usually perceptual) judgments. We assume, however, that the decision to conform or deviate even on nonmoral issues grows, in part, out of moral cognitions. Several studies (e.g., Costanzo & Shaw, 1966; Iscoe, Williams, & Harvey, 1963) have found a curvilinear (inverted U shape) relationship between social influence and age, with children at or about early adolescence conforming the most to group judgments on perceptual tasks. Saltzstein, Diamond, and Belenky (1972) found a similar curvilinear relationship between seventh-graders' conformity to erroneous peer judgments of the relative lengths of lines and independently assessed Kohlberg-type moral reasoning. Stage 3 ("good boy, good girl," moral reasoning) children conformed to the erroneous group judgment more than children at lower Stages 1 and 2 and more than children at higher Stages 4 and 5, with the latter subjects being the least likely to conform. The authors' explanation of these results is based on the assumption that in such situations, where the group is clearly making erroneous judgments, the experimenter stands for accuracy in the eyes of the child (Schulman, 1967). Less mature children are disinclined to conform because of their deference to the experimenter (Stage 1) or desire to be accurate and thus achieve the prize for accuracy (Stage 2), while more mature children (Stages 4 and 5) are disinclined to conform because of their implicit agreement with the experimenter to do the best they can, as well as their general commitment to accuracy. Stage 3 children, however, are committed above all to good socioemotional relations, and thus are inclined to conform to known peers in contrast to the unknown experimenters. The relationship between the level of moral development and conformity is no doubt more complicated than this analysis would imply, and depends also on the accuracy of the group's judgment and ambiguity of the task (Hoving, Hamm, & Galvin, 1969). But in general the moral development of the child should determine the kind and amount of the child's susceptibility to peer and adult influence.

A recent study (Saltzstein & Osgood, 1975) bears upon the second hypothesis: With development, interdependence among members of a group increasingly serves as a basis for conformity to peers. Children aged 5 to 14 were interviewed about hypothetical work-play situations in which they were members of a team in competition with another team. The interview centered on the rights and wrongs of conforming to or deviating from teammates' requests. These group requests did not involve perceptual judgments, but behaviors necessary for the group's performance on the task. Should a team member, for example, continue at his particular subtask even if he finds it boring or difficult? In general, the children's reasoning about these social obligations developed with age in a way that, at least in part, paralleled the development of reasoning about Kohlberg-type moral dilemmas. The younger children, for example, argued that one should comply only if the group request coincides with one's individual interests and desires; there is no group obligation, only an "obligation" to serve oneself, a right that everyone has—a mentality paralleling Kohlberg's Stage 2. The older children typically justified conforming to the group's request in terms of personal loyalty to the group, because the group depended on them or because of the prior agreement or social contract they had made with the group—a mentality paralleling Kohlberg's Stages 3 or 4. The reasoning underlying a decision to conform or deviate from the expectations of others in a hypothetical peer-group situation thus develops in morally relevant stages. Research is needed to determine whether these social-moral stages, in fact, determine the child's actual overt behavioral response to peer and adult influences in interdependent situations.

Summary

The central points of this chapter may be summarized as follows:

1. Studies of discipline and moral development should elucidate the processes by which transitions in moral development

are accomplished. Gross discipline categories are not as useful for this end as refined categories. To make sense of the diverse findings in this area it is necessary to distinguish not only between different kinds of moral measures (behavioral, sociometric, cognitive, projective, etc.) but also between different kinds of internalized morality (e.g., morality as conformity to rules in deference to authority versus morality as consideration for others; conventional versus humanistic morality).

2. Theories of social influence processes may be useful in examining the relationship between moral development stages and discipline techniques, for parental discipline is only one arena in which social influence is exerted. This chapter has proposed parallels between three major types of discipline and Kelman's social influence processes (1958), and between these influence processes and Kohlberg's three levels of moral development (Chap. 2, 1969b).

3. Until recently, it was too often assumed only that parents influence children. The interactive process whereby parents and children influence each other must be examined.

4. The concept of role taking offers an especially promising approach to understanding how parents and society influence the development of children's conception of social relationships and thus their moral thought and behavior.

PART 4

MORALITY AND SOCIAL ISSUES

CHAPTER 15

The Responsive Bystander

WHY HE HELPS[1]

Ted L. Huston and Chuck Korte

Introduction

Consider the following incidents, each of which involved bystanders who failed to come to the aid of a person in distress. These events were widely reported in the mass media, and each elicited a good deal of editorial comment decrying the condition of contemporary morality.

—Carmen Colon, a 10-year-old kidnapped while she was on an errand for her mother, temporarily escaped from her captor along a busy highway near Rochester, New York. Halfclad and obviously distraught, she cried out for help. More than a hundred motorists passed her by. Shortly thereafter, Carmen was murdered ("A Social Disaster," 1971).

—Herman Glaser, a 56-year-old lawyer, was mugged and robbed on the streets of New York City before scores of onlookers, none of whom came to his aid. Glaser, recounting the experience at Lenox Hill Hospital said: "It was like a jungle. . . . I can't understand the apathy of all the people on that street" (Arnold, 1972).

—Wolfgang Friedmann, a Columbia University professor, did not live to talk about his ordeal

in the city streets; he had been stabbed to death the week before the Glaser incident while attempting to protect himself from a mugging. The *New York Times* (Perlmutter, 1972) editorialized: "for some time passersby stared and went on their way before any fellow human being had the decency to call the police. Creatures of the jungle could not be more unfeeling."[2]

Layman and social scientist alike have been shocked by incidents such as these: A victim of misfortune stands in desperate need of help; witnesses to the person's plight fail to offer aid. Such a disturbing phenomenon prompted two social psychologists, Bibb Latané and John Darley, to set out in the 1960s in search of the causes of onlooker inaction (see Chap. 13). Their research indicated that inactive bystanders, far from being apathetic, were paralyzed by uncertainty and conflict. Latané and Darley also concluded that the character of the emergency situation, including such things as the number and demeanor of other bystanders, was a more accurate predictor of onlooker response than personality dispositions, such as those measured by social responsibility and Machiavellianism scales (see Table 15.2 for sample items from such scales).

Latané and Darley's research (1970) is summarized in their excellent monograph, *The Unresponsive Bystander: Why Doesn't He Help?* We have taken the title of this influential book and turned it about in order to shift the focus of social scientists away from analyses of why people do not help to determinations of why they do provide assistance to others.

The aim of this chapter is to determine the methods for increasing effective bystander intervention. Since this obviously is not a scientific goal—and even its desirability is arguable—the first part of the chapter outlines our rationale for advocating it. If it is granted that bystander intervention ought to be encouraged, then the development of social programs toward this end involves practical considerations as well as an appreciation of the conclusions and limitations of available research on emergency intervention. To gain a more complete understanding of bystander helpfulness, we will review existing literature, attempting to identify its biases and inadequacies, and profile the "Good Samaritan," indicating factors that prompt him to intervene. Finally, we will consider what is being done in this country and in others to increase the degree to which onlookers feel responsible for taking action in emergencies, and we will suggest useful strategies for enhancing such intervention.

The Morality of Bystander Intervention

The biblical parable of the Good Samaritan contains many ingredients of what may be regarded as the ideal moral response to emergency situations:

A man was going from Jerusalem to Jericho, and he fell among robbers, who stripped him and beat him, and departed, leaving him half dead. Now by chance a priest was going down that road; and when he saw him he passed by on the other side. So likewise a Levite, when he came to the place and saw him, passed by on the other side. But a Samaritan, as he journeyed, came to where he was; and when he saw him, he had compassion, and went to him and bound up his wounds, pouring on oil and wine; then he set him on his own beast and brought him next to an inn, and took care of him. And the next day he took out two denarii and gave them to the innkeeper, saying, "Take care of him; and whatever you spend, I will repay you when I come back" (Luke 10:29–37).

The parable of the Good Samaritan represents a line of thinking in the "highest" Judeo-Christian moral tradition. Most social psychologists researching bystander intervention appear to have implicitly subscribed to this positive view of helping others in distress. Some social philosophers (e.g., Rand, 1943; 1957; Stirner, 1912), however, maintain that the noblest purpose of human life is for each individual to look out only for himself or herself, and to let others fend for themselves as best they may. It has also been argued (e.g., Bartlett, 1966) that laypeople should not interject themselves into situations that can be handled with more acumen and ability by those with special expertise, such as medical or law enforcement experience.

The moral issues underlying bystander intervention become even more complex when we expand our perspective to a cross-cultural scene. In some social milieus, for instance, the encouragement of bystander intervention can threaten other higher-priority commitments and values in the social system. For example, Bloodworth (1969) writes of pre-Communistic Chinese society, "As a family man the Good Samaritan is suspect: how much might he have endangered himself and his kin by irresponsibly helping an unknown man who had been mixed up with brutal thieves?" (p. 118).

Fundamentally, the question of whether active intervention leads to greater social benefit than bystander inactivity is an empirical issue with a heavy value overlay. First, of course, it is necessary to determine what social aims are sought and how various kinds of onlooker behaviors enhance or detract from the achievement of such aims. Our tentative bias is toward the limited encouragement of bystander intervention; more importantly, however, we are concerned that the fundamental moral questions not be shunned or ignored, since we believe that they have had a strong historical influence on the direction and form of bystander intervention research.

Why Do Bystanders Help?

Available research on bystander behavior provides a substantive lode that can be mined extensively for insight regarding the degree to which various social programs designed to enhance such intervention are likely to be effective. It is important from a practical standpoint to determine the degree to which bystander helpfulness is prompted or inhibited by factors in the emergency situation as opposed to the relatively stable characteristics of persons. If the degree to which onlookers help depends primarily on situational factors, then programs can be designed to modify the physical and social environment, as well as to provide consequences for onlookers' various lines of action. But, on the other hand, if personal qualities are more important than situational considerations, then programs fostering the development of the former could be encouraged. Such efforts might include, for instance, systematic attempts to modify parental socialization practices, to change the content of television programs, and to alter the social climate of the schools.

Determining the relative importance of situational as compared to personal characteristics in regard to bystander behavior is admittedly a difficult task (see Bowers, 1973, and Mischel, 1973, for discussions of the interpretive perils involved). This effort is further complicated by the shortcomings of research strategies in vogue—strategies which we believe may place undue emphasis on the importance of situational factors in accounting for bystander response to emergency situations.

THE NATURE AND LIMITATIONS OF RESEARCH ON BYSTANDER INTERVENTION

There is a large body of research literature on helping behavior from which to cull insights on emergency intervention. In addition to Latané and Darley's monograph (1970) on bystander intervention, two collections of original writings (Macaulay & Berkowitz, 1970; Wispé, 1972), and at least seven reviews (Berkowitz, 1972, 1973a; Bryan & London, 1970; M. L. Hoffman, Chap. 7; D. L. Krebs, 1970a; Midlarsky, 1968; Staub, 1974) of research on altruistic behavior have been published. Much of the reported work, however, has looked at responses to nonemergency situations, such as requests for street directions or for aid in carrying out some task, rather than at responses to emergencies. Given that data exist suggesting that the correlates of helping behavior differ in terms of the nature of the help required (e.g., Gergen, Gergen, & Meter, 1972), we will limit our discussion where possible to research studying emergency intervention which includes elements similar to those in the Good Samaritan parable.

Emergency situations that concern us generally have two basic qualities: (1) The distressed person's need is potentially severe; (2) bystander action is required if the distressed person is to be spared a worse fate. Researchers have not lacked imagination in creating and/or exploring such emergency situations. Dramatic instances have included field studies investigating the rescue of Jews in Nazi Germany (London, 1970), donations of bone marrow (Schwartz, 1970a) and kidneys (Fellner & Marshall, 1970), and civil rights work in the South during the early dangerous period of the civil rights movement (Rosenhan, 1970). Other field experiments have confronted onlookers with a collapsed subway rider (I. Piliavin, Rodin, & Piliavin, 1969; J. Piliavin & Piliavin, 1972), a person groaning and lying in a doorway (Darley & Batson, 1973), and an individual who has twisted an ankle or knee and fallen to the ground (Shotland & Johnson, 1974).

Laboratory research on emergency intervention has also faced bystanders with a variety of horrors, including a physical assault (Borofsky, Stollak, & Messé, 1971), signs of a fire (Latané & Darley, 1968; Ross, 1971), a loud crash in an adjacent room followed by severe sobbing (Staub, 1970a, 1970b, 1971a, 1971b, 1972), as well as various simulated mishaps, such as someone falling from a ladder (Bickman, 1971, 1972; Clark & Word, 1972; Darley, Teger & Lewis, 1973; Latané & Rodin, 1969; Ross, 1971; Ross & Brabend, 1973; Yakimovich & Saltz, 1971), collapsing from a fainting spell (R. Smith, Smythe, & Lien, 1972; R. Smith, Vanderbilt, & Callen, 1973), suffering an epileptic seizure (Darley & Latané, 1968; Horowitz, 1971; Schwartz & Clausen, 1970), having an asthmatic attack (Korte, 1971), undergoing severe electric shock (Clark & Word, 1974; Kaufman, 1968; Tilker, 1970), or experiencing severe stomach cramps (Staub, 1974).

The applicability of the findings of these studies to real-life emergencies is undercut by several considerations. For one, it is questionable whether the situations selected for study are representative of emergencies of major social concern. Though scientific interest in the subject area of bystander intervention was instigated by the murder of a young woman (Kitty Genovese) in New York City (A. M. Rosenthal, 1964), only one study (Borofsky, Stollak, & Messé, 1971) of the cited literature has investigated bystander response to a person who is being physically assaulted. Bystander unresponsiveness to events such as muggings and rapes may be significantly influenced by fear of retaliation and the degree to which bystanders are unable to overcome such a fear,

but it would be difficult to draw such a conclusion from available research.

Two other important considerations limit the generalizability of the research findings on bystander intervention to naturally occurring emergencies. First, approximately 80 percent of such research has been conducted in college laboratories. Typically, students are brought to the laboratory to participate in studies ostensibly concerned with things such as psychodrama, impression formation, and the validation of mental tests. Once there, they become witnesses to a simulated emergency staged by the experimenter. Whether students in laboratory experiments act the same as they would in naturalistic settings is ultimately an empirical question; it would be incautious, however, to conclude that the variables operative in the laboratory and in real-life emergencies parallel one another. Participants in laboratory experiments, for instance, may be more attentive and reactive to the behavior of other onlookers than they would be in naturalistic settings.

Second, social science research has primarily focused on detailing situational determinants of onlooker behavior, with a correspondingly lesser interest in studying the role of personal characteristics of onlookers as they relate to intervention. Since empirical interest in the phenomenon of bystander behavior was stimulated by a social problem, the relative emphasis on studying situational parameters probably reflects the view that such factors are more powerful influencers of bystander behavior than are personal characteristics. This may be the case, or, as we hope to demonstrate in the following section, such a conclusion may be premature, given the available evidence.

DETERMINANTS OF EMERGENCY INTERVENTION: AN INTERPRETIVE EXAMINATION OF THE LITERATURE

Bystander intervention, according to Latané and Darley (1970), hinges on a series of interlocked decisions that the bystander must make in order to take action. The bystander must (1) notice the event, (2) interpret it as an emergency, (3) ascribe personal responsibility to himself for intervention, (4) consider the form his assistance should take, and (5) decide how to implement his decision.

Much of the research on bystander behavior examines the role of situational parameters (e.g., the characteristics, number, and demeanor of other bystanders) as they affect the degree to which onlookers interpret an event as an emergency situation (decision 1 above) and feel responsible to intervene to alleviate the victim's distress (decision 3 above). We will undertake a selective review of this research in order to capture its flavor and to provide background material for assessing its value and shortcomings in regard to providing an understanding of what prompts effective bystander behavior (see Rosenhan, Moore, & Underwood, Chap. 13, for another interpretation of this literature).

This research has shown (Darley & Latané, 1968; Latané & Rodin, 1969; R. Smith, Smythe, & Lien, 1972) that onlookers typically provide help when they are alone in observing a potential emergency situation develop, presumably because they would suffer little embarrassment should their interpretation prove wrong, and, perhaps more importantly, because they recognize that they are the only one who can spare the victim a worse fate.

When a bystander is one individual among many, a variety of factors apparently influence whether he or she will intervene. Several studies investigating these factors simulated an emergency situation in which a female experimenter, after getting research participants started on a task unrelated to helping behavior, left the laboratory to work in an adjoining room. Shortly thereafter, she apparently fell from a ladder, crying in distress (in some experiments she fainted). Some of these studies have concentrated on showing how onlookers influence one another in deciding whether to provide the distressed

woman with help. One such study (Darley, Teger, & Lewis, 1973) has found that when bystanders were seated so that they could see one another's initial reaction to the event, most of them (80 percent) helped, whereas when they were seated out of each other's sight, relatively few (20 percent) provided aid. R. Smith, Smythe, and Lien (1972), in another study, found that bystanders who were led to believe that they had much in common with an impassive onlooker—(who was really an actor) only rarely helped (5 percent); those paired with onlookers with whom they thought they had little in common intervened more often (35 percent of the time). The authors suggested that participants paired with the similar, rather than the dissimilar, bystander probably placed more trust in the interpretation of the emergency event implied by the other onlooker's impassivity and, as a consequence, intervened less often.

Several studies suggest that situational forces serve either to focus responsibility for intervention on a particular bystander or to diffuse it among many bystanders. Research indicates, for instance, that a bystander who finds himself in a better position to help—as when he is less encumbered or is in much closer proximity to the victim than others—tends to help much more than when he and others can help with equal ease (Bickman, 1972; Korte, 1971). Also, an adult is more likely to help if the only other bystander is a child rather than another adult (Ross, 1971) or is blind rather than sighted (Ross & Brabend, 1973). However, should a bystander believe another observer is apt to be more capable of dealing with the emergency situation—as would be the case if one of the onlookers were a doctor and the distressed individual were in need of medical care—the bystander usually defers to such a person (Schwartz & Clausen, 1970).

In contrast to such studies, which are primarily concerned with uncovering how the behavior of one bystander interacts with the behavior of others, a few investigations have examined the characteristics of emergency events and how such characteristics relate to intervention. Persons have been found, as one might expect, to respond more readily and frequently to unambiguous as compared to ambiguous emergencies (Clark & Word, 1972, 1974; Yakimovich & Saltz, 1971), and to provide help more often to a man who collapses on a subway because of apparent sickness rather than seeming drunkenness (I. Piliavin, Rodin, & Piliavin, 1969).

Given this array of studies, there is some temptation to assign major responsibility to situational factors in accounting for bystander intervention. After all, fluctuations of 50 percent or more in the frequency of intervention have been found to result from variations in situational parameters. But serious problems may be involved in unqualified acceptance of this conclusion. Take, for instance, the study by Ross and Brabend (1973) which concludes that onlookers are more likely to intervene when the only other bystander present is blind rather than sighted, presumably because in the former situation responsibility for intervention is more focused on the sighted onlooker. Actual emergency conditions which pose issues of felt responsibility in such a dramatic fashion are obviously rare. If research variables are selected as they were in the Ross and Brabend study, isolated from other variables that might detract from their impact, and then made extreme to strengthen the probability of significant findings, the results must be interpreted cautiously. Before we accept the overriding importance of situational factors on the basis of available experimental research, we must know more about the kinds of emergency events that occur in the natural environment, and be able to determine the manner in which various elements affect bystanders. Situational extremes may also wash out individual differences which would occur in less extraordinary conditions. For example, people who differ in feelings of social responsibility (see Berkowitz & Lutterman, 1968, for a scale which measures this), may respond differently to emergency situations—but only when situational parameters neither strongly focus nor diffuse these feelings of responsibility.

Research designs that attempt simultaneously to tap situational and personality correlates of bystander intervention have generally failed to uncover many systematic relationships between the two (see, e.g., Darley & Batson, 1973; Korte, 1971; Latané & Darley, 1968; Yakimovich & Saltz, 1971); however, such research has been beset by several problems. A study by Darley and Batson (1973), for instance, set up a modern-day version of the emergency situation found in the Good Samaritan parable. The parable, it may be remembered, illustrates callous disregard of suffering on the part of religious persons who would presumably behave in especially moral ways. The Samaritan, without a formal religious role, might reasonably be seen to have behaved in a humanistic, atheological manner. On the basis of these ideas, Darley and Batson decided to determine the character of the religious commitment of their experimental subjects— students at Princeton Theological Seminary. Some seminarians, they found, were committed to religion largely as a means to other ends ("The primary purpose of prayer is to gain relief and protection"), while others' involvement was based on the intrinsic value of religion ("I try hard to carry my religion over into all my other dealings in life") or on religion as a quest for meaning in their psychosocial world.[3]

Each student, upon arriving for the experiment, was told that he was to deliver a lecture from prepared notes on one of two topics: the parable of the Good Samaritan or the job opportunities for seminary graduates. Half of those assigned to each of the lectures were told that they would have to hurry to be on time, while the other half were informed that they had more than ample time. On the way across campus, the students came upon a person in distress (actually an actor) who sat slumped motionless in a doorway, coughing and groaning with his head down and eyes closed.

The seminary students, regardless of the nature of their religious conviction, behaved more like the priest and Levite than the Samaritan. Of the 40 subjects, only 16 stopped to help the victim. Those who helped were primarily from the group given more than ample time to get to their lecture. Perhaps most surprising was the fact that students who were to deliver a lecture on the Good Samaritan were no more likely to help than those asked to lecture on job opportunities. "Indeed on several occasions," Darley and Batson (1973) note, "a seminary student going to give his talk on the parable of the Good Samaritan literally stepped over the victim as he hurried on his way" (p. 107).

It is quite possible that religiosity is not a strong predictor of whether bystanders will provide help, but such an interpretation is risky on several grounds. The study sample, for one thing, is probably more homogeneous with regard to the nature of its religiosity than the general population; and, as researchers know, homogeneous populations do not provide promising contexts in which to conduct correlational research. Darley and Batson's study (1973), however, is not alone in this regard. Studies on bystander intervention almost invariably have used college students, who are more similar among themselves than the general population with regard to personal characteristics such as self-confidence, prosocial attitudes, empathic ability, and feelings of responsibility—all traits that may relate to bystander intervention.

Since Darley and Batson used volunteer subjects, all of whom were paid a token sum for their participation, the problems are further compounded; persons who fail to "volunteer" under such circumstances may have been even lower in altruism than the generally unresponsive bystanders Darley and Batson successfully enlisted. Like Darley and Batson, researchers studying bystander intervention have almost invariably chosen to use "random" —or more accurately "volunteer"—samples of participants rather than to employ stratified samples in which participants are preselected in terms of personality characteristics. Presumably, sampling procedures have been chosen in order to maximize the degree to which the subjects are representative of the populations from which they are drawn. But such a concern with representativeness is not paralleled in regard to the experimental conditions; therefore, it becomes notably difficult to estimate the relative importance of situational versus dispositional factors in emergency intervention (see Bowers, 1973, for a discussion of the problems this bias poses in the interpretation of social-psychological research).

Darley and Batson's sample (1973) of 40 persons was quite small, and its members were distributed among three varieties of religiosity and assigned to four experimental conditions. Such a small sample, which is typical of intervention research studying individual differences, does not allow for statistically powerful tests. The within-cell N's for instance, drop to 3 or 4 persons, and potentially useful conclusions concerning the interaction of situational and personality variables become lost.

Finally, it can be noted that Darley and Batson measured only one personal characteristic. A more comprehensive approach would have looked at several characteristics and determined their relationships, singly and in combination, to helping behavior. It may be true, for instance, that type of religiosity is correlated with bystander intervention when the onlooker is also high in empathic ability, but not when he is low in such ability.

Is there, then, a Good Samaritan personality? Are personality dispositions important determinants of bystander intervention? Current social-psychological methodology, as noted, provides strong tests of situational factors and weak tests of the role of personality and dispositional parameters. But the handful of studies to be discussed below has avoided some of these problems and has found strong and mutually consistent personality correlates of bystander helpfulness in emergency situations. They suggest that Good Samaritans are among us—and that they can be characterized.

Profiling the Good Samaritan

Research providing the source material for sketching a profile of the Good Samaritan is summarized in Table 15.1. This table includes studies that have found significant personality correlates as well as those that have failed to do so. The studies failing to find significant correlates of bystander behavior have problematic meanings and tend to be marked by methodological shortcomings. We will concentrate on the studies that have discovered personality factors related to bystander intervention. This research, of course, is not without its own methodological problems; but the results fit into a coherent package, and the variety of research designs tends to compensate somewhat for the weakness in methodology in any particular study.

In one study using interview data, London (1970) found that persons who rescued Jews in Nazi Germany during World War II shared a spirit of adventurousness, a sense of being on the margin of society, and a close identification with a morally committed and sometimes moralistic parent. One rescuer's recollections illustrate the moral upbringing of many of London's interviewees (1970):

You inherit something from your parents, from the grandparents. My mother said to me when we were small, and even when we were bigger, she said to me. . . . "Regardless of what you do with your life, be honest. When it comes to the day you have to make a decision, make the right one. It could be a hard one. But even the hard ones should be the right ones" (p. 247).

This person, London (1970) notes, "went on to talk about his mother in glowing terms, about how she told him how to live, how she had taught him morals, and how

she had exemplified morality for him" (p. 247).

London emphasizes the limitations of his data, indicating that the reports are retrospective, that his sample is small, and that the respondents—all of whom had emigrated to the United States from Germany—may not be representative of rescuers of Jews in Nazi Germany. Nonetheless, several of London's observations about the familial antecedents of high-risk altruistic behavior have been confirmed by Rosenhan's study (1970) of civil rights workers who participated in activities such as freedom rides and voter registration drives in the South during the early 1960s. Rosenhan contrasted "fully committed" civil rights workers (those whose involvement spanned a year or more) with "partially committed" civil rights workers (those whose efforts were limited to no more than a couple of freedom rides) in regard to their recollections of their moral upbringing. Members of the two groups were similar in perceiving their parents as having had strong moral concerns; but fully committed activists tended to see their parents as having backed their concerns with action, while partially committed ones tended to note discrepancies between what their parents said they believed and what they actually did. One fully committed activist, for instance, indicated that his father, moved by the atrocities of Nazi Germany, joined the military during World War II, even though he had originally been exempted from the service because of his age and health. Another recalled being carried on his father's shoulders during the Sacco-Vanzetti protest parades. In contrast, a partially committed activist "went into a lengthy tirade against his father, who had preached stern honesty but vigorously condoned dishonesty toward members of a cultural outgroup" (Rosenhan, 1970, p. 262).

London's rescuers and Rosenhan's civil rights workers subjected themselves to considerable risk in order to carry out their altruistic endeavors. Faced with accepting what they regarded as moral wrongs or taking risks in order to correct the evils they perceived, these individuals chose the latter course.

Several experimental investigations have faced bystanders with emergencies similar to, though less threatening than, those studied by London and Rosenhan, and have attempted to ascertain personal characteristics related to intervention. This line of research has the advantage over interview studies in that it allows for predictive tests of intervention. McNamee (in prep.), in one of these studies, attempted to relate differences in moral reasoning as measured by Kohlberg's scale (see Chap. 2) to bystander response. McNamee's study faced participants with this dilemma: They could follow an experimenter's lead and ignore pleas for help from a subject who seemed to be "freaked out" on a psychedelic drug, or they could ignore the implicit demands of the experimenter to proceed with the experiment and offer to help the distressed individual, even though this would delay the experiment and perhaps anger the experimenter. The bystander's response was categorized first in terms of whether or not he or she offered assistance, and then, if assistance was offered, in terms of the nature of the aid, using three categories: (1) statements of sympathy or protest; (2) offers of information about where the person could go for help, and (3) provisions of personal assistance, such as taking the person home or to a place where help could be secured.

Each participant was scored for stage of moral reasoning on the basis of interview responses to moral dilemmas designed by Kohlberg and his colleagues. Results showed that the frequency of help giving increased with each higher level of moral development: Persons at Stage 2 helped 11 percent of the time; those at Stage 3 27 percent; Stage 4, 38 percent; Stage 5, 68 percent; and Stage 6, 100 percent. The nature of the help offered also differed as a function of stages. Persons at the principled level of moral development (Stages 5 and 6) sometimes offered personal assistance, whereas individuals at lower levels never offered such assistance.

Two studies have also shown that individual differences in the degree to which bystanders feel sympathetic and responsible for the welfare of others relate to intervention. Liebhart (1972), in one of these studies, measured individual differences in both sympathetic orientation (using Lenrow's 1965 measure) and the tendency to take instrumental action to reduce personal discomfort (using a scale he constructed). The emergency in this case involved a person in an adjoining room who appeared to have suffered a mishap and was crying and moaning. The results showed that bystanders high in sympathetic orientation helped more quickly, but only when they were also highly disposed to take instrumental action to reduce their own distress. Such a finding underlines the importance of looking at combinations of bystander characteristics as they relate to intervention rather than considering them one at a time.

Schwartz and Clausen (1970), in the second study, first obtained scores on an index of the tendency of individuals to ascribe responsibility to themselves for others' welfare (see Table 15.2, for sample items). These scores were then correlated with the persons' behavior when confronted with a staged emergency in which a confederate of the experimenter feigned an epileptic fit. Bystanders high as compared to low in the tendency to define their social responsibilities in broad terms were found to help more often, more rapidly, and more directly.

The studies by London (1970), Rosenhan (1970), McNamee (in prep), Liebhart (1972), and Schwartz and Clausen (1970) indicate, first, that Good Samaritans exist—that there are indeed persons who will help others at some cost to themselves; second, that impetus to Good Samaritanism is likely rooted in early socialization experiences; and, third, that Good Samaritan behavior in general is

TABLE 15.1 Relationships between Personality Characteristics and Intervention in Emergencies

Author and Date	Subjects			Nature of Emergency	Personality Characteristics	Findings
	Sex	Age	N			
Latané & Darley (1968)	M–F	College	72	Epileptic seizure	Social responsibility; need for approval, Machiavellianism, authoritarianism, alienation.	None of the personality measures correlated significantly with frequency of reporting the seizure.
London (1970)	no data	no data	27	Rescue of Jews in Nazi Germany	Personality characteristics gleaned from interview data.	Rescuers were characterized as possessing a spirit of adventurousness, social marginality, and an intense identification with highly moralistic parent(s).
Rosenhan (1970)	M–F	17–51	46	Active civil rights work in the South, Late 1950s to 1961	Personality-socialization dimensions gleaned from interview data.	Fully committed activists as compared to partially committed activists had more often maintained a positive, warm, and respecting relationship with their parents. Fully committed activists viewed their parents as both having preached and practiced moral altruism, whereas partially committed activists viewed their parents as preaching but not practicing moral altruism.
Schwartz & Clausen (1970)	M–F	College	189	Epileptic seizure	Ascription of responsibility (AR), awareness of consequences (AC), Internal–external control (I–E).	Persons high in AR aided the victim more often, more quickly, and more directly than those low in AR; AC and I–E were unrelated to helping.
Horowitz (1971)	M	College	80	Epileptic seizure	Service group membership vs. social fraternity membership.	Members of service groups intervened more often than fraternity group members.
Korte (1971)	M	College	60	Asthma attack	Autonomy, deference, ascendance–submissiveness.	Interveners and noninterveners did not differ on any of the personality measures; a cluster of items from the autonomy scale which appear to tap unconventionality, did differentiate the two groups.

Study	Sex	Population	N	Variable	Emergency	Results
(1971a)				of activity, need for approval, expression of positive affection, and competence.	in adjoining room; sobbing and crying	...ratings of boys' imitation of activities correlated positively with helping; ratings of girls' need for approval correlated negatively with helping. All other ratings were non-significantly correlated with helping.
Staub (1971b)	F	18–28	56	Need for approval.	Loud crash in adjoining room; sobbing and crying	Need for approval was unrelated to helping behavior.
Yakimovich & Saltz (1971)	M	College	33	Trustworthiness, independence, altruism, agreement with New Left beliefs.	Fall from ladder	None of the personality measures was related to helping behavior.
Liebhart (1972)	M	High school students	102	Sympathetic orientation; instrumental activity.	Violent bang in adjoining room; shrill cry and moan	Bystanders high in both sympathetic orientation and the disposition to take action instrumental to the reduction of their own discomfort helped faster than bystanders low either in one or both of these characteristics.
Darley & Batson (1973)	M	Seminary students	40	Type of religiosity.	Victim slumped in doorway	Seminary students whose commitment to religion was based on social reasons (religion as a means), the intrinsic value of religion, and religion as a quest for meaning did not differ in frequency of helping.
Clark & Word (1974)	M	College	108	Competence in electronics.	Accident: person electrically shocked	Competent bystanders intervened both more quickly and more safely than incompetent bystanders.
Staub (1974)	M	College	130	Belief in moral and prosocial values; activity–passivity; speed in making judgments.	Severe stomach cramps	Belief in moral and prosocial values was significantly related to helping behavior; activity–passivity (reaction time) and speed in making judgments were unrelated to helping.
McNamee (In prep.)	M–F	18–25	124	Stage of moral development.	Drug reaction	Persons at higher stages on Kohlberg's scale of moral judgment helped more often and more directly than did persons at lower stages.

TABLE 15.2   Correlations of Personality Measures with Prosocial Orientation Index and Bystander Helpfulness[a]

Measure	Sample Items	Factor Loading on Index of Prosocial Orientation	Correlation with Helpfulness
Machiavellianism (Christie & Geis, 1968)	A: "Most men are brave." D: "Anyone who completely trusts anyone else is asking for trouble."	.70	.30
Ascription of Responsibility for Other's Welfare (Schwartz, 1968)	A: "If a good friend of mine wanted to injure an enemy of his, it would be my duty to stop him." D: "When a man is completely involved in valuable work, you can't blame him if he is insensitive to those around him."	.59	.27
Social Responsibility (Berkowitz & Lutterman, 1968)	A: "I am the kind of person people can count on." D: "In school my behavior has gotten me into trouble."	.51	.34
Moral Reasoning (Kohlberg, 1969b)	Moral dilemmas such as whether a man should steal a drug he cannot afford in order to save his dying wife.	.46	.25
Values (Rokeach, 1969)	Individuals are asked to rank-order 18 values,[b] including		
	(1) Helpful (ranked high)	.58	.24
	(2) Equality (high)	.56	n.s.
	(3) Courageous (high)	n.s.	.26
	(4) Comfortable life (ranked low)	.58	n.s.
	(5) Clean (neat, tidy) (low)	.33	.32
Index of Prosocial Orientation			.45

Source: Adapted from Staub (1974).

[a] Correlations are based on scoring each scale so that high scores are indicative of a prosocial orientation; hence, all correlations are positive. Similarly, the items sampled from the scales show the direction of the responses (A = Agree, D = Disagree) a person high in prosocial orientation would give.

[b] The correlations for the Rokeach values are between the rank-order for the value and (1) the index of prosocial orientation, and (2) the degree of bystander helpfulness.

correlated with sympathetic attitudes toward the welfare of others.

Such a view is supported in a recent study by Staub (1974), which compares persons of differing levels of "prosocial orientation" (a composite measure of several personality scales, described below), with regard to helpfulness toward a person in another room apparently suffering from progressively worsening stomach cramps.

Subjects in the experiment were instructed to make personality judgments of characters portrayed in a series of written vignettes. Depending on the session, participants were (1) given no information about the appropriateness of going into the other room, (2) told they were to time themselves with a stopwatch they had been given and to work fast and without interruption, or (3) told that coffee was brewing in the other room and that they should feel free to get some when it was ready. The experimenter then left. About four minutes later, sounds of distress emanated from the adjoining room; the distressed person then mentioned the extent of his pain, next offered to go to another room so as not to disturb the worker, and finally directly requested the subject to go to the drugstore and get him some pills. Persons observing through a one-way mirror coded the subject's reactions to the unfolding emergency and, from these coded data, derived a composite index of bystander helpfulness.

Three to six weeks prior to their involvement in the experimental session the participants had filled out a series of paper-and-pencil tests of personality. A factor analysis indicated that the measures were highly loaded on a single factor; Staub, therefore, weighted them by their factor loadings and summed them to provide a composite score, an index of "prosocial orientation," for each subject. Table 15.2 summarizes the measures making up this overall index and indicates (1) the factor loading of each measure and (2) the correlation of each measure with helpfulness in the emergency situation.

Several notable conclusions which show the advantages of studying multiple aspects of personality in regard to bystander behavior may be drawn from Staub's analysis (1974). First, the relationship between the composite index of prosocial orientation and the degree that onlookers provided help was stronger than the correlation between helpfulness and any of the personality measures taken independently. Second, the relationship between prosocial orientation and helpfulness was unaffected by the different instructions given to the subjects concerning the appropriateness of entering the room from which the victim called. Third, some of the personality measures, when considered alone, interacted with situational parameters in determining bystander response.[4] The Good Samaritan, these findings indicate, has a variety of personal characteristics which appear to complement one another in producing a predisposition to help others.

A summary profile reveals the Good Samaritan to have a strong sense of moral and social responsibility, a spirit of adventurousness and unconventionality, sympathy for others, and a tendency to reduce his or her own distress by social actions designed to reduce the distress of another. This last characteristic suggests that people who are *capable* of effective intervention and who feel competent to deal with emergencies are more likely than others to provide help. Clark and Word (1974), for instance, found that persons knowledgeable as compared to individuals naive about electronics provided safer and more rapid help to a man who had apparently suffered an accident in which he became entangled in electrical wires. The Good Samaritan is more likely to be male than female (Borofsky, Stollak, & Messé, 1971; I. Piliavin, Rodin, & Piliavin, 1969; J. Piliavin & Piliavin, 1972), especially when other potential helpers are present (Schwartz & Clausen, 1970). This finding may be due to the sexes' different socialization experiences, which produce in males a greater feeling of competence and responsibility when confronted with emergencies. There is also evidence that Good Samaritans are more likely to be firstborns than laterborns (Staub, 1970a), and to come from small rather than large families (Staub, 1971a). The data are inconsistent, however, regarding whether persons who have grown up in small communities are more helpful than those who have grown up in large ones (Latané & Darley, 1970; Schwartz & Clausen, 1970).

The profile we have drawn of the Good Samaritan is based on laboratory and field studies that have tended to use rather idiosyncratic emergency situations. A major unresolved issue concerns the degree to which the profile will accurately predict bystander behavior across a much wider spectrum of varying emergency situations. At the moment, too, we do not possess adequate information about the prevalence of persons possessing the composite characteristics defining the Good Samaritan. If increasing the number of Good Samaritan interventions is desirable, more and better data bearing on these issues need to be gathered.

Strategies for Enhancing Bystander Responsiveness

On the basis of what is known and suspected about bystander intervention, what practical steps can be taken to support the Good Samaritan impulse and to increase the likelihood of helpful intervention?

One approach is to provide socialization experiences that enhance altruism or emphasize prosocial values (see, for example, M. L. Hoffman, Chap. 7; Liebert & Poulos, Chap. 16; Staub, 1975). A more direct attempt to modify bystander behavior has been through legal means: the enactment of statutes designed to decrease the risks and increase the rewards of providing help to others. Community-based programs that support similar goals, such as volunteer auxiliary police patrol groups, have also been initiated, especially in New York City.

LEGAL SUPPORTS

In many parts of continental Europe (Dawson, 1966; Rudzinski, 1966), the responsibility to rescue persons in need is legally prescribed. In France, for instance,

"A person who abstains from giving assistance to somebody in danger, when he can give this assistance without risk to himself or to other persons, either by his personal action or by prompting rescue, incurs a punishment of three months at least and five years at most in jail, and a fine of 360 francs at least and 15,000 francs at most" (Tunc, 1966, p. 47). The French law, which was enacted in the early 1940s, not only compels bystanders to intervene but also protects them from liability when they do so. This statute also holds the person in need of rescue, regardless of whether he requests help, liable for damages incurred by a Good Samaritan who attempts to help him (Tunc, 1966).

Anglo-American law, though abstaining from compelling altruism, nonetheless has begun to move in the direction of providing incentives in support of Good Samaritan behavior. First, a few states—including Georgia, Texas, and Mississippi—have enacted legislation granting immunity from liability to persons who inadvertently cause damage when attempting to help (Holland, 1967). Second, several states have followed the lead of France and other European countries and passed legislation providing public compensation to Good Samaritans for losses suffered as a consequence of rendering aid (Culhane, 1965; Edelhertz & Geis, 1974; Holland, 1967; Kaplan, 1972).

No data are available, however, comparing the relative frequency and effectiveness of onlooker intervention in jurisdictions governed by the different kinds of Good Samaritan laws and those without such legislation. It is possible that most people will either intervene or not, regardless of whether they will be compensated or held potentially liable for their efforts. It also seems that few people are aware that Good Samaritan behavior will qualify them for aid; they are ignorant until they act to help and find themselves in need of the compensation. For laws designed to promote Good Samaritanism to be effective, the general public must be better informed of their existence. Moreover, incentives such as financial rewards or bonuses (rather than reparative compensation) and public recognition may more effectively encourage bystanders to intervene. Kaplan (1972), for instance, has proposed that Good Samaritans be rewarded through compensation or by having their name placed in a lottery, with a cash payment given the winning Good Samaritan. Such a lottery would provide public affirmation of the cultural value placed on helpful intervention, and would offer dramatic recognition of persons who had helped others in distress.

MODIFICATION OF THE SOCIAL ENVIRONMENT

In recent years groups of citizens have begun to organize themselves in order to decrease crime in their communities and to increase mutual aid in times of emergency. In New York City, for example, protective groups, often called "block associations" (usually involving a one- to three-block square), have been formed to foster a sense of community. These block associations have initiated citizen patrols (Baumgold, 1973; Shepherd, 1973), implemented alarm systems that alert the community and the police to the fact that a resident is in need of help ("Lower East Side Group," 1973; Shepherd, 1973), and fostered activities designed to get people to know one another better. The police, in addition, have trained more than 6000 unarmed auxiliary volunteers as well as 10,000 street watchers, who watch the streets from their windows and report anything unusual (Shepherd, 1973). These programs are designed to maximize collaboration between citizens and police with the dual aim of making neighborhoods safer places and forestalling the formation of vigilante groups.

Evidence regarding the effectiveness of community-based programs in preventing crime and stimulating bystander responsiveness is primarily anecdotal. A member of a New York City citizen patrol which nabbed ten muggers during a four-month period provided the following testimonial:

Before we had the civilian patrol no one knew anyone else. . . . Now they're talking to each other, and there's the beginning of a community feeling. We started learning about safety. If someone was screaming, we'd go for help. I liked it. It was a great feeling.[5] And I met people and it got me out of the house and onto the street. Best of all, we caught muggers left and right (Shepherd, 1973, p. 63).

The fact that the latter part of the testimonial is in the past tense provides a clue to the problems that may be involved in sustaining community action groups. This action group, for instance, fell apart during the winter months when the weather turned raw, citizens spent less time outdoors, and the frequency of muggings and other distress situations presumably decreased. Since the impetus for communities to organize is apt to be collective fear, the effectiveness of the programs they develop is likely to be self-limiting: Any success such programs experience reduces citizen fear and undermines the basis of the commitment to the action programs. Nonetheless, involvement in such efforts may increase the degree to which people are willing to provide assistance to others in need. The New York City citizen action programs offer a model of a method to increase bystander intervention. The need to assess the impact of efforts such as Good Samaritan legislation and citizen patrols, and to integrate and expand this knowledge with laboratory field studies, is basic to the development of more sophisticated programs dealing with bystander intervention.[6]

CHAPTER 16

Television As a Moral Teacher

Robert M. Liebert and Rita Wicks Poulos

Introduction

Until relatively recently developmental psychologists paid scant heed to the role of television in socialization. Then, beginning in the early 1960s, there was an enormous surge of interest in the effects of this medium upon the young (e.g., Bandura, 1963; Maccoby, 1964). A look at television's spectacular commercial rise may partially explain the shift. In 1948 less than 1 percent of all American homes had television sets; by 1972 virtually every dwelling, even the humblest, had a working receiver. In fact there seems little doubt that more children now have television available than have adequate heating or indoor plumbing.

The spectacular rise of the medium would not justify its mention in this volume, though, unless its content were pertinent to morality and moral development. A. H. Stein (1972), in a thoughtful review for the National Society for the Study of Education, addressed this issue in a summary of recent analyses of television content:

Aggression and illegal actions are often portrayed as successful and morally justified. . . . Law enforcement officers and other heroes use violence as frequently as villains and often break laws and moral codes as well. In both adults' and children's programs, these socially disapproved methods of attaining goals are more often successful than socially approved methods. . . While criminal and illegal activities frequently escape punishment, goodness alone is rarely sufficient to achieve success. . . . The fundamental philosophy manifest in most current television programming is that the end justifies the means, and the successful means are often immoral, illegal, or violent. . . (p. 186).

Does this enormous diet of morally relevant television affect the child in more than transient or trivial ways? This question has been asked about all the pictorial media—movies, comic books, and television—at one time or another. It is undeniable that television has emerged as a significant agent of socialization. One team of psychiatrists has even stated bluntly that "it is a matter of fact and concern that television has increasingly replaced parents as a definitive adult voice and national shaper of views" (Heller & Polsky, 1971, pp. 279–280).

But what specific role does—and can—television play in the development of moral values and behavior? While few people doubt that television viewing has some influence, its impact is not easy to analyze. The child is continually interacting with his environment—soaking up, weighing, and judging all kinds of information from an array of sources. How can the effects of television be separated from a multitude of other influences? How can its impact be followed over time when there is so much interference? How can the differential effects of so great a variety of programs be sorted out? It is no wonder that our ability to analyze television's effects is commonly described as primitive, and that many researchers have been discouraged completely from the task.

On closer inspection, though, the problem of understanding this medium is no more complicated than that of analyzing the effects of parental nurturance, academic encouragement, or socioeconomic factors. Recent studies of the effects of television are no more primitive, and probably somewhat more advanced, than investigations of most other influences on a child's development. And the solution to the dilemmas raised above has been the same for television research as for other areas: We do not ask for or attempt definitive superstudies or a single methodology, but rely on converging and complementary theory and research approaches. Only in this way can we hope to produce information relevant to the long-term effects of television and the complex interaction of forces that doubtless come into play in the real world.

In trying to make sense out of TV's effect on children, we need a basic theoretical model, a superordinate framework to account for the various data. Our view focuses on observational learning as the critical process underlying television as an instrument of socialization.

A Theoretical Framework: The Process of Observational Learning

Observational learning is, first of all, a vicarious process in which the behavior of children (or adults) changes as a function of exposure to the actions of others. These other individuals may be viewed directly *(live modeling)* or indirectly *(symbolic modeling);* in the latter case the model's actions are displayed through media such as books, newsprint, motion pictures, and television. Thus, a range of situations far too vast to be experienced directly by the average person is made available. Investigations over the last fifteen years have firmly established that observational learning is a basic means by which the human acquires and modifies his behavior, standards, values, and attitudes (for relevant reviews, see Bandura, 1969a; Flanders, 1968; Zimmerman & Rosenthal, 1974).

THE THREE STAGES OF OBSERVATIONAL LEARNING

How exactly does observational learning occur? It is useful to conceptualize the process as involving three major stages (cf. Liebert, 1972, 1973): *exposure, acquisition,* and *acceptance* (see Figure 16.1).

For observational learning to occur the observer must first be exposed to the specific acts or *modeling cues* of the exemplar. Note, however, that *exposure* to a particular behavioral example can occur without necessarily leading to learning or retention. A child may simply fail to attend to what is being shown, or he may fail to process and store this information effectively. Yet it is only if the second stage, *acquisition,* also occurs that modeling cues can have a further effect.

The third and final stage of observational learning is *acceptance*. Does a child who has been exposed to and has acquired the modeling cues now accept this information as a guide for his own subsequent actions? Acceptance effects can be grouped

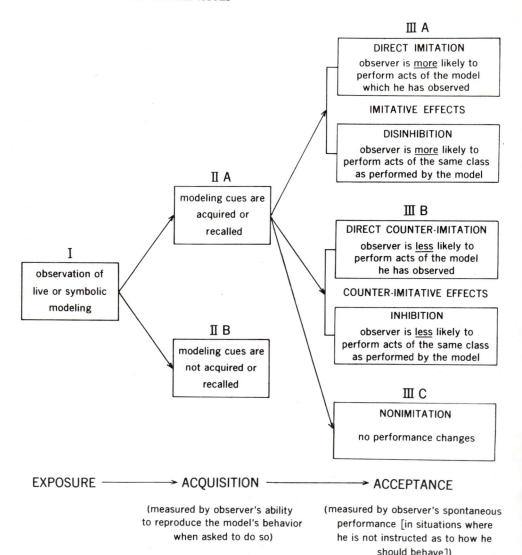

Figure 16.1 Schematic presentation of the stages of observational learning.

into two broad categories: observer actions that are *imitative*, in which case the viewer's behavior becomes more like that of the model than it would otherwise be, and actions that are *counterimitative*, in which case the viewer's behavior becomes less like that of the model. Counterimitative behavior is illustrated by the child who, upon seeing a friend bitten by a dog, becomes less likely to approach the animal than he might have been previously. In this situation the viewer accepts the exemplar's actions as a guide for what action to avoid.

Modeling cues may also serve to bring about acceptance of a more general class of behaviors of which the cues are perceived as being only an instance. For example, the child who sees her parent donate money to a variety of charities may subsequently be more willing to share her toys with other children or to divide a piece of chocolate cake with her little brother. In like manner, a youngster who observes a variety of peers punished for handing in homework late or talking back to the teacher may avoid other school "transgressions" which he has not seen modeled. In the former example, *disinhibition* has occurred; in the latter example *inhibition*.

OBSERVATIONAL LEARNING AS APPLIED TO TELEVISION VIEWING

We assume that the foregoing analysis, derived from a variety of studies on live and symbolic modeling, is equally applicable to television. Beyond potentially accounting for television effects, this analysis can also guide and refine the nature of the inquiry itself. Note, for example, that the emphasis on exposure to specific modeling cues directs our attention to the television content seen by individual children; overall exposure to television per se, as a medium, would tell us little about what any particular youngster might have been exposed to, learned, and accepted from television.[1]

An important aspect of the application of the three-stage analysis to television is derived from a distinction traceable to Bandura and Walters (1963). While only a small percentage of viewers may show immediate acceptance effects, others who have been exposed to the content may also have acquired some, or all, of what they have seen. If so, they will be able to activate their knowledge when a more favorable occasion arises, thereby manifesting delayed acceptance.

An experiment by Bandura (1965a) provides a clear demonstration. Children were shown one of three films which began with identical modeling cues: an adult female model behaving aggressively toward a Bobo doll. The films differed in their endings, however, as the model's actions had various consequences: in the first, she was rewarded with food treats and praise; in the second, she was castigated verbally for her untoward action; and, in the third, she had nothing done to her (no consequences). An immediate test of imitative aggression in the playroom revealed that children who had watched the model being punished produced fewer imitative aggressive responses than those in the other two groups. Did the punishment-viewing youngsters fail to *acquire* the model's aggressive repertoire or did they simply fail to *adopt* her hostile course of action because of the unacceptable consequences it would bring?

In the experiment, children were offered attractive rewards if they would demonstrate all they could remember of what the model had done. Now the differences between the groups disappeared entirely; those who had witnessed the punished model had indeed absorbed her exemplary hostilities and were quite able to perform them when the circumstances were altered to make their performance acceptable and profitable.

Bandura and Walters (1963) thus argued that although measures of acceptance necessarily indicate some of what the observer has acquired, they do not always indicate all of the knowledge gained. Acquisition can be evaluated using any procedure that demonstrates learning from modeling cues. The child can be asked to choose between alternative behaviors (one of which has been modeled), to describe what a model did, or to perform on a test that permits extrapolation from the exemplary performance. Without broad assessment, though, caution must be exercised in judging the limits of acquisition.

The previous sections have described the theoretical perspective we have used to organize and understand television as a possible moral teacher. Employing this framework, we can turn now to an examination of the medium itself.

Exposure to Television

Television obviously cannot be an important teacher of moral lessons unless children are exposed to it. In fact, virtually every American home has at least one television set and soon a majority will have at least two. It seems incongruous now that warnings were once frequently voiced that TV would be just another fad because people could not use it, as they did radio, while they went about their everyday work and rest.

What has happened, instead, is that other activities have been sacrificed to the television set. In the United States television has affected the lives of the entire family; by the mid-1960s 55 percent of American families had changed their sleeping habits for television, 55 percent had altered their mealtimes, and 78 percent had begun to use television as an "electronic baby-sitter" (N. Johnson, 1967). Visiting others and entertaining at home also have reportedly decreased (e.g., Cunningham & Walsh, 1958), and the use of other media such as radio and movies has been adversely affected (e.g., Baxter, 1961).

These kinds of changes have been demonstrated wherever television exists. Robinson (1972), for example, compared the daily activities of TV owners and nonowners in fifteen locations in eleven countries by having his subjects fill out diaries concerning all of their activities throughout a full, twenty-four-hour day. Such time budgets showed decreases in radio listening, book reading, and movie viewing. Sleep, social gatherings away from home, other leisure activities (correspondence and knitting), conversation, and some types of household care also decreased. From his results Robinson (1972) concluded that "at least in the temporal sense, television appears to have had a greater influence on the structure of daily life than any other innovation in this century" (p. 428).

But what about more specific viewing habits? How much television do children actually watch? It is estimated that in America the average set is on for 6 hours and 18 minutes daily (*Broadcasting Yearbook,* 1971). This does *not* mean that it is being watched for all of those hours. Still, the usual figure for children's viewing is between 2 and 3 hours daily. A recent major study, for example, looked at the viewing habits of children in a small town in southern California (Lyle & Hoffman, 1972). Interviews, viewing records, and TV diaries for over 250 first-graders, about 800 sixth-graders, and 500 tenth-graders revealed that most children watched every day for at least 2 hours, and significant numbers (especially of younger children) were exposed to twice that amount of viewing.

Lyle and Hoffman's findings concerning the time of day when children watched is of additional interest. Although first-grade viewing peaked at 8:00 P.M., 10 to 15 percent of these youngsters were still watching at 9:30 P.M. About half the older children were watching at 9:00 P.M. and over 25 percent were still watching at 10:30 P.M. It would appear, then, that children view a great deal of entertainment that is sometimes justified as being shown only at "adult hours." The reality is seen most clearly in the report of other investigators that "on one Monday during the period covered, over five million children under the age of 12 . . . were still watching between 10:30 and 11:00 P.M." (McIntyre & Teevan, 1972, p. 384).

So television seems to have become part and parcel of daily life. It now serves children, for better or worse, as a constant informer, a faithful teacher, a window on the world. Exactly what is seen through this window? As far as we know there have been no attempts to characterize all the potential lessons of a sample of television shows at once. Instead, certain aspects of broadcast entertainment have been surveyed and counted according to the interests of the investigators or the times. It is perhaps not surprising that violence and aggression have been carefully and repeatedly surveyed. Some attention has been paid to the presence of national, ethnic, and social stereotypes which may convey undesirable prejudices. On the other hand, there have been few attempts to identify and systematically study the positive lessons of television entertainment, even though there is little doubt that these can be found. Our subsequent discussion therefore continues by first considering within the context of observational learning the effects of televised aggression and violence. Other relevant, and often related, content areas such as rule breaking and prejudicial stereotypes will be discussed more briefly; and, finally, consideration will be given to positive moral lessons that television might provide. Despite this division, it is important to remember that the basic process of observational learning underlies effects in all of these domains. *What* moral lessons television teaches depends simply on what is shown.

Aggression and Violence

A great deal has been written about violence and aggression on television: research, critique, speculation, and defense. In discussing this area, it is first necessary to define terms. By *aggression* we mean any action that is harmful to others; such behavior often, but not always, contains a component of hostility or antisocial means of goal seeking. While this definition is admittedly broad, it excludes behavior that is simply of high magnitude or energetic. A child (or a television character) can be bold and assertive without being aggressive as defined here.

VIOLENCE IN TELEVISION ENTERTAINMENT

Since television's beginning, violence and aggression have been part of American TV fare, but they have gradually and consistently increased. The National Association of Educational Broadcasters, reporting to a Senate subcommittee on juvenile delinquency, noted a 15 percent increase in violent incidents in television entertainment from 1951 to 1953. In 1954 about 17 percent of prime time was given to violence-saturated adventure programs; by 1961 this figure had risen to 60 percent. Two-thirds of the violence in 1964 was aired before 9:00 P.M., indicating that it was available even to children not among the late viewers (Liebert, Neale, & Davidson, 1973). In 1968 it was estimated that "the average child between the ages of 5 and 15 watches the violent destruction of more than 13,400 persons on TV" (Sabin, 1972).

George Gerbner (1972, 1973), Dean of the Annenberg School of Communications, has provided one of the most compelling estimates of the amount of violence appearing during the five-year period from 1967 to 1972. Gerbner's trained observers recorded the number of violent episodes on prime-time and Saturday morning cartoons during one week in October which was representative of each year's programming.

The major results of this research are startling. In 1969, for example, eight in ten plays contained violence, with five violent episodes per play. Further, the most violent programs were cartoons designed exclusively for children. The average cartoon hour in 1967, according to the Gerbner studies, contained more than three times as many violent episodes as the average adult dramatic hour. By 1969 there was a violent episode at least every two minutes in all Saturday morning cartoon programming, including the least violent and also commercial time. The average cartoon had nearly twelve times the vio-

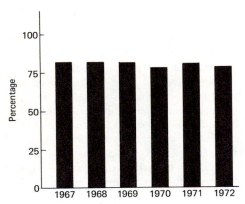

Figure 16.2   The percentage of network programming (prime time and Saturday morning) containing violence, 1967 to 1973. (Source: Gerbner, 1973.)

lence rate of the average movie hour. This same pattern of high-level violence has held for several years, as can be seen in Figure 16.2.

ACQUISITION OF TELEVISED VIOLENCE AND AGGRESSION

As Bandura (1965a) has shown, a single exposure to novel aggressive actions portrayed on a television screen is often sufficient for children to learn how to be exact "carbon copies" of their exemplars, precisely imitating complex sequences of verbal and physical aggression. What is more, behavior learned in this way is often retained for long periods of time; after a single viewing many children can reproduce what they have seen six to eight months later (Hicks, 1965, 1968).

Recall of physical acts portrayed in specially prepared film sequences must, however, be distinguished from the acquisition of the somewhat more subtle themes and relationships characterizing television stories. There is a growing body of evidence that young children respond to television dramas quite differently from adults, both cognitively and affectively, and thus learn quite different things than

their elders from the same content. Children, for example, may inaccurately perceive the underlying plot even if it is a simple one; or they may fragment the overall content into discrete and unrelated segments (cf. Collins, 1970).

In view of these findings, it is reasonable to ask whether children perceive the motives and consequences of a television character's aggression as accurately as they perceive the aggressive actions themselves. The issue is an extremely important one in light of the industry's claim that televised violence is usually negatively sanctioned, inasmuch as "bad guys" are not rewarded for antisocial behavior. Unfortunately, though, the evidence shows rather clearly that commercial entertainment does *not* communicate the negative effects of "bad" violence to young viewers, whatever the broadcaster's intent.

Leifer and Roberts (1972) have attempted to identify age differences in the comprehension of motives and consequences surrounding aggressive acts shown on actual television programs. Almost 300 children, ranging in age from kindergarteners to twelfth-graders, served in their study. Striking age differences were found. Kindergarteners answered only about one-third of the questions correctly, third-graders about one-half, and twelfth-graders about 95 percent. Clearly, then, younger subjects did not learn or retain much about the motives and consequences involved in the story lines. Consistent with these findings is the work of A. H. Stein and Friedrich (1972), which has showed that preschoolers could remember some details of the programs they had viewed, but their recall was far from perfect. Stein and Friedrich's data suggest that "nonaction" detail observed only once was not easily remembered.

In contrast to the consequences reaped by villains, televised violence by heroes is not punished. Rather, it is justified by moral pronouncements about the rectitude of aggressing for "good" reasons. We might also ask, then, about what children acquire from exposure to televised heroes who pronounce virtuous statements as they break laws and thrash their opponents. In a series of experiments Bryan and his associates (e.g., Bryan & Walbek, 1970a, 1970b) have documented that a child's moral statements bear little relationship to his actual behavior. "[These] investigations," write Bryan and Schwartz (1971) in a thoughtful review, "suggest the possibility that the aggressive hero who verbalizes socially sanctioned norms may well be teaching the observer how to be brutal and what to verbalize" (p. 58).

CHILDREN'S ACCEPTANCE OF TELEVISED AGGRESSION

Findings described in the previous sections show that children in our society are exposed to a substantial amount of violent televised material, and that repeated exposure to such symbolic modeling can teach specific responses and convey more general impressions about society at large and how people deal with each other. The remaining, and perhaps most important, question is whether children actually accept what they see in television's symbolic format as a guide for their own attitudes and actions in the moral sphere.

Correlational field studies. To obtain a broad view of the possibility that television violence contributes to aggressiveness, correlational field studies are particularly useful. In general, these investigations involve determining the relationship between the amount of TV violence viewed in the home and the degree to which observers engage in, or otherwise express approval and acceptance of, aggressive acts. While it is widely recognized that the method cannot definitively establish causality, it does provide suggestive evidence while maximizing the naturalness of the events of interest.

Many correlational studies have been conducted. They converge in showing that for youngsters from a variety of backgrounds and ages, television violence viewing is related positively to many aspects of aggressive behavior, from petty meanness to delinquency. Although detailed discussion of this work is beyond the scope of this paper, a simplified tabular summary offered by Chaffee (1972) appears in Table 16.1, and provides a measure of its breadth. (For a more extensive review, see Chaffee, 1972, and Liebert, Neale, & Davidson, 1973.)

Experimental studies. Recent experimental studies have further confirmed the correlational findings described above. In one already mentioned study, Leifer and Roberts (1972) presented 271 children (40 kindergarteners, 54 third-, 56 sixth-, 51 ninth-, and 70 twelfth-graders) with television programs containing varying amounts of aggression. These programs covered the range usually watched by children of these ages and were taken directly off the air and shown without editing. Immediately after viewing, the child was questioned about his understanding of the motivations and consequences for the violence in each program; then he was asked to choose among various behavioral options in hypothetical conflict situations that were presented in story and slide form. The amount of aggression in the program watched was one of the best predictors of how aggressive the child's behavioral choices were, while the context of what he had seen, defined in terms of motivations and consequences, did not relate to aggression at all and thus failed to serve as a "controlling cue."

That the successful aggressive acts of heroes may outweigh the motives and intentions underlying them will not be surprising to students of cognitive development; Piaget (e.g., 1932) and Kohlberg (e.g., Chap. 2) have long argued that for the young, and for older individuals who are less mature, morality is judged largely by outcomes rather than intentions. Thus, by showing that violence, lawbreaking and other antisocial means of goal attainment

TABLE 16.1   Summary of Correlations between Violence Viewing and Aggressiveness

Locale	Grade	N	Self-Report Aggressive Behavior	Other-Report Aggressive Behavior
		Samples of Boys		
New York	3	211	no data	++
Michigan	4–5–6	434	no data	++
Wisconsin	6–7	38	+	+
Maryland	7	122	+	0
Maryland	8–9	80	0	no data
Wisconsin	9–10	43	+	++
Maryland	10	107	++	++
		Samples of Girls		
New York	3	216	no data	0
Michigan	4–5–6	404	no data	+++
Wisconsin	6–7	30	++	++
Maryland	7	108	++	++
Wisconsin	9–10	40	+	++
Maryland	10	136	+	+

Source: Chaffee (1972) who notes, "Cell entries indicate presence of positive (+) or null (0) correlation between the amount of violence viewing reported by the adolescent, and an aggressiveness index based on the type of report listed in the column heading. Stronger or more consistent positive relationships are indicated by repeating the sign (++). These are very approximate estimates of the strength of the evidence that the correlation is non-zero" (p. 25).

are successful, television is also simultaneously, if inadvertently, imparting to the young child the impression that these actions are also morally right (cf. A. H. Stein, 1972).

The question is often raised whether aggressive *behavior*, as well as attitudes and hypothetical choices, can also be affected directly by violence viewing. The question is a difficult one, because acting on what one has learned through exposure to aggression probably occurs most often in the absence of adult witnesses and only in situations that are otherwise conducive to the success of antisocial behavior. Given these qualifications, it is impressive that many studies have shown the immediate instigation of overt aggressive actions after children's exposure to violent television fare.

Numerous older studies (for example, Bandura, Ross, & Ross, 1963a, 1963b; Hicks, 1965; Rosekrans & Hartup, 1967)

have shown that aggressive acts seen on a television screen will be copied spontaneously by young children when they subsequently interact with inanimate victims such as toys or plastic Bobo dolls. More recently, this basic finding has been amplified by a series of studies showing that preschool and young elementary school children who have seen televised aggression will respond similarly to real people—for example, by hitting a human clown with a mallet, sometimes forcefully (Hanratty, Liebert, Morris, & Fernandez, 1969; Hanratty, O'Neal, & Sulzer, 1972; Savitsky, Rogers, Izard, & Liebert, 1971). Even more striking, such effects have now been shown for peer aggression. Liebert and Baron (1972) exposed boys and girls aged 5 to 6 and 8 to 9 years to either a sports sequence (neutral content) or a violent sequence taken from the television program *The Untouchables*. When given an opportunity to help or hurt another child who was presumably seated in the next room, the youngsters who had seen the violent film chose to hurt the other child for a longer period of time than those who had viewed the neutral program.

Other studies have also shown such effects in the more natural situation of children's play. A. H. Stein and Friedrich (1972) showed violent cartoons or neutral or prosocial fare to 3- to 5-year-old children over a period of four weeks (twenty minutes a day, three times a week). Children who had been above the median in interpersonal aggressiveness on a pretest became significantly more aggressive against peers on the playground and in the nursery school if they had watched the aggressive cartoons. Steuer, Applefield, and Smith (1971), in another study of preschoolers, found that children who watched aggressive cartoons for eleven days became significantly more aggressive toward others than a control group, and in some cases showed increases in overt aggression (e.g., kicking and pushing) of 200 to 300 percent. Ellis and Sekyra (1972) showed first-grade children either an aggressive or neutral animated cartoon, both selected from the film library of a local TV station. The aggressive film featured hitting, tackling, and kicking within the context of a football contest; the neutral film depicted a musical variety show in which the characters sang and danced. Youngsters who had viewed the aggressive cartoon engaged in significantly more aggressive behavior when they returned to their classrooms than those in either the neutral or no-TV control groups. This finding is of particular importance because it was demonstrated in a classroom setting, and the stimulus material was regularly broadcast TV films of the cartoon variety so popular in children's programming.

Longitudinal data. Experimentation has shown that the impact of controlled violence viewing endures for several weeks, even when the subjects' home viewing diets are uncontrolled (A. H. Stein & Friedrich, 1972). But a more direct basis for suggesting that television violence does have a cumulative, adverse effect on the young has been provided by a longitudinal correlational study which spanned a ten-year period (Lefkowitz, Eron, Walder, & Huesmann, 1972).

Lefkowitz and his associates obtained data from more than 400 youngsters at 9 years of age and again at 19 years. The measures included peer ratings of aggression, self-reports of aggression, self-reports of various aspects of television viewing, and information on family background and parental practices. The results of this longitudinal study disclosed that, for boys, exposure to television violence at age 9 was significantly linked to aggressive behavior ten years later, at age 19. In fact, of the great variety of other socialization and family background factors measured, viewing of television violence was the best single predictor of aggressive behavior in late adolescence. Complex statistical analyses by the investigators and others (Kenny, 1972; Neale, 1972) have revealed that this relationship is most likely a causal one, not a spurious association. What is more, careful inspection of the evidence shows that television violence effects were not limited to a small number of boys who were already highly aggressive at age 9, but affected the entire spectrum of youngsters with an impact that was socially as well as statistically significant (Huesmann, Eron, Lefkowitz, & Walder, 1973), as shown in Figure 16.3.

Other Moral Lessons of Television and Their Effects on Behavior

The previous section focused almost entirely on the possibility that exposure to televised violence would increase young viewers' overt aggressiveness. Clearly, this is one result that has been repeatedly demonstrated by the research. Other ef-

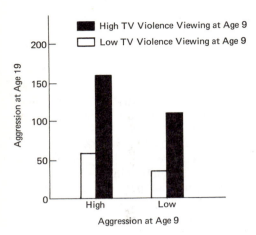

Figure 16.3 Mean aggression scores for boys at age 19. (Source: Based on data reported in Huesmann, Eron, Lefkowitz, & Walder, 1973.)

fects of television viewing, related in various degrees to the violence issue, may be equally or even more important in the child's moral development.

WILLINGNESS TO BREAK ESTABLISHED RULES

We have already noted that one correlate of violence on television is that both "bad guys" and "good guys" use violence to break established rules. Robert Lewis Shayon (1966) gives this example:

. . . it is difficult to recall an instance in which the wraps have been taken off popular entertainment's international morality so callously as in the case of *Mission: Impossible*. . . . It tends to legitimatize unilateral force for solving international problems. . . . It pretends that individual Americans are morally impeccable when they break the laws of a foreign nation. . . . The fact that they are not punished endorses the propriety of their acts. . . . Finally, it argues to viewers that a nation may enjoy a double standard— one for domestic, the other for exterior rela-

tionships . . . television writers too long have taken the easy way out, solving their problems by dubious moral standards. In a world at the door of satellite communications, it is time to introduce some international dimensions of ethical sensitivity (p. 34).

What are the effects of televised rule breaking on young viewers? An extensive literature discloses that observational learning can play a potent role in shaping responses to situations in which breaking an established rule will bring immediate gratifications or benefits to the transgressor. It has been repeatedly shown that children exposed to an exemplar who breaks an established rule will themselves break the rule more often in the absence of adult surveillance than will those who have no such example (M. K. Allen & Liebert, 1969; Bandura & Kupers, 1964, A. H. Stein, 1967). On the other hand, it has been equally well established that live exposure to exemplars who adhere to established rules increases the likelihood that children will also adhere to rules, even when they are highly tempted and seem to be able to transgress the rules without being detected (J. H. Hill & Liebert, 1968; McMains & Liebert, 1968; Rosenkoetter, 1973).

Investigators have recently determined that the above pattern of findings also applies to the effects of televised models. Exposure to a deviant television model induces more rule violation in elementary school youngsters than exposure to no example (Walters & Parke, 1964; Wolf, 1973; Wolf & Cheyne, 1972) or exposure to a conforming model (G. M. Stein & Bryan, 1972; Wolf, 1972). Wolf and Cheyne's comparison (1972) of live and televised rule deviations is a particularly important one because a one-month follow-up was included. They found that the effect of televised example was generally as potent as that of live example; both of these types of observational experiences were more important influences on the child's rule breaking than live verbal statements presented by an adult. Impressively, youngsters exposed to a deviant televised example in simulated television programs lasting less than three minutes were more likely to break the rule when tested one month later than were youngsters in the no-television control group. This demonstration that a brief television exposure can instill a remarkably stable tendency to transgress provides strong refutation of the argument that television examples exert only highly transitory influences on moral behavior.

BLUNTING SENSITIVITY TO VIOLENCE

Whether exposure to television violence leads young viewers to accept aggression as a mode of behavior is not limited to the direct performance of aggressive acts. An equally important outcome is that children's sensitivities may be blunted to aggressive and violent actions performed by others.

Support for this possibility has emerged from a correlational study by Cline, Croft, and Corrier (1972). These investigators divided a sample of 5- to 12-year old boys into high and low TV users on the basis of interviews with the parents and the children themselves. All youngsters were then exposed to a film containing both violent and nonviolent segments while a variety of physiological measures of arousal (GSR, blood volume, pulse amplitude) were obtained. High users of TV showed less emotional reactivity to the violent scenes than low users. This finding suggests that television violence had indeed blunted the sensitivity of the former group.

As in other areas discussed in this chapter, experimental research is beginning to converge with correlational evidence. In one study (Rabinovitch, McLean, Markham, & Talbott, 1972), sixth-grade children watched either a violent program (a *Peter Gunn* episode) or a neutral one (from the series *Green Acres*).

Then, to determine the youngsters' sensitivity to violence perpetrated by others, each child was simultaneously exposed to a pair of slides (one to each eye) using a stereoscopic projector which presented the images so quickly that only one could be seen. In each pair one slide was violent and the other was not. In all other respects the two slides were similar. For example, in one slide pair, the first slide showed a man hitting another person with a book, while the second slide showed a man pointing out something in a book to someone. After each pair was presented, the child was asked to describe in writing what he had seen. Those who had previously watched the violent TV show were less likely to report seeing violence in the slides than those who had watched the neutral program; this suggests that the former group had at least temporarily been desensitized to violent actions by others. Extending these results further, Drabman and Thomas (1974) have recently shown that children exposed to an aggressive television program were subsequently slower to intervene when observing a fight between other youngsters than were children who had not seen violent television fare.

STEREOTYPES

Beyond acquiring information about the perpetration and justification of violence, children may also acquire stereotypes about aggressor and victim that will extend beyond the sphere of aggression itself. In this regard it is significant that the white American male is the leading character in half of all television programs. Usually young, middle-class, and unmarried, he is frequently an aggressor. Women, regardless of ethnic or racial background, make up about one-fourth of television characters. Two of every three women are married or engaged; employed women are more likely to be depicted as villains than are housewives.

Similar stereotypes can be found in

regard to ethnic or national background. Minority groups are underrepresented and certain national groups are more likely than white Anglo-Saxon Protestants to be lawbreakers. One study has reported that Italians-Americans were represented as lawbreakers in over half the times they appeared on TV (Smythe, 1954). Until recently blacks were hardly portrayed, and then only in minor roles or as lovable clowns. Now blacks appear as stars, but the black experience in America is portrayed no more realistically than before. The black hero is a middle-class white with a dark complexion—a dauntless policeman or an ardent professional supporter of the status quo.

In presenting these stereotypes, TV does not portray the world as it is. Still, it may convey information, accurate or not, to children about what is expected of others and themselves:

Several times a day, seven days a week, the dramatic pattern defines situations and cultivates premises about power, people, and issues. Just as casting the dramatic population has a meaning of its own, assigning "typical" roles and fates to "typical" groups of characters provides an inescapable calculus of chances and risks for different kinds of people (Gerbner, 1972, p. 44).

In real life, of course, people are not simply good or bad, and estimates of an individual's moral stance can rarely be made from sex, occupational, or ethnic characteristics. Facial scars, voluptuous moustaches, and black or white hats are useless predictors of a person's decency or worth. Yet these very flat, simplistic categorizations are those that television most often presents. Rather than helping youngsters to outgrow simplistic stereotypes, TV seems to foster them (cf. DeFleur and DeFleur, 1967).

Given the stereotypic portrayals that dominated television in the late 1950s, it is perhaps not surprising that one of the earliest studies showed that boys who were high users of pictorial media (television, movies, and comic books) were more likely to invoke social stereotypes than were low users, even after the researchers statistically controlled for such third-variable explanations as social class and IQ (Bailyn, 1959). Similarly, an early study conducted by Siegel (1958) illustrated the same process experimentally. She asked second-grade children to listen to a radio program in which taxicab drivers were aggressive or to a similar radio play in which the drivers did not act aggressively. When questioned later about the likely behavior of cab drivers, children exposed to the more aggressive story were more likely to believe that drivers in their own town would act aggressively. This effect occurred after a single exposure, and may be only a weak reflection of the impact of repeatedly presented stereotypes through the more captivating audiovisual format of television.

REDUCTION IN COOPERATIVE BEHAVIOR

Televised violence may also teach children by implication that people do not cooperate with each other, that negotiation and working together are not the usual (or effective) ways to settle differences or divide resources. If this is a fact, TV's influence should "spread" to other areas of behavior. The manner in which such spreading may occur has been demonstrated by Hapkiewicz and Roden (1971). In this study children saw either an aggressive cartoon, a nonaggressive cartoon, or no cartoon. Shortly thereafter they had an opportunity, in pairs and in the presence of an adult, to look at a movie through a "peephole" so that only one member of the pair could look at a time. Those who had seen the aggressive cartoon were dramatically less likely to share the peephole. Specifically, those in the nonaggressive cartoon group shared an average of 34 times during the observation period. Among the boys in the aggressive cartoon group there was an average of less than 9 instances of sharing during the same period—almost a fourfold difference.

Implications and a Look to the Future of Television as a Moral Teacher

At the simplest level one implication of the research reviewed above is clear: Television *is* a moral teacher, and a powerful one. Contemporary television entertainment is saturated with violence and related antisocial behavior and lessons, which have a clear and, by most standards, adverse effect on young viewers' moral development and behavior.

But what are the further implications of these facts? Some might be tempted to damn the medium entirely, urging parents and educators to take private and public steps to reduce television usage by the young. We feel, however, that beyond the questionable practicality of such a plan—all indications are that massive exposure of children to television is here to stay—a blanket condemnation misses the more fundamental lesson of the research: Television does not stimulate antisocial behavior, *certain types of television content stimulate antisocial behavior*. And if certain content can teach undesirable moral lessons, there is good reason to believe that other content might be equally potent in teaching positive, prosocial, moral lessons instead.

Loosely paralleling the exploration of aggressive and antisocial acts through observational learning, an equally impressive body of literature shows that desirable, prosocial forms of behavior can be acquired and shaped through exactly the same processes. It has been demonstrated repeatedly, for example, that exposure to live exemplars can increase children's sharing and stimulate cooperative behavior (Bryan & London, 1970; D. L. Krebs, 1970a; Poulos & Liebert, 1972).

Furthermore, as was the case for observational learning and aggression, the accumulated findings suggest a continuity between live modeling and television formats. Elliot and Vasta (1970), for example, have shown that sharing can be stimulated by exposure to a televised model, and that sharing may generalize to forms other than that demonstrated. Children who viewed a peer model give away some of his candy on television were more willing to share their money than children who observed no model. An extensive series of investigations by Bryan and his associates (e.g., Bryan, 1971; Bryan & Walbek, 1970a, 1970b) has provided further evidence of the potency of televised behavioral examples of generosity on young observers. Subjects were given the opportunity to play and win gift certificates. They then viewed a televised model who, upon winning certificates in the same manner, either kept all of them or gave some away to a charity. Subjects who viewed the charitable model were more likely to share than those who viewed the selfish exemplar. It is noteworthy that Bryan has tested hundreds of children in several geographic locations, and has consistently found this result. And generosity is not the only prosocial behavior influenced by televised models. Friendly, cooperative acts can be transmitted via a television format (Fechter, 1971; Fryrear & Thelen, 1969), as can adherence to a rule (G. M. Stein & Bryan, 1972; Wolf & Cheyne, 1972).

Nor are we limited in this realm to laboratory demonstrations. As noted earlier, A. H. Stein and Friedrich (1972) exposed 3- to 5-year-olds to one of three conditions. Children saw either aggressive programming (Batman and Superman cartoons), prosocial programming (episodes taken from *Mister Rogers' Neighborhood*), or neutral fare (scenes such as children working on a farm). Effects were measured by observing the youngsters' naturally occurring behavior for two weeks prior to the viewing period, four weeks during the viewing, and two weeks after the viewing. Prosocial behavior was categorized into two classes: *self-control,* including rule obedience, tolerance of delay, and persistence; *interpersonal prosocial behavior,* including cooperation, nurturance, and verbalization of feelings. The results generally showed that self-control was increased by the prosocial programs and decreased by the aggressive ones as compared to the neutral programming; for youngsters in lower socioeconomic ranges, exposure to the prosocial shows increased positive interpersonal behavior as well.

Experimental demonstrations of what television *could* do, of course, will have little social significance until broadcasters know how to produce such programs and are convinced that these shows will enjoy popularity among young viewers in the competitive world of commercial television. It is here that we feel concerned social scientists can play one of their most significant roles in the future. In our own work we are proceeding in several ways.

One of our efforts involves an attempt to construct a code that can evaluate regular television programs for prosocial content. Such a code is necessary in the selection of programs for research purposes, but could also provide parents with a tool for assessing current programming—thus enabling them to meaningfully monitor their children's viewing. Feedback to the industry, in turn, could be an effective way to influence broadcasters' decisions about the kinds of programs they will air.

Our second thrust involves an effort to demonstrate further the positive impact of commercial programs high in prosocial content. From data recently collected there is no doubt that such an effort will be fruitful. In conjunction with this work we are also investigating children's attention to, and liking for, specific aspects of a variety of programs. This information can be fed into the production of prosocial shows which will be compelling in their lessons and enjoyable in their format and style of presentation.

Finally, as the culmination of our other efforts, we are collaborating in the production of children's programs. The first of these projects, now under way, involves miniature, commercial-message-length stories depicting nonaggressive, prosocial solutions to conflict situations. In this work, the full battery of knowledge regarding observational learning, vicarious consequences, and modeling techniques is being employed; equally important, children's understanding and reactions are being tested throughout production, a procedure rarely, if ever, employed in making standard fare for the young.

CHAPTER 17

Social-Cognitive Understanding

A GUIDE TO EDUCATIONAL AND CLINICAL PRACTICE[1]

Robert L. Selman

Introduction

The notion that the human capacity for judgment about morals proceeds according to a predictable series of universal stages is not new. As long ago as 1909 John Dewey pointed to the significance of such a concept. Yet even today few professionals directly concerned with social development, social adjustment, or social intervention in the lives of children view such cognitive-moral stages as applicable to the day-to-day business of the psychological handling of children's social and emotional behavior.

One example of this attitude can be found in the recent movement within schools toward affective education, aimed at children's development of humanistic values, altruism, sympathy, and increased social awareness. Many adherents of this movement feel that a moral judgment stage approach, concerned with rational issues such as justice and fairness, is too cold and calculating for use within a humanistic or affectively oriented context. Likewise, for the professionals wedded to the psy-

chodynamic approach traditionaly used in clinics for children with emotional or behavioral difficulties, the cognitive-developmental stage approach seems to disregard nonjudgmental or irrational factors such as fantasy, interpersonal dynamics, and unconscious drives in the explanation of interpersonal behavior.

My research has indicated, however, that descriptions of social-cognitive stages, within the context of a theory of ego development, can be usefully applied to both educational and clinical intervention. The base of these stages is sufficiently broad to be valuable in diagnosing children's behavior and in planning and evaluating efforts to improve children's social functioning.

Consider a short clinical vignette. An 8-year-old boy is referred to a guidance clinic or a school psychologist because he is continually getting into fights with his classmates. His teacher is particularly upset because she observes that when classmates accidentally bump him in the hall or during recess, he reacts by getting angry, fighting, and accusing his peers of starting the trouble. The teacher's concern extends beyond the child's development to the well-being of the entire class.

In such a case, different theoretical approaches to the understanding of human development, particularly to social behavior, would stress different steps in trying to understand this child. For example, a dynamically oriented viewpoint might first focus on the child's anger and aggression and try to analyze their source. Such an approach might assume that the child was projecting his own aggressive feelings and hostility onto his peers and then reacting in kind, or that he was displacing feelings really directed toward his father or some other important Oedipal figure.

A cognitive-developmentalist, however, would take a different approach to understanding this child's behavior. He would try first to see things through the child's eyes. He might ask whether this troubled 8-year-old has differentiated cognitively between purposive and unintentional behavior. Most children understand by the age of 6 or 7 that other people usually have reasons underlying their actions, and that their actions can be partially explained or justified in terms of these reasons. At this stage, children can distinguish between willed, purposive activity (psychological causality) and strictly mechanical, overt behavior (physical causality). Before this stage of understanding, children often decide the rightness or wrongness of an act on the basis of its observable consequences rather than on the intentions of the actor. They are unable to differentiate one viewpoint from another, or even the reasons behind the actions of others from the actions themselves.

Determining the stage of cognitive or social development of a particular child leads the professional to understand how the child looks at the world, and to avoid expectations of conceptual and emotional abilities that the child has not yet developed. Far from disdaining the value of understanding the child's interpersonal

dynamics, this approach enhances that understanding by exploring the stage underlying his behavior and by identifying the next stage toward which his development can be directed.

For the past several years I have used the Piagetian structuralist-developmental approach in focusing my research on the description of successive stages in the development of the ability to take the perspective of another (social role taking), and on the relation of this ability to theoretically parallel stages in the development of moral thought. This chapter begins by devoting considerable space to defining a developmental sequence of role-taking ability (using reasoning about moral dilemmas as the context), in the hope of clarifying the logical structures that underlie important aspects of this large sphere of social development. It then speculates about how role taking and moral judgment stages may fit within the context of a cognitive-developmental theory of ego development, and then goes on to discuss various implications of the cognitive-developmental approach for social intervention.

Social Role-Taking Stages and Their Relation to the Development of Moral Judgment

SOME THEORETICAL COMMENTS

Over the years role-taking has been studied from a variety of theoretical orientations. Research findings have indicated that role-taking ability and accuracy of social perception improve with age (Ausubel, 1952; Feffer & Gourevitch, 1960; Flavell, 1968) and that development in this area continues into adolescence (Flavell, 1968; O. K. Moore, 1958; Taft, 1955). Other research has correlated role-taking ability with psychometric measures of intelligence (DeVries, 1970; Neale, 1966; Selman, 1971a, 1971b) and with emotional balance (Chandler, 1971; Solomon, 1963; Taft, 1955).

These findings have shown that role-taking is clearly a developed capacity, but none of them has illustrated the qualitative nature of this development. In my research, I have used structural analysis to define developmental transformations (or stages) in order to describe the development of role-taking ability. Therefore, instead of viewing progression in role taking simply as the result of a quantitative accumulation of social knowledge, I have viewed it in terms of qualitative changes in the child's structuring of his understanding of the relation between the perspectives of self and others.

In defining the *structural aspect* of a particular stage of role taking the following questions are asked: How does the child differentiate the perspectives of self and other? How does the child coordinate or relate his perspective to that of another? In what way are the new differentiations and coordinations of a given stage based upon, but more advanced than, those of the previous stage? The answers to these questions define the structure of each successive role-taking stage.

My analysis of role taking also considers *content,* which is defined by the following: What is the child's conception of the subjective aspects of self and other? What is his understanding of another's capabilities, personality attributes, expectations and desires, feelings and emotions, motives, potential reactions, and social judgments? These categories of role-taking content are seen as developing concepts about basic categories of social experience. They are closely related to role-taking structure because their own form is partially defined for the child by his structural role-taking stage.

In other words, a child's development from a structural stage in which he can take only one point of view at a time to a stage in which he can see another's view as related to his own, is paralleled by a change in his conceptions of personality development, motivation, and other elements of social relations.

Role-taking development plays an important part in a wide range of human social behaviors. In our research we have studied the part it plays in four general areas of application: (1) children's general social problem-solving ability (e.g., ability to play cooperative or competitive games, such as hide-and-seek); (2) children's communicative and persuasive abilities; (3) children's understanding of the feelings of others (sympathy, empathy); and (4) children's understanding of fairness and justice, and the development of moral reasoning. This last aspect is the focus of this paper.

A BRIEF DESCRIPTION OF ROLE-TAKING STAGES IN THE CONTEXT OF MORAL REASONING

A structural analysis of stages attempts to look for the organization and order underlying thought or behavior, and to formalize the organization according to mathematical or logical models (Gardner, 1973). The utility of such an analysis rests upon the ability of others to see the logic of the stage sequences, and thereby to recognize the order as described. Stages of social and moral judgment must justify their application to social intervention and education by being readily understandable to teachers, therapists, and educators. (If only stage theorists can see the stages in everyday life, useful application is a long way off.) Therefore, it seems appropriate to describe in detail each of the successive stages of role taking as they play a part in reasoning about moral issues.

In studying the development of role taking and in devising this analysis, I have followed the open-ended clinical method first used by Piaget (1929) in his study of children's understanding of physical concepts and later applied by Kohlberg (1969b) to the study of moral thought. This method entails the use of dilemmas to engage the child in social or moral thought. Although the dilemmas are standardized, the ensuing discussion is open-ended (hence clinical). The following are some examples of sociomoral dilemmas and types of role-taking probe questions used in determining stage definition. The first two are taken from Kohlberg's original method (1969b).

Heinz's dying wife needs a special drug. He has offered the druggist who discovered the drug half-payment now (all the money he has) and the rest at a later date. The druggist-inventor has refused. Heinz must decide whether or not to steal the drug.

Role-Taking Questions:

1. Would a good husband steal the drug for his wife?
2. What do you think the husband would do if he didn't love his wife?
3. What would his wife think if he did not steal it? What would she want him to do?
4. Would you steal the drug to save your own life?
5. What would you do if you were the husband?

The second dilemma is also from Kohlberg (1969b):

Two young brothers are in serious trouble, and need money to leave town in a hurry. Karl, the older one, breaks into a store and steals 500 dollars. Bob, the younger one, goes to an old retired man who had been known to help others. Bob tells the man that he is very sick and needs $500 to pay for an operation. He wasn't really sick at all, and he has no intention of paying the man back. Although the man doesn't know Bob very well, he loans him the money. So Bob and Karl skip town, each with $500.

Role-Taking Questions:

1. Who would feel worse, the man who lent his money but didn't get it back, or the man whose store was robbed?
2. How would you feel in this situation if you lent some money and didn't get it back?
3. Why is trust so important to people?
4. What will the lender do when he finds out that he won't get his money back?

The next example of an open-ended sociomoral dilemma is for younger children (aged 4 to 10) and taps the lower stages of role taking:

Holly is an 8-year-old girl who likes to climb trees. She is the best tree climber in the neighborhood. One day while climbing down from a tall tree, she falls off the bottom branch but does not hurt herself. Her father sees her fall. He is upset and asks her to promise not to climb trees any more. Holly promises.

Later that day, Holly and her friends meet Shawn. Shawn's kitten is caught up in a tree and can't get down. Something has to be done right away, or the kitten may fall. Holly is the only one who climbs trees well enough to reach the kitten and get it down, but she remembers her promise to her father.

Role-Taking Questions:

1. Does Holly know how Shawn feels about the kitten?
2. How will Holly's father feel if he finds out she climbed the tree?
3. What does Holly think her father will do if he finds out that she climbed the tree?
4. What would you do in this situation?

Role-taking stages within moral reasoning are scored on the basis of the subject's responses to both standardized and open-ended probe questions which focus on three structural aspects of role taking: (1) the subject's own point of view, (2) the different viewpoints of each character in the dilemma, and (3) the relationships among these various perspectives. In addition, an analysis is made of the subject's conception of persons and of the social nature of human behavior, particularly his conception of the motives and feelings of others as this applies to his ethical judgments.

Stage 0: Egocentric Role Taking (About Ages 4 to 6)[2]

STRUCTURAL ASPECTS

Distinguishing perspectives. Stage 0 is characterized by the child's inability to make a distinction between a personal interpretation of social action (either by self or other) and what he considers the true or correct perspective. Therefore, although the child can differentiate self and other as entities, he does not differentiate their points of view.

Relating perspectives. Just as the child does not differentiate points of view, he does not relate perspectives. He is very likely to give his mother a bag of jelly beans for her birthday, not necessarily because he likes jelly beans or because he thinks that she will like jelly beans, but because "jelly beans are liked." At this egocentric level the child does not reflect upon thoughts of self or other. For example:

Q *What do you think Holly will do, Save the kitten or keep her promise?*
A She will save the kitten because she doesn't want the kitten to die.
Q *How will her father feel when he finds out?*
A Happy, he likes kittens.
Q *What would you do if you were Holly?*
A Save the kitten so it won't get hurt.
Q *What if Holly doesn't like kittens? What will she do?*
A She won't get it.
Q *What if her father punishes her if she gets the kitten down?*
A Then she will leave it up there.
Q *Why?*
A Because she doesn't want to get in trouble.
Q *How will she feel?*
A Good, she listened to her father.

Analysis. A child at Stage 0 is unable to conceptualize differences between one character's perspective (Holly's) of the situation and that of another (Holly's father). The child focuses on the act of rescuing the kitten, and thinks all the participants do likewise. If the interviewer refocuses the child's attention on the punitive consequences of breaking the promise to the father, the child orients to the father's viewpoint, still maintaining a consensus among characters and showing no awareness of inconsistency.

CONCEPTION OF PERSONS

At Stage 0 the child is able to "predict" or read off another's emotions (such as sad, mad, happy) in those situations where the child knows his own response. He bases his judgments of others on observable action, not covert psychological data. He lacks the social-cognitive ability to get under the skin of another person and to see the cause-effect relation between someone's reasons and their actions. For example:

Q *Would you climb the tree to get the kitten down?*
A Yes, it might get hurt.
Q *How will Holly feel if her father punishes her for climbing the tree?*
A Sad.
Q *Why?*
A Because her father hit her.
Q *How do you know she will feel sad?*
A She'll cry.
Q *Why did her father hit her?*
A Because she climbed the tree.
Q *Did Holly have a good reason for climbing the tree?*
A I don't know.
Q *Would you climb the tree?*
A No, I don't want to get hit.

Analysis. At no point does the child at Stage 0 refer to a possible explanation of action on a covert psychological level, for example, at the level of intentions (which emerges at the next stage). The psychological state of sadness is simply "read off" from the overt behavior of crying.

Stage 1: Social-Informational Role Taking (About Ages 6 to 8)

STRUCTURAL ASPECTS

Distinguishing perspectives. At Stage 1 the child sees himself and the other as actors with potentially different interpretations of the same social situation, largely determined by the data each has at hand. He realizes that people feel differently or think differently because they are in different situations or have different information.

Relating perspectives. The child is still unable to maintain his own perspective and simultaneously put himself in the place of others in attempting to judge their actions. Nor can he judge his own actions from their viewpoint. He has yet to see reciprocity between perspectives, to consider that his view of the other is influenced by his understanding of the other's view of him (Stage 2). He understands the subjectivity of persons, but does not understand that persons consider each other as subjects. As he makes moral applications at Stage 1, the child still assumes that only one perspective is "right" or "true"—the authority's or his own—even though he recognizes the existence of different viewpoints. For example:

Q *Who would feel worse, someone who lent money and was not going to get it back, or a storeowner who was robbed of the same amount?*
A The storeowner who was robbed. Because the storeowner knows somebody stole it, but the man who loaned the $500 doesn't know for sure that he won't get it back.

Analysis. The child reasons from the social fact that the storeowner knows immediately that he has been robbed to the "objective" conclusion that the storeowner will "subjectively" feel bad, but that the lender will not feel as bad because he does not realize that he will lose his money. At stages of role taking higher than Stage 1, the focus will be less on who knows what and more on the relative points of view of the storeowner viewing an impersonal robbery as compared to the old man viewing a broken trust.

CONCEPTION OF PERSONS

Whereas at Stage 0 the child considers others persons as information collectors, that is, perceivers of social data, at Stage 1 the child sees other persons as information processors, that is, interpreters of social situations. The child now understands that to be a person means to have evaluative abilities. He consequently realizes that both himself and another, as persons, can make distinctions between intentional and unintentional actions. This understanding of intentionality is a marked change from Stage 0, and it leads to the understanding of the concept of personal reasons as cause for choices or actions. For example:

Q *Do you think Holly's father would get angry if he found out she climbed the tree?*
A If he didn't know why she climbed the tree, he would be angry. But if Holly tells him why she did it, he would realize she has a good reason.[3]

Stage 2: Self-Reflective Role Taking (About Ages 8 to 10)

STRUCTURAL ASPECTS

Distinguishing perspectives. At Stage 2 the child is aware that people think or feel differently, because each person has his own uniquely ordered set of values or purposes. In moral terms this role-taking development leads to a relativistic belief that no person's perspective is absolutely right or valid.

Relating perspectives. A major development at Stage 2 is the ability to reflect on the self's behavior and motivation as seen from outside the self, from the other's point of view. The child recognizes that the other can also put himself in the child's shoes, so the child is able to anticipate the other's reactions to his own motives or purposes. However, these reflections do not occur simultaneously or mutually. They occur only sequentially. Thus the child cannot "get outside" the two-person situation and view it from a third-person perspective. For example:

Q *What punishment does Holly think is fair if she climbs the tree?*

A None.

Q *Why not?*

A She knows that her father will understand why she climbed the tree, so she knows that he won't want to punish her at all.

Analysis. The subject takes the perspective of the daughter who realizes that the father will in turn understand the daughter's reasoning (motives). At Stage 2 therefore the subject realizes that his taking of another's point of view is directly influenced by his own assumption of how another will take his perspective.

CONCEPTION OF PERSONS

At Stage 2 the child understands that the motives of one individual can be in conflict or can be ordered by the individual in a relativistic hierarchy. Because the child begins to think of others as multimotivated rather than unimotivated, he begins to see that altruistic (other-oriented) and instrumental (self-interested) motives may conflict in his mind and another's. The child can now conceive of persons doing things they may not want to do, and vice versa. For example:

Q *Do you think Holly would climb the tree?*

A Yes. She knows her father will understand why she did it.

Q *What do you think Holly's father would want Holly to do? In this situation would he want her to go up and get the kitten or not?*

A No.

Q *Why not?*

A Because he would be changing his order, and he wouldn't be a good father if he changed his mind. The father may think breaking a promise is worse, but he'd understand that Holly thinks saving the kitten's life is more important.

Q *Would all fathers think this way?*

A No, it all depends on what they think is more important.

Stage 3: Mutual Role Taking (About Ages 10 to 12)

STRUCTURAL ASPECTS

Distinguishing perspectives. At Stage 3 the child can differentiate the self's perspective from the generalized perspective, that is, the point of view taken by an average member of a group. In a dyadic situation the child distinguishes each party's point of view from that of a third person. He can be an impartial spectator and maintain a disinterested point of view.

Relating perspectives. The child at Stage 3 discovers that both self and other can consider each party's point of view simultaneously and mutually. Each can put himself in the other's place and view himself from that vantage before deciding how to react (the Golden Rule). In addition, each can consider a situation from the perspective of a third party who can also assume each individual's points of view and consider the relationships involved. Such an endless chain of role taking leads in the moral domain to the development of conventional rules for deciding between the claims of individuals. For example:

Q *Would the judge think Heinz was right to steal the drug?*

A I think the judge would have thought that it wasn't right for Heinz to steal, but now that he had done it and the judge had heard his side of the story, the judge would feel that Heinz was doing what he thought was right. Heinz realizes that the judge will consider how he felt.

Analysis. Two aspects of this example indicate Stage 3 reasoning. First, the subject attributes to each party the ability to consider each other's point of view. Second, he understands that the judge is aware of Heinz's self-reflection ("the judge would feel that Heinz was doing what he thought was right"). This awareness that each of the participants in a dyad is mindful of the self-reflective process in the other characterizes Stage 3 role taking.

CONCEPTION OF PERSONS

A child at Stage 3 knows that all persons have a conception of the shared nature of social facts and interpersonal relationships. Trust, friendship, and mutual respect and expectations are viewed as dyadic or mutual. At Stage 2, the concept of friend is defined from only one perspective: A friend is someone who does the self a favor and acts kindly from the self's perspective. At Stage 3, the concept of friend is defined in interpersonal or mutual terms, which go beyond simple reciprocity. A temporal component also emerges as the child begins to perceive consistency of actions by each member of the relationship over time as necessary to the definition of mutual relations. For example:

Q *Suppose it wasn't Heinz's wife who was dying of cancer, but it was Heinz's best friend; his friend didn't have any money and there was no one in his family who wanted to steal the drug; do you think Heinz would steal the drug for his friend in that case?*

A He'd really have to be the top friend to do it. Because I mean, you put yourself in your friend's place and you think, "Would he do it for me?" I guess it would depend on what kind of friends they have been. If they each have proven their friendship to each other, then maybe he would do it. It all depends on how strong a relationship it is, how long they've been friends.

Analysis. At Stage 3 the child is aware that social relations have a certain depth, consistency, and temporal dimension. Friendship is not viewed as an immediate process of reciprocal back scratching, but as the product of a series of interchanges over time that validate mutuality. The child also realizes that certain actions may have different meanings for different persons, based on each one's previous social experiences. Understanding of a person's subjectivity is much more complex than, for example, the Stage 1 realization of different perspectives based simply on different social information. Thus mutuality at Stage 3 is evidenced in both structure (a simultaneous coordination of perspectives) and concept of the person (the understanding that both self and other hold mutual expectations).

Stage 4: Social and Conventional System Role Taking (About Ages 12 to 15+)

STRUCTURAL ASPECTS

Perspective taking. At Stage 4 perspective taking is raised from the level of the dyad to the level of a general social system involving a group or social perspective. The adolescent at Stage 4 views the social system within which he operates as a construction of conventional perspectives which all members share in mutual relationship with his own. At Stage 3 the subject considers the activity of the impartial observer as taking the perspective of both the self and the other; at Stage 4 the subject realizes that each self considers the shared point of view of the *generalized other* (the social system) in order to facilitate accurate communication with and understanding of others. For example:

Q *What do you think the judge would do in Heinz's case?*

A I'm afraid he'd have to convict him. When Heinz stole the drug, he knew it was wrong from society's point of view. He also knew that if he were caught, he'd be convicted because he'd realize the judge would have to uphold the law.

Q *Why?*

A The judge has to think about the way it would look to everybody else. If they see Heinz getting no punishment, they might think they can get away with stealing. Heinz should realize this and take some form of punishment.

Q *Would the judge think Heinz was right or wrong to do what he did?*

A The judge is not supposed to be a philosopher. Even if the judge thought Heinz was morally right, from the legal point of view, the judge has to consider the law of the people.

Analysis. Conceptions such as law and morality are based upon the idea of a consensual group perspective. The mutuality which first developed at Stage 3 is expanded at Stage 4 to subordinate the dyadic relation to the group perspective.

CONCEPTION OF PERSONS

At Stage 4 the relationship between judgment and action within each individual's social decision-making process is now viewed as a complex intrapersonal system analogous in nature to an interpersonal social system The developing conception of personality (or character) reflects the subject's understanding that the other's thoughts and actions are a function of an intrapsychic organization of developing beliefs, values, and attitudes, and that this allows the prediction of the other's future actions and the understanding of his past actions. People may have different perspectives on internal values as well as on external social actions. For example:

Q *Who would feel worse, the storeowner who was robbed or the man who was cheated out of a loan?*

A Well that's really hard to say. You would have to know what each guy is really like. Like maybe the guy who

lent the money was the kind of guy who realized that he might not get it back. He might not expect thanks or stuff like that. Then he might not be upset at all, or just a little sad because he realizes that people may not be honest. On the other hand, if he is the kind of guy who expects a lot from people, he may really be hurt, or it may break his faith in human nature. In general, I'd say the guy who lent the money would feel a broken personal trust. You'd have to know the guys to be sure.

Some Empirical Findings

Recent studies (Colby & Kohlberg, in prep.) indicate a general correspondence between moral stages and Piagetian stages of cognitive development. The Piaget cognitive stages appear to be necessary but not sufficient conditions for the parallel moral stages. The same necessary-but-not-sufficient relation seems to exist between role-taking stages and moral stages (Selman, 1971a; Selman, 1972). Conceptually, role taking can be described as a form of social cognition intermediate between logical and moral thought.

According to this outlook the child's cognitive stage indicates his level of understanding of physical and logical problems, while his role-taking stage indicates his level of understanding of the nature of social relations, and his moral judgment stage indicates the manner in which he decides how to resolve social conflicts between people with different points of view. Moral judgment considers how people *should* think and act with regard to each other, while social role taking considers how and why people do *in fact* think about and act toward each other. The stage at which the moral claims of self and others are considered builds on the structurally parallel role-taking stage of understanding the relationship between the perspectives of self and others. If the subject has not reached a given stage of role taking, he cannot apply this stage of social cognition to the moral domain. Table 17.1 presents the parallel stage sequences for role taking and moral judgment.

My own empirical evidence, as well as that of others (Giraldo, 1973; Hickey, 1972; Kuhn, 1973; Moir, 1972; Thrower, 1972), supports this analysis of the relationship between role taking and moral judgment. For example, these studies, using a variety of role-taking measures, found subjects whose role-taking reasoning exceeded their structurally parallel moral judgments. The reverse, significantly, was not true. These measures have shown that in normal populations, role-taking stage generally paralleled moral stage or exceeded it by only one stage. In a study of young adult delinquents, however, the role taking of many subjects was far superior (by two or more stages) to their moral thinking. These subjects had a relatively mature conception of the way the social world operated, but a retarded sense of what it should be like (Hickey, 1972).

In a study (Thrower, 1972) of institutionalized orphanage children ranging in age from 10 to 18, both moral and role-taking stages were depressed well below levels achieved by normal control groups. Just as in the study of delinquents, each role-taking stage was found to be a necessary but not sufficient condition for the corresponding moral stage.

Theory to Practice: Applications of Social-Cognitive Analyses to Intervention

Because Piagetian developmental theory has been thought by many to apply only to cognitive development, its potential application to clinical and social education areas has not been realized. The chapter turns now to this question: How can universal stages of social development (role taking and moral judgment) serve pro-fessionals such as educators and clinical psychologists directly concerned with enhancing social and cognitive development in children?

From a cognitive-developmental perspective, both education and psychotherapy seek the optimal rate of development of children through social-cognitive and cognitive stages. This developmental stage perspective becomes an invaluable and unique tool, a common concept that can coordinate the different outlooks and terminologies of the clinician, educator, and developmentalist.

IMPLICATIONS FOR SOCIAL AND AFFECTIVE EDUCATION

The most common criticism of the cognitive-developmental approach is that the individual's social or moral judgments do not necessarily determine his actual behavior. Critics frequently charge cognitive-developmental psychology with a failure to consider the role of a person's affective or "gut" reactions in shaping his social conduct. Would he really do what he says he ought to do or will do? Might he not be too frightened, too self-interested, too concerned about his family? Where do feelings fit in?

While the adequacy of the cognitive-developmental approach to deal with these questions could be debated on theoretical grounds, the answer to the above criticism is in part empirical. A number of recent studies of a variety of different populations at various ages has shown that the cognitive-developmental approach in moral discussion groups stimulates movement to higher moral stages (Blatt & Kohlberg, in prep.; Colby, Fritz, & Kohlberg, 1974; Hickey, 1972). How this movement relates to behavior and to feelings about the self has also been explored (see Kohlberg & Selman, 1972; Scharf, Hickey, & Kohlberg, 1973). A summary of these studies indicates that although the correspondence of judgment and action is never simple, better judgment *may* lead to more con-

TABLE 17.1 Parallel Structured Relations between Social Role-Taking and Moral Judgment Stages

Social Role-Taking Stage	Moral Judgment Stage
Stage 0—Egocentric Viewpoint (Age Range 3–6)[a]	**Stage 0—Premoral Stage**
Child has a sense of differentiation of self and other but fails to distinguish between the social perspective (thoughts, feelings) of other and self. Child can label other's overt feelings but does not see the cause and effect relation of reasons to social actions.	Judgments of right and wrong are based on good or bad consequences and not on intentions. Moral choices derive from the subject's wishes that good things happen to self. Child's reasons for his choices simply assert the choices, rather than attempting to justify them.
Stage 1—Social-Informational Role Taking (Age Range 6–8)	**Stage 1—Punishment and Obedience Orientation**
Child is aware that other has a social perspective based on other's own reasoning, which may or may not be similar to child's. However, child tends to focus on one perspective rather than coordinating viewpoints.	Child focuses on one perspective, that of the authority or the powerful. However, child understands that good actions are based on good intentions. Beginning sense of fairness as equality of acts.
Stage 2—Self-Reflective Role Taking (Age Range 8–10)	**Stage 2—Instrumental Orientation**
Child is conscious that each individual is aware of the other's perspective and that this awareness influences self and other's view of each other. Putting self in other's place is a way of judging his intentions, purposes, and actions. Child can form a coordinated chain of perspectives, but cannot yet abstract from this process to the level of simultaneous mutuality.	Moral reciprocity is conceived as the equal exchange of the intent of two persons in relation to one another. If someone has a mean intention toward self, it is right for self to act in kind. Right defined as what is valued by self.
Stage 3—Mutual Role Taking (Age Range 10–12)	**Stage 3—Orientation to Maintaining Mutual Expectations**
Child realizes that both self and other can view each other mutually and simultaneously as subjects. Child can step outside the two-person dyad and view the interaction from a third-person perspective.	Right is defined as the Golden Rule: Do unto others as you would have others do unto you. Child considers all points of view and reflects on each person's motives in an effort to reach agreement among all participants.
Stage 4—Social and Conventional System Role-Taking[b] (Age Range 12–15+)	**Stage 4—Orientation to Society's Perspective**
Person realizes mutual perspective taking does not always lead to complete understanding. Social conventions are seen as necessary because they are understood by all members of the group (the generalized other) regardless of their position, role, or experience.	Right is defined in terms of the perspective of the generalized other or the majority. Person considers consequences of actions for the group or society. Orientation to maintenance of social morality and social order.

[a] Age ranges for all stages represent only an average approximation based on our studies to date.
[b] Higher stages of role taking and their relation to Kohlberg's Stages 5 and 6 have been defined by Byrne (1975).

sistent social behavior and more realistic feelings about the self.

My own experience with intervention (Selman & Lieberman, in press) has been with children going through what is often called latency (roughly ages 6 to 12). Whereas late adolescence can be seen as a critical period for the development of principled moral thought (Kohlberg's Stages 5 and 6; see Chap. 2), the ages of 8 or 9 to 12 can be seen as an important period for the development of general social thought and interpersonal experience. Therefore my goals have been different from those of previous efforts with adolescents (Blatt & Kohlberg, in prep.), although upward movement through social-cognitive stages remains a common criterion for all intervention.

Both adolescents and adults may frequently choose not to take another's perspective, but the younger child often lacks the ability to do so. Because of the conviction that moral thought rests on the ability to take another's perspective, our intervention programs for preadolescents have focused on helping children to understand the social reasoning of others and to relate others' social points of view to their own. To this end, we have developed a filmstrip series of moral value dilemmas—dealing with issues such as rules, trust, property rights, and fairness—to help children aged 6 to 12 move through the lower stages of social-cognitive development (to Stage 3).[4] The dilemmas are used by the teacher to stimulate discussion of values in a variety of formats ranging from small "buzz groups" to structured classroom debate.

The emphasis of this filmstrip series is primarily on social cognition—getting children to understand more and reason better about the mutual aspects of social relationships. Educating children to understand and evaluate the reasoning of others in relation to their own depends on a great deal of role taking; in this sense, our program is very cognitively oriented. Nevertheless, children's feelings become inescap-able issues when they begin to think about their own reactions and relationships to others. What would they do, for example, if they had to decide whether to rescue a kitten or keep a promise not to climb trees? The actual social and moral conflicts of the classroom, as the second- and third-grade teachers who have worked with the filmstrip program came to realize, prove to be most natural material for stimulating both affective and cognitive involvement in moral issues. In fact, our evaluation of this approach (Selman & Lieberman, in press) indicates that social educational gains were greatest in classrooms where teachers maintained the cognitive-developmental methods defined in our program, even after the actual program had ended.

Recognizing the social-cognitive stages of each child helps the teacher in several ways. First, she can better understand the behavior of her class by understanding how her children view social relationships, rights, and obligations. This kind of diagnosis also helps the teacher to determine her own expectations for her students' developmental goals. Most of all, it helps the teacher not to overestimate the affective as well as cognitive capacity of children. For example, before attaining Stage 3 role taking and moral judgment, children do not have adequate understanding of such central interpersonal concepts as trust, love, friendship, and their concomitant affective attitudes. They achieve this affective awareness only as they achieve the parallel social-cognitive stage awareness. This does not mean that children cannot act in a trusting or loving way before they reach certain social-cognitive stages. It does imply, however, that children must reach these stages before they can reflect upon and truly understand the meaning and reason for their actions in a mature sense.

The basic integration of cognition and affect is perhaps best summarized by Hirst and Peters (1970):

In most of the standard works on child development, studies are classified under the heading of physical, intellectual, social, and emotional development; but what distinguishes, say, emotional development from social development? And how is intellectual development to be distinguished from either of them? . . . Emotions such as jealousy, guilt, pity, and envy cannot be characterized without reference to moral and social concepts such as rules, ownership, and rights. . . . The tendency to disregard the importance of cognition in this area has led to the neglect of the specific features of interpersonal understanding as a mode of experience which is of manifest importance in the recognition of emotions and motives in oneself and others. . . . The result is that the development of stages in interpersonal understanding remains uncharted in any precise way; so also does the development of emotions and motives (pp. 49–50).

It is my belief that the integrated conception of role-taking and moral judgment stages constitutes a first step in the development of what Hirst and Peters call "stages of interpersonal understanding," and that role taking links cognitive to both emotional and moral functioning. To take the perspective of others is to begin to understand their feeling and emotions as well as their motives and reasons.

This approach can be just as useful for understanding the social development of inadequately functioning children in the clinic as for educating normal children in the classroom.

COGNITIVE-DEVELOPMENTAL APPLICATIONS TO CLINICAL DIAGNOSIS

Child clinicians do not usually conceptualize children's social-emotional deficits in terms of retarded moral thinking, or define role-taking gains as the aim of therapeutic intervention. Most clinicians would, however, accept "ego development" as a valid therapeutic goal. Indeed, clinical, educational, and developmental psychologists generally agree that ego develop-

ment as a concept provides a fundamental definition of the person, his core beliefs about himself, and his relation to the social and physical world.

From the cognitive-developmental point of view, ego-development research looks for structural levels in the growth of the child's understanding of the following basic categories of knowledge:

1. *The physical domain:* Conceptions of physical objects and of the relation of the self to these objects (for example, the relation of the self to time, space, and movement of objects).
2. *The logical domain:* Conceptions of classes and subclasses, relations, and the ordering of relations between classes.
3. *The social domain:* Conceptions of the self, the relation of self to others (role taking), and the means for resolving conflicts of different selves (moral reasoning).

Picture a rectangular ego-development grid. Across the horizontal axis of the grid is an array of content categories (1, 2, 3, above) to be understood and acted upon by the child. On the vertical axis is a developmental sequence of stages for each of the content areas. Theoretically, at each stage a common structural unity runs across the different content areas.

A clinical analysis of horizontal aspects of development can be of value at two levels. At the superordinate level, a child's stage of functioning can be compared *across* the basic horizontal dimensions of ego development, for example, the logical, the social (role taking), and the moral. In my own research, investigation is under way to see whether a wide discrepancy between a child's moral judgment and role-taking stage (instances where the role-taking stage exceeds the moral judgment stage by two or more levels) indicates behavioral problems (e.g., boredom in school, fighting, and other antisocial behavior) as well as structural signs of disequilibrium. Similar analyses are possible comparing cognitive and social-cognitive stage development.

At the subordinate level, a scatter analysis can be made of subissues within a given category. At this level the interplay of content and structure is most visible. In our research on role taking (Selman, in press), for example, we have divided role-taking content into various concepts and defined stage development for each of them. Our concepts revolve around the two basic categories of social experience defined and elaborated by George Herbert Mead in his book *Mind, Self, and Society* (1934): (1) conceptions of the nature of the *self* (conceptions of personality, motives, and self-reflection) and (2) conceptions of the nature of *society* (conceptions of roles and relations, the nature of "social reality"). A stage developmental analysis across concepts can yield a specific clinical profile that shows the areas in which the child is lagging and those in which he is functioning at an age-typical stage. Even more important, such an analysis can indicate areas of difficulty in the child's social and emotional functioning; these findings will complement the information gained from other clinical tools which do not focus on children's social and physical concepts.

TWO CASE STUDIES: A WINDOW ON THE WORLD OF THE CHILD

For the past several years I have been attempting to prove to my own satisfaction the actual substance of cognitive-developmental stages. Do they really exist in the minds of children as well as in the minds of cognitive-developmentalists? Can the same consistent patterns of thought be identified in children's day-to-day activities as well as in their verbal responses to the standardized questionnaires of research?

Because my interest has been the application of developmental approaches by teachers and clinicians who must deal directly with children, I decided on the case study approach of using dialogue with children as a medium for "real-life" stage analysis. Working with children with a variety of social and emotional problems at the Judge Baker Child Guidance Center in Boston, I sought to understand the functioning of the child from a cognitive-developmental as well as from a psychodynamic viewpoint.

Undertaking to substantiate a pet theory by the clinical approach proves a humbling experience. A child, in all his complexity, has a way of overwhelming the clinician with data—so much so that theory appears to have less and less to do with the total "variance of behavior" of the child. A child's developmental stage of reasoning often seems of little use in explaining all the causes of deviant behavior (and probably "normal" behavior as well). Nevertheless, my clinical experience leads me to believe that describing the child's developmental stage does provide one kind of understanding of the child. Developmental stages also provide criteria for the evaluation of a therapeutic or interventive effort by observing whether or not there has been movement to a higher stage (Kohlberg & Mayer, 1972).

As an illustration of clinical stage analysis, let us consider the case histories of two children whose behavior can in part be better understood by the application of social-cognitive stages. These are children whom I saw over several weeks in diagnostic work at the Judge Baker clinic.

Case 1: Tommy B. Tommy B. was an extremely hyperactive and aggressive 8-year-old boy with a chaotic family background. He was unable to function in a traditional public school. Since he seemed able to learn in one-to-one tutoring and treatment, he was placed in a special class with four or five other children his age. Although he was able to do well academically in this special class, he exhibited patterns of social behavior with his teacher and with his therapists that were indicative of social-cognitive arrest.

During our diagnostic sessions, Tommy would come into my office and insist that I buy him a present or give him one of the toys in the office. When I refused or was unable to meet his request, he became furious. First, he would attempt to gain his objective by saying that he wouldn't be my friend. When I asked him in various ways to define what he meant by "friend," or how else I could be his friend, he was unable to consider anything but the immediate situation.

If I complied with Tommy's wishes, his anger would quickly dissipate, and for some time he would play with his toy. But as soon as another request was refused, he would insist once again that I hated him, and that he wouldn't be my friend. No continuity of relationship seemed possible; Tommy's social relations seemed, rather, a series of individual encounters, each with its own social meaning. When I asked him questions or tried in other ways to ascertain his conception of what our or any relationship meant, he would always refer to some concrete desired object and say that he would not be my friend if I didn't give it to him. When I asked him if he ever thought about what I might want him to do for me in order to be his friend (reciprocal role taking), he showed no comprehension of the question. When I tried to help him understand his own reasons for his actions, I could elicit no signs of improved understanding.

Similarly, if the teacher in Tommy's special class did not pay extra attention to him, he would sulk and claim she hated him. When he discovered her home phone number, he began to call her up at 6:00 A.M. on weekdays and Sundays in a pathetic effort to gain more individual attention. When the teacher could no longer meet or comply with this aspect of Tommy's behavior and tried to explain to him that such calls were annoying to her, Tommy, furious and unable to see her side, claimed she hated him.

Clearly, the boy felt strong affective deprivation and, from a dynamic view, was behaving much like a narcissistic infant. However, in addition to suffering powerful affective needs and tragic desperation, Tommy lagged at Stage 0 social logic from a cognitive-developmental point of view at an age when most children are in transition between Stages 1 and 2 in both role-taking and moral judgments. In the moral domain, Tommy's justification for the judgment, "I should get X," was "Because I want it." In other words, Tommy showed no conception of reasons as justifications or causes of actions or desires. Good was what he wanted; bad was what he did not want (moral Stage 0).

In the role-taking domain Tommy had one perspective: not his or another's perspective, but *the* perspective. His accusation that teacher and therapist hated him could be understood in terms of his inability to see our social perspectives, to view the situation as we might view it, for example, to consider the teacher's perspective on receiving early morning phone calls. Not to meet his needs was, according to his precausal logic, to hate him. In this sense, Tommy's social-cognitive development was at least temporarily arrested at Stage 0. Interestingly, his cognitive (conceptions of physical and logical) development, as assessed by Piagetian cognitive measures, had progressed to a transitional, operational stage beyond the precausal level. This cognitive assessment also contained evidence of slight developmental retardation, but was taken diagnostically as evidence that Tommy had the capacity for social-cognitive development.

As Tommy's social world became more chaotic, meaningful interaction with others was becoming more difficult—a difficulty that might be expected to affect all spheres of his ego development, including the cognitive. As he isolated himself, he began to maintain his own primitive system of logic, unchecked or unchallenged by the thoughts of others (peer or parental).

Even though Tommy wanted to relate

to the other children in the class, he literally did not know how (basically, because for him friendship meant simply that other children would do things for him or be nice to him). When the other children asked for some basic evidence of interpersonal reciprocity—for example, that he share class material equally with others (Stage 1 moral judgment)—he did not comprehend, so he could not comply. Reciprocity to him meant action for the self (Stage 0 role taking); it had no meaning in terms of understanding others' subjective needs as separate and different from his own.

Tommy was functioning at a level most children pass through at ages 4 and 5. Through close contact with this child—watching him play, watching him interact with others, listening to his requests, and focusing on how he justified his actions—it was possible to see the nature of his stage of social and logical thought, and to understand something of the logic behind his behavior. Therapeutic treatment with Tommy could in turn be evaluated in terms of his progress to higher moral and role-taking stages.

Given that his cognitive level exceeded his social level, it seemed as though Tommy could make social-cognitive gains in a milieu in which he could be helped to comprehend social situations, their implicit rules, and the expectations of others. He was enrolled over the summer in a therapeutic camp at which the counselors' strategy with Tommy was to continually emphasize the reasons behind their social actions and to make as clear as possible for him the structure of the social interaction at the camp. The reasons behind the nature and rules of social games were carefully explained to him, as were the motives of counselors and other campers.

Apparently the strategy was successful. At the beginning of camp, sociometric peer ratings showed Tommy to be one of the least liked children. By the end of the eighth week, he not only had improved his conception of friendship but also had managed to win the friendship of many of the children in his cabin. A reanalysis of his social thinking indicated that he had developed a functioning conception of social and moral intentionality from Stage 0 to Stage 1.

Our structural-developmental analysis does not "explain" Tommy's behavior, but it helps to define his behavior so that a therapeutic plan of action can be chosen. It also provides a guideline for eventual evaluation of the treatment program.

Case 2: Marty S. Marty S. was an adolescent of 14 years who was brought to the clinic by his mother because she felt he was isolated and friendless. The previous year he had developed a school phobia, which caused him to miss half the year, to repeat a grade, and to have almost no peer relations. Marty's phobia seemed to be related to a very low sense of self-esteem and a related fear of the natural social environment, including peers and teachers. He saw the world as a frightening place. We asked Marty to respond to the standard Kohlberg dilemma about Heinz, the man whose wife was dying of cancer. His answers follow:

Q *Should Heinz steal the drug to save his wife's life?*
A If he loves her, he should. If he doesn't love her, he won't. He doesn't want to get in trouble and end up in jail.
Q *Why is loving her important?*
A Because, if he needs her he should steal it. If he doesn't, why take the chance?
Q *Should Heinz steal the drug if he were dying? Should he steal it to save his own life?*
A No.
Q *Why not?*
A I wouldn't . . . I wouldn't steal it to save myself.
Q *Why not?*
A I'm not worth that much. I'd be all sick and wouldn't want to be alive.

Q *What do you mean, you're not worth that much?*

A Well, I'm not important, I don't have a lot of money, for example.

Q *Would you steal it to save a pet?*

A Sure, a pet wants to live as much as the wife. A pet is a friend so I would steal it for the pet.

Q *What about for a friend?*

A I don't have any friends.

At a later point in treatment, Marty expounded his ideas on the death penalty for convicted murderers.

A I don't see why they have life imprisonment. They should just kill them. If I were sent up for life, I wouldn't want to live. Besides the government would save lots of money. Life imprisonment is a dumb law.

Q *What about from the prisoner's point of view? How would they like that law?*

A They don't want to spend their whole life in jail. They probably would want to die.

Although most 14-year-olds have developed to Stage 3 or 4 in their role-taking ability and to Stage 3 in moral judgment, Marty appeared to be functioning at Stages 1 and 2 in both areas. Although he was aware that others may have a different viewpoint, his attempt to take the inmate's perspective regarding life imprisonment was not clearly separated from and then related to his own; hence it was characteristic of Stage 1. Marty gave no evidence that he could consider the reciprocity of perspective involved in understanding that some prisoners might prefer life imprisonment even if he didn't, nor did he seem able to weigh the perspectives of self and other (Stage 2).

His moral judgment appeared to be a mixture of Stages 1 and 2. He had a very instrumental orientation (Stage 2) concerning what Heinz's attitude toward his wife should be. More significant from a clinical point of view, however, his conception of the value of his own life appeared to be at Stage 1: an equation of moral with material worth ("I'm not important, I don't have a lot of money"). This Stage 1 materialistic conception of the value of his own life corresponds to and helps us understand the cognitive basis for Marty's extremely low level of self-esteem and self-worth. The implication here is not that cognition is cause and feelings are effect, but that cognition and feelings about the self and about others are inseparable.

Differences between the level of Marty's view of the social world and the level of his conceptions of the physical world proved particularly interesting. He had good scientific ability. On physics tests similar to those used by Piaget and Inhelder (1958) to test for cognitive operations, Marty showed the ability to think at at least a low level of formal operations (Piaget's highest stage). However, his social isolation was so complete that he apparently had little opportunity to test his own social-cognitive theories against those of his peers and thus performed at a concrete operational level in the social area.

Marty's inadequate social development was clear in the content as well as the structure of his thought. He believed that the Army was watched over by the President, and that if he, Marty, were to enlist and the Army did not uphold its contracts with him, the President would sue the Army for him. Such a simplistic conception of the social system is not uncommon in children half Marty's age, and is another indication of his social-cognitive retardation.

Marty's judgmental stage scores across all moral issues were not uniformly low. He held some Stage 3 conceptions on issues of family relations. However, his Stage 1 conception of the value of (his own) life was an accurate structural reflection of the content area of his personality, which was quite fragile and immature.

Our point in presenting these cases is not to claim that cognitive and social-cognitive developmental measures should replace other clinical tools or conceptions, but that the cognitive-developmental approach has a place in the diagnosis and treatment of children.

Conclusion

One way cognitive-developmental theory may be of use in enriching the clinical understanding of social and emotional development of individuals or in providing guidelines for social or moral intervention, is to take the direction of what Loevinger (1973) has called a *strand theory of ego development*. This theoretical approach construes ego development as consisting of various conceptual domains, each with its own set of interrelated stages, together defining an ego-development grid as discussed earlier. The notion of different concept domains does not imply that ego development occurs without some unifying, binding force. A host of studies has shown that various stage measures of ego, moral, and social development are highly correlative in both a conceptual and empirical sense.

The application of cognitive-developmental theory to social issues also requires the clarification of the relation of judgment to action. A structural-developmental approach does not predict specific actions, but describes the general form of thinking most likely to underlie a wide range of an individual's judgments in a particular issue domain or across several domains. It may be true that both adults and children can say one thing (reflecting perhaps their highest level of judgment) and do another, but this does not mean that they do

not have a reason for what they do, or that there is not a structure underlying their reasons. Although there is no simple one-to-one correspondence between action and structure, the cognitive-developmental approach makes it clear that an analysis of reasoning is one necessary condition for the complete understanding of social behavior.

In essence, cognitive-developmental and social-cognitive analyses do not "explain" the causes of behavior; rather, they present a way of organizing and "describing" behavior, and this description then becomes useful for intervention because of the invariant and hierarchical nature of the stages. The stages provide the criteria that allow us to make claims about the adequacy of any structural change in reasoning.

It is also clear that applying social-cognitive stages to educational and clinical practice requires a shift in emphasis from the study of the development of concepts across persons to the study of the particular quality of an individual's thinking. This is not an easy task, but it is an essential one. Stages of cognitive and social-cognitive development will become as sterile (and probably as abused) as IQ points if the structural level of an individual's judgment is taken as a product, rather than understood as a process of social reasoning within the broader context of a given *individual child's* social experience. Stage analysis will best serve teachers and clinicians interested in child development if it deemphasizes reliance on standardized assessment and emphasizes the professional's need to understand the child's view of his life experience and to maintain with him an open-ended and mutual dialogue.

CHAPTER 18

Moral Reasoning and Public Policy Debate

Alan L. Lockwood

Introduction

Much debate about public policy issues is cast in the language of morality. We still discuss the morality or immorality of the war in Vietnam; we are concerned with truth telling or lying by government officials; we are variously urged to reorganize our value priorities; we deliberate the rights and obligations of citizens; we raise questions about the proper distribution of social goods; we consider how various ethnic groups should relate to one another.

This chapter will consider the relationship between normative moral philosophy and public policy controversy. First, I will briefly comment on why we may expect moral reasoning to be applicable to public policy debate. Second, I will present some psychological research that attempts to describe the relationship between individuals' ethical views and their policy positions and actions. Third, and finally, I will discuss the adequacy of certain moral points of view for resolving public policy disputes.

Similarities between Moral and Public Policy Issues

Certain issues are topics of both moral debate and public policy debate. Consequently, similarities exist between some types of moral questions and some types of public policy questions.

1. Both types of questions use "should" or "ought" concepts. For example, should we have bombed North Vietnam? Should capital punishment be outlawed? Should busing be employed to establish racial balance in schools? Should Socrates have escaped from prison? Should we ever take another's life?

2. Both types of questions involve consideration of what we normally call *values*. In other words, they involve defining and justifying our adherence to concepts such as equality, freedom, honesty, pluralism, and respect for others. Both are similarly concerned with defining and justifying our *rights* to life, property, due process, and so on.

3. Both ethical and public policy

questions are concerned with ascertaining and justifying the effects of proposed or present actions.

4. Both types of questions involve adjudicating between competing interests and values; that is, they are concerned with determining whose interests will be served in a situation or which value should take priority in a situation. For example, when should national security take priority over free speech? Is it right to give special tax privileges to oil companies? Should racial integration be given greater priority than freedom of choice in busing disputes? Is it right to lie to protect another's life?

5. Both ethical and public policy questions are concerned with determining "good reasons" for a course of action, and they both presume that people will abide by a decision even if it goes against their personal preferences.

There is enough similarity between the questions of ethical philosophy and public policy controversy to expect a relationship between one's ethical positions and his public policy positions. The following section discusses research that explores this relationship between people's ethical views and their views on public issues. The notion of "people's ethical views" is quite broadly construed in this context. The assumption is that everyone has a "moral philosophy"; that is, each person has a point of view about what values are superior to others, and uses reasons to justify his positions on moral and public issues. This does not imply that such views are formally elegant or the product of rigorous conscious deliberation.

Social Science Research on Ethical Views and Public Policy Positions

One aspect of a person's ethical system consists of the behaviors or ideals which he values as morally good or right. Among nineteenth-century philosophers, for example, we find John Stuart Mill (1910) valuing an open marketplace of ideas over a more controlled system of public expression, and Kant (1785) arguing for the valuing of life and truth telling. We often assume that values such as these will be significant determinants of a person's position on public policy issues. This assumption leads to the inference that public officials who advocate and practice surreptitious wiretapping do so because they value order over citizens' rights to privacy or free speech; that a mayor orders his police to shoot looters because he values property rights over human life; or that a person opposes busing because he values freedom of choice over equal opportunity.

A systematic connection between a person's values, on the one hand, and his public policy positions or behavior, on the other hand, has not been established by research. Two studies (Prothro & Grigg, 1960; Westie, 1965) which used a similar methodology assessed the agreement between what subjects said they generally valued and what practices (policy positions) they would accept. Both studies showed large discrepancies between subjects' acceptance of general values and their acceptance of particular practices derived from these values. In the study by Westie (1965), for example, 98 percent of the subjects agreed that everyone "should have an equal opportunity to get ahead," but only 60 percent said they would accept having a black supervisor on their job. Similarly, 97 percent agreed that each individual "should be judged according to his own individual worth," but only 66 percent said they would be willing to have a black teacher for their children. And 94 percent said they believed in "brotherhood among men," but only 29 percent said they would be willing to invite a black family into their homes for dinner.

Prothro and Grigg (1960) found similar discrepancies on more obviously political questions. For example, they obtained high agreement (94 to 98 percent) on such general value statements as "Every citizen should have an equal chance to influence government policy, and public officials should be chosen by a majority." However, 51 percent said that only citizens who were well informed on an issue should be allowed to vote on that issue; 54 percent said a legally elected Communist should be barred from taking office; and, depending on education and region of country, 10 to 35 percent said a legally elected black should be barred from taking office.

Both of these investigations found high verbal agreement with general value statements, but little verbal agreement with policies intended to represent those values. Attempts to find correlations between observed behavior and stated values have been even more problematic. The following two studies illustrate the difficulty.

La Piere's classic study (1970) showed a discrepancy between verbal statements and observed behavior. Attitude surveys in the 1920s and 30s consistently reported widespread white antipathy toward Chinese, and it was with some trepidation that La Piere made an extensive automobile trip around the United States with a foreignborn Chinese couple. He expected that they would run into difficulty obtaining service in restaurants and places of lodging. During their trip, however, they were refused only once out of 251 instances in which they requested service. Some months after the journey La Piere sent questionnaires to the places they had visited, asking "will you accept members of the Chinese race as guests in your establishment?" Only one respondent said he would accept Chinese patrons.

Hartshorne, May, and others (1927) carried out a series of studies attempting to find a relationship between what they called "moral knowledge" and behavior. Included in their notion of moral knowledge was the extent to which subjects adhered to various ethical values such as honesty. They devised a number of ingenious methods for observing deceptive behavior such as cheating on tests and stealing money. Hartshorne, May, and others (1927) found that "general moral knowledge as measured by the tests described, and the specific behaviors classified as deception are only slightly related" (p. 53). Commenting on recent similar experiments, Kohlberg (1969a) starkly concluded, "People's verbal moral values about honesty have nothing to do with how they act. People who cheat express as much or more moral disapproval of cheating as those who don't cheat" (p. 5).

It is clear from these studies that we lack insight into the nature of the relationship between verbal values and public policy positions or actions. The studies do not show us how people enact or operationalize their values. Loubser (1970) has claimed, "Moral reason . . . is the mechanism by which the specific action implications of a general moral principle are derived for a given concrete situation" (p. 115). But in the studies cited, we have not seen people's moral reasoning, or what Baier (1965) would call their practical moral deliberation. Perhaps insight into the *reasoning* underlying people's ethical statements would help us better understand the source of their public policy positions or actions.

Kohlberg (1963a), extending the work of Piaget (1932), has developed a system for categorizing the moral reasoning of individuals into six broad categories called stages. He has found that as people mature, they move through these stages in an invariant sequence, beginning at Stage 1. Not all people attain the highest stages, but they reach their present stage by moving sequentially through prior stages. Each of the stages is constructed as a generally complete moral philosophy with an internally consistent point of view on how ethical problems should be resolved. (Kohlberg describes his psychology of moral development and the six stages of moral reasoning in Chap. 2). If we know an individual's stage of moral reasoning, can we predict his point of view about questions of public policy and/or his public behavior? Research on this question has only recently begun, but some of the results are promising.

A brief digression is needed to identify three components of what I have been vaguely calling a person's public policy position. One component is his particular conclusion, or *choice,* about what policy should or should not be adopted in a situation. A decision to vote for one candidate over another or to support or oppose busing would be an example of a choice. A second component is the *reasons* a person offers to justify his choice. For example, one might vote for a particular presidential candidate because he believes that nominee will best be able to restore vitality to the economy, or one might support busing because he believes children should have multiethnic contacts in public schools. The final component of one's public policy position is *action*. Obviously, everyone does not take action in regard to every issue about which he has a point of view, but most people act on some public policy issues at least some of the time. The following studies relate stage of moral reasoning to the above three components.

RELATIONSHIP OF MORAL REASONING TO PUBLIC POLICY CHOICES

Kohlberg (1971a) has stressed that his stages should be construed as forms of reasoning and not as an arrangement of particular choices: "[A] stage is a way of thinking which may be used to support either side of an action choice, that is, it illustrates the distinction between moral form and moral content (action choice)" (p. 169). Theoretically, then, there is no reason to assume that persons who share the same stage of reasoning will necessarily come to the same conclusion about a particular public policy question. Empirically, however, there may be correlations between stage and choice in specific situations where the issues are clear and the consequences of alternative actions generally agreed upon. To my knowledge,

for example, no subject reasoning at Stage 6 has ever concluded on Kohlberg's Heinz dilemma that a poor man should not steal an overpriced drug to save his dying wife.

Most public issues, however, may be construed as complexes of different value issues and varied or uncertain consequences. As a result, same-stage reasoning subjects cannot be expected to agree that busing is a good policy, that a wage freeze should be employed, or that a particular gun-control law should be enacted. Nevertheless, certain gross choice-stage correlations have been found. Rest (1971), for example, found that principled subjects (those who reasoned at Stages 5 and 6) were more likely to make attitude choices that would commonly be labeled *liberal* as opposed to *law and order*. In Rest's study, examples of liberal choices were opposing a mayor's orders to shoot to kill looters, and favoring nondiscrimination in the selling of private homes.

It would be rash to conclude from this study that principled moral reasoning is necessarily equated with liberal choices. One reason for this is that some liberal choices may be justified on other than principled moral grounds. For example, one might oppose shoot-to-kill orders on the grounds that they will unite certain social groups and provoke confrontations leading to social disorder or chaos (a stereotypical Stage 4 reason), or one might favor nondiscrimination because being discriminatory exhibits mean motives and is not consistent with what most good people think (a stereotypical Stage 3 reason). Another reason to avoid hasty equation of principled reasoning with liberal choices is related to the various, and ofttimes inconsistent, meanings of the word *liberal*. To define a range of particular public policy choices as liberal, another range of choices as conservative, and another range of choices as radical, and so on is too arbitrary. The adjectival usage of the word *liberal* is subject to volatile shifts depending upon the speaker's attitude and the political climate in which an issue is raised. Consider, for example, the history of opposition to the war in Vietnam. Polls indicate that, over time, groups with various political identifications came to feel United States involvement was a mistake. If there is agreement among same-stage reasoners on some public policy choices, it is not because the choices are "liberal" or "conservative," but because particularly clear issues are raised by the policy choices.

RELATIONSHIP OF MORAL REASONING TO REASONING ON PUBLIC POLICY ISSUES

Kohlberg's system (Chap. 2) for categorizing reasoning on his classic moral dilemmas can also be used to characterize persons' reasoning on contemporary public issues. In one study (Lockwood, in press) subjects were presented with three of Kohlberg's moral dilemmas and three (then current) public policy dilemmas. The public policy dilemmas were descriptions of a student take-over of a campus building, a racial discrimination incident, and an attempt to regulate the editorial content of a high school newspaper. Subjects' reasoning on the public policy dilemmas was readily scorable in Kohlberg's stage categories. For example, regarding the students' newspaper, one subject argued, "They should have it because school is where you get ideas. It's just ideas, as long as he doesn't advocate all-out revolt. As long as an authority, a teacher or principal, is over it." This instance of reasoning can be classified as Stage 4 because of the concern for order and maintenance of conventional authority. In the racial discrimination case, one subject said a landlord should rent a room to a black because if she didn't "he would have taken her to court." This instance of reasoning may be characterized as Stage 2 because of the exclusive emphasis on punitive consequences likely to affect the landlord. Moral reasoning, as defined by Kohlberg's stages, is involved in a subject's position on public policy issues.

Many questions of public policy in-volve considerations of what laws or rules should be established as well as what sanctions should be enacted upon persons who violate existing rules or laws. A study by Tapp and Kohlberg (1971) found that orientation to the general issues of law and justice paralleled the Kohlbergian stages of moral development. Subjects were interviewed on a number of questions such as "What would happen if there were no rules?"; "Why should people follow rules?"; "Can rules be changed?"; "Are there times when it might be right to break a rule?" An examination of age trends in subjects' reasoning on these questions showed developmental stages consonant with Kohlberg's moral development stages. The researchers were "struck by the astonishing similarities" between their findings and moral stage development (p. 73). For example, from primary school children to college students, the reasons for obeying laws developed from simple avoidance of punishment through social conformity to notions of laws as having beneficial, rational purposes. Similarly, on the questions of ever breaking a rule, there was movement from the younger children's unqualified adherence to rules, to the college students' notion that moral considerations can take precedence over legal considerations. Subjects' positions on particular public policy issues were not ascertained in the study, but it is fair to assume that these general moral orientations are partly determinant of one's point of view on relevant public policy issues.

In short, the research does provide support for the idea that the moral reasoning domain of a person's ethical philosophy is an important component of his reasoning on matters of public policy.

RELATIONSHIP OF MORAL REASONING TO DECISIONS TO ACT

The relationship between a person's moral reasoning and his public policy points of view as manifested in his behavior has not been adequately researched. There is evidence that suggests that principled moral reasoning subjects behave differently from nonprincipled subjects in certain circumstances. For example, Kohlberg (1970) reports that 75 percent of Stage 6 principled reasoning subjects disobeyed orders to continue shocking a "victim" in Milgram's laboratory experiment on obedience to authority, while only 13 percent of lower-stage subjects disobeyed. Kohlberg (1970) also reports that replications of Hartshorne, May, and others' cheating experiments (1927) showed that Stage 5 and 6 subjects cheated much less than lower-stage subjects. In one study only 20 percent of the principled reasoning subjects cheated; in another only 11 percent.

Honesty or disobedience to authority in controlled experimental situations may or may not have anything to do with subjects' decisions to take action in regard to public policy questions. A major study that attempted to assess the relationship between stage of moral reasoning and "naturally occurring" social action was conducted by Haan, Smith, and Block (1968). They studied participants and nonparticipants in the original free speech movement sit-ins at Berkeley, which were a response to administration attempts to control the expression of different political views on campus. Kohlberg (1970) has summarized their findings: "About 50 percent of the Stage 5 subjects sat in. For Stage 6 subjects, the issue was clear-cut and 80 percent of them sat in" (p. 79). Finally, 60 percent of Stage 2 subjects also participated in the sit-in.

On the issue of civil disobedience, the stages of reasoning used by the persons interviewed "fit" the observed behavior quite well. Conventional (Stages 3 and 4) reasoning tended to support and maintain the existing system of rules and role expectations and led one to choose not to engage in civil disobedience. Stage 5 principled reasoning was concerned with the utility of anticipated consequences, due

process, and the contractual arrangement between the university and the students who freely chose to attend the university. As such, Stage 5 reasoning could support participation or nonparticipation in the sit-in, depending on the student's view of these contingencies. Stage 2 reasoning could also support either action, depending on how the student saw the consequences for his own personal welfare. Stage 6 reasoning, presumably untrammeled in this situation by self-interest or exclusive concern with consequences or social contract, could define the issue clearly as one of the University's violation of the right to free expression—a right which would take precedence over any particular institutional arrangements.

Leming (1974), in a situation analogous to the Berkeley sit-ins, assessed the moral reasoning of high school students who participated in a sit-in opposing the Cambodian invasion in spite of a principal's warning of suspension if they failed to clear the area. His findings were consistent with those of the Berkeley study, with the striking exception that 65 percent of the high school protesters reasoned at Stage 3.

It should be clear that particular actions in particular situations may be justified by a variety of forms of moral reasoning. Whether a specific action is mandated by a stage of reasoning depends, in part, upon how the individual defines or perceives the issues in the situation and consequences he sees related to available alternative actions. Most public questions are highly complex and lack the clarity of issues apparent in the Milgram (1963) laboratory. Therefore, a single course of action, at least for the first five stages, is difficult to predict from stage of moral reasoning.

Before proceeding to the next section, let me summarize the points made so far. I have discussed the extent to which individuals' ethical philosophies provide guidance in the determination of their views on matters of public policy. A cursory review of research suggests that a person's general values are inadequate as predictors of his public policy positions. There is, however, a relationship between a person's reasoning about public policy questions and his moral reasoning as defined by the Kohlberg stages—although the relationship between moral stage and choice of action is problematic.

Decision-Making Principles for the Moral Justification of Public Policy Positions

Most public policy issues are formulated in normative terms: Should we engage in a policy of busing? Was it right for Daniel Ellsberg to release secret documents to the public? Is it fair to use property taxes for the support of public schools? And the advocates of particular public policy positions must offer us reasons for their policy—not just any reasons, but compelling reasons which convince us that the recommended policy is morally preferable. The demand for good reasons implies that some justifications for policies are better than other justifications. In the remainder of this chapter I will discuss three types of reasons that might be used as justifications for public policy positions.

PREVAILING MORES AS JUSTIFICATION FOR PUBLIC POLICY

One might take the position that good reasons for public policy should conform with what most people think are good reasons. In politics this notion would represent strict adherence to the principle that the majority rules. Therefore, one might argue, "I am opposed to busing because the latest polls show 62 percent of the public believes busing is wrong." In a similar way, one might argue, "The latest polls show 62 percent of the people believe that children should be allowed to go to the school nearest their home. Busing involves transporting children away

from the nearest school; therefore, busing is wrong."

This conformist reasoning presents a number of difficulties. From a moral point of view, the most significant weakness of this type of reasoning is that it could support policies that we would generally believe to be morally wrong. Suppose, for example, the prevailing mores permitted genocide or slavery. Using prevailing mores to justify policy would rule out the possibility of questioning whether the majority is right or wrong—which is precisely what we often wish our moral reasoning to question. As Baier (1965) has argued, "we could not properly speak of *a morality,* as opposed to a system of conventions, customs, or laws, unless the question of the correctness or incorrectness, truth or falsity, of the rules prevalent in a community is asked, unless, in other words, the prevalent rules are subjected to certain tests" (p. 84). "The morality of the group may be wrong. The moral convictions of the group may be mistaken" (p. 89).

UTILITARIANISM AS JUSTIFICATION FOR PUBLIC POLICY

A second justification for public policy is offered by utilitarianism. The classic maxim of utilitarianism urges us to promote the greatest balance of good over evil. In this view, "the sole ultimate standard of right, wrong, and obligation is the *principle of utility* or *beneficence,* which says quite strictly that the moral end to be sought in all that we do is *the greatest possible balance of good over evil* (or the least possible balance of evil over good)" (Frankena, 1963, p. 29). The principle of utility, however, does not provide a definition of the good or goods to be promoted. These must be defined in some other way.

The major objection to the principle of utility is that it does not provide guidance as to how the good should be distributed. That is, one may be able to promote a great amount of good, say, pleasure, among a small proportion of the population through policies that promote only minimal pleasure or even minimal pain among the rest of the population. To continue with the question of busing, for example, if we stipulate racial harmony as the good to be promoted by busing, and we find that busing promotes a great amount of racial harmony among 20 percent of the population and either no racial harmony or small amounts of racial discord among the remaining 80 percent, then the policy would be morally justified by the principle of utility.

Formulating the principle of utility as the greatest good for the greatest number (as opposed simply to the greatest amount of good over evil) still does not provide a satisfactory rationale for public policy, although it does partially avoid the problem of distributing the good to only a small portion of the population. This revised formulation would still argue that it is right to promote the greatest amount of good over evil, but add the condition that this good must be distributed to the greatest number of people. The difficulty with this version of utilitarianism is that it can justify policies which, while promoting good for the majority of the population, can inflict evil on a minority of the population. For example, if we find busing promotes a great amount of racial harmony among 51 percent of the population and a great amount of racial discord among the remaining 49 percent, and all other balances of good and evil are unaffected, then busing would be morally justified according to the principle of utility.

Another problem with the principle of utility—as can be seen in the two hypothetical examples used so far—is that all questions of rightness are cast in instrumental, means-to-an-end considerations (Hampshire, 1973). Such a view does not provide criteria for ruling out some policies, *even if they can* promote the greatest amount of good over evil.

In a similar way, utilitarianism does not provide for deciding between alternative policies reasonably expected to produce the same amount of good. If, for example, racial harmony would be promoted equally by a policy of busing or a policy of placing a mild euphoria-producing drug in the nation's water supplies, how would the principle of utility aid us in determining which policy, if either, to choose? Rawls (1971) has argued that in utilitarianism, "The correct decision is essentially a question of efficient administration" (p. 27). In this view, then, utilitarianism could justify a policy of drugging the citizenry in our hypothetical situation, if, as seems plausible, that policy could be cheaply and rapidly carried out.

TWO DEONTOLOGICAL PRINCIPLES AS JUSTIFICATION FOR PUBLIC POLICY

Utilitarianism is a moral theory that is *teleological*. These theories determine the rightness of an act of policy by assessing its consequences for the promotion of good or evil. Moral theories which have been defined in opposition to teleological views are generally called *deontological* moral theories. Deontologists contend "that it is possible for an action or rule of action to be the morally right or obligatory one even if it does not promote the greatest possible balance of good over evil for self, society, or universe" (Frankena, 1963, p. 14).

Two relatively well-known deontological principles are (1) An act or policy is right if the principle it embodies may be acted upon without contradiction in all similar situations; and (2) An act or policy is right if it would be acceptable to all parties affected were they to change roles. The first principle is roughly derived from Kant's categorical imperative (1785) and the second is a variant of the Golden Rule similar to that found in Baier (1965) and R. D. Hare (1965b).

The general value of these orientations is that they require us to judge the *kind* of policy or action under consideration, not simply its known or probable *effects.* Thus, where utilitarianism might allow us to justify genocide, a principle based on role exchange would not.

The use of these principles for justification of public policies is difficult largely because of the nature of public policy decisions. For one thing, it is not always clear what principle or principles are embodied in particular policy choices; and, for another, most policy decisions will have different effects on persons in the same roles and on persons in different roles.

The problem of determining what principle is embodied in a policy choice is illustrated in the case of busing. One might argue that the principle embodied in busing is equal educational opportunity; that such a principle can pass our deontological tests; and, therefore, busing is morally acceptable as a public policy. On the other hand, one might argue that the principle embodied in busing is the state overriding the will of its citizens; that such a principle is unacceptable to our deontological tests; and, therefore, busing is morally unacceptable as a public policy. Different perceptions of embodied principles can occur in most public policy debates, and we need some way of resolving these differences in perception in order to satisfactorily determine whether a policy is morally acceptable.

The variable effects of public policies on people in various roles can also be illustrated by the case of busing. Some students will be better off, others will not; some parents will be better off, others will not; some teachers will be better off, others will not; and so on. It is also possible that most people in one type of role, say, students, will be better off, while most people

in another role will be worse off. (I have purposely used the vague terms *better off* and *worse off* because of the general nature of the point I wish to make.) The problems of role exchange as a test for moral acceptability become clear when we consider the variable effects of most public policy decisions.

In this section I have tried to show some of the difficulties encountered when one attempts to find principles adequate for making morally acceptable public policy decisions. Reliance upon prevailing mores is clearly inadequate because it does not permit us to question the rightness of the majority's views. The principle of utility allows us to judge the rightness of an act or policy, but is overly dependent on the consequences of the act or policy and may be used to justify actions that result in inequitable distributions of good or in important violations of human rights. The sample deontological principles allow us to examine the "character" of an action as well as its consequences, but are difficult to apply to public policy questions because of differences in people's perceptions about what principles are embodied in policies, and differential effects of various policies on persons in various roles.

We should not assume that moral principles can yield clearly acceptable public policies or "right answers" to all controversial public issues; however, we should not conclude that we ought to stop asking questions about the morality of public policies. Developing a satisfactory moral philosophy for public policy, particularly in a complex pluralistic society, is a formidable task, but few other tasks can be more important.

A Paradigmatic Analysis of Psychological Issues at the Interface of Jurisprudence and Moral Conduct

James C. Mancuso and Theodore R. Sarbin

Changing Paradigms in Behavior Sciences

Psychologists have noted and described the paradigm revolution (Kuhn, 1971) that is redirecting their discipline (Braginsky & Braginsky, 1971; Dember, 1974; Price, 1972). This chapter assays and prognosticates the effects that the revolution will have on the field of behavior science that treats rule-following behavior.

Future historians of psychology, we believe, will note that Kuhn's description of a paradigm revolution imprecisely depicts psychology's upheaval. Psychology's current paradigm revolution, unlike other scientific revolts, represents a rebellion against paradigm forms, rather than an effort to supplant precisely stated, formalized systems. Psychology's revolutionists protest the explaining of persons through analyzing and naming the basic "forms" of human behavior, as is done by factor analysts searching out core human "traits." Nor are the revolutionists satisfied with descriptions of an individual as an externally guided machine, through which energies are distributed to various "be-

haviors." And, except among committed devotees, Freud's effort to combine mechanist and formist metaphors has rapidly acquired mythlike status. Trait theories, drive-elaborated associationism, and psychodynamic instinct theories poorly guide the normal science of psychology. The revolutionaries turn to models that treat man as *a being in a system*.

PEPPER'S CLASSES OF WORLD HYPOTHESES AND BEHAVIOR THEORY

We hold that the paradigms prevalent in modern behavior science are exemplars of the metaphysical models that Pepper (1942) described as "formist" and "mechanist" models. Further, the current student of rule-following behavior, trying to work within these models, confronts puzzles that do not yield solutions through continued application of formist and mechanist metaphors. "Contextualist" metaphors, by contrast, promise a means of integrating the data produced by studies of rule-following behavior. Without such integrations behavior scientists will continue to provide low tragicomedy in the dramas of criminal justice systems. (Pepper also identified a fourth major world view, "organicism." Though modern behavior scientists such as Ornstein, 1972, reflect this last organic world view, we defer comment on it.)

Each world-metaphysical system approaches an understanding of events with particular metaphoric representations. The root metaphor of *formism* is *similarity*. The world is full of isolable events which a person may regard as similar. Formism speaks of truth as the identification of a similarity or correspondence between two or more things, so that statements pertaining to one member of a set may be applied to the remaining member, or members, of the set. A criminologist, following formism, might say, for example, "Sociopaths are identified by a lesion in the sympathetic nervous system." *Mechanistic* world views, on the other hand, metaphorize by references to energy-transferring machines. Further, mechanists venerate efficient causal statements (see Rychlak, 1968, pp. 96–131, chap. 5), especially when they describe energy sources as causes. To explain crime, a mechanist might say, "Arousal of the sympathetic nervous system mobilizes aggressive energies, which become the source of antisocial action."

The *contextualist* view takes the presently occurring historical event as its root metaphor. The integrated event, in its totality, is the unit of study. Contextualism assumes, for example, that a behavior scientist cannot speak of a personality as if it exists outside the context in which its behavior is transacted. One runs the least risk of violating the root metaphor of contextualism by describing behavior only with present participles: *cognizing* an event as desirable, *performing* an act, which someone is *judging* to be bad. Further, the irreducible contextualist categorical statements assert *change* and *novelty*. The very integration of conditions in the contextually perceived event will alter the context (meaning) of a future

event that appears to have a similarity to the preceding one. Neisser (1967) reflects a contextualist's approach to behavior when he describes *familiarity* by stating that "we experience familiarity to the extent that the present act of visual synthesis is identical to an earlier one" (p. 98).

Piaget's overall developmental theory, to which he relates his theory of moral judgments (1932), represents a contextualist theory in behavior science (see Lickona, Chap. 12). In Piaget's theory, stimuli cannot be treated in isolation from a person's cognitive system. Any incorporation (assimilation) of a stimulus situation into a person's existing cognitive structures implies adjustments (accommodations) which will, in turn, alter the conditions defining the context of a similar future event. Moreover, the act of designating an event as bad reflects a judgment process dependent on the cognitions of the judging person. The cognitive systems of the judge, then, are no less the subject of study than is the behavior which he has judged. No arbitrarily chosen part of the context "explains" the event.

Traditional formistic and/or mechanistic analyses of public unwanted acts have focused on the transgressor and the conditions antecedent to his conduct. Contextual paradigms treat crime as a manifestation of an individual's struggle to maintain a valid role within a social complex (Kittrie, 1971; Matza, 1964; Ryan, 1971).

FOREVIEW

Our discussion first focuses on some core problems found in traditional attempts to relate behavior science to jurisprudence. We begin by considering behavioral scientists' propensity to equate law with transcendental rightness. We then consider behavior scientists' implicit or explicit assumption of the superiority of particular approaches to moral functioning and how such an assumption intrudes into theories about the development of rule-following behavior. Finally, we consider the relationship of the first two issues to the adjudging of culpability as a function of "mental soundness." The discussion of the last matter includes an attempt to show that somewhat tenuous assumptions, emanating from reliance on the paradigms that have traditionally guided behavior sciences, have introduced almost insoluble puzzles into the most prevalent, current treatments of culpability and mental soundness.

Paradoxes of the Theory of Law as "Rightness"

Although behavior scientists have long been interested in establishing criteria for assessing an individual's ability to stand trial (see Macdonald, 1969; Szasz, 1965), we cannot find a comparable interest in establishing criteria for assessing a legislator's ability to make law. Theories are built, hypotheses constructed, and observations are made on the assumption that laws are rules that all sound people should accept, for laws are identified with being *right*.[1] Writers would present vastly different theories of law-related behavior, however, if they gave serious consideration to the position that law is *evil*.

If a behavior theorist took into account, for example, the arguments of the rebels of Attica prison during the tragic confrontation in September, 1971, he would pursue his enterprise differently from theorists who regarded the Attica rebels as crackpots using rhetoric of social revolutionaries. Contrast the language in the following statements, the first paraphrasing a statement from a student's term paper, the second coming from a standard psychiatric commentary on "crime and the mind."

People in prisons are often political prisoners. A man who is put into prison for stealing is the victim of a law that was created by those who own property, and the law was made only because it protects their property. When a law protects property and property is distributed inequitably, the man who receives less than his fair share of the property is the victim of that law. When he steals, he is not a criminal in any absolute sense; he is a revolutionary. When he is apprehended for stealing and put into prison, he is not put into prison for stealing; he is put into prison for his revolutionary activity—his announcement of his detestation for a one-sided and unfair protection of property (Anonymous, 1971).

The traditional explanation [of crime] is that hunger and economic pressure drive men to burglary and shoplifting. This may shed a dubious light on the psychodynamic explanation of burglary and shoplifting: that they are motivated by deeper unconscious drives for revenge on the orally depriving mother (Bergler, 1949) or the denying father. In our time, however, the romantic view that such crimes as burglary and shoplifting are responsive to reality needs is not justified (Bromberg, 1965, p. 231).

Bromberg (1965) sees stealing, in its many forms, as one expression of aggression, a "fundamental characteristic of humankind" (p. 95). Laws aimed at protecting property, then, become society's means of attempting to curb human aggression. If laws do not exactly embody *rightness*, they do protect society's members from our basic, naturally formed, built-in *wrongness!*

But Bromberg's implicit willingness to accept the law's definitions of events as reflections of rightness leads him into interesting dilemmas. In 1965, for example, when Bromberg published his text on crime and the mind, termination of pregnancy was a crime in most states, unless performed under closely circumscribed medical auspices. Bromberg (1965) wrote, "The problem of induced abortion is tangential to that of infanticide, . . . those elements of aggression toward infants uncovered by psychiatric scrutiny of female abortionists borrow their strength and persistence from the mythic preoccupation of women with creation and destruction" (pp. 171, 172).

Since Bromberg's discussion (1965) of abortion—"that primitive matriarchal aggression which places woman's function beyond the reach of man's law" (p. 175)—legal restrictions on abortion have been sharply modified: first by legislation in New York State and then by the sweeping United States Supreme Court ruling, which in January, 1973, overturned all state laws that restricted a "woman's right" to abortion during the first three months of pregnancy. New York State's Health Department (1972) reported that during 1971, the first full year following the state's revised code, 262,807 abortions had been performed in the state by Bromberg's medical colleagues. We are now faced with the perplexing question: Does one apply Bromberg's psychodynamic explanation to the physicians who performed these legal abortions, particularly to the female physicians?

We must conclude that laws are rules, and that as rules they represent agreed-upon conceptualizations of propriety. Laws change just as any other concensually validable conceptualization may change. Behavior scientists must not fall into the error of drawing up derogating explanations of criminal conduct. A review of history tells us that the crime of today may be the heroic deed of tomorrow, and vice versa. George Washington would have been hanged as a traitor if England had won the War of Independence.

Rather than remaining preoccupied with explaining why *individuals* fail to accept laws as rules, behavior scientists should seek to understand the antecedent processes of rule making, the dissemination of rule information, the personal acceptance of rules, and rule enforcement. They can make their best contribution to the study of law-related conduct by treating law as a *totally human enterprise*. A suitable approach would begin by inquiring into the nature of law-related behaviors in the same manner that one inquires into any other kinds of behavior. From a psychological standpoint, for example, the person defining *appropriateness* of conceptions in the social ecology is similar to the person defining appropriateness in the numerical ecology. Just as a thorough psychological explanation of how a child learns to add and subtract should give attention to the development and promulgation of the cultural number system within which the child works, so a thorough psychological explanation of how a child learns legal definitions of behavior should give attention to the development of the culture's legal system. The judgment systems of the persons who *define* appropriateness are as important to the discussion of law-related behavior as are the judgment systems of the persons being asked to *accept* legally defined rules. The behavior scientist must explain the construct system of the learner or actor in the same terms as he explains the construct system of the teacher or judge. Adequate psychological principles will explain the motivational systems, the inference systems, and general information-processing systems of both parties of the moral-legal interpersonal behavior system.

To summarize, we subscribe to the view that laws are rules, that moral judgments are rules, and that all rules represent positively valued conceptualizations of events within a person's social ecology. As *good* or *proper* conceptualizations of events, laws and moral judgments do not differ from any other *good* conceptualizations. Behavior science analysis of law-related behavior will best proceed by adopting a contextualist paradigm wherein laws are treated as conceptualizations, and within which the conceptual functioning system of the lawgiver and judge are as important as the conceptual systems of the subject of the law.

The Study of Psychological Development and Law-related Behavior

Imagine a midtwentieth-century anarchist, an advocate of political nihilism. What a frustrating experience he would have were he to search for behavior science principles to aid him in subverting efforts to educate children in law-following behavior. He would uncover many discourses, treatises, and books on how to *socialize children, prevent delinquency,* and *develop conscience* in children. Students of developmental psychology clearly are concerned not only with the isolation of behavior science principles but also with maintaining an existing social order.

The role definition of *scientist* as it applies to developmental psychologists, however, requires no commitment to constructing a behavior-engineering technology. Instead, developmental psychologists should engage in the scientific enterprise of constructing theories to account for the ways in which children behave, regardless of whether such behavior is deemed appropriate or inappropriate. A nonscientific commitment, however, can be detected within most paradigms employed to explain law-related behavior. The most troubling assumptions of these paradigms relate to the tendency to accept the premises that (1) rules relate to "classes" of behavior that are somehow readily identified, and (2) certain rule-related behaviors assume a status of necessity; that is, certain rule-related behaviors are considered to be *more mature, more rational,* or *more psychologically advanced.* This latter assumption is often tied to the former, and moral development is then conceived as a process of leaving behind one "class" of moral behaviors and adopting a new category of morally "better" behaviors, which will in turn be abandoned for a still "higher" class of conduct, and so on.

THE ASSUMPTION THAT RULES COVER IDENTIFIABLE "CLASSES" OF CONDUCT

Hartshorne and May (1928) provide the classic illustration of a study of rule-following behavior in which the subject is expected to respond consistently to a supposedly identifiable class of behaviors, "deceit." The study, sponsored by the Character Education Inquiry, implicitly endorsed the proposition that people

should not engage in deceitful behaviors. *Deceit* included (1) copying from another pupil, (2) making illegitimate use of a key or answer sheet while doing or scoring one's work, (3) claiming achievement beyond that possible, (4) taking a dime that another appeared to have left behind inadvertently, (5) keeping a coin from a large array of coins, and (6) lying to gain approval. Hartshorne and May (1928) employed a series of tests to assess thousands of children on conduct related to these "deceitful" behaviors. When the scores on these various tests were intercorrelated, the coefficients clustered in a range around .25. These figures do not support the proposition that "deceit" labels a general class of behavior, although to the experimenters (and to formist thinkers), deceit *was* a general conceptual class.

On considering the implications of their findings for the engineering of appropriate moral behaviors, Hartshorne and May (1928) reasoned:

The large place occupied by the "situation" in the suggestion and control of conduct, not only in its larger aspects, such as the example of other pupils, the personality of the teacher, etc., but also in its more subtle aspects, such as the nature of the opportunity to deceive, the kind of material or test on which it is possible, the relation of the child to this material, and so on, points to the need of a careful educational analysis of all such situations for the purpose of making explicit the nature of the direct or honest mode of response *in detail,* so that when a child is placed in these situations, there may be a genuine opportunity for him to practice direct methods of adjustment (p. 413).

This statement implies that forms, capable of bearing trait labels such as honesty, directness, or deceit, could be ultimately discovered in the situations these investigators had tested. Hartshorne and May apparently believed that the child was not properly trained to identify deceit in the multitudes of life situations in which it occurs. In spite of their findings of situational specificity, they held on to the notion that deceit does exist as a form of the "out there" behaviors, and thereby continued the grand formist metaphysic of Plato: By exercising one's reasoning powers, a person discovers the abstract good, and thus becomes a moral man.

A more fruitful approach would look not into the child's capacity to identify the good in the universe, but into his ability to define the social dimension good–bad, and his ability to place behavioral events on that dimension according to varying social prescriptions. One social group might regard copying from another pupil as morally indifferent; another might locate the pilfering of a coin at the good end of a good–bad judgmental dimension and place public self-acclaim at the bad end of the continuum. *Mission: Impossible* television scenarios make clear that acts ordinarily considered unlawful and dishonest, such as burglary, bribery, larceny, safe-cracking, and counterfeiting, are considered good when performed in the service of national security or to confound the bad guys.

The society, then, determines whether stealing a small coin, copying on a test, and counterfeiting are prohibited and therefore bad. There is a societally defined classifying dimension, good–bad, and each person learns to apply this dimension to specific acts. A paradigm built on these premises would investigate, and could offer explanations of, the probable validity of the popular view that people are generally honest or generally deceitful. The classifying system, however, derives from the context surrounding the person during his social interactions, and not from an a priori form presumably inherent in the acts. The behavior scientist needs to study the child's development of skill at working within the social context as he or she makes judgments along a personalized, but socially influenced, good–bad dimension.

The formist metaphysic exhibited by Hartshorne and May (1928) also enters psychoanalytic explanation through the assumption that bad behaviors represent a manifestation of the basic armamentarium of the biologically adaptive organism. The person's id-directed impulses, ever-present and ever-watchful for opportunities to burst forth, must be subdued by the repressive counterforces supplied by agents of society, the collectivity that seeks to protect and preserve its own integrity. The legacy of Freud's morality making has infused our court systems. Professional witnesses, trained only in the Freudian viewpoint, attempt to trace bad behavior to its roots in biological structures. Criminal acts—from violations of traffic regulations (Schuman, Pelz, Ehrlich, & Selzer, 1967) to forging checks (Macdonald, 1969) and assassination (Bromberg, 1965, p. 149)—are explained by positing a driving, unconscious, biological force that, when out of control, leads to illegal acts.

THE ASSUMPTION OF THE PSYCHOLOGICAL SUPERIORITY OF CERTAIN MORAL CONCEPTIONS

Piaget (1932) weaves his explanations of the development of moral judgments into a general theory of cognitive development and provides an excellent model for the contextualist paradigm that promises to generate the best explanations of moral judgment development. He writes:

Society is the sum of social relations, and among these relations we can distinguish two extreme types: relations of constraint, whose characteristic is to impose upon the individual from outside a system of rules with obligatory content, and relations of cooperation, whose characteristic is to create within people's minds the consciousness of ideal norms at the back of all rules. Arising from the ties of authority and unilateral respect, the relations of constraint therefore characterize most of the features of society as it exists, and in particular the relations of the child to its adult surrounding. Defined by equality and mutual respect, the relations of cooperation on the contrary, constitute an equilibrial limit rather than a static system. Constraint, the source of duty and heteronomy, cannot, therefore, be reduced to the good and to autonomous rationality, which are the fruits of reciprocity . . . (pp. 395–396).

Piaget clearly regards relations of cooperation as the impetus for the development of a personal moral judgment system which is more desirable than the system that develops through relations of constraint. Piaget goes on to elaborate his use of the contextualist's position by showing that moral judgment development also depends on the cognitive structures which the child brings to the interactive context. He proposes that a child cannot incorporate a morality system based on relations of cooperation until he first develops the stage of cognitive functioning in which he shows use of *concrete operational* thinking. Before acquiring this latter mode of information processing, the child cannot recognize his egocentrism; and he believes that his psychological perspective bears a direct correspondence to external events. This belief causes the peroperational child to treat his viewpoint as the only possible construction of events. Within this egocentric cognitive system, he cannot regard rules as a resolution of conflict in conceptualizations of regulated events; if all conceptualizations are synonymous with each other, then there can be no understanding of rules as consensually validated conceptualizations.

Rules, as guides to the judgment of what is to be regarded as good, are seen by Piaget as developing from the mutual, cooperative efforts of individuals to understand each other; the child comes to understand that rules have the character of a social contract. But Piaget, as well as others who posit a sequential stage model, unduly assumes the superiority of the developmentally more advanced conception of rules. The same assumption can be found in a study by Tapp and Kohlberg (1971) concerned with the development of conceptualizations of law and legal justice. These investigators found that the levels of a child's cognitive development

parallel his views of legal processes; they conclude their report as follows:

Those who reached the postconventional level of legal development describe a far more flexible perception of man's relationship to his legal or rule system, one oriented to principles of morality and justice directing compliance. Thus, postconventional youth viewed rules and laws as norms mutually agreed on by individuals for maximizing personal and social welfare. They judged laws should be obeyed either because of rational considerations or because they are coincident with universal principles of justice. This perspective offered a coherent, responsive guide to social change and the creation of new norms (p. 85).

Tapp and Kohlberg (1971) then declare that "The role of the educator or socializer is to stimulate and facilitate youth to higher cognitive positions. The joint concern of social scientists and law operatives alike remains: what procedures seem key or instrumental in moving individuals toward principled legal development?" (p. 85).

Tapp and Kohlberg appear to believe that principled legal development represents the most desirable form of rule-related behavior. They disparage an "obedience and punishment orientation to rules" but fail to give evidence that "moving individuals toward principled legal development" is more-or-less effective in achieving an agreed-upon criterion of successful socialization. Perhaps the achievements of certain goals in some societies during unique historical epochs depends upon these societies' members functioning within an obedience-and-punishment orientation. On the other hand, it might be found that humans cannot be prevented from developing toward principled orientations, and that efforts to produce rule-following automatons, will result only in failure to achieve their goals.

Our efforts to understand the development of rule-followng behavior, therefore, must avoid the trap of believing that a psychologically later-developing form of behavior approaches an approximation of an ultimately good behavior. Piaget and

Kohlberg provide a superb framework for understanding the development of *conceptions* about rule following, but they have not yet informed us about the development of *good* conceptions. While we might yearn to see a society of persons who understand rules within a morality of reciprocity, the fact that this kind of morality develops later in the course of psychological growth does not show that once we have achieved it, we are farther along the road to "ultimate goodness." The prescription to achieve a morality of reciprocity is no more of an a priori obligation than is the prescription to obey authority.

We would advise behavior scientists to avoid lending support to the ultimate validity of certain classes of ethical and moral behaviors. The pursuit of ultimate validity has proven to be unproductive. Scientists can more productively work from the safe assumption that societies establish the moral criteria they regard as desirable through their regulations of individual behaviors, and that societies must support the study of which social regulations best achieve those criteria, as well as the study of how to promote individual acceptance of suitable rules.

Behavior Theory and Culpability before the Law

Our society becomes particularly concerned about an individual's acceptance of social regulation when the person shows signs of having failed to consider and to comprehend the necessity of his compliance. At such points the legal systems raise questions about the "mental soundness" of the nonconformist. A person's mental soundness is a definite legal issue in such events as the drafting of wills and other agreements, as well as in assessments of a person's ability to stand trial (Szasz, 1965). In jurisdictions that have instituted indeterminate sentences, release from incarceration is often dependent upon a person's "rehabilitation"; and behavior scientists are frequently called upon to offer judgments about release from custody. The mental soundness concept is particularly significant in determining a defendant's criminal culpability. The theories of behavior science experts—usually psychiatrists—become more than academic word spinning when such experts render testimony in court, frequently on matters of life and death. Yet few scenes in the whole drama of meting out justice are more ludicrous than the dialogues produced in trials in which the "mental soundness" of the defendant elicits conflicting testimony from "expert" witnesses.

Useful clarifications of the issues surrounding determinations of culpability have been written by numerous legal scholars (see, for example, R. C. Allen, Ferster, & Weihofen, 1968; Goldstein, 1967; Goulett, 1965; Weihofen, 1957), and by behavior scientists (see, for example, Halleck, 1967; Livermore & Meehl, 1967; Robitscher, 1966; Whitlock, 1963). According to Whitlock (1963), the distinctions between criminality and insanity were hardly noted in English law until the beginning of the seventeenth-century. During the seventeenth and eighteenth centuries, the relation of culpability to "soundness of mind" became an important feature of juridical discussions. The question was directly addressed as a result of the trial of Daniel M'Naghten (Bousfield, 1843), who had murdered the private secretary of Prime Minister Robert Peel in a misdirected attempt on Peel's life. M'Naghten was acquitted on the grounds of insanity. The defense, facing the problem of postulating a disease process that affected only a part of a person's mind, had made much of the concept of *partial insanity* during M'Naghten's trial. The political significance of such an appeal caused, in the opinion of Biggs (1955), "the Queen [Victoria] and the Lords to put a hot fire to the feet of the judges of England" (p. 107).[2] The lords addressed a series of questions to fifteen judges of the common law courts; the judges' answers established the famous M'Naghten rules.

The most significant of the judges' responses were in answer to the second and third of the lords' questions:

What are the proper questions to be submitted to the jury, where a person alleged to be afflicted with insane delusion respecting one or more particular subjects or persons, is charged with the commission of a crime (murder, for example) and insanity is set up as a defense?

In what terms ought the question be left to the jury as to the prisoner's state of mind at the time when the act was committed? ("Daniel M'Naghten's Case," 1901, p. 720)

The judges responded:

As these two questions appear to us to be more conveniently answered together, we have to submit our opinion to be that the jurors ought to be told in all cases that every man is to be presumed to be sane, and to possess a sufficient degree of reason to be responsible for his crimes, until the contrary be proved to their satisfaction; and that to establish a defence on the ground of insanity, it must be clearly proved that, at the time of committing the act, the party accused was labouring under such a defect of reason, and from disease of the mind, as not to know the nature and quality of the act he was doing or, if he did know it, that he did not know he was doing what was wrong. The mode of putting the latter part of the question to the jury on these occasions has generally been, whether the accused at the time of doing the act knew the difference between right and wrong: which mode, though rarely, if ever, leading to any mistake with the jury, is not, as we conceive, so accurate when put generally and in the abstract, as when put with reference to the party's knowledge of right and wrong in respect to the very act with which he is charged . . . ("Daniel M'Naghten's Case," 1901, pp. 722–723).

With this statement in hand, the legal systems of the English-speaking nations began the task of clarifying the meaning of the M'Naghten rules. The greatest confusion has come from the terms *disease of the mind, know,* and *wrong.* Behavior scientists have tried to lift the curtain of obscurity from the first two terms, while

legal scholars have wrestled with the third. The vocabulary is derived from psychological models that, for the most part, were unchallenged. For example, scholars persist in regarding *mind* as a formistic entity, rather than as a convenient metaphor. The confusions surrounding the M'Naghten rules can be traced to the failure to replace the outworn psychological conceptions underlying English law with the more useful paradigms being developed through viewing behaving people as cognizers, or information processors.

DEFINING THE TERM "WRONG"

Perhaps as long as men become attached to particular theological or ethical beliefs, there will be philosophers who postulate an "ultimate morality." Similarly, judges will be found to defend the position that some ultimate morality underlies the law and that people ought to "know" it. Thus, judges will sometimes try to define the term *wrong.* The following quotation from Robitscher (1966) is illustrative; the case involved a man who had killed a prostitute and who averred that he had responded to the Divine's will that she be sacrificed in atonement.

In this case (*People* v. *Schmidt*), which has since been the law of New York, the court concluded that the "wrong" of the M'Naghten rule ought not be and was not meant to be limited to legal wrong. (The defendant, appealing his conviction, said that his real offense had not been murder, but manslaughter, and that he had confessed to the greater crime and then feigned insanity in order to protect abortion ring confederates.) Judge Cardozo ruled that the lower court had erred in finding him guilty because it should have been dealing with the concept of moral wrong not legal wrong—and it is not morally wrong to murder if voices say this is a religious necessity. (But, since in his appeal the defendant had admitted feigning insanity, Cardozo did not set aside the conviction.) (p. 58)

N. Morris and Hawkins (1970) propose a very clean solution to the issue of defining "wrong" in instances involving the insanity plea. They would issue the following "ukase": "The defense of insanity shall be abolished. The accused's mental condition will be relevant to the question of whether he did or did not, at the time of the crime, have the *mens rea* of the crime of which he is charged" (p. 174). In short, these writers would ask only, as would the proponents of the American Law Institute's *Model Penal Code*, "Did the transgressor appreciate the *criminality* of his conduct?" (American Law Institute, 1962, p. 66; emphasis added). This approach, as Weihofen (1957) notes, "would resolve one big ambiguity in the right-and-wrong test by abandoning the vague word 'wrong' and substituting 'criminality' " (p. 64).

To substitute the term "criminal" for the term "wrong" rejects the formist and mechanist paradigms which have traditionally guided the discussion of inability to differentiate right from wrong. This substitution would, by no means, eliminate all the problems related to determinations of a transgressor's ability to cognize the illegality of his act. Such a resolution does, once again, remind us of the comprehensiveness of explanations from a contextual paradigm. Judgments of the soundness of a person's cognizing abilities, relative to his ability to discriminate *legal* from *illegal* acts, might force considerations of the clarity with which law givers have drawn the distinction between legal and illegal. Additionally, this approach promotes recognition that laws result from a human enterprise, rather than being a formalization of objective goodness.

BEHAVIOR SCIENCE AND THE "DISEASED MIND"

Lacking an unequivocal definition of *diseased mind* and *mental illness* sorely complicates the behavior scientist's task of determining the extent to which these presumed entities can interfere with a person's ability to understand and deal with legal issues. At one time, most alienists (the name for the precursors of modern forensic psychiatrists) might have agreed that aberrant behavior derived from pathological physiological substrata. The hope then could be maintained that some day an accurate test for a diseased mind would be found and administered as easily as counting heartbeats or recording body temperatures. The results of such a test would allow a physician to declare confidently whether a defendant's mental state could or could not interfere with his judgment regarding the propriety of a given act.

Such hope has not completely died. Today, some behavior theorists offer complex formulations regarding the presumed connections between improper behavior and biology. H. J. Eysenck (Chap. 6) stands as one of the foremost of these theorists, but even he has not been able to develop convincing evidence that variations in individual conditionability are associated in any clear-cut way with physiological functioning. These theorists can, of course, maintain that a vast plexus of mystery remains to be unravelled by their physiological research.

Meehl (1970) offers a colorful set of hypotheses linking crime and physiology in a way that enhances optimism about the potential of physiological psychology for solving the culpability problem:

Given only a little advancement in our knowledge of the brain and our electronic instrumentation, it will be feasible to have implanted electrodes appropriately placed in the brain of a chronic recidivist that will reveal the fact that he is approaching a potentially dangerous state of rage readiness, or sexual arousal, or anxiety level nearing panic, or other states which in his case are a major factor in producing episodes of antisocial conduct. This cerebral "danger signal" could either be monitored by a central receiving station—sort of a computerized parole officer!—or the patient trained to respond to his own electro-therapist by pushing the right button on his equipment to "turn off the undesirable state." He might even be wired directly so that such a dangerous brain-signal would give rise, in the apparatus worn, to an appropriate "turn-off" electronic input, thus bypassing the patient's own volition as well as any decision by the central monitoring agency (p. 14).

When the kinds of linkages envisioned by Meehl are more thoroughly researched and understood, behavior scientists will be better able to discuss culpability in criminal behavior. Following Meehl's theory (1970), a person who commits a sex crime while impelled by a "potentially dangerous state of . . . sexual arousal" would not be held culpable where the principle of irresistible impulse is legally admissible—particularly if a pathologist could show that such dangerous sexual arousal developed through the functioning of anomalously formed central nervous system nuclei.

Unfortunately, we can only cautiously endorse the optimism that leads Meehl to believe that "only a little advancement in our knowledge" separates the current parole system from the "computerized parole officer." Many gaps in the theory need to be filled, and considerably more research is necessary to establish the accuracy of Meehl's assumptions. For example, research has yet to show that rage in a human interaction is preceded by a detectable cerebral danger signal. Furthermore, several investigations have called into question the utility of so hallowed a mechanistic concept as direct "sexual arousal" (Fisher, 1962; Fowler & Whalen, 1961).

Psychological assumptions similar to Meehl's ideas about "dangerous brain signals" underlie the work of other crime theorists. Bromberg's psychoanalytic theory (1965) that improper and illegal behavior derives from impulses has been used by many other behavior scientists to explain the etiology of criminal acts. In a sense, then, Meehl's position, a mixture of formism and mechanism, follows the view that a "diseased mind" represents an anomaly of the centers where impulses are generated. Should a direct relationship between the psychoanalytic concept of *impulse* and physiological function or anatomical structure be empirically demonstrated, "diseased mind" might then be used as an appropriate causal entity.

A student of criminal behavior could dispense with the mechanist metaphors of psychoanalysis which liken an uncontrolled impulse to a team of spirited horses dragging off a helpless driver, and instead speak of a diseased mind as a matter of malfunctioning neural structures. The court expert, when theory advances to the point envisioned by Meehl, could offer into evidence the kinds of electrical readings that are the stock in trade of neurophysiologists, as well as x-ray films and similar studies.

The notion of physiological substrata, we hasten to add, is not widely held as an explanation of criminal behavior. Most commentary on the association between "mental disease" and crime reflects the continuing struggle surrounding the definition of "mental illness." This debate, reflecting a major paradigm revolution in the behavior sciences, addresses itself to the question, Has the medical metaphor "diagnosis" any utility when we confront instances of unwanted conduct?

We note one point from the arguments against the continued use of the medical metaphor. Any careful observer of the "mental health" scene must concur that the diagnosis of "mental illness" derives mainly from the diagnostician's observations of behavior. Interview and clinical tests used by the psychodiagnostician do no more than produce behavior which is then used as data. The diagnostician may also review historical material to further assess the behavior of the subject. The diagnostic procedure then requires that the expert draw inferences about the "etiology" which might underlie the behaviors, now called "symptoms." In medical practice, further clinical tests frequently reveal reliable evidence of other associated symptoms and etiological factors. In psychodiagnosis, however, there simply are no instances where symptoms (the "pathological" behavior) can be reliably related to cause. Psychodiagnosis, then, reduces to a process which simply allows a behavior analyst to pronounce the presence of a deviant behavior, and to state that such behavior is "illness." In other words, psychodiagnosis is a professional justification of stigmatization.

The infelicity of using the medical metaphor in this fashion can be observed in the use of the diagnostic category *antisocial personality*. Current textbooks of psychiatry and abnormal psychology (L. C. Kolb, 1968, pp. 503–508; Vetter, 1972, chap. 9), as well as the American Psychiatric Association's *Diagnostic and Statistical Manual of Mental Disorders* (1968), discuss the "syndrome" associated with this label. "This term," the manual notes, "is reserved for individuals who are basically unsocialized and whose behavior pattern brings them repeatedly into conflict with society" (p. 43). Thus, the very fact that one commits an act adjudged to be a crime may serve as evidence for the psychodiagnostician that the actor suffers from a mental disorder. Any further diagnostic effort, we have argued, merely catalogs the other unwanted behaviors, whereupon the diagnostician tautologically confirms the presence of an underlying disease.

The well-known ruling in *Durham* v. *United States* (1954) epitomizes the circularity of efforts to clarify the term *diseased mind* as it affects legal culpability.

The rule we now hold [is] simply that an accused is not criminally responsible if his unlawful act was the product of mental disease or mental defect.

We use "disease" in the sense of a condition which is considered capable of either improving or deteriorating and which may be either congenital or the result of injury or the residual effect of a physical or mental disease (pp. 874–875).

How would a diagnostician decide that the defendant has a mental disease? Presumably he would ask questions that give the defendant an opportunity to demonstrate that he believes strange things. The diagnostician might question others or read records compiled about the defendant.

Information would be sought to show that the crime was not a singular piece of undesirable behavior. If convinced that the defendant regularly behaves badly, the diagnostician would announce that his subject suffers a "condition which is considered capable of either improving or deteriorating"; that is, that the defendant either will desist, henceforth, from performing illegal acts or will continue to perform illegal acts. In short, the diagnostician will determine whether the defendant is a chronic norm violator. If he is, the courts which follow *Durham* v. *United States* should decide that the defendant is not criminally responsible.

The disease model, which had its greatest utility, and success, in establishing the efficient cause statements required in mechanistic paradigms, has served poorly in explaining unwanted behavior. The causes of "diseases of the mind" have not been established, and one cannot draw much encouragement from progress toward establishing causal connections between malformed or malfunctioning neural systems and particular "resultant" behaviors. Specifically, there has been no evidence for the proposition that any particular class of criminal behavior is "the product of a mental disease or mental defect." And, having failed to duplicate the mechanist's success in stating efficient causality, behavior scientists must beware of slipping into using tautological formist causal statements such as "criminal behavior is caused by a person's criminal tendencies," or "aggression is caused by XYY types" (see Sarbin, 1967, 1969, for discussion of the concept of criminal types).

THE CONDITIONS OF "KNOWING"

The third obfuscating item in the M'Naghten formula is the term *know*. How does a behavior scientist determine if a person *knows*, or *knew*, the difference between right and wrong? Classically, one could test whether a person has a construct such as right–wrong through a discrimination task, such as that used by Kendler and Kendler in their investigations of reversal shift learning (see Kendler & Kendler, 1962, 1969, for reviews of these studies). In the Kendler task, a person is required to learn to choose from a set of stimuli the stimulus that the experimenter indicates to be "correct." The subject demonstrates that he knows when he successfully discriminates along a particular dimension by continually choosing the correct stimulus. In the typical reversal shift experiment, a child might be asked to select the approval-obtaining stimulus from an array of four stimuli. Two of the stimuli might be small, one might be black, the other white. The array might also contain one large black stimulus and one large white stimulus. If the child can on instruction continuously choose the small stimulus, regardless of color, an investigator can reasonably claim that the child knows the difference between small and large.

A similar procedure could test a defendant's ability to cognize events in terms of right and wrong. A defendant might, for example, view filmed behavior sequences and then be asked to arrange such stimulus material along a legal right–wrong continuum. Jurists and psychologists presumably would embrace such a straightforward test of ability to discriminate along a right–wrong dimension.

Apparently, however, the test of ability to differentiate right from wrong measures, to most jurists, an ability to know which acts *should* be considered wrong and which acts *should* be considered right. The test, then, is not to determine whether an individual discriminates along a personal right–wrong construct, but whether the defendant can succeed in sorting right acts from wrong acts by using an arbitrary moral sorting criterion that is considered "proper" by those who make and enforce the rules.

In the case of the *People* v. *Schmidt* (1965), discussed above, Schmidt's attorney claimed that his client had heard voices which had instructed him to murder the victim. This defense did not persuade the lower court, which decided that Schmidt had the ability to discriminate between *legal* definitions of right and wrong. Cardozo ruled that the court should have ruled on the basis of whether the defendant could discriminate between *moral* definitions of right and wrong.

Suppose the court had initially followed Cardozo's ruling. The fact that Schmidt claimed that a prostitute deserved death as an expiation for her wrong indicates that he was, indeed, discriminating along some right–wrong continuum. If so, Schmidt would not be excused from culpability.

Could Schmidt differentiate *the* right from *the* wrong? Would he, in applying his personal construct of right–wrong, obtain general agreement from others regarding his judgment of the rightness of *his* murderous act? These, obviously, are questions of a different order. Following our earlier assumptions, we would hold that Schmidt, like every other human, was unable to differentiate *the* right from *the* wrong. He could only say what was right and wrong to him.

Unfortunately, in their liberalizing efforts, behavior scientists and legal scholars have not been asking whether an accused can discriminate along a personal right–wrong continuum. They have been asking rather, "Can the defendant conceptualize his behavior along a right–wrong continuum defined by the agents of the power structure?" Writers have rather blindly assumed that the personal right–wrong continuum of powerful others represents a reasonable facsimile of a transcendent right–wrong continuum. By responding to questions about disease and culpability as formulated in traditional models, behavior scientists ingenuously enter the political arena. What is more, by accepting the basic formist assumption that people whose minds are rightly formed have a naturally given human ability to distinguish right from wrong, behavior scientists abandon their basic responsibility to make explicit their understanding of *knowing*. Psychological explanation no longer can naively accept the realist's position that judgments, or any other kinds of cognizing experiences, reflect a passive—if representationally transformed—and direct mirroring of stimulus events. A behavior scientist must face his obligation to state what he means by *know* when he speaks of knowing right from wrong. And legal professionals are obligated to recognize that the behavior scientist must explicate his position on *knowing*.

RECAPITULATION

Confusion permeates efforts to determine the mental conditions that might mitigate legal culpability. This confusion derives, for the most part, from failure to clarify whether law represents rightness. There would be less confusion if the behavior science expert were called upon to determine the defendant's responsibility by deciding if he could recite the law—thus testing whether the person possessed the ability to discriminate *legal* from *illegal*. Current developmental psychology offers theoretical outlines through which such assessment can be approached (Tapp, 1971).

Conclusions Regarding Jurisprudence and Moral Conduct

This discourse had observed three recurring sources of ambiguity in the area where behavior science theory relates to jurisprudence. These sources are (1) the treatment of law as a reflection of universal *goodness*, (2) the related practice of discussing the development of personal rule-following behavior as the development of an ultimately superior approach to proper conduct, and (3) the delimiting of the conditions under which an individual can be exempted from being accountable for his failure to act in accordance with the law.

Throughout this discussion we have argued that the failures to reach clarity on these issues reflect deficiencies in the paradigms traditionally used to formulate experimental questions and responses. Psychological theory has been understandably improvisational. It has borrowed heavily from paradigms existing in the common language structure, and has sought its scientific accreditation by tying into the mechanistic formulas of physics and biology. The current language of ethics and of the law, moreover, is founded on several thousand years of formistic thought. Goodness and its counterpart, the law, have been seen to emanate from extrahuman, universal regulatory powers. Man's ability to identify immanent goodness has also been regarded as a gift granted by universal powers.

Behavior scientists, being called to explain how persons develop or fail to develop positive regard for rules, have haplessly offered explanations from within the same paradigms used by the guardians of moral propriety. Explanations of failures to achieve social conformity have frequently relied on formist constructs such as "weakness of the will." With the triumph of Darwinism, a scientist could "biologize sin" and discourse on ethics by speaking of the "human nature to aggress." The psychologist, then, has no difficulty moving from Darwinism to a mixed formist-mechanist model by treating aggression, for example, as an energic quantum that resists repression.

Either the formist or the mechanist paradigm can be translated into a seemingly liberalized position on crime. To save a body from the flames, the ax, or the noose, the behavior theorist can draw an analogy between bloody sputum and bloody murder. The criminal is no more responsible for his "symptom," the murder, than is the tubercular for his symptom, the bloody sputum; both symptoms are the result of identifiable causes, and both have been predetermined in mechanistic terms.

Having become uneasy with these overextended metaphors, the behavior scientist can turn to a paradigm that frees him from many of the dilemmas created by formist and mechanist approaches, and that also promises a coherent explanation of law-following behavior. Contextualist paradigms are available as useful guides to the study of rule following.

Let it first be clear that the advocacy of a contextualist metaphysic as a guide to the conduct of the behavior scientist, *qua* scientist, is not an advocacy of a contextual metaphysic as a guide to evaluating the moral behavior of those being studied. We have taken the position that our science does not lead us into recommending the superiority of any ethical system. We are recommending procedural contextualism, not doctrinaire contextualism. The ethical systems of social groups, our contextualist approach suggests, are best studied by considering the group's goals. Thus, the group's constructions of morality become the focus of our study, and our position is one of relativism. If the group, nevertheless, espouses an authoritarian approach to morality, the scientist meets his obligation as a citizen by opposing this orientation. As a *scientist,* however, he is required to study the *process* of moral functioning, whatever the goals of the society.

Contextualist theorists like G. Kelly (1955), G. H. Mead (1934), and Piaget (1932) have stressed the undesirability of isolating the person from his context as we attempt to explain his individual psychology. Piaget's classic work (1932; see also Lickona, Chap. 12) best exemplifies the applications of contextualism in explanations of moral judgment. Within this theory, which stresses differences in personal modes of processing morality-related information, one must consider the individual's cognitive orientations toward the rules promulgated. The theory also emphasizes the social contexts that generate both the rules and the person's cognitive orientations. Further, use of Piaget's theory forces behavior analysts to recognize the importance of a person's

perceptions of other people's perceptions during rule-making and rule-enforcing interactions. It is from the empirical verifications of Piaget's theory, for example, that we conclude that a child who operates in the egocentric mode, as a prisoner of his own perceptions, cannot conceptualize rule making as facilitating social interaction among persons who have different perspectives on a particular event.

The repeated confirmations of the explanatory utility of Piaget's theory argues for its utility as a contextualist's guide to discussions of legal culpability. From this paradigm an expert witness would ask and try to respond to such questions as, Was the individual able to judge the rightness or wrongness of an event by taking into account the perspectives of other persons? Can the transgressor recognize that another person's conceptualizations might be as valid as his own? Did the lawmakers make clear the efficacy of following the course of action prescribed by their evaluation of the goodness or badness of the behavioral events circumscribed by the law? Indeed, can such efficacy be claimed for existing laws? And, in what ways did the lawmakers assure that an accused would have access to explanations of the purposes of the law?

To advocate the use of a contextualist paradigm asks for *consideration of the total ecology of rule-following conduct.* Analytic judgments of a behaving person who has been charged with theft, for example, must scrutinize the context within which the concept of theft was invented; the conditions under which legislators and jurists have defined certain acts, and not others, as theft; the multifarious conditions under which law enforcement personnel categorize and react to an act as theft.

The recognition of the complexities of practically implementing a contextualist view of moral conduct may lead to despair among behavior scientists charged with putting order into a confusing realm of events. Our support of a contextualist view stems basically from being convinced of the emptiness of mechanist and formist views of rule following. The concept of legal culpability, for example, needs to be totally revised; but we see little promise of revision so long as the current timeworn and tattered concepts of formist and mechanistic determinism shackle our thought (see Mancuso, 1972a, 1972b). As a last resort, the despairing behavior scientist can declare that he will not participate in legal processes that require him to respond to questions derived from such outworn paradigms.

Our closing commentary on the interfaces of behavior science and jurisprudence cites a recent dramatic example of using the illness metaphor to explain the act of a man accused of fratricide, a violation of a most ancient law. Lester Zygmaniak shot his older brother George to death, because George's spinal cord had been severed at the cervical level following a motorcycle accident. Lester, in moving testimony, recounted his response to his brother's plea for death. Two defense psychiatrists—facing the opposition of a prosecution psychiatrist—declared that Lester had suffered a temporary psychotic reaction at the time of the transgression and therefore was not accountable for his act, since he had been deprived of his ability to understand its nature. One of the defense psychiatrists was quoted as follows in the New York Times (Johnston, 1973): "His brain was functioning under an impaired condition and it could not function normally" (p. 41). The jury acquitted Lester Zygmaniak on the ground of his temporary insanity, and released him from custody on the ground that he had regained his sanity.

Do behavior scientists advance their discipline by such strange public acts? Has the functioning of the legal system been enhanced by the expedient of stigmatizing Zygmaniak as temporarily insane? Is Zygmaniak's conduct effectively explained by speaking about debilitated organic structures? This chapter presses the point that behavior scientists, when collaborating with legal professionals, must insist that acts such as Zygmaniak's be considered within the perspective of the purpose and origins of law about homicide, within the conception of living held by persons such as the closely tied brothers, and in terms of the compassion that the man felt toward his incapacitated brother. Indeed, from this perspective, Zygmaniak's defense might better have been, "Not guilty by reason of love."

CHAPTER 20

The Social Ecology of Violence[1]

Gilbert Geis and John Monahan

Introduction

"I was trying to learn to write, commencing with the simplest things," Ernest Hemingway (1932, p. 2) notes in *Death in the Afternoon,* "and one of the simplest things of all and the most fundamental is violent death." Hemingway's preoccupation with violence—both in his fiction and in his personal life—has been traced to his severe wounding during World War I while he was serving on the Fossalta front with the Italian Army (Young, 1966). Thereafter, Hemingway catharsized his terrible anxiety about violent death as best he could by vicarious expeditions on paper and real encounters in life against that specter that seemed to threaten at any moment to overwhelm him. Violence, as Hemingway saw it, forced a human to demonstrate grace in the face of terror, and dignity in the face of devastation; to be wanting in these qualities was for Hemingway the most desperate and despicable thing that could happen to a person. At the end, Hemingway almost inevitably chose to meet death violently; to kill himself rather than to face continuing physical and mental deterioration (Baker, 1969).

The challenge that violence poses to its objects, the theme that fascinated Hemingway, is one of its major elements. There are other facets too: violence can be viewed in terms of its perpetrators, its goals, its achievements, its manifestations as a collective phenomenon, and its situational context. It can also be regarded in terms of its social and legal definitions and in terms of attempts to predict and head off its occurrence. Components such as these constitute what we call here *the social ecology of violence.*

Our aim is to examine attributes of violence in order to generalize about some of the relationships between morality and violence. We will attempt to persuade readers that definitions of what constitutes violence provide telling information about the distribution and employment of power. We will argue that violence is a multi-faceted activity (S. Feshbach, 1971), of which only some kinds have been singled out for elaborated definition and retributive response. Violence, as Skolnick (1969) points out, "is an ambiguous term whose meaning is established through political processes" (p. 4). In our judgment, some of today's meanings of violence are reasonable, as when the law proscribes traditional criminal offenses such as murder, forcible rape, and armed robbery, and allows a reasonable degree of retaliatory violence to be employed for self-defense. However, when other kinds of devastating and often lethal consequences fail to be embraced and understood within definitions of violence, the situation seems to us both unreasonable and immoral. To illustrate this point we will advert to a case involving the deaths of more than a dozen persons because executives of a light aircraft manufacturing company did not see to it that the fuel tank on several of their models was safe, despite sufficient forewarnings of danger.

The victims of the aircraft crashes suffered from a form of violence by omission; they were killed because those who should have been responsible for protecting their lives failed to act. Our argument suggests that the perpetrators of street murder and the instigators by default of suite murder are at least equally culpable morally. Habitués of executive offices and street criminals, however, clearly are not equally vulnerable to the consequences of their violent misdeeds; the former readily find sanctuary behind concepts such as intent, proximate cause, and knowledge— all devices for anesthetizing the obloquy that their death dealing deserves. In this endeavor to avoid responsibility they are aided by the law, by archaic historical precedents, and by the fact that in considerable measure they are able to define and defend their own behavior in a manner best suited to their own self-interest (Dicey, 1905). Conceptualizations of morality that fail to attach responsibility to power and prestige contribute to the social ethic that winks at white-collar violence committed at a distance while swiftly condemning crime in the street.

Murder Known to the Police

Primarily to limit our realm of discourse, we are concentrating largely on violence that produces death, Hemingway's "simplest" and "most fundamental" realm. Obviously, there are other forms of violence that are more terrible and, perhaps in some respects, that go more directly to the major points we make. But death is dramatic, readily and clearly definable, and generally contradictory to major social and personal goals of American society (Fulton & Geis, 1965).

The crime of murder, the killing of a human being without justification and with malice aforethought, is the most discernible form of death-producing personal violence. In the United States, 18,520 murders became known to the police in 1972, representing perhaps 75 to 90 percent of the total that occurred. Some murders remain undetected because they are confused with accidents: the husband backing out of the garage, running over his wife, and claiming that he did not know she was there; or the placing of a comatose drunken person in front of an open window in a freezing climate so that he contracts a fatal case of pneumonia.

All told, though, the reported information about the crime of murder seems relatively accurate. That information (Kelley, 1973) indicates a national murder rate for 1972 of 8.9 per 100,000 inhabitants, varying from a high of 19.7 in cities with populations of more than 250,000 to 4.6 in suburban areas and 7.4 in rural locales. Victims of murder are male in approximately 4 out of 5 instances. Approximately 45 out of every 100 murder victims are white, 53 are black, and 2 from other races. The largest number of murders (3 out of ten) occurring in any ten-year-age bracket is in the 20- to 29-year-old group.

Murder occurs most often in the southern states (12.6 per 100,000), where 7 out of 10 killings are accomplished by the use of firearms; the South also has the highest rate for use of such weapons in the country. "Criminal homicide," the FBI reports (Kelley, 1973), "is largely a societal problem which is beyond the control of the police. . . . In 1972, murder within the family made up approximately one-fourth of all murder offenses. Over one-half of these family killings involved spouse killing spouse. The remainder were parents killing children and other in-family killings" (p. 8). In murders involving husband and wife, the wife was the victim in 52 percent of the incidents, and the husband in the remaining 48 percent. During 1972, another 7 percent of murders were the result of romantic triangles or lovers' quarrels. In lovers' quarrels, when the husband discovers his wife with another man, he almost invariably kills the other man, if he kills anybody. There are also so-called felony murders, defined as killings resulting from robbery, sex motives, gangland slayings, and other felonious activities. In 1972, these constituted 27 percent of all murders. The remaining murders were largely the result of what the FBI calls "other arguments" (Kelley, 1973, p. 9).

Cross-cultural material puts some of the American information into better perspective. In England, for instance, where the murder rate is about one-tenth that in the United States, guns account for only 10 percent of the murders (Gibson & Klein, 1961), and one-third of the persons who commit murder thereafter kill themselves (West, 1966). This last figure compares with a 4 percent murder-suicide rate reported in three American studies (Gibbens, 1958; Guttmacher, 1960; Wolfgang, 1958, pp. 269–283). Lastly, it is worth noting that the murder rate in the United States, which is fifteenth out of sixty-one countries reporting their rates to the United Nations, is exceeded by that in a number of South American countries, including Colombia, Nicaragua, and Guatemala (Wolfgang & Ferracuti, 1967, pp. 274–275).

Interpretative forays regarding this factual material can take a number of paths. The most productive, we believe, would examine the offenders' self-percepts and value systems (see, for example, Wolfgang & Ferracuti, 1967). Murderers presumably have derived from their social life a sense of the moral acceptability—indeed, perhaps even the necessity—of their recourse to death-dealing behavior instead of alternative actions. If this is so, it also becomes important to note that, regardless of how fundamental the impulse toward murder may be or may not be, the moral restraints controlling this impulse vary greatly under different social conditions and in different social groups.

The Unsubtle Violences

The very heavy concentration of tabulated kinds of murder among the poor, the dispossessed, and the socially pressured (Wolfgang, 1958) provides a basic key to the relationship between violence and morality. Those who do not have what they have been led and have led themselves to believe that they ought to, have to maintain some sense of their own worth—be it defined as *machismo* in South American countries or masculine self-image in the United States—and are more likely than self-respecting persons to respond aggressively when they feel particularly threatened (Ilfeld, 1970). This is true, however, only if murder is seen as a permissible behavior, or, at least, as one less taboo than the consequences that will accrue if it is not carried out (Geis, 1967). If a social system does not include acceptance of death dealing as a way to resolve a problem, then murder will not be done, except by the few who are uniquely inventive and fairly impervious to social influence. The effect of social attitudes on the probability of violent behavior is well illustrated by M. Mead's observation (1950, pp. 80–81) that among the Arapesh, a Papuan tribal group, there is sexual frustration, but the idea of forcible rape is inconceivable and incomprehensible to men because their conception of male nature simply does not embrace the idea of taking a female sexually by force. Indeed, among the Arapesh it is not the aggressor who is disapproved and punished, but anyone who arouses anger and violence in another person (M. Mead, 1972, p. 197).

A dramatic illustration of social-class–related imperatives to commit the type of murder reported in crime statistics appears in a case we followed during research on the establishment of the California program to compensate victims of violent crime (Geis, 1966). The case was the first in the United States in which a crime victim received public aid as a consequence of her loss of support from a murdered husband. It is likely that many thousands of the recorded murders in the country do not differ significantly from this one in their basic ingredients.

The crime built to its climax after John Rodgers (the names are fictitious) telephoned his girl friend, and was answered by a visiting neighbor, Mrs. Evans. Mrs. Evans told Rodgers that his girl friend no longer wished to have anything to do with him. Rodgers called Mrs. Evans a number of names, including—her written statement to the police indicates— "a Fucken Hor." That evening, Mrs. Evans told her husband that she had been insulted by Rodgers. Later, when Rodgers came around to try to see his girl friend, he found himself confronted by Mr. Evans's demand that he apologize to Evans's wife for his verbal effrontery. Rodgers, predictably, refused; Evans then took off his belt and went after Rodgers (testimony is in conflict as to whether this was before or after Rodgers pulled a gun,

which he had just gotten that day for a new job as a night watchman, or before or after Rodgers began retreating to his car). Rodgers shot Evans. He then walked to a nearby bar, and was sitting there when the police came for him.

At the station house, after being warned of his rights, which he waived out of hand, Rodgers told the police his story. He did *not* insist that he had been provoked, and he did *not* emphasize self-defense. Instead, he belligerently maintained that the police were very wrong in suggesting that it had taken him three shots to hit Evans. In his written statement, Rodgers put it this way:

When I arrived at the House, a guy came out of the house swinging a belt buckle at me. I reached for my gun in the holster on my left front and pumped some lead in that son of a bitch and dropped him. I shot the young punk first.[2] I shot him right in the gut. I shot two times, that is all, because if you don't think I can handle a .38 better than that, it is something else.

The accused offered as his motive the fact that he "just got tired of being pushed around by those people," and added: "If I'm turned loose I'll go back and finish the job." Rodgers didn't need to; Evans died of his wounds less than a week later. The public defender, though convinced that Rodgers had a good case of self-defense, ultimately pled Rodgers guilty to second-degree murder because he was fearful of putting him on the witness stand to rebut the first-degree murder charge, with a possible death penalty, that had been brought by the district attorney.

The murdering imperative shown in the Rodgers case, the mentality that manhood demands violent action, only very infrequently impels similar behavior in members of the middle and higher classes. In their case, something more than the simplistic ingredients of the Rodgers–Evans confrontation is often involved. Members of the "have" classes are usually verbally adept and possess a certain grace that can be employed to avoid and, if necessary, to extricate themselves from such potentially explosive circumstances as those created by Mrs. Evans's insistence that she had been insulted and was owed an apology.

THE PREDICTION OF VIOLENCE

John Rodgers is obviously the kind of person who might be predicted to be "violence-prone." The circumstances under which a political authority may exercise its power to deprive such individuals of their liberty constitutes a fundamental moral issue. Inevitably, certain infringements on freedom are undertaken for what is defined and defended as the common good; mandatory education for youngsters is one example. For one thing, youngsters are deemed incapable of possessing sufficient judgment to decide what is best for them; and, for another, a functioning social system is seen as needing to formally transfer its lore and accumulated knowledge to the next generation in order to move forward and maintain the elements believed to distinguish the society. This type of societal imposition, as well as other inroads on total liberty, are based upon implicit statistical estimates of the probability of certain harms ensuing if constraints are not introduced.

In regard to the prediction of violence, the value equation goes essentially like this: If we can predict with x amount of success that certain persons will commit harmful acts, then by isolating all persons predicted to be dangerous, we will spare innocent potential victims from harm. If the predictions of violence are but 10 percent accurate for a cohort of 100 individuals, then 10 potential victims will be protected (presuming one dangerous act per offender), while the liberty of 90 wrongly accused will be sacrificed to achieve this end. If the predictions are 90 percent accurate, then the injustice quotient is reduced appreciably. When and whether the end is worth the means is, of course, a moral question, and moral questions can rarely be resolved satisfactorily by categorical pronouncements. It is generally accepted that societies must infringe on the freedom of some (but how many is tolerable?) who would fare better without such constraints, such as persons who would be more inventive if not formed so rigidly by public education. Presumably, however, few persons weighing these considerations would follow the dictate of an English cleric who stoutly maintained that it would be immoral for an innocent person about to be hanged to protest his plight, because by doing so he would undermine the citizenry's faith in their judicial system (Paley, 1838, p. 388).

Predictions of violence are made, among other reasons, because they are viewed as protecting "good" people from the aggression of "undersocialized" elements in the population. That almost all murder has as its victims persons located in more or less similar social circumstances as the offenders (Wolfgang, 1958) is of little policy importance, for enough death is regarded as likely to spill over as to threaten respectable burghers.

Illustrative of the more intense advocacies of massive programs to screen and then isolate the potentially violent is the proposal by Hutschnecker (Maynard, 1970), a psychiatric consultant to the National Commission on the Causes and Prevention of Violence, who recommended that psychological tests be administered to all 6-year-olds in the United States to determine their likelihood of criminal behavior. Those identified as potentially antisocial should, in Hutschnecker's words (quoted by Maynard, 1970), undergo "massive psychological and psychiatric treatment." The approach was heralded by him as "a better short-term solution to the crime problem than urban reconstruction." Under its provisions, "teen-age boys later found to persist in incorrigible behavior would be remanded to camps" (p. 9).

That other purposes are being served by proposals such as Hutschnecker's is suggested by Morris and Hawkins's observation (1970) that there is no operable concept of dangerousness, and that the term is usually employed for retributive purposes. The validity of this pronouncement may be gathered from an examination of the accuracy of predictions of dangerousness and the efficacy of efforts to deal with persons deemed to be dangerous.

In the United States, a diagnosis of dangerousness often is the determinative step for entrance into a mental hospital, a prison, or a facility for the criminally insane. California's Lanterman-Petris-Short Act, for example, provides three criteria for involuntary hospitalization: dangerousness to self, grave disablement, and dangerousness to others. The first two criteria are defined with some clarity, though the likelihood of the eventualities they are designed to protect against is something less than carefully documented. The meaning of "dangerousness to others," however, is left to the discretion of the mental health examiner. Indeed, in one jurisdiction it was determined—and upheld by a federal appelate court in *Overholser* v. *Russell* (1960)—that writing a bad check is sufficiently "dangerous" to justify incarceration in a mental health facility.[3]

The most sophisticated study of the accuracy of predictions of dangerousness is the ten-year inquiry conducted by Kozol, Boucher, and Garofalo (1972) at the Massachusetts Center for the Diagnosis and Treatment of Dangerous Persons. Independent clinical examinations by at least two psychiatrists, two psychologists, and a social worker were supplemented by an elaborate psychological test battery and "a meticulous reconstruction" of the person's life history. Of the 592 patients admitted to the facility for observation, 435 were released. The diagnostic team recommended the release of 386 as nondangerous and opposed the release of 49 as dangerous (with the court deciding otherwise). During a five-year follow-up

period, 8 percent of those predicted by the diagnostic team to be *not* dangerous committed a serious assaultive act, while 35 percent of those deemed to be dangerous (but released by the court) committed such an act.

The diagnostic team's assessment obviously had some power, but the false positives are what stand out. Of the individuals identified as dangerous, 65 percent did not commit a dangerous act. Despite the extensive and meticulous examinations, the diagnostic team was wrong in two out of three of their predictions for this group of persons.

Other predictive studies have shown even poorer results. An attempt by a research group working with California Department of Corrections' clients (Wenk, Robison, & Smith, 1972) to develop and use a "violence prediction scale" to aid in parole decisions found that 86 percent of the persons identified on this scale as potentially dangerous did not commit a violent act while on parole. A second study (Wenk, Robison, & Smith, 1972) of 7712 parolees assigned to various categories of "potential aggressiveness" ended wtih 326 incorrect predictions of violent behavior for each correct prediction. In a third study (Wenk, Robison, & Smith, 1972), involving 4146 California Youth Authority wards, the authors concluded that the parole decision maker who used a history of actual violence as his sole predictor of future violence would have 19 false positives in every 20 predictions, and yet "there is no other form of simple classification available thus far that would enable him to improve on this level of efficiency [i.e., accuracy]" (p. 400).

A naturalistic test of the accuracy of dangerous predictions was provided when the U.S. Supreme Court in *Baxstrom* v. *Herold* (1966) held that the plaintiff had been denied equal protection of the law by being detained in an institution for criminally insane beyond his maximum sentence without the benefit of a new hearing to determine his current dangerousness. The court's ruling resulted in the transfer of nearly one thousand persons, "reputed to be some of the most dangerous mental patients" (Steadman, 1972, p. 266), from hospitals for the criminally insane to civil mental hospitals. Four follow-up reports on the transferred patients (Halfon, David, & Steadman, 1972; Hunt & Wiley, 1968; Steadman & Halfon, 1971; Steadman & Keveles, 1972) all agreed that the level of violence experienced in the civil mental hospitals was much less than had been feared, though the transferred patients were treated the same as the other patients. At some time during the four-year period following their admittance, 26 percent of the female and 20 percent of the male transferred patients were assaultive to persons in the civil hospital. Thus, 74 percent of the females and 80 percent of the males who were committed to hospitals for the criminally insane on the basis of their alleged potential dangerousness were probably unnecessarily committed. Furthermore, only 3 percent of the transferred patients proved sufficiently dangerous to be returned to a hospital for the criminally insane during the four years following the Supreme Court's decision (Steadman & Halfon, 1971). And among the 121 transferred patients who ultimately were released into the community and followed as part of the research effort, only 9 were convicted of a crime during thirty months of freedom, and only one of the convictions was for an act of violence (Steadman & Keveles, 1972).

There are several factors associated with violence that make its prediction very difficult. The first is the complex causal nature of the criterion event, the violent act itself. The eruption of violence, like the occurrence of any other behavior, is determined in substantial part by the situation confronting an individual (Mischel, 1968, 1973). To predict individual acts of violence accurately, therefore, requires a foreknowledge of the ingredients of every situation that an individual will en-

counter. In addition, research that claims to be predictive of violence is in fact research based only on discovered violence. The accuracy of information that becomes available on the extent of violent behavior is quite questionable. In fact, the very poor results achieved in predictive efforts could be considered spuriously good in view of the likelihood that only ineptly violent and easily caught persons typically come to official attention and are included in such studies; the more skillfully violent are likely to elude detection in the first place and would be difficult to catch in repeated violence even if they were included in prediction studies.

The low base rate of violence further complicates the task of prediction studies. If the base rate of an event is high, predicting it without too many false positives is easy. If nine out of ten persons commit murder, the shrewd prognosticator, in order to be correct 90 percent of the time, would merely need to indicate that everyone will commit murder. As the base rate becomes lower, however, the issue gets much more complicated, as Livermore, Malmquist, and Meehl (1968) illustrate:

Assume that one person out of a thousand will kill. Assume also that an exceptionally accurate test is created which differentiates with 95 percent effectiveness those who will kill from those who will not. If 100,000 persons were tested, out of the 100 who would kill, 95 would be isolated. Unfortunately, out of the 99,000 who would not kill, 4,995 people would also be isolated as potential killers. In these circumstances, it is clear that we could not justify incarcerating all 5,090 people. If, in the criminal law, it is better that ten guilty men go free than that one innocent man suffer, how can we say in the civil commitment area that it is better that 54 harmless people be incarcerated lest one dangerous man be free? (p. 84).

THE TREATMENT OF VIOLENCE

Treatment programs directed toward the violent also show notably poor results. The Massachusetts study discussed earlier

(Kozol, Boucher, & Garofalo, 1972), for instance, presents data regarding 100 subjects diagnosed as violent and then treated with various combinations of eclectic group and individual psychotherapy. Of the 82 persons recommended for release as not dangerous after an average of forty-three months of treatment, 5 persons (6 percent) later committed a violent act. Of the 18 persons released by the court after an average of thirty months of treatment despite the staff's insistence that they were still dangerous, 5 (28 percent) committed an act of violence. On the basis of the violence rate among those treated and recommended for release by the staff, Kozol, Boucher, and Garofalo (1972) conclude that "treatment was successful in modifying the dangerous potential of 94 percent of the patients recommended for discharge" (p. 392).

On closer examination, however, this conclusion is a good deal less persuasive than it is meant to be. For one thing, subjects were not randomly assigned to treatment or control groups. Everyone received the same eclectically oriented therapy for several years. The patients who, in the eyes of the staff, performed well in therapy were considered to have been treated. The patients who were judged not to have performed adequately were considered the comparison group. The findings, therefore, more than likely reflect preexisting differences between the two groups, rather than any effect of treatment. That the good get better and the bad get worse is by now one of the commonplace observations about traditional psychotherapeutic interventions. Even if the subjects had been randomly assigned to a treatment group and a control group, attributing success to the treatment can be done only in relation to the base rates for success among controls. Considering that the "control group" in this instance (persons released by the court against the staff's recommendation) remained nonviolent in 72 percent of the cases, at best only 22 percent (94 percent less 72 percent) of the success was in response to treatment. The fundamental (and avoidable) methodological flaws in the study, however, render even so tempered a conclusion suspect.

The Massachusetts study, plus a variety of other investigations (Bailey, 1966; Jew, Clanon, & Mattocks, 1972; Martinson, 1972; Kassebaum, Ward, & Wilner, 1971) dealing with the treatment of numerous alleged behavior disorders and difficulties that bring a person into contact with the criminal justice system or auxiliary agencies, indicate clearly that no currently available treatment is even minimally effective in reducing violence. Thus, both rationales that are given to deprive individuals of their liberty in regard to violent acts or proclivities prove to be chimerical: Violence cannot be predicted and those incarcerated in order to reduce their supposed violence potential cannot successfully be treated to accomplish this end.

Since this is so, then why allow the continuation of efforts to predict violence and to isolate those deemed violence-prone? It is possible, of course, that such endeavors are most fundamentally directed toward deterrence, particularly of others who might be inclined to duplicate the proscribed behavior. If this is the purpose of such predictions, they ought to be promulgated as serving such an end; then they can be debated in terms of their value and morality as deterrent efforts (see Zimring & Hawkins, 1973). More likely, however, regimens mounted to supposedly abate violence persist for two basic reasons. First, the persons involved as patients or prisoners almost invariably are located in social positions where they do not have adequate political or financial resources to protest effectively against what is being done to them. That is, they lack things such as ready media access and funds to hire good lawyers. Second, since the clients are vulnerable and quiescent, it is far safer to incarcerate as many as possible and thus avoid the risk that someone left free might commit a violent offense which would then be blamed on officials who had failed to keep him incarcerated.

If society's aim is really to isolate the violent and violence-prone and protect the innocent, then why are those who allow faulty fuel tanks to continue to be installed in the planes they market, and those who are or ought to be responsible for things such as an unconscionably high national infant mortality rate (Gross, 1967, p. 24), not similarly "diagnosed" and "rehabilitated"?

Answers to questions such as the above seem more complicated than Marxist platitudes about class injustice and proletariat exploitation, but less complicated than bursts of sophistry that maintain that air and infant deaths are altogether different events from murder—as if death from a plane crash or death in the smog belt is more acceptable to victims than death from street crimes. "Our revulsion against murder," as Cohen (1961) suggests, "is rather against direct and messy forms of it" (p. 68).

The Subtle Violences

The tendency of our social system to truncate the reach of its logic regarding violence is well illustrated by Szasz's observation (1963) that thousands of persons are deprived of liberty each year on the suppositious ground that they are potential suicides (that is, that they constitute a danger to themselves), while automobile-racing drivers, whose behavior is much more of a threat to their own existence than that of the diagnosed would-be suicides, are celebrated as courageous and skillful athletes.

It is sometimes said that in evaluating and dealing with violence, the most fundamental social value upheld, regardless of how imperfectly it is realized, is the protection of life. We would argue that this goal is often only a camouflage and that, indeed, many social policies are self-evidently destructive of the value of life

which they are grandiloquently proclaimed to protect. Laws against opiate drugs clearly illustrate this theme. Such laws are defended on the ground that heroin is an extremely dangerous drug, likely to produce severe physical deterioration or death. Studies (e.g., Cherubin, 1967; Nyswander, 1965, p. 60) indicate clearly, however, that few, if any, detrimental physical sequelae ensue if the drug is pure and if it is mixed with distilled rather than tap water and injected with a sterile hypodermic needle. Indeed, the analgesic quality of opiates is apt to produce a passive life-style that may keep the addict alive longer than otherwise. Thus, death from opiate overdoses (Arnold, 1970), from neglect of personal hygiene, from criminal activity to support a habit (Hughes, 1961), and from diseases such as hepatitis (Batonbacal & Slipyan, 1959), are largely the consequence of the illegal nature of opiates. The law, justified as protective, becomes the agency of disaster. That opiate use is almost exclusively located among the lower classes, and that it undercuts the Puritan ethic, may reasonably be regarded as more adequate foci of explanation for its continuing criminalization than any regard for the life and health of the user or potential user (cf. Geis, 1972, pp. 105–172).

Note might be made, too, of the secondary position of life protection when this value collides with considerations deemed more important. Several thousand persons could be spared death and many thousands more serious injury if highway speed limits below those presently in force were established (O'Connell & Myers, 1966). With lower limits, the convenience of moving rapidly from one place to another obviously would be diminished. In this sense, victims of highway slaughter may be regarded as offerings sacrificed on an altar of superordinate values: speed, convenience, vitality, automobile sales, highway construction. That this argument is not altogether spurious—after all, no matter what the speed limit, we can always say that a lower ceiling might be safer—is indicated by the 1974 nationwide decrease of the limit to 55 miles an hour to conserve fuel and to render us less vulnerable to Arab-state blackmail. Clearly, while lifesaving considerations were not persuasive, economic and political considerations were able to carry the day.

THE FAULTY FUEL TANK CASES

A case history concerned with one of the subtler violences can be read as complementary to our earlier account of a run-of-the-mill murder. This episode (G. Hill & Eisenberg, 1971; Jesilow & Meredith, 1973)[4] involved thirteen persons killed between 1964 and 1968 in crashes of light aircraft produced by the same manufacturer. The crashes apparently resulted from sloshing of fuel to one side of the tank when the plane tipped and the resultant failure of the fuel to feed into the engine. Judgments and out-of-court settlements resulted in the payment of several million dollars to survivors of the crash victims.

The facts brought forth during the suits for damages appear to indicate willful negligence on the part of the company's policy makers. The damage suits were won, of course, with proof "preponderantly" favorable to the plaintiff's cases. Had the evidence been brought in a case of criminal neglect against the manufacturer, it might not have been sufficient ("beyond a reasonable doubt") for a conviction. These differing standards are themselves illustrative of the redoubts within which the subtler violences can be hidden. Why should plaintiffs try to meet a more demanding criminal standard of proof against an aircraft manufacturer when a lesser civil standard will suffice for the award of considerable amounts of money (none of it belonging to the company officials), while the tougher standard will bring no financial gains? On the other hand, in commonplace street crime deaths, no money is to be had by the

victim from the offender, and the burden of proof is usually not overly difficult to meet, given the generally uncomplicated nature of the death-dealing event.

The first notice within the manufacturing company that fuel tanks on certain of its planes were defective apparently came at least three years prior to the first fatal crash. In an interoffice memorandum that went to five company officials, including two vice-presidents, the Western division manager wrote:

A condition [exists] which is extremely dangerous and corrective action should be taken immediately. . . . When making a rolling take-off when the tanks are half full, the centrifugal force throws the gas to the outside of the tanks and the engine quits dead after the airplane is airborne. [The test pilot] has tried this several times and found it to happen each and every time. . . .

I submit the information for your help and recommendation. It looks to me like our Quality Control and/or Flight Department, when testing and checking these airplanes, are letting a lot of things through that certainly should not be.

Follow-up tests supported this warning. In late 1961 a project engineer filed the following information with the company:

Efforts to incorporate a suitable and effective baffle into the fuel cell have been unsuccessful. . . .

It is suggested that mention could be made of this operating problem in a service letter. People should be again warned against taking off on practically empty tanks.[5] Also some people make short-field take-offs by making an extremely fast turn around on the ground as part of their take-off run. With less than eight gallons of fuel in the tank on the outside of the turn, this can result in an interruption of the fuel supply, if the turn around is made too fast.

Nothing was done to correct the defect. In 1964, a company-made plane crashed on approach to the Tacoma Industrial Airport, killing the pilot and three passengers. In 1965, another plane crashed, this time while approaching the airport in Salinas, California. Two men were killed. On May 6, 1966, the company received a letter from a customer, again noting the inadequacy of its fuel mechanism:

After taking off with 80 gallons of gas aboard, cruising at 65% power for 1 hour and 20 minutes, I was descending when the engine stopped. . . .
    To increase my rate of descent, I lowered the left wing into a side-slip and shortly thereafter the engine quit. The engine was restarted in approximately 7 seconds by simultaneously relieving the side-slip and turning on the booster pump. The gasoline selector valve was on . . . the low tank due to the side-slip. I am concerned about this situation, since I can see a duplication of these effects when landing in a strong cross wind with both tanks low on fuel. . . .

The company responded by conducting another series of tests, which confirmed the experience of the customer. No action was taken, however, until the Federal Aviation Agency determined that the Salinas crash might have been due to inadequate fuel feeding. The FAA report was not filed until 1967, and it took another two years before an airworthiness directive required that a number of models manufactured by the company carry the following placard:

Take off and land on main tanks only—turning type take-offs or take-offs immediately following fast taxi turns prohibited. Refer to FAA flight manual for other fuel system limitations.

What accounted for the long-term indifference to federal safety regulations and, as juries saw the matter, a lack of concern or care within the company that led to the fatal crashes? An attorney for one of the plaintiffs offered a simple explanation: "I guess they wanted to sell those aircraft."
    Another plaintiff's attorney said in his final argument to the jury:

. . . for no reason other than profit, what else can you conclude, what other alternative is there than to say the choice of fixing the hundred if not thousands of [planes] that were

already amongst the consuming public, and altering the fuel cells by putting baffles in them on future models was a cost the manufacturer decided would interfere with his profit picture and instead they decided to gamble. They decided and hoped this accident and others will not and have not occurred, but unfortunately this has not been the case.

Another attorney also noted in an interview (Jesilow & Meredith, 1973):

The only conclusion I can reach after so much time and reviewing so much evidence is that [the company's] top management concluded that the crashes would look like pilot error instead of design error. To me, this was a case of corporate manslaughter (p. 18).

COMMERCE IN DEATH

There is little doubt that commercial manslaughter kills more people than are murdered by acts listed in the official crime statistics. But only rarely are such acts viewed in terms synonymous with the tough judgments of the traditional criminal law. Ralph Nader undoubtedly is the major exponent of the need for symmetry in public and official response to all forms of violence. "If you want to talk about violence," Nader has noted, "Don't talk of Black Panthers. Talk of General Motors" (quoted in "White-Collar Crime," 1970, p. 10). Nader has accused the American automobile industry of "criminal negligence" in building and selling potentially lethal cars, and in this regard he has underlined our failure to appreciate and to deal congruently with acts that produce similar harm:

If there are criminal penalties for the poor and deprived when they break the law, then there must be criminal penalties for the automobile industry when its executives knowingly violate standards designed to protect citizens from injuries and systematic fraud ("Angry Senator Shouts," 1971, p. 26).

Similarly, Nader (1971) returns to the idea of violence in a polemic against unchecked air pollution:

The efflux from motor vehicles, plants, incinerators of sulfur oxides, hydrocarbons, carbon monoxide, oxides of nitrogen, particulates, and many more contaminants amounts to compulsory consumption of violence by most Americans. . . . "Smogging" a city or town has taken on the proportions of a massive crime wave, yet federal and state statistical compilations of crime pay attention to "muggers" and ignore "smoggers" . . . (p. viii).

Whether verdicts of criminal manslaughter could be achieved against many of the commercial offenders such as the plane company officials remains arguable, especially since the effort is almost never made or, apparently, even passingly considered.[6] In regard to civil suits, it is clear that those who can offer up money or status (as did former Vice President Agnew) can trade such wherewithal for immunity from imprisonment, much as in earlier periods violent acts were recompensed by payments by the offender's clan to placate the ire of the victim's survivors.

Several historical, cultural, and legal conditions and traditions have served to maintain inapt distinctions between commercial deaths and deaths from traditional forms of criminal violence. These conditions put an extraordinary emphasis on the nature of the death-dealing actor rather than focusing more directly on the fact of death itself. If the moral and legal system were to dictate that preventable death is the basic evil, and to concentrate its powers on attempting to deter and to punish such outcomes, it would employ different approaches than those now in effect. Why it does not do so, and suggestions regarding how it might change, are matters we will specify in our concluding section.

Conclusions Regarding the Social Ecology of Violence

We have sought to demonstrate that the social ecology of violence logically embraces at least two distinct kinds of death-dealing behaviors: (1) those officially recognized and reacted to and (2) those that tend to remain beyond the ken of official notice and response. This distinction can be examined further in terms of the following two factors: (1) the criminal law's commitment to the doctrine of free will and (2) the libertarian tradition that allows individuals extraordinary freedom to pursue their own ends without imposing on them a concomitant responsibility to their fellows.

THE CRIMINAL LAW AND THE DOCTRINE OF FREE WILL

The concepts of intent and criminal capacity as they appear in Anglo-American jurisprudence inexorably lead to disparate concern with certain forms of death dealing as opposed to others. The free will emphasis insists that virtually all persons are equally responsible for their behavior. "Criminal intent," as McGrath (1957, p. 37) notes, "has reference to free will in action." Holmes (1881) pithily encapsulated the thrust of the doctrine in his famous aphorism: "Even a dog distinguishes between being stumbled over and being kicked" (p. 3). We would prefer, "A person today distinguishes between being stabbed and being polluted to death." And we would add, "But he ought not." The obvious force of the idea of intent in criminal law is that it excludes from retaliation persons who inadvertently inflict injury, through mistake or accident or for similar reasons. Differing culpability ought to adhere, of course, in any reasonable moral system to lethal acts which involve, on the one hand, slipping on a slick floor and accidentally dislodging a death-dealing flower pot from the window sill of a sixteenth-floor hotel room and, on the other, aiming the flower pot at a passerby below. But injustice comes about when intent becomes extraordinarily difficult to prove legally—both in commercial dealings which produce death (e.g., faulty car planning to pare costs) and in run-of-the-mill, more traditional crimes whose intent is more readily inferred though not necessarily any more involved than in the commercial episode.

Not only do the concepts of intent and responsibility lead to disparate concern with certain forms of death dealing as opposed to others, but they also lead to disparate concern with death dealing by certain kinds of people rather than others. The anomaly of exempting the insane from penal consequences while embracing the deprived has been spelled out by Morris (1968):

It too often is overlooked that one group's exculpation from criminal responsibility confirms the inculpation of other groups. Why not permit the defense of dwelling in a Negro ghetto? Such a defense would not be morally indefensible. Adverse social and subcultural background is statistically *more* crimogenic than is psychosis. . . You argue that insanity destroys, undermines, diminishes man's capacity to reject what is wrong and to adhere to what is right. So does the ghetto—more so (p. 520).[7]

When courts are presented with Morris's argument they typically acknowledge its rationality but dismiss it. In the recent decision in *United States* v. *Brawner* (1972), the Washington, D.C., Circuit Court stated that while "there may be logic" in exculpating those whose incapacity to control their behavior arose from social as well as psychological conditions, the court would not do so. It warned that the recognition of psychiatric excuses "is not to be twisted, directly or indirectly, into a device for exculpation of those without an abnormal condition of the mind" (p. 995).

It may well be that necessity, if not ethics, obligates the law to retain its adherence to free will principles until such time as an alternate and more viable set of guiding metaphors is articulated (Monahan, 1973a). More suitable, in our viewpoint, than the intricate web of proof necessary to establish criminal intent might be doctrines explicating the aim of social

protection, seen as the shielding of innocent persons from preventable injury. Under such an approach, guilt would accompany failure to inhibit outcomes that might have been and should have been averted, regardless of the offender's mental or social status.

THE LIBERTARIAN ETHIC AND THE FREEDOM TO GET RICH

The doctrine of laissez-faire places a high priority on the unfettered use of power by the powerful. As Tawney (1920, pp. 80–81) noted, under sufferance of the doctrine, mill owners could poison workers and customers, and get off with a warning or a nominal fine; landowners could draw rents from slums in which children were dying from crowding and disease, and still be welcome in polite society. Property had no obligations and therefore it could do no wrong. Tawney (1920) described the appeal of laissez-faire industrialism as follows:

To the strong it promises unfettered freedom for the exercise of their strength; to the weak the hope that they, too, one day may be strong. . . . It assures men that there are no ends other than their own ends, no law other than their desires, no limit other than that which they think advisable. . . . It relieves communities of the necessity of discriminating . . . between enterprise and service, energy and unscrupulous greed, property which is legitimate and property which is theft . . . because it treats all economic activities as standing upon the same level, and suggests that excess or defect, waste or superfluidity, requires no conscious effort of social will to avert them (pp. 30–31).

Today, more than half a century after Tawney wrote, there has been some abatement of the more glaring excesses of the laissez-faire doctrine, but these inroads have been counterbalanced by the appearance of many mechanisms that more effectively screen entrenched malevolence from public view, and that render it more dangerous than ever before.

While the libertarian ethic abets the subtler violences, we are not proposing the wholesale discard of libertarianism. Libertarian principles are invoked to justify a person's rights to remain free of coerced psychiatric hospitalization (Szasz, 1963; Monahan, 1973b) and to be free to engage in "crimes" (such as homosexual relations between consenting adults) for which there are no complaining victims (Geis, 1973), as well as to justify his "right" to abuse others in the pursuit of his own ends. We are opposed only to the last of these invocations. While it is generally accepted that the right to swing one's own arm ends where the nose of another begins, we would also add that the right to pollute the air ends where another's health begins and that the right to build an unsafe product ends as soon as the manufacturer tries to sell it.

Summary

We suggest that a moral approach to violence must establish satisfactory means to see that persons now nakedly vulnerable to the subtler violences are afforded adequate protection. At times, such protection can be focused on arrangements which render more potential victims inaccessible to harm, just as locks protect cars from being stolen. At other times, such protection must take the classical form of responses against perpetrators of violence which seek to deter them and others similarly inclined. Such approaches certainly have potential for injustice, if they are not implemented cautiously, carefully, and compassionately. Otherwise, they are apt, like current attempts to predict violence and to isolate and treat the potentially violent, to be vindictive and in vain.

Our remarks may at times have had the flavor of muckraking, carrying the implication that power is invariably accompanied by corruption, and that commerce is inevitably attended by subtle forms of violence against the larger public. There is considerable tradition for this view (e.g., Ecclesiastes 27:2; Lewis, 1961). But we do not desire to enroll ourselves with those who in broad strokes blacken indiscriminantly the behavior and intentions of large groups of persons and organizations. It is no more accurate to say that all power is violence-prone than it is to repeat the calumny that all ghetto residents are violence-prone and apt to kill. But it is true that power tends to corrupt; and it is almost absolutely true that absolute power corrupts absolutely (Acton, 1948, p. 365). And it is also true that traditional ways of thinking about things such as violence tend to be inaugurated under certain social conditions and to resist redefinition and fresh interpretation long past the time when they have lost whatever legitimacy they may originally have possessed.

Two quotations from Nader serve to supplement the thrust of the argument put forward here. In the first, Nader notes his anger at "the tremendous amount of injustice and brutality in industrialized society without any accountability, without any responsibility . . . that people sitting in executive suites can make . . . decisions which will someday result in tremendous carnage. And because they are remote in time and space between their decision and the consequences of the decision, there is no accountability" (quoted by Whiteside, 1972, p. 82). In the other, Nader generalizes on the basis of his experiences while attempting to alert the public to lethal characteristics of certain General Motors cars:

The requirement of a just social order is that responsibility shall lie where the power of decision rests. But the law has never caught up with the development of the large corporate unit. Deliberate acts emanate from the sprawling and indeterminate shelter of the corporate organization. Too often the responsibility for an act is not imputable to those whose decision enables it to be set in motion (quoted by Whiteside, 1972, p. 224).

Essentially this has been the nature of our theme. We have tried to explicate its dimensions and its validity by examining in panoramic fashion the spectrum of behavior leading to violent consequences, and the skewed character of social and legal efforts to predict, inhibit, and control violence. And we have sought to set forth and to support the thesis that a more morally acceptable approach to violence than we now have must cut through present structures of thought and response in order to examine more logically the entire realm of socially harmful actions and to establish operable and equitable methods for dealing with all such behaviors.

FOOTNOTES

Chapter 1. Critical Issues in the Study of Moral Development and Behavior

[1] From "Education for justice: A modern statement of the platonic view," by L. Kohlberg, in N. F. Sizer and T. R. Sizer (Eds.), *Moral Education*, Cambridge, Mass.: Harvard University Press, 1970, pp. 69–70. Copyright 1970 by Harvard University Press.

[2] The five primary values found by Morris (1956, cited by Wright, 1971) emphasize, respectively, (1) responsible, conscientious, and intelligent participation in human affairs, and appreciating and conserving what has been achieved rather than initiating change; (2) vigorous action for the overcoming of obstacles, and the initiation of change rather than preserving what has been achieved; (3) a rich inner life of heightened self-awareness, insight, a deep sympathy with all living things, and the repudiation of control over persons and things; (4) receptivity and sympathetic responsiveness to others, service to them, and submission to their needs; and (5) sensuous enjoyments of all kinds.

[3] For a recent round in this debate, see Kurtines and Greif's evaluation (1974) of Kohlberg's work, which challenges both the reliability and standardization of his moral judgment scale and the predictive and constructive validity of his six-stage model—and Kohlberg's reply (1975).

[4] From "Education for moral responsibility," by J. M. Gustafson, in N. F. Sizer and T. R. Sizer (Eds.), *Moral Education,* Cambridge, Mass.: Harvard University Press, 1970, pp. 16–17. Copyright 1970 by Harvard University Press.

[5] The gap between moral reasoning and behavior may yawn wide even in history's moral heroes. Gore Vidal's *Burr* (1973) levels this charge against Thomas Jefferson: "Proclaiming the unalienable rights of man for everyone (excepting slaves, Indians, women and those entirely without property), Jefferson tried to seize the Floridas by force, dreamed of a conquest of Cuba, and after his illegal purchase of Louisiana sent a military governor to rule New Orleans against the will of its inhabitants. . . . It was of course Jefferson's gift at one time or another to put with eloquence the 'right' answer to every moral question. In practice, however, he seldom deviated from an opportunistic course, calculated to bring him power" (p. 202).

[6] From "Concrete principles and the rational passions," by R. D. Peters, in N. F. Sizer and T. R. Sizer (Eds.), *Moral Education*, Cambridge, Mass.: Harvard University Press, 1970, p. 51. Copyright 1970 by Harvard University Press.

[7] From "Moral education," by B. Bettelheim, in N. F. Sizer and T. R. Sizer (Eds.), *Moral Education,* Cambridge, Mass.: Harvard University Press, 1970, p. 94. Copyright 1970 by Harvard University Press.

Chapter 2. Moral Stages and Moralization

[1] Major portions of this chapter are reproduced with permission from L. Kohlberg (Ed.), *Recent research in moral development.* New York: Holt, Rinehart and Winston, in preparation.

[2] If it is true that moralization may be described as a process of sequential irreversible changes in structure, then the concepts useful for describing age-developmental changes *within* individuals should also be useful for describing differences *between* individuals of a given age in terms of developmental advance or arrest.

Chapter 4. The Socialization of Moral Judgment and Behavior in Cross-Cultural Perspective

[1] Of particular importance cross-culturally is the distribution of different kinds of moral orientations and levels within a society, as well as the model types. This is because such a distribution may be thought of as describing the salient structure and ideology of the social system. By examining the patterns and paths of moral development within a particular culture, an index of the social system is obtained. By further noting the relative frequency with which typical and atypical patterns are manifested by persons within that culture—as a function of sex, socioeconomic status, age, ethnic affiliation, and so on—we may obtain a relatively complete picture of the culture's moral system and at the same time gain important clues about its overall strategy of socialization.

Chapter 5. A Cognitive Social-Learning Approach to Morality and Self-Regulation

[1] Preparation of this paper was facilitated by National Institute of Mental Health grant M-6830 and National Science Foundation grant GS-32582 to Walter Mischel.

[2] In the present view, just because a particular cognitive or behavioral tendency occurs later in development does not necessarily mean that it is superior to its predecessors. As Alston (1971, p. 275) has noted, the concept of arbitrary exceptions to rules logically depends on the concept of rules, but it enjoys no moral superiority on those grounds. An example in the realm of moral reasoning is Kohlberg's "Stage 3" conception of the value of human life based on social sharing, community, and love, which may depend logically on the instrumental and hedonistic value of life more characteristic of "Stage 2." This sequence does not necessarily mean, however, that moral thinking involving the former is superior to moral thinking involving the latter.

[3] One also wonders about the degree to which age-related changes in moral reasoning are unique to moral development or are merely one aspect of age-related changes in the cognitive and verbal styles used to explain and justify choices. For example, would similar changes (in terms of use of increasingly general, "universal," abstract rules) be found if one studied age-related changes in the reasons given for esthetic preferences, vocational choices, peer preferences, and so on? Moreover, the links between moral maturity, IQ, and mental age also suggest the need for a scale of verbal intellectual sophistication as a control instrument. On such a scale answers might be scored in terms of their increasing use of higher-order abstractions and generalizations (i.e., references to universals) versus less intellectually sophisticated (i.e., more concrete) self-references and personal preferences and feelings.

[4] Staub (1974) found significant correlations between several indices of prosocial orientation, including moral reasoning and helping behavior; but these associations depend on the specific conditions, the particular measures used, and the exact nature of the help needed.

[5] Noting the grossness of standard IQ tests, Aronfreed (1968c) perceptively questions "whether any significant variation in principles of conscience would be apparent among children who, regardless of their age, had been identified as comparable in general cognitive capacity by techniques which were more sensitive to the specific operations of their thought processes" (p. 266).

Chapter 6. The Biology of Morality

[1] We may ask whether the need to specify parameter conditions for optimal conditioning of extraverts and introverts does not make it unlikely that such a laboratory-based scheme could have any great relevance to ordinary life, where such parameter conditions are extremely unlikely to be encountered. The answer seems to be linked with the fact that conditions must be optimal for conditioning to occur in extraverts, whereas introverts condition almost as well in conditions which are far from optimal. (An optimal situation is here defined as one in which an unselected sample of subjects produces the largest number of conditioned responses over a given number of pairings). In other words, everyday situations are not likely to be optimal, and consequently extraverts are not likely to produce many conditioned responses; introverts, not requiring optimal situations, will condition quite readily under variable circumstances.

[2] Walter (1964, 1966, 1967) has shown several times that individuals described as recidivist delinquents with psychopathic personality have shown only very meager evidence of CNVs. (CNVs are slow, surface-negative shifts in the EEG baseline that typically depend on the contingency of two successive stimuli). CNVs have much in common with conditioned responses, but are of course, quite involuntary; indeed, hardly any subjects would know of CNVs' existence. CNVs are almost certainly linked with the state of arousal of the cortex, and their failure to show up in the groups studied by Walter is therefore in good agreement with the theory under discussion.

[3] Persons who are accident-prone also tend to congregate in this quadrant (Shaw & Sichel, 1971). The reason appears to be that such people are more likely to indulge in the sensation-seeking behavior, and less likely to perform socialized safe-driving behavior. We have here a type of antisocial behavior which is often subcriminal, although occasionally it may actually become punishable by law.

[4] Some children became stimulated by the drug rather than showing more subdued behavior: "Such children became more alert, accomplished their daily tasks with more initiative and dispatch, became more aggressive in competitive activity, and showed an increased interest

in what was going on about them. As a result of these changes, they gave the impression of being more self-sufficient and mature. They also appeared happier and more contented." This paradoxical effect appeared mostly in children who were pathologically shy, withdrawn, and underactive. Too little is known about these withdrawn children and the particular effects observed to make it possible to state to what extent their reactions to the drugs contradict the general theory we have formulated above.

Chapter 7.   Empathy, Role Taking, Guilt, and Development of Altruistic Motives

[1] This paper was prepared in conjunction with grant HD-02258 from the National Institute of Child Health and Human Development. It is an expansion of a paper presented initially at the NICHHD Workshop "The Development of Motivation in Childhood" in Elkridge, Maryland, 1972 and, in revised form, at the meeting of the American Psychological Association Honolulu, 1972.

[2] Once a person has experienced it, empathic distress may be elicited subsequently as a secondary conditioned affective response to distress cues. This possibility contributes an additional component to future experiences of empathic distress.

[3] Furthermore, the complexity of the tasks varies, and this affects the results. Thus Selman (1971) found perceptual role taking in 5-year-olds whereas Piaget and Inhelder (1956) did not find it before age 8 or 9. This discrepancy is probably due to the fact that shortly before administering the task Selman showed the subjects the entire experimental setup, in the course of which they undoubtedly had the opportunity to view the stimulus materials from the same vantage point as the other child. As a result their estimate of the latter's perception may have been aided by short-term memory. Piaget and Inhelder's subjects lacked such an opportunity and thus had to rely entirely on their imagination in constructing what the other child would perceive.

[4] The amount of feedback needed varies with the child's developmental level. A less mature child than Michael would require more specific and direct feedback, which may contribute to his very first stirrings of awareness that people's perspectives and needs differ. A more mature child requires less feedback, and at some point can supply his own; though his first tendency might still be to attribute his needs to the other person, he may correct himself internally before acting. Eventually the entire feedback process is short-circuited, the person's initial response tendency being based on a more veridical interpretation of the other person's state. Even the fully mature person may project his own perspective, however, if he lacks the necessary information. But this projection will be done with the advance expectation of corrective feedback—an expectation lacking in a young child like Michael.

In a recent laboratory study of communicative role taking (Peterson, Danner, & Flavell, 1972), 4-year-olds readily reformulated their initial messages when explicitly requested to do so by the listener, but they failed to do so in response to nonverbal, facial expressions of listener incomprehension and implicit verbal requests for additional help, such as "I don't understand."

[5] The plight of the group and of the individual are often consonant. When they conflict, the group's plight will ordinarily be more compelling, since group well-being is the more inclusive indicator of human well-being. When the distress cues from the individual are more salient, however, they may be largely instrumental in determining the observer's response.

[6] Another possible contributing factor is that empathic distress is from the beginning and perhaps through life largely, if not entirely, an involuntary response. The resulting awareness that other people's distress is inevitably accompanied by unpleasant feelings in oneself, given the basic positive orientation discussed above, may add to the child's sense of oneness with others.

[7] A study by R. F. Weiss et al. (1973) suggests a direct way to test the assumption that sympathetic distress predisposes the individual to act. They found a positive correlation between intensity of distress cues and speed of the subject's helping response. The subjects also sweated a lot when exposed to the distress cues. It should be possible to find out, using systematic physiological measures of emotional arousal, if arousal precedes the overt helping response, if its intensity relates positively to the speed of the response, and if it diminishes right afterwards— all of which would be expected if sympathetic distress predisposes the person to act.

[8] We deal here with the general structural basis for guilt. There are obviously individual differences. Some people feel guilty even when they have no choice, and some avoid guilt even when they have a choice.

[9] This was true only when the parent was generally not power assertive in his discipline

pattern. When highly power-assertive parents pointed out harmful consequences from the child's behavior, the child showed little considerate behavior. This finding suggests a possible "reactance" effect.

[10] In relating existential guilt to social activism I do not mean to imply that it was the only, or even the primary, motive for activism, only that it may have been a contributing factor.

[11] In L. W. Hoffman's study over two-thirds of the male subjects responded to Horner's items with responses indicating a negative attitude toward success. In Horner's original work (1968), done seven years earlier, less than 10 percent of the males gave such responses. Two-thirds of the females gave such responses in both studies.

[12] There are limits to how far the parent should go in making sacrifices. If parental generosity is overdone and not balanced with appropriate demands, the child, instead of identifying with the parental model, may grow to expect others to continue to make sacrifices for him.

Chapter 9.   A Holistic Approach to Moral Development and Behavior

[1] That stage structure alone is the subject of Kohlberg's research, rather than structure and cultural content, has been questioned (see Simpson, 1974). An interesting field example may be drawn from an account of Twin Oaks, a commune modeled after Skinner's *Walden II*, in which the communards attempt to live Stage 6 lives based on universal principles of equality, reciprocity, and justice—in this case, the subprinciples of free choice and sharing. In the sexual sphere possessiveness and jealousy are seen as faults. Whereas monogamy is acceptable if both parties choose it, it is certainly not encouraged by the community (Kinkade, 1973). In this group, as in any other, the specific applications of values and principles are culturally defined.

[2] An attempt to locate Eichmann on Kohlberg's hierarchy of moral reasoning on the basis of his testimony at the Jerusalem trials illustrates the operation of unconscious influences on reasoning. Like Hannah Arendt (1963), scorers who were given materials from which clues to identity were carefully omitted placed his moral judgments at the conventional level, Stage 4, where belief in authority and the maintenance of the social order dominate. Scorers who knew Eichmann's identity classified his moral reasoning as Stage 2—instrumental reciprocity in which actions are taken only to get what is wanted from others.

[3] A master of contemporary fiction, Jorge Luis Borges, has been quoted as saying that the censorship of his art had the tremendous advantage of making him "find metaphors." Thus far the censors have not discovered that there is a *solid* ethical argument for their work.

Chapter 10.   Honesty and Dishonesty

[1] This average r is based on data from column 6 of the tables on pp. 130–132, book II, *Studies in Deceit* (Hartshorne & May, 1928). The summed score consisted of 24 to 27 specific test scores.

[2] The findings for the factor analysis should be considered very tentative because of the small n of 44.

Chapter 11.   New Approaches in the Assessment of Moral Judgment

[1] Piaget and Kohlberg, in addition to investigating judgments of hypothetical stories, collect information on subjects' explanations of terms (e.g., What is a "lie"?).

[2] Another improvement in Kohlberg's method would be to include stories on moral topics other than those usually covered, for example, stories on the distribution of wealth, power, and opportunity.

[3] Much work needs to be done in specifying stage characteristics, in explaining why each characteristic is logically a part of its stage, and in explaining how the characteristics of later stages are conceptually more adequate than those of earlier stages. On the basis of available research, some hypotheses about stage characteristics seem to be less valid than others. Kohlberg's review (1964) of Piaget's stage characteristics, for example, reports that only about half of them were supported by empirical studies. Similarly, some of Kohlberg's stage characteristics seem likely to be confirmed and others disconfirmed by empirical studies. However, Kohlberg's current methods of data collection and scoring make it difficult, if not

impossible, to study stage characteristics individually. Consequently, one cannot evaluate individual parts of the scoring system.

[4] Recent discussions of stage characteristics (Kohlberg, 1972; Rest & Kohlberg, in preparation) have postulated an antiestablishment moral orientation which rejects conventional morality but has no positive principles for deriving obligations (Stage "4½"), an intuitive humanist orientation which derives obligations from certain ideals (Stage 5B), and a social contract moral orientation (Stage 5A).

[5] Carroll's work also includes an attempt to devise an objective test of moral judgment for use with subjects younger (below eighth grade) than those for whom the DIT is designed. Using rejection data may furnish a valuable index of moral judgment development.

[6] Kohlberg (1964, p. 404) reported a correlation of his measure with age (IQ controlled) of .59.

[7] Kohlberg's measure has an average correlation of .60 with a measure of comprehension of moral concepts (Rest, 1969).

[8] For example, a correlation of —.52 with his scale and the California F-scale, a measure of authoritarianism on which a high score reflects low-level moral judgment, has been reported by Kohlberg (1964, p. 422; 1969b, p. 390).

Chapter 12. Research on Piaget's Theory of Moral Development

[1] Research on moral development during the preschool years is in its infancy. McNamee and Peterson (1973) are constructing a Preschool Moral Judgment Scale which uses a forced-choice picture test designed to avoid some of the problems with verbally interviewing very young children. Damon (1973) has developed a measure of young children's conception of justice, while Irwin (Irwin & Moore, 1971) has investigated early role taking.

Chapter 13. The Social Psychology of Moral Behavior

[1] Supported by the National Institutes of Mental Health grant MH 21987-01. We thank T. Lickona for his helpful comments on an earlier draft of this paper.

Chapter 14. Social Influence and Moral Development

[1] The author wishes to thank Dr. Martin L. Hoffman for making some unpublished findings available to him and Dr. Sylvia Saltzstein for her helpful suggestions. Some of the original research reported here was supported by a grant from the National Institute of Child Health and Human Development, HD-06519, and a Faculty Research Award from the City University of New York.

[2] Of course, power assertion and induction also have a love withdrawal component. It is perfectly clear to a child whose parent has slapped him or taken away his privileges or even told the child that he has hurt the parent's feelings that the parent's love has been withdrawn, at least temporarily. The presumed difference between love withdrawal and the other two techniques is that in the case of love withdrawal, loss of affection alone is made focal.

[3] I do not mean to imply that honesty is ultimately unrelated to consideration for others, but only that in the typical experimental situation the connection may not be apparent to the child. Honesty then may reduce to more-or-less blind conformity to rules.

[4] One critical question about the above theorizing and the Hoffman and Saltzstein research is, Are the conventional and humanistic types different end-results of personality development, or are they different sequential stages of development? If the latter is the case, we might expect clearer relationships between parental discipline and moral types if the types were more refined to coincide with Kohlberg's developmental stages.

[5] M. L. Hoffman (1975) has offered a vigorous and interesting defense of the parent-discipline-influencing child proposition. Unfortunately it came to my attention too late to incorporate it into my discussion. While in my opinion it does not disprove the child's potential for influencing the parent's discipline under many conditions, it does strongly support the idea that parent discipline may and does influence the child. It is a central argument of the present chapter that the parent–child interaction involves mutual and circular influence.

[6] Recently Kohlberg has revised his stage descriptions, particularly Stage 3. Most of the relevant research discussed in this chapter was based on the earlier stage description, and we have relied on that earlier conceptualization throughout.

Chapter 15. The Responsive Bystander

[1] We express a special thanks to Tom Lickona and Gil Geis for their editorial commentary which, on many occasions, forced us to rethink issues. Carl Ridley, Liz Susman, and Dean Tjosvold read an earlier draft of the paper and offered numerous constructive suggestions.

[2] The Carmen Colon incident was the subject of an editorial which appeared in the *Poughkeepsie Journal* on January 23, 1971. The Glaser and Friedmann incidents, which, when considered together, aroused almost as much concern in New York City as did the well-known Kitty Genovese murder (see A. M. Rosenthal, 1964), were reported in the *New York Times* on September 28 and 21, 1972, respectively.

[3] No sample items for the last variety of religiosity are available in published works.

[4] Interactions between personality dimensions and situational factors were uncommon, however. Only 6 of 56 interactions were statistically significant.

[5] A similar illustration regarding the power of helping behavior in creating a sense of value in the helper is provided by the comments of a Danish woman who helped smuggle Jews out of her country during World War II: "We helped the Jews because it meant that for once in your life you were doing something worth-while. There has been a lot of talk about how grateful the Jews should be to their fellow Danes for having saved their lives, but I think the Danes should be equally grateful to the Jews for giving them an opportunity to do something decent and meaningful. It was a terrible time, but I must confess that it was also a wonderful time. Yes, I don't think that we were ever happier. Our activities gave us a special feeling of oneness. We were together. Nowhere were we refused" (Flender, 1964, p. 110).

[6] The senior author is currently collaborating with Dr. Gilbert Geis (Huston, Geis, Wright, & Garrett, 1976) on a two-year field study, supported by the National Institute of Mental Health, of the determinants of bystander intervention in crime in California (where the law provides compensation for injuries sustained by interveners). An early finding is that those who intervene in criminal events appear to be motivated more by anger toward the offender than by compassion for the victim.

Chapter 16. Television As a Moral Teacher

[1] The point is important because the first major studies of television effects on children did simply look at television per se, and generally found the overall presence of the medium at that time to have little impact. Industry spokesmen have misused these reports to claim that contemporary offerings (e.g., highly violent cartoons) regardless of content are also innocuous.

Chapter 17. Social-Cognitive Understanding

[1] This paper was written with the support of the Spencer Foundation, Chicago, Illinois.

[2] Age ranges for all stages represent only an average approximation based on our studies to date.

[3] Excerpting sentences from the open-ended interviews in order to provide examples of role-taking stages is always dangerous. It is, in a way, antithetical to the nature of a structural analysis, which searches for the organization of thought underlying a wide range of the child's ideas, not an isolated instance. Because higher stages incorporate lower ones, it is more likely that scoring errors will be made in the direction of scoring a child's thinking too low rather than too high. Therefore in this particular example, the statement is indicative of thinking that is at least Stage 1. Only through the examination of the entire protocol can one be sure that higher-stage role-taking is not present.

[4] The filmstrips, entitled *First Things: Social Reasoning* (1974) and *First Things: Values* (1971), are published by Guidance Associates, New York.

Chapter 19. A Paradigmatic Analysis of Psychological Issues at the Interface of Jurisprudence and Moral Conduct

[1] We can identify writers who accept the premise of "law as rightness" by their omissions. Glueck and Glueck (1970, 1972) readily create categories of transgressions, but take little trouble to analyze and categorize the laws that have been transgressed. Kidnapping and the use of marijuana appear to have equal utility as validating data for their hypotheses. Toch (1969) recognizes that "collective violence cannot be remedied when there is no other way to

achieve dignity and status" (p. 239). Yet his remedies for violence focus on his psychodynamic interpretations of violent men. He does not give derogatory explanations of politicians, for example, who limit redress by voting to discontinue public funds that support legal counsel for the indigent. Abrahamsen (1973) concludes, after his study of American assassins, that they "all showed surprising similarities in their family background, their personality make-up and their pattern of behavior" (p. 18). One wonders if Toch and Abrahamsen would be willing to extend their dynamic interpretations of violent men and assassins to cover the lawbreakers who gave us the Boston Tea Party, Bastille Day, the attempt on the lives of Hitler and Chiang.

[2] Biggs's account (1955, pp. 97–100) of the M'Naghten matter provides a valuable historical perspective. Behavioral scientists frequently overlook the rich historical context of the affair. Conservative British factions promoted the belief that the assassination attempt had been fomented by the Anti-Corn-Law League, and were happy to allow the inference that M'Naghten was part of the radical movements troubling Great Britain at that time. Queen Victoria's interest in the case is well documented. One can easily believe that the posttrial promulgation of the famous M'Naghten rules by the House of Lords resulted largely from the strong concern that the radicals "were getting away with something dangerous" by appealing for acquittal on grounds of insanity.

Chapter 20.   The Social Ecology of Violence

[1] The authors wish to express their appreciation to Linda Monahan, Peter Scharf, Robley Geis, and Carol Whalen for their comments on a previous draft of this chapter, and to Susan Miller for her editorial assistance.

[2] Evans was about ten years older than Rodgers. One of the bullets ricocheted off Evans's body and inflicted a glancing wound on his father-in-law, who was standing nearby.

[3] The curious reasoning of the decision is worth noting: "The danger to the public need not be possible physical violence or a crime of violence. It is enough if there is competent evidence that he may commit any criminal act, for any such act will injure others and will expose the person to arrest, trial and conviction. There is always additional possible danger—not to be discounted even if remote—that a non-violent criminal act may expose the perpetrator to violent retaliatory acts by the victim of the crime" (p. 198).

[4] Details and quotations are taken from the transcripts of the civil suits and from exhibits introduced during their adjudication.

[5] Service letters had been sent earlier to owners of single-engine planes, but were not dispatched to owners of other vulnerable models, nor was notice of the problem inserted into the owner's manual.

[6] A telling exception (*Commonwealth* v. *Welansky,* 1944) was the manslaughter conviction of the owner of the Cocoanut Grove nightclub in Boston after the disastrous 1942 fire for failure to meet safety regulations, stated as "intentional failure to take such care in disregard of the harmful possible consequences." The club owner was in the hospital at the time of the fire and claimed corporate, not personal, responsibility. We may assume that the somewhat unsavory nature of his enterprise—compared with manufacturing airplanes—made him particularly vulnerable to the negligence charge.

[7] It should be evident that neither Morris nor the present authors are advocating that poverty itself should be a criminal defense.

REFERENCES

A social disaster. *Poughkeepsie Journal*, Jan. 23, 1971.

Abel, T. M. Moral judgments among subnormals. *Journal of Abnormal and Social Psychology*, 1941, *36*, 378–392.

Abelson, R. Are attitudes necessary? In B. T. King & E. McGinnes (Eds.), *Attitudes, conflicts, and social change*. New York: Academic, 1972.

Abraham, K. *Selected papers*. London: Hogarth, 1928.

Abrahamsen, D. *The murdering mind*. New York: Harper & Row, 1973.

Abram, M. B. America's mute conscience. *New York Times*, Dec. 26, 1971, 9.

Acton, J. *Essays on freedom and power*. Boston: Beacon Press, 1948.

Aderman, D. Elation, depression, and helping behavior. *Journal of Personality and Social Psychology*, 1972, *24*, 91–101.

Alexander, F. The relation of structural and instinctual conflicts. *Psychoanalytic Quarterly*, 1933, *2*, 76–90.

Alexander, F. Remarks about the relation of inferiority feelings to guilt feelings. *International Journal of Psychoanalysis*, 1938, *19*, 41–49.

Allen, H. Bystander intervention and helping on the subway. In L. Bickman & T. Henchy (Eds.), *Beyond the laboratory: Field research in social psychology*. New York: McGraw-Hill, 1972.

Allen, M. K. & Liebert, R. M. Children's adoption of self-reward patterns: Model's prior experience and incentive for nonimitation. *Child Development*, 1969, *40*, 921–926.

Allen, M. S. *Morphological creativity*. Englewood Cliffs, N.J.: Prentice-Hall, 1962.

Allen, R. C., Ferster, E. Z., & Wiehofen, H. *Mental impairment and legal incompetency*. Englewood Cliffs, N.J.: Prentice-Hall, 1968.

Allinsmith, W. The learning of moral standards. In D. R. Miller and G. E. Swanson (Eds.), *Inner conflict and defense*. New York: Holt, Rinehart and Winston, 1960, pp. 141–176.

Allport, G. W. *Becoming*. New Haven, Conn.: Yale University Press, 1955.

Allport, G. W., Vernon, P. E., & Lindzey, G. *Study of values*. Boston: Houghton Mifflin, 1960.

Almond, G. & Verba, S. *The civic culture: Political attitudes and democracy in five nations*. Boston: Little, Brown, 1963.

Alston, W. P. Comments on Kohlberg's "From is to ought." In T. Mischel (Ed.), *Cognitive development and epistemology*. New York: Academic, 1971, pp. 269–284.

American Law Institute. *Model penal code*. Philadelphia: American Law Institute, 1962.

American Psychiatric Association. *Diagnostic and statistical manual of mental disorders* (2d ed). Washington, D.C.: American Psychiatric Association, 1968.

Anderson, J. The prediction of adjustment over time. In I. Iscoe & H. Stevenson (Eds.), *Personality development in children*. Austin: University of Texas Press, 1960.

Anderson, N. H. Information integration theory: A brief survey. *Center for human information processing, technical report no. 24*. University of California at San Diego, 1972.

Andres, D. & Walters, R. H. Modification of delay of punishment effects through cognitive restructuring. *Proceedings of the 78th Annual Convention of the American Psychological Association*, 1970, 483–484.

Angry Senator shouts at Nader in hearing. *Los Angeles Times*, May 11, 1971, 26.

Argyle, M. & Little, B. R. Do personality traits apply to social behavior? *Journal of Theory of Social Behavior (Great Britain)*, 1972, *2*, 1–35.

Anonymous. Shall mental health personnel be added to New York State's prisons? Unpublished student paper, State University of New York at Albany, 1971.

Arendt, H. *Eichmann in Jerusalem*. New York: Viking, 1963.

Armsby, R. E. A reexamination of the development of moral judgments in children. *Child Development*, 1971, *42*, 1241–1248.

Arnold, M. Narcotic deaths put at over 1,050. *New York Times*, December 20, 1970, 32.

Arnold, M. Many look on as 3 youths here mug and rob prominent lawyer. *New York Times*, Sept. 28, 1972, 1, 31.

Aronfreed, J. The nature, variety and social patterning of moral responses to transgression. *Journal of Abnormal and Social Psychology*, 1961, *63*, 223–240.

Aronfreed, J. The effects of experimental socialization paradigms upon two moral responses to transgression. *Journal of Abnormal and Social Psychology*, 1963, *66*, 437–448.

Aronfreed, J. The origins of self-criticism. *Psychological Review*, 1964, *71*, 193–218.

Aronfreed, J. Aversive control of internalization. In W. J. Arnold (Ed.), *Nebraska Symposium on Motivation* (Vol. 16). Lincoln: University of Nebraska Press, 1968, pp. 271–320. (a)

Aronfreed, J. The concept of internalization. In D. A. Goslin & D. C. Glass (Eds.), *Handbook of socialization theory*. New York: Rand-McNally, 1968. (b)

Aronfreed, J. *Conduct and conscience: The socialization of internalized control over behavior.* New York: Academic, 1968. (c)

Aronfreed, J. The socialization of altruistic and sympathetic behavior: Some theoretical and experimental analyses. In J. Macaulay & L. Berkowitz (Eds.), *Altruism and helping behavior*. New York: Academic, 1970. Pp. 103–126.

Aronfreed, J. Some problems for a theory of the acquisition of conscience. In C. M. Beck, B. S. Crittenden, & E. V. Sullivan (Eds.), *Moral education: Interdisciplinary approaches.* Toronto: University of Toronto Press, 1971. Pp. 183–199.

Aronfreed, J. & Leff, R. The effects of intensity of punishment and complexity of discrimination upon the generalization of an internalized inhibition. Unpublished manuscript, University of Pennsylvania, 1963.

Aronfreed, J. & Paskal, V. Altruism, empathy, and the conditioning of positive affect. Unpublished manuscript, University of Pennsylvania, 1965.

Aronfreed, J. & Paskal, V. The development of sympathetic behavior in children: An experimental test of a two-phase hypothesis. Unpublished manuscript, 1966.

Aronfreed, J. & Reber, A. Internalized behavioral suppression and the timing of social punishment. *Journal of Personality and Social Psychology*, 1965, *1*, 3–16.

Aronoff, J. *Psychological needs and cultural systems*. New York: Van Nostrand, 1967.

Aronson, E. & Mettee, D. R. Dishonest behavior as a function of differential levels of induced self-esteem. *Journal of Personality and Social Psychology*, 1968, *9*, 121–127.

Atkins, B. E. & Atkins, R. E. A study of the honesty of prospective teachers. *The Elementary School Journal*, 1936, *36*, 595–603.

Ausubel, D. P. *Ego development and the personality disorders.* New York: Grune & Stratton, 1952.

Ausubel, D. P. *Theory and problems of child development.* New York: Grune & Stratton, 1958.

Ayllon, T. & Azrin, N. *The token economy.* New York: Appleton, 1968.

Bacon, M. K., Child, I. L., & Barry, H., III. A cross-cultural study of correlates of crime. *Journal of Abnormal and Social Psychology*, 1963, *66*, 291–300.

Baier, K. *The moral point of view.* New York: Random House, 1965.

Bailey, W. Correctional treatment: An analysis of one hundred correctional outcome studies. *Journal of Criminal Law, Criminology, and Police Science*, 1966, *57*, 153–160.

Bailyn, L. Mass media and children: A study of exposure habits and cognitive effects. *Psychology Monographs*, 1959, *73* (1, Whole No. 471).

Bakan, D. *On method: Toward a reconstruction of psychological investigation.* San Francisco: Jossey-Bass, 1969.

Baker, C. *Ernest Hemingway: A life story.* New York: Scribner, 1969.

Baldwin, A. L. *Theories of child development.* New York: Wiley, 1967.

Baldwin, J. M. *Social and ethical interpretations in mental development.* New York: Macmillan, 1906.

Bandura, A. Social learning through imitation. In M. R. Jones (Ed.), *Nebraska Symposium on Motivation* (Vol. 10). Lincoln: University of Nebraska Press, 1962. Pp. 211–269.

Bandura, A. What TV violence can do to your child. *Look*, Oct. 22, 1963, *27*, 46–52.

Bandura, A. Influence of models' reinforcement contingencies on the acquisition of imitative responses. *Journal of Personality and Social Psychology*, 1965, *1*, 589–595. (a)

Bandura, A. Vicarious processes: A case of no-trial learning. In L. Berkowitz (Ed.), *Advances in experimental social psychology*, Vol. 2. New York: Academic, 1965. Pp. 1–55. (b)

Bandura, A. *Principles of behavior modification.* New York: Holt, Rinehart and Winston, 1969. (a)

Bandura, A. Social learning theory of identificatory processes. In D. A. Goslin (Ed.), *Handbook of socialization theory and research.* Chicago: Rand-McNally, 1969. (b)

Bandura, A. Analysis of modeling processes. In A. Bandura (Ed.), *Psychological modeling: Conflicting theories.* Chicago: Aldine-Atherton, 1971. (a)

Bandura, A. *Social learning theory.* New York: General Learning, 1971. (b)

Bandura, A. Vicarious and self-reinforcement processes. In R. Glaser (Ed.), *The nature of reinforcement.* New York: Academic, 1971. (c)

Bandura, A. *Aggression: A social learning analysis.* Englewood Cliffs, N.J.: Prentice-Hall, 1973.

Bandura, A. & Harris, M. B. Modification of syntactic style. *Journal of Experimental Child Psychology,* 1966, *4,* 341–352.

Bandura, A. & Kupers, C. J. Transmission of patterns of self-reward through modeling. *Journal of Abnormal and Social Psychology,* 1964, *69,* 1–9.

Bandura, A. & McDonald, F. J. The influence of social reinforcement and the behavior of models in shaping children's moral judgments. *Journal of Abnormal and Social Psychology,* 1963, *67,* 274–281.

Bandura, A. & Perloff, B. Relative efficacy of self-monitored and externally imposed reinforcement systems. *Journal of Personality and Social Psychology,* 1967, *7,* 111–116.

Bandura, A., Ross, D., & Ross, S. A. Imitation of film-mediated aggressive models. *Journal of Abnormal and Social Psychology,* 1963, *66,* 3–11. (a)

Bandura, A., Ross, D., & Ross, S. A. Vicarious reinforcement and imitative learning. *Journal of Abnormal and Social Psychology,* 1963, *67,* 601–607. (b)

Bandura, A. & Walters, R. H. *Adolescent aggression.* New York: Ronald, 1959.

Bandura, A. & Walters, R. H. *Social learning and personality development.* New York: Holt, Rinehart and Winston, 1963.

Bandura, A. & Whalen, C. K. The influence of antecedent reinforcement and divergent modeling cues on patterns of self-reward. *Journal of Personality and Social Psychology,* 1966, *3,* 373–382.

Bar-Yam, M., Reimer, J., & Kohlberg, L. Development of moral reasoning in the kibbutz. In L. Kohlberg (Ed.), *Recent research in moral development.* New York: Holt, Rinehart and Winston, in preparation.

Barbu, Z. Studies in children's honesty. *Quarterly Bulletin of the British Psychological Society,* 1951, *2,* 53–57.

Barker, R. & Gump, P. *Big school, small school.* Stanford, Ca.: Stanford University Press, 1966.

Barr, R. F. & McConaghy, N. A general factor of conditionability: A study of galvanic skin responses and penile responses. *Behavior Research and Therapy,* 1972, *3,* 215–228.

Bartlett, R. Testimony before *Meeting of Governor's committee on the compensation of victims of violent crime.* New York: Association of the Bar of City of New York, Jan. 3, 1966. Pp. 74–88.

Bateson, G., Jackson, D., Haley, J., & Weakland, J. Toward a theory of schizophrenia. *Behavioral Science,* 1956, *1,* 251–264.

Batonbacal, I. & Slipyan, A. Transmission of serum hepatitis in heroin addicts. *New York State Journal of Medicine,* 1959, *59,* 320–323.

Battle, E. & Rotter, J. Children's feelings of personal control as related to social class and ethnic group. *Journal of Personality,* 1963, *31,* 482–490.

Baumgold, J. The new community of victims. *New York,* Sept. 1973, *6,* 54.

Baumrind, D. Child care practices anteceding three patterns of preschool behavior. *Genetic Psychology Monographs,* 1967, *75,* 43–88.

Baumrind, D. Current patterns of parental authority. *Developmental Psychology,* 1971, *4,* 1–103.

Baumrind, D. & Black, A. E. Socialization practices associated with dimensions of competence in pre-school boys and girls. *Child Development,* 1967, *38,* 291–327.

Baxstrom v. Herold. *U.S. Reports*, 1966, *383*, 107.

Baxter, W. The mass media and young people. *Journal of Broadcasting*, 1961, *5*, 49–58.

Becker, W. Consequences of different kinds of parental discipline. In M. L. Hoffman & L. W. Hoffman (Eds.), *Review of Child Development Research*, Vol. I. New York: Russell Sage Foundation, 1964. Pp. 169–208.

Bell, R. Q. A reinterpretation of the direction of effects in studies of socialization. *Psychological Review*, 1968, *75*, 81–95.

Bell, S. M. The development of the concept of object as related to infant–mother attachment. *Child Development*, 1970, *41*, 291–311.

Benedict, R. *Patterns of culture.* New York: New American Library, 1958. (Originally published, 1934.)

Benedict, R. *The chrysanthemum and the sword.* Boston: Houghton Mifflin, 1946.

Benton, A. A. Effects of the timing of negative response consequences on the observational learning of resistance to temptation in children. Unpublished doctoral dissertation, University of California at Los Angeles, 1966.

Berger, S. M. Conditioning through vicarious instigation. *Psychological Review*, 1962, *69*, 450–466.

Bergler, E. *Basic neurosis.* New York: Grune & Stratton, 1949.

Berkowitz, L. *Aggression: A social psychological analysis.* New York: McGraw-Hill, 1962.

Berkowitz, L. *Development of motives and values in a child.* New York: Basic Books, 1964.

Berkowitz, L. Social norms, feelings, and other factors affecting helping and altruism. In L. Berkowitz (Ed.), *Advances in experimental social psychology,* Vol. 6. New York: Academic, 1972.

Berkowitz, L. Reactance and the unwillingness to help others. *Psychological Bulletin*, 1973, *79*, 310–317. (a)

Berkowitz, L. Words and symbols as stimuli to aggressive responses. In J. Knutson (Ed.), *The control of aggression.* Chicago: Aldine-Atherton, 1973. (b)

Berkowitz, L. & Connor, W. H. Success, failure and social responsibility. *Journal of Personality and Social Psychology*, 1966, *4*, 664–669.

Berkowitz, L. & Lutterman, K. The traditionally socially responsible personality. *Public Opinion Quarterly*, 1968, *32*, 169–187.

Berscheid, E. & Walster, E. When does a harm-doer compensate a victim? *Journal of Personality and Social Psychology*, 1967, *6*, 435–441.

Berscheid, E. & Walster, E. *Interpersonal attraction.* Reading, Mass.: Addison-Wesley, 1969.

Bettelheim, B. Individual and mass behavior in extreme situations. *Journal of Abnormal and Social Psychology*, 1943, *38*, 417–452.

Bettelheim, B. *The informed heart.* New York: The Free Press, 1960.

Bettelheim, B. Moral education. In N. F. Sizer & T. R. Sizer (Eds.), *Moral education: Five lectures.* Cambridge, Mass.: Harvard University Press, 1970. Pp. 85–108.

Bickman, L. The effect of another bystander's ability to help on bystander intervention in an emergency. *Journal of Experimental Social Psychology*, 1971, *7*, 367–379.

Bickman, L. Social influence and diffusion of responsibility in an emergency. *Journal of Experimental Social Psychology*, 1972, *8*, 438–445.

Biggs, J. *The guilty mind.* Baltimore, Md.: Johns Hopkins, 1955.

Blatt, M. & Kohlberg, L. The effects of classroom moral discussion upon children's level of moral development. In L. Kohlberg (Ed.), *Recent research in moral deveopment.* New York: Holt, Rinehart, and Winston, in preparation.

Block, J. *The challenge of response sets.* New York: Appleton, 1965.

Block, J. Some reasons for the apparent inconsistency of personality. *Psychological Bulletin*, 1968, *70*, 210–212.

Block, J. Some antecedents of ego-control: A longitudinal analysis. Paper presented at the NIMH Conference on Development Aspects of Self-Regulation, La Jolla, California, Feb. 1972.

Block, J. & Martin, B. Predicting the behavior of children under frustration. *Journal of Abnormal and Social Psychology*, 1955, *51*, 281–285.

Block, Jeanne. Personal communication, 1972.

Block, Jeanne. The role of ego-conrol and ego resiliency in cognitive processing. Paper presented at the NIMH Conference on Developmental Aspects of Self-Regulation, La Jolla, California, Feb. 1972.

Bloodworth, D. *The Chinese looking glass*. New York: Dell, 1969.

Boas, F. *General anthropology*. Boston: D. C. Heath, 1938.

Boas, F. *Kwakiutl ethnology*. Unpublished study, quoted in Codere, 1950, p. 99. (n. d.)

Boehm, L. The development of independence: A comparative study. *Child Development*, 1957, *28*, 85–92.

Boehm, L. The development of conscience: A comparison of American children of different mental and socio-economic levels. *Child Development*, 1962, *33*, 575–590.

Boehm, L. Conscience development in mentally retarded adolescents. *Journal of Special Education*, 1967, *2*, 93–103.

Boehm, L. & Nass, M. L. Social class differences in conscience development. *Child Development*, 1962, *33*, 565–574.

Bolt, R. *A man for all seasons*. New York: Random House, 1960.

Bonhoeffer, D. *Letters and papers from prison*. New York: Macmillan, 1953.

Bonjean, C. M. & McGee, R. Scholastic dishonesty among undergraduates in differing systems of social control. *Sociology of Education*, 1965, *38*, 127–137.

Borke, H. Interpersonal perception of young children: Egocentrism or empathy? *Developmental Psychology*, 1971, *5*, 263–269.

Borke, H. Chandler and Greenspan's "Ersatz Egocentrism": A rejoinder. *Developmental Psychology*, 1972, *7*, 107–109.

Borkovec, T. D. Autonomic reactivity to sensory stimulation in psychopathic, neurotic and normal juvenile delinquents. *Journal of Consulting and Clinical Psychology*, 1970, *35*, 217–222.

Borofsky, G., Stollak, G., & Messé, L. Sex differences in bystander reactions to physical assault. *Journal of Experimental Social Psychology*, 1971, *7*, 313–318.

Bousfield, R. M. *Report of the trial of Daniel M'Naghten*, London: Henry Renshaw, 1843.

Bower, G. H. Organizational factors in memory. *Cognitive Psychology*, 1970, *1*, 18–46.

Bowers, K. S. Situationism in psychology: An analysis and a critique. *Psychological Review*, 1973, *80*, 307–336.

Bowers, W. J. *Student dishonesty and its control in college*. New York: Columbia University, the Bureau of Applied Social Research, 1964.

Bowlby, J. *Forty juvenile thieves: Their character and home life*. London: Hogarth, 1946.

Bradley, C. & Bowen, M. Amphetamine therapy of children: Behavior disorders. *American Journal of Orthopsychiatry*, 1941, *11*, 92–103.

Braginsky, D. D. & Braginsky, B. M. *Hansels and Gretels*. New York: Holt, Rinehart and Winston, 1971.

Bramel, D. Interpersonal attraction, hostility, and perception. In J. Mills (Ed.), *Experimental social psychology*. London: Macmillan, 1969. Pp. 1–120.

Breznitz, S. & Kugelmass, S. Intentionality in moral judgment: Developmental stages. *Child Development*, 1967, *38*, 469–479.

Bridges, K. M. B. *The social and emotional development of the preschool child*. London: Kegan Paul, 1931.

Broadbent, D. E. *Perception and communication*. Oxford: Pergamon, 1958.

Broadcasting Yearbook, 1971. Washington, D.C.: Broadcasting Publications, 1971.

Brock, T. C. & Becker, L. A. "Debriefing" and susceptibility to subsequent experimental manipulations. *Journal of Experimental Social Psychology*, 1966, *2*, 314–323.

Brock, T. C. & DelGiudice, C. Stealing and temporal orientation. *Journal of Abnormal and Social Psychology*, 1963, *66*, 91–94.

Brodsky, S. L. & Jacobson, L. S. The study of deceptive and antisocial behavior in the laboratory. Paper presented at the 78th annual meeting of the American Psychological Association, Miami Beach, 1970.

Brogden, H. E. A factor analysis of forty character tests. *Psychological Monographs*, 1940, *52*, 39–55.

Bromberg, W. *Crime and the mind*. New York: Macmillan, 1965.

Bronfenbrenner, U. Some familial antecedents of responsibility and leadership in adolescents. In L. Petrullo & B. Bass (Eds.), *Leadership and interpersonal behavior*. New York: Holt, Rinehart and Winston, 1961. Pp. 239–272.

Bronfenbrenner, U. The role of age, sex, class and culture in studies of moral development. *Religious Education*, 1962, *57* (4, Research Supplement), 3–17. (a)

Bronfenbrenner, U. Soviet methods of character education. *American Psychologist*, 1962, *17*, 550–564. (b)

Bronfenbrenner, U. Reaction to social pressure from adults versus peers among Soviet day-school and boarding-school pupils in the perspective of an American sample. *Journal of Personality and Social Psychology*, 1970, *15*, 179–189. (a)

Bronfenbrenner, U. *Two worlds of childhood*. New York: Russell Sage Foundation, 1970. (b)

Bronfenbrenner, U. Developmental research and public policy. In J. M. Romanshin (Ed.), *Social science and social welfare*. New York: Council of Social Work Education, 1973.

Brown, R. W. *Social psychology*. New York: The Free Press, 1965.

Bryan, J. H. Model affect and children's imitative altruism. *Child Development*, 1971, *42*, 2061–2065.

Bryan, J. H. & London, P. Altruistic behavior by children. *Psychological Bulletin*, 1970, *73*, 200–211.

Bryan, J. H. & Schwartz, T. Effects of film material upon children's behavior. *Psychological Bulletin*, 1971, *75*, 50–59.

Bryan, J. H. & Test, M. A. Models and helping: Naturalistic studies in aiding behavior. *Journal of Personality and Social Psychology*, 1967, *6*, 400–407.

Bryan, J. H. & Walbek, N. H. The impact of words and deeds concerning altruism upon children. *Child Development*, 1970, *41*, 747–757. (a)

Bryan, J. H. & Walbek, N. H. Preaching and practicing generosity: Children's actions and reactions. *Child Development*, 1970, *41*, 329–353. (b)

Buchanan, J. P. & Thompson, S. K. A quantitative methodology to examine the development of moral judgment. *Child Development*, 1973, *44*, 186–189.

Bull, N. J. *Moral education*. London: Routledge, 1969.

Burgess, P. K. Eysenck's theory of criminality: A new approach. *British Journal of Criminology*, 1972, *12*, 74–82.

Burns, N. & Cavey, L. Age differences in empathic ability among children. *Canadian Journal of Psychology*, 1957, *11*, 227–230.

Burt, C. Factorial studies of personality and their bearing on the work of the teacher. *British Journal of Educational Psychology*, 1965, *35*, 368–378.

Burton, R. V. Research on the processes of internalization of rules, standards, and values. Unpublished project report for NIMH Intramural Research, 1960.

Burton, R. V. Generality of honesty reconsidered. *Psychological Review*, 1963, *70*, 481–499.

Burton, R. V. Socialization: Psychological aspects. In D. L. Sills (Ed.), *International encyclopedia of the social sciences*, Vol. 14. New York: Crowell-Collier and Macmillan, 1968, pp. 534–545.

Burton, R. V. Validity of retrospective reports assessed by the multitrait–multimethod analysis. *Developmental Psychology Monograph*, 1970, *3*, 3, Part 2.

Burton, R. V. Correspondence between behavioral and doll-play measures of conscience. *Developmental Psychology*, 1971, *5*, 320–332.

Burton, R. V. & Goldberg, F. G. Cheating related to maternal pressures for achievement. Unpublished paper, n.d.

Burton, R. V., Maccoby, E. E., & Allinsmith, W. Antecedents of resistance to temptation in four-year-old children. *Child Development*, 1961, *32*, 689–710.

Burton, R. V. & Whiting, J. W. M. The absent father and cross-sex identity. *Merrill-Palmer Quarterly of Behavior and Development*, 1961, *7*, 85–95.

Byrne, D. Role-taking in adolescence and adulthood. Unpublished doctoral dissertation, Harvard University, 1975.

Campbell, D. T. Conformity in psychology's theories of acquired behavioral dispositions. In I. A. Berg & B. M. Bass (Eds.), *Conformity and deviation.* New York: Harper & Row, 1961. Pp. 101–142.

Campbell, D. T. & Fiske, D. Convergent and discriminant validation. *Psychological Bulletin,* 1959, *56,* 81–105.

Canning, R. Does an honor system reduce classroom cheating? An experimental answer. *Journal of Experimental Education,* 1956, *24,* 291–296.

Carini, P. Studying thinking in children. Unpublished monograph, The Prospect School, North Bennington, Vermont, 1968.

Carlsmith, J. M. The effect of punishment on avoidance responses: The use of different stimuli for training and punishment. Paper presented at the annual meeting of the Eastern Psychological Association, Philadelphia, 1961.

Carlsmith, J. M. & Gross, A. Some effects of guilt on compliance. *Journal of Personality and Social Psychology,* 1969, *11,* 240–244.

Carroll, J. Children's judgments of statements exemplifying different moral stages. Unpublished doctoral dissertation, University of Minnesota, 1974.

Carroll, W. R., Rosenthal, T. L., & Brysh, C. Socially induced imitation of grammatical structures. Paper presented at the meeting of the Society for Research in Child Development, Santa Monica, March 1969.

Caruso, I. H. La notion de responsabilité et de justice immanente chez l'enfant. *Archives de Psychologie,* 1943, *29* (Whole no. 114).

Cautela, J. R. Covert conditioning. In A. Jacobs & L. B. Sachs (Eds.), *The psychology of private events.* New York: Academic, 1971. Pp. 112–130.

Chaffee, S. H. Television and adolescent aggressiveness (overview). In G. A. Comstock & E. A. Rubinstein (Eds.), *Television and social behavior, Vol. III: Television and adolescent aggressiveness.* Washington, D.C.: U.S. Government Printing Office, 1972. Pp. 1–34.

Chandler, M. J. Egocentrism and childhood psychopathology. Paper presented at the meeting of the Society for Research in Child Development, Minneapolis, April 1971.

Chandler, M. J. & Greenspan, S. Ersatz egocentrism: A reply to H. Borke. *Developmental Psychology,* 1972, *7,* 104–106.

Cherubin, C. The medical sequelae of narcotic addiction. *Annals of Internal Medicine,* 1967, *67,* 23–33.

Cheyne, J. A. Some parameters of punishment affecting resistance to deviation and generalization of a prohibition. *Child Development,* 1971, *42,* 1249–1261.

Cheyne, J. A. Punishment and "reasoning" in the development of self-control. In R. D. Parke (Ed.), *Recent trends in social learning theory.* New York: Academic, 1972.

Cheyne, J. A., Goyeche, J. R. M., & Walters, R. H. Attention, anxiety, and rules in resistance to deviation in children. *Journal of Experimental Child Psychology,* 1969, *8,* 127–139.

Cheyne, J. A. & Walters, R. H. Intensity of punishment, timing of punishment, and cognitive structure as determinants of response inhibition. *Journal of Experimental Child Psychology,* 1969, *7,* 231–244.

Child, I. Socialization. In G. Lindzen (Ed.), *Handbook of social psychology.* Reading, Mass.: Addison-Wesley, 1954.

Chittenden, G. E. An experimental study in measuring and modifying assertive behavior in young children. *Monographs of the Society for Research in Child Development,* 1942, *7,* no. 1 (Serial No. 31).

Christie, R. & Geis, G. (Eds.) *Studies in Machiavellianism.* New York: Academic, 1968.

Church, R. M. The varied effects of punishment on behavior. *Psychological Review,* 1963, *70,* 369–402.

Clark, R. & Word, L. Why don't bystanders help? Because of ambiguity? *Journal of Personality and Social Psychology,* 1972, *24,* 392–400.

Clark, R. & Word, L. Where is the apathetic bystander? Situational characteristics of the emergency. *Journal of Personality and Social Psychology,* 1974, *29,* 279–287.

Cleckley, H. *The mask of sanity.* St. Louis: Mosley, 1964.

Cline, V. B., Croft, R. G., & Corrier, S. The desensitization of children to television violence. *Proceedings of the American Psychological Association*, 1972, *80*, 99–100.

Clore, G. L. & Jeffery, K. M. Emotional role playing, attitude change, and attraction toward a disabled person. *Journal of Personality and Social Psychology*, 1972, *23*, 105–111.

Coder, R. Moral judgment in adults. Unpublished doctoral dissertation, University of Minnesota, 1975.

Codere, H. *Fighting with property.* New York: J. J. Augustin, 1950.

Coffin, W. S., Jr. Not yet a good man. *New York Times*, June 19, 1973, 39.

Cohen, M. *Reason and the law.* New York: Collier, 1961.

Colby, A. Logical operational limitations on the development of moral judgment. Unpublished doctoral dissertation, Columbia University, 1972.

Colby, A., Fritz, B., & Kohlberg, L. The relation of logical and moral judgment stages. Unpublished manuscript, Harvard University, Cambridge, Mass., 1974.

Colby, A. & Kohlberg, L. The relation between the development of formal operations and moral judgment. In D. Bush & S. Feldman (Eds.), *Cognitive development and social development: Relationships and implications.* New York: Lawrence Earlbaum Associates, in preparation.

Collins, W. A. Learning of media content: A developmental study. *Child Development*, 1970, *41*, 1133–1142.

Commonwealth *v.* Welansky. *Northeast Reports* (2d), 1944, *55*, 902.

Condry, J. Freedom, choice and the development of individuation. Unpublished manuscript, Cornell University, 1971.

Condry, J. & Siman, M. An experimental study of adult versus peer orientation. Unpublished manuscript, Cornell University, Ithaca, N.Y., 1968.

Cooper, D. The analysis of an objective measure of moral development. Unpublished doctoral dissertation, University of Minnesota, 1972.

Costanzo, P. R., Coie, J. D., Grument, J. F., & Farnill, D. A reexamination of the effects of intent and consequences on children's moral judgment. *Child Development*, 1973, *44*, 154–161.

Costanzo, P. R. & Shaw, M. E. Conformity as a function of age level. *Child Development*, 1966, *37*, 967–975.

Cowan, P., Langer, J., Heavenrich, J., & Nathanson, M. Social learning and Piaget's cognitive theory of moral development. *Journal of Personality and Social Psychology*, 1969, *11*, 261–274.

Cox, H. *The feast of fools.* New York: Harper & Row, 1969.

Craft, M., Stephenson, G., & Granger, C. A controlled trial of authoritarian and self-governing regimes with adolescent psychopaths. *American Journal of Orthopsychiatry*, 1964, *34*, 543–554.

Craig, K. D. & Weinstein, M. S. Conditioning vicarious affective arousal. *Psychological Reports*, 1965, *17*, 955–963.

Crider, K. & Lunn, R. Personality correlates of electrodermal lability. *Psychophysiology* (Abstracts), 1970, *60*, 633–634.

Cronbach, L. J. & Meehl, P. E. Construct validity in psychological tests. *Psychological Bulletin*, 1955, *52*, 281–302.

Crowley, P. Effect of training upon objectivity of moral judgment in grade-school children. *Journal of Personality and Social Psychology*, 1968, *8*, 228–232.

Culhane, J. California enacts legislation to aid victims of criminal violence. *Stanford Law Review*, 1965, *18*, 266–273.

Cunningham & Walsh. *Videotown, 1948–1957.* New York: Cunningham & Walsh, 1958.

Curdin, J. A study of the development of immanent justice. Unpublished doctoral dissertation, University of North Carolina at Chapel Hill, 1966.

Cutts, K. K. & Jasper, H. H. Effect of benzedrine sulfate on behavior problem children with abnormal electroencephalograms. *Archives of Neurology and Psychiatry*, 1949, *41*, 1138–1145.

Damon, W. Children's conception of justice. Paper presented at the annual meeting of the Society for Research in Child Development, Philadelphia, March 1973.

D'Andrade, R. G. Cognitive structures and judgment. Paper prepared for T.O.B.R.E. Research Workshop on *Cognitive Organization and Psychological Processes*, Huntington Beach, California, August 16–21, 1970.

Daniel M'Naghten's case. *The English Reports*, 1901, *8*, 718–724.

Darley, J. & Batson, C. "From Jerusalem to Jericho": A study of situational and dispositional variables in helping behavior. *Journal of Personality and Social Psychology*, 1973, *27*, 100–108.

Darley, J. & Latané, B. Bystander intervention in emergencies: Diffusion of responsibility. *Journal of Personality and Social Psychology*, 1968, *8*, 377–383.

Darley, J., Teger, A., & Lewis, L. Do groups always inhibit individuals' responses to potential emergencies? *Journal of Personality and Social Psychology*, 1973, *26*, 395–399.

Darlington, R. B. & Macker, C. E. Displacement of guilt-produced altruistic behavior. *Journal of Personality and Social Psychology*, 1966, *4*, 442–443.

David, K. H. Sex differences in cheating and judgment discrepancy on Barron's ES scale. *Perceptual and Motor Skills*, 1967, *24*, 1154.

Davies, J. C. *Human nature in politics*. New York: Wiley, 1963.

Davis, K. E. & Jones, E. E. Changes in interpersonal perception as a means of reducing cognitive dissonance. *Journal of Abnormal and Social Psychology*, 1960, *61*, 402–410.

Davis, R., Sutherland, N. S., & Judd, B. R. Information content in recognition and recall. *Journal of Experimental Psychology*, 1961, *61*, 422–429.

Dawson, J. Rewards for the rescue of human life? In J. Ratcliffe (Ed.), *The good Samaritan and the law*. New York: Doubleday Anchor, 1966.

Death at Donora. *Time Magazine*, Nov. 8, 1948, *52*, 25.

DeFleur, M. & DeFleur, L. The relative contribution of television as a learning source for children's occupational knowledge. *American Sociological Review*, 1967, *32*, 777–789.

Delay, J., Deniker, P., & Green, A. Le milieu familial des schizophréniques. *L'Encephale* (Paris), 1957, *46*, 189–232.

Dember, W. N. Motivation and the cognitive revolution. *American Psychologist*, 1974, *29*, 161–168.

DeMille, R. *Put your mother on the ceiling*. New York: Walker, 1967.

Dennis, W. Animism and related tendencies in Hopi children. *Journal of Abnormal and Social Psychology*, 1943, *38*, 21–37.

Dermine, A. M. Relationship between values and behavior: An experiment. Unpublished doctoral dissertation, Cornell University, 1969.

Deur, J. L. & Parke, R. D. Resistance to extinction and continuous punishment in humans as a function of partial reward and partial punishment training. *Psychonomic Science*, 1968, *13*, 91–92.

Deur, J. L. & Parke, R. D. Effects of inconsistent punishment on aggression in children. *Developmental Psychology*, 1970, *2*, 403–411.

Deutsch, M. & Gerard, H. B. A study of normative and informational social influences upon individual judgment. *Journal of Abnormal and Social Psychology*, 1955, *51*, 629–636.

Devereux, E. C. The role of peer-group experience in moral development. In J. P. Hill (Ed.), *Minnesota Symposia on Child Psychology*, Vol. 4. Minneapolis: University of Minnesota Press, 1970. Pp. 94–140.

Devereux, E. C., Bronfenbrenner, U., & Rodgers, R. Child rearing in England and the United States: A cross-national comparison. *Journal of Marriage and the Family*, 1969, *31*, 257–270.

Devereux, E. C., Bronfenbrenner, U., & Suci, G. Patterns of parent behavior in America and West Germany: A cross-national comparison. *International Social Science Journal*, 1962, *14*, 488–506.

DeVries, R. The development of role-taking as reflected by behavior of bright, average, and retarded children in a social guessing game. *Child Development*, 1970, *41*, 759–770.

Dewey, J. *Moral principles in education.* New York: Philosophical Library, 1954.

Dewey, J. & Tufts, J. H. *Ethics.* (Revised edition) New York: Holt, 1932.

Dicey, A. *Lectures on the relations between law and public opinion in England during the nineteenth century.* London: Macmillan, 1905.

Dilling, C. A. A study of moral orientation in relation to the Piagetian concept of egocentrism. Unpublished doctoral dissertation, Michigan State University, 1967.

DiLollo, V. & Berger, S. M. Effects of apparent pain in others on observer's reaction time. *Journal of Personality and Social Psychology,* 1965, *2,* 573–575.

Dion, K. K. Physical attractivenss and evaluation of children's transgressions. *Journal of Personality and Social Psychology,* 1972, *24,* 207–213.

Dodds, E. *The Greeks and the irrational.* Boston: Beacon Press, 1957.

Drabman, R. S. & Thomas, M. H. Does media violence increase children's toleration of real life aggression? *Developmental Psychology,* 1974, *10,* 418–421.

Dulany, D. E., Jr. The place of hypotheses and intentions: An analysis of verbal control in verbal conditioning. In C. W. Eriksen (Ed.), *Behavior and awareness.* Durham, N.C.: Duke University Press, 1962. Pp. 102–129.

Durham *v.* United States. *Federal Reporter* (2d). St. Paul, Minn.: West, 1954, *214,* 862–876.

Durkheim, E. *Moral education.* Glencoe, Ill.: The Free Press, 1961.

Durkin, D. Children's acceptance of reciprocity as a justice principle. *Child Development,* 1959, *30,* 289–296. (a)

Durkin, D. Children's concepts of justice: A comparison with the Piaget data. *Child Development,* 1959, *30,* 59–67. (b)

Durkin, D. Children's concepts of justice: A further comparison with the Piaget data. *Journal of Educational Research,* 1959, *52,* 252–257. (c)

Durkin, D. The specificity of children's moral judgments. *Journal of Genetic Psychology,* 1961, *98,* 3–14.

Dworkin, E. The effects of imitation, reinforcement, and cognitive information on the moral judgments of children. Unpublished doctoral dissertation, University of Rochester, 1966.

Eaton, J. W. & Weil, R. J. *Culture and mental disorders.* Glencoe: The Free Press, 1955.

Edel, A. Scientific research and moral judgment: A philosophical perspective. Paper presented at the Conference on Studies of the Acquisition and Development of Values, sponsored by the National Institute of Child Health and Human Development, May 1968.

Edelhertz, H. & Geis, G. *Public compensation to victims of crime.* New York: Praeger, 1974.

Einhorn, J. A. test of Piaget's theory of moral judgment. *Canadian Journal of Behavioral Science,* 1971, *3,* 102–113.

Eisen, M. Characteristic self-esteem, sex, and resistance to temptation. *Journal of Personality and Social Psychology,* 1972, *24,* 68–72.

Eisenberg, L., Lachman, R., Molling, P. A., Lockner, A., Mizelle, J. D., & Conners, C. K. A psychopharmacological experiment in a training school for delinquent boys: Methods, problems, findings. *American Journal of Orthopsychiatry,* 1963, *33,* 431–447.

Elliott, R. & Vasta, R. The modeling of sharing: Effects associated with vicarious reinforcement, symbolization, age, and generalization. *Journal of Experimental Child Psychology,* 1970, *10,* 8–15.

Ellis, G. T. & Sekyra, F. The effect of aggressive cartoons on the behavior of first-grade children. *Journal of Psychology,* 1972, *81,* 37–43.

Elms, A. & Milgram, S. Personality characteristics associated with obedience and defiance toward authoritative command. *Journal of Experimental Research and Personality,* 1966, *1,* 282–289.

Emmerich, W. Models of continuity and change. Paper presented at the annual meeting of the Society for Research in Child Development, March 27, 1969, Santa Monica, California.

Epstein, R. The development of children's conceptions of rules in the years four to eight. Unpublished senior paper, University of Chicago, 1965.

Erikson, E. H. *Childhood and society.* New York: Norton, 1950.

Erikson, E. H. *Insight and responsibility.* New York: Norton, 1963.

Erikson, E. H. *Identity: Youth and crisis.* New York: Norton, 1968.

Essen-Möller, E. The concept of schizoida. *Monatschrift für Psychiatrie und Neurologie*, 1946, *112*, 258–271.

Eysenck, H. J. Schizothymia-cyclothymia as a dimension in personality. *Journal of Personality*, 1952, *20*, 345–384. (a)

Eysenck, H. J. *The scientific study of personality.* London: Routledge, 1952. (b)

Eysenck, H. J. *The dynamics of anxiety and hysteria.* London: Routledge, 1957.

Eysenck, H. J. (Ed.) *Experiments with drugs.* Oxford: Pergamon, 1963.

Eysenck, H. J. *The biological basis of personality.* Springfield, Ill.: Charles C Thomas, 1967.

Eysenck, H. J. Clinical psychology. In J. G. Howels (Ed.), *Modern perspectives in world psychiatry.* Edinburgh: Oliver & Boyd, 1968, pp. 353–390.

Eysenck, H. J. *Crime and personality.* London: Paladin Books, 1970. (a) (Originally published, 1964.)

Eysenck, H. J. A dimensional system of psychodiagnostics. In A. R. Mahrer (Ed.), *New approaches to personality classification and psychodiagnosis.* New York: Columbia University Press, 1970, pp. 169–207. (b)

Eysenck, H. J. Personality and sexual adjustment. *British Journal of Psychiatry*, 1971, *118*, 593–608.

Eysenck, H. J. An experimental and genetic model of schizophrenia. In A. R. Kaplan (Ed.), *Genetic factors in schizophrenia.* Springfield, Ill.: Charles C Thomas, 1972. (a)

Eysenck, H. J. *Psychology is about people.* London: Allen Lane, Penguin Press, 1972. (b)

Eysenck, H. J. & Eysenck, S. B. G. A factorial study of psychoticism as a dimension of personality. *Multivariate Behavioral Research*, Special Issue, 1968, 15–32.

Eysenck, H. J. & Eysenck, S. B. G. *Personality structure and measurement.* San Diego, Ca.: R. R. Knapp, 1969.

Eysenck, H. J. & Eysenck, S. B. G. A comparative study of criminals and matched controls on three dimensions of personality. *British Journal of Social and Clinical Psychology*, 1971, *10*, 362–366.

Eysenck, H. J. & Eysenck, S. B. G. Prisoners of XYY constitution. *British Journal of Psychiatry*, 1972, *120*, 124.

Eysenck, H. J., Granger, G. W., & Brengelmann, J. C. *Perceptual processes and mental illness.* London: Oxford, 1957.

Eysenck, H. J. & Levey, A. Alternation in choice behavior and extraversion. *Life Sciences*, 1965, *4*, 115–119.

Eysenck, H. J. & Levey, A. Könditionierung, Introversion-extraversion und die Starke des Nervensystems. *Zeit. für Psychol.*, 1967, *174*, 96–106.

Eysenck, S. B. G. & Eysenck, H. J. The measurement of psychoticism: A study of factor stability and reliability. *British Journal of Social and Clinical Psychology*, 1968, *7*, 286–294.

Eysenck, S. B. G. & Eysenck, H. J. Scores on three personality variables as a function of age, sex and social class. *British Journal of Social and Clinical Psychology*, 1969, *8*, 69–76. (b)

Eysenck, S. B. G. & Eysenck, H. J. "Psychoticism" in children: A new personality variable. *Research in Education*, 1969, *1*, 21–37. (a)

Eysenck, S. B. G. & Eysenck, H. J. Crime and personality: An empirical study of the three-factor theory. *British Journal of Criminology*, 1970, *10*, 225–239.

Eysenck, S. B. G. & Eysenck, H. J. Crime and personality: Item analysis of questionnaire responses. *British Journal of Criminology*, 1971, *11*, 44–62.

Eysenck, S. B. G. & Eysenck, H. J. The questionnaire measurement of psychoticism. *Psychological Medicine*, 1972, *2*, 50–55.

Farley, F. H. & Farley, S. V. Extraversion and stimulus seeking motivation. *Journal of Consulting Psychology*, 1967, *31*, 215–216.

Farley, F. H. & Farley, S. V. Impulsiveness, sociability and the preference for varied experience. *Perceptual and Motor Skills*, 1970, *31*, 47–50.

Feather, N. T. Effects of prior success and failure on expectations of success and subsequent performance. *Journal of Personality and Social Psychology*, 1966, *3*, 287–298.

Fechter, J. V., Jr. Modeling and environmental generalization by mentally retarded subjects of televised aggressive or friendly behavior. *American Journal of Mental Deficiency*, 1971, *76*, 266–267.

Feffer, M. H. & Gourevitch, V. Cognitive aspects of role-taking in children. *Journal of Personality*, 1960, *28*, 383–396.

Feldman, S. E. & Feldman, M. T. Transition of sex differences in cheating. *Psychological Reports*, 1967, *20*, 957–958.

Fellner, C. & Marshall, J. Kidney donors. In J. Macaulay & L. Berkowitz (Eds.), *Altruism and helping behavior*. New York: Academic, 1970.

Fenichel, O. *The psychoanalytic theory of neurosis*. New York: Norton, 1945.

Ferguson, J. *Moral values in the ancient world*. London: Methuen, 1958.

Feshbach, N. D. & Roe, K. Empathy in six and seven year olds. *Child Development*, 1968, *39*, 133–145.

Feshbach, S. Dynamics and morality of violence and aggression: Some psychological considerations. *American Psychologist*, 1971, *26*, 281–292.

Festinger, L. *A theory of cognitive dissonance*. Stanford, Ca.: Stanford University Press, 1957.

Festinger, L. Behavioral support for opinion change. *Public Opinion Quarterly*, 1964, *28*, 404–417.

Festinger, L. & Freedman, J. L. Dissonance reduction and moral values. In P. Worchel & D. Byrne (Eds.), *Personality change*. New York: Wiley, 1964. Pp. 220–243.

Fischer, C. T. Levels of cheating under conditions of informative appeal to honesty, public affirmation of values, and threats of punishment. *The Journal of Educational Research*, 1970, *64*, 12–16.

Fisher, A. E. Effects of stimulus variation on sexual satiation in the male rat. *Journal of Comparative Psychology*, 1962, *55*, 614–620.

Fishkin, J., Keniston, K., & MacKinnon, C. Moral reasoning and political ideology. *Journal of Personality and Social Psychology*, 1973, *27*, 109–119.

Flanders, J. P. A review of imitative behavior. *Psychological Bulletin*, 1968, *69*, 316–337.

Flavell, J. H. The development of inferences about others. Paper presented at the Interdisciplinary Conference on Our Knowledge of Persons: Personal Perception and Inter-Personal Behavior, State University of New York at Binghamton, December 1971.

Flavell, J. H., Botkin, P., Fry, C., Wright, J., & Jarvis, P. *The development of role-taking and communication skills in children*. New York: Wiley, 1968.

Flavell, J. H. & Wohlwill, J. Formal and functional aspects of cognitive development. In D. Elkind & J. Flavell (Eds.), *Studies in cognitive development*, New York: Oxford, 1969, 67–120.

Flender, H. *Rescue in Denmark*. New York: Manor Books, 1964.

Flugel, J. C. *Man, morals, and society: A psychoanalytic study*. New York: International Universities, 1955.

Fodor, E. M. Resistance to social influence among adolescents as a function of level of moral development. *Journal of Social Psychology*, 1971, *85*, 121–126.

Fowler, H. & Whalen, R. E. Variation in incentive stimulus and sexual behavior in the male rat. *Journal of Comparative Physiological Psychology*, 1961, *54*, 68–71.

Fox, R. & Lippert, W. Spontaneous GSR and anxiety level in sociopathic delinquents. *Journal of Consulting Psychology*, 1963, *27*, 368.

Fraiberg, S. Libidinal object constancy and mental representation. *The Psychoanalytic Study of the Child*, 1969, *24*, 9–47.

France, A. *The red lily (Le lys rouge, 1894)*. Trans. by W. Stephens. New York: Dodd, Mead, 1927.

Frankena, W. K. *Ethics*. Englewood Cliffs, N. J.: Prentice-Hall, 1963.

Fraser, C., Bellugi, U., & Brown, R. Control of grammar in imitation, comprehension, and production. *Journal of Verbal Learning and Verbal Behavior*, 1963, *2*, 121–135.

Freedman, J. L., Wallington, S. A., & Bless, E. Compliance without pressure: The effect of guilt. *Journal of Personality and Social Psychology*, 1967, *7*, 117–124.

Freud, A. *Ego and the mechanisms of defense.* London: Hogarth, 1937.

Freud, A. & Dann, S. An experiment in group upbringing. In *The psychoanalytic study of the child,* Vol. VI. New York: International Universities, 1951. Pp. 127–168.

Freud, S. A child is being beaten. *Standard Edition, 17.* London: Hogarth, 1955. (Originally published, 1919.)

Freud, S. The economic problem of masochism. *Standard Edition, 19.* London: Hogarth, 1961. (Originally published, 1924.)

Freud, S. *The ego and the id.* London: Hogarth, 1927.

Freud, S. Civilization and its discontents. *Standard Edition, 21.* London: Hogarth, 1961. (Originally published, 1930.)

Freud, S. *The problem of anxiety.* New York: Norton, 1936.

Freud, S. Moses and monotheism. *Standard Edition, 23.* London: Hogarth, 1964. (Originally published, 1939.)

Fryrear, J. L. & Thelen, M. H. Effects of sex of model and sex of observer on the imitation of affectionate behavior. *Developmental Psychology,* 1969, *1,* 298.

Fulton, R. & Geis, G. Death and social values. In R. Fulton (Ed.), *Death and identity.* New York: Wiley, 1965. Pp. 67–75.

Gale, A., Coles, M., & Blaydon, J. Extraversion-introversion and the EEG. *British Journal of Psychology,* 1969, *60,* 209–233.

Garbarino, J. Political and religious authority and the democratic political system. Unpublished manuscript, St. Lawrence University, Canton, New York, 1968.

Gardner, H. *The quest for mind.* New York: Knopf, 1973.

Geer, J. H., Davison, G. C., & Gatchel, R. I. Reduction of stress in humans through nonveridical perceived control of aversive stimulation. *Journal of Personality and Social Psychology,* 1970, *16,* 731–738.

Geiger, H. *The family in Soviet Russia.* Cambridge, Mass.: Harvard University Press, 1968.

Geis, G. Experimental design and the law: A prospectus for research on victim-compensation in California. *California Western Law Review,* 1966, *2,* 85–91.

Geis, G. Violence in American society. *Current History,* 1967, *52,* 354–358.

Geis, G. Not the law's business? An examination of homosexuality, abortion, prostitution, narcotics, and gambling in the United States. *Crime and Delinquency Issues: A Monograph Series,* Center for Studies of Crime and Delinquency, National Institute of Mental Health. Washington, D.C.: U.S. Government Printing Office, 1972.

Geniesse, J. Blockwork orange. *New York,* 1973, *6* (Sept.), 56.

Gerbner, G. Measures and indicators of violence on prime-time and Saturday network television drama, 1967–1972. Unpublished manuscript, University of Pennsylvania, 1973.

Gerbner, G. Violence in television drama: Trends and symbolic functions. In G. A. Comstock & E. A. Rubinstein (Eds.), *Television and social behavior, Vol. I: Media content and control.* Washington, D.C.: U.S. Government Printing Office, 1972. Pp. 28–187.

Gergen, K. J. Personal consistency and the presentation of self. In C. Gordon & K. J. Gergen (Eds.), *The self in social interaction.* New York: Wiley, 1968. Pp. 299–308.

Gergen, K. J., Gergen, M. M., & Meter, K. Individual orientations to prosocial behavior. *Journal of Social Issues,* 1972, *28,* 105–130.

Gheselin, B. The creative process and creative talent. In C. W. Taylor & F. Barron (Eds.), *Scientific creativity: Its recognition and development.* New York: Wiley, 1963.

Gibbens, T. Sane and insane homicide. *Journal of Criminal Law, Criminology, and Police Science,* 1958, *49,* 110–115.

Gibbon, E. *The decline and fall of the Roman empire.* In *Great Books of the Western World,* 40. Chicago: Encyclopaedia Britannica, 1952. (Originally published, 1787.)

Gibson, E. & Klein, S. *Murder.* London: Her Majesty's Stationery Office, 1961.

Gilligan, C. F. Responses to temptation: An analysis of motives. Unpublished doctoral dissertation, Harvard University, 1963.

Gilligan, C. F. Kohlberg, L., Lerner, J., & Belenky, M. Moral reasoning about sexual dilemmas: The development of an interview and scoring system. In *Technical report of the commission on obscenity and pornography,* Vol. 1 (No. 5256–0010). Washington, D.C.: Superintendent of Documents, U.S. Government Printing Office, 1971.

Gilligan, J. Shame and guilt in schizophrenic and paranoid psychoses and the psychotic depressions. Unpublished M.D. thesis, School of Medicine, Case Western Reserve University, Cleveland, Ohio, 1965.

Giraldo, M. Egocentrism and moral development. Unpublished doctoral dissertation, Catholic University, Washington, D.C., 1972.

Glueck, S. & Glueck, E. *Toward a typology of juvenile offenders.* New York: Grune & Stratton, 1970.

Glueck, S. & Glueck, E. (Eds.) *Identification of pre-delinquents.* New York: International Medical Book Corporation, 1972.

Goldstein, A. S. *The insanity defense.* New Haven: Yale University Press, 1967.

Goodman, M. *The individual and culture.* Homewood, Illinois: Dorsey, 1967.

Gordon, R., Short, J., Cartwright, D., & Strodtbeck, F. Values and gang delinquency. *American Journal of Sociology,* 1963, *69,* 109–128.

Gordon, W. J. J. *Synectics.* New York: Harper & Row, 1961.

Goulett, H. M. *The insanity defense in criminal trials.* St. Paul, Minn.: West, 1965.

Greenglass, E. R. A cross-cultural study of the relationship between resistance to temptation and maternal communication. *Genetic Psychology Monographs,* 1972, *86,* 119–139.

Greer, S. Study of parental loss in neurotics and sociopaths. *Archives of General Psychiatry,* 1964, *11,* 177–180.

Gregory, C. The good Samaritan and the bad: The Anglo-American law. In J. Ratcliffe (Ed.), *The good Samaritan and the law.* New York: Doubleday Anchor, 1966.

Gregory, I. Studies of parental deprivation in psychiatric patients. *American Jounral of Psychiatry,* 1958. *115,* 432–442.

Grim, P. F., Kohlberg, L., & White, S. H. Some relationships between conscience and attentional processes. *Journal of Personality and Social Psychology,* 1968, *8,* 239–252.

Grinder, R. E. Parental childrearing practices, conscience, and resistance to temptation of sixth-grade children. *Child Development,* 1962, *33,* 803–820.

Grinder, R. E. Relations between behavioral and cognitive dimensions of conscience in middle childhood. *Child Development,* 1964, *35,* 881–893.

Gross, M. *The doctors.* New York: Dell, 1967.

Grusec, J. & Ezrin, S. A. Techniques of punishment and the development of self-criticism. *Child Development,* 1972, *43,* 1273–1288.

Grusec, J. & Mischel, K. Model's characteristics as determinants of social learning. *Journal of Personality and Social Psychology,* 1966, *4,* 211–215.

Guardo, C. J. & Bohan, J. B. Development of a sense of self-identity in children. *Child Development,* 1971, *42,* 1909–1921.

Gunsberg, L. Conflict training and the development of moral judgment in children. Unpublished doctoral dissertation, Yeshiva University, 1973.

Gustafson, J. M. Education for moral responsibility. In N. F. Sizer and T. R. Sizer (Eds.), *Moral education.* Cambridge, Mass: Harvard University Press, 1970.

Guttmacher, M. *The mind of the murderer.* New York: Farrar, Straus, 1960.

Haan, N., Smith, B., & Block, J. Moral reasoning of young adults. *Journal of Personality and Social Psychology,* 1968, *10,* 183–201.

Halfon, A., David, M., & Steadman, H. The Baxstrom women: A four year follow-up of behavior patterns. *Psychiatric Quarterly,* 1972, *45,* 1–10.

Halleck, S. L. *Psychiatry and the dilemmas of crime: A study of causes, punishment and treatment.* New York: Harper & Row, 1967.

Hamilton, D. L. Implicit personality theories: Dimensions of interpersonal cognition. Paper presented at APA convention, Washington, D.C., Sept., 1971.

Hampshire, S. Morality and pessimism. *New York Review of Books,* 1973, *XIX,* 26–33.

Haney, C., Banks, C., & Zimbardo, P. Interpersonal dynamics in a simulated prison. *International Journal of Criminology and Penology,* 1973, *1,* 69–97.

Hanratty, M. A., Liebert, R. M. Morris, L. W., & Fernandez, L. E. Imitation of film-mediated aggression against live and inanimate victims. *Proceedings of the 77th Annual Convention of the American Psychological Association*, 1969, *77*, 457–458.

Hanratty, M. A., O'Neal, E., & Sulzer, J. L. The effects of frustration upon the imitation of aggression. *Journal of Personality and Social Psychology*, 1972, *21*, 30–34.

Hapkiewicz, W. G. & Roden, A. H. The effects of aggressive cartoons on children's interpersonal play. *Child Development*, 1971, *42*, 1583–1585.

Hare, R. D. Acquisition and generalization of a conditioned-fear response in psychopathic and non-psychopathic criminals. *Journal of Psychology*, 1965, *59*, 367–370. (a)

Hare, R. D. *Freedom and reason.* New York: Oxford, 1965. (b)

Hare, R. D. Temporal gradient of fear arousal in psychopaths. *Journal of Abnormal Psychology*, 1965, *70*, 442–445. (c)

Hare, R. D. Detection threshold for electric shocks in psychopaths. *Journal of Abnormal Psychology*, 1968, *73*, 268–272.

Hare, R. D. *Psychopathy.* London: Wiley, 1970.

Harp, J. & Taietz, P. Academic integrity and social structure: A study of cheating among college students. *Social Problems*, 1966, *13*, 365–373.

Harris, H. Development of moral attitudes in white and Negro boys. *Developmental Psychology*, 1970, *2*, 376–383.

Harrower, M. Social status and moral development. *British Journal of Educational Psychology*, 1934, *4*, 75–95.

Hart, H. C. Piaget's test of immanent justice responses compared for several patient–nonpatient populations. *Journal of Genetic Psychology*, 1962, *101*, 333–341.

Hartshorne, H., May, M. A., *et al. Testing the knowledge of right and wrong.* New York: Religious Education Association, 1927.

Hartshorne, H. & May, M. A. *Studies in the nature of character. Vol. I: Studies in deceit.* New York: Macmillan, 1928.

Hartshorne, H., May, M. A., & Maller, J. B. *Studies in the nature of character. Vol. II: Studies in self-control.* New York: Macmillan, 1929.

Hartshorne, H., May, M. A., & Shuttleworth, F. K. *Studies in the nature of character. Vol. III: Studies in the organization of character.* New York: Macmillan, 1930.

Harvey, O. J., Hunt, D., & Schroeder, D. *Conceptual systems and personality organization.* New York: Wiley, 1961.

Havighurst, R. J. & Neugarten, B. L. *American Indian and white children: A sociological investigation.* Chicago: University of Chicago Press, 1955.

Hayden, T. & Mischel, W. Maintaining trait consistency in the resolution of behavioral inconsistency: The wolf in sheep's clothing. Unpublished manuscript, Stanford University, 1972.

Hebb, D. O. Comment on altruism: The comparative evidence. *Psychological Bulletin*, 1971, *76*, 409–410.

Hebb, D. O., & Thompson, W. R. The social significance of animal studies. In G. Lindzey (Ed.), *Handbook of social psychology, Vol. I: Theory and method.* Cambridge: Addison-Wesley, 1954, pp. 532–561.

Heider, F. *The psychology of interpersonal relations.* New York: Wiley, 1958.

Heilman, M. E., Hodgson, S. A., & Hornstein, H. A. Effects of magnitude and rectifiability of harm and information value on the reporting of accidental harm-doing. *Journal of Personality and Social Psychology*, 1972, *23*, 211–218.

Heller, M. S. & Polsky, S. Television violence—guidelines for evaluation. *Archives of General Psychiatry*, 1971, *24*, 279–285.

Helson, H. *Adaptation-level theory.* New York: Harper & Row, 1964.

Hemingway, E. *Death in the afternoon.* New York: Charles Scribner's, 1932.

Henshel, A. The relationship between values and behavior: A developmental hypothesis. *Child Development*, 1971, *42*, 1997–2007.

Heston, L. L. Psychiatric disorders in foster home reared children of schizophrenic mothers. *British Journal of Psychiatry*, 1966, *112*, 833–839.

Hetherington, E. M. & Feldman, S. E. College cheating as a function of subject and situational variables. *Journal of Educational Psychology*, 1964, *55*, 212–218.

Hickey, J. Stimulation of moral reasoning in delinquents. Unpublished doctoral dissertation, Boston University, 1972.

Hicks, D. J. Imitation and retention of film-mediated aggressive peer and adult models. *Journal of Personality and Social Psychology*, 1965, *2*, 95–100.

Hicks, D. J. Short- and long-term retention of affectively varied modeled behavior. *Psychonomic Science*, 1968, *11*, 369–370.

Hill, D. EEG in episodic psychotic and psychopathic behaviour. *Electroencephalography and Clinical Neurophysiology*, 1952, *4*, 419–442.

Hill, G. & Isenberg, B. Testimony documents indicate Beech Models had unsafe fuel tanks. *Wall Street Journal*, July 30, 1971, pp. 1, 6.

Hill, J. H. & Liebert, R. M. Effects of consistent or deviant modeling cues on the adoption of a self-imposed standard. *Psychonomic Science*, 1968, *13*, 243–244.

Hill, J. P. & Kochendorfer, R. A. Knowledge of peer success and risk of detection as determinants of cheating. *Developmental Psychology*, 1969, *1*, 231–238.

Hirst, P. & Peters, R. *The logic of education*. London: Routledge, 1970.

Hitler, A. *Mein kampf*. Boston: Houghton Mifflin, 1962. (Originally published, 1943.)

Hobbhouse, L. T. *Morals in evolution*. London: Chapman & Hall, 1906.

Hoffman, L. Fear of success in males and females: 1965 and 1971. *Journal of Consulting and Clinical Psychology*, 1974, *42*, 353–358.

Hoffman, M. L., Some psychodynamic factors in compulsive conformity. *Journal of Abnormal and Social Psychology*, 1953, *48*, 383–393.

Hoffman, M. L. Power assertion by the parent and its impact on the child. *Child Development*, 1960, *31*, 129–143.

Hoffman, M. L. Child rearing practices and moral development: Generalizations from empirical research. *Child Development*, 1963, *34*, 295–318. (a)

Hoffman, M. L. Parent discipline and the child's consideration for others. *Child Development*, 1963, *34*, 573–588. (b)

Hoffman, M. L. Conscience, personality, and socialization techniques. *Human Development*, 1970, *13*, 90–126. (a)

Hoffman, M. L. Moral development. In P. H. Mussen (Ed.), *Carmichael's manual of child psychology*. (Third ed.) Vol. 2. New York: Wiley, 1970. Pp. 261–359. (b)

Hoffman, M. L. Causal inference in correlational research: Discipline and moral development. *Developmental Reports*, No. 35, Department of Psychology, University of Michigan, Ann Arbor, 1973.

Hoffman, M. L. Personal communication, 1974.

Hoffman, M. L. Altruistic behavior and the parent–child relationship. *Journal of Personality and Social Psychology*, 1975, *31*, 937–943. (a)

Hoffman, M. L. Moral internalization, parental power, and the nature of parent–child interaction. *Developmental Psychology*, 1975, *11*, 228–239. (b)

Hoffman, M. L. Sex differences in moral internalization. *Journal of Personality and Social Psychology*, in press.

Hoffman, M. L. & Saltzstein, H. D. Parent practices and the development of children's moral orientations. In W. E. Martin (Chm.), *Parent behavior and children's personality development: Current project research*. Symposium presented at annual meeting of the American Psychological Association, Chicago, Sept. 1, 1960.

Hoffman, M. L. & Saltzstein, H. D. Parent discipline and the child's moral development. *Journal of Personality and Social Psychology*, 1967, *5*, 45–47.

Hogan, R. Moral conduct and moral character: A psychological perspective. *Psychological Bulletin*, 1973, *79*, 217–232.

Holland, L. The good Samaritan laws: A reappraisal. *Journal of Public Law*, 1967, *16*, 128–137.

Holmes, O., Jr. *The common law*. Boston: Little, Brown, 1881.

Holstein, C. B. Parental determinants of the development of moral judgment. Unpublished doctoral dissertation, University of California at Berkeley, 1968.

Holstein, C. B. Moral judgment change in early adolescence and middle age: A longitudinal study. Paper presented at the Society for Research in Child Development, Philadelphia, 1973.

Holt, E. B. *Animal drive and the learning process.* Vol. I. New York: Holt, 1931.

Horner, M. Sex differences in achievement motivation and performance in competitive and non-competitive situations. Unpublished doctoral dissertation, University of Michigan at Ann Arbor. University Microfilms, 1968.

Horowitz, I. The effect of group norms on bystander intervention. *Journal of Social Psychology*, 1971, *83*, 265–273.

Hoving, K. L., Hamm, N., & Galvin, P. Social influence as a function of stimulus ambiguity at three age levels. *Developmental Psychology*, 1969, *1*, 631–636.

Howells, T. H. Factors influencing honesty. *The Journal of Social Psychology*, 1938, *9*, 97–102.

Huesmann, L. R., Eron, L. D., Lefkowitz, M. M., & Walder, L. O. Television violence and aggression: The causal effect remains. *American Psychologist*, 1973, *28*, 617–620.

Hughes, H. (Ed.) *The fantastic lodge.* Boston: Houghton Mifflin, 1961.

Hume, D. *Treatise on human nature*, 1739.

Hume, D. *An inquiry concerning the principles of morals.* C. W. Hendel, ed. New York: Liberal Arts Press, 1957. (Originally published, 1751.)

Hume, D. *An inquiry concerning human understanding.* C. W. Hendel, ed. New York: Liberal Arts Press, 1955. (Originally published, 1758.)

Hunt, D. E. Matching models and moral training. In C. M. Beck, B. S. Crittenden, & E. V. Sullivan (Eds.), *Moral education: Interdisciplinary approaches.* Toronto: University of Toronto Press, 1971, pp. 231–251.

Hunt, J. McV. Intrinsic motivation and its role in psychological development. In D. Levine (Ed.), *Nebraska Symposium on Motivation.* Lincoln: University of Nebraska Press, 1965. Pp. 189–282.

Hunt, R. & Wiley, E. Operation Baxstrom after one year. *American Journal of Psychiatry*, 1968, *124*, 947–978.

Huston, T., Geis, G., Wright, R., & Garrett, T. Good Samaritans as crime victims. In E. Viano (Ed.), *Crimes, victims, and society.* Leiden, the Netherlands: Sijthoff International, 1976.

Ilfeld, F., Jr. Environmental theories of violence. In D. Daniels, M. Gilula, & F. Ochberg (Eds.), *Violence and the struggle for existence.* Boston: Little, Brown, 1970, pp. 79–95.

Irwin, D. & Moore, S. The young child's understanding of social justice. *Developmental Psychology*, 1971, *5*, 406–410.

Isaacs, S. S. *Social development in young children.* London: Routledge, 1933.

Iscoe, I., Williams, M., & Harvey, J. Modification of children's judgments by a simulated group technique: A normative developmental study. *Child Development*, 1963, *34*, 963–978.

Isen, A. M. Success, failure, attention, and reaction to others: The warm glow of success. *Journal of Personality and Social Psychology*, 1970, *15*, 294–301.

Isen, A. M., Horn, N., & Rosenhan, D. L. Effects of success and failure on children's generosity. *Journal of Personality and Social Psychology*, 1973, *27*, 239–247.

Isen, A. M. & Levin, P. Effect of feeling good on helping: Cookies and kindness. *Journal of Personality and Social Psychology*, 1972, *21*, 384–388.

Jackson, J. M. & Saltzstein, H. D. The effect of person–group relationships on conformity processes. *Journal of Abnormal and Social Psychology*, 1958, *57*, 17–24.

Jacobsen, R. & Halle, M. *Fundamentals of language.* The Hague: Mouton, 1956.

Jacobson, L. I., Berger, S. E., & Millham, J. Individual differences in cheating during a temptation period when confronting failure. *Journal of Personality and Social Psychology*, 1970, *15*, 48–56.

Jahoda, G. Immanent justice among West African children. *Journal of Social Psychology*, 1958, *47*, 241–248.

James, W. *Principles of psychology*. New York: Holt, Rinehart and Winston, 1890.

Jeffery, K. & Mischel, W. The layman's use of traits to predict and remember behavior. Unpublished manuscript, Stanford University, 1972.

Jesilow, P. & Meredith, M. Unpublished paper, Program in Social Ecology, University of California at Irvine, 1973.

Jew, C., Clanon, T., & Mattocks, A. The effectiveness of group psychotherapy in a correctional institution. *American Journal of Psychiatry*, 1972, *129*, 602–605.

Jinks, J. L. & Fulker, D. W. Comparisons of the biometrical genetical, MAVA and classical approaches to the analysis of human behavior. *Psychological Bulletin*, 1970, *73*, 311–349.

Johnson, C. D. & Gormly, J. Academic cheating: The contribution of sex, personality, and situational variables. *Developmental Psychology*, 1972, *6*, 320–325.

Johnson, N. *How to talk back to your television set*. Boston: Little, Brown, 1967.

Johnson, R. C. A study of children's moral judgments. *Child Development*, 1962, *33*, 327–354.

Johnston, R. J. H. M.D.'s split on "mercy" killer's sanity. *New York Times*, Nov. 2, 1973, 45.

Jones, E. E. *Ingratiation: A social psychological analysis*. New York: Appleton, 1964.

Jones, E. E. & Davis, K. E. From arts to dispositions. In L. Berkowitz (Ed.), *Advances in experimental social psychology*, Vol. 2. New York: Academic, 1965, pp. 220–266.

Jones, E. E. & Nisbett, R. E. *The actor and observer: Divergent perceptions of the causes of behavior*. New York: General Learning Press, 1971.

Kagan, J. *Change and continuity in infancy*. New York: Wiley, 1971.

Kahlbaum, K. Über Heboidophrenie. *Allgemeine Zeitschrift für Psychiatrie*, 1890, *46*, 461–483.

Kahneman, D. & Tversky, A. On the psychology of prediction. *Psychological Review*, 1973, *80*, 237–251.

Kanfer, F. H. Influence of age and incentive conditions on children's self-rewards. *Psychological Reports*, 1966, *19*, 263–274.

Kanfer, F. H. The maintenance of behavior by self-generated stimuli and reinforcement. In A. Jacobs & L. B. Sachs (Eds.), *Psychology of private events*. New York: Academic, 1971.

Kanfer, F. H., Cox, L. E., Greiner, J. M., & Karoly, P. Contracts, demand characteristics and self-control. *Journal of Personality and Social Psychology*, 1974, *30*, 605–619.

Kanfer, F. H. & Duerfeldt, P. H. Age, class standing, and commitment as determinants of cheating in children. *Child Development*, 1968, *39*, 545–557.

Kanfer, F. H. & Marston, A. R. Determinants of self-reinforcement in human learning. *Journal of Experimental Psychology*, 1963, *66*, 245–254.

Kanfer, F. H. & Phillips, J. S. *Learning foundations of behavior therapy*. New York: Wiley, 1970.

Kant, I. *The critique of pure reason*. In *Great books of the western world*, 42. Chicago: Encyclopedia Britannica, 1952. (Originally published, 1787.)

Kant, I. *The critique of practical reason*. In *Great books of the western world*, 42. Chicago: Encyclopedia Britannica, 1952. (Originally published, 1788.)

Kaplan, J. A legal look at prosocial behavior: What can happen for failing to help or trying to help someone. *Journal of Social Issues*, 1972, *28*, 219–226.

Kaplan, J. & Plaut, T. *Personality in a communal society*. Lawrence: University of Kansas, 1956.

Karpman, B. The structure of neurosis. *Archives of Criminal Psychodynamics*, 1961, *4*, 599–646.

Kassebaum, G. G., Ward, D., & Willner, D. *Prison treatment and parole survival*. New York: Wiley, 1971.

Katz, D. The functional approach to the study of attitudes. *The Public Opinion Quarterly*, 1960, *24*, 163–204.

Kaufman, H. The unconcerned bystander. *Proceedings of the 76th annual convention of the American Psychological Association*, 1968, *3*, 387–388.

Kazdin, A. E. & Bryan, J. H. Competence and volunteering. *Journal of Experimental Social Psychology*, 1971, *7*, 87–97.

Keasey, C. B. Social participation as a factor in the moral development of preadolescents. *Developmental Psychology*, 1971, *5*, 216–220.

Kelley, C. *Crime in the United States—1972*. Washington, D.C.: U.S. Government Printing Office, 1973.

Kellmer Pringle, M. L. & Edwards, J. B. Some moral concepts and judgments of junior school children. *British Journal of Social and Clinical Psychology*, 1964, *3*, 196–215.

Kelly, E. L. Consistency of the adult personality. *American Psychologist*, 1955, *10*, 659–681.

Kelly, G. A. *The psychology of personal constructs*. Vols. I and II. New York: Norton, 1955.

Kelman, H. Compliance, identification and internalization: Three processes of attitude change. *Journal of Conflict Resolution*, 1958, *2*, 51–60.

Kelman, H. C. & Lawrence, L. H. Assignment of responsibility in the case of Lt. Calley: Preliminary report on a national survey. *Journal of Social Issues*, 1972, *28*, 177–212.

Kelsen, H. *General theory of law and state*. New York: Russell & Russell, 1945.

Kendler, H. H. & Kendler, T. S. Vertical and horizontal processes in problem-solving. *Psychological Review*, 1962, *69*, 1–16.

Kendler, H. H. & Kendler, T. S. Reversal-shift behavior: Some basic issues. *Psychological Bulletin*, 1969, *72*, 229–232.

Keniston, K. *Young radicals*. New York: Harcourt, 1968.

Keniston, K. Student activism, moral development and morality. *American Journal of Orthopsychiatry*, 1970, *40*, 577–592.

Kenny, D. A. Threats to the internal validity of cross-lagged panel inference, as related to "Television violence and child aggression: A followup study." In G. A. Comstock & E. A. Rubinstein (Eds.), *Television and social behavior. Vol. III: Television and adolescent aggressiveness*. Washington, D.C.: U.S. Government Printing Office, 1972, pp. 136–140.

Kessen, W., Haith, M. M., & Salapatek, P. H. Infancy. In P. Mussen (Ed.), *Carmichael's manual of child psychology*. New York: Wiley, 1970, pp. 287–446.

Kierkegaard, S. *Fear and trembling*. (W. Lowrie, trans.) Princeton: Princeton University Press, 1941.

Kinkade, K. *A Walden II experiment: The first five years of Twin Oaks community*. New York: Morrow, 1973.

Kittrie, N. N. *The right to be different*. Baltimore: Johns Hopkins Press, 1971.

Klineberg, S. L. Future time perspective and the preference for delayed reward. *Journal of Personality and Social Psychology*, 1968, *8*, 253–257.

Knott, J. R., Platt, E. B., Ashby, M. C., & Gottlieb, J. S. A familial evaluation of the electroencephalograph of patients with primary behavior disorders and psychopathic personality. *Electroencephalography and Clinical Neurophysiology*, 1953, *5*, 363–370.

Knowlton, J. Q. & Hamerlynck, L. A. Perception of deviant behavior: A study of cheating. *Journal of Educational Psychology*, 1967, *58*, 379–385.

Knutson, J. N. *The human basis of the polity*. Chicago: Aldine, 1972.

Kohlberg, L. The development of modes of moral thinking and choice in the years ten to sixteen. Unpublished doctoral dissertation, University of Chicago, 1958.

Kohlberg, L. The development of children's orientations toward a moral order. I: Sequence in the development of human thought. *Vita Humana*, 1963, *6*, 11–33. (a)

Kohlberg, L. Moral development and identification. In H. Stevenson (Ed.), *Child Psychology*, 62nd Yearbook of the National Society for the Study of Education. Chicago: University of Chicago Press, 1963, pp. 277–332. (b)

Kohlberg, L. Development of moral character and moral ideology. In M. L. Hoffman and L. W. Hoffman (Eds.), *Review of child development research*. Vol. I. New York: Russell Sage Foundation, 1964, pp. 383–432.

Kohlberg, L. Relationships between the development of moral judgment and moral conduct. Paper presented at biannual meeting of the Society for Research in Child Development, Minneapolis, Minn., 1965.

Kohlberg, L. A. cognitive-developmental analysis of children's sex-role concepts and attitudes. In E. Maccoby (Ed.), *The development of sex differences*. Stanford, Ca.: Stanford University Press, 1966, pp. 82–172.

Kohlberg, L. The impact of cognitive maturity on the development of sex-role attitudes in the years four to eight. *Genetic Psychology Monographs*, 1967, *75*, 91–165. (a)

Kohlberg, L. Moral and religious education and the public schools: A developmental view. In T. Sizer (Ed.), *Religion and public education*. Boston: Houghton-Mifflin, 1967, pp. 164–183. (b)

Kohlberg, L. The child as a moral philosopher. *Psychology Today*, Sept. 1968, 25–30. (a)

Kohlberg, L. An evaluation of Piaget's theory of moral judgment development. Unpublished manuscript, Harvard University, 1968. (b)

Kohlberg, L. Moral development. *International Encyclopedia of the Social Sciences*. New York: Macmillan and Free Press, 1968. (c)

Kohlberg, L. The relations between moral judgment and moral action: A developmental view. Unpublished paper, presented at Institute of Human Development, University of California at Berkeley, March 1969. (a)

Kohlberg, L. Stage and sequence: The cognitive-developmental approach to socialization. In D. A. Goslin (Ed.), *Handbook of socialization theory and research*. Chicago: Rand McNally, 1969, pp. 347–480. (b)

Kohlberg, L. Education for justice: A modern statement of the Platonic view. In N. F. Sizer and T. R. Sizer (Eds.), *Moral education: Five lectures*. Cambridge, Mass.: Harvard University Press, 1970, pp. 57–83.

Kohlberg, L. From is to ought: How to commit the naturalistic fallacy and get away with it in the study of moral development. In T. Mischel (Ed.), *Cognitive development and epistemology*. New York: Academic, 1971, pp. 151–235. (a)

Kohlberg, L. Stages of moral development as a basis for moral education. In C. M. Beck, B. S. Crittenden & E. V. Sullivan (Eds.), *Moral education: Interdisciplinary approaches*. Toronto: University of Toronto Press, 1971, pp. 23–92. (b)

Kohlberg, L. The concepts of developmental psychology as the central guide to education. In M. C. Reynolds (Ed.), *Psychology and the process of schooling in the next decade*. Minneapolis, Minn.: Department of Audio-Visual Extension (University of Minnesota), 1972, pp. 1–55.

Kohlberg, L. The cognitive-developmental approach: New developments and a response to criticisms. Paper presented in the Symposium on Moral Development and Behavior, biannual convention of the Society for Research in Child Development, Denver, April 1975.

Kohlberg, L. (Ed.) *Recent research in moral development*. New York: Holt, Rinehart and Winston, in preparation.

Kohlberg, L., Colby, A., Speicher-Dubin, B., & Lieberman, M. *Standard form scoring manual*. Cambridge: Moral Education Research Foundation, 1975.

Kohlberg, L. & DeVries, R. Relations between Piaget and psychometric assessments of intelligence. Paper presented at the Conference on the Natural Curriculum, Urbana, Ill., 1969.

Kohlberg, L. & Gilligan, C. F. The adolescent as philosopher: The discovery of the self in a postconventional world. *Daedalus*, 1971, *100*, 1051–1086.

Kohlberg, L. Gilligan, C., Hickey, J., Jennings, W., Kohlberg, L., Lieberman, M., Scharf, P., & Selman, R. Workshop in moral development, Harvard University, June 1972.

Kohlberg, L., Havighurst, R., & Neugarten, B. A further analysis of cross-cultural moral judgment data. Unpublished manuscript, Harvard University, 1967.

Kohlberg, L. & Kramer, R. B. Continuities and discontinuities in childhood and adult moral development. *Human Development*, 1969, *12*, 93–120.

Kohlberg, L. & Mayer, R. Development as the aim of education. *Harvard Educational Review*, *42* (4) November 1972.

Kohlberg, L., Scharf, P., & Hickey, J. The justice structure of the prison: A theory and an intervention. *The Prison Journal*, Autumn–Winter, 1972, *LI* (no. 2).

Kohlberg, L. & Selman, R. *Preparing school personnel relative to values: A look at moral education in the schools*. Washington, D.C.: ERIC Clearinghouse on Teacher Education, Jan., 1972.

Kohlberg, L. & Turiel, E. Moral development and moral education. In G. S. Lesser (Ed.), *Psychology and educational practice.* Glenview, Ill.: Scott Foresman, 1971, pp. 410–465.

Kohlberg, L. & Zigler, E. The impact of cognitive maturity on sex-role attitudes in years four to eight. *Genetic Psychology Monographs,* 1967, *75,* 89–165.

Kohnstamm, G. A. Experiments on teaching Piagetian thought operations. In J. Hellmeth (Ed.), *Cognitive studies,* Vol. 1. New York: Brunner/Mazel, 1970, pp. 370–382.

Kolb, D. A. Achievement motivation for underachieving high school boys. *Journal of Personality and Social Psychology,* 1965, *2,* 783–792.

Kolb, L. C. *Modern clinical psychiatry.* Philadelphia: Saunders, 1968.

Korte, C. Effects of individual responsibility and group communication on help-giving in an emergency. *Human Relations,* 1971, *24,* 149–159.

Kozol, H., Boucher, R. & Garofalo, R. The diagnosis and treatment of dangerousness. *Crime and Delinquency,* 1972, *18,* 371–392.

Kraepelin, E. *Psychiatrie* (8th ed., Vol. 3, Part 2) Leipzig: Barth, 1913.

Kramer, R. *Moral development in young adulthood.* Unpublished doctoral dissertation, University of Chicago, 1968.

Krebs, D. L. Altruism: An examination of the concept and a review of the literature. *Psychological Bulletin,* 1970, *73,* 258–303. (a)

Krebs, D. L. Empathically-experienced affect and altruism. Unpublished doctoral dissertation, Harvard University, 1970. (b)

Krebs, D. L. Infrahuman altruism. *Psychological Bulletin,* 1971, *76,* 411–414.

Krebs, R. L. The development of intentional and sanction-independent moral judgment in the years four to eight. Unpublished master's thesis, University of Chicago, 1965.

Krebs, R. L. Some relations between moral judgment, attention, and resistance to temptation. Unpublished doctoral dissertation, University of Chicago, 1967.

Krebs, R. L. Teacher perceptions of children's moral behavior. *Psychology in the Schools,* 1969, *6,* 394–395.

Krebs, R. L., Brener, B., & Kohlberg, L. The development of moral judgments in the years four to eight. Unpublished manuscript, Harvard University, 1967.

Kroeber, A. *Anthropology.* New York: Harcourt, 1948.

Kugelmass, S. & Breznitz, S. The development of intentionality in moral judgment in city and kibbutz adolescents. *Journal of Genetic Psychology,* 1967, *111,* 103–111.

Kuhn, D. The development of role-taking ability. Unpublished manuscript, Columbia University, 1972.

Kuhn, D., Kohlberg, L., Langer, J., & Haan, U. The development of formal operations in logical and moral judgment. *Genetic Psychology Monographs,* in press.

Kuhn, D., Langer, J., & Kohlberg, L. Relations between logical and moral development. In L. Kohlberg (Ed.), *Recent research in moral development.* New York: Holt, Rinehart and Winston, in preparation.

Kuhn, T. S. *The structure of scientific revolutions.* Chicago: University of Chicago Press, 1971.

Kurtines, W. & Greif, E. B. The development of moral thought: Review and evaluation of Kohlberg's approach. *Psychological Bulletin,* 1974, *81,* 453–470.

Langer, J. Disequilibrium as a source of development. In P. Mussen, J. Langer, & M. Covington (Eds.), *Trends and issues in developmental psychology.* New York: Holt, Rinehart and Winston, 1969, pp. 22–37.

Landauer, T. K., Carlsmith, J. M., & Lepper, M. Experimental analysis of the factors determining obedience of 4-year old children to adult females. *Child Development,* 1970, *41,* 601–611.

La Piere, R. T. Attitudes vs. actions. In D. Forcese & S. Richer (Eds.), *Stages of social research: Contemporary perspectives.* Englewood Cliffs, N. J.: Prentice-Hall, 1970, 93–100.

Latané, B. & Darley, J. Group inhibition of bystander intervention. *Journal of Personality and Social Psychology,* 1968, *10,* 215–221.

Latané, B. & Darley, J. *The unresponsive bystander: Why doesn't he help?* New York: Appleton, 1970.

Latané, B. & Rodin, J. A lady in distress: Inhibiting effects of friends and strangers on by-stander intervention. *Journal of Experimental Social Psychology*, 1969, *5*, 189–202.

Laungani, D. The effect of previously learned habits and personality variables on verbal conditioning. Unpublished study, 1970.

LaVoie, J. C. The effect of type of punishment on resistance to temptation. Paper presented at the biannual meeting of the Society for Research in Child Development, Philadelphia, 1973.

Lee, L. C. The concomitant development of cognitive and moral modes of thought: A test of selected deductions from Piaget's theory. *Genetic Psychology Monographs*, 1971, *83*, 93–146.

Leff, R. Effects of punishment intensity and consistency on the internalization of behavioral suppression in children. *Developmental Psychology*, 1969, *1*, 345–356.

Lefkowitz, M. M., Eron, L. D., Walder, L. O., Huesmann, L. R. Television violence and child aggression: A follow-up study. In G. A. Comstock & E. A. Rubinstein (Eds.), *Television and social behavior. Vol. III: Television and adolescent aggressiveness*. Washington, D.C.: U.S. Government Printing Office, 1972, pp. 35–135.

LeFurgy, W. G. & Woloshin, G. W. Immediate and long-term effects of experimentally induced social influence in the modification of adolescents' moral judgments. *Journal of Abnormal and Social Psychology*, 1969, *12*, 104–110.

Leifer, A. & Roberts, D. Children's responses to television violence. In J. P. Murray, E. A. Rubinstein, & G. A. Comstock (Eds.), *Television and social behavior. Vol. II: Television and social learning*. Washington, D.C.: U.S. Government Printing Office, 1972, pp. 43–180.

Leming, J. Moral reasoning, sense of control and social-political activism among adolescents. *Adolescence*, 9 (No. 36), Winter 1974, pp. 507–528.

Lenrow, P. Studies of sympathy. In S. Tomkins & C. Izard (Eds.), *Affect, cognition, and personality: Empirical studies*. New York: Springer, 1965.

Lepper, M. R. Dissonance, self-perception, and honesty in children. *Journal of Personality and Social Psychology*, 1973, *25*, 65–74.

Lepper, M. R., Green, D., & Nisbett, R. E. Undermining children's intrinsic interest with extrinsic reward: A test of the "overjustification" hypothesis. *Journal of Personality and Social Psychology*, 1973, *28*, 129–137.

Lerner, E. *Constraint areas and the moral judgment of children*. Menasta, Wis.: George Banta, 1937. (a)

Lerner, E. The problem of perspective in moral reasoning. *American Journal of Sociology*, 1937, *43*, 249–269. (b)

Lerner, M. J. Desire for justice and reactions to victims. In I. Macaulay & L. Berkowitz (Eds.), *Altruism and helping behavior*. New York: Academic, 1970, pp. 205–229.

Lerner, M. J. & Simmons, C. H. Observer's reaction to the "innocent victim": Compassion or rejection? *Journal of Personality and Social Psychology*, 1966, *4*, 203–210.

Leveque, K. L. & Walker, R. E. Correlates of high school cheating behavior. *Psychology in the Schools*, 1970, *7*, 159–163.

Levey, A. B. *Eyeblink conditioning, extraversion and drive*. Unpublished doctoral dissertation, University of London, 1972.

Lewis, C. S. *The screwtape letters and screwtape purposes*. New York: Macmillan, 1961.

Lickona, T. The development of the child's conception of moral responsibility from 6 to 12. Research paper presented at the annual meeting of the Psychological Association of Northern New York, Albany, 1967.

Lickona, T. Piaget misunderstood: A critique of the criticisms of his theory of moral development. *Merrill-Palmer Quarterly of Behavior and Development*, 1969, *16*, 337–350.

Lickona, T. The acceleration of children's judgments about responsibility: An experimental test of Piaget's hypotheses about the causes of moral judgmental change. Unpublished doctoral dissertation, State University of New York at Albany, 1971.

Lickona, T. An experimental test of Piaget's theory of moral development. Paper presented at annual meeting of the Society for Research in Child Development, Philadelphia, April 1973.

Lickona, T. A cognitive developmental approach to interpersonal attraction. In T. L. Huston (Ed.), *Foundations of interpersonal attraction*. New York: Academic, 1974, pp. 31–59.

Liebermann, M. Estimation of a moral judgment level using items whose alternatives form a graded scale. Unpublished doctoral dissertation, University of Chicago, 1971.

Liebert, R. M. Television and social learning: Some relationships between viewing violence and behaving aggressively (overview). In J. P. Murray, E. A. Rubinstein, & G. A. Comstock (Eds.), *Television and social behavior. Vol. II: Television and social learning.* Washington, D.C.: U.S. Government Printing Office, 1972, pp. 1–42.

Liebert, R. M. Observational learning: Some social applications. In P. J. Elich (Ed.), *Fourth Western Symposium on Learning*. Bellingham, Wash.: Western Washington State College, 1973.

Liebert, R. M. & Baron, R. A. Some immediate effects of televised violence on children's behavior. *Developmental Psychology*, 1972, *6*, 469–475.

Liebert, R. M., Neale, J., & Davidson, E. *The early window: Effects of television on children and youth.* New York: Pergamon, 1973.

Liebhart, E. Empathy and emergency helping: The effects of personality, self-concern, and acquaintance. *Journal of Experimental Social Psychology*, 1972, *8*, 404–411.

Lindsley, D. B. & Henry, C. E. The effects of drugs on behavior and the electro-encephalogram of children with behavior disorders. *Psychosomatic Medicine*, 1942, *4*, 140–149.

Lippert, W. W. & Sentner, R. J. Electrodermal responses in the sociopath. *Psychonomic Science*, 1966, *4*, 25–26.

Lipset, S. M. *Political man*. Garden City, N.Y.: Doubleday, 1959.

Liu, C. The influence of cultural background on the moral judgments of children. Unpublished doctoral dissertation, Columbia University, 1950.

Livermore, J. M., Malmquist, C., & Meehl, P. On the justifications for civil commitment. *University of Pennsylvania Law Review*, 1968, *117*, 75–96.

Livermore, J. M. & Meehl, P. E. The virtues of McNaghten. *Minnesota Law Review*, 1967, *51*, 789–856.

Locke, E. A. Relationship of success and expectation to affect on goal-seeking tasks. *Journal of Personality and Social Psychology*, 1967, *7*, 125–134.

Lockwood, A. L. Relations of political and moral thought. Unpublished doctoral dissertation, Harvard University, 1970.

Lockwood, A. L. Stages of moral development and students' reasoning about public policy issues. In L. Kohlberg (Ed.), *Recent research in moral development*. New York: Holt, Rinehart and Winston, in preparation.

Loevinger, J. The meaning and measurement of ego development. *American Psychologist*, 1966, *21*, 195–206.

Loevinger, J. Recent research on ego development. Invited address, at the annual meeting of the Society for Research in Child Development, March 31, 1973.

Loevinger, J. & Wessler, R. *Measuring ego development*. Vols. 1 & 2. San Francisco: Jossey-Bass, 1970.

London, P. The rescuers: Motivational hypotheses about Christians who saved Jews from the Nazis. In J. Macaulay & L. Berkowitz (Eds.), *Altruism and helping behavior*. New York: Academic, 1970.

Loubser, J. The contribution of schools to moral development: A working paper in the theory of action. *Interchange*, 1970, *1*, 99–115.

Loughran, R. A pattern of development in moral judgments made by adolescents derived from Piaget's schema of its development in childhood. *Educational Review*, February 1967.

Lovell, K. A. follow-up of some aspects of the work of Piaget and Inhelder on the child's conception of space. *British Journal of Educational Psychology*, 1959, *29*, 107–117.

Lower East Side group to use "panic button" against muggers. *New York Times*, Nov. 18, 1973; 32.

Lykken, D. T. A study of anxiety in the sociopathic personality. Unpublished doctoral dissertation, University of Minnesota, 1955. Quoted by Hare, 1970.

Lyle, J. & Hoffman, H. R. Children's use of television and other media. In E. A. Rubinstein, G. A. Comstock, & J. P. Murray (Eds.), *Television and social behavior. Vol. IV: Television in day-to-day life: Patterns of use.* Washington, D.C.: U.S. Government Printing Office, 1972, pp. 129–256.

Macaulay, J. & Berkowitz, L. (Eds.) *Altruism and helping behavior.* New York: Academic, 1970.

Maccoby, E. Effects of the mass media. In M. Hoffman & L. Hoffman (Eds.), *Review of child development research,* Vol. I. New York: Russell Sage Foundation, 1964, pp. 323–348.

Maccoby, E. The development of moral values and behavior in childhood. In J. A. Clauson (Ed.), *Socialization and society.* Boston: Little, Brown, 1968, pp. 227–269.

Macdonald, J. M. *Psychiatry and the criminal.* Springfield, Ill.: Charles C Thomas, 1969.

MacKinnon, D. W. Violation of prohibitions. In H. A. Murray et al. (Eds.), *Explorations in personality.* New York: Oxford, 1938, pp. 491–501.

MacRae, D., Jr. The development of moral judgment in children. Unpublished doctoral dissertation, Harvard University, 1950.

MacRae, D., Jr. A test of Piaget's theories of moral development. *Journal of Abnormal and Social Psychology,* 1954, *49,* 14–18.

Magowan, S. A. & Lee, T. Some sources of error in the use of the projective method for the assessment of moral judgment. *Briitsh Journal of Psychology,* 1970, *61,* 535–543.

Makarenko, A. S. *The road to life.* Moscow: Foreign Languages Press, 1955.

Maller, J. B. General and specific factors in character. *Journal of Social Psychology,* 1934, *5,* 97–102.

Mancuso, J. C. Culpability: A psychological, social, and legal concept. *CPCU Annals,* 1972, *25,* 127–140. (a)

Mancuso, J. C. The utility of the concept of culpability in promoting proper driving behavior. *Marquette Law Review,* 1972, *55,* 85–101. (b)

Mandler, G. Organization and memory. In K. W. Spence & J. T. Spence (Eds.), *The psychology of learning and motivation: Advances in research and theory.* New York: Academic Press, 1967.

Mandler, G. Association and organization: Facts, fancies and theories. In T. R. Dixon & D. L. Horton (Eds.), *Verbal behavior and general behavior theory.* Englewood Cliffs, N.J.: Prentice-Hall, 1968.

Martinson, R. Can corrections correct? *New Republic,* April 8, 1972, *167,* 13–15.

Maslow, A. *Motivation and personality.* New York: Harper & Row, 1954.

Maslow, A. *Toward a psychology of being.* Princeton: Van Nostrand, 1962.

Masters, J. C. Effects of success, failure and reward outcome upon contingent and noncontingent self-reinforcement. *Developmental Psychology,* 1972, *7,* 10–118. (a)

Masters, J. C. Social comparison by young children. In W. W. Hartup (Ed.), *The young child,* Vol. 2. Washington, D.C.: National Association for the Education of Young Children, 1972, pp. 320–339. (b)

Masters, J. C. & Peskay, J. Effects of race, socioeconomic status, and success or failure upon contingent and noncontingent self-reinforcement in children. *Developmental Psychology,* 1972, *7,* 139–145.

Matza, D. *Delinquency and drift.* New York: Wiley, 1964.

May, R. *Love and will.* New York: Norton, 1969.

Maynard, R. Doctor would test children to curb crime. *Los Angeles Times,* April 5, 1970, Sect. A, 9.

McClelland, D. C., Atkinson, J. W., Clark, R. A., & Lovell, E. L. *The achievement motive.* New York: Appleton, 1953.

McCord, W. & McCord, J. *Psychopathy and delinquency.* New York: Grune & Stratton, 1956.

McCord, W., McCord, J., & Howard, A. Familial correlates of aggression in nondelinquent male children. *Journal of Abnormal and Social Psychology,* 1961, *62,* 79–83.

McCord, J., McCord, W., & Howard, A. Family interaction as antecedent to the direction of male aggressiveness. *Journal of Abnormal and Social Psychology,* 1963, *66,* 239–242.

McDougall. W. *An introduction to social psychology.* London: Methuen, 1908.

McGeorge, C. The fakability of the Defining Issues Test of moral judgment. Unpublished manuscript, University of Canterbury, New Zealand, 1973.

McGrath, J. *Comparative study of crime and its imputability in ecclesiastical law, and in American criminal law.* Washington, D.C.: Catholic University Press, 1957.

McIntyre, J. J. & Teevan, J. J., Jr. Television violence and deviant behavior. In G. A. Comstock & E. A. Rubinstein (Eds.), *Television and social behavior. Vol. III: Television and adolescent aggressiveness.* Washington, D.C.: U.S. Government Printing Office, 1972, pp. 383–435.

McMains, M. J. & Liebert, R. M. Influence of discrepancies between successively modeled self-reward criteria on the adoption of a self-imposed standard. *Journal of Personality and Social Psychology*, 1968, *8*, 166–171.

McNamee, S. Relation of moral reasoning to experimental helping behavior. In L. Kohlberg (Ed.), *Recent research in moral development.* New York: Holt, Rinehart and Winston, in preparation.

McNamee, S. & Peterson, J. Proposal for research in preschool curriculum in moral development and role-taking. Case Western Reserve University, 1973.

McQueen, R. Examination deception as a function of residual, background, and immediate stimulus factors. *Journal of Personality*, 1957, *25*, 643–650.

Mead, G. H. M*ind, self and society.* Chicago: University of Chicago Press, 1934.

Mead, M. *Sex and temperament in three primitive societies.* New York: New American Library, 1950.

Mead, M. *Blackberry winter: My earliest years.* New York: Morrow, 1972.

Medinnus, G. R. Immanent justice in children: A review of the literature and additional data. *Journal of Genetic Psychology*, 1959, *94*, 253–262.

Medinnus, G. R. Objective responsibility in children: A comparison with the Piaget data. *Journal of Genetic Psychology*, 1962, *101*, 127–133.

Medinnus, G. R. Age and sex differences in conscience development. *Journal of Genetic Psychology*, 1966, *109*, 117–118. (a)

Medinnus, G. R. Behavioral and cognitive measures of conscience development. *Journal of Genetic Psychology*, 1966, *109*, 147–150. (b)

Medow, W. Zür Erblichkeit in der Psychiatrie. *Zeitschrift der Gesumten Neurologie Psychiatrie*, 1914, *26*, 493.

Meehl, P. E. Psychology and the criminal law. *University of Richmond Law Review*, 1970, *5*, 1–30.

Meggendorfer, R. Klinische und genealogische Untersuchung über "moral insanity." *Zeitschrift der Gesumten Neurologie Psychiatrie*, 1921, *66*, 208.

Meichenbaum, D. H. Cognitive factor in behavior modification: Modifying what clients say to themselves. Research Report No. 25, University of Waterloo, Ontario, July 23, 1971.

Melden, S. I. *Ethical theories.* Englewood Cliffs, N. J.: Prentice-Hall, 1967.

Merelman, R. M. *Political socialization and educational climates.* New York: Holt, Rinehart and Winston, 1971.

Merritt, C. B. & Fowler, R. G. The pecuniary honesty of the public at large. *Journal of Abnormal Social Psychology*, 1948, *43*, 90–93.

Merton, R. K. *Social theory and social structure.* Glencoe, Ill.: Free Press, 1957.

Meyer, W. & Thompson, G. The differences in the distribution of teacher approval and disapproval among sixth grade children. *Journal of Educational Psychology*, 1956, *47*, 385–396.

Midlarsky, E. Aiding responses: An analysis and review. *Merrill-Palmer Quarterly*, 1968, *14*, 229–260.

Milgram, S. Behavioral study of obedience. *Journal of Abnormal and Social Psychology*, 1963, *67*, 371–378.

Milgram, S. Group pressure and action against a person. *Journal of Abnormal and Social Psychology*, 1964, *69*, 137–143.

Milgram, S. Some conditions of obedience and disobedience to authority. *Human Relations,* 1965, *18,* 57–76.

Milgram, S. The experience of living in cities. *Science,* 1970, *167,* 1461–1468.

Mill, J. S. On liberty. In M. Lerner (Ed.), *Essential works of John Stuart Mill.* New York: Bantam, 1961, 249–360. (Originally published, 1910.)

Miller, D. & Swanson, G. *Inner conflict and defense.* New York: Holt, Rinehart and Winston, 1960.

Miller, G. A., Galanter, E., & Pribram, K. H. *Plans and the structure of behavior.* New York: Holt, Rinehart and Winston, 1960.

Miller, J. G. Eyeblink conditioning of primary and neurotic psychopaths. Unpublished doctoral dissertation, University of Missouri, 1964. Cited by R. D. Hare, 1970.

Miller, N. E. & Dollard, J. *Social learning and imitation.* New Haven, Conn.: Yale University Press, 1941.

Miller, P. H., Kessel, F. S., & Flavell, J. H. Thinking about people thinking about . . .: A study of social cognitive development. *Child Development,* 1970, *41,* 613–623.

Mills, J. Changes in moral attitudes following temptation. *Journal of Personality,* 1958, *26,* 517–531.

Mischel, W. Preference for delayed reinforcement: An experimetnal study of a cultural observation. *Journal of Abnormal and Social Psychology,* 1958, *56,* 57–61.

Mischel, W. Delay of gratification, need for achievement, and acquiescence in another culture. *Journal of Abnormal and Social Psychology,* 1961, *62,* 543–552. (a)

Mischel, W. Father-absence and delay of gratification: Cross-cultural comparisons. *Journal of Abnormal and Social Psychology,* 1961, *63,* 116–124. (b)

Mischel, W. Preference for delayed reinforcement and social responsibility. *Journal of Abnormal and Social Psychology,* 1961, *62,* 1–7. (c)

Mischel, W. Delay of gratification in choice situations. NIMH Progress Report (mimeo.), Stanford University, 1962.

Mischel, W. Theory and research on the antecedents of self-imposed delay of reward. In B. A. Maher (Ed.), *Progress in experimental personality research,* Vol. 3. New York: Academic, 1966.

Mischel, W. *Personality and assessment.* New York: Wiley, 1968.

Mischel, W. Continuity and change in personality. *American Psychologist,* 1969, *24,* 1012–1018.

Mischel, W. *Introduction to personality.* New York: Holt, Rinehart and Winston, 1971.

Mischel, W. Toward a cognitive social learning reconceptualization of personality. *Psychological Review,* 1973, *80,* 252–283.

Mischel, W. Processes in delay of gratification. In L. Berkowitz (Ed.), *Advances in social psychology,* Vol. 7. New York: Academic, 1974.

Mischel, W. & Baker, N. Cognitive appraisals and transformations in delay behavior. *Journal of Personality and Social Psychology,* 1975, *31,* 254–261.

Mischel, W., Coates, D. B., & Raskoff, A. Effects of success and failure on self-gratification. *Journal of Personality and Social Psychology,* 1968, *10,* 381–390.

Mischel, W., Ebbesen, E. B., & Zeiss, A. R. Cognitive and attentional mechanisms in delay of gratification. *Journal of Personality and Social Psychology,* 1972, *21,* 204–218.

Mischel, W., Ebbesen, E., & Zeiss, A. R. Selective attention to the self: Situational and dispositional determinants. *Journal of Personality and Social Psychology,* 1973, *27,* 129–142.

Mischel, W. & Gilligan, C. Delay of gratification, motivation for the prohibited gratification, and response to temptation. *Journal of Abnormal and Social Psychology,* 1964, *69,* 411–417.

Mischel, W. & Grusec, J. Determinants of the rehearsal and transmission of neutral and aversive behaviors. *Journal of Personality and Social Psychology,* 1966, *3,* 197–205.

Mischel, W., & Grusec, J. Waiting for rewards and punishments: Effects of time and probability on choice. *Journal of Personality and Social Psychology,* 1967, *5,* 24–31.

Mischel, W. & Liebert, R. M. Effects of discrepancies between observed and imposed reward criteria on their acquisition and transmission. *Journal of Personality and Social Psychology*, 1966, *3*, 45–53.

Mischel, W. & Liebert, R. M. The role of power in the adoption of self-reward patterns. *Child Development*, 1967, *38*, 673–683.

Mischel, W., Mailer, J., & Zeiss, A. Attribution of internal-external control for positive and negative events: Developmental and stimulus effects. Unpublished manuscript, Stanford Univ., 1973.

Mischel, W. & Masters, J. C. Effects of probability of reward attainment on response to frustration. *Journal of Personality and Social Psychology*, 1966, *3*, 390–396.

Mischel, W. & Moore, B. S. Effects of attention to symbolically-presented rewards upon self-control. *Journal of Personality and Social Psychology*, 1973, *28*, 172–179.

Mischel, W., Moore, B. S., & Zeiss, A. Cognitive transformations of the stimulus in delay of gratification. Unpublished manuscript, Stanford Univ., 1973.

Mischel, W. & Staub, E. Effects of expectancy on working and waiting for larger rewards. *Journal of Personality and Social Psychology*, 1965, *2*, 625–633.

Mischel, W., Zeiss, R., & Zeiss, A. R. Internal-external control and persistence: Validation and implications of the Stanford Preschool Internal-External Scale (SPIES). *Journal of Personality and Social Psychology*, 1974, *29*, 265–278.

Moir, D. J. Egocentrism and the emergence of conventional morality in preadolescent girls. A Master of Arts in Education thesis, University of Canterbury, Christchurch, New Zealand, 1971.

Monahan, J. Abolish the insanity defense? Not yet. *Rutgers Law Review*, 1973, *26*, 719–741. (a)

Monahan, J. The psychiatrization of criminal behavior. *Hospital and Community Psychiatry*, 1973, *24*, 105–107. (b)

Monahan, J. & O'Leary, K. D. Effects of self-instruction on rule-breaking behavior. *Psychological Reports*, 1971, *29*, 1059–1066.

Moore, B. S., Underwood, B., & Rosenhan, D. L. Affect and altruism. *Developmental Psychology*, 1973, *8*, 99–104.

Moore, G. & Stephens, W. B. Two year gains in moral conduct by normals and retardates. Paper delivered at the biannual meeting of the Society for Research in Child Development, Minneapolis, 1971.

Moore, O. K. Problem-solving and the perception of persons. In R. Tagiuri and L. Petrullo (Eds.), *Person perception and interpersonal behavior*. Stanford: Stanford University Press, 1958, pp. 131–150.

Morris, C. *Varieties of human value*. Chicago: University of Chicago Press, 1956.

Morris, N. Psychiatry and the dangerous criminal. *Southern California Law Review*, 1968. *41*, 514–547.

Morris, N. & Hawkins, G. *The honest politician's guide to crime control*. Chicago: University of Chicago Press, 1970.

Mowrer, O. H. *Learning theory and personality dynamics*. New York: Ronald, 1950.

Mowrer, O. H. *Learning theory and the symbolic processes*. New York: Wiley, 1960.

Mulaik, S. A. Are personality factors raters' conceptual factors? *Journal of Consulting Psychology*, 1964, *28*, 506–511.

Murdock, G. *Social structure*. New York: Macmillan, 1949.

Murphy, L. B. *Social behavior and child personality*. New York: Columbia University Press, 1937.

Mussen, P. H. (Ed.) *Carmichael's manual of child psychology*. (3d Ed.) New York: Wiley, 1970.

Mussen, P. H., Rutherford, E., Harris, S., & Keasey, C. B. Honesty and altruism among preadolescents. *Developmental Psychology*, 1970, *3*, 169–194.

Nader, R. Foreword. In J. Esposito, *Vanishing air*. New York: Grossman, 1971.

Najarian-Svajian, P. H. The idea of immanent justice among Lebanese children and adults. *Journal of Genetic Psychology*, 1966, *109*, 57–66.

Nakasato, Y. & Aoyama, Y. Resistance to temptation of girls in reformatory school. *Reports of the National Research Institute of Police Science: Research on Prevention of Crime and Delinquency*, 1970, *11*, 18.

Nakasato, Y. & Aoyama, Y. Some relations between children's resistance to temptation and their moral judgment. *Reports of the National Research Institute of Police Science: Research on Prevention of Crime and Delinquency*, 1972, *13*, 70.

Napalm inventor discounts "guilt." *New York Times*, Dec. 27, 1967, 8.

Nass, M. L. The development of conscience: A comparison of the moral judgments of deaf and hearing children. *Child Development*, 1964, *35*, 1073–1080.

Neale, J. M. Egocentrism in institutionalized and noninstitutionalized children. *Child Development*, 1966, *37*, 97–101.

Neale, J. M. Comment on "Television violence and child aggression: A followup study." In G. A. Comstock & E. A. Rubinstein (Eds.), *Television and social behavior. Vol. III: Television and adolescent aggressiveness.* Washington, D.C.: U.S. Government Printing Office, 1972, pp. 141–148.

Neisser, U. *Cognitive psychology.* New York: Appleton, 1967.

Nelsen, E. A., Grinder, R. E., & Biaggio, A. M. B. Relationships among behavioral, cognitive-developmental, and self-support measures of morality and personality. *Multivariate Behavioral Research*, 1969, *4*, 483–500.

Nelsen, E. A., Grinder, R. E., & Mutterer, M. L. Sources of variance in behavioral measures of honesty in temptation situations: Methodological analyses. *Developmental Psychology*, 1969, *1*, 265–279.

The New Republic, November 28, 1970, p. 11.

New York State Department of Health. *Report of Selected Characteristics on Induced Abortions Recorded in New York: January–December, 1971.* Albany: New York State Department of Health, 1972.

Newsweek, October 9, 1972, 27.

Nietzsche, F. Beyond good and evil. *The philosophy of Nietzsche.* New York: Modern Library, 1927. (Originally published, 1886.)

Nietzsche, F. The genealogy of morals. *The philosophy of Nietzsche.* New York: Modern Library, 1927. (Originally published, 1887.)

Nissen, H. W. & Crawford, M. P. A preliminary study of food-sharing behavior in young chimpanzees. *Journal of Comparative Psychology*, 1936, *22*, 383–419.

Norman, W. T. "To see ourselves as others see us!": Relations among self-perceptions, peer-perceptions, and expected peer-perceptions of personality attributes. *Multivariate Behavioral Research*, 1969, *4*, 417–443.

Nyswander, M. *The drug addict as a patient.* New York: Grune & Stratton, 1965.

O'Connell, J. & Myers, A. *Safety last: An indictment of the auto industry.* New York: Avon, 1966.

Ödegard, O. The psychiatric disease entities in the light of a genetic investigation. *Acta Psychiatrica Scandinavia Supplement*, 1963, *169*, 94–104.

Odom, R. D., Liebert, R. M. & Hill, J. H. The effects of modeling cues, reward, and attentional set on the production of grammatical and ungrammatical syntactic constructions. *Journal of Experimental Child Psychology*, 1968, *6*, 131–140.

O'Leary, K. D. The effects of self-instruction on immoral behavior. *Journal of Experimental Child Psychology*, 1968, *6*, 297–301.

Oliver, D. W. & Bane, M. J. Moral education: Is reasoning enough? In C. M. Beck, B. S. Crittenden, & E. V. Sullivan (Eds.), *Moral education: Interdisciplinary approaches.* Toronto: University of Toronto Press, 1971, pp. 252–271.

Olson, D. R. From perceiving to performing the diagonal. *Ontario Journal of Educational Research*, 1968, *10*, 171–179.

Oltman, J. & Friedman, S. Parental deprivation in psychiatric conditions. *Diseases of the Nervous System*, 1967, *28*, 298–303.

Opton, E. It never happened and besides they deserved it. In N. Sanford & C. Comstock (Eds.), *Sanctions for evil.* San Francisco: Jossey-Bass, 1971, 49–70.

Ornstein, R. E. *The psychology of consciousness.* New York: Viking, 1972.

Orris, J. B. Visual monitoring performance in three sub-groups of male delinquents. Unpublished master's thesis, University of Illinois, 1967. Cited by R. D. Hare, 1970.

Osborn, A. F. *Applied imagination.* New York: Scribner, 1963.

Osgood, C. E., Suci, G. J., & Tannenbaum, P. H. *The measurement of meaning.* Urbana, Ill.: University of Illinois Press, 1957.

Overholser *v.* Russell. *Federal Reporter* (2d), 1960, *282*, 195.

Paley, W. *The works of William Paley.* London: Longmans, 1838.

Palmore, E. B. *Normal aging.* Durham, N.C.: Duke University Press, 1970.

Panowitsch, H. Change and stability in the Defining Issues Test. Unpublished doctoral dissertation, University of Minnesota, 1975.

Parke, R. D. Nurturance, nurturance withdrawal, and resistance to deviation. *Child Development,* 1967, *38*, 1101–1110.

Parke, R. D. Effectiveness of punishment as an interaction of intensity, timing, agent nurturance, and cognitive structuring. *Child Development,* 1969, *40*, 213–235.

Parke, R. D. The role of punishment in the socialization process. In R. A. Hoppe, G. A. Milton, & E. C. Simmel (Eds.), *Early experiences and the processes of socialization.* New York: Academic, 1970, pp. 81–108.

Parke, R. D. & Walters, R. H. Some factors influencing the efficacy of punishment training for inducing response inhibition. *Monographs of the Society for Research in Child Development,* 1967, *32*, 1 (Serial No. 109).

Parnes, S. J. & Harding, H. F. (Eds.) *A source book for creative thinking.* New York: Scribner, 1962.

Parr, F. W. The problem of student honesty. *Journal of Higher Education,* 1936, *7*, 318–326.

Passingham, R. E. Crime and personality: A review of Eysenck's theory. In V. D. Nebylitsyn & J. Gray (Eds), *Biological bases of behavior.* New York: Academic, 1972, 342–351.

Patrick, J. Political education and democratic political orientations of 9th-grade students across four community types. Unpublished manuscript, Indiana University, 1971.

Pearlin, L. I. *Class context and family relations: A cross-national study.* Boston: Little, Brown, 1971.

Pearlin, L. I., Yarrow, M. R., & Scarr, H. A. Unintended effects of parental aspirations: The case of children's cheating. *The American Journal of Sociology,* 1967, *73*, 73–83.

Peck, R. F. & Havighurst, R. J. *The psychology of character development.* New York: Wiley, 1960.

Pepper, S. *World hypotheses.* Berkeley, Ca.: University of California Press, 1942.

Perlmutter, E. Professor slain in mugging here. *New York Times,* Sept. 21, 1972, 1, 39.

Peters, R. D. Concrete principles and the rational passions. In N. F. Sizer and T. R. Sizer (Eds.), *Moral education.* Cambridge, Mass.: Harvard University Press, 1970.

Peterson, C. L., Danner, F. W., & Flavell, J. H. Developmental changes in children's responses to three indications of communicative failure. *Child Development,* 1972, *43*, 1463–1468.

Pfeiffer, S. Is Eichmann in all of us? *New York Times,* June 30, 1974, 10. (Letter to the editor.)

Piaget, J. *Judgment and reasoning in the child.* New York: Harcourt, 1926. (a)

Piaget, J. *The language and thought of the child.* London: Routledge, 1959. (Originally published, 1926.) (b)

Piaget, J. *The child's conception of the world.* London: Routledge, 1929.

Piaget, J. *The moral judgment of the child.* (M. Gabain, Trans.) New York: Free Press, 1965. (First published in English, London: Kegan Paul, 1932.)

Piaget, J. *The construction of reality in the child.* New York: Basic Books, 1954.

Piaget, J. *Six psychological studies.* New York: Random House, 1967.

Piaget, J. & Inhelder, B. *The child's conception of space.* London: Routledge, 1956.

Piaget, J. & Inhelder, B. *The growth of logical thinking from childhood to adolescence.* New York: Basic Books, 1958.

Piaget, J. & Inhelder, B. *The psychology of the child.* New York: Basic Books, 1969.

Piers, G. & Singer, M. B. *Shame and guilt: A psychoanalytic and a cultural study.* Springfield, Ill.: Charles C Thomas, 1953.

Piliavin, I., Rodin, J., & Piliavin, J. Good Samaritanism: An underground phenomenon? *Journal of Personality and Social Psychology,* 1969, *13*, 289–299.

Piliavin, J. & Piliavin, I. Effects of blood on reactions to a victim. *Journal of Personality and Social Psychology*, 1972, *23*, 353–361.

Pinard, A. & Laurendeau, M. *The development of the concept of space in the child*. New York: International Universities, 1970.

Pittel, S. M. & Mendelsohn, G. A. Measurement of moral values: A review and critique, *Psychological Bulletin*, 1966, *66*, 22–35.

Planansky, K. Conceptual boundaries of schizoidness: Suggestions for epidemiological and genetic research. *Journal of Nervous and Mental Diseases*, 1966, *142*, 318–331. (a)

Planansky, K. Phenotypic boundaries of schizophrenia in twins. *Mutation in population*. Proceedings of the Prague Symposium, 1965. Prague: Academia, 1966. (b)

Planansky, K. Schizoidness in twins. *Acta Genetica Medica Gemelli (Roma)*, 1966, *15*, 151–159. (c)

Podd, M. H. Ego identity status and morality: The relationship between two developmental constructs. *Developmental Psychology*, 1972, *6*, 497–507.

Porteus, B. & Johnson, R. C. Children's responses to two measures of conscience development and their relation to sociometric nomination. *Child Development*, 1965, *36*, 703–711.

Poulos, R. W. & Liebert, R. M. Influence of modeling, exhortive verbalization, and surveillance on children's sharing. *Developmental Psychology*, 1972, *6*, 402–408.

Prentice, N. M. The influence of live and symbolic modeling on promoting moral judgment of adolescent delinquents. *Journal of Abnormal Psychology*, 1972, *80*, 157–161.

Price, R. *Abnormal behavior: Perspectives in conflict*. New York: Holt, Rinehart and Winston, 1972.

Pringle, K. M. & Gooch, S. Chosen ideal person personality development and progress in school subjects: A longitudinal study. *Human Development*, 1965, *8*, 161–180.

Proshansky, H. M. The development of intergroup attitudes. In L. W. Hoffman and M. L. Hoffman (Eds.), *Review of child development research*, Vol. 2. Russell Sage Foundation, New York, 1966, pp. 311–372.

Prothro, J. & Grigg, C. Fundamental principles of democracy: Bases of agreement and disagreement. *Journal of Politics*, May 1960, 276–294.

Rabinovitch, M. S., McLean, M. S., Jr., Markham, J. W., & Talbott, A. D. Children's violence perception as a function of television violence. In G. A. Comstock, E. A. Rubinstein, & J. P. Murray (Eds.), *Television and social behavior. Vol. V: Television effects: Further explorations*. Washington, D.C.: U.S. Government Printing Office, 1972, pp. 231–252.

Rachlin, H. Self-control. Unpublished manuscript, State University of New York at Stony Brook, 1973.

Rand, A. *The fountainhead*. Indianapolis: Bobbs-Merrill, 1943.

Rand, A. *Atlas shrugged*. New York: Random House, 1957.

Rawlings, E. T. Reactive guilt and anticipatory guilt in altruistic behavior. In J. Macaulay & L. Berkowitz (Eds.), *Altruism and helping behavior*. New York: Academic, 1970, pp. 163–177.

Rawls, J. *A theory of justice*. Cambridge: Harvard University Press, 1971.

Regan, D. T., Williams, M., & Sparling, S. Voluntary expiation of guilt: A field experiment. *Journal of Personality and Social Psychology*, 1972, *24*, 42–45.

Regan, J. W. Guilt, perceived injustice, and altruistic behavior. *Journal of Personality and Social Psychology*, 1971, *18*, 124–132.

Reich, W. *Character analysis*. New York: Orgone Institute Press, 1948. (Originally published, 1933.)

Rest, J. Hierarchies of comprehension and preference in a developmental stage model of moral thinking. Unpublished doctoral dissertation, University of Chicago, 1969.

Rest, J. The development of moral-political evaluation, comprehension and attitude assessed by objective measures. Unpublished mimeo, University of Minnesota, 1971.

Rest, J. Comprehension of Social Moral Concepts Test. Unpublished test, University of Minnesota, 1972.

Rest, J. Patterns of preference and comprehension in moral judgment, *Journal of Personality*, 1973, *41*, 86–109.

Rest, J., Cooper, D., Coder, R., Masanz, J., & Anderson, D. Judging the important issues in moral dilemmas. *Developmental Psychology*, 1974, *10* (4), 491–401.

Rest, J. & Kohlberg, L. Comprehension, preference, and spontaneous usage in moral judgment. In L. Kohlberg (Ed.), *Recent research in moral development*. New York: Holt, Rinehart and Winston, in preparation. (a)

Rest, J. & Kohlberg, L. The hierarchical nature of stages of moral judgment. In Kohlberg, L. (Ed.), *Recent research in moral development*. New York: Holt, Rinehart and Winston, in preparation. (b)

Rest, J., Turiel, E., & Kohlberg, L. Relations between level of moral judgment and preference and comprehension of the moral judgment of others. *Journal of Personality*, 1969, *37*, 225–252.

Ricoeur, P. *The symbolism of evil*. Boston: Beacon Press, 1967.

Riedel, H. Zür empirischen erbprognose der psychopathie. *Zeitschrift der Gesumten Neurologie Psychiatrie*, 1937, *159*, 597.

Robertson, J. M. *A short history of morals*. London: Watts, 1920.

Robertson, J. M. *Morals in world history*. London: Watts, 1947.

Robins, L. N. *Deviant children grow up*. Baltimore: Williams & Wilkins, 1966.

Robins, L. N. Dissecting the "broken home" as a predictor of deviance. Paper presented at the *NIHM Conference on Developmental Aspects of Self-Regulation*, La Jolla, California, February 19, 1972.

Robinson, J. P. Television's impact on everyday life: Some cross-national evidence. In E. A. Rubinstein, G. A. Comstock, & J. P. Murray (Eds.), *Television and social behavior. Vol. IV: Television in day-to-day life: Patterns of use*. Washington, D.C.: U.S. Government Printing Office, 1972, pp. 410–431.

Robitscher, J. B. *Pursuit of agreement: Psychiatry and the law*. Philadelphia: Lippincott, 1966.

Rokeach, M. *The open and closed mind*. New York: Basic Books, 1960.

Rose, R. J. Preliminary study of three incidents of arousal: Measurement, interrelationship, and clinical correlates. Unpublished doctoral dissertation, University of Minnesota, 1964. Cited by R. D. Hare, 1970.

Rosekrans, M. A. & Hartup, W. W. Imitative influences of consistent and inconsistent response consequences to a model on aggressive behavior in children. *Journal of Personality and Social Psychology*, 1967, *7*, 429–434.

Rosenhan, D. L. Determinants of altruism: Observations for a theory of altruistic development. Unpublished paper presented at APA Symposium on Prosocial Behavior in Children, September 1969. (a)

Rosenhan, D. L. Some origins of concern for others. In P. Mussen, J. Langer, & M. Covington (Eds.), *Trends and issues in developmental psychology*. New York: Holt, Rinehart and Winston, 1969, pp. 132–153. (b)

Rosenhan, D. L. The natural socialization of altruistic autonomy. In J. Macaulay & L. Berkowitz (Eds.), *Altruism and helping behavior*. New York: Academic Press, 1970.

Rosenhan, D. L. Learning theory and pro-social behavior. In L. Wispé (Ed.), *Positive forms of social behavior. Journal of Social Issues*, 1972, *28* (Whole No. 3), 151–163.

Rosenhan, D. L., Underwood, B. & Moore, B. S. Affect moderates self-gratification and altruism. *Journal of Personality and Social Psychology*, 1974, *30*, 546–552.

Rosenhan, D. L. & White, G. M. Observation and rehearsal as determinants of prosocial behavior. *Journal of Personality and Social Psychology*, 1967, *5*, 424–431.

Rosenkoetter, L. I. Resistance to temptation: Inhibitory and disinhibitory effects of models. *Developmental Psychology*, 1973, *8*, 80–84.

Rosenthal, A. M. *Thirty-eight witnesses*. McGraw-Hill, 1964.

Rosenthal, T. L. & Whitebook, J. S. Incentives versus instructions in transmitting grammatical parameters with experimenter as model. *Behaviour Research and Therapy*, 1970, *8*, 189–196.

Rosenthal, T. L. Zimmerman, B. J., & Durning, K. Observationally induced changes in children's interrogative classes. *Journal of Personality and Social Psychology*, 1970, *16*, 681–688.

Roskens, R. W. & Dizney, H. F. A study of unethical academic behavior in high school and college. *The Journal of Educational Research*, 1966, *59*, 231–234.

Ross, A. Effect of increased responsibility on bystander intervention: The presence of children. *Journal of Personality and Social Psychology*, 1971, *19*, 306–310.

Ross, A. & Brabend, J. Effect of increased responsibility on bystander intervention II: The cue value of a blind person. *Journal of Personality and Social Psychology*, 1973, *25*, 254–258.

Ross, S. A. The effect of deviant and nondeviant models on the behavior of preschool children in a temptation situation. Unpublished doctoral dissertation, Stanford University, 1962.

Ross, S. A. A test of the generality of the effects of deviant preschool models. *Developmental Psychology*, 1971, *4*, 262–267.

Rotter, J. B. *Social learning and clinical psychology*. Englewood Cliffs, N.J.: Prentice Hall, 1954.

Rotter, J. B. Generalized expectancies for internal versus external control of reinforcement. *Psychological Monographs*, 1966, *80* (1, Whole No. 609).

Rotter, J. B. Beliefs, social attitudes, and behavior: A social learning analysis. In J. B. Rotter, J. E. Chance, & E. J. Phares (Eds.), *Applications of a social learning theory of personality*. New York: Holt, Rinehart and Winston, 1972.

Rubenstein, R. L. *The religious imagination*. Boston: Beacon Press, 1968.

Rüdin, E. *Zurverebung und neuentstehung der dementia praecox*. Berlin: Springer, 1916.

Rudzinski, A. The duty to rescue: A comparative analysis. In J. Ratcliffe (Ed.), *The good Samaritan and the law*. New York: Doubleday Anchor, 1966.

Rumelhart, D. E., Lindsay, P. H., & Norman, D. A. A process model for long-term memory. *Technical Report No. 17, Center for Human Information Processing,* University of California at San Diego, 1971.

Ryan, W. *Blaming the victim*. New York: Vintage Books, 1971.

Rychlak, J. *A philosophy of science for personality theory*. Boston: Houghton Mifflin, 1968.

Sabin, L. Why I threw out my TV set. *Today's Health*, February 1972.

Saltzstein, H. D. Social influence on children's standards. Public Health Service Research Grant, No. HD06519, 1974.

Saltzstein, H. D. Role-taking as a method of facilitating moral development. Symposium on *Role-taking and Moral Development*. New York: Eastern Psychological Association, April 4, 1975.

Saltzstein, H. D., Diamond, R. M., & Belenky, M. Moral judgment level and conformity behavior. *Developmental Psychology*, 1972, *7*, 327–336.

Saltzstein, H. D. & Osgood, S. The development of children's understanding of group interdependence and obligation. *Journal of Psychology*, 1975, *90*, 147–155.

Sanford, N. & Comstock, C., et al. *Sanctions for evil*. San Francisco: Jossey-Bass, 1971.

Sarbin, T. R. The dangerous individual an outcome of social identity transformation. *British Journal of Criminology*, 1967, *7*, 285–295.

Sarbin, T. R. *The myth of the criminal type*. Middletown, Conn.: Wesleyan University, Center for Advanced Studies, 1969.

Savage, R. D. Electro-cerebral activity, extraversion and neuroticism. *British Journal of Psychiatry*, 1964, *110*, 98–100.

Savitsky, J. C., Rogers, R. G., Izard, C. E., & Liebert, R. M. Role of frustration and anger in the imitation of filmed aggression against a human victim. *Psychological Reports*, 1971, *29*, 807–810.

Scarr, S. The inheritance of sociability. *American Psychologist*, 1965, *20*, 524. (Abstract)

Schab, F. Honor and dishonor in the secondary schools of three cultures. *Adolescence*, 1971, *6*, 145–154.

Schachter, S. The interaction of cognitive and physiological determinants of emotional state. In L. Berkowitz (Ed.), *Advances in experimental social psychology*, Vol. 1. New York: Academic Press, 1964, pp. 49–80.

Schachter, S. & Latané, R. Crime, cognition and the autonomic nervous system. In M. R.

Jones (Ed.), *Nebraska Symposium on Motivation*. Lincoln: University of Nebraska Press, 1964, 221–275.

Schachter, S. & Singer, J. E. Cognitive, social and physiological determinants of emotional states. *Psychological Review*, 1962, *69*, 379–399.

Schafer, R. *The clinical application of psychological tests*. New York: International Universities, 1951.

Schalling, D. & Levander, G. Rating of anxiety proneness and responses to electrical pain stimulation. *Scandinavian Journal of Psychology*, 1964, *5*, 1–9.

Scharf, P., Hickey, J., & Kohlberg, L. Moral stages and their application to work in prisons. Unpublished manuscript, Harvard University, 1973.

Schmauk, F. A. study of the relationships between kinds of punishment, automatic arousal, subjective anxiety and avoidance learning in the primary sociopath. Unpublished doctoral dissertation, Temple University, 1968. Cited by R. D. Hare, 1970.

Schneider, D. J. Tactical self-presentation after success and failure. *Journal of Personality and Social Psychology*, 1969, *13*, 262–268.

Schneider, D. J. Implicit personality theory: A review. *Psychological Bulletin*, 1973, *73*, 294–309.

Schoenherr, J. C. Avoidance of noxious stimulation in psychopathic personality. Doctoral dissertation, University of California, 1964. Cited by R. D. Hare, 1970.

Schulman, G. I. Asch conformity studies: Conformity to the experimenter and/or to the group. *Sociometry*, 1967, *30*, 26–40.

Schuman, H. & Harding, J. Prejudice and the norm of rationality. *Sociometry*, 1964, *27*, 353–371.

Schuman, S. H., Pelz, D. C., Ehrlich, N. J., & Selzer, M. L. Young male drivers. *Journal of the American Medical Association*, 1967, *200*, 1026–1030.

Schwartz, S. Words, deeds, and the perceptions of consequences and responsibility in action situations. *Journal of Personality and Social Psychology*, 1968, *10*, 232–242.

Schwartz, S. Elicitation of moral obligation and self-sacrificing behavior: An experimental study of volunteering to be a bone marrow donor. *Journal of Personality and Social Psychology*, 1970, *15*, 283–293. (a)

Schwartz, S. Moral decision making and behavior. In J. Macaulay & L. Berkowitz (Eds.), *Altruism and helping behavior*. New York: Academic, 1970, pp. 127–142. (b)

Schwartz, S. & Clausen, G. Responsibility, norms, and helping in an emergency. *Journal of Personality and Social Psychology*, 1970, *16*, 299–310.

Schwartz, S., Feldman, K. Brown, M., & Heingartner, A. Some personality correlates of conduct in two situations of moral conflict. *Journal of Personality*, 1969, *37*, 41–58.

Scott, P., Burton, R. V., & Yarrow, M. R. Social reinforcement under natural conditions. *Child Development,* 1967, *38*, 53–63.

Scott, W. A. Rationality and non-rationality of international attitudes. *Journal of Conflict Resolution*, 1958, *2*, 8–16.

Sears, R. R. A theoretical framework for personality and social behavior. *American Psychologist*, 1951, *6*, 476–483.

Sears, R. R., Maccoby, E. E., & Levin, H. *Patterns of child rearing*. Evanston, Ill.: Row, Peterson, 1957.

Sears, R. R., Rau, L., & Alpert, R. *Identification and child rearing*. Stanford, Ca.: Stanford University Press, 1965.

Sears, R. R., Whiting, J. W. M., Nowlis, V., & Sears, P. S. Some child-rearing antecedents of aggression and dependency in young children. *Genetic Psychology Monographs*, 1953, *47*, 135–234.

Selman, R. L. The relation of role-taking to the development of moral judgment in children. *Child Development*, 1971, *42*, 79–91. (a)

Selman, R. L. Taking another's perspective: Role-taking development in early childhood. *Child Development*, 1971, *42*, 1721–1734. (b)

Selman, R. L. The relation of role-taking and moral judgment stages: A theoretical and empirical analysis. Unpublished manuscript, Harvard University, Cambridge, Mass., 1972.

Selman, R. L. *First things: Social reasoning.* New York: Guidance Associates, 1974.

Selman, R. L. A structural-developmental analysis of interpersonal conceptions: Peer relations concepts in poorly adjusted and well adjusted preadolescents. In A. Pick (Ed.), *Tenth Annual Minnesota Symposium on Child Development,* University of Minnesota Press, in press.

Selman, R. L. The importance of reciprocal role-taking for the development of conventional moral thought. In L. Kohlberg (Ed.), *Recent research in moral development.* New York: Holt, Rinehart and Winston, in preparation.

Selman, R. L. & Byrne, D. Manual for scoring role-taking in social and moral judgment interviews. Unpublished manuscript, Harvard University, 1973.

Selman, R., Byrne, D., & Kohlberg, L. Role taking development and its relation to moral judgment. In L. Kohlberg (Ed.), *Recent research in moral development.* New York: Holt, Rinehart and Winston, in preparation.

Selman, R. L. & Kohlberg, L. *First things: Values.* New York: Guidance Associates, 1971.

Selman, R. L. & Lieberman, M. Moral education in the primary grades: An evaluation of a developmental curriculum. *Journal of Educational Psychology,* in press.

Severy, L. J. & Davis, K. E. Helping behavior among normal and retarded children. *Child Development,* 1971, *42,* 1017–1031.

Shagass, C. & Schwartz, M. Observations on somatosensory cortical reactivity in personality disorders. *Journal of Nervous and Mental Disease,* 1962, *135,* 44–51.

Shapiro, D. *Neurotic styles.* New York: Basic Books, 1965.

Shaw, L. & Sichel, H. *Accident proneness.* Oxford: Pergamon, 1971.

Shayon, R. L. Mission: Immoral. *Saturday Review,* November 19, 1966.

Shelton, J. & Hill, J. P. Effects on cheating of achievement anxiety and knowledge of peer performance. *Developmental Psychology,* 1969, *1,* 449–455.

Shenker, I. An awesome reliving of Auschwitz unfolds at St. John's. *New York Times,* June 4, 1974, 39.

Shepherd, J. West side report. *New York,* 1973, *6* (September), 56–59.

Sherrill, D., Horowitz, B., Friedman, S. T., & Salisbury, J. L. Seating aggregation as an index of contagion. *Educational and Psychological Measurement,* 1970, *30,* 663–668.

Shirer, W. *The rise and fall of the third reich.* New York: Simon & Schuster, 1960.

Shoffeitt, P. G. The moral development of children as a function of parental moral judgments and childrearing. Unpublished doctoral dissertation: George Peabody College for Teachers, Nashville, Tenn., 1971.

Shotland, L. & Johnson, M. Bystander intervention: Victim and incident characteristics. Unpublished manuscript, The Pennsylvania State University, 1974.

Sidgwick, H. *Outlines of the history of ethics.* Boston: Beacon Press, 1960.

Siegel, A. The influence of violence in the mass media upon children's role expectations. *Child Development,* 1958, *29,* 35–36.

Siegler, R. S., Liebert, D. E., & Liebert, R. M. Inhelder and Piaget's pendulum problem. *Developmental Psychology,* 1973, *9,* 97–101.

Simpson, E. L. *Democracy's stepchildren: A study of need and belief.* San Francisco: Jossey-Bass, 1971. (a)

Simpson, E. L. The integrated person: Cognitive development and the creative unconscious. Paper presented at the Second International Conference of Humanistic Psychologists, University of Würzberg, Germany, July 1971. (b)

Simpson, E. L. Correlates of moral development in a secondary school sample. Unpublished study. Center for International Education, University of Southern California, 1972.

Simpson, E. L. Moral development research: A case of scientific cultural bias. *Human Development,* 1974, *17* (No. 2), 81–106.

Sizer, N. F., & Sizer, T. R. *Moral education: Five lectures.* Cambridge, Mass.: Harvard University Press, 1970.

Skinner, B. F. *Science and human behavior.* New York: Macmillan, 1953.

Skinner, B. F. *Walden II.* New York: Macmillan, 1962.

Skinner, B. F. *Beyond freedom and dignity.* New York: Knopf, 1971.

Skolnick, J. *The politics of protest.* New York: Simon & Schuster, 1969.

Skrzypek, G. J. The effects of perceptual isolation and arousal on anxiety: Complexity preference and novelty preference in psychopathic and neurotic delinquents. *Journal of Abnormal Psychology,* 1969, *74,* 321–329.

Smedslund, J. The acquisition of conservation of substance and weight in children: V. Practice in conflict situations without external reinforcement. *Scandinavian Journal of Psychology,* 1961, *2,* 156–160.

Smith, C. P., Ryan, E. R., & Diggins, D. R. Moral decision making: Cheating on examinations. *Journal of Personality,* 1972, *40,* 640–660.

Smith, M. B., Bruner, J. S., & White, R. *Opinions and personality.* New York: Wiley, 1956.

Smith, R., Smythe, L., & Lien, D. Inhibition of helping behavior by a similar or dissimilar nonreactive fellow bystander. *Journal of Personality and Social Psychology,* 1972, *23,* 414–419.

Smith, R., Vanderbilt, K., & Callen, M. Social comparison and bystander intervention in emergencies. *Journal of Applied Social Psychology,* 1973, *3,* 186–196.

Smythe, D. W. Reality as presented by television. *Public Opinion Quarterly,* 1954, *18,* 143–156.

A social disaster. *Poughkeepsie Journal,* Jan. 23, 1971.

Soloman, L. Experimental studies of tacit coordination: A comparison of schizophrenic and normal samples. Paper presented at the Brockton Veteran's Administration Hospital Colloquium Series, 1963.

Solomon, R. L. Letter in O. H. Mowrer, *Learning theory and the symbolic processes.* New York: Wiley, 1960.

Solomon, R. L. Punishment. *American Psychologist,* 1964, *19,* 239–253.

Solomon, R. L., Turner, L. H., & Lessac, M. S. Some effects of delay punishment on resistance to temptation in dogs. *Journal of Personality and Social Psychology,* 1968, *8,* 233–238.

Solomon, R. L. & Wynne, L. C. Traumatic avoidance learning: The principles of anxiety conservation and partial irreversibility. *Psychological Review,* 1954, *61,* 353–385.

Spiro, M. *Children of the kibbutz.* Cambridge, Mass.: Harvard University Press, 1958.

Spitz, R. A. Anxiety in infancy: A study of its manifestations in the first year of life. *International Journal of Psychoanalysis,* 1950, *31,* 138–143.

Staub, E. A child in distress: The effect of focusing responsibility on children on their attempts to help. *Developmental Psychology,* 1969, *2,* 152–153.

Staub, E. A child in distress: The influence of age and number of witnesses on children's attempts to help. *Journal of Personality and Social Psychology,* 1970, *14,* 130–140. (a)

Staub, E. A child in distress: The influence of focusing responsibility on children on their attempts to help. *Developmental Psychology,* 1970, *2,* 152–153. (b)

Staub, E. A child in distress: The influence of nurturance and modeling on children's attempts to help. *Developmental Psychology,* 1971, *5,* 124–132. (a)

Staub, E. Helping a person in distress: The influence of implicit and explicit "rules" of conduct on children and adults. *Journal of Personality and Social Psychology,* 1971, *17,* 137–144. (b)

Staub, E. The use of role-playing and induction in children's learning of helping and sharing behavior. *Child Development,* 1971, *42,* 805–816. (c)

Staub, E. Interpersonal influences on helping in emergencies. Paper presented at the annual meeting of the Eastern Psychological Association, Boston, May 1972.

Staub, E. Helping a distressed person: Social, personality, and stimulus determinants. In L. Berkowitz (Ed.), *Advances in experimental social psychology,* Vol. 7. New York: Academic, 1974.

Staub, E. *The development of prosocial behavior in children.* New York: General Learning Press, 1975.

Staub, E., & Sherk, L. Need for approval, children's sharing behavior, and reciprocity in sharing. *Child Development,* 1970, *41,* 243–253.

Stayton, D., Hogan, R., & Ainsworth, M. Infant obedience and maternal behavior: Origins of socialization reconsidered. *Child Development*, 1971, *42*, 1057–1069.

Steadman, H. The psychiatrist as conservative agent of social control. *Social Problems*, 1972, *20*, 263–271.

Steadman, H. & Halfon, A. The Baxstrom patients: Backgrounds and outcomes. *Seminars in Psychiatry*, 1971, *3*, 376–386.

Steadman, H. & Keveles, G. The community adjustment and criminal activity of the Baxstrom patients: 1968–1970. *American Journal of Psychiatry*, 1972, *129*, 304–310.

Stein, A. H. Imitation of resistance to temptation. *Child Development*, 1967, *38*, 159–169.

Stein, A. H. Mass media and young children's development. *71st Yearbook of the National Society for the Study of Education*, 1972, 191–202.

Stein, A. H. & Friedrich, L. K. Television content and young children's behavior. In J. P. Murray, E. A. Rubinstein, & G. A. Comstock (Eds.), *Television and social behavior. Vol. II: Television and social learning.* Washington, D.C.: U.S. Government Printing Office, 1972, pp. 202–317.

Stein, G. M. & Bryan, J. H. The effect of a televised model upon rule adoption behavior of children. *Child Development*, 1972, *43*, 268–273.

Stephens, W. B., Miller, C. K., & McLaughlin, J. A. The development of moral conduct in retardates and normals. Paper presented at the biannual meeting of the Society for Research in Child Development, Santa Monica, Calif., 1969.

Stern, W. *Psychology of early childhood.* New York: Holt, 1924.

Steuer, F. B., Applefield, J. M., & Smith, R. Televised aggression and the interpersonal aggression of preschool children. *Journal of Experimental Child Psychology*, 1971, *11*, 442–447.

Stirner, M. *The ego and his own* (S. Byington, Trans.) London: Field, 1912. (Originally published, 1882.)

Stotland, E. Exploratory investigations of empathy. In L. Berkowitz (Ed.), *Advances in experimental social psychology.* Vol. 4. New York: Academic, 1969, pp. 271–313.

Stouwie, R. J. Inconsistent verbal instructions and children's resistance-to-temptation behavior. *Child Development*, 1971, *42*, 1517–1531.

Stroh, C. M. *Vigilance: The problem of sustained attention.* Oxford: Pergamon, 1971.

Stuart, R. B. Decentration in the development of children's concepts of moral and causal judgments. *Journal of Genetic Psychology*, 1967, *111*, 59–68.

Stumpfl, F. Untersuchungen an psychopathischen zerillingen. *Zeitschrift der Gesumten Neurologie Psychiatrie*, 1936, *158*, 480–482.

Sullivan, E. V., McCullough, G., & Stager, M. A developmental study of the relationship between conceptual, ego, and moral development. *Child Development*, 1970, *41*, 399–411.

Szasz, T. S. *Law, liberty, and psychiatry.* New York: Macmillan, 1963.

Szasz, T. S. *Psychiatric justice.* New York: Macmillan, 1965.

Szasz, T. S. Justice in the therapeutic state. In F. A. Freyhan (Ed.), *Comprehensive psychiatry*, New York: Grune & Stratton, 1970.

Taft, R. The ability to judge people. *Psychological Bulletin*, 1955, *52*, 1–23.

Tapp, J. L. (Ed.) Socialization, the law, and society. *The Journal of Social Issues*, 1971, *27*, 65–91.

Tapp, J. L. & Kohlberg, L. Developing sense of law and legal justice. *The Journal of Social Issues*, 1971, *27*, 65–91.

Tawney, R. *The acquisitive society.* New York: Harcourt, 1920.

Taylor, S. P. & Lewit, D. W. Social comparison and deception regarding ability. *Journal of Personality*, 1966, *34*, 94–104.

Terman, L. M. Genetic studies of genius. *Mental and physical traits of a thousand gifted children.* Vol. I. Stanford, Calif.: Stanford University Press, 1925.

Terman, L. M. & Tyler, L. Psychological sex differences. In L. Carmichael (Ed.), *Manual of child psychology.* New York: Wiley, 1946.

Thorndike, E. L. *Animal intelligence.* New York: Macmillan, 1911.

Thrower, J. S. The effects of group home and foster care on development of moral judgment. Unpublished doctoral dissertation, Harvard University, Cambridge, Mass., 1972.

Thrower, J. S. Effects of orphanage and foster home care on development of moral judgment. In L. Kohlberg (Ed.), *Recent research in moral development*. New York: Holt, Rinehart and Winston, in preparation.

Tilker, H. Socially responsible behavior as a function of observer responsibility and victim feedback. *Journal of Personality and Social Psychology*, 1970, *14*, 95–100.

Toch, H. *Violent men*. Chicago: Aldine Atherton, 1969.

Tomes, H. The adaptation, acquisition, and extinction of empathically mediated emotional responses. *Dissertation Abstracts*, 1964, *24*, 3442–3443.

Tomlinson-Keasey, C. & Keasey, C. B. The mediating role of cognitive development in moral judgment. *Child Development*, 1974, *45*, 291–298.

Tunc, A. The volunteer and the good Samaritan. In J. Ratcliffe (Ed.), *The good Samaritan and the law*. New York: Doubleday Anchor, 1966.

Turiel, E. An experimental test of the sequentiality of developmental stages in the child's moral judgments. *Journal of Personality and Social Psychology*, 1966, *3*, 611–618.

Turiel, E. Developmental processes in the child's moral thinking. In P. Mussen, J. Langer, & M. Covington (Eds.), *Trends and issues in developmental psychology*. New York: Holt, Rinehart and Winston, 1969, pp. 92–133.

Turiel, E. Conflict and transition in adolescent moral development. Unpublished manuscript, Harvard University, Cambridge, Mass., 1973.

Turiel, E. A comparative analysis of moral knowledge and moral judgment in males and females. Unpublished manuscript, University of California at Santa Cruz, 1974.

Turnbull, C. *Mountain people*. New York: Simon & Schuster, 1972.

Ugurel-Semin, R. Moral behavior and moral judgment of children. *Journal of Abnormal and Social Psychology*, 1952, *47*, 463–474.

Underwood, B., Moore, B. S., & Rosenhan, D. L. Affect and self-gratification. *Developmental Psychology*, 1973, *8*, 209–214.

United States *v.* Brawner, *Federal Reporter* (2d), 1972, *471*, 969.

Van den Daele, L. A developmental study of ego-ideals. *Genetic Psychology Monographs*, 1968, *78*, 191–256.

Verma, R. & Eysenck, H. J. Severity and type of psychotic illness as a function of personality. *British Journal of Psychiatry*, 1973.

Vernon, P. E. *Personality assessment: A critical survey*. New York: Wiley, 1964.

Vetter, H. J. *Psychology of abnormal behavior*. New York: Ronald, 1972.

Vich, M. & Rhyne, J. Psychological growth and the use of art materials: Small group experiments with adults. *Journal of Humanistic Psychology*, 1967, Fall, 163–170.

Vidal, G. *Burr*. New York: Random House, 1973.

Vincent, J. Scaling the universe of states on certain useful multivariate dimensions. *The Journal of Social Psychology*, 1971, *85*, 261–283.

Vitro, F. T. The effects of probability of test success, opportunity to cheat and test importance on the incidence of cheating. Unpublished doctoral dissertation, University of Iowa, Ames, Iowa, 1969.

Von Wright, G. H. *The varieties of goodness*. London: Routledge, 1963.

Vygotsky, L. S. *Thought and speech*. Cambridge, Mass.: M.I.T. Press, 1962.

Wallace, J. An abilities conception of personality: Some implications for personality measurement. *American Psychologist*, 1966, *21*, 132–138.

Wallace, J. & Sadalla, E. Behavioral consequences of transgression: The effects of social recognition. *Journal of Experimental Research in Personality*, 1966, *1*, 187–194.

Wallas, G. *Human nature in politics*. Lincoln: University of Nebraska Press, 1921.

Waller, W. *Sociology of teaching*. New York: Russel, 1961.

Walsh, R. P. Sex, age, and temptation. *Psychological Reports*, 1967, *21*, 625–629.

Walsh, R. P. Generalization of self-control in children. *The Journal of Educational Research*, 1969, *62*, 464–466.

Walter, W. G. Slow potential waves in the human brain associated with expectancy, attention and decision. *Archives Psychiatrie Nervenkrankheit*, 1964, *206*, 309–322.

Walter, W. G. Electropsychiatric contributions to psychiatric therapy. In J. H. Masserman

(Ed.), *Current psychiatric therapies*, Vol. 6. New York: Grune & Stratton, 1966, pp. 13–25.

Walter, W. G. Slow potential changes in the human brain associated with expectancy, decision and intention. In W. Cobb & C. Morocuth (Eds.), *The evoked potentials.* Amsterdam: Elsevier, 1967, pp. 123–130.

Walters, R. H. & Cheyne, J. A. Some parameters influencing the effects of punishment on social behavior. Paper presented at the annual meeting of the American Psychological Association, New York, 1966.

Walters, R. H. & Parke, R. D. Influence of response consequences to a social model on resistance to deviation. *Journal of Experimental Child Psychology*, 1964, *1*, 269–280.

Walters, R. H., Parke, R. D., & Cane, V. Timing of punishment and the observation of consequences to others as determinants of response inhibition. *Journal of Experimental Child Psychology*, 1965, *2*, 10–30.

Warren, A. B. & Grant, D. A. The relations of conditioned discrimination to MMPI and personality variable. *Journal of Experimental Psychology*, 1955, *49*, 23–27.

Weinberger, G. Manifestations of conscience development as a function of experimenter permissiveness. Unpublished doctoral dissertation, Stanford University, 1961.

Weiner, B. & Peter, N. A cognitive-developmental analysis of achievement and moral judgments. Unpublished manuscript, University of California at Los Angeles, 1973.

Weiss, R. F., Boyer, J. L., Lombardo, J. P., & Stich, M. H. Altruistic drive and altruistic reinforcement. *Journal of Personality and Social Psychology*, 1973, *25*, 390–400.

Weiss, W. Effects of the mass media on communication. In G. Lindzey & E. Aronson (Eds.), *Handbook of social psychology.* (2d ed.) Boston: Addison-Wesley, 1968.

Wender, P. N. *Minimal brain dysfunction in children.* New York: Wiley-Interscience, 1971.

Wenk, E., Robinson, J., & Smith, G. Can violence be predicted? *Crime and Delinquency*, 1972, *18*, 393–402.

Werner, H. *The comparative psychology of mental development.* Chicago: Wilcox & Follett, 1948.

West, D. *Murder followed by suicide.* Cambridge, Mass.: Harvard University Press, 1966.

Westie, F. The American dilemma: An empirical test. *American Sociological Review*, August, 1965, 527–538.

White, G. M. Immediate and deferred effects of model observation and guided and unguided rehearsal on donating and stealing. *Journal of Personality and Social Psychology*, 1972, *21*, 139–148.

White, R. Ego and reality in psychoanalytic theory. *Psychological Issues, 3* (No. 3). New York: International Universities, 1963.

"White-collar crime": Must all U.S. citizens pay for the sins of a few? *Barron's*, March 30, 1970, *1*, 10.

Whiteman, P. H. & Kosier, K. P. Development of children's moralistic judgments: Age, sex, IQ, and certain personal-experiential variables. *Child Development*, 1964 *35*, 843–850.

Whiteside, T. *The investigation of Ralph Nader.* New York: Arbor House, 1972.

Whiting, B. B. Sex identity conflict and physical violence: A comparative study. *American Anthropologist*, 1965, *67*, 123–140.

Whiting, J. W. M. Fourth presentation. In J. M. Tanner & B. Inhelder (Eds.), *Discussions on child development.* Vol. 2. London: Tavistock, 1954.

Whiting, J. W. M. Sorcery, sin, and the superego: A cross-cultural study of some mechanisms of social control. In M. R. Jones (Ed.), *Nebraska Symposium on Motivation: 1959.* Lincoln: University of Nebraska Press, 1959, pp. 174–195.

Whiting, J. W. M. & Child, I. L. *Child training and personality: A cross-cultural study.* New Haven, Conn.: Yale University Press, 1953.

Whiting, J. W. M. & Mowrer, O. H. Habit progression and regression: A laboratory study of some factors relevant to human socialization. *Journal of Comparative Psychology*, 1943, *36*, 229–253.

Whiting, J. W. M. & Whiting, B. B. *Children of six cultures.* Cambridge, Mass.: Harvard University Press, 1974.

Whiting, L. M. W. & Whiting, B. The behavior of children in six cultures. Unpublished manuscript, Harvard University, Cambridge, Mass., 1969.

Whitlock, F. A. *Criminal responsibility and mental illness.* London: Butterworths, 1963.

Wiehofen, H. *The urge to punish.* London: Victor Gollancz, 1957.

Wiggins, J. Interconsistent socialization. *Psychological Reports,* 1968, *23,* 303–336.

Willner, D. *Nation building and community in Israel.* Princeton, N. J.: Princeton University Press, 1969.

Wispé, L. (Ed.) Positive forms of social behavior. *Journal of Social Issues,* 1972, *28* (Whole No. 3).

Wittgenstein, L. *Tractatus logico-philosophicus.* London: Routledge, 1921.

Wolf, T. M. A developmental investigation of televised modeled verbalizations on resistance to deviation. *Developmental Psychology,* 1972, *6,* 537.

Wolf, T. M. Effects of televised modeled verbalizations and behavior on resistance to deviation. *Developmental Psychology,* 1973, *8,* 51–56.

Wolf, T. M. & Cheyne, J. A. Persistence of effects of live behavioral, televised behavioral, and live verbal models on resistance to deviation. *Child Development,* 1972, *43,* 1429–1436.

Wolfgang, M. *Patterns in criminal homicide.* Philadelphia: University of Pennsylvania Press, 1958.

Wolfgang, M. & Ferracuti, F. *The subculture of violence.* London: Tavistock, 1967.

Worell, J. & Worell, L. Sex: The character of punishment and resistance to transgression. Paper delivered at the annual meeting of the Southeastern Psychological Association, Miami Beach, Fla.,, 1971.

Wren-Lewis, J. Love's coming of age. In C. Rycroft (Ed.), *Psychoanalysis observed.* New York: Coward-McCann, 1966, pp. 85–118.

Wright, D. *The psychology of moral behavior.* Baltimore, Md.: Penguin Books, 1971.

Wurtz, K. R. The expression of guilt in fantasy and reality. *Journal of Genetic Psychology,* 1959, *95,* 227–238.

Yakimovich, D. & Saltz, E. Helping behavior: The cry for help. *Psychonomic Science,* 1971, *23,* 427–428.

Yarrow, M. R., Campbell, J. D., & Burton, R. V. *Child rearing: An inquiry into research and methods.* San Francisco: Jossey-Boss, 1968.

Yarrow, M. R., Scott, P. M., & Waxler, C. Z. Learning concern for others. *Developmental Psychology,* 1973, *8,* 240–260.

Yarrow, M. R., Waxler, C. Z. & Scott, P. M. Child effects on adult behavior. *Developmental Psychology,* 1971, *5,* 300–311.

Yerkes, R. M. & Dodson, J. D. The relation of strength of stimulus to rapidity of habit formation. *Journal of Comparative Neurological Psychology,* 1908, *18,* 459–482.

Young, P. *Ernest Hemingway: A reconsideration.* University Park: Pennsylvania State University Press, 1966.

Zimmerman, B. J. & Rosenthal, T. L. Observational learning of rule-governed behavior by children. *Psychological Bulletin,* 1974, *81,* 29–42.

Zimring, F. & Hawkins, G. *Deterrence: The legal threat in crime control.* Chicago: University of Chicago Press, 1973.

Zuckerman, M. *Manual and research reports for the sensation-seeking scale.* Newark: University of Delaware, 1972.

Zuckerman, M., Kolin, E. A., Price, L., & Zorb, I. Development of a sensation-seeking scale. *Journal of Consulting Psychology,* 1964, *28,* 477–482.

Indexes

Name Index

E

F

Subject Index

Contributors' Biographies

Justin Aronfreed directs the Doctoral Program in Developmental Psychology at the University of Pennsylvania. He previously taught at Yale and the University of Michigan, and in 1966 received a National Science Foundation Senior Postdoctoral Fellowship Award. His book *Conduct and Conscience* and many related articles analyze the cognitive and affective processes by which children develop internalized control over their social–moral conduct. Currently, his research deals with the development of children's naturalistic concepts, the representation of thought in language, and the process of imitation in young children.

Urie Brofenbrenner is a Professor in the Department of Human Development and Family Studies at Cornell University, where he has taught since 1948. His interest in how societies approach the task of educating and caring for children has taken him to Russia and China and led to the book *Two Worlds of Childhood: U.S. and U.S.S.R.* and a film comparing the socialization of children in Russia, China, and the United States. He is Director of the Program on the Ecology of Human Development for the Foundation for Child Development, a frequent consultant to the Office of Child Development of H.E.W., and a nationally recognized spokesman for the needs of children. In 1975 he received the American Education Research Association Award for Distinguished Contributions to Educational Research.

Roger V. Burton is Professor and Director of Developmental Psychology at the State University of New York at Buffalo. Previously, he worked for 15 years as a research psychologist with the Laboratory of Socioenvironmental Studies at the National Institute of Mental Health. He is author of several studies on resistance to temptation and guilt, and is presently investigating moral conduct, the socialization of self-control, and sex-identity development. His co-authored book *Child-Rearing: An Inquiry into Research and Methods* and other papers on research methodology and analysis have gained him respect as an authority in this area.

H. J. Eysenck founded in 1950 and continues to direct the Department of Psychology at the University of London's Institute of Psychiatry. He has written approximately 400 articles spanning a vast range of human interests and activities. More than 20 books bear his name, including *The Effects of Psychotherapy, The Biological Basis of Personality*, and *Crime and Personality*. The journal *Behavior Research and Therapy*, which he founded in 1962 and edits, reflects his long-standing interest in the application of the principles of behaviorism to the treatment of neurosis. Central among his current interests are the genetics of personality and the construction of an experimental model of intelligence.

James Garbarino tutors adults in developmental psychology and related subjects as a faculty member of New York's Empire State College at Ithaca. He was a Woodrow Wilson Fellow at Cornell University, where he earned his doctorate in 1973. His studies of human development have examined television and sex-role stereotyping, the roots of alienation in adolescence, and the ecological correlates of child abuse. He has been research director and consultant for a variety of educational projects, and is at work on a monograph on "The School as a Context for Human Development in Ecological Perspective."

Gilbert Geis is a Professor in the Program in Social Ecology at the University of California at Irvine. During a previous tenure with the California State University at Los Angeles, he received a state award for excellence in teaching. He has authored several books, the most recent being *Public Compensation to Victims of Crime*, and scores of articles and reports on violent crime, white-collar crime, victimless crime, delinquency, corrections, and the criminal law. He has also directed several funded projects for innovations in the treatment of narcotics offenders, and is a frequent consultant to national commissions on drug abuse, law enforcement, and the causes and prevention of violence.

James Gilligan, a psychiatrist, received his medical training at Case Western Reserve and his psychiatric training at the Massachusetts Mental Health Center. He also did postgraduate work at the Boston Psychoanalytic Institute, and has maintained a private practice in the Boston area since 1969. He is now writing a book entitled *The Death of Morality*, which presents a psychoanalytic theory of the psychology of shame and guilt.

Martin L. Hoffman has been a Professor of Psychology at the University of Michigan since 1965. Prior to that he spent 12 years as a Research Associate at The Merrill-Palmer Institute. During that time he became editor of the *Merrill-Palmer Quarterly of Behavior and Development*, a position that he still holds. The two-volume *Review of Child Development Research*, which he co-edited, received the Child Study Association Book Award in 1964. He is well known for his contributions to understanding the role of the parent in the child's moral growth and for several state-of-the-art chapters on moral development theory and research. His current writing focuses on the process of moral internalization and the bases of altruistic behavior.

Ted L. Huston, a social psychologist, is editor of *Foundations of Interpersonal Attraction* and the principal investigator for a two-year field study of the determinants of bystander intervention in crime. After teaching in the Departments of Psychology at the State University of New York at Albany and Vassar College, he joined the faculty of the Division of Individual and Family Studies at the Pennsylvania State University in 1972. His research has investigated why and when people like each other, and currently centers on interpersonal competence and strategies of interaction in first encounters. He is also writing a book *Marriage and Family Relationships*.

Lawrence Kohlberg is a Professor of Education and Social Psychology at Harvard University. He obtained his Ph.D. in 1958 at the University of Chicago, where he began his still-continuing longitudinal study of the moral reasoning of then pre-adolescent and adolescent boys. In 1969 he received the Research Scientist Award from the National Institute of Mental Health. His research and theoretical writings have encompassed psychosexual development and the growth of logical thinking as well as moral development, and his stage theory of moral reasoning has stimulated scores of studies by other researchers. In 1974 he founded at Harvard a Center for Moral Development and Moral Education, which sponsors moral development research and numerous intervention projects with schools and prisons in the New England area. He has also recently co-authored a book on a cognitive-developmental approach to early education.

Chuck Korte is a Lecturer in Social Psychology at the University of St. Andrews in Scotland. He earned his doctorate at Harvard in 1969, then spent six years with the Department of Psychology at Vassar College before moving to Scotland. His research has examined group effects on help-giving in an emergency and is presently focused on urban social behavior.

Thomas Lickona is an Associate Professor of Education at the State University of New York at Cortland. Previously, he taught for two years in the Department of Psychology at SUNY at Albany, where he did research on the moral development theory of Jean Piaget and earned his doctorate in 1971. For the last five years he has directed Project Change, a graduate teacher education program that received the 1973 national Distinguished Achievement Award from the American Association of Colleges for Teacher Education. He is editor of two sourcebooks on humanistic education and has written articles on moral education, human development, and a person-centered approach to teacher education. Presently, he is co-authoring a book on marriage and parenting with Ted Huston.

Robert M. Liebert is the senior author of *The Early Window: Effects of Television on Children and Youth*, a book that grew out of his work as investigator for the National Institute of Mental Health's program on Television and Social Behavior. He is a Professor of Psychology at the State University of New York at Stony Brook, founder and director of the Media Action Research Center, and an international spokesman for the need to develop television's potential for promoting prosocial behavior. He was a Senior Investigator at the Fels Research Institute before moving to Stony Brook in 1970. He has written on a wide range of topics and co-authored several books, including *Personality* and *Developmental Psychology*.

Alan Lockwood teaches social studies education with an emphasis on moral development in the Department of Curriculum and Instruction at the University of Wisconsin. He received his doctorate in education from Harvard University in 1970. Prior to that he had helped both to train teachers in inner-city Boston and to plan an alternative high school in Cambridge. He has spoken widely on values education, and his booklet *Moral Reasoning: The Value of Life* is used in many schools throughout the country.

James C. Mancuso has sought to apply the psychology of personal constructs to an understanding of moral judgment, personality, and deviant behavior that disturbs others. He is a Professor of Psychology at the State University of New York at Albany, where he has taught since 1961. He has also served as a school psychologist and a consultant to community agencies dealing with deviance. His published writing includes a book on a cognitive theory of personality, and several articles on attitudes toward mental illness and culpability and the law. Among his present projects is a book on schizophrenia with Ted Sarbin.

Harriet N. Mischel is a Lecturer in Psychology at Stanford University. She has written about the origins of sex differences and carried out a project for the federal government that applied social learning principles to the reduction of racism and sexism. Her publications in this area have also dealt with sex-role stereotyping in early readers, and sex bias in the evaluation of professional achievements. She is co-author of the book *Readings in Personality*.

Walter Mischel taught at Harvard and the University of Colorado before joining the Department of Psychology at Stanford in 1962. His research and writing have applied a cognitive social-learning approach to the analysis of sex differences, observation learning, delay of gratification, perceived locus of control, and continuity and change in personality. He is a Fellow with the Center for Advanced Study in the Behavioral Sciences, and a consulting editor for several professional journals. His numerous publications include three books on personality.

John Monahan holds a joint appointment with the Department of Psychiatry and the Program in Social Ecology at the University of California at Irvine. In 1972 he received the Young Psychologist Award of the American Psychological Association. He is the editor of two books and author of several chapters and articles on community mental health, criminal justice, and the prediction of violence. His testimony on dangerousness and civil commitment has influenced the passage of laws in two states.

Bert S. Moore obtained his Ph.D. in psychology from Stanford University in 1973 with a specialization in personality and experimental psychopathology. Since then, he has taught in the Department of Psychology at Wellesley College, where he is doing research on aggression, competition and cooperation, and personality correlates of persons who use the concept of mental illness to explain behavior. His publications include several articles on the relationship between affect and altruism, and four chapters for the book *Developmental Psychology Today*.

Rita Wicks Poulos is Associate Director of the Media Action Research Center and a member of the Department of Psychology at Stony Brook, where she obtained her Ph.D. in 1971. She is co-author of *Developmental Psychology* and several articles, chapters, and reports on the effects of television on the social behavior of children. Her work is aimed at spotlighting the capacity of television to be either a positive or a negative influence on the young. Current interests include the development of achievement motivation in females.

James R. Rest describes his major interest as the development of moral judgment and applications to value education programs. After a year as a postdoctoral fellow at Harvard, he joined the Department of Social, Psychological, and Philosophical Foundations of the University of Minnesota in 1970, and is presently an Associate Professor. A frequent speaker at moral development conferences, he has published nearly a score of papers on issues in the assessment of moral stages and on research he has carried out with his objective measure of moral reasoning. Over 300 investigators from 11 different countries have thus far requested the use of his test in their research.

D. L. Rosenhan is a Professor of Psychology and Law at Stanford University. In addition to serving as consulting or associate editor for three psychological journals, he has co-edited two books on abnormal psychology and authored numerous articles and chapters. His teaching and research interests encompass prosocial and altruistic behavior, personality theory, and the social-psychological structure of institutions. His 1973 essay for *Science*, "On Being Sane in Insane Places," has been reprinted in over 30 other publications.

Herbert D. Saltzstein has studied the role of parental discipline in children's moral development and the impact of social influence on children's moral and perceptual judgments. He teaches developmental and social psychology at Lehman College of the City Univerity of New York, having previously held several other faculty appointments and a position as research associate at the Merrill-Palmer Institute. His current research interests include the contribution of role-taking training to children's moral thinking, and the effect of social influence on the legal judgments of children and adults. He is also at work on a book, *The Social and Moral Development of Children*.

Theodore R. Sarbin has been a Professor of Psychology at the University of California at Santa Cruz since 1969. He has received numerous fellowships and spent a year at Oxford University under a Senior Fulbright Award. Among his many publications are several books and chapters dealing with topics such as hypnosis, clinical inference, and role theory, all contributing to what he calls the "demythification" of psychological thinking about subjects such as mental illness. In 1975 he was the keynote speaker at the meeting of the American Association for the Abolition of Involuntary Mental Hospitalization. His recent interests include imagination, ethical decision-making, and connections between morality and the law.

Robert L. Selman identifies his major research interest as analyzing the logical and interpersonal concept development of well-adjusted and poorly adjusted children. He has designed and evaluated moral education curricula for the elementary school, and continues to apply cognitive-developmental theory to education in his present position as Director of Boston's Judge Baker Guidance Center school for children with learning and behavior problems. For the last several years he has been a Lecturer at Harvard University's Laboratory of Human Development and a practicing clinical psychologist. His current projects involve developing a life-span description of levels of understanding interpersonal relations, a manual for scoring early developmental levels, and a book on his research and interventions in this area.

Elizabeth Léonie Simpson has taught at several California universities. Her professional experience also includes the associate directorship of the Center for International Education, and consultancies with the National Institute of Education, the Ford Foundation, and the Constitutional Rights Foundation. In 1970 she received the Pi Lambda Theta National Distinguished Research Award. Among her publications are *Democracy's Stepchildren: A Study of Need and Belief*, a social studies text, and various articles and chapters on topics ranging from political socialization to cognitive development and the creative unconscious. She is also a published poet and short-story writer.

Bill Underwood, a Ph.D. graduate of Stanford University, teaches personality and developmental psychology at the University of Texas at Austin. Previously he was an Assistant Professor of Psychology at Boston College. His research has focused on the role of affective factors in prosocial behavior and cognitive factors in delay of gratification. He has co-authored several chapters on personality and social development.

DATE DUE

DEC 1 4 1981			
APR 7 1983			
APR 1 6 1984			
DEC 3 1987			